T5-BBB-201

American Political Science Series

GENERAL EDITOR

EDWARD S. CORWIN

Professor of Jurisprudence in Princeton University

American Political Science Series

Under the Editorship of

Edward S. Corwin

REPRESENTATIVE GOVERNMENT
HENRY JONES FORD

AMERICAN CITY GOVERNMENT
WILLIAM ANDERSON, *University of Minnesota*

INTERNATIONAL RELATIONS
RAYMOND L. BUELL, *Foreign Policy Association*

NEW GOVERNMENTS OF CENTRAL AND EASTERN EUROPE
MALBONE W. GRAHAM, JR., *University of California at Los Angeles*

AMERICAN PARTIES AND POLITICS
HAROLD R. BRUCE, *Dartmouth College*

INTERNATIONAL LAW
ELLERY C. STOWELL, *American University*

STATE GOVERNMENT
FINLA G. CRAWFORD, *Syracuse University*

GOVERNMENT AND POLITICS ABROAD
HENRY R. SPENCER, *Ohio State University*

MYTHS AND REALITIES OF AMERICAN FOREIGN POLICIES
HAROLD H. SPROUT, *Princeton University*, and MARGARET T. SPROUT

A HISTORY OF POLITICAL THEORY

GEORGE H. SABINE

Professor of Philosophy
Cornell University

REVISED EDITION

Henry Holt and Company
New York

Printed in the United States of America

To

THE MEMORY OF

WALTER JAMES SHEPARD

IUSTUM ET TENACEM PROPOSITI VIRUM
NON CIVIUM ARDOR PRAVA IUBENTIUM,
NON VOLTUS INSTANTIS TYRANNI,
MENTE QUATIT SOLIDA.

PREFACE TO THE SECOND EDITION

In this revision the text of Chapters I to XXIX (down to Hegel) remains unchanged, save for a few verbal corrections and the addition to the notes of some important publications that have appeared since 1937. These unfortunately have been relatively few, since so many important projects of historical publication were delayed or postponed or even abandoned on account of the war; hence this limited way of revising the earlier part of the book seemed justified. It is interesting that the largest number of additions had to be made to the chapters on the English Civil Wars, where the work of Professors A. S. P. Woodhouse, William Haller, and Don M. Wolfe, together with the author's study of Gerrard Winstanley, have made accessible many sources that were difficult or impossible to see in this country twelve years ago. In all the chapters of the book, however, the titles listed at the end under the heading, Selected Bibliography, have been re-examined and additions or substitutions have been made. The pagination down to page 619 remains the same as in the first edition.

The chapters from Hegel to the end of the book, on the other hand, have been completely rewritten and considerably enlarged. As was suggested in the Preface to the first edition, the author was never satisfied with these chapters, and twelve eventful years have certainly not made them a better representation of the great issues at stake between liberal democracy, fascism, and communism. Much is now certain that in 1937 was doubtful, and some hopes that then seemed reasonable are now much less so. At the same time the author is not aware of having changed in fundamental respects his philosophical interpretation of the subjects included in these chapters. The classification of subject-matter in the subdivisions is not greatly different, though some additions have been made.

In certain respects that are somewhat less than fundamental, however, considerable changes have been made. The most important of these are as follows. First, the author now believes that the connection made in the first edition between national socialism and the Hegelian theory of the state was hasty and superficial. For this change of view he should express his indebtedness to analyses of national socialism and Hegelianism by German critics, especially to Herbert Marcuse's *Reason and Revolution.* The change entails a somewhat different estimate of Hegelianism itself, especially with respect to the connotations that the word "state" had for Germans prior to the rise of national socialism, and also a different estimate of the Hegelian element in the theory of Italian fascism. The latter now appears to the author to be little better than a caricature of Hegel. In consequence the conclusion is re-enforced that the true affinity of national socialism was thoroughgoing irrationalism, best expressed in the mysticism and pseudo-science of the racial theory.

Second, the original chapter on liberalism has been expanded into two. The purpose of this change is twofold. It makes possible a fuller account of the very substantial achievements of early liberalism and also of its very serious philosophical deficiencies. Possibly the author should here acknowledge what may be a double bias: the conviction on the one hand that substantial social and political improvement depends on painstaking, matter-of-fact research rather than on inspiration, and on the other hand that research needs to be supplemented by penetrating philosophical analysis of its methods and objectives. The change makes possible also a clearer statement at once of the differences and the continuity between the earlier and the later forms of liberalism. This appears to the author to be important because he is convinced that liberalism, or what is now more commonly called democracy, depends both on maintaining its connection with the tradition of civil liberty and constitutional government and also on continually readapting itself to new problems set by rapidly changing economic and political situations.

Third, the chapter on communism, though not changed in essentials, has been considerably expanded and has perhaps been changed in emphasis. A good deal more information is available today than in 1937 about the development of Leninism, its dependence on specifically Russian ideas and conditions, and its differences from the tradition of Marxism in Western Europe.

In respect to these matters the author should acknowledge a general indebtedness to Bertram D. Wolfe's biography of Lenin, Trotsky, and Stalin. Moreover, twelve years' experience of communism in action, in Russia and elsewhere, has considerably modified the expectations that can reasonably be entertained about its concrete meaning and consequences. On this point the author ought perhaps to record his opinion that at present no democratic movement can expect anything but disaster from an alliance with communism.

In general the author can only reaffirm his belief in the point of view from which the book was originally written: viz., that any clear-headed theory of politics requires discrimination between states of fact, causal connections, formal implications, and the values or ends that a policy is designed to achieve. In any political philosophy all these factors are combined, but no combination can alter the fact that they are logically different and that conclusions about them are differently warranted. The author is even more deeply convinced than he was in 1937 that neither he nor any man can stand apart from the values and the convictions of the culture in which he was reared. But he is also convinced that there is in intelligence and good will a power of discrimination and of intellectual honesty that is not wholly limited either by nationality or by social class. He is aware that for this conviction he is indebted to the tradition of liberalism itself, and hence he is forced to see in that tradition the most hopeful prospect for social and political improvement by peaceful means.

G. H. S.

Seattle, Washington
December 19, 1949

PREFACE TO THE FIRST EDITION

This history of political theory is written in the light of the hypothesis that theories of politics are themselves a part of politics. In other words, they do not refer to an external reality but are produced as a normal part of the social *milieu* in which politics itself has its being. Reflection upon the ends of political action, upon the means of achieving them, upon the possibilities and necessities of political situations, and upon the obligations that political purposes impose is an intrinsic element of the whole political process. Such thought evolves along with the institutions, the agencies of government, the moral and physical stresses to which it refers and which, one likes at least to believe, it in some degree controls.

Thus conceived, the theory of politics no more reaches an end than politics itself, and its history has no concluding chapter. If there is a divine, far-off event toward which human history moves, the author of this book makes no pretense of knowing what it is. Taken as a whole a political theory can hardly be said to be true. It contains among its elements certain judgments of fact, or estimates of probability, which time proves perhaps to be objectively right or wrong. It involves also certain questions of logical compatibility respecting the elements which it tries to combine. Invariably, however, it includes valuations and predilections, personal or collective, which distort the perception of fact, the estimate of probability, and the weighing of compatibilities. The most that criticism can do is to keep these three factors as much as possible distinct: to prevent preferences from claiming the inevitableness of logic or the certainty of fact.

It cannot be supposed that any political philosophy of the present time, more than those of the past, can step out of the relationships in which it stands to the problems, the valuations, the habits, or even the prejudices of its own time. A writer of history, at least, ought to avoid the egoism that makes every generation fancy that it is the heir of all the ages. On the other hand, he can make no profession of impartiality beyond that fidelity to sources which is the obligation of every serious historian, or beyond that avowal of conscious preferences which should be expected of every honest man. In any other sense the claim of detachment is a superficiality or a pretense.

A reader is entitled, if he is interested, to an avowal of an historian's own philosophical preferences. Those of the author are in general agreement with the results of Hume's criticism of natural law described in the first part of Chapter XXIX. So far as he can see, it is impossible by any logical operation to excogitate the truth of any allegation of fact, and neither logic nor fact implies a value. Consequently he believes that the attempt to fuse these three operations, whether in Hegelian idealism or in its Marxian variant, merely perpetuated an intellectual confusion inherent in the system of natural law. The substitution of the belief that there is a determinate order of evolution or historical progress for the belief in rational self-evidence displaced an unverifiable idea with one still less verifiable. So far as there is any such thing as historical "necessity," it seems to belong to the calculation of probabilities, and in application this calculation is usually impossible and always highly uncertain. As for values, they appear to the author to be always the reaction of human preference to some state of social and physical fact; in the concrete they are too complicated to be generally described even with so loose a word as utility. Nevertheless, the idea of economic causation was probably the most fertile suggestion added to social studies in the nineteenth century.

To write the whole history of Western political theory from the point of view of this sort of social relativism is probably a greater task than a careful scholar ought to have attempted. It implies a range of knowledge which the author is painfully aware that he does not possess. For, on the one hand, political theory has always been a part of philosophy and science, an application to politics of the relevant intellectual and critical apparatus which is at the moment available. And, on the other hand, it is a reflection upon morals, economics, government, religion, and law — whatever there may be in the historical and institutional situation that sets a problem to be solved. It is of the essence of the point of view here adopted that neither factor should be neglected.

The intellectual apparatus is important, at least for political theory, only in so far as it is really applied to some state of the facts, and the institutional realities are important only so far as they evoke and control reflection. Ideally both should be conceived and presented by an historian with equal clearness; political theory in action ought to receive equal treatment with political theory in books. The demand thus made on the historian's scholarship is impossibly heavy.

In dealing with the large mass of literature that makes up the sources for a history of political theory, the author has tried to avoid so far as possible the mere mention of men and books that for lack of space could not be described in their setting. The fact that a man existed or that a book was written is, in itself, no part of the history of political theory as it is here conceived. In many cases it has been necessary frankly to select a specimen to stand for a considerable group, omitting other possible representatives. After a selection has been made the preserving of reasonable proportions between the subjects included presents the greatest difficulties. Especially as one approaches the present time the problem of knowing what to include and what to omit, and of deciding upon the relative importance of the items selected for inclusion, becomes nearly insoluble in view of the space at one's disposal. To be specific, the author is gravely in doubt whether the chapters following that on Hegel do not omit much that ought to have been included, if a proportion consonant with that observed in the earlier chapters were to be maintained. If the author were to offer an excuse, it would be that a friend, Professor Francis W. Coker, has recently done this task better than he in any case could have done it.

The author owes a heavy debt to the many scholars who have dealt, more adequately than he could do, with specific phases or limited parts of the subject.

G. H. S.

Ithaca, New York
April 10, 1937

CONTENTS

PART I

THE THEORY OF THE CITY-STATE

CHAPTER I

THE CITY-STATE

Most modern political ideals — such, for example, as justice, liberty, constitutional government, and respect for the law — or at least the definitions of them, began with the reflection of Greek thinkers upon the institutions of the city-state. But in the long history of political thought the meaning of such terms has been variously modified, and always that meaning has to be understood in the light of the institutions by which the ideals were to be realized and of the society in which those institutions did their work. The Greek city-state was so different from the political communities in which modern men live that it requires no small effort of the imagination to picture its social and political life. The Greek philosophers were thinking of political practices far different from any that have prevailed commonly in the modern world, and the whole climate of opinion in which their work was done was different. Their problems, though not without analogies in the present, were never identical with modern problems, and the ethical apparatus by which political life was evaluated and criticised varied widely from any that now prevails. In order to understand at all accurately what their theories meant, it is necessary first to realize at least roughly what kind of institutions they had in view and what citizenship connoted, as a fact and as an ideal, to the public for whom they wrote. For this purpose the government of Athens is especially important, partly because it is the best known but chiefly because it was an object of special concern to the greatest of the Greek philosophers.

SOCIAL CLASSES

As compared with modern states the ancient city-state was exceedingly small both in area and in population. Thus the whole territory of Attica was only a little more than two-thirds the area of Rhode Island, and in population Athens was comparable with such a city as Denver or Rochester. The numbers are exceedingly uncertain but a figure somewhat in excess of three hundred thousand would be approximately correct. Such an arrangement of a small territory dominated by a single city was typical of the city-state.

This population was divided into three main classes that were politically and legally distinct. At the bottom of the social scale were the slaves, for slavery was a universal institution in the ancient world. Of all the inhabitants of Athens perhaps a third were slaves. Consequently as an institution slavery was as characteristic of the city-state economy as wage-earning is of the modern. It is true of course that the slave did not count politically in the city-state. In Greek political theory his existence was taken for granted, just as the feudal ranks were taken for granted in the Middle Ages or as the relation of employer and employee is taken for granted now. Sometimes his lot was deplored and sometimes the institution (though not its abuses) was defended. But the comparatively large number of slaves — and still more the exaggeration of their numbers — has given rise to a myth that is seriously misleading. This is the idea that the citizens of the city-state formed a leisure class and that its political philosophy was therefore the philosophy of a class exempt from gainful labor.

This is an almost complete illusion. The leisure class in Athens could hardly have been larger than it is in an American city of equal size, for the Greeks were not opulent and lived upon a very narrow economic margin. If they had more leisure than the moderns, it was because they took it — their economic machine was not so tightly geared — and they paid for it with a lower standard of consumption. The simplicity and plainness of Greek living would be a heavy burden to the modern American. Certainly the overwhelming majority of Athenian citizens must have been tradesmen or artisans or farmers who lived by working at their trades. There was no other way for them to live. Consequently, as with most men in modern communities, their political activities had to take place in such time as they could spare from their private occupations. It is true that Aristotle deplored this fact and thought it would be desirable to have all manual work done by slaves, in order that citizens might have the leisure to devote themselves to politics. Whatever may be thought of the wisdom of this ideal, it is certain that Aristotle was not describing what existed but was proposing a change for the improvement of politics. Greek political theory sometimes idealized a leisure class, and in aristocratic states the governing class might be a landed gentry, but it is quite false to imagine that in a city like Athens the citizens were typically men whose hands were unsoiled by labor.

The slaves being put aside, the second main group in a Greek city was composed of the resident foreigners, or metics. In a commercial city like Athens the number of such persons might be large and many of them would not be transients. But there was no form of legal naturalization, and residence extending over several generations would still leave a metic outside the citizen-body, unless indeed he were taken in by inadvertence or connivance. The metic like the slave had no part in the political life of the city, though he was a freeman and his exclusion implied no social discrimination against him.

Finally, there was the body of citizens or those who were members of the city and entitled to take part in its political life. This was a privilege attained by birth, for a Greek remained a citizen of the city to which his parents belonged. Moreover, what citizenship entitled a man to was *membership;* that is, some minimum share of political activity or participation in public business. This minimum might be no more than the privilege of attending town-meeting, which itself might be of greater or less importance according to the degree of democracy that prevailed, or it might include eligibility to a narrower or a wider range of offices. Thus Aristotle, obviously thinking of Athenian practice, considered that eligibility to jury-duty is the best criterion of citizenship. Whether a man were eligible to many offices or only a few would again depend upon the degree of democracy that prevailed in his city. But the point to be noted is that, for a Greek, citizenship always meant some such participation, much or little. The idea was therefore much more intimate and much less legal than the modern idea of citizenship. The modern notion of a citizen as a man to whom certain rights are legally guaranteed would have been better understood by the Roman than by the Greek, for the Latin term *ius* does partly imply this possession of private right. The Greek, however, thought of his citizenship not as a possession but as something shared, much like membership in a family. This fact had a profound influence upon Greek political philosophy. It meant that the problem as they conceived it was not to gain a man his rights but to insure him the place to which he was entitled. Somewhat differently stated, it meant that, in the eyes of Greek thinkers, the political problem was to discover what place each kind or class of men merited in a wholesome society so constituted that all the significant sorts of social work could go on.

POLITICAL INSTITUTIONS

The institutions by which this body of citizen-members undertook to transact its political business can be illustrated by taking Athens as the best-known type of the democratic constitution.[1] The whole body of male citizens formed the Assembly or Ecclesia, a town-meeting which every Athenian was entitled to attend after he had reached the age of twenty years. The Assembly met regularly ten times in the year and in extraordinary sessions at the call of the Council. The acts of this town-meeting corresponded, as nearly as anything in the system did, to modern enactments in which the whole public authority of the body-politic is embodied. This is not to say, however, that the formation of policies and the effective discussion of measures took place, or was intended to take place, in this body. Direct democracy conducted by the whole people assembled is rather a political myth than a form of government. Moreover, all forms of Greek government (except extralegal dictatorship), whether aristocratic or democratic, included some sort of assembly of the people, even though its share in government might actually be small.

The interesting thing about Athenian government is therefore not the Assembly of the whole people but the political means which had been designed to make the magistrates and officials responsible to the citizen-body and answerable to its control. The device by which this was effected was a species of representation, though it differed in important ways from modern ideas of representation.

[1] The constitution of Cleisthenes, whose reforms were adopted in 507 B.C. Minor changes were made from time to time, largely in the direction of increasing the number of magistrates chosen by election and lot and also the number of paid services, both devices of popular government, but the reforms of Cleisthenes established the constitution of Athens as it was during the period of Athens' greatest power and as it remained. There was a brief oligarchic reaction at the close of the Peloponnesian war but the old forms were restored in 403.

What was aimed at was the selection of a body sufficiently large to form a sort of cross-section or sample of the whole body of citizens, which was permitted in a given case or for a short term to act in the name of the people. The terms were short; there was usually a provision against re-election; and thus the way was open for other citizens to have a turn at the management of public affairs. In line with this policy the magistracies were held as a rule not by individuals but by boards of ten, one chosen from each of the tribes into which the citizens were divided. The magistrates, however, had for the most part little power. The two bodies which formed the keys to popular control of government in Athens were the Council of Five Hundred and the courts with their large popular juries.

The manner in which the members of these governing bodies were chosen explains the sense in which they could be said to represent the whole people. For purposes of local government the Athenians were divided into about a hundred demes, or, as they might be called, wards or parishes or townships. These demes were the units of local government. There was one respect, however, in which they were not comparable strictly to local units; membership in them was hereditary, and even though an Athenian moved from one locality to another, he remained a member of the same deme. Accordingly, though the deme was a locality, the system was not purely one of local representation. The demes had, however, some measure of local autonomy and certain local police-duties of rather trifling importance. They were, moreover, the door by which the Athenian entered into citizenship, for they kept the register of their members and every Athenian boy was enrolled at the age of eighteen. But their really important function was the presentation of candidates to fill the various bodies by which the central government was carried on. The system was a combination of election and lot. The demes elected candidates, roughly in proportion to their size, and the actual holders of office were chosen by lot from the panel thus formed by election. To the Greek understanding this mode of filling offices by lot was the distinctively democratic form of rule, since it equalized everyone's chances to hold office.

There was, however, one important body of Athenian officials which remained outside this scheme of choice by lot and which retained a much larger measure of independence than the others. These were the ten generals who were chosen by direct election and were, moreover, eligible to repeated re-elections. The generals were, of course, in theory purely military officers but especially in imperial days they actually exercised not only important powers in foreign parts of the Athenian Empire but also very great influence over the decisions of the Council and the Assembly at home. The office therefore was not really a military post but in certain cases a political office of the highest importance. It was as general that Pericles acted year after year as the leader of Athenian policy, and his position with reference to the Council and Assembly was much more like that of prime minister in a modern government than that of a mere commander of troops. But his power lay in the fact that he could carry the Assembly with him; a failure to do so would have disposed of him as effectively as an adverse vote disposes of a responsible minister.

As was said above, the really essential governing bodies at Athens were the Council of Five Hundred and the courts with their large popularly chosen juries. Some sort of council was a characteristic part of all forms of the Greek city-state but in the aristocratic states, as at Sparta, the council was a senate composed of elders chosen for life and without responsibility to the assembly. Membership in such a council would normally be the prerogative of a well-born governing class and hence quite different from the popularly chosen Council at Athens. The Council of the Areopagus was the remnant of an aristocratic senate which had been shorn of its powers by the rising democracy. In substance the Council of Five Hundred was an executive and steering committee for the Assembly.

The actual work of government was really centered in this committee. But five hundred was still far too large for the transaction of business and it was reduced to a working size by the favorite device of rotation in office. Each of the ten tribes into which the Athenians were divided furnished fifty of the members and the fifty members from a single tribe were active for one-tenth of the yearly term of office. This committee of fifty, augmented by one councilman from each of the nine tribes not in office, was in actual control and transacted business in the name of the entire Council. A president was chosen by lot from the fifty for a single day and no

Athenian could hold this honor for more than one day in his entire life. The Council was charged with the very important duty of proposing measures for the consideration of the general Assembly of the citizens, which only acted upon matters coming to it through the Council. At the time when the Athenian constitution was at its best, it would appear that the Council rather than the Assembly was the body which effectively formulated measures. At a later date it seems to have confined itself rather to the duty of drafting measures to be debated in the Assembly. In addition to these legislative duties the Council was also the central executive body in the government. Foreign embassies had access to the people only through the Council. The magistrates were largely subject to its control. It could imprison citizens and even condemn them to death, acting itself as a court or committing offenders to one of the ordinary courts. It had entire control of finances, the management of public property, and taxation. The fleet and its arsenals were directly controlled by it, and a multitude of commissions and administrative bodies or servants were attached more or less closely to it.

The great powers of the Council, however, were always dependent upon the good will of the Assembly. It passed upon matters which the Council presented to it, enacting, amending, or rejecting them as it saw fit. A proposal originating in the Assembly might be referred to the Council, or the latter body might present a proposal to the Assembly without recommendation. All major matters, such as declarations of war, the concluding of peace, the forming of alliances, the voting of direct taxes, or general legislative enactments, were expected to go before the Assembly for popular approval, but it was apparently not expected, at least in the best days of Athenian politics, that the Council should be a mere drafting body. At all events decrees were passed in the name of the Council *and* the people.

It was through the courts, however, that popular control both of magistrates and of the law itself was consummated. The Athenian courts were undoubtedly the keystone of the whole democratic system. They occupied a position not comparable to that held by the courts in any modern government. Their duty, like that of any other court, was of course to render judicial decisions in particular cases either civil or criminal; but in addition they had powers vastly beyond this, which to modern ideas were clearly of an executive or legislative rather than of a judicial nature.

The members of these courts, or jurymen, were nominated by the demes, a panel of six thousand being elected each year, and were then told off by lot to sit in particular courts and upon particular cases. Any Athenian citizen thirty years old might be chosen for this duty. The court was a very large body, scarcely ever less than 201, commonly as many as 501, and sometimes much larger. These citizens were indifferently judge and jury, for the Athenian court had none of the machinery that goes with a technically developed form of law. Parties in litigation were obliged to present their cases in person. The court simply voted, first upon the question of guilt, and then, if the verdict had been guilty, upon the penalty to be assessed, after each party had proposed a punishment which he deemed just. A decision by a court was final, for there was no system of appeals. This was indeed perfectly logical, for it was the theory of the Athenian courts that the court acted and decided in the name of the whole people. The court was not merely a judicial organ; it was conceived to be literally the Athenian people for the purpose in hand. A decision in one court was therefore in no way binding upon any other court. In fact, a court was in some respects coordinate with the Assembly itself. Both the Assembly and the court were the people. Hence the courts were utilized to secure a popular control both over officials and over the law itself.

The control of the courts over magistrates was secured in three main ways. In the first place, there was a power of examination before a candidate could take office. An action might be brought on the ground that a given candidate was not a fit person to hold office and the court could disqualify him. This process made the choice of magistrates by lot less a matter of chance than it might at first appear to be. In the second place, an official could be made subject at the conclusion of his term of office to a review of all the acts performed by him, and this review also took place before a court. Finally, there was a special auditing of accounts and a review of the handling of public money for every magistrate at the end of his term. The Athenian magistrate, ineligible as he was to reelection and subject to examination before and after his term by a court composed of five hundred or more of his fellow citizens chosen by lot, had little independence of action. In the case of the generals, the fact that their re-election enabled them to escape the review no doubt largely explains why they were the most independent of Athenian officials.

The control of the courts by no means stopped with magistrates. They had a control over the law itself which might give them real legislative power and raise them to a position in particular cases coordinate with the Assembly itself. For the courts could try not only a man but a law. Thus a decision of the Council or of the Assembly might be attacked by a peculiar form of writ alleging that it was contrary to the constitution. Any citizen could bring such a complaint and the operation of the act in question was then suspended until it was acted upon by a court. The offending law was tried exactly as if it were a person and an adverse decision by the court quashed it. In practice there was apparently no limit to the ground of such an action; it might merely be alleged that the law in question was inexpedient. Again it is obvious that the Athenians thought of the jury as identical, for the purposes in hand, with the whole people.

POLITICAL IDEALS

The popularly chosen Council and its responsibility to the Assembly, and the independent and popularly chosen juries, were the characteristic institutions of Athenian democracy. As in any system of government, however, there were, behind the institutions, certain conceptions of what the institutions ought to embody, ideals of a valuable political life to which the institutions ought to be instrumental. Such ideals are less easy to discover and less tangible to describe, but they are no less important than the institutions themselves for an understanding of political philosophy. Fortunately, the historian Thucydides has stated, in a passage of incomparable brilliance, this meaning which democracy had for thoughtful Athenians. This is the famous Funeral Oration, appropriately attributed to Pericles, who was the leader of the democracy, and represented as having been delivered in honor of the soldiers who had fallen in the first year of the great war with Sparta.[2] Probably never in historical literature has there been a statement equally fine of a political ideal. The

[2] Thucydides, Bk. II, 35–46. The quotations are taken from Benjamin Jowett's translation, second edition, Oxford 1900.

pride with which the Athenian contemplated his city, the love with which he cherished his share in her civic life, and the moral significance of Athenian democracy are written in every line.

The main purpose of Pericles's speech was evidently to awaken in his hearers' minds the consciousness of the city itself as their supremely valuable possession and as the highest interest to which they could devote themselves. The purpose of the address is a patriotic appeal and the occasion is a funeral, so that the speaker might be expected to dwell upon traditional pieties and ancestral greatness. In fact, Pericles has little to say of tradition or of the past. It is the present glory of a united and harmonious Athens upon which he dwells. What he asks of his hearers is to see Athens as she really is, to realize what she means in the lives of her citizens, as if she were a supremely beautiful and worthy mistress.

> I would have you day by day fix your eyes upon the greatness of Athens, until you become filled with the love of her; and when you are impressed by the spectacle of her glory, reflect that this empire has been acquired by men who knew their duty and had the courage to do it, who in the hour of conflict had the fear of dishonour always present to them, and who, if ever they failed in an enterprise, would not allow their virtues to be lost to their country, but freely gave their lives to her as the fairest offering which they could present at her feast.

Their citizenship is, then, the Athenians' highest glory. "In magnifying the city I have magnified them." For what treasure can the thoughtful man prefer to that? What possession has he which he can hold in higher esteem or for which he will risk and sacrifice more? Shall he prefer his property or his family? Of what use is property except to enable a man to enjoy that higher good which comes from having an active share in the city's life? And of what value is family, even though it be of ancient and honorable lineage, except as it gives one an entrance into that higher form of social relationship represented by civil life? Above all faction, above all lesser groups of any sort, stands the city, which gives to all of them their meaning and their value. Family and friends and property are to be enjoyed at their best only if they form elements in that supreme good, which consists in having a place in the life and activities of the city itself.

When all due allowance is made for the rhetorical exaggeration natural to the occasion, the fact remains that the Funeral Oration was expressing a perfectly genuine ideal of Greek political life. This life had a quality of intimacy which it is very difficult for the modern man to associate with politics. Modern states are relatively so large, so remote, so impersonal, that they cannot fill the place in modern life that the city filled in the life of a Greek. The Athenian's interests were less divided, fell less sharply into compartments unconnected with one another, and they were all centered in the city. His art was a civic art. His religion, in so far as it was not a family matter, was the religion of the city, and his religious festivals were civic celebrations. Even his means of livelihood were dependent upon the state far more frequently than is the case in modern life. For the Greek, therefore, the city was a life in common; its constitution, as Aristotle said, was a "mode of life" rather than a legal structure; and consequently the fundamental thought in all Greek political theory was the harmony of this common life. Little distinction was made between its various aspects. For the Greek the theory of the city was at once ethics, sociology, and economics, as well as politics in the narrower modern sense.

The pervasiveness of this common life and the value which the Athenians set upon it is apparent upon the face of their institutions. Rotation in office, the filling of offices by lot, and the enlargement of governing bodies even to unwieldiness were all designed to give more citizens a share in the government. The Athenian knew the arguments against all these devices as well as anyone, but he was prepared to accept the drawbacks for the sake of the advantages as he conceived them. His government was a democracy, "for the administration is in the hands of the many and not of the few." In modern politics such an expression is likely to be taken not quite literally, unless it be understood of the rather colorless right to cast a ballot. Certainly the holding of office counts for little in the calculations of modern democrats, other than those few for whom politics is a career. For the Athenian it might be a normal incident in the life of almost any citizen. On the strength of figures given by Aristotle in his *Constitution of Athens* it has been estimated that in any year as many as one citizen in six might have some share in the civil government, even though it might amount to no more than jury-service. And if he held no office, he might still take part, regularly ten times each year, in the discussion of political questions at the general assembly of the citizens. The discussion, formal or informal, of public matters was one of the main delights and interests of his life.

Accordingly, the proudest boast of Pericles is that Athens, better than any other state, has found the secret of enabling her citizens to combine the care of their private affairs with a share of public life.

> An Athenian citizen does not neglect the state because he takes care of his own household; and even those of us who are engaged in business have a very fair idea of politics. We alone regard a man who takes no interest in public affairs, not as a harmless, but as a useless character; and if few of us are originators, we are all sound judges of policy.

To have absorbed his entire time with his private business would have seemed to the Athenian of Pericles's time a monstrous perversion of values; Athenian manufacture, especially of pottery and arms, was indeed in its time the best in the Greek world, but even the artisan would have been revolted by a life which left no leisure for an interest in the common business, the affairs of the city.

With this desire that all should participate went necessarily the ideal that none should be excluded because of extraneous differences of rank or wealth.

> When a citizen is in any way distinguished, he is preferred to the public service, not as a matter of privilege, but as the reward of merit. Neither is poverty a bar, but a man may benefit his country whatever be the obscurity of his condition.

In other words, no man is born to office and no man buys office, but by an equal opportunity he is sifted down to the position to which his natural gifts entitle him.

Finally, this ideal of a common life in which all might actively share presupposed an optimistic estimate of the natural political capacity of the average man. On the negative side it assumed that severe training and intense specialization were not required in order to form an intelligent judgment of political and social questions. There is no clearer note in Pericles's speech than the pride which the democratic Athenian takes in his "happy versatility."

> We rely not upon management or trickery, but upon our own hearts and hands. And in the matter of education, whereas they [the Spartans] from early youth are always undergoing laborious exercises which are to make them brave, we live at ease, and yet are equally ready to face the perils which they face.

This is, of course, a fling at Sparta with its rigid military discipline, but it is more than that. The spirit of the amateur, both for good and ill, is written large upon Athenian political practice. Athenian wits were sharp and the Athenian was prepared to believe — to his cost — that sharpness of wit might be a substitute for expertness of knowledge and the skill of specialization. Nevertheless, there was truth in the Athenian's boast that by sheer intellectual ability he could surpass all other nations — in art, in craftsmanship, in naval warfare, and in statesmanship.

In the Athenian conception, then, the city was a community in which its members were to live a harmonious common life, in which as many citizens as possible were to be permitted to take an active part, with no discrimination because of rank or wealth, and in which the capacities of its individual members found a natural and spontaneous and happy outlet. And in some considerable measure — probably more than in any other human community — the Athens of Pericles succeeded in realizing this ideal. Nevertheless, it was an ideal and not a fact. Even at its best the democracy had its seamy side which had as much to do with the beginnings of political theory as its successes. The *Republic* of Plato might almost be described as a commentary upon the democratic notion of "happy versatility," a notion which seemed to Plato nothing less than the ineradicable defect of any democratic constitution. And indeed, with the disastrous outcome of the Peloponnesian War before his eyes, the values might well appear more questionable to him than they had to Pericles. In Thucydides's *History,* too, there is a dreadful irony about the Funeral Oration, when it is placed against the story of Athenian defeat that followed.

On the wider issue of achieving a harmonious common life, also, it must be admitted that the city-state was only a qualified success. The very intimacy and pervasiveness of its life, which was responsible for much of the moral greatness of the ideal, led to defects which were the reverse of its virtues. In general the city-states were likely to be a prey to factional quarrels and party rivalries whose bitterness was as intense as only a rivalry between intimates can be. Thucydides draws a terrible picture of the march of revolution and faction through the cities of Greece as the war progressed.

> Reckless daring was held to be loyal courage; prudent delay was the excuse of a coward; moderation was the disguise of unmanly weakness; to know everything was to do nothing. Frantic energy was the true quality of a man. . . . The lover of violence was always trusted. . . . The tie of party was stronger than the tie of blood. . . . The seal of good faith was not divine law, but fellowship in crime.[3]

At a later date, after the war was over, Plato sadly said that, "Any city, however small, is in fact divided into two, one the city of the poor, the other of the rich."[4]

It is precisely because the ideal of harmony was only partly or precariously realized that it forms so persistently a part of Greek political thought. Loyalty tended constantly to be paid to a particular form of government or to a party rather than to the city, and this too easily opened the way to sheer political egoism which was not even loyal to a party. In this respect Athens was certainly better than the average and yet the career of Alcibiades illustrates both the dangers of faction and the unscrupulous selfishness which were possible in Athenian politics.

Though but precariously realized, this ideal of a harmonious common life in which it should be the chief joy of every citizen to have a part remains the guiding thought in Greek political theory. This more than anything else explains the unfamiliarity which a modern reader immediately feels when he first takes up the political writings of Plato and Aristotle. Our commonest political concepts are not there; in particular, the conception of individual citizens endowed with private rights and a state which, by means of the law, protects citizens in their rights and exacts from them the obligations required for this purpose. Our most familiar political thought contemplates some balance of these two opposed tendencies, enough power to make the state effective but enough liberty to leave the citizen a free agent. The philosopher of the city-state envisaged no such opposition and no such balance. Right or justice means for him the constitution or the organization of a

[3] Bk. III, 82.

[4] *Republic,* Bk. IV, 422e.

life common to citizens, and the purpose of law is to find for every man his place, his station, his function in the total life of the city The citizen has rights, but they are not attributes of a private personality; they belong to his station. He has obligations, too, but they are not forced on him by the state; they flow from the need to realize his own potentialities. The Greek was happily free both from the illusion that he had an inherent right to do as he pleased and from the pretension that his duty was the "stern daughter of the voice of God."

Within the circle thus set by the conception of civic harmony and a life in common the Athenian ideal found a place for two fundamental political values, always closely connected in the Greek mind, which formed as it were the pillars of the system. These were freedom and respect for law. It is important to notice how Pericles unites the two almost in the same sentence.

> There is no exclusiveness in our public life, and in our private intercourse we are not suspicious of one another, nor angry with our neighbour if he does what he likes; we do not put on sour looks at him which, though harmless, are not pleasant. While we are thus unconstrained in our private intercourse, a spirit of reverence pervades our public acts; we are prevented from doing wrong by respect for the authorities and for the laws, having an especial regard to those which are ordained for the protection of the injured as well as to those unwritten laws which bring upon the transgressor of them the reprobation of the general sentiment.

The activities of the city are carried on with the voluntary cooperation of the citizens, and the main instrumentality of this cooperation lies in the free and full discussion of policy in all its aspects.

> The great impediment to action is, in our opinion, not discussion, but the want of that knowledge which is gained by discussion preparatory to action. For we have a peculiar power of thinking before we act and of acting too, whereas other men are courageous from ignorance but hesitate upon reflection.

It was just this belief in discussion as the best means to frame public measures and to carry them into effect — this faith that a wise measure or a good institution could bear the examination of many minds — that made the Athenian the creator of political philosophy. It was not that he despised custom, but he never believed that a customary code was binding merely because it was ancient. He preferred to see in custom the presumption of an underlying principle that would bear rational criticism and be the clearer and more intelligible for it. This problem of the interrelation of custom and reason ran through all the theory of the city-state. Thus the skepticism which sees in right nothing but blind custom and which therefore sees in political institutions only a way of gaining advantages for the beneficiaries of the system seemed to Plato the deadliest of all social poisons. But in this respect Plato stood for the native Greek faith that government rests in the last resort upon conviction and not on force, and that its institutions exist to convince and not to coerce. Government is no mystery reserved for the Zeus-born noble. The citizen's freedom depends upon the fact that he has a rational capacity to convince and to be convinced in free and untrammeled intercourse with his fellows. The Greek had, indeed, a somewhat naive belief that he alone of all men was gifted with such a rational faculty, and that the city-state alone of all governments gave free play to it. This was the ground for his somewhat supercilious attitude toward "barbarians," who, as Aristotle said, were slaves by nature.

Freedom thus conceived implies respect for law. The Athenian did not imagine himself to be wholly unrestrained, but he drew the sharpest distinction between the restraint which is merely subjection to another man's arbitrary will and that which recognizes in the law a rule which has a right to be respected and hence is in this sense self-imposed. There is one point upon which every Greek political thinker is agreed, namely, that tyranny is the worst of all governments. For tyranny means just the application of unlawful force: even though it be beneficent in its aims and results, it is still bad because it destroys self-government.

> No worse foe than the despot hath a state,
> Under whom, first, can be no common laws,
> But one rules, keeping in his private hands
> The law.[5]

In the free state the law and not the ruler is sovereign, and the law deserves the citizen's respect, even though in the particular case it injures him. Freedom and the rule of law are two supplementing aspects of good government, the secret, as the Greek be-

[5] Euripides, *The Suppliants,* ll. 429–432 (Way's trans.).

lieved, of the city-state and the prerogative of the Greek alone of all the peoples of the world.

This is the meaning of Pericles's proud boast that, "Athens is the school of Hellas." The Athenian ideal might be summed up in a single phrase as the conception of free citizenship in a free state. The processes of government are the processes of impartial law which is binding because it is right. The citizen's freedom is his freedom to understand, to discuss, and to contribute, not according to his rank or his wealth but according to his innate capacity and his merit. The end of the whole is to bring into being a life in common, for the individual the finest training-school of his natural powers, for the community the amenities of a civilized life with its treasures of material comfort, art, religion, and free intellectual development. In such a common life the supreme value for the individual lies just in his ability and his freedom to contribute significantly, to fill a place however humble in the common enterprise of civic life. It was the measure of the Athenian's pride in his city that he believed that here, for the first time in human history, the means for realizing this ideal had been approximately realized. It is the measure of his success that no later people has set before itself the ideal of civic freedom uninfluenced by his institutions and his philosophy.

SELECTED BIBLIOGRAPHY

Greek Political Theory: Plato and his Predecessors. By Ernest Barker. 2nd ed. London, 1925. Chs. 1, 2.

Lawyers and Litigants in Ancient Athens: The Genesis of the Legal Profession. By Robert J. Bonner. Chicago, 1927.

Aspects of Athenian Democracy. By Robert J. Bonner. Berkeley, California, 1933.

Griechische Staatskunde. By Georg Busolt. 3 vols. Munich, 1920–26.

Greek Imperialism. By W. S. Ferguson. Boston, 1913.

Thucydides. By John H. Finley, Jr. Cambridge, Mass., 1942.

The Greek City and Its Institutions. By G. Glotz. Eng. trans. by N. Mallinson. London, 1929.

Essays in Greek History and Literature. By A. W. Gomme. Oxford, 1937. Chs. 4, 5, 9, 11.

A Handbook of Greek Constitutional History. By A. H. J. Greenidge. London, 1896.

"Democracy at Athens." By George M. Harper, Jr. In *The Greek*

Political Experience: Studies in Honor of William Kelly Prentice. Princeton, N. J., 1941.

"Cleisthenes and the Development of the Theory of Democracy at Athens." By J. A. O. Larsen. In *Essays in Political Theory.* Ed. by Milton R. Konvitz and Arthur E. Murphy. Ithaca, New York, 1948.

"Athens: The Reform of Cleisthenes." By E. M. Walker. In the *Cambridge Ancient History,* Vol. IV (1926), ch. 6.

"The Periclean Democracy." By E. M. Walker. In the *Cambridge Ancient History,* Vol. V (1927), ch. 4.

Greek Oligarchies, their Character and Organization. By Leonard Whibley. New York, 1896.

A Companion to Greek Studies. Ed. by Leonard Whibley. 3rd ed. rev. and enlarged. Cambridge, 1916. Ch. 6.

Staat und Gesellschaft der Griechen. By Ulrich von Wilamowitz-Moellendorff. 2nd ed., 1923. In *Die Kultur der Gegenwart.* Ed. by P. Hinneberg. Berlin, 1906–1925.

The Greek Commonwealth: Politics and Economics in Fifth-century Athens. By Alfred E. Zimmern. 5th ed. rev. Oxford 1931.

CHAPTER II

POLITICAL THOUGHT BEFORE PLATO

The great age of Athenian public life fell in the third quarter of the fifth century B.C., while the great age of political philosophy came only after the downfall of Athens in her struggle with Sparta. Here, as in so many cases in history, reflection followed achievement, and principles were abstractly stated only after they had long been acted upon. The Athenian of the fifth century was not much given either to the reading or the writing of books and, moreover, even if political treatises were written before the time of Plato, not much has been preserved. Nevertheless there are clear indications that much active thought and discussion were expended upon political problems during the fifth century and also that many of the conceptions found later in Plato and Aristotle had already crystallized. The origin and development of these ideas cannot be properly traced, but the atmosphere of opinion must be suggested in which the more explicit political philosophy of the next century could evolve.

POPULAR POLITICAL DISCUSSION

That the Athenians of the fifth century were immersed in the discussion of politics need scarcely be said. Public concerns and the conduct of public affairs were their great topics of interest. The Athenian lived in an atmosphere of oral discussion and conversation which it is difficult for the modern man to imagine. It is certain that every sort of interesting political question was actively canvassed by the curious and inquiring minds of Athenian citizens. Indeed, the circumstances could hardly have been more favorable to certain sorts of political inquiry. The Greek was almost forced to think of what would now be called comparative government. Throughout the length and breadth of the Greek world he found a great variety of political institutions, all indeed of the city-state type, but still capable of very great differences. At the very least there was one contrast which every Athenian must have heard discussed from the time he was old enough to follow conversation at all, that between Athens and Sparta, the types of the progressive and the conservative state, or of the democratic and the aristocratic state. Then in the east there was always the terrible shadow of Persia which could never be long out of any Greek's consciousness. He hardly counted it, indeed, as a genuine government, or at all events he counted it such a government as only the barbarian merited, but it formed the dark background upon which he projected his own better institutions. As his travels took him still farther afield — to Egypt, to the western part of the Mediterranean, to Carthage, to the tribes of the Asiatic hinterland — he found continually new material for comparison.

That the Greek of the fifth century had formed already a lively curiosity about the queer laws and institutions which filled his world is amply proved by the fund of anthropological lore embodied by Herodotus in his *History*. The strange customs and manners of foreign peoples form a regular part of his stock in trade. Behavior which in one country is looked upon as expressing the greatest piety and goodness is regarded in another with indifference or perhaps even with loathing. Each man naturally prefers the customs of his own country, and though there may be little in these customs which is intrinsically superior to those of another country, the life of every man must be lived in accord with some standards. Human nature needs the piety that belongs to some sort of observance. Herodotus looked with a curious and a tolerant eye, but withal respectfully, upon the strange medley that he revealed. He considers it the most certain evidence of Cambyses's madness that he despised and insulted the religious rites of other nations besides the Persians. "It is, I think, rightly said in Pindar's poem that 'use and wont is lord of all.'"[1]

Even in this very unphilosophical book there is one rather startling bit of evidence of the lengths to which popular thought in Greece had gone in theorizing about government. This is the passage[2] in which seven Persians are represented as discussing the relative merits of monarchy, aristocracy, and democracy. Most of the stock arguments appear: The monarch tends to degenerate into a tyrant, while democracy makes all men equal

[1] Herodotus, Bk. III, 38. [2] Bk. III, 80–82.

before the law. But democracy readily becomes mob-rule and a government by the best men is certainly preferable. And nothing can be better than the rule of the one best man. This is a genuine Greek touch which Herodotus certainly did not learn in Persia. This standard classification of the forms of governments, then, was a bit of popular theorizing long antedating anything known as political philosophy. When it occurs in Plato and Aristotle it is already a commonplace which need not be taken too seriously.

In the beginnings of political thought no doubt disinterested curiosity about foreign countries counted for something, but this was certainly not the main motive. The essential condition was the rapidity with which Athenian government itself had changed and the tenseness of the struggles by which the changes had come about. At no date within the historical era had there been a time when Athenian life — or indeed Greek life — had been mainly regulated by unquestioned custom. Sparta indeed could pose as a marvel of political stability but the Athenian had perforce to take pride in progress, since not much could be said for the antiquity of his institutions. The final triumph of democracy was not much older than the political career of Pericles; the constitution itself went back only to the last years of the sixth century; and the beginning of the democracy, counting from the establishment of popular control over the courts by Solon, was less than a century older. Moreover, from Solon on the general issues of Athenian domestic politics had been the same. The underlying causes were economic and the issue was between aristocracy, dominated by the old and well-born families whose property was in land, and democracy, dominated by the interests of foreign trade and aiming to develop Athenian power upon the sea. Already Solon could boast that the purpose of his legislation was to see fair play between the rich and the poor, and this difference of interest was still for Plato the fundamental cause of disharmony in Greek government. Athenian history, and indeed the history of the Greek cities generally, had been for at least two centuries the arena of active party-struggle and the scene of rapid constitutional change.

Only occasionally is it possible to catch a glimpse that enables one to guess how intense the discussion of political questions must have been that accompanied these struggles. In particular, the triumph of the democracy at Athens was the occasion of at least one astonishing bit of political description which probably did not stand alone and which serves to show how well the underlying economic causes of the political changes were understood. This is the little essay on the *Constitution of Athens,* written by some disgruntled aristocrat and formerly attributed (falsely) to Xenophon.[3] The author sees in the Athenian constitution at once a perfect instrument of democracy and a thoroughly perverted form of government. He sees also that the roots of democratic power are in overseas commerce and in the consequent importance of the navy which, under ancient conditions, was the typically democratic branch of the military system, just as the heavy-armed infantry was the typically aristocratic branch. Democracy is a device for exploiting the rich and putting money into the pockets of the poor. The popular courts he regards as merely a clever way of distributing pay to the six thousand jurymen and of compelling Athens's allies to spend their money in Athens while they wait to get their judicial business transacted. Like Plato later he complains that in a democracy one cannot even tell a slave when he jostles one in the street. It is obvious that Plato's satirical picture of the democratic state in Book VIII of the *Republic* was no new theme.

There is other evidence also that the Athenian public was no stranger to the discussion of the most radical programs of social change. Thus Aristophanes in his *Ecclesiazusae,* which was performed about 390, was able to make a comedy out of the idea of women's rights and the abolition of marriage, which has strongly suggested a relation to the communism put forward seriously by Plato at about the same time. Women are to oust men from politics; marriage is to be discarded, children are to be kept in ignorance of their true parents and are to be all equally the sons of their elders; labor is to be performed only by slaves; and gambling, theft, and lawsuits are to be abolished. The relation of all this to the *Republic* is obscure, since it is not known whether Aristophanes or Plato published first.[4] But this is not the really interesting

[3] Translated by H. G. Dakyns in *Xenophon's Works,* Vol. II; also by F. Brooks in *An Athenian Critic of Athenian Democracy,* London, 1912. The probable date is about 425 B.C.

[4] Various hypotheses are discussed by James Adam in his edition of the *Republic,* Vol. I, pp. 345 ff. Communism of women might be sufficiently familiar to readers of Herodotus. See Bk. IV, 104, 180. See also Euripides, Fr. 655 (Dindorf).

point. Aristophanes seems to be lampooning not a speculative philosophy but the utopian ideas of a radical democracy. And since the primary requirement of comedy is that it should go over the footlights, his audience must have known what he was talking about. It is an obvious inference that, early in the fourth century at least, an Athenian audience found nothing incomprehensible in a thoroughly subversive criticism of their political and social system. Again Plato was not an innovator; he was merely trying to take the social position of women seriously, a serious question then as now in spite of the hare-brained treatment it may receive.

ORDER IN NATURE AND SOCIETY

It is clear, then, that active thought and discussion of political and social questions preceded explicit political theory and that isolated political ideas, of more or less importance in themselves, were matters of common knowledge before Plato tried to incorporate them in a well-rounded philosophy. But there were current also certain general conceptions, not exclusively political in their nature, but forming a kind of intellectual point of view, within which political thought developed and which for the first time it made explicit. Here too the conceptions were present and had been expressed before they were abstractly stated as philosophical principles. Such assumptions are elusive but important, for they largely determine what sort of explanations are felt to be intellectually satisfying and therefore the direction that later theories will try to take.

As was said in the preceding chapter, the fundamental thought in the Greek idea of the state was the harmony of a life shared in common by all its members. Solon commended his legislation as producing a harmony or a balance between the rich and the poor in which each party received its just due.[5] The part which ideas of harmony and proportion played in Greek conceptions both of beauty and of morals has been too often emphasized to need repeating. These ideas appeared at the very beginning of Greek philosophy, when Anaximander tried to picture nature as a system of opposite properties (like heat and cold, for instance) which are " divided off " from an underlying neutral substance. Harmony

[5] The poem is quoted by Ernest Barker, *Greek Political Theory* (1925), pp. 43 f.

or proportion or, if one prefers, "justice" is an ultimate principle in all the earliest attempts at a theory of the physical world. "The sun will not overstep his measures," said Heraclitus; "if he does, the Erinyes, the handmaids of Justice, will find him out." The Pythagorean philosophy in particular regarded harmony or proportion as a basic principle in music, in medicine, in physics, and in politics. In a figure of speech that still persists in English, justice is described as a "square" number. This regard for measure or proportion as an ethical quality is registered in the famous proverb, "Nothing too much." The same ethical idea in a literary form appears in Euripides's *Phoenician Maidens* when Jocasta urges her son to moderation, begging him to honor

> Equality, which knitteth friends to friends,
> Cities to cities, allies unto allies.
> Man's law of nature is equality.
>
> . . . .
>
> Measures for men equality ordained
> Meting of weights and number she assigned.[6]

At the start, then, the fundamental idea of harmony or proportionality was applied indifferently as a physical and as an ethical principle and was conceived indifferently as a property of nature or as a reasonable property of human nature. The first development of the principle, however, took place in natural philosophy and this development reacted in turn upon its later use in ethical and political thought. In physics measure or proportion came to have a definite and somewhat technical significance. It meant that the details or the particular events and objects that made up the physical world were to be explained on the hypothesis that they were variations or modifications of an underlying substance which in essence remained the same. The contrast here is between fleeting and ever-changing particulars and an unchangeable "nature" whose properties and laws are eternal. This conception as a physical principle culminated in the formulation (late in the fifth century) of the atomic theory, according to which the unchanging atoms, by various combinations, produce all the variety of objects that the world holds.

The interest in physical nature which produced this brilliant first approximation to a scientific point of view lasted right through

[6] Ll. 536–542 (Way's trans.).

the fifth century, but at about the middle of that century a change of interest began to make its appearance. This was a swing in the direction of humanistic studies, such as grammar, music, the arts of speech and writing, and ultimately psychology, ethics, and politics. The reasons for this change, which came to have its chief center at Athens, were in the first place a growth of wealth, an increasing urbanity of life, and the feeling that a higher level of education was needed, especially in those arts, like public speaking, which had a direct relation to a successful career in a democratic government. The instruments by which the change was initiated were those itinerant teachers known as Sophists, who made their living — sometimes a very opulent living — by offering instruction to such as were able to pay for it. But the force by which the change of interest was consummated was the tremendous personality of Socrates, supplemented by the incomparable representation of that personality in the Dialogues of Plato. This change amounted in its results to an intellectual revolution, for it turned philosophy definitely away from physical nature and toward humanistic studies — psychology, logic, ethics, politics, and religion. Even where the study of the physical world persisted, as with Aristotle, the explanatory principles were drawn largely from the observation of human relationships. Never again, from the death of Socrates down to the seventeenth century, was the study of external nature for its own sake, irrespective of its relation to human affairs and interests, a matter of primary concern to the great mass of thinkers.

So far as the Sophists were concerned, they had no philosophy; they taught what well-to-do students were willing to pay for. But none the less some of them at least stood for a new point of view as compared with the hitherto prevailing interest of philosophy in the discovery of a permanent substratum for physical change. On its positive side this new point of view was simply humanism — the twisting of knowledge toward man as its center. On the negative side it implied a kind of skepticism toward the older ideal of a detached knowledge of the physical world. This is the most plausible understanding of Protagoras's famous saying that, "Man is the measure of all things, of what is that it is and of what is not that it is not." In other words, knowledge is the creation of the senses and other human faculties and so is a strictly human enterprise. Nothing that Plato says about Protagoras justifies the notion that he meant really to teach that anything is true which anyone chooses to believe, though Plato himself thought that this was what he ought to mean. This would be, indeed, a suicidal doctrine for a professional teacher. What Protagoras presumably meant is that "the proper study of mankind is man."

If, however, it was really the object of the new humanism to set entirely aside the ways of thinking followed by the older physical philosophy, it failed utterly. What it succeeded in doing was to give a new interest and a new direction. The earlier philosophers had gradually come to conceive of physical explanation as the discovery of simple and unchanging realities to the modification of which they might attribute the changes that everywhere appear upon the face of concrete things. But the Greeks of the fifth century had become familiar — through their contacts with foreign peoples and through rapid changes of legislation in their own states — with the variety and the flux of human custom. What more natural, then, than that they should find in custom and convention the analogue of fleeting appearances and should seek again for a "nature" or a permanent principle by which the appearances could be reduced to regularity? The substance of the physical philosophers consequently reappeared as a "law of nature," eternal amid the endless qualifications and modifications of human circumstance. If only such a permanent law could be found, human life might be brought to a degree of reasonableness. Thus it happened that Greek political and ethical philosophy continued along the ancient line already struck out by the philosophy of nature — the search for permanence amid change and for unity amid the manifold.

The question remained, however, as to what form this permanent element in human life should take. What really is the unchanging core of human nature which all men have in common, whatever may be the veneer of "second nature" which habit and custom have laid over the surface? What are the permanent principles of human relationship which remain after due allowance has been made for all the curious forms in which conventionality has clothed it? Obviously, the mere presumption that man has a nature and that some forms of relationship are right and proper in no way settles what the principle shall be. Moreover, what will be the consequence of finding it? How will the customs and the laws of one's own nation look when compared with the standard? Will it enforce the substantial wisdom and reasonableness of the traditional pieties or will it be subversive and destructive? If men discover how to be "natural," will they still be faithful to their families and loyal to their states? Thus was thrown into the caldron of political philosophy that most difficult and ambiguous of all conceptions, the natural, as the solvent for the complications, psychological and ethical, which actual human behavior presents. Many solutions were offered, depending on what was conceived to be natural. Except for the skeptics, who finally declared in utter weariness that one thing is as natural as another and that use and wont are literally "lord of all," everyone agreed that something is natural. That is to say, some law does exist which, if understood, would tell why men behave as they do and why they think some ways of doing are honorable and good, others base and evil.

NATURE AND CONVENTION

There is ample evidence that this great discussion about nature *versus* convention was spread wide among the Athenians of the fifth century. It might, of course, as frequently it has done since, form the defense of the rebel, in the name of a higher law, against the standing conventions and the existing laws of society. The classic instance of this theme in Greek literature is the *Antigone* of Sophocles, perhaps the first time that an artist exploited the conflict between a duty to human law and a duty to the law of God. Thus when Antigone is taxed with having broken the law by performing the funeral rites of her brother, she replies to Creon:

> Yea, for these laws were not ordained of Zeus,
> And she who sits enthroned with gods below,
> Justice, enacted not these human laws.
> Nor did I deem that thou, a mortal man,
> Could'st by a breath annul and override
> The immutable unwritten laws of Heaven.
> They were not born to-day nor yesterday;
> They die not; and none knoweth whence they sprang.[7]

[7] Ll. 450–457 (F. Storr's trans.). A passage in Lysias (*Against Andocides*, 10) suggests that the idea came from a speech by Pericles.

This identification of nature with the law of God and the contrast of convention with the truly right was destined to become almost a formula for the criticism of abuses, a rôle in which the law of nature has appeared again and again in the later history of political thought. In this rôle the contrast occurs also in Euripides, who uses it to deny the validity of social distinctions based on birth, even in that critical case for Greek society, the slave:

> There is but one thing bringeth shame to slaves,
> The name: in all else ne'er a slave is worse
> Than free men, so he bear an upright soul.[8]

And again,

> The honest man is Nature's nobleman.[9]

The critical Athenian of the fifth century was quite aware that his society had its seamy side and the critic was prepared to appeal to natural right and justice as against the adventitious distinctions of convention.

On the other hand, it is by no means necessary that nature should be conceived as setting a rule of ideal justice and right. Justice may itself be thought of as a convention having no other basis than the law of the state itself, and nature may figure as, in any usual sense, non-moral. Such a view is associated with the later Sophists who apparently found it profitable to shock conservative sensibilities by denying that slavery and nobility of birth are "natural." Thus the orator Alcidamas is credited with saying, "God made all men free; nature has made no man a slave." Most shocking of all, the sophist Antiphon denied that there was "naturally" any difference between a Greek and a barbarian. The end of the fifth century was a time when the dearest prejudices of the fathers were being dissected by and for a not-too-reverent younger generation.

Fortunately something is known of the political ideas of this sophist Antiphon since a small fragment remains of his book *On Truth*.[10] He asserted flatly that all law is merely conventional

[8] *Ion*, ll. 854–6 (Way's trans.).

[9] Fr. 345 (Dindorf); trans. by E. Barker.

[10] *Oxyrhinchus Papyri*, No. 1364, Vol. XI, pp. 92 ff. Also in Ernest Barker, *Greek Political Theory, Plato and his Predecessors* (1925), pp. 83 ff. The Sophist Antiphon is not to be confused with the Antiphon who led the oligarchical revolt at Athens in 411, though he was a contemporary.

and hence contrary to nature. The most advantageous way to live is to hold the law in respect before witnesses, but when one is not observed to " follow nature," which means to consult one's own advantage. The evil of breaking the law is in being seen and rests only " on opinion," but the bad consequences of going against nature are inevitable. Most of what is just according to law is against nature, and men who are not self-assertive usually lose more than they gain. Legal justice is of no use to those who follow it; it does not prevent injury or correct the injury afterward. For Antiphon " nature " is simply egoism or self-interest. But obviously he was setting up self-interest itself as a moral principle in opposition to what is called moral. The man who followed nature would always do the best he could for himself.

These fragments show clearly that the radical speculation about justice with which Plato begins the *Republic* were not the inventions of his own imagination. The argument of Thrasymachus, that justice is only " the interest of the stronger," since in every state the ruling class makes those laws which it deems most conducive to its own advantage, is quite in the same spirit. Nature is not a rule of right but a rule of strength. A similar point more elaborated is made by Callicles in the *Gorgias,* when he argues that natural justice is the right of the strong man and that legal justice is merely the barrier which the multitude of weaklings puts up to save itself. " If there were a man who had sufficient force . . . he would trample under foot all our formulas, and spells, and charms, and all our laws which are against nature." [11] In the same vein was the famous speech of the Athenian ambassadors to Melos in Thucydides: " Of the gods we believe, and of men we know, that by a necessary law of their own nature they rule wherever they can." [12] It seems quite clear that Thucydides meant this speech to express the spirit of Athens's policy toward her allies.

Of course, the theory which identifies nature with egoism need not carry quite such anti-social implications as it seems to have in Antiphon or as Plato gives it in speeches of Callicles. Glaucon in Book II of the *Republic* develops it more moderately as a kind of social contract, by which men agree together not to do injuries, in order that they may escape injury at the hands of their fel-

[11] 484a (Jowett's trans.). [12] Bk. V, 105.

lows. The rule would still be egoism, but enlightened self-interest might be compatible with law and justice, as the most feasible way of living together. This view, though not an invitation to lawlessness, is still not compatible with the idea that the city is a life in common. This cool way of holding a fellow citizen at arm's length until one is sure he can get as much as he gives is not in the spirit of a "community." Accordingly, Aristotle argues against it in the *Politics*,[13] where he attributes it to the Sophist, Lycophron. Since Lycophron was a Sophist of the second generation, a pupil of Gorgias, it is possible that a sort of contract-theory — a utilitarian development of the principle of self-interest — existed early in the fourth century. At a later date this kind of political philosophy reappeared in the Epicureans.

Before the close of the fifth century, then, the contrast of nature and convention had begun to develop in two main directions. The one conceived nature as a law of justice and right inherent in human beings and in the world. This view necessarily leaned to the assumption that the order in the world is intelligent and beneficent; it could be critical of abuses but it was essentially moralist and in the last resort religious. The other conceived nature non-morally, and as manifested in human beings it was self-assertion or egoism, the desire for pleasure or for power. This view might be developed as a kind of Nietzschean doctrine of self-expression, or in its more moderate forms it might become a kind of utilitarianism; the extreme forms could become theories of a definitely anti-social complexion. Already in the fifth century, therefore, there were ideas, not as yet systematic or abstract, which contain suggestions of most of the philosophical systems which were produced in the fourth century. Perhaps it needed only that Athens should fall upon evil days, as she did at the close of the Peloponnesian War, to make her people contemplative rather than active, and to make her a "school for Hellas" in a sense of which Thucydides never dreamed.

SOCRATES

The personal agency by which suggestive ideas were turned into explicit philosophy was Socrates, and, curiously enough, all the possibilities were equally indebted to him. The profoundly ex-

[13] 1280 b 12.

citing quality of his personality influenced men of the most different character and induced conclusions which were logically quite incompatible though obviously all derivative from Socrates. Thus Antisthenes could find the secret of his personality in his self-command and could enlarge this into an ethics of misanthropy, while Aristippus could see the secret of the same personality in a boundless power to enjoy and could enlarge this into an ethics of pleasure — two quite different versions of Callicles's strong man who could trample under foot the weakness of sociability. For the time being these philosophies seemed of minor importance, eclipsed as they were by the splendor of Plato and Aristotle, but in the event each set up its ideal of the philosopher and that ideal, in both cases, was Socrates. Nevertheless, it seems certain that more of Socrates's personality and a juster conception of his ideas must have gone into the teaching of his greatest pupil, Plato. But in all of Socrates's pupils was consummated the humanistic reaction which the Sophists began. The great interest of his mature years at least was ethics, in short, the puzzling question about the multitude of local and changeable conventions and the true and abiding right.

Unlike the Sophists, however, he carried into his humanism the rational tradition of the older physical philosophy. This is the meaning of the doctrine most characteristically imputed to him, the belief that virtue is knowledge and so can be learned and taught, and also of the method which Aristotle attributes to him, the pursuit of precise definition. For given these two, the discovery of a valid general rule of action is not impossible, and imparting it by means of education is not impracticable. Or to state it in somewhat different words, if ethical concepts can be defined, a scientific application of them in specific cases is possible, and this science may then be used to bring about and maintain a society of demonstrable excellence. It is this vision of a rational, demonstrable science of politics, which Plato pursued throughout his life.

What exactly were Socrates's conclusions about politics is not known. But in general the implications of identifying virtue with knowledge are too clear to be missed. Socrates must have been an outspoken critic of the Athenian democracy, with its presumption that any man can fill any office. This is broadly suggested in the *Apology* and practically stated by Xenophon in the *Memorabilia;* [14] and in any case Socrates's trial and conviction are a little hard to understand unless there was " politics " somewhere behind it. It may very well be, then, that some considerable measure of the political principles developed in the *Republic* really belonged to Socrates and were learned directly from him by Plato. However this may be, the intellectualist cast of the *Republic,* the inclination to find salvation in an adequately educated ruler, is certainly an elaboration of Socrates's conviction that virtue, political virtue not excluded, is knowledge.

SELECTED BIBLIOGRAPHY

Greek Political Theory: Plato and his Predecessors. By Ernest Barker. 2nd ed. London, 1925. Chs. 3–5.

Greek Philosophy. Part I. From Thales to Plato. By John Burnet. London, 1920. Book II.

" The Age of Illumination." By J. B. Bury. In the *Cambridge Ancient History,* Vol. V (1927), ch. 13.

Before and after Socrates. By F. M. Cornford. Cambridge, 1932.

The People of Aristophanes: A Sociology of Old Attic Comedy. By Victor Ehrenberg. Oxford, 1943.

" The Old Oligarch." By A. W. Gomme. In *Athenian Studies Presented to William Scott Ferguson.* Cambridge, Mass., 1940.

Greek Thinkers: A History of Ancient Philosophy. By Theodor Gomperz. Vol. I. Eng. trans. by Laurie Magnus. New York, 1901. Book III, chs. 4–7. Vol. II. Eng. trans. by G. G. Berry. New York, 1905. Book IV, chs. 1–5.

Paideia: The Ideals of Greek Culture. By Werner Jaeger. Eng. trans. by Gilbert Highet. 3 vols. New York, 1939–44. Book II.

Society and Nature: A Sociological Inquiry. By Hans Kelsen. Chicago, 1943. Part II.

Greek Thought and the Origin of the Scientific Spirit. By Léon Robin. Eng. trans. by M. K. Dobie. New York, 1928. Book III, chs. 1, 2.

Socrates. By A. E. Taylor. London, 1933.

[14] Bk. I, ch. ii, 9.

CHAPTER III

PLATO: THE *REPUBLIC*

The imperial ambitions of Athens perished with her defeat in the Peloponnesian War, but though her rôle was changed, her influence upon Greece, and ultimately upon the whole of the ancient world, was by no means diminished. After the loss of her empire she became more and more the educational center of the Mediterranean world, a position which she retained even after her political independence had vanished and indeed far down into the Christian Era. Her schools of philosophy and science and rhetoric were the first great institutions in Europe devoted to higher education and to the research which necessarily accompanies advanced instruction, and to them came students from Rome and all parts of the ancient world. Plato's Academy was the first of the philosophical schools, though Isocrates, who taught especially rhetoric and oratory, probably opened his school a few years earlier. Aristotle's school at the Lyceum was opened some fifty years later, and the two other great schools, the Epicurean and the Stoic, began some thirty years after Aristotle.

Those who have mastered the fine spontaneity, both of life and of art, in the Periclean Age can hardly avoid looking upon this academic specialization of Athenian genius as a decline. Probably it is true that the Greeks would not have turned to philosophy, at least in the manner they did, had the life of Athens remained as happy and as prosperous as it seemed to be when Pericles's Funeral Oration struck its dominant note. And yet no one can doubt that the teaching of the Athenian Schools played as large a part in European civilization as the art of the fifth century. For these Schools mark the beginning of European philosophy, especially in its relations with politics and the other social studies. In this field the writings of Plato and Aristotle were the first great pioneering operations of the European intellect. At the start they have only rudimentary beginnings and nothing that can properly be called a body of sciences, distinguished and classified in the way that now seems obvious. The subjects and their interrelations were in process of creation. But by the time the *corpus* of Aristotelian writings was completed in 323, the general outline of knowledge — into philosophy, natural science, the sciences of human conduct, and the criticism of art — was fixed in a form that is recognizable for any later age of European thought. Certainly no scholar can afford to belittle the advancing specialization and the higher standard of professional accuracy which came with the Schools, even though it brought something academic and remote from civic activity.

THE NEED FOR POLITICAL SCIENCE

Plato was born about 427 B.C. of an eminent Athenian family. Many commentators have attributed his critical attitude toward democracy to his aristocratic birth, and it is a fact that one of his relatives was prominently connected with the oligarchic revolt of 404. But the fact can be perfectly well explained otherwise; his distrust of democracy was no greater than Aristotle's, who was not noble by birth nor even Athenian. The outstanding fact of Plato's intellectual development was his association as a young man with Socrates, and from Socrates he derived what was always the controlling thought of his political philosophy — the idea that virtue is knowledge. Otherwise stated, this meant the belief that there is objectively a good life, both for individuals and for states, which may be made the object of study, which may be defined by methodical intellectual processes, and which may therefore be intelligently pursued. This in itself explains why Plato must in some sense be an aristocrat, since the standard of scholarly attainment can never be left to numbers or popular opinion. Coming to manhood at the conclusion of the Peloponnesian War, he could hardly be expected to share Pericles's enthusiasm for the "happy versatility" of democratic life. His earliest thought on politics, that recorded in the *Republic,* fell just at the time when an Athenian was most likely to be impressed by the discipline of Sparta and before the hollowness of that discipline was made evident by the disastrous history of the Spartan Empire.

In the autobiography attached to the Seventh Letter[1] Plato

[1] The account of Plato's adventure in Sicily presumes the historical reliability, if not the actual authenticity, of Letters III, VII, and VIII. For this there is now ample authority.

tells how, as a young man, he had hoped for a political career and had even expected that the aristocratic revolt of the Thirty (404 B.C.) would bring substantial reforms in which he might bear a part. But experience with oligarchy soon made the democracy seem like a golden age, though forthwith the restored democracy proved its unfitness by the execution of Socrates.

> The result was that I, who had at first been full of eagerness for a public career, as I gazed upon the whirlpool of public life and saw the incessant movement of shifting currents, at last felt dizzy . . . and finally saw clearly in regard to all states now existing that without exception their system of government is bad. Their constitutions are almost beyond redemption except through some miraculous plan accompanied by good luck. Hence I was forced to say in praise of the correct philosophy that it affords a vantage-point from which we can discern in all cases what is just for communities and for individuals; and that accordingly the human race will not see better days until either the stock of those who rightly and genuinely follow philosophy acquire political authority, or else the class who have political control be led by some dispensation of providence to become real philosophers.[2]

It is exceedingly tempting to see in this passage an important reason for the founding of Plato's School, though rather curiously the School is not mentioned in the Letter. The date must have been within a few years after the conclusion of his rather extensive travels and his return to Athens in 388. Doubtless the Academy was not founded exclusively for any single purpose and therefore it would be an exaggeration to say that Plato intended to build an institution for the scientific study of politics and the training of statesmen. Specialization had not yet reached this point, and Plato hardly thought of the need for the philosopher in politics as a need for men trained *ad hoc* in the professions of administration and legislation. He thought of it rather as a need for men in whom an adequate intellectual training had sharpened the perception of the good life and who were therefore prepared to discriminate between true and false goods and between adequate and inadequate means of attaining the true good. The problem was an outgrowth of the distinction between nature and convention which had been before the minds of reflective Greeks during the second half of the fifth century. It was, therefore, in

[2] Letter VII, 325 d–326 b; L. A. Post's trans. Plato was writing in 353 B.C. The last sentence echoes the famous passage in the *Republic* (473 d) about philosophers becoming kings.

Plato's conception, an important part of the general problem of discriminating true knowledge from appearance, opinion, and downright illusion. To it no branch of advanced study, such for example as logic or mathematics, was irrelevant. At the same time it would be hard to believe that Plato, convinced as he was that such knowledge and its acquisition by rulers was the only salvation for states, did not hope and expect that the Academy would disseminate true knowledge and philosophy, not spurious arts such as rhetoric. Certainly he believed later that statesmanship is the supreme or " kingly " science.

In 367 and 361 Plato made his famous journeys to Syracuse to aid his friend Dion in the education and guidance of the young king Dionysius in whose accession he saw what he hoped was the auspicious occasion for a radical political reform — a youthful ruler with unlimited power and a willingness to profit by the combined advice of a scholar and of an experienced statesman. The story is told with great vividness in the Seventh Letter. Plato soon found that he had been wholly misled by the report of Dionysius's willingness to take advice and to apply himself either to study or to business. The project was a complete failure, and yet it does not appear that there was anything essentially visionary about Plato's purposes. The advice contained in his letters to Dion's followers is sound and moderate, and it seems clear that Dion's plans were wrecked by his own failure to meet the Syracusans with a conciliatory policy. Some parts of Plato's Seventh Letter imply that he perceived the great importance for the whole Greek world of a strong Greek power in Sicily to offset the Carthaginians,[3] which was certainly a statesman-like project, and if he believed that an adequate power was impossible without monarchy, this was a conclusion which the Hellenization of the East by Alexander did much to justify. So far as the Sicilian adventure concerned Plato personally, he manifestly felt that no serious scholar who, for a generation, had been preaching the doctrine that politics required philosophy could refuse the support which Dion asked.

> I feared to see myself at last altogether nothing but words, so to speak, — a man who would never willingly lay hand to any concrete task.[4]

[3] 332e–333a.

[4] Letter VII, 328c.

Matters more or less connected with political philosophy are discussed in many of Plato's Dialogues, but there are three which deal mainly with the subject and from these his theories must be mainly gathered. These are the *Republic,* the *Statesman,* and the *Laws.* The *Republic* was written in Plato's mature but comparatively early manhood, probably within a decade of the opening of his School. Though it was certainly intended to be a unit and has so impressed its best critics, its composition may well have extended over several years, and there is good stylistic evidence that the discussion of justice in Book I is relatively early. The *Laws,* on the other hand, was the work of Plato's old age and according to the tradition he was still at work on it when he died in 347. Thirty years (or possibly even more) elapsed, therefore, between the writing of the *Republic* and the writing of the *Laws.* It is plausible to see in the former work the enthusiasm of Plato's first maturity, of the time which saw the founding of the School, and in the latter the disillusionment which came with age, perhaps accentuated by the failure of his venture in Syracuse. The *Statesman* was written between the other two dialogues, but probably nearer the *Laws* than the *Republic.*

VIRTUE IS KNOWLEDGE

The *Republic* is a book which defies classification. It fits into none of the categories either of modern social studies or of modern science. In it practically every side of Plato's philosophy is touched upon or developed, and its range of subject-matter is such that it may be said to deal with the whole of human life. It has to do with the good man and the good life, which for Plato connoted life in a good state, and with the means for knowing what these are and for attaining them. And to a problem so general no side of individual or social activity is alien. Hence the *Republic* is not a treatise of any sort, nor does it belong to politics, or ethics, or economics, or psychology, though it includes all these and more, for art and education and philosophy are not excluded. For this breadth of subject-matter, which is a little disconcerting to an academically trained reader, several facts account. The mere literary mechanics of the dialogue-form which Plato used permitted an inclusiveness and a freedom of arrangement which a treatise could not tolerate. Moreover, when Plato wrote, the various "sciences" mentioned above did not yet have the distinctness that was later somewhat artificially assigned to them. But more important than either literary or scientific technique is the fact to which reference has already been made, that in the city-state life itself was not classified and subdivided so much as it now is. Since all of a man's activities were pretty intimately connected with his citizenship, since his religion was the religion of the state, and his art very largely a civic art, there could be no very sharp separation of these questions. The good man must be a good citizen; a good man could hardly exist except in a good state; and it would be idle to discuss what was good for the man without considering also what was good for the city. For this reason an interweaving of psychological and social questions, of ethical and political considerations, was intrinsic to what Plato was trying to do.

The richness and variety of the problems and subject-matter that figure in the *Republic* did not prevent the political theory contained in the work from being highly unified and rather simple in its logical structure. The main positions developed, and those most characteristic of Plato, may be reduced to a few propositions, and all these propositions were not only dominated by a single point of view but were deduced pretty rigorously by a process of abstract reasoning which was not, indeed, divorced from the observation of actual institutions but did not profess to depend upon it. To this statement the classification of forms of government in Books VIII and IX is in some degree an exception, but the discussion of actual states was introduced to point the contrast with the ideal state and may therefore be neglected in considering the central argument of the *Republic.* Aside from this the theory of the state is developed in a closely concatenated line of thought which is both unified and simple. Indeed, it is necessary to insist that this theory is far too much dominated by a single idea and far too simple to do justice to Plato's subject, the political life of the city-state. This explains why he felt obliged to formulate a second theory — without however admitting the unsoundness of the first — and also why the greatest of his students, Aristotle, while accepting some of the most general conclusions of the *Republic,* stood much closer on the whole to the form of political philosophy developed in the

Statesman and the *Laws* than to the ideal state of the *Republic.* The over-simplification of the political theory contained in the earlier work made it, except in respect of very general principles, an episode in the development of the subject.

The fundamental idea of the *Republic* came to Plato in the form of his master's doctrine that virtue is knowledge. His own unhappy political experience reenforced the idea and crystallized it in the founding of the Academy to inculcate the spirit of true knowledge as the foundation for a philosophic statecraft. But the proposition that virtue is knowledge implies that there is an objective good to be known and that it can in fact be known by rational or logical investigation rather than by intuition, guesswork, or luck. The good is objectively real, whatever anybody thinks about it, and it ought to be realized not because men want it but because it is good. In other words, will comes into the matter only secondarily; what men want depends upon how much they see of the good but nothing is good merely because they want it. From this it follows that the man who knows — the philosopher or scholar or scientist — ought to have decisive power in government and that it is his knowledge alone which entitles him to this. This is the belief which underlies everything else in the *Republic* and causes Plato to sacrifice every aspect of the state that cannot be brought under the principle of enlightened despotism.

Upon examination, however, this principle is more broadly based than might at first be supposed. For it appears upon analysis that the association of man with man in society depends upon reciprocal needs and the resulting exchange of goods and services. Consequently the philosopher's claim to power is only a very important case of what is found wherever men live together, namely, that any co-operative enterprise depends upon everyone attending to his own part of the work. In order to see what this involves for the state, it is necessary to know what sorts of work are essential, an investigation which leads to the three classes of which the philosopher-ruler will obviously be the most important. But this dividing of tasks and securing the most perfect performance of each — the specialization of function which is the root of society — depends upon two factors, natural aptitude and training. The first is innate and the second is a matter of experience and education. As a practical enterprise the state depends on controlling and interrelating these two factors; in other words, upon getting the best human capacity and developing it by the best education. The whole analysis reenforces the initial conception: there is no hope for states unless power lies in the hands of those who know — who know, first, what tasks the good state requires, and, second, what heredity and education will supply the citizens fitted to perform them.

Plato's theory is therefore divisible into two main parts or theses: first, that government ought to be an art depending on exact knowledge and, second, that society is a mutual satisfaction of needs by persons whose capacities supplement each other. Logically the second proposition is a premise for the first. But since Plato presumably derived the first almost ready-formed from Socrates, it is reasonable to suppose that temporally the second was a generalization or extension of the first. The Socratic principle that virtue is knowledge proved to have a larger applicability than appeared on its face.

THE INCOMPETENCE OF OPINION

The thesis that the good is a matter of exact knowledge descends to Plato directly from the already ancient distinction of nature and convention and the quarrel between Socrates and the Sophists. Unless something is good, really and objectively, and unless reasonable men can agree about it, there is no standard for an art of statesmanship such as Plato hoped to found. The question in its various ramifications is spread at large over Plato's earlier dialogues, in the continually recurring analogy between the statesman and the physician or the skilled artisan, in the counter comparison in the *Gorgias* of oratory to the pampering of appetite by cookery, in the lack of method and the pretentiousness attributed to the teaching of the Sophists in the *Protagoras*, and on a more speculative level in the frequently recurring question about the relative positions of reason and inspiration, or of methodical knowledge and intuition. In the same category belong the long discussions of art in the *Republic* and the not very flattering estimate of artists as men who get an effect without knowing how or why. This parallels precisely the charge that statesmen, even the greatest of them, have governed by a kind of "divine madness." Obviously no one can seriously hope to teach divine madness.

The difficulties of the city-state, however, are not in Plato's opinion the result of defective education alone and still less of moral deficiencies in its statesmen or its teachers. They arise rather from a sickness of the whole body-public and of human nature itself. The public itself, he said, is the great sophist. A constantly recurring note in his ethics is the conviction that human nature is at war with itself, that there is a lower man from whom the higher man must at all costs save himself. It was this which made Plato seem to the Fathers of the Church "almost a Christian." Quite gone is the faith in "happy versatility" so magnificently praised in the Funeral Oration. The happy confidence of a generation that had created both spontaneously and successfully has given place to the doubt and uncertainty of a more critical age. In Plato the hope still persisted that it may be possible to recapture the happier frame of mind, but only through methodical self-examination and rigid self-discipline. In origin, therefore, the *Republic* was a critical study of the city-state as it actually was, with all the concrete defects that Plato saw in it, though for special reasons he chose to cast his theory in the form of an ideal city. This ideal was to reveal those eternal principles of nature which existing cities tried to defy.

Chief among the abuses that Plato attacked was the ignorance and incompetence of politicians, which is the special curse of democracies. Artisans have to know their trades, but politicians know nothing at all, unless it be the ignoble art of pandering to the "great beast." After the disastrous outcome of the Peloponnesian War, the generation in which the *Republic* was written was peculiarly a time in which Athenians would be likely to admire the thoroughness and discipline of Sparta. Xenophon went farther than Plato in this direction, and indeed Plato never could have admired whole-heartedly a one-sided military education like that at Sparta, however much he might admire the devotion to duty that it produced. But it is noticeable that he was more sharply critical of Sparta at the end of his life, when he wrote the *Laws,* than he was in the *Republic.* Moreover, the idea of expert skill professionally trained was one which, in Plato's day, was just dawning upon Greece. Not many years before the Academy was opened a professional soldier, Iphicrates, had astonished the world by showing what a body of light-armed, professionally trained troops could do even against the heavy infantry of Sparta. Professional oratory may be said to have started about the same time with the School of Isocrates. Thus Plato was merely making explicit an idea that was already growing up. What he rightly perceived was that the whole question is much larger than the training of soldiers or orators, or even than training itself. Behind training lies the need of knowing what to teach and what to train men to do. It cannot be assumed that someone already has the knowledge which shall be taught; what is most urgently needed is more knowledge. The really distinctive thing in Plato is the coupling of training with investigation, or of professional standards of skill with scientific standards of knowledge. Herein lies the originality of his theory of higher education in the *Republic* and something of this sort, it is tempting to believe, he must have tried to realize in the founding of the Academy.

Incompetence is a special fault of democratic states but there is another defect which Plato saw in all existing forms of government equally. This is the extreme violence and selfishness of party-struggles, which might at any time cause a faction to prefer its own advantage above that of the state itself. The harmony of political life — that adjustment of public and private interests which Pericles boasted had been achieved in Athens — was indeed, as Plato perceived, for the most part an ideal. Loyalty to the city was at best a precariously founded virtue, while the political virtue of ordinary custom was likely to be loyalty to some type of class-government. The aristocrat was loyal to an oligarchical form of constitution, the man of common birth to a democratic constitution, and both alike were only too likely to make common cause with their own kind in another state. Practices which by standards of modern political ethics would be counted treasonable were in Greek politics rather common. The best-known example, but by no means the worst, is Alcibiades, who did not hesitate to intrigue against Athens both with Sparta and Persia, in order to re-establish his own political influence and that of his party. Sparta, which was oligarchic in its form of government, was regularly looked to for support by the oligarchic party of all the cities within her sphere of influence, and in the same way Athens made common cause with the popular factions.

This fierce spirit of factionalism and party-selfishness was manifestly a chief cause of the relative instability of government in the city-state. Plato attributed it largely to the discrepancy of economic interests between those who have property and those who have none. The oligarch is interested in the protection of his property and the collection of his debts whatever hardship this works upon the poor. The democrat is prone to schemes for supporting idle and indigent citizens at public expense, that is, with money taken from the well-to-do. Thus in even the smallest city there are, Plato said, two cities, a city of the rich and a city of the poor, eternally at war with each other. So serious is this condition that Plato can see no cure for factionalism in Greek politics unless there is a profound change in the institution of private property. As a root-and-branch remedy he would abolish it outright, but at the very least he believes it necessary to do away with the great extremes of poverty and wealth. And the education of citizens to prefer civic welfare before everything else is hardly less important than the education of rulers. Incompetence and factionalism are two fundamental political evils that any plan for perfecting the city-state must meet.

THE STATE AS A TYPE

The theoretical or scientific implications of Plato's principle are not less important for him than the critical. There is a good both for men and for states and to grasp this good, to see what it is and by what means it may be enjoyed, is a matter of knowledge. Men have, indeed, all sorts of opinions about it and all sorts of impressionistic notions about how to reach it, but of opinions there is no end and among them there is little to choose. Knowledge about the good, if it could be attained, would be quite a different sort of thing. There would, in the first place, be some rational guarantee for it; it would justify itself to some faculty other than that by which men hold opinions. And in the second place, it would be one and unchanging, not one thing at Athens and another at Sparta, but the same always and everywhere. In short, it would belong to nature and not to the shifting winds of custom and convention. In man as in other parts of the world there is something permanent, a "nature" as distinct from an appearance, and to grasp nature is just what discriminates knowledge from opinion. When Plato says that it is the philosopher who knows the good, this is no boast of omniscience; it is merely the assertion that there is an objective standard and that knowledge is better than guess-work. The analogy of professional or scientific knowledge is never far from Plato's mind. The statesman ought to know the good of a state as the physician knows health, and similarly he should understand the operation of disturbing or preserving causes. It is knowledge alone which distinguishes the true statesman from the false, as it is knowledge that distinguishes the physician from the quack.

To Plato when he wrote the *Republic* this determination to be scientific implied that his theory must sketch an ideal state and not merely describe an existing state. Though it may seem paradoxical, it is literally true that the *Republic* pictures a utopia not because it is a "romance," as Dunning imagines,[5] but because Plato intended it to be the start of a scientific attack upon the "idea of the good." The statesman was really to know what the good is and consequently what is required to make a good state. He must know also what the state is, not in its accidental variations but as it is intrinsically or essentially. Incidentally, the philosopher's right to rule could only be vindicated if this were shown to be implied by the nature of the state. Plato's state must be a "state as such," a type or model of all states. No merely descriptive account of existing states would serve his purpose, and no merely utilitarian argument would vindicate the philosopher's right. The general nature of the state as a kind or type is the subject of the book, and it is a secondary question whether actual states live up to the model or not. This procedure accounts for the rather cavalier way in which Plato treats questions of practicability, which are likely to bother the modern reader. It is easy to exaggerate his remoteness from actual conditions, but as he understood the problem, the question whether his ideal state could be produced really was irrelevant. He was trying to show what in principle a state *must be;* if the facts are not like the principle, so much the worse for the facts. Or to put it a little differ-

[5] *History of Political Theories, Ancient and Mediaeval* (1905), p. 24.

ently, he was assuming that the good is what it objectively is; whether men like it or can be persuaded to want it is another matter. To be sure, if virtue is knowledge, it may be presumed that men will want the good when they find out what it is, but the good will be none the better for that.

Plato's way of proceeding here will be much more intelligible if it is realized that his conception of what would make a satisfactory science of politics is built upon the procedure of geometry. The relation of his philosophy to Greek mathematics was exceedingly close, both because of the influence upon him of the Pythagoreans and because of the inclusion in his own School of at least two of the most important mathematicians and astronomers of the day. There is a tradition, indeed, that he refused to admit students who had not studied geometry. Moreover, Plato himself propounded to his students the problem of reducing the apparently erratic motions of the planets to simple geometric figures and the problem was solved by Eudoxus of Cnidos.[6] This feat produced the first scientific theory of the planetary system and also the first approximation to a mathematical explanation of any natural phenomenon. In short, the method and the ideal of exact scientific explanation, which first appeared in Greek geometry and astronomy and which reappeared in the astronomy and mathematical physics of the seventeenth century, is one strand in the great Platonic tradition. It has its beginning precisely in the generation which saw the founding of the Academy and the writing of the *Republic*.

It is in no way surprising, therefore, that Plato should have imagined that progress in the rational understanding of the good life lay along a similar line. It was obvious to him that the precision of exact science depended upon a grasp of types; there is no geometry unless one is content to deal with idealized figures, neglecting the divergences and complications that occur in every representation of the type. All that empirical fact can claim, for example in astronomy, is that the types used shall "save the appearances"; in short, that the astronomer's deductions shall yield a result in agreement with what apparently is happening in the heavens. Manifestly the astronomer's types — his true

[6] Sir Thomas Heath, *Aristarchus of Samos* (1913), chs. xv, xvi.

circles and triangles — tell what is "really" happening.[7] In the same manner the *Republic* aims not to describe states but to find what is essential or typical in them — the general sociological principles upon which any society of human beings depends, in so far as it aims at a good life. The line of thought is substantially similar to that which caused Herbert Spencer to argue for a deductive "Absolute Ethics," applying to the perfectly adapted man in the completely evolved society, as an ideal standard of reference for descriptive social studies.[8] The utility or even the possibility of such a project, as conceived either by Plato or Spencer, may be doubted, but it is a gross error to think that Plato intended to loose his imagination for a flight into the regions of fancy.

RECIPROCAL NEEDS AND DIVISION OF LABOR

The proposition that the statesman should be a scientist who knows the idea of the good supplied Plato with a point of view from which he could criticise the city-state and also with a method that led to the ideal state. From this point he was led directly to his analysis of the typical state, and here again he found that he could follow the rule of specialization. The frequent analogies between the statesman and other kinds of skilled workers, artisans, or professional men, are in truth more than analogies. This is true because societies arise in the first place out of the needs of men, which can be satisfied only as they supplement each other. Men have many wants and no man is self-sufficient. Accordingly they take helpers and exchange with one another. The simplest example is, of course, the production and exchange of food and the other means of physical maintenance, but the argument can be extended far beyond the economic needs of a society. For Plato it afforded a general analysis for all association of men in social groups. Wherever there is society there is some sort of satisfaction of needs and some exchange of services for this purpose.

This analysis, introduced so simply and unobtrusively by Plato into his construction of the ideal state, was one of the pro-

[7] Cf. the contrast of real astronomy and "star-gazing" (*Republic,* 529b–530c) and of science with computation throughout Plato's account of the higher education in mathematics (522c–527c).

[8] *Data of Ethics*, ch. xv.

foundest discoveries which his social philosophy contains. It brought to light an aspect of society which is admittedly of the greatest importance for any social theory and it stated once for all a point of view which the social theory of the city-state never abandoned. Briefly stated it amounts to this: society is to be conceived as a system of services in which every member both gives and receives. What the state takes cognizance of is this mutual exchange and what it tries to arrange is the most adequate satisfaction of needs and the most harmonious interchange of services. Men figure in such a system as the performers of a needed task and their social importance depends upon the value of the work they do. What the individual possesses, therefore, is first and foremost a status in which he is privileged to act, and the freedom which the state secures him is not so much for the exercise of his free will as for the practice of his calling.

Such a theory differs from one which pictures social relations in terms of contract or agreement and which therefore conceives the state as primarily concerned with maintaining liberty of choice. A theory of the latter sort occurs, as was pointed out in the last chapter, both in the fragment of Antiphon the Sophist and in the remarks on justice by Glaucon early in the second book of the *Republic*.[9] But Plato rejected it because agreement, resting solely upon the will, can never show that justice is intrinsically a virtue. Social arrangements can be shown to rest on nature rather than convention only if it can be shown that what a man does has meaning beyond the mere fact that he wants to do it. How convincing the argument was found is shown by the fact that Aristotle, who was not greatly influenced by most of Plato's argument for his ideal state, was quite at one with him in this. The analysis of the community in the opening pages of the *Politics* was merely a new version of Plato's argument that a society depends upon mutual needs.

But exchange of services implies another principle of almost equal importance, the division of labor and the specializing of tasks. For if needs are satisfied by exchange, each must have more than he needs of the commodity which he offers, just as he must have less than he needs of that which he receives. It is clearly necessary, therefore, that there should be some specializa-

[9] 358e ff.

tion. The farmer produces more food than he needs while the shoemaker produces more shoes than he can wear. Hence it is advantageous to both that each should produce for the other, since both will be better fed and better clothed by working together than by each dividing his work to make all the various things he needs. This rests, according to Plato, upon two fundamental facts of human psychology, first, that different men have different aptitudes and so do some kinds of work better than others and, second, that skill is gained only where men apply themselves steadily to the work for which they are naturally fitted.

> We must infer that all things are produced more plentifully and easily and of a better quality when one man does one thing which is natural to him and does it at the right time, and leaves other things.[10]

Upon this brief but exceedingly penetrating analysis of society and of human nature Plato's further construction of the state depends.

It turns out, therefore, that the philosopher-ruler is not peculiar but that his claim to power is justified by the same principle which is at work throughout all society. Banish specialization entirely and all social interchange is banished with it. Imagine men with no difference of natural aptitude and the basis for specialization is gone. Take away all training by which natural aptitude is perfected into developed skill and specialization becomes meaningless. These, then, are the forces in human nature upon which society and with it the state have to rely. The question, then, is not whether they shall be used but only whether they shall be used well. Shall men be divided according to their real aptitudes? Shall these aptitudes be wisely and adequately trained to bring them to their most perfect form? Shall the needs which men seek to satisfy co-operatively be their highest and most genuine needs, or merely the wants of their lower and more luxurious natures? These questions can be answered only in the light of what Plato calls inclusively a knowledge of the good. To know the good is to know how to answer them. And this is the special function of the philosopher. His knowledge is at once his right and his duty to rule.

[10] *Republic,* 370c.

CLASSES AND SOULS

It will be clear upon reflection that this argument makes an important assumption which is not explicitly stated by Plato. Individual capacities are assumed to be of such a sort that, when developed by a properly devised and controlled education, they will result in a harmonious social group. The difficulty with existing states has been that education has been wrong; or at all events, if better breeding is needed — and Plato believes that it is — an improvement of existing strains will accomplish the purpose. In other words, he takes for granted that there is nothing radically unsocial or antisocial in well-bred human beings which might result in disharmony precisely because of a complete and perfect development of individual powers. This assumption is not obviously true and many thinkers since Plato have questioned it; some have even gone to the length of supposing the opposite, namely, that socialized training must be more or less repressive of individual self-expression. But this possibility does not enter into Plato's calculations. While the assumption just mentioned is not explicitly stated, it does enter into the argument of the *Republic* at one point which is likely, without explanation, to be a little puzzling. This is the point at which the state is assumed to be merely the individual " writ large "[11] and at which, accordingly, the question about justice is transformed from the search for an individual virtue into the search for a property of the state. The difficulty of the transition, which seems to a modern reader a little artificial, is masked for Plato by the presumption that there is an inherent fitness of human nature for society and of society for human nature, and this fitness he interprets as a parallelism. Both man and the state have a single underlying structure which prevents the good for one from being essentially different from the good for the other.

It must be admitted that this assumption is responsible for much that is most attractive in the ethical ideal of the city-state and in Plato's representation of it. It explains why, in Plato's ethics, there is no ultimate cleft between inclination and duty or between the interests of individuals and those of the society to which they belong. Where such conflicts arise — and the *Re-*

[11] 368d.

public was written because they do arise — the problem is one of development and adjustment, not of repression and force. What the unsocial individual needs is a better understanding of his own nature and a fuller development of his powers in accordance with that knowledge. His internal conflict is not an unappeasable strife between what he wants to do and what he ought to do, because in the last resort the full expression of his natural powers is both what he really wants and what he is entitled to have. On the other hand, what the inharmonious society needs is to provide just those possibilities of complete development for its citizens which their needs demand. The problem of the good state and of the good man are two sides of the same question, and the answer to one must at the same time give the answer to the other. Morality ought to be at once private and public and if it is not so, the solution lies in correcting the state and improving the individual until they reach their possible harmony. It may very well be doubted whether, in general terms, any better moral ideal than this has ever been stated.

At the same time Plato's attempt to make one analysis do duty for both the state and the individual yields him a theory much too simple to solve his problem. The analysis of the state shows that there are three necessary functions to be performed. The underlying physical needs must be supplied and the state must be protected and governed. The principle of specialization demands that essential services should be distinguished, and it follows that there are three classes: the workers who produce and the "guardians," who in turn are divided, though not so sharply, into the soldiers and the rulers, or the philosopher-king if he be a single ruler. But since division of functions rests on difference of aptitude, the three classes depend upon the fact that there are three kinds of men, those who are fitted by nature to work but not to rule, those who are fit to rule but only under the control and direction of others, and finally those who are fit for the highest duties of statesmanship such as the final choice of means and ends. These three aptitudes imply on the psychological side three vital powers or "souls," that which includes the appetitive or nutritive faculties and which Plato supposes to reside below the diaphragm, that which is executive or "spirited" and which resides in the chest, and that which knows or thinks, the rational soul which is situated in the head. It would seem natural that each soul should have its own special excellence or virtue, and Plato does in fact carry out this plan in part. Wisdom is the excellence of the rational soul and courage of the active, but he hesitates to say that temperance can be confined to the nutritive soul. Justice is the proper interrelation of the three functions, whether of the classes in the state or of the faculties in an individual.

It would probably be a mistake to put too much stress upon this theory of the "three souls." Plato seems never to have tried seriously to develop it, and often in psychological discussion he does not use it. Moreover, it is certainly not true that in the *Republic* the three classes are so sharply separated as his schematic statement of the theory would lead one to expect. The classes are certainly not castes, for membership in them is not hereditary. On the contrary his ideal seems to be a society in which every child born is given the highest training that his natural powers permit him to profit by, and in which every individual is advanced to the highest position in the state that his achievements (his capacity *plus* his education and experience) enable him to fill adequately. Plato in the *Republic* showed himself remarkably free from temperamental class-prejudice, much freer than Aristotle, for example, and freer than he seems to be in the outline of the second-best state in the *Laws*. But when all these allowances are made, the fact remains that the parallelism assumed between mental capacities and social classes is a restricting influence which prevented him from doing justice in the *Republic* to the complexity of the political problems under discussion. The theory obliged him to assume that all the intelligence in the state was concentrated in the rulers, though his repeated references to the skill of the artisans in their own kind of work shows that he did not literally believe this. On the other hand, in their political capacity the workers have nothing to do but obey, which is nearly the same thing as to say that they have no properly political capacity at all. The position to which they are assigned cannot be corrected even by education, because they seem not to need education for civic activity or for participation in the self-governing activities of the community. In this part of the state's life they are onlookers.

This result has often been attributed, as for example by Edward

Zeller,[12] to a contempt for artisans and the handicrafts as compared with intellectual labor, but in truth Plato showed a more genuine admiration for manual skill than Aristotle. The explanation is to be found rather in the assumption that good government is nothing but a matter of knowledge and that knowledge is always the possession of a class of experts, like the practice of medicine. According to Plato most men are permanently in the relation to their rulers of a patient to his physician. Aristotle asked a pertinent question on this point when he inquired whether there are not cases where experience is a better guide than the knowledge of an expert.[13] A man who has to live in a house need not rely on a builder to tell him whether it is commodious or not. But Plato's ideas about sound knowledge when he wrote the *Republic* allowed little importance to experience. The result was that he failed to grasp one of the most significant political aspects of the city-state whose civil life he desired to perfect. His distrust of "happy versatility" was so great that he swung to the opposite extreme and allowed to artisans no capacity for public service except their trades. The old free give and take of the town-meeting and the council is utterly gone, and this side of human personality, which the Athenian democrat valued above everything, must be quite eradicated from the masses. So far as the higher activities of life are concerned, they live in a state of tutelage to wiser men.

JUSTICE

The theory of the state in the *Republic* culminates in the conception of justice. Justice is the bond which holds a society together, a harmonious union of individuals each of whom has found his life-work in accordance with his natural fitness and his training. It is both a public and a private virtue because the highest good both of the state and of its members is thereby conserved. There is nothing better for a man than to have his work and to be fitted to do it; there is nothing better for other men and for the whole society than that each should thus be filling the station to which he is entitled.

[12] *Plato and the Older Academy.* Trans. by S. F. Alleyne and Alfred Goodwin, 1888, p. 473.

[13] *Politics,* 3, 11; 1282a 17 ff.

> Social justice thus may be defined as the principle of a society, consisting of different types of men . . . who have combined under the impulse of their need for one another, and by their combination in one society, and their concentration on their separate functions, have made a whole which is perfect because it is the product and the image of the whole of the human mind.[14]

This is Plato's elaboration of the *prima facie* definition of justice as " giving to every man his due." For what is due *to* him is that he should be treated as what he is, in the light of his capacity and his training, while what is due *from* him is the honest performance of those tasks which the place accorded him requires.

To a modern reader such a definition of justice is at least as striking for what it omits as for what it includes. In no sense is it a juristic definition. For it lacks the notion, connoted by the Latin word *ius* and the English word right, of powers of voluntary action in the exercise of which a man will be protected by law and supported by the authority of the state. Lacking this conception Plato does not mean by justice, except remotely, the maintenance of public peace and order; at least, external order is but a small part of the harmony which makes the state. What the state provides its citizens is not so much freedom and protection as a life — all the opportunities for social interchange which make up the necessaries and the amenities of a civilized existence. It is true that in such a social life there are rights, just as there are duties, but they can hardly be said to belong in any peculiar sense to individuals. They are inherent rather in the services or functions that individuals perform. Resting as it does upon the principle that the state is created by mutual needs, the analysis runs necessarily in terms of services and not of powers. Even the ruler is no exception, for he has merely the special function to which his wisdom entitles him. The notion of authority or sovereign power, such as the Roman attached to his magistracies, has practically no part in Plato's political theory, nor indeed in that of any Greek philosopher.

This completes the general outline of Plato's theory of the state. Starting from the conception that the good must be known by methodical study, the theory constructs society around this

[14] E. Barker, *Greek Political Theory, Plato and his Predecessors* (1925), pp. 176 f.

idea by showing that the principle is implicit in all society. The division of labor and the specialization of tasks are the conditions of social co-operation, and the problem of the philosopher-king is to arrange these matters in the most advantageous way. Because human nature is innately and inherently social, the maximum advantage to the state means also the maximum advantage to citizens. The goal is therefore a perfect adjustment of human beings to the possibilities of significant employment which the state affords. The remainder of Plato's argument might almost be described as a corollary. The only remaining question concerns the means by which the statesman can bring about the adjustment required. Broadly speaking there are only two ways to take hold of this problem. Either the special hindrances to good citizenship may be removed or the positive conditions of good citizenship may be developed. The first results in the theory of communism and the second in the theory of education.

PROPERTY AND THE FAMILY

Plato's communism takes two main forms which meet in the abolition of the family. The first is the prohibition of private property, whether houses or land or money, to the rulers and the provision that they shall live in barracks and have their meals at a common table. The second is the abolition of a permanent monogamous sexual relation and the substitution of regulated breeding at the behest of the rulers for the purpose of securing the best possible offspring. This bracketing of the two social functions of procreating children and of producing and owning goods was more obvious in a society that lived mainly under a household economy than it is now. A radical innovation in respect to the one coalesced readily with an innovation in respect to the other. Communism in the *Republic,* however, applies only to the guardian class, that is, to the soldiers and rulers, while the artisans are to be left in possession of their private families, both property and wives. How this is to be made consistent with promotion from the lower rank to the higher is not explained. But the truth is that Plato does not take the trouble to work out his plan in much detail. Still more striking is the fact that, in connection with his theory of private property, he does not have anything to say about slaves. It is a fact that Plato's state seemingly might exist without slavery, since no work especially to be done by slaves is mentioned, a respect in which the state of the *Laws* is strikingly different. This has led Constantin Ritter to argue that in the *Republic* slavery is "in principle abolished." [15] But it is almost incredible that Plato intended to abolish a universal institution without mentioning it. It is more probable that he merely regarded slavery as unimportant.

Plato was in no way unique in believing that an economic cleavage between the citizens of a state is a most dangerous political condition. In general, the Greeks were quite frank in admitting that economic motives are very influential in determining political action and political affiliation. Long before the *Republic* was written Euripides had divided citizens into three classes, the useless rich who are always greedy for more, the poor who have nothing and are devoured by envy, and the middle class, the sturdy yeomanry, who "save states." [16] The oligarchical state to a Greek meant a state governed by, and in the interest of, the well-born among whom the possession of property is hereditary, while a democratic state was one governed by and for the "many," who have neither birth nor property. The economic difference was the key to the political distinction, as is quite clear from Plato's account of oligarchy.[17] The importance of economic causes in politics was therefore no new idea, and in believing that great diversity of wealth was inconsistent with good government Plato was following a common conviction which represented Greek experience through many generations. The causes of civic unrest in Athens had been mainly of this sort from at least the days of Solon.

So firmly was Plato convinced of the pernicious effects of wealth upon government that he saw no way to abolish the evil except by abolishing wealth itself, so far as soldiers and rulers are concerned. To cure the greed of rulers there is no way short of denying them the right to call anything their own. Devotion to their civic calling admits no private rival. The example of Sparta, where citizens were denied the use of money and the privilege of engaging in trade, doubtless weighed with Plato in reaching this

[15] *Platon, sein Leben, seine Schriften, seine Lehre* (1923), Vol. II, p. 596.
[16] *The Suppliants*, ll. 238–245.
[17] *Republic*, 551d.

conclusion. His reasons, however, should be carefully noted. He was not in the least concerned to do away with inequalities of wealth because they are unjust to the individuals concerned. His purpose was to produce the greatest degree of unity in the state, and private property is incompatible with this. The emphasis is characteristic of Greek thought, for when Aristotle criticises communism, he does so not on the ground that it is unfair but on the ground that it would not in fact produce the unity desired. Plato's communism has, therefore, a strictly political purpose. The order of ideas is exactly the reverse of that which has mainly animated modern socialist utopias; he does not mean to use government to equalize wealth, but he equalizes wealth in order to remove a disturbing influence in government.

The same is true also of Plato's purpose in abolishing marriage, since he regards family affection, directed toward particular persons, as another potent rival to the state in competing for the loyalty of rulers. Anxiety for one's children is a form of self-seeking more insidious than the desire for property, and the training of children in private homes he regards as a poor preparation for the whole-souled devotion which the state has a right to demand. But in the case of marriage Plato had other purposes as well. He was appalled at the casualness of human mating, which, as he says, would not be tolerated in the breeding of any domestic animal. The improvement of the race demands a more controlled and a more selective type of union. Finally, the abolition of marriage was probably an implied criticism of the position of women in Athens, where her activities were summed up in keeping the house and rearing her children. To Plato this seemed to deny to the state the services of half its potential guardians. Moreover, he was unable to see that there is anything in the natural capacity of women that corresponds to the Athenian practice, since many women are as well qualified as men to take part in political or even military duties. The women of the guardian class will consequently share all the work of the men, which makes it necessary both that they shall receive the same education and be free from strictly domestic duties.

To a modern taste there is something a little startling about the coolly unsentimental way in which Plato argues from the breeding of domestic animals to the sexual relations of men and women. It is not that he regards sex casually, for the reverse is emphatically true; in fact, he demands a degree of control and of self-control that has never been realized among any large population. The point is rather that he carries out a line of thought relentlessly and with little regard for difficulties that are manifest to feeling even when they are not explicitly stated. The unity of the state is to be secured; property and family stand in the way; therefore property and marriage must go. There can be no doubt that here Plato spoke the authentic language of doctrinaire radicalism, which is prepared to follow the argument where it may lead. On the score of common sense Aristotle's answer left nothing to be said. It is possible, he pointed out, to unify a state to the point where it ceases to be a state. A family is one thing and a state is something different, and it is better that one should not try to ape the other.

EDUCATION

However much importance Plato attached to communism as a means for removing hindrances from the path of the statesman, it was not upon communism but upon education that he placed his main reliance. For education is the positive means by which the ruler can shape human nature in the right direction to produce a harmonious state. A modern reader cannot fail to be astonished at the amount of space devoted to education, at the meticulous care with which the effect of different studies is discussed, or at the way in which Plato frankly assumes that the state is first and foremost an educational institution. He himself called it "the one great thing"; if the citizens are well educated they will readily see through the difficulties that beset them and meet emergencies as they arise. So striking is the part played in Plato's ideal state by education that some have considered this to be the chief topic of the *Republic.* Rousseau said that the book was hardly a political work at all, but was the greatest work on education ever written. Obviously this was no accident but a logical result of the point of view from which the work was written. If virtue is knowledge, it can be taught, and the educational system to teach it is the one indispensable part of a good state From Plato's point of view, with a good system of education almost any improvement is possible; if education is neglected, it matters little what else the state does.

This degree of importance being conceded, it follows as a matter of course that the state cannot leave education to private demand and a commercialized source of supply but must itself provide the needed means, must see that citizens actually get the training they require, and must be sure that the education supplied is consonant with the harmony and well-being of the state. Plato's plan is therefore for a state-controlled system of compulsory education. His educational scheme falls naturally into two parts, the elementary education, which includes the training of young persons up to about the age of twenty and culminates in the beginning of military service,[18] and the higher education, intended for those selected persons of both sexes who are to be members of the two ruling classes and extending from the age of twenty to thirty-five. It is necessary to consider these two branches of education separately, as Plato himself does.

The plan for a compulsory, state-directed scheme of education was probably the most important innovation upon Athenian practice which Plato had to suggest, and his insistence upon it in the *Republic* may be interpreted as a running criticism upon the democratic custom of leaving every man to purchase for his children such education as he fancies or as the market affords. In the *Protagoras* he broadly implied that often they give less thought to training their children than to breaking a good colt. The Athenian exclusion of women from education falls under the same criticism. Since Plato believed that there was no difference in kind between the native capacities of boys and girls, he logically concluded that both should receive the same kind of instruction and that women should be eligible to the same offices as men. This, of course, is in no sense an argument for women's rights but merely a plan for making the whole supply of natural capacity available to the state. In view of the importance which education has in the state, it is extraordinary that Plato never discusses the training

[18] The compulsory military service of Athenian boys between the ages of eighteen and twenty was probably not yet in force when Plato wrote, though it was adopted not many years after, as Wilamowitz supposes, because of the *Laws* (*Aristoteles und Athen,* 1893, Vol. I, pp. 191 ff.).

of the artisans and does not even make clear how, if at all, they are to be included in the plan of elementary instruction. This fact illustrates again the surprising looseness and generality of his conclusions, since his unquestionable intention to promote promising children born of artisan parents seems to be wholly unworkable unless a competitive educational system made selection possible. On the other hand, he did not exclude the artisans and it is an open question whether those commentators, especially Zeller, are right who regard the omission as evidence of Plato's aristocratic contempt for the workers. It is at least true that he set no great store by general education, much as he relied on selective education for the more gifted youth.

The plan of elementary education sketched in the *Republic* was rather a reform of existing practice than the invention of a wholly new system. The reform may be said roughly to consist in combining the training usually given to the son of an Athenian gentleman with the state-controlled training given to a youthful Spartan and in revising pretty drastically the content of both. The curriculum was therefore divided into two parts, gymnastics for training the body and "music" for training the mind. By music Plato meant especially the study and interpretation of the masterpieces of poetry, as well as singing and playing the lyre. It is easy to exaggerate the influence of Sparta upon Plato's theory of education. Its most genuinely Spartan feature was the dedication of education exclusively to civic training. Its content was typically Athenian, and its purpose was dominated by the end of moral and intellectual cultivation. This is true even of gymnastics, which aims only secondarily at giving physical prowess. Gymnastics might be called a training of the mind through the body, as distinguished from direct training of the mind by music. It is meant to teach such soldierly qualities as self-control and courage, a physical keenness tempered by gentleness, as Plato himself defines it. Plato's plan of training represents therefore an Athenian, not a Spartan, conception of what constitutes an educated man. Any other conclusion would have been unthinkable for a philosopher who believed that the only salvation for states lay in the exercise of trained intelligence.

But while the content of elementary education was mainly poetry and the higher forms of literature, it cannot be said that

Plato desired particularly an esthetic appreciation of these works. He regarded them rather as a means of moral and religious education, somewhat in the way that Christians have regarded the Bible. For this reason he proposed not only to expurgate drastically the poets of the past, but to submit the poets of the future to censorship by the rulers of the state, in order that nothing of bad moral influence might fall into the hands of the young. For a man who was a consummate artist himself Plato had a singularly philistine conception of art. Or perhaps it would be truer to say that when he wrote about the moral purpose of art a certain puritanical, almost an ascetic, strain is apparent which seems in general out of character for a fourth-century Greek, though it is a strain which appears elsewhere in Plato. Philosophically this is connected with the very sharp contrast of mind and body, most evident in the *Phaedo,* which passed from Plato to Christianity. The poverty which Plato exacts of his rulers perhaps shows the same tendency, as do also the preference which he expressed for a very primitive (non-luxurious) sort of state at the beginning of his construction of the ideal state, and the suggestion accompanying the Myth of the Den that the philosopher may have to be forced to descend from a life of contemplation to take part in the affairs of man. Obviously the rule of philosophers might easily become a rule of the saints. Probably the closest analogue that has ever existed to Plato's ideal state is a monastic order.

Undoubtedly the most original as well as the most characteristic proposal in the *Republic* is the system of higher education, by which selected students are to be prepared, between the ages of twenty and thirty-five, for the highest positions in the guardian class. The relation of such a conception of higher education to the founding of the Academy and to the whole plan for a science and art of statemanship has been sufficiently stressed. Unless it be the Academy, there was nothing in Greek education upon which Plato could have built; the idea was entirely and characteristically his own. The higher education of the guardians was in purpose professional and for his curriculum Plato chose the only scientific studies known to him — mathematics, astronomy, and logic. Beyond doubt he believed that these most exact studies are the only adequate introduction to the study of philosophy, and there is little reason to doubt that he expected the philosopher's special object of study — the idea of the good — to yield results of comparable precision and exactness. For this reason the outline of the ideal state properly culminates in the plan for an education in which such studies would be fostered, in which new investigations would be undertaken and new knowledge placed at the disposal of rulers. In order to appreciate the greatness of such a conception it is not necessary to believe that Plato was right in hoping for a science of politics as exact as mathematics. It is hardly fair to demand more of him than that he should have tried to follow the lead which, in his own hands and those of his students, was creating in mathematics perhaps the truest monument to human intelligence.

THE OMISSION OF LAW

Few books that claim to be treatises on politics are so closely reasoned or so well co-ordinated as the *Republic*. None perhaps contains a line of thought so bold, so original, or so provocative. It is this quality which has made it a book for all time, from which later ages have drawn the most varied inspiration. For the same reason its greatest importance is general and diffused, rather than the result of specific imitation. The *Republic* was the greatest of utopias and the whole tribe of utopian philosophers followed it, but this phase of the book interested Plato so little that he was almost careless in carrying through the details of the plan. The true romance of the *Republic* is the romance of free intelligence, unbound by custom, untrammeled by human stupidity and self-will, able to direct the forces even of custom and stupidity themselves along the road to a rational life. The *Republic* is eternally the voice of the scholar, the profession of faith of the intellectual, who sees in knowledge and enlightenment the forces upon which social progress must rely. And indeed, who can say what are the limits of knowledge as a political force, and what society has yet brought to bear upon its problems the full power of trained scientific intelligence?

Yet it is impossible to avoid the conclusion that in the *Republic* Plato, like most intellectuals, simplified his problem beyond what the province of human relations will bear. An enlightened despotism — and Plato is right when he concludes that government by intelligence must be government by the few — cannot be merely assumed to be the last word in politics. The presumption that government is purely a matter of scientific knowledge, which the mass of men can resign into the hands of a few highly trained experts, leaves out of account the profound conviction that there are some decisions which a man must make for himself. This is no argument certainly for " muddling through " in cases where muddling means only the bungling choice of means for recognized ends. But Plato's argument assumes that the choice of ends is exactly comparable with the choice of means for an end already agreed upon, and this appears to be simply not true. His comparison of government to medicine, carried through to its farthest extreme, reduces politics to something that is not politics. For an adult, responsible human being, even though he be something less than a philosopher, is certainly not a sick man who requires nothing but expert care. Among other things he requires the privilege of taking care of himself and of acting responsibly with other like responsible human beings. A principle which reduces political subordination to one type, the relation of those who know to those who do not know, is simpler than the facts.

Not the least significant aspect of the *Republic* is what it omits, namely, law and the influence of public opinion. The omission is perfectly logical, for Plato's argument is unanswerable if his premise is granted. If rulers are qualified merely by their superior knowledge, either the judgment of public opinion upon their acts is irrelevant or else the pretense of consulting it is a mere piece of political Jesuitry by which the " discontent of the masses " is held in check. Similarly, it is as foolish to bind the hands of the philosopher-king with the rules of law as to force an expert physician to copy his prescription from the recipes in a medical textbook. But in reality the argument begs the question. For it assumes that public opinion is nothing but a muddled representation of what the ruler already knows more clearly, and that law has no meaning other than to give the least bungling rule that will fit an average case. And this is not a description but a caricature. As Aristotle said, the knowledge of a thing in use and by direct experience is different in kind from a scientist's knowledge about it, and presumably it is just this immediate experience of the pressures and burdens of government, of their bearing upon human interests and ends, that public opinion expresses. Presumably also the law contains not merely an average rule but also an accumulation of the results of applying intelligence to concrete cases and also an ideal of equitable treatment of like cases.

At all events the ideal state of the *Republic* was simply a denial of the political faith of the city-state, with its ideal of free citizenship and its hope that every man, within the limits of his powers, might be made a sharer in the duties and privileges of government. For this ideal was founded on the conviction that there is an ineradicable moral distinction between subjection to the law and subjection to the will of another human being, even though that other be a wise and benevolent despot. The difference is that the first is compatible with a sense of freedom and dignity while the second is not. The sense of his own freedom under the law was precisely the element in the city-state upon which the Greek set the highest moral valuation and which made the difference, to his mind, between a Greek and a barbarian. And this conviction, it must be acknowledged, has passed from the Greeks into the moral ideals of most European governments. It was expressed in the principle that " governments derive their just powers from the consent of the governed," and vague as the meaning of consent is, it is hard to imagine that the ideal itself will disappear. For this reason Plato's omission of law from his ideal state cannot be interpreted otherwise than as a failure to perceive a striking moral aspect of the very society which he desired to perfect.

At the same time it is clear that Plato could not have included the law as an essential element of the state without reconstructing the whole philosophical framework of which the ideal state is a part. Its omission was not a matter of caprice but a logical consequence of the philosophy itself. For if scientific knowledge has always the superiority to popular opinion which Plato supposes, there is no ground for that respect for law which would make it the sovereign power in the state. Law belongs to the class of convention; it rises through use and wont; it is the product of experience growing slowly from precedent to precedent. A wisdom which arises by rational insight into nature cannot abdicate its claims before the claim of law unless law itself has access to a kind of wisdom different from that which scientific reason possesses. If, then, Plato is wrong in trying to make the state over into an educational institution, if this puts a load upon education which it is not able to bear, the philosophical principles — especially the sharp contrast of nature and convention and of reason and experience — need to be reexamined. It is the suspicion that this might be the case, at least the sense that the theory in the *Republic* had not got to the bottom of all the problems involved, that led Plato in his later years to canvass the place of law in the state and to formulate in the *Laws* another type of state in which law rather than knowledge should be the ruling force.

CHAPTER IV

PLATO: THE *STATESMAN* AND THE *LAWS*

The later form of Plato's political philosophy, contained in the *Statesman* and the *Laws,* belongs a good many years after that contained in the *Republic.* The two later works show a resemblance and the theory which they contain is in marked contrast with that of the *Republic;* together they present the final results of Plato's reflection upon the problems of the city-state. The *Laws* was definitely a work of his old age, and all critics agree in finding in it evidence of declining powers, though this has very often been exaggerated. In respect to literary quality there is no comparison between the *Republic* and the *Laws.* The earlier work is conceded to be the greatest literary masterpiece in the whole range of philosophical writing. The *Laws,* on the other hand, is distinctly hard reading. It is rambling, even when all allowance is made for the liberties in this regard that the dialogue-form permitted; it is wordy and it is repetitious. The tradition that it lacked the author's final revision is plausible. It contains fine passages — passages which competent scholars consider as fine as any in Plato's works — but he has lost either the capacity for, or the interest in, sustained literary effect.

Because of its defects of style the *Laws* has been little read, as compared with the *Republic,* and there has perhaps been a tendency to confuse its decline in literary quality with a decline in intellectual power. This is certainly a mistake. The political philosophy of the *Laws* has not the bold sweep of speculative construction that is found in the *Republic,* but on the other hand in the later form of his theory Plato tried to come to grips with political actualities in a way that he never approached in the earlier work. This accounts in part for its lack of order; it is developed less upon a single train of thought and more upon the complexities of its subject-matter. The *Republic* is a book for all time, because the generality of its principles is almost timeless. But the later form of Plato's thought was more influential in the development of political philosophy by his successors in the ancient world. This is evident in the case of Aristotle, since it is the *Statesman* and the *Laws,* rather than the *Republic,* which formed the point of departure for the *Politics*. In respect to its influence on the discussion of specifically political questions in their theoretical aspects — such, for example, as the constitution of states, their political organization, and especially the theory of the so-called "mixed" state — it would be hard to exaggerate the importance of the *Laws*.

THE READMISSION OF LAW

The line of thought which Plato followed in the *Republic* yielded a theory in which everything was subordinated to the ideal of the philosopher-king, whose unique claim to authority is the fact that he alone knows what is good for men and states. The working-out of this line of reflection resulted in the exclusion of law altogether from the ideal state and the conception of the state as an educational institution only, in which the majority of the citizens are in a condition of permanent tutelage to the philosopher-ruler. This ran quite contrary to the deepest convictions of the Greeks about the moral value of freedom under the law and of participation by the citizens in the task of self-government. In this sense the first form of Plato's political theory was one-sided in its devotion to a single principle and inadequate to express the ideals of the city-state. This suspicion in the mind of its author was responsible for the direction which his later thought took. As the name of the dialogue indicates, the *Laws* was written in an attempt to restore law to the place which it occupied in the moral estimation of the Greeks and from which Plato had tried to remove it. The fundamental difference between the theory of the *Republic* and that of the *Laws* is that the ideal state of the former is a government by specially chosen and specially trained men, quite untrammeled by any general regulations, while the state sketched in the latter is a government in which law is supreme, ruler and subject alike being subject to it. But this difference implied drastic changes in all the underlying principles of government, more drastic changes than Plato succeeded in carrying through to a logical conclusion.

It is not uncommon to impute the change from the earlier

to the later form of his political theory to the disillusionment which he must have suffered as a consequence of the failure in his attempt to take part in the affairs of Syracuse, and it may well be that this experience brought home to Plato the actualities of political life in an especially poignant fashion. At the same time it is impossible to suppose that he went to Syracuse with the expectation of founding an ideal state ruled by a philosopher-king and then modified his views because he failed. Plato himself in the Seventh Letter says the contrary. In his advice to Dion's followers he says:

> Let not Sicily nor any city anywhere be subject to human masters — such is my doctrine — but to laws. Subjection is bad both for masters and for subjects, for themselves, for their children's children, and for all their posterity.[1]

And though this was written in 353, Plato says also that the plan which he recommends for a legislative commission to draw up new laws is akin to what he and Dion had intended to carry through together.[2] It is clear therefore that the venture at Syracuse was from the start designed to issue in a state under the forms of law. The legislative commission — a common device in Greece for formulating a code for a colony — is the literary device which offers the excuse for the *Laws*. And if the *Statesman* was written about the time of Plato's association with Dion (367–361), the discussion of the relative merits and demerits of law in government evidently marks a doubt in his mind about the feasibility of his conclusions in the *Republic*. It is safe to conclude, therefore, that Plato never made any sudden change in his convictions and that he was aware over a long period of years that the omission of law from the ideal state was a cardinal difficulty.

On the other hand, it is also a fact that Plato never definitely decided that the theory developed in the *Republic* was erroneous and had to be abandoned. He says repeatedly that his purpose in the *Laws* is to describe a second-best state and he sometimes puts this assertion into conjunction with his strongest statements about the importance of law. Without laws men "differ not at all from the most savage beasts," and yet if a competent ruler should arise, they would have no need to be ruled by laws, "for no law

[1] 334 c–d; L. A. Post's trans.

[2] 337 d.

or ordinance is mightier than knowledge."[3] To the end, therefore, Plato was convinced that in a truly ideal state the rule of pure reason, embodied in the philosopher-king and unhampered by law or custom, ought to prevail. Perhaps he was never very sure that such an ideal could be realized, but as time went on he became convinced that it could not. The state ruled by law was always a concession to the frailty of human nature and never something which he was willing to accept as having a right to stand on a parity with the ideal. Still, if the knowledge necessary to make the philosopher-king is unattainable, then Plato is clear that the common moral consciousness is right in believing that a government according to law is better than a government by men, rulers being what they are. The relation between the two theories is highly unsatisfactory; the ideal is logically irreproachable but not attainable in fact, while the second-best state is not impossible to attain but is shaky in respect to its credentials.

Now the truth is that this difficulty about the best and the second-best state grew directly out of a fundamental problem in Plato's philosophy which he had to face at many points during the latter part of his life and which he never succeeded in solving. It was not a question merely of making up his mind whether he did or did not have a high opinion of the law as an element in government. If the line of reasoning followed in the *Republic* (together with the general body of philosophical principles) was sound, there was no place in the state for law. Conversely, if a place had to be made for law, then there was nothing for it but to modify profoundly the whole philosophical structure and to admit principles which, to say the least, would greatly complicate it. The situation presented a dilemma and the fact that Plato himself saw and stated it is the true measure of his intellectual greatness. Probably no critic from Aristotle on has ever stated an objection against Plato which he could not have learned from reading Plato.

The exclusion of law from the ideal state resulted from the twofold fact that statesmanship is defined as an art depending upon an exact science and that this science is conceived, after the manner of mathematics, as a rational apprehension of the type to which factual knowledge contributes nothing, or at least nothing

[3] 874 e; 875 c.

beyond illustration. Behind this theory is the presumption that intelligence and perception are at least disparate and perhaps opposed; knowledge of the type is impossible so long as a thinker is hemmed in and restricted by all the insignificant variability that the senses show, just as true astronomy is impossible so long as the real motions of the planets are believed to be what they seem to be. On the side of ethics a knowledge of the good implies a like independence of the inclinations and appetites that are most closely associated with the body; this distinction of body and soul, which occasionally grows into an out-and-out opposition of a lower and higher nature, is a troublesome factor in Plato's thought, though he is never committed to all the implications of once for all accepting it. Now in the field of politics, the positive law — law as it actually exists and is practiced by men in an actual community — must be counted on the side of the senses and the inclinations. This was perhaps more obvious to a Greek than it is now, since Greek law was more completely a matter of use and wont than is the case where there exists a professional judiciary and the elements of a more or less scientific jurisprudence. But in any case the wisdom of the law is the wisdom of experience, feeling its way from precedent to precedent, making its rules to fit cases as they arise and never arriving at a very clear-cut knowledge of its principles. In short, it is quite different from what Plato conceived an art to be — the self-conscious application of scientifically ascertained causes to produce a clearly foreseen end. The problem was inherent in the contrast of nature and convention from which he started. For if the law belongs to convention (in Greek the words are the same) and cannot be ruled out as a factor in government, how can institutions ever be got on a rational basis where they are sure to realize the maximum natural good?

This is no antiquarian problem even today. How is a planned and managed society to make its peace with such enormous psychological forces as those represented by the genius of the Roman Law or the English Common Law? The ordinary business of life, its everyday valuations and expectations, goes on in a matrix of use and wont which changes indeed but changes slowly and which has never been planned or even envisaged as a whole, precisely because it is the matrix in which planning and valuation go on. In the mass it is not irrational but non-rational, though parts of it are continually coming to the front as precisely the irrational forces of mere convention or custom which stand in the way of any intelligent modification of the existing order. Is the customary basis of life — the habitual valuations and ideals by which men regulate their personal ambitions and their dealings with other men — to be interpreted as the enemy of intelligence and the great obstacle in the way of an art of living and governing? In effect this is the assumption behind the ideal state of the *Republic,* and that presumption forced Plato to become a rebel against the most cherished political ideal of the state which he desired to save. But if use and wont are not the great enemy, if convention is not the opposite of nature, how can the two be interpreted as supplementing one another? Can a man serve two masters? Or must he not hold to one and despise the other? Plato had learned from Socrates — and he never changed his mind — that he must hold to reason, but he became less certain that he must despise convention. And this is the problem of his later political theory, the problem of the place that must be assigned to law in the state.

THE GOLDEN CORD OF THE LAW

It is the emergence of this problem that can be seen in the *Statesman.* The dialogue is not indeed primarily a political work but an exercise in definition, the statesman being the subject-matter with which Plato chose to work, but the choice was hardly an accident. It is true also that the conclusion reached is that the statesman is a kind of artist whose chief qualification is knowledge. The figure used is that of the shepherd who has the control and management of a human flock, or more specifically the head of a household who directs his family for the good of all the members. This argument, it should be noted in passing, forms the starting-point of Aristotle's *Politics,* which opens with an attempt to show that the household and the state are distinct kinds of groups and that the family is therefore not a fair analogue for civil government. The issue is broader than it seems, and it became traditionally a bone of contention between the defenders of absolute government on the one hand and of liberal government on the other. The question, of course, is whether subjects shall be assumed to be dependent upon rulers, as children must be dependent upon their parents, or whether they shall be assumed to be responsible and self-governing. The important point, however, is not so much the sense in which Plato answered the question as the fact that he discussed it. The *Republic* had assumed that the statesman is an artist who has the right to rule because he alone knows what is good. In the *Statesman* the question is canvassed and the assumption of the *Republic* is made the subject of an elaborate definition.

The definition is backed up by a strong argument in favor of political absolutism, in case the ruler is really an artist at his work:

> Among forms of government that one is preeminently right and is the only real government, in which the rulers are found to be truly possessed of science, not merely to seem to possess it, whether they rule by law or without law, whether their subjects are willing or unwilling. . . .[4]

It is indeed a " hard saying " that government should be carried on without law, but law has to deal roughly with average cases and it is preposterous that a really expert ruler should thus have his hands bound, just as it is preposterous that a physician should be forced to prescribe by the book, if he knows enough about medicine to have written the book. The argument is that by which enlightened despotism has been justified from Plato's day to our own. If people are forced, " contrary to the written laws and inherited traditions, to do what is juster and nobler and better than what they did before,"[5] it is absurd to say that they are ill-used. For not many men can be expected to know what is good for the state. The assumption of the *Republic* is thus made explicit and its conclusion is fully accepted. In the ideal state the consent of subjects is no part of the ruler's equipment, since the subject's liberty according to the customs and traditions of the law can only work to hamper the free artistry of the ruler who knows his art.

And yet Plato is not quite willing to take all the consequences of his conclusion, or at least he is well aware that there is another side to the matter. This is apparent from the fact that his definition of the statesman draws a sharp distinction between the

[4] *Statesman,* 293 c; H. N. Fowler's trans.

[5] 296 c–d

king and the tyrant upon precisely the point at issue. A tyrant rules by force over unwilling subjects, while the true king or statesman has the art of making his rule voluntary.[6] There is no way in which the two positions can be made compatible, but it is apparent that Plato is not willing to abandon either. It is not unjust to force men to be better than their traditions, and yet he cannot conquer the Greek detestation of government that has to depend frankly upon force. The passage recalls the eloquent denunciation of tyranny and the tyrant in Books VIII and IX of the *Republic*, not least because of the tyrant's utter lack of piety and reverence toward all normal human relations.

The classification of states which Plato includes in the *Statesman* shows also that he has moved some distance from the position taken in the *Republic*. The two noticeable points are, first, that the ideal state is set off definitely from the class of possible states and, second, that democracy is given a more favorable place than in the *Republic*. In the earlier work, where little or no attention is given to an effort to classify, the ideal state is placed at the top and actual states are arranged as successive degenerations the one from the other. Thus timocracy, or the military state, is a corruption of the ideal state; oligarchy, or government by the rich, is a corruption of timocracy; democracy arises by the corruption of oligarchy; and tyranny, which is at the bottom of the list, is a corruption of democracy. In the *Statesman* a more elaborate classification is attempted. The ideal state, or a pure monarchy ruled by the philosopher-king, is "divine" and therefore too perfect for human affairs. It is distinguished from all actual states by the fact that in it knowledge rules and there is no need for law. It is the state of the *Republic* now definitely relegated to its place as a "model fixed in the Heavens" for human imitation but not for attainment. The classification of actual states is reached by crossing two classifications on each other. The traditional threefold division is subdivided in each of its parts into a lawless and a law-abiding form. In this way Plato reaches the sixfold classification, of three law-abiding states and their corresponding lawless corruptions, which Aristotle afterward adopted in the *Politics*. Thus the rule of one yields monarchy and tyranny; the rule of a few, aristocracy and oli-

[6] 276 e.

garchy; while for the first time Plato recognizes two types of democracy, a moderate and an extreme form. More striking still, he now makes democracy the best of the lawless states, though the worst of the law-abiding states. Both forms of democracy are therefore better than oligarchy. Evidently Plato has moved toward the position later taken in the *Laws,* in which the second-best state is described as an attempt to combine monarchy with democracy. It is a tacit admission that in the actual state the factors of popular assent and participation cannot be overlooked.

Plato's new theory, then, is to be frankly a second-best, involving the unsatisfactory contrast of the heavenly with the earthly city. The available stock of human intelligence is not great enough to make the philosopher-king a possibility. The humanly best solution, therefore, is to rely upon such wisdom as can be embodied in the law and upon the natural piety of men toward the wisdom of use and wont. The bitterness with which Plato accepts this compromise is apparent in the irony with which he remarks that now the execution of Socrates must be justified.[7] The state, with its inherited law, must be conceived as somehow an imitation of the heavenly city. At least there can be no doubt that law is better than caprice and the piety of the law-abiding ruler than the arbitrary will of a tyrant, a plutocracy, or a mob. Nor is it to be doubted that law is in general a civilizing force without which, human nature being what it is, man would be the worst of savage beasts. And yet this saying, so suggestive of Aristotle. is for Plato an act of faith for which his philosophy, in so far as it contrasts knowledge and opinion, can offer no real justification.

In one of the most striking passages of the *Laws* he does not hesitate to say that it is an act of faith:

> Let us suppose that each of us living creatures is an ingenious puppet of the gods, whether contrived by way of a toy of theirs or for some serious purpose — for as to that we know nothing; but this we do know, that these inward affections of ours, like sinews or cords, drag us along and, being opposed to each other, pull one against the other to opposite actions; and herein lies the dividing line between goodness and badness. For, as our argument declares, there is one of these pulling forces which every man should always follow and nohow leave hold of, counteracting thereby the pull of the other sinews: it is the leading-string, golden and

[7] *Statesman,* 299 b–c.

holy, of "calculation", entitled the public law of the State; and whereas the other cords are hard and steely and of every possible shape and semblance, this one is flexible and uniform, since it is of gold. With that most excellent leading string of the law we must needs co-operate always; for since calculation is excellent, but gentle rather than forceful, its leading-string needs helpers to ensure that the golden kind within us may vanquish the other kinds.[8]

The state of Plato's later theory, then, is to be held together by the "golden cord of the law" and this implies that its ethical principle of organization is different from that in the *Republic.* The law is now, so to speak, the surrogate for that reason which Plato had sought to make supreme in the ideal state and which he still regarded as the supreme force in nature. The chief virtue in the ideal state had accordingly been justice, the division of labor and the specialization of functions which puts every man in his proper place and "gives him his due" in the sense that he is enabled to bring all his faculties to their highest development and allowed to put them to the fullest use. In the state of the *Laws* wisdom is crystallized — perhaps one might even say frozen — in the law; no such flexible adjustment of the individual to the state is possible, but the regulations made by the law are assumed to be the best possible "on the whole." Consequently the supreme virtue in such a state is temperance or self-control, which means a law-abiding disposition or a spirit of respect toward the institutions of the state and a readiness to subordinate oneself to its lawful powers.

In the early books of the *Laws* Plato criticises pretty sharply those states, like Sparta, which have adopted the fourth virtue, courage, as the chief end of their training and so have made all civic virtue subordinate to military success. The estimate of Sparta is distinctly less favorable than that implied by the account of the timocracy in the *Republic* and is outspoken in its condemnation of the futility of war as an end for states. The end is harmony, both in domestic and foreign relations, and short of the perfect harmony which would issue from specialization of functions in the ideal state, its best guarantee is obedience to law. The state of the *Laws,* therefore, is a state constructed upon temperance or moderation as its chief virtue and seeking to achieve harmony by fostering the spirit of obedience to law.

[8] *Laws,* 644d–645a. R. G. Bury's trans.

THE MIXED STATE

It is evident, then, that Plato requires a principle of political organization designed to bring about this desired result, one which shall play the part for his later theory that the division of labor and the division of citizens into three classes had played in the *Republic*. In point of fact he discovered [9] a principle which passed into the later history of political theory and succeeded in gaining the adherence of the majority of thinkers who dealt with the problem of organization over a period of many centuries. This was the principle of the "mixed" state, which is designed to achieve harmony by a balance of forces, or by a combination of diverse principles of different tendency in such a way that the various tendencies shall offset each other. Stability is thus a resultant of opposite political strains. This principle is the ancestor of the famous separation of powers which Montesquieu was to rediscover centuries later as the essence of political wisdom embodied in the English constitution. In the case of Plato the mixed state sketched in the *Laws* is said to be a combination of the monarchic principle of wisdom with the democratic principle of freedom. It cannot be said, however, that he succeeded in making the combination which he had in mind or even that he always remained faithful to the ideal of the mixed constitution. Plato's allegiance was hopelessly divided and in the end he reverted to the more congenial line of thought already developed in the *Republic*.

Nevertheless, his manner of introducing and defending the principle of the mixed state was in the highest degree significant for the later development of the study. The *Laws* deals with actual states. Plato accordingly sees that the method of free logical or speculative construction which he had consciously adopted in the *Republic* is out of place. The problem concerns now the rise and fall of states and the actual rather than the ideal causes of their greatness and decay. In the third book of the *Laws*, therefore, Plato makes the first suggestion of the innumerable attempts at a kind of philosophic history, which shall trace the development of human civilization, mark its critical

[9] Possibly Plato did not discover the mixed state. See Aristotle's reference to other theories of mixed states (*Politics*, 1265 b 33) which may refer to earlier writers. The *Laws* is at any rate the earliest extant form of the theory.

stages, note the causes of progress and decay, and by analysis of the whole derive the laws of political stability which the wise statesman will observe in order to control and direct the changes that beset human society. He remarks, in a passage that suggests Aristotle, that human life is controlled by God, chance, and art, and art must co-operate with occasion.[10] It is true that Plato's mythological history contained nothing suggesting canons of accurate investigation. And yet this suggestion in the *Laws,* that the study of politics is to be attached to the history of civilization, had more possibilities of fruitfulness than the analytic and deductive method which governed the *Republic.* It formed the beginning of the authentic tradition of social studies and in particular of the mode of investigation which was to be taken up and perfected by Aristotle.

The plan of Plato's philosophic history of the race is not very clear-cut because it has more than one purpose and combines more than one principle. In the first place it utilizes what was doubtless the current Greek conception of the direction in which their own institutions had developed. In the beginning men lived as herdsmen in solitary families, lacking the arts that use the metals and also the social distinctions and many of the vices of a civilized life. Plato imagines it to have been a kind of " natural " age, in which men lived at peace since the causes of war that mark a more ambitious society had not yet appeared. Already in Plato the " state of nature " — that long-drawn myth of later political philosophers — has made its appearance. As men increase in numbers, and as agriculture grows and new manual arts are devised, families are gathered in villages, and finally statesmen arise who unite the villages into cities. It is this line of evolution that Aristotle used in the opening chapters of the *Politics* to mark off the distinctive function of the city as the bearer of the possibilities of a civilized life.

Plato has, however, at least two other purposes, the one somewhat incidental and the other more closely connected with the emergence of the mixed constitution. Incidentally he points his criticism of Sparta by tracing its downfall to its exclusively military organization, since " ignorance is the ruin of states." But what he mainly wishes to do is to show how the arbitrary power of monarchy and the tyranny that goes with it has been a cause

[10] *Laws,* 709 a–c.

of decay, as exemplified especially in Persia, and how an unbridled democracy at Athens ruined itself by an excess of liberty. Either might have been prosperous had it been content to remain moderate, to temper power with wisdom or liberty with order. It is the extreme in both cases that proved ruinous. Here then is the principle upon which a good state must be formed. If not a monarchy it must at least contain the principle of monarchy, the principle of wise and vigorous government subject to the law. But equally, if not a democracy, it must contain the democratic principle, the principle of freedom and of power shared by the masses, again of course subject to law.

The argument may be generalized. Men have admitted historically several claims to power — the right of parents over children, of age over youth, of freemen over slaves, of well-born over base-born, of strong over weak, and of rulers chosen by lot over other citizens [11] — some incompatible with others and hence the cause of factions. In Plato's opinion, of course, the only "natural" claim to power is that of the wise over the less wise, but this belongs to the ideal state. In the second-best state the problem is to select and combine these admitted claims in order to get on the whole the most law-abiding rule. In effect this means some approximation to wisdom by favoring age, good birth, or property, which may be taken perhaps as *prima facie* symptoms of better than average ability, with some concession to the lot for the sake of democracy. This Plato describes, not very aptly, as a mixture of monarchy and democracy.

The founding of a city to meet these specifications evidently requires attention to the underlying physical, economic, and social factors upon which the political constitution depends, since Plato's mixed state is not a balance of merely political forces. He begins accordingly by discussing the geographical situation of the city and the conditions of climate and soil which are most favorable. Here again he introduced what became a favorite and indeed almost a traditional part of the political theory of the philosophic historian, the influence of which was immediate, as may be seen in Aristotle's remarks preparatory to sketching the best state.[12] The best site is not, Plato thinks, upon the coast, because of the cor-

[11] 690 a–d. Cf. the similar list of claims in Aristotle's *Politics,* 3, 12–13, 1283 a 14 ff.

[12] *Politics,* Bk. VII (the traditional arrangement of books).

ruptions introduced by foreign commerce and more especially because foreign trade means a navy and a navy means power for the democratic masses. This view is built upon the history of Athens and the condemnation of the abuses of naval power is a companion piece to the earlier condemnation of the abuse of military power by Sparta. The ideal is a mainly agricultural community, on a soil that is self-sufficing but rugged, since this is the nurse of the hardiest and most temperate kind of population. This recalls the admiration which many theorists of the eighteenth century felt for the Swiss and shows the same distrust of commercialism and industrialism. He believes also that common race, language, law, and religion are desirable, provided they do not give too great a weight to custom.

SOCIAL AND POLITICAL INSTITUTIONS

Of all social institutions that which is politically most significant is the ownership and use of property. This had been Plato's view in the *Republic* — though there he had tried to make a state that would put education into first place — and it is doubly true where he is trying to deal with actual states. In the *Laws* he makes no secret of the fact that he still thinks communism the ideal arrangement but too good for human nature. Accordingly he concedes to human frailty the two chief points and leaves private ownership and the private family standing. He still retains his plan for the equal education of women and for their sharing in military and other civic duties, though he now says nothing of their holding office. Permanent monogamous unions — with an intolerable amount of public supervision — are accepted as the lawful form of marriage. With his concession of the private ownership of property Plato unites the most stringent regulation of its amount and use, following in general the regulations in effect at Sparta. The number of citizens is fixed at 5040 and the land is divided into an equal number of allotments, which pass by inheritance but can be neither divided nor alienated. The produce of the land is to be consumed in common at a public mess. Property in land is therefore equalized. The cultivation of the land is to be done by slaves, or possibly a more descriptive word would be serfs, who pay a rental in the form of a share of the produce.

Personal property, on the other hand, is permitted to be unequal but its amount is limited; that is, Plato would prohibit to any citizen the ownership of personal property in excess of four times the value of a lot of land.[13] The purpose is to exclude from the state those excessive differences between rich and poor which Greek experience had shown to be the chief causes of civic contention. In fact, however, the use of personal property is restricted as stringently as its amount. Citizens are not to be permitted to engage either in industry or trade, to have a craft or a business. All these activities, in so far as they cannot be dispensed with, are to be in the hands of resident aliens, who are freemen but not citizens. The state is to have only a token-currency (perhaps like the iron money of Sparta); the taking of interest for loans is prohibited; even the possession of gold and silver is forbidden. The citizen's "ownership" of his property is made by every restriction that Plato can think of strictly a Barmecide feast.

Analysis of the social arrangements described in the *Laws* shows that Plato has not really abandoned the division of labor which, in the *Republic,* he had offered as the basic principle of all society. He has merely offered a new division of labor, replacing the three classes of citizens in the earlier theory. The new division is broader in that it applies to the whole population of the state but it is just as exclusive. Thus agriculture is set down as the special function of the slaves, trade and industry as that of a class of freemen who are not citizens, while all political functions are the prerogative of the citizens. It is evident also that this plan, like the one in the *Republic,* gives up the fundamental problem instead of solving it. The problem is one of participation; as Pericles had said in the Funeral Oration, to find a way by which the mass of men can attend to their private affairs and yet have a hand in the public business. Nominally this is the solution that Plato is seeking, but what he arrives at is a state in which citizenship is frankly restricted to a class of privileged persons who can afford to turn over their private business — the sordid job of earning a living — to slaves and foreigners. And this is what the democracy of Pericles's day emphatically was not. The lines of class-cleavage in the *Republic* are less overtly significant than those in the *Laws,* for the former were lines between citizens, even if Plato

[13] 744 e.

had not thought the problem through very carefully. In the *Laws* the economic part of the population is not composed of citizens at all, and the state is therefore based frankly on economic privilege. This is none the less true because the kind of privilege that Plato prefers is security rather than wealth.

It is unnecessary to go into the details of the political constitution which Plato erects upon his social system. He provides for the main kinds of institutions — town-meeting, council, and magistrates — which existed in every Greek city. The point to be noted is the way in which he tries to carry out the idea of a mixed constitution. The mode of choosing magistrates is by election — according to Greek ideas an aristocratic method — and the duties of the general assembly of citizens are practically exhausted in these elections. The chief board of magistrates — called now by Plato the "guardians of the law" instead of guardians — is a group of thirty-seven, chosen by a threefold election consisting of a nominating ballot by which three hundred candidates are selected, a second ballot by which a hundred are selected from the three hundred, and a final ballot by which thirty-seven are selected from the hundred. But the most characteristic bit of electoral machinery is that by which the council of 360 is chosen. This plan is frankly devised to weight the votes of the better-to-do. The citizens are divided into four classes according to the amount of their personal property, a device which Plato adopted from the Athenian constitution introduced by Solon and antedating the democracy. Since personal property may not exceed four times the value of a lot of land, there are four property-classes, the lowest class being composed of those whose personal property does not exceed the value of their land, the next of those above this amount but not exceeding twice the value of their land, and so on. Presumably the lowest class would be much the most numerous, and the highest much the smallest, yet Plato assigns to each class one-fourth of the members of the council,[14] much as the former Prussian constitution allocated the choice of electors for members of the chamber of deputies to three groups each of which paid one-third of the taxes. He further weights the votes of the more opulent citizens by providing a penalty for non-voting which does not

[14] 744e; 756b–e; cf. the Servian Constitution at Rome described by Cicero, *Republic,* Bk. II, 22, 39–40.

apply to the lowest property-classes. The system of property-classes has an effect on the constitution also because certain offices can be filled only from the highest group or groups. In the case of the council there is only one concession to democracy: the number of persons elected is double the number of places to be filled and the final choice is made by lot.

It is rather incomprehensible that Plato should have regarded this constitution, the practically effective part of which is surely the system of property-classes, as a combination of monarchy and democracy. The concession to democracy was certainly very slight and was grudgingly made " on account of the discontent of the masses." Moreover, Aristotle, at least, thought that there was no element of monarchy whatever in the constitution described in the *Laws*. " It is nothing but oligarchy and democracy, leaning rather to oligarchy."[15] It is true that what Plato intends is to secure the preponderance of the law-abiding elements and an equality proportioned to merit, but the effect of his constitution is to give the preponderance to those who have the most personal property. Yet he himself says that a niggardly man, who is certainly not good, will probably be richer than a good man who likes spending for noble purposes.[16] It is not clear, therefore, that he would have agreed with Aristotle, who also used the property-qualification for his middle-class state, in believing that the well-to-do are on the average better than the poor. It is a fact also, as has been pointed out, that in the *Statesman* he places even the lawless democracy higher than the oligarchy. It is impossible to make Plato's plan of government square with his intentions. Apparently when he came to constitution-making he found that differences of property are overt and usable while differences of virtue are not.

EDUCATIONAL AND RELIGIOUS INSTITUTIONS

It is unnecessary to say much about Plato's later plan of education, which still occupies a great share of his attention in the *Laws*. The general outline of the curriculum, as including music and gymnastic, remains very similar to that in the *Republic;* his distrust of the poets still issues in the most rigorous censorship of literature and art; the education of women equally with men re-

[15] *Politics,* 2, 6; 1266 a 6.

[16] 743 a–b.

mains an important part of the plan; and the education of all citizens is still compulsory. The changes are chiefly that he gives more attention to the organization of education and, since the whole state is no longer an educational institution, that he is obliged to consider the articulation of the system of education with the rest of government. In respect to the first it is noteworthy that he now undertakes to outline a system of publicly regulated schools with paid teachers to provide a fully outlined course of instruction for the elementary and secondary grades. In respect to the relations of this system to the state, he makes the magistrate who has charge of the schools the chief of all the magistrates. The theory of education in the *Laws,* unlike that of the *Republic,* is the theory of a system of educational institutions.

A similar inclination to institutionalize appears in Plato's account of religion and its relation to the state. Perhaps it was a sign of old age that he should have showed so much more interest in religion, a subject which he had passed over with scarcely more than a reference in the *Republic.* Certainly the rather extended development of religious law in the tenth book of the *Laws,* while not without the impressiveness that goes with intense conviction, is the most lamentable thing that his genius produced. Religion, from the point of view of the *Laws,* must be subject to the regulation and supervision of the state, just as education is. Consequently Plato forbids any kind of private religious exercises and enacts that rites may be performed only in public temples and by authorized priests. In this he is influenced partly by his dislike of certain disorderly forms of religion to which, as he remarks, hysterical persons and especially women are prone, and partly by the feeling that a private religion withdraws men from their allegiance to the state. His regulation of religion does not stop with ceremonial. He has become convinced that religious belief is closely related to moral behavior or, more specifically, that certain forms of disbelief are definitely of an immoral tendency. Accordingly he thinks it necessary to provide religion with a kind of creed and the state with a law of heresy for the punishment of disbelievers. The creed is simple. What it forbids is atheism, of which Plato distinguishes three kinds: denial of the existence of the gods, denial that they concern themselves with human conduct, and the belief that they are easily placated for a sin committed. Imprisonment and, for the worst cases, death are the penalties attached to atheism. These proposals are strongly out of keeping with the practice of the Greeks and give to the *Laws* the bad pre-eminence of being the first reasoned defense of religious persecution.

The *Laws* closes on a note which is entirely out of keeping with the purpose which Plato has been following and with the state which he has sketched in accordance with that purpose. In the last few pages he adds to the state another institution, barely mentioned before, which not only fails to articulate in any way with the other institutions of the state but also contradicts the purpose of planning a state in which the law is supreme. This Plato calls the Nocturnal Council — a body composed of the ten eldest of the thirty-seven guardians, the director of education, and certain priests chosen specially for their virtue. This Council is quite outside the law and yet is given a power to control and direct all the legal institutions of the state. Its members are supposed to have the knowledge needed for the salvation of the state and Plato's final conclusion is that the Council must first be founded and the state placed in its hands. It is evident that the Nocturnal Council stands in the place of the philosopher-king of the *Republic* and that its inclusion in the *Laws* is a flagrant violation of loyalty to the second-best state. But it is not quite the philosopher-king. Coming as it does after the creation of a crime of heresy and a class of authorized priests there is a disagreeable flavor of clericalism about the Nocturnal Council which is heightened by the evidently religious nature of the wisdom which Plato imputes to its members.

THE *REPUBLIC* AND THE *LAWS*

If Plato's political philosophy be considered as a whole and in relation to the immediate development of the subject, the theory of the state contained in the *Republic* must be regarded as having made a false start. What the *Republic* supplied to the theory of the city-state was a consummate analysis of the most general principles underlying society — its nature as a mutual exchange of services in which human capacity is developed equally to the end of personal satisfaction and of achieving the highest type of social life. In the *Republic*, however, this conception was developed almost wholly in terms of the Socratic doctrine that virtue is knowledge of the good, and knowledge was conceived upon the analogy of the exact, deductive procedure of mathematics. For this reason Plato thought of the relation between rulers and subjects as a relation between the learned and the ignorant. This in turn resulted in eliminating law from the state, since there was no place in Plato's theory of knowledge at this stage of his thought for the gradual growth of wisdom through experience and custom. Yet the omission of law falsified the moral ideal of free citizenship which was the very essence of the city-state.

The effort in Plato's later philosophy to restore law to its place in the state was always in some degree half-hearted and inconclusive, as was indicated by the unsatisfactory compromise which made him describe the later version as only a second-best. The real difficulty was that the revision called for a complete reconstruction of his psychology to make a significant place for habit and of his theory of knowlege to make a place for experience and custom. Yet it was the study of the state in the *Laws* that suggested the nature of the revisions required. For here Plato turned to a really careful analysis of actual institutions and laws, and suggested the attachment of such studies to history. In the *Laws* also he suggested the principle of balance — of a mutual adjustment of claims and interests — as the proper means for forming a constitutional state. Far more than the abstract type-state of the *Republic,* this was a serious attack upon the problem of the city-state — the conciliation of the interests of property with the democratic interest represented by numbers. It was from these beginnings in the *Laws* that Aristotle started. Without abandoning the general principles stated in the *Republic,* which still provide the materials for his theory of the community, he adopted in almost every case the hints thrown out in the *Laws,* enriching them with more painstaking and more extensive examinations of the empirical and historical evidence. And in the general system of his philosophy Aristotle sought to provide a consistent body of logical principles to explain and justify the procedure which he followed.

SELECTED BIBLIOGRAPHY

" Greek Political Thought and Theory in the Fourth Century." By Ernest Barker. In the *Cambridge Ancient History,* Vol. VI (1927), ch. 16.

Greek Political Theory: Plato and his Predecessors. By Ernest Barker. 2nd ed. London, 1925. Chs. 6–17.

" Fact and Legend in the Biography of Plato." By George Boas. In the *Philos. Rev.,* Vol. LVII (1948), p. 439.

" The Athenian Philosophical Schools." By F. M. Cornford. In the *Cambridge Ancient History,* Vol. VI (1927), ch. 11.

The Laws of Plato. Ed. by E. B. England. 2 vols. Manchester, 1921. Introduction.

Plato and his Contemporaries: A Study in Fourth-century Life and Thought. By G. C. Field. London, 1930.

Greek Thinkers: A History of Ancient Philosophy. By Theodor Gomperz. Vol. III. Eng. trans. by G. G. Berry. New York, 1905. Book V, chs. 13, 17, 20.

Plato's Thought. By G. M. A. Grube. London, 1935. Ch. 8.

The Authorship of the Platonic Epistles. By R. Hackforth. Manchester, 1913.

Paideia: The Ideals of Greek Culture. By Werner Jaeger. Eng. trans. by Gilbert Highet. 3 vols. New York, 1939–44. Book IV.

Essays in Ancient and Modern Philosophy. By H. W. B. Joseph. Oxford, 1935. Chs. 1–5.

Knowledge and the Good in Plato's Republic. By H. W. B. Joseph. London, 1948.

Discovering Plato. By Alexandre Koyré. Eng. trans. by Leonora C. Rosenfield. New York, 1945.

Studies in the Platonic Epistles. By Glenn R. Morrow. Illinois Studies in Language and Literature. Urbana, Illinois, 1935.

" Plato and the Law of Nature." By Glenn R. Morrow. In *Essays in Political Theory.* Ed. by Milton R. Konvitz and Arthur E. Murphy. Ithaca, New York, 1948.

Lectures on the Republic of Plato. By Richard L. Nettleship. Ed. by Lord Charnwood. London, 1914.

The Open Society and its Enemies. By K. R. Popper. 2 vols. London, 1945. Vol. I.

The Essence of Plato's Philosophy. By Constantin Ritter. Eng. trans. by Adam Alles. London, 1933.

What Plato Said. By Paul Shorey. Chicago, 1933.

Plato, the Man and His Work. By A. E. Taylor. 3rd ed. New York, 1929.

CHAPTER V

ARISTOTLE: POLITICAL IDEALS

About the time when Plato was asked by Dion to undertake the venture in Syracuse for the education of the young Dionysius and the improvement of Syracusan government, the greatest of Plato's students joined the Academy. Aristotle was not an Athenian but a native of Stagira in Thrace, where he was born in 384. His father was a physician, which probably contributed to the prevailing interest in biological studies that Aristotle's work shows, and had been attached in that capacity to the Macedonian court. Aristotle was probably attracted to Plato's school in the first place because it was the best place in Greece to carry on advanced studies. Once there, he remained a member of the school as long as Plato lived — a period of twenty years — and his mind received indelibly the impression of Plato's teaching. Every page of his later philosophical writing bears witness to this connection. After Plato's death in 347 Aristotle left Athens and during the next twelve years was variously employed. To this period belongs the first of his independent writing. In 343 he became the instructor of the young prince Alexander of Macedon, but one looks in vain in his political writings for any effect of his Macedonian connection upon his ideas. He seems to have lacked the imagination necessary to see the revolutionary importance of Alexander's conquest of the East, with the consequent mingling of Greek and oriental civilization. The choice of such a policy was directly contrary to everything that he must have taught his royal pupil about politics. In 335 Aristotle opened his own School in Athens, the second of the four great philosophical Schools, and during the next twelve years most of his books were written, though they probably included work begun during the earlier period. Aristotle survived his great pupil by a year; he died in Euboea in 322, after leaving Athens to escape the anti-Macedonian disturbances that followed Alexander's death.

THE NEW SCIENCE OF POLITICS

The Aristotelian writings present a problem very different from that of Plato's Dialogues. His extant works, neglecting fragments of early popular writings, were for the most part not books completed and prepared for publication. They were used in connection with his teaching, though important parts of them were probably written before the Lyceum was opened. In fact, they were not published in their present form until four centuries after his death but remained the property of the School and were doubtless used by later instructors. It seems probable that the twelve years of Aristotle's life as head of the Lyceum were largely occupied in directing a number of extensive projects of research, shared by his students, such as the famous investigation of the constitutional history of a hundred and fifty-eight Greek cities, of which the *Constitution of Athens* (discovered in 1891) is the only surviving example. These researches, of which the study of the constitutions was only one, were mainly historical rather than philosophical; they were genuinely empirical investigations and in the light of them Aristotle from time to time made additions to the body of writings which he already had by him when the School was opened.

The great political treatise which goes by the name of the *Politics* cannot therefore be regarded as a finished book such as Aristotle would have produced had he been writing for a general public. It has been doubted, in fact, whether Aristotle himself arranged it in its existing form or whether it may not have been put together by his editors from several bodies of manuscript.[1] The difficulties lie upon the surface and could hardly be missed by any attentive reader, but the solution of them is another matter. Later editors have shifted the books about in an attempt to improve the order, but no rearrangement of the text will make a unified and finished work of the *Politics*.[2] Thus Book VII, in

1 Thus, for example, Ernest Barker (*Political Thought of Plato and Aristotle,* 1906, p. 259) believes that notes of three distinct sets of lectures are combined in the *Politics,* while W. D. Ross (*Aristotle,* 1924, p. 236) calls it a "conflation of five separate treatises."

2 References to the books by number mean the order of the manuscript; so many experiments have been tried that, beyond Books I to III, the numbers are very ambiguous. There is a table giving the order in the principal editions in Immisch's Teubner text, p. vii.

which Aristotle takes up the construction of an ideal state, apparently goes on from the end of Book III, while Books IV, V, and VI, dealing with actual and not ideal states, form a group by themselves. For this reason Books VII and VIII are usually put after Book III, and Books IV to VI at the end; yet there is a connection between the discussion of monarchy near the end of Book III and the discussion of oligarchy and democracy in Book IV. So far as the reading of the text goes, there are difficulties in any order, and probably Ross is right when he says that the reader might as well take it as it stands traditionally.

The best hypothesis which has so far been advanced to explain the *Politics* is that by Werner Jaeger [3] and while this is not demonstrated, it at least offers a reasonable way of envisaging the development of Aristotle's political philosophy. According to Jaeger the *Politics* as it stands is Aristotle's work and not that of an editor. But the text belongs to two stages and therefore falls into two main strata. There is, in the first place, a work dealing with the ideal state, and with previous theories of it. This includes Book II, an historical study of earlier theories and chiefly notable for the criticism of Plato; Book III, a study of the nature of the state and of citizenship but intended to be introductory to a theory of the ideal state; and Books VII and VIII on the construction of the ideal state. These four books Jaeger assigns to a date not long after Aristotle's departure from Athens following the death of Plato. There is, in the second place, a study of actual states, mainly democracy and oligarchy, together with the causes of their decay and the best means of giving them stability, which makes up Books IV, V, and VI. This Jaeger assigns to a date after the opening of the Lyceum,[4] supposing that it represents a return to political philosophy after or during the investigation of the hundred and fifty-eight constitutions. Books IV, V, and VI were inserted by Aristotle in the middle of the original draft, and result in enlarging the work on the ideal state into a general treatise on political science. Finally, Jaeger believes, Book I was written last of all as a general introduction to the enlarged treatise, though it was joined hastily and imperfectly to Book II.

[3] *Aristoteles* (1923); Eng. trans. by Richard Robinson, 1934, ch. 10.

[4] Note the reference to the murder of Philip of Macedon in 336; 5, 10; 1311 b 2. He puts the collection of constitutions between 329 and 326.

According to Jaeger's conception, therefore, the *Politics* was intended to form a treatise on a single science, but was never subjected to the rewriting that would have been necessary to bring the parts, written as they were over a period of perhaps fifteen years, into a well-unified form.

If this hypothesis be correct, the *Politics* represents two stages in Aristotle's thought which are distinguished by the distance that he has travelled in emancipating himself from the influence of Plato, or perhaps it would be better to say, in striking out a line of thought and investigation characteristically his own. In the first he still thinks of political philosophy as the construction of an ideal state upon lines already laid down especially in the *Statesman* and the *Laws*. Plato's prevailingly ethical interest in the subject still predominates; the good man and the good citizen are one and the same, or at all events they ought to be, and the end of the state is to produce the highest moral type of human being. It is not to be supposed that Aristotle consciously abandoned this point of view, since the treatise on the ideal state was left standing as an important part of the *Politics*. At some date not far removed from the opening of the Lyceum, however, he conceived a science or art of politics on a much larger scale. The new science was to be general; that is, it should deal with actual as well as ideal forms of government and it should teach the art of governing and organizing states of any sort in any desired manner. This new general science of politics, therefore, was not only empirical and descriptive, but even in some respects independent of any ethical purpose, since a statesman might need to be expert in governing even a bad state. The whole science of politics, according to the new idea, included the knowledge both of the political good, relative as well as absolute, and also of political mechanics employed perhaps for an inferior or even a bad end. This enlargement of the definition of political philosophy is Aristotle's most characteristic conception.

The description of Aristotle's political theory can therefore be advantageously divided into two parts. The source for the first is Books II, III, VII, and VIII. The questions to be considered here are the relations of his thought to Plato's in his first attempt at an independent philosophy and especially the suggestions, in so far as they can be discerned, that presage the final step which took him quite beyond Plato. The source for the second is Books IV, V, and VI, and the questions here are his final thoughts on the kinds of government, his conception of the social forces behind political organization and change, and his description of the means with which the statesman has to work. Finally, in the opening chapters of Book I he said his last word about the great philosophical problem upon which both he and Plato had been engaged, the distinction of nature from appearance or convention, and suggested the conception of nature to which his ripest political reflection led him.

THE KINDS OF RULE

True to a custom which he follows in works on other subjects, Aristotle begins his book on the ideal state with a survey of what other writers have written on the subject. The point of greatest interest here is his criticism of Plato, since one would expect to find the key to the differences of which he was conscious between himself and his master. The result is rather disappointing. So far as the *Republic* is concerned he is emphatic in his objections to the abolition of private property and the family. These objections have already been referred to and nothing further need be said about them. His criticism of the *Laws*, on the other hand, is difficult to interpret. It refers largely to matters of detail and moreover it is sometimes astonishingly inaccurate. This is surprising in view of the fact that, in his construction of the ideal state, almost every subject discussed is suggested by the *Laws* and there are many parallelisms (even verbal) in small points.[5] Evidently when the passage was written he did not regard it as worth while to analyze the *Laws* and state his dissent from its principles. The tone of his criticism suggests what may be the reason. Apparently he felt about both Plato's political works, and perhaps about his philosophy in general, that they are brilliant and suggestive but too radical and speculative. They are, as he says, never commonplace and always original. But the query in his mind seems to be, Are they reliable? The general ground of his dissent is stated in a dryly humorous remark which sums up better than pages of comment the fundamental difference of temper between Aristotle and his master:

[5] A considerable list of parallels is given by E. Barker, *Greek Political Theory, Plato and his Predecessors* (1925), pp. 380 ff.

Let us remember that we should not disregard the experience of ages; in the multitude of years these things, if they were good, would certainly not have been unknown; for almost everything has been found out, although sometimes they are not put together; in other cases men do not use the knowledge which they have.[6]

In short, Aristotle's is the soberer if less original genius. He feels that too great a departure from common experience probably has a fallacy in it somewhere, even though it appears to be irreproachably logical.

One essential difference between Plato and Aristotle is apparent in all parts of the *Politics* that have to do with the ideal state: what Aristotle calls the ideal state is always Plato's second-best state. The rejection of communism just referred to shows that the ideal state of the *Republic* was never entertained by Aristotle, even as an ideal. His ideal was always constitutional and never despotic rule, even though it were the enlightened despotism of the philosopher-king. Consequently, Aristotle accepted from the start the point of view of the *Laws*, that in any good state the law must be the ultimate sovereign and not any person whatsoever. He accepted this not as a concession to human frailty but as an intrinsic part of good government and therefore as a characteristic of an ideal state. The relation of the constitutional ruler to his subjects is different in kind from any other sort of subjection because it is consistent with both parties remaining free men, and for this reason it requires a degree of moral equality or likeness of kind between them, despite the undoubted differences which must exist.

This distinction between different kinds of rule is so important for Aristotle that he returns to it again and again, and it had evidently been an object of early interest with him.[7] The authority of a constitutional ruler over his subjects is quite different from that of a master over his slaves, because the slave is presumed to be different in nature, a lower sort of being who is inferior from birth and incapable of ruling himself. Aristotle admits, to be sure, that this is often not true in fact, but at all events it is the theory upon which slavery is justified. For this reason the slave

[6] *Politics,* 2, 5; 1264 a 1 ff. (Jowett's trans).

[7] Cf. *Politics* 3, 6; in 1278 b 31 he refers to his early popular dialogues, while only a few lines before, 1278 b 18, he refers to the discussion of household authority in Book I, though the subject is evidently the same.

is the master's living tool, to be kindly used, but still used for the master's good. Political authority differs also from that which a man exercises over his wife and children, though the latter is certainly for the good of the dependent as well as for that of the father. The failure to distinguish household from political authority Aristotle regarded as one of Plato's serious errors, since it led him in the *Statesman* to assert that the state is like the family only larger. The child is not an adult and even though he is ruled for his own good, he is still not in a position of equality. The case of the wife is not so clear but apparently Aristotle believed that women were too different in nature from men (though not necessarily inferior) to stand with them on the peculiar footing of equality which alone permits the political relationship. The ideal state, therefore, if not a democracy, at least includes a democratic element. It is "a community of equals, aiming at the best life possible"[8] and it ceases to be constitutional or genuinely political if the discrepancy between its members is so great that they cease to have the same "virtue."

THE RULE OF LAW

Constitutional rule in the state is closely connected, also, with the question whether it is better to be ruled by the best man or the best laws, since a government which consults the good of its subjects is also government in accordance with law. Accordingly the supremacy of law is accepted by Aristotle as a mark of a good state and not merely as an unfortunate necessity. His argument for this position is that Plato is mistaken when, in the *Statesman,* he makes government by law and government by wise rulers alternatives. Even the wisest ruler cannot dispense with law because the law has an impersonal quality which no man, however good, can attain. The law is "reason unaffected by desire";[9] and the analogy which Plato was accustomed to draw between politics and medicine is wrong. The political relationship, if it is to permit of freedom, must be of such a kind that the subject does not wholly resign his judgment and his responsibility, and this is possible provided both the ruler and the ruled have a legal status. The "passionless" authority of law does not take the place of a magistrate, but it gives to the magistrate's authority a moral

[8] 7, 8; 1328 a 36. [9] 3, 16; 1287 a 32.

quality which it could not otherwise have. Constitutional rule is consistent with the dignity of the subject, whereas a personal or despotic rule is not. The constitutional ruler, as Aristotle sometimes says, rules over willing subjects; he rules by consent and is quite different from a dictator. The precise moral property which Aristotle means to point out is as elusive as the consent of the governed in modern theories, but no one can doubt its reality.

Constitutional rule as Aristotle understands the expression has three main elements: First, it is rule in the public or general interest as distinguished from a factional or tyrannous rule in the interest of a single class or individual. Second, it is lawful rule in the sense that government is carried on by general regulations and not by arbitrary decrees, and also in the vaguer sense that the government does not flout standing customs and conventions of the constitution. Third, constitutional government means the government of willing subjects as distinguished from a despotism that is supported merely by force. Though these three properties of constitutional rule are clearly mentioned by Aristotle, he nowhere examines them systematically, to find out either if the list is complete or what is the relationship between the three. He was aware that one of the properties might be absent from a government while the others were present; for example, a tyrant may act despotically and yet in the public interest, or a lawful government may be unjustly favorable to one class. But constitutional rule was never really defined by Aristotle.

The emphasis upon constitutional rule is the consequence of taking seriously the suggestion in the *Laws* that law may be regarded not as a makeshift but as an indispensable condition of a moral and civilized life. An introductory passage in the *Politics* was evidently written with one of Plato's remarkable utterances in mind: "Man, when perfected, is the best of animals, but, when separated from law and justice, he is the worst of all."[10] But this view of law is impossible unless it be supposed that there is a gradual increase of wisdom through the accumulation of experience and that this growing stock of social intelligence is embedded in law and custom. The point is of fundamental philosophical importance because if wisdom and knowledge are the prerogatives of scholars, the experience of the ordinary man never

[10] 1, 2; 1253 a 31 ff. Cf. *Laws*, 874 e.

brings him more than unreliable opinion, and Plato's reasoning is unanswerable. To put the case the other way about, if Plato's philosophy is mistaken in neglecting the experience of the ages, then that experience must represent a genuine growth in knowledge, though this growth registers itself in custom rather than in science and is produced by common sense rather than by learning. Public opinion must be admitted to be not only an unavoidable force but also, up to a point, a justifiable standard in politics.

It is possible to argue, Aristotle says, that in the making of law the collective wisdom of a people is superior to that of even the wisest lawgiver. He develops the argument still farther in connection with his discussion of the political ability of popular assemblies. Men in the mass supplement each other in a singular fashion, so that by one understanding one part of a question and another another part, they all together get around the whole subject. He illustrates this by the assertion (perhaps not quite obvious) that popular taste in the arts is reliable in the long run, while experts make notorious blunders at the moment. To somewhat the same effect is his marked preference for customary as compared with written law. He is even prepared to admit that possibly Plato's plan for abolishing law would be an advantage if only the written law were at stake. But he holds it clearly impossible that the knowledge of the wisest ruler can be better than the customary law. The rigid distinction between nature and convention, with the extreme intellectualism or rationalism to which this distinction had committed Socrates and Plato, was thus broken down by Aristotle. The reason of the statesman in a good state cannot be detached from the reason embodied in the law and custom of the community he rules.

At the same time, Aristotle's political ideal was quite at one with Plato's in setting up an ethical purpose as the chief end of the state. He never changed his opinion on this point, even after he had enlarged his definition of political philosophy to include a practical manual for statesmen who have to do with governments which are very far from ideal. The real purpose of a state ought to include the moral improvement of its citizens, because it ought to be an association of men living together to achieve the best possible life. This is the " idea " or meaning of a state; Aristotle's ultimate effort at a definition turns upon his conviction that the state alone is "self-sufficing," in the sense that it alone provides all the conditions within which the highest type of moral development can take place. Like Plato, also, Aristotle confined his ideal to the city-state, the small and intimate group in which the life of the state is the social life of its citizens, overlapping the interests of family, of religion, and of friendly personal intercourse. Even in his examination of actual states there is nothing to show that his connection with Philip and Alexander enabled him to perceive the political significance of the Macedonian conquest of the Greek world and of the East. The political failure of the city-state did not, in his eyes, take from it the character of an ideal.

Aristotle's theory of political ideals, therefore, stands upon ground which he had clearly occupied because of his association with Plato. It follows from an effort to adopt and take seriously the chief elements of the theory developed in the *Statesman* and the *Laws,* with such changes as were required to make that theory clear and self-consistent. This applies particularly to the distinctive feature of Plato's later theory, that law must be treated as an indispensable constituent of the state. This being true, it is necessary to take account of the conditions of human nature which make it true. Law must be admitted to include real wisdom, and the accumulation of such wisdom in social custom must be allowed for. And the moral requirements which make law necessary must be incorporated as part of the moral ideals of the state. True political rule must therefore include the factors of subordination to law and of freedom and consent on the part of its subjects. These become factors not of a second-best state but of the ideal state itself.

About Aristotle's ideal state itself not much need be said. In truth his avowed purpose to construct an ideal state never eventuated, and the reader feels that the task was really little to his taste. What he does is to write a book not on an ideal state but upon the ideals of the state. The sketch of an ideal state, begun in Books VII and VIII, was apparently never finished, which is significant, especially if it be correct to suppose that these books belong to the earlier draft of the *Politics.* The good life requires conditions both physical and mental, and it is upon these that Aristotle expends his attention. The list of conditions is derived from the *Laws*. It includes specifications regarding the population needed, both its amount and character, the territory most suitable in size, nature, and situation. It is not the case that Aristotle always agrees with Plato. He is distinctly more favorable to a situation on or near the sea, for example, but the differences are matters of detail, and the list of relevant conditions is substantially that which Plato had proposed. Aside from physical conditions of the good life, the most important force in molding citizens is, for Aristotle as for Plato, a compulsory system of education. In his general theory of education Aristotle differs from Plato, as might be expected, in allowing greater weight to the formation of good habits. Thus he places habit between nature and reason among the three things which make men virtuous. Such a change was necessary in view of the importance which custom must have in a state subject to law. Aristotle's discussion is wholly devoted to liberal education and shows, far more than Plato's, an actual contempt for the useful. A plan of higher education such as had formed so notable a part of the *Republic* is conspicuous by its absence — an omission which may of course be due to the fact that the book is unfinished. The government of the ideal state also suggests the *Laws*. Property is to be privately owned but used in common. The soil is to be tilled by slaves, and artisans are to be excluded from citizenship on the ground that virtue is impossible for men whose time is consumed in manual labor.

CONFLICT OF THE IDEAL AND THE ACTUAL

So far Aristotle's political ideals have been outlined without raising any questions about the discrepancies and difficulties that would be encountered if these ideals were brought into relation with the actual institutions and practices of cities. The ideal is in itself almost as deductive as Plato's and apparently it had been formed by a kind of dialectical analysis of the defects of the earlier theory. But it is obvious that discrepancies with practice and with ends actually pursued in government are much more serious for Aristotle than for Plato. The latter had never supposed that an ideal need be embodied in practice to be valid, and he had never allowed to custom any such claim to wisdom as Aristotle's theory required. If facts fail to square with ideal truth, Plato could always say, like the mathematician or the mystic, so much the worse for facts. Aristotle, with a heavy obligation to common sense and the wisdom of the ages, is in no position to be so radical. He might be reformist but never revolutionary. The whole bent and bias of his thought must be toward the view that the ideal, while conceded to be an effective force, must still be a force within the actual current of affairs and not dead against it. The wisdom inherent in custom must, so to speak, be a guiding principle that takes advantage of such plasticity as actual conditions include to lift them gradually to a better conformation. This is the view of nature which Aristotle finally evolved as a result of his reflection upon both social and biological problems.

That Aristotle was by no means at peace with this problem, even when he wrote the treatise on the ideal state, is written large in the complexities of Book III, in which the crucial questions of the whole work are discussed. The conclusion of the book shows that it was designed as an introduction to an ideal state. Books VII and VIII, however, show that Aristotle found the carrying out of this project so unsatisfactory that he never completed it, and when the first draft was enlarged, it was not by proceeding with the sketch of the ideal state but by the insertion of Books IV to VI. These are conspicuously realistic in their purpose and tone but carry forward lines of thought that are started in Book III. It is safe to conclude that the construction of an ideal state became less and less congenial to Aristotle's mode of thought as he grew older, and also that he finally found in Book III an introduction to a line of investigation which he had not originally intended to pursue. This conclusion is borne out by the reading of Book III itself. Its complexities are due, in part at least, to the fact that an introduction to the ideal state involves, to Aristotle's mind, a rather extended study of existing kinds of states. Often he is evidently more interested in the empirical study than in the purpose that he had set himself. In short, the reasons which led Aristotle to insert Books IV to VI after Book III were sound, though presumably they were not the reasons which led him to write Book III in the first place. The plan outgrew its original scope, but it grew from interests that were present at the start.

The general nature of the difficulty which Aristotle confronts is not difficult to see. The political ideal which came to him from Plato presumed that city and citizen are strictly correlative terms. This accounts for three questions which he places at the opening of Book III: What is a state? Who is a citizen? Is the virtue of a good man the same as the virtue of a good citizen? A state is an association of men for the sake of the best moral life. The type of life which a group of men will live in common depends upon what kind of men they are and what ends they design to realize, and reciprocally the end of the state will determine who can be members of it and what kind of life they can individually live. From this point of view a constitution is, as Aristotle says, an arrangement of citizens, or, as he says elsewhere, a kind of life, and a form of government is the expression of the kind of life which the state is designed to foster. The ethical nature of the state not only dominates but, so to speak, completely overlaps its political and legal nature. Thus Aristotle concludes that a state lasts only so long as its form of government endures, since a change in form of government would signify a change in the constitution or the underlying " kind of life " that the citizens are trying to realize. Law, constitution, state, form of government all tend to coalesce, since from a moral point of view they are all equally relative to the purpose which causes the association to exist.

In so far as the object is to formulate an ideal state, this is not an insuperable objection. For such a state would be dominated by the highest possible kind of life, and Plato, at least, had supposed that an understanding of the idea of the good would show what this is. But to arrive at the idea of the good first and then to use this as a standard for criticising and evaluating actual lives and actual states, was just what made Aristotle despair. If, on the other hand, one begins with the observation and description of actual states, distinctions evidently have to be made. The good man and the good citizen cannot be quite identical, as Aristotle points out, except in an ideal state. For unless the purposes of the state are the best possible, their realization will require a kind of life in the citizens which falls below the best possible. In actual states there must be different kinds of citizens with different kinds of " virtue." Similarly, when Aristotle defines the citizen as one who is eligible to take part in the assembly and to serve on juries — a definition based upon Athenian practice — he is obliged to point out at once that the definition will not fit any but a democratic state. Or again, when he concludes that the identity of the state changes with its form of government, he has to add a warning that the new state is not therefore justified in defaulting the debts and other obligations contracted by the previous state. Distinctions must in practice be made. A constitution is not only a way of life for the citizens but also an organization of officers to carry on public business, and therefore its political aspects cannot be forthwith identified with its ethical purpose. Merely to observe these complexities is to feel a difficulty about the construction of an ideal state to serve as a standard for them all.

A similar sense of the complexities of his problem is apparent when Aristotle passes on to discuss the classification of forms of government. Here he adopts the sixfold classification already used by Plato in the *Statesman*. Having distinguished constitutional from despotic rule by the principle that the former is for the good of all and the latter for the good of the ruling class only, he crosses this division upon the traditional threefold classification and thus gets a group of three true (or constitutional) states — monarchy, aristocracy, and moderate democracy (polity) — and three perverted (or despotic) states — tyranny, oligarchy, and extreme democracy or mob-rule. The only difference between Plato's treatment and Aristotle's — and it appears to be unimportant — is that the former describes his true states as law-abiding while the latter describes them as governed for the general good. In view of his analysis of what constitutional government means, Aristotle must have thought that the two descriptions came to nearly the same thing. No sooner does he complete the sixfold classification, however, than he points out that there are serious difficulties about it. The first of these is that the popular classification by the number of rulers is superficial and does not say, except by accident, what those who use it mean. What everybody means by an oligarchy is a government by the rich, just as a democracy is a government by the poor. It is true that there are many poor and few rich, but this does not make the relative numbers descriptive of the two kinds of state. The essence of the matter is that there are two distinct claims to power, one based upon the rights of property and the other upon the welfare of the greater number of human beings.

CONFLICTING CLAIMS TO POWER

This correction of the formal classification carries Aristotle a long way, for it raises the question, What are the justifiable claims to power in the state? And if there are more than one, how can they be adjusted to each other in such a way as to save them all? Similar questions, as has been said, had already presented themselves to Plato.[11] These questions, be it noted, do not really concern an ideal state — and Plato had not supposed that they did — but the relative merits of actual states, and the relative claims of various classes in the same state. Wisdom and virtue might be said to have an absolute claim to power; at least Plato had thought so and Aristotle did not deny it. But this point is academic. The dispute is not about a general moral principle but about the way to approximate it in practice. Everyone will admit, Aristotle says, that the state ought to realize the largest measure of justice possible and also that justice means some kind of equality. But does equality mean that everybody is to count for one and nobody for more than one, as the democrat supposes? Or does it mean that a man with large property-interests and perhaps a good social position and education ought to count for more than one, as the oligarch believes? Granted that government ought to be carried on by wise and virtuous rulers, where must you lodge power to get wisdom and virtue, or at least the best available approximation to them?

When the question is put in this way Aristotle immediately perceives that a relative question requires a relative answer. He shows easily enough that wealth has no absolute moral claim to power, for the state is not a trading company or a contract, as Lycophron the Sophist had said. It is easy to show also that counting everybody for one is at most a convenient fiction. But on the other hand, can it be said that property has no rights? Aristotle was convinced that Plato's venture in that direction had proved disastrous, and in any case, as he points out, a plundering democracy is no more honest than an exploiting oligarchy. Property has moral consequences and for this reason is too important to be left entirely out of the picture by anyone who is trying to be realistic. Good birth, good education, good associations, leisure

[11] *Laws,* 690 a ff.

— and these go in some degree with wealth — are not negligible as claims to political influence. The democrat also has something to say relatively for his claim. The number of persons affected surely is a moral consideration in estimating political consequences, and moreover a sober public opinion, Aristotle is convinced, often is right where professedly wise persons are wrong. The upshot of the discussion is that there are objections against every claim to power that can be advanced and also that all the usual claims have a certain amount of merit. It is hard to see just how this conclusion can advance the construction of an ideal state, but it is also obvious that Aristotle has treated a perennial dispute in political ethics with incomparable common sense. In fact, this examination of the conflicting claims of democracy and oligarchy led Aristotle later to lay aside the search for an ideal state and to take up the more modest problem of the best form of government attainable by most states.

The conclusion that no class has an absolute claim to power re-enforces the principle that the law must be supreme, since its impersonal authority is less subject to passion than men can claim to be. But Aristotle recognizes that even this, one of his most deeply-held convictions, cannot be asserted quite absolutely. For the law is relative to the constitution and consequently a bad state will be likely to have bad laws. Legality itself then is only a relative guarantee of goodness, better than force or personal power, but quite possibly bad. A good state must be ruled according to law but this is not the same as saying that a state ruled according to law is good.

Apparently Aristotle believed that monarchy and aristocracy alone have any claim to be regarded as ideal states. He has very little to say about aristocracy but he treats monarchy at some length. It is precisely this discussion of a supposedly ideal state that shows clearest how little he has to say on the subject and connects most clearly with the quite realistic rediscussion of democracy and oligarchy placed in Book IV. The monarchy ought theoretically to be the best form of government if it be assumed that a wise and virtuous king can be found. Plato's philosopher-king would come nearest to having an absolute claim to his power. But then, he would be a god among men. To allow other men to make law for a mortal god would be ridiculous and to ostracize him would not be quite just. The only alternative is to allow him to rule. And yet Aristotle is not perfectly certain that even such a man has an indefeasible right to rule. So much importance does he attach to the equality which ought to exist between citizens of the same state that he questions whether even perfect virtue would be an exception. The problem of equality concerns every form of government, good as well as perverted. Still, Aristotle is willing to admit that monarchy would be suitable for a society in which one family was far superior to all others in virtue and political skill. The truth is that the ideal monarchy is for Aristotle perfectly academic. Except for the authority of Plato he probably would never have mentioned it. He remarks that monarchy according to law is not really a constitution at all, and if this be taken literally, the fact that good government must recognize the supremacy of law really puts the monarchy out of consideration as a true form of government. A monarchy of the ideal type would belong to domestic rather than political rule. Nothing but his acceptance of Plato's sixfold classification brings it into consideration.

When Aristotle turns to an examination of existing monarchies he drops the consideration of an ideal state entirely. Two legal forms of monarchy he knows, the Spartan kingship and the dictatorship, but neither of these is a constitution, and two kinds of monarchical constitution, the Oriental monarchy and the monarchy of the heroic age. The latter, of course, is conjectural and really outside Aristotle's experience. The Oriental monarchy is more truly a form of tyranny, though it is lawful after a barbarian fashion, since Asiatics are slaves by nature and do not object to despotic government. Substantially, therefore, actual monarchy, as Aristotle knows it, is equivalent to such government as that of Persia. However, the significance of this discussion is less in what he says about monarchy than in the fact that he distinguishes the different kinds. Evidently the sixfold classification of states had already lost its meaning for him as compared with an empirical study of the actual working of governments. It was precisely at this point that he took up again the examination of oligarchy and democracy — that is to say, Greek forms of government — in Book IV.

The reasons should now be clear why Aristotle's political ideals did not eventuate in the construction of an ideal state. The ideal state represented a conception of political philosophy which he inherited from Plato and which was in fact little congenial to his genius. The more he struck out an independent line of thought and investigation, the more he turned toward the analysis and description of actual constitutions. The great collection of one hundred and fifty-eight constitutional histories made by him and his students marks the turning point in his thought and suggested a broader conception of political theory. This did not mean that Aristotle turned to description alone. The essence of the new conception was the uniting of empirical investigation with the more speculative consideration of political ideals. Moral ideals — the sovereignty of law, the freedom and equality of citizens, constitutional government, the perfecting of men in a civilized life — are always for Aristotle the ends for which the state ought to exist. What he discovered was that these ideals were infinitely complicated in the realization and required infinite adjustment to the conditions of actual government. Ideals must exist not like Plato's pattern in the Heavens but as forces working in and through agencies by no means ideal.

CHAPTER VI

ARISTOTLE: POLITICAL ACTUALITIES

The opening paragraphs of Book IV of the *Politics* show a significant enlargement of Aristotle's conception of political philosophy. Any science or art ought, he says, to cover the whole of a subject. A gymnastic trainer ought indeed to be able to produce a finished athlete, but he ought also to be able to supervise the physical education of those who cannot become athletes or select suitable exercises for those who need a special kind of training. The same should be true of the political scientist. He needs to know what would be the best government if there were no impediments to be overcome, in other words, how to construct an ideal state. But he should know also what is best relative to circumstances and what will succeed in any given conditions even though it is neither the best abstractly considered nor the best under the circumstances. Finally, on the strength of this knowledge he should be able to judge what form of government is best suited to most states and attainable without presuming more virtue and intelligence than men commonly possess. With this knowledge he can suggest the measures that will be most likely to correct the defects of existing governments. In other words, the complete art of the statesman must take governments as they are and do the best it can with the means it has. It might even divorce itself from moral considerations altogether and tell the tyrant how to succeed in tyranny, as Aristotle actually does later.

No such radical separation of politics from ethics was intended, but nevertheless the new view of the statesman's art makes it a different subject of investigation from the ethics of individual and personal morality. At the beginning of Book III of the *Politics* Aristotle had discussed the virtue of a good man and the virtue of a citizen and had treated their non-identity as a problem. In the closing pages of the *Nicomachean Ethics* he takes for granted that they are not identical and presents the problem of legislation as a branch of investigation distinct from the study of the noblest form of ethical ideal. The subject, he says, has been too much neglected but is necessary to complete a philosophy of human nature. Significantly also he refers to his collection of constitutions as a source for studying the causes which preserve or destroy states and which bring good or bad government; it can hardly be doubted that the proposed study is that which ended in the writing of Books IV to VI of the *Politics*.

> When these have been studied we shall perhaps be more likely to see with a comprehensive view, which constitution is best, and how each must be ordered, and what laws and customs it must use, if it is to be at its best.[1]

This discrimination of ethics and politics, which marks the beginning of the two as distinct but connected subjects of investigation, is of a piece with the astounding power of logical organization displayed by his philosophy as a whole. By virtue of this capacity, in which he far surpassed Plato, he was able to outline the main branches of scientific knowledge as they have remained even to modern times.

THE POLITICAL AND ETHICAL CONSTITUTIONS

The analysis of actual forms of Greek government undertaken in Book IV is attached to the sixfold classification of constitutions in Book III. Perhaps more truly it is connected with the treatment of monarchy in the latter part of that Book. Aristotle now refers to monarchy and aristocracy as belonging to the class of ideal states, though this does not correspond very accurately with the discussion of them in Book III, and he proposes to pass on to a closer examination of oligarchy and democracy. It is commonly supposed, he says, that there is only one form of each of these but this is a fallacy, a remark which recalls his comment on the difficulty of seeing that there are several kinds of monarchy.[2] What the practical statesman needs to know, in order to work with actual government, is how many kinds of oligarchy and democracy there are and what laws are suitable to each kind of constitution. This will enable him to tell what form of government is best for most states, what is best for a state that has to exist under some special condition, what is needed to make any

[1] *Nic. Eth.*, 10, 9; 1181 b 20 (Ross' trans.).
[2] 3, 14; 1285 a 1.

given form of government practicable, and what causes make for stability or instability in different kinds of states.

The reopening of the question of classification with respect to oligarchy and democracy requires a re-examination of the general nature of the constitution. The view which had on the whole prevailed in Book III is that the constitution is an " arrangement of citizens " or a mode of life which more or less dictates the external organization of the state. This is a normal point of view so long as the ethical aspect of the state was uppermost in Aristotle's mind. For the determining factor in any state would be the ethical values which the association of citizens was designed to realize; the moral purposes of the citizens in living together would be the essential thing that they had in common and hence, so to speak, " the life of the state." Aristotle had, however, defined a constitution also as the arrangement of offices or magistracies, which is closer to a political view of the state in the modern sense. In Book IV the latter definition is restated and the constitution is distinguished from the law, which is the body of rules to be followed by magistrates in performing the duties of their offices. Aristotle also adds still a third analysis of states into social classes, or united groups smaller than the state itself, such as families, or the rich and poor, or occupational groups such as farmers, artisans, and merchants. The economic structure of the state is not spoken of as a constitution, but its influence is often decisive in determining what form of political constitution (arrangement of offices) is suitable or feasible. Aristotle compares economic classes to an animal's organs and says that there are as many kinds of states as there are ways of combining the classes necessary to support a social life.

At the outset, therefore, Aristotle has introduced into the discussion of actual states several important distinctions, which to be sure he has not made explicit but which show clearly how far he has progressed in the assessment of real political forces. In the first place, reference has already been made to the discrimination of politics from ethics. This was involved in the plan of treating the actual apart from the ideal constitution, and is marked by the greater importance given to the definition of the constitution as an arrangement of offices. He now distinguishes also the law from the political structure of the organized government. Still more important is the discrimination of political structure from the social and economic structure which lies behind it. The modern distinction between the state and society is one which no Greek thinker made clearly and adequately, and which perhaps could not be clearly made until the state was conceived as a legal structure, but Aristotle at least reached a very good first approximation to it. Moreover, he was able to use the distinction in a highly realistic fashion when he shrewdly remarked that a political constitution is one thing and the way the constitution actually works is another. A government democratic in form may govern oligarchically, while an oligarchy may govern democratically.[3] Thus a democracy with a prevailingly agricultural population may be quite changed by the addition of a large urban trading class, though the political structure of the state — the offices and the political rights of its citizens — is quite unchanged.

The use which Aristotle made of this twofold analysis of the state — into political agencies and classes united by similarity of economic interest — would have been easier to follow if he had always distinguished his use of the one from his use of the other, and if he had discriminated both from the interaction of one upon the other. In his enumeration of the kinds of democracy and oligarchy it is often hard to see what principle of classification he is following; in fact he offers two lists of each [4] without explaining wherein the two differ, though in one he seems to be thinking mainly of the political constitution and in the other of the economic constitution. Moreover, the classification is complicated by the distinction between lawless and law-abiding governments, though this ought not to apply to oligarchy at all and in any case would have to be regarded as a result derivative from the arrangement of offices or classes. But though the treatment is not schematic, it is substantially clear and unquestionably it represents a mastery of its subject — the internal working of the Greek city-states — such as has rarely been displayed by any later political scientist over any other form of government. Substantially the thought is as follows: There are certain political regulations — such for instance as qualifications for voting and

[3] 4, 5; 1292 b 11 ff.

[4] Of democracy, 4, 4; 1291 b 30 ff; 4, 6; 1292 b 22 ff . Of oligarchy, 4, 5; 1292 a 39 ff; 4, 6; 1293 a 12 ff.

eligibility to office — which are characteristic of democracy and others which are characteristic of oligarchy. There are also economic conditions — such for instance as the way in which wealth is distributed or the predominance of one or another economic class — which predispose a state toward democracy or oligarchy and determine what kind of political constitution will be most likely to succeed. Both the political and the economic arrangements vary in degree, some tending to a more extreme and some to a less extreme form of the two types. The possible number of combinations is large, since states may be formed not only from democratic or oligarchic elements but also from elements of both types, as for instance it would be if the assembly were democratically organized while the judiciary was chosen with some sort of oligarchical qualification. The way a government actually works depends in part on the combination of political factors, in part on the economic factors, and also on the way both sets of factors are combined with each other. Finally, some of the economic factors tend to produce a lawless state and others a law-abiding state, and the same is true of the political factors. Such a conclusion is hard to state in a formal classification, but it has the merit of recognizing a great mass of political and social complexity.

THE DEMOCRATIC AND OLIGARCHIC PRINCIPLES

It will be enough to indicate how in general Aristotle follows out these lines of classification, without giving in detail all the subdivisions of oligarchy and democracy that he mentions. Thus democracies differ in their political constitutions according to their inclusiveness, and this usually follows from the way they use, or fail to use, a property qualification. There may be no qualification at all, either for voting in the assembly or for holding office, or the qualification may be lower or higher, or it may apply to some offices but not to others. On the other hand, a democracy may not only impose no qualification but may pay its citizens a fee (as at Athens) for jury-service or even for attending the town-meeting, which puts a premium on attendance by the poor. Democracies will differ also according to the economic structure of the state. A democracy composed of farmers may impose no qualification and yet the management of affairs may be wholly in the hands of the gentry, since the mass of people have little time and little inclination to trouble themselves with public business. Aristotle considers this to be the best kind of democracy; the people have a considerable power and hold the governing class in check by the possibility that they may use it, but so long as the rulers proceed moderately the people leave them free to do much as they think best. A very different sort of democracy results when there is a large urban population who not only have power but use it by trying to transact public business in the town-meeting. This opens an arena to the demagogues, and such a democracy is nearly certain to become lawless and disorderly. In practice it is hardly different from tyranny. The problem of a democracy is to unite popular power with intelligent administration and the latter is not possible by a large assembly.

The kinds of oligarchy are distinguished upon the same general lines. For oligarchy a property qualification or some condition of eligibility, both for citizenship and for office, is normal, but the qualification may be higher or lower. The oligarchy may be broadly based in the population or power may be confined to a small faction. Such a faction may form a self-perpetuating corporation which fills public offices from its own ranks without even a show of election, and in extreme cases a few families, or even a single family, may have practically hereditary power. What kind of oligarchical government is possible will depend in turn upon the distribution of property. If there is a fairly large class of property owners with no great extremes of wealth, the oligarchy is likely to be broadly based, but if there is a small class of the very wealthy, government will be likely to fall into the hands of a clique. And when this happens it will be hard to prevent the abuses of factional rule. At the extreme, oligarchy, like democracy, becomes practically indistinguishable from tyranny. The problem in an oligarchy is the converse of that in a democracy: it is to keep power in the hands of a comparatively small class without allowing this class to become too oppressive to the masses, for oppression is nearly certain to breed disorder. In Aristotle's judgment aggression by the rich is more probable than aggression by the masses, and consequently oligarchy is harder to regulate than democracy. At the same time an oligarchy broadly based in a population where wealth is pretty evenly distributed may be a law-abiding form of government.

This examination of the kinds of democracy and oligarchy is later elaborated by Aristotle in a more systematic analysis of the political constitution or political organs of government. He distinguishes three branches which are present in some form in every government. First, there is the deliberative branch, which exercises the ultimate legal power of the state in such acts as the making of war and peace, the concluding of treaties, the auditing of magistrates' accounts, and legislation. Second, there are various magistrates or administrative officers, and third, there is the judiciary. Each of these branches may be organized democratically or oligarchically, or more or less democratically or oligarchically. The deliberative body may be more or less inclusive and may exercise a larger or a smaller number of functions. The magistrates may be chosen by a larger or smaller electorate, or in more democratic governments by lot; they may be chosen for longer or shorter terms; they may be more or less responsible to the deliberative branch and may have a larger or a smaller measure of power. In the same way the courts may be popular, chosen by lot from a large panel, and may exercise powers co-ordinate with the deliberative branch itself, as at Athens, or they may be restricted in power or numbers and chosen in a more selective way. Any given constitution may be organized more democratically in one of its branches and more oligarchically in another.

THE BEST PRACTICABLE STATE

The analysis of the political factors in democracy and oligarchy has put Aristotle in a position where he can consider the question which now takes the place of the construction of an ideal state, viz., what form of government is best for most states, leaving aside special circumstances that may be peculiar to a given case and assuming no more virtue or political skill than states can usually muster? Such a form of government is in no sense ideal; it is merely the best practicable average which results from avoiding the extremes in democracy and oligarchy that experience has shown to be dangerous. This sort of state Aristotle calls the polity, or constitutional government, a name applied in Book III to moderate democracy; Aristotle would not be averse to adopting the word aristocracy (previously used in its etymological meaning for an ideal state) in those cases where the constitution leans away from popular government too much to be called a moderate democracy.

In any case the distinctive feature of this best practicable state is that it is a mixed form of constitution in which elements are judiciously combined from oligarchy and democracy. Its social foundation is the existence of a large middle class composed of those who are neither very rich nor very poor. It is this class which, as Euripides had said years before, "saves states." For they are not poor enough to be degraded or rich enough to be factious. Where such a body of citizens exists they form a group large enough to give the state a popular foundation, disinterested enough to hold the magistrates responsible, and select enough to avoid the evils of government by the masses. Upon such a social foundation it is possible to build a political structure drawing upon institutions typical of both democracy and oligarchy. There may be a property qualification but only a moderate one, or there may be no property qualification with no use of lot in selecting magistrates. Aristotle regarded Sparta as a mixed constitution. He was probably thinking also of the government attempted at Athens in 411 — in reality a paper constitution — which aimed to form a citizen-body restricted to five thousand able to supply themselves with heavy armor and which in the *Constitution of Athens* Aristotle said was the best government that Athens had ever had. Like Plato, Aristotle is obliged by practical considerations to fall back upon property as a surrogate for virtue. Neither thinker believed on principle that property is a sign of goodness but both reached the conclusion that for political purposes it offers the best practicable approximation to it.

The principle of the middle-class state is balance, balance between two factors that are certain to count for something in every political system. These factors grow from the claims to power discussed in Book III but Aristotle now treats them less as claims than as forces. These two he describes as quality and quantity. The first includes political influences such as arise from the prestige of wealth, birth, position, and education; the second is the sheer weight of numbers. If the first predominates the government becomes an oligarchy; if the second, a democracy. In order to produce stability it is desirable that the constitution should allow for both and balance the one against the other. It is because this is most easily done where there is a large middle class that this kind of state is the most secure and the most law-abiding of practicable constitutions. In some respects Aristotle sees safety in numbers, because he believes in the collective wisdom of a sober public opinion and thinks that a large body is not easily corrupted. But especially for administrative duties men of position and experience are the best. A state that can combine these two factors has solved the chief problems of stable and orderly government. Undoubtedly Greek history bears out this diagnosis of the internal difficulties which the city-state had to meet. On the other hand, Aristotle has little to say about an equally pressing difficulty which the course of history in his own lifetime ought to have suggested to him — the difficulty of foreign affairs and the fact that the city-state was too small successfully to govern a world in which powers like Macedon and Persia had to be coped with.

In Book V Aristotle discusses at length the causes of revolution and the political measures by which it can be prevented, but the details may be passed over. His political penetration and his mastery of Greek government are apparent on every page. But the theory of the subject is already apparent in the discussion of the middle-class state. Both oligarchy and democracy are in a condition of unstable equilibrium, and as a result each runs the risk of being ruined by being too much itself. A statesman whose practical problem is to govern a state of either kind has to prevent it from carrying out the logic of its own institutions. The more oligarchical an oligarchy becomes the more it tends to be governed by an oppressive faction, and similarly, the more democratic a democracy becomes, the more it tends to be governed by a mob. Both tend to degenerate into tyranny, which is bad in itself and also unlikely to be successful. The almost cynical freedom with which Aristotle advises the tyrant presages Machiavelli. The traditional tactics are to degrade and humiliate all who might be dangerous, to keep subjects powerless, and to create divisions and mistrust among them. A better way is to rule as little like a tyrant as possible, to pretend at least to an interest in the public welfare, and at all events to avoid the public exhibition of a tyrant's vices. In the long run no form of government can be permanent unless it has the support of the major political and economical forces in the state — regard being given both to quality and quantity — and for this reason it is usually good policy to gain the loyalty of the middle class. It is the extreme in any direction that ruins states. In short, if not actually a middle-class government, the state must be as like middle-class government as it can, always of course allowing for any special circumstances which may be decisive in a given case.

THE NEW ART OF THE STATESMAN

Aristotle's conception of a new and more general type of political science, including not only a study of the ethical meaning of the state but also an empirical study of the elements, both political and social, of actual constitutions, their combination, and the consequences which are found to follow from these combinations, represented in no sense an abandonment of the fundamental ideas which he had derived from Plato. It did represent, however, an important modification and readjustment of them. The objective is still the same in so far as it looks to an art of statesmanship able to direct political life to morally valuable ends by means rationally chosen. The state is still to realize its true meaning as a factor in a civilized life and the discovery of this meaning is therefore still of vital importance. The direction of political life along the lines best adapted to give the state its true meaning is a work to be performed by intelligence; it is the subject of a science and an art, and therefore as different for Aristotle as for Plato from the mere sharpness of a designing politician, the bungling of a popular assembly, or the rhetorical cleverness of a demagogue or a sophist. What Aristotle did was not to abandon the ideal but to work forward to a new conception of the science and of the art based on it. Plato had believed that politics could be made the subject of a free intellectual or speculative construction by grasping once for all the idea of the good, though the writing of the *Laws* is enough to show that in the end he was forced substantially beyond this conception of the task. Aristotle's association with Plato fell in the years when this readjustment of his political thought was taking place, and in any case the native bent of Aristotle's mind would probably have forced him along a line different from that upon which Plato had started.

The method of free intellectual construction — suitable enough for a philosophy that adopted mathematics as the type of all knowledge — was therefore closed to Aristotle from the start. This is proved by his inability to carry out the project for a sketch of an ideal state. But it was a slow and difficult task to adapt the ideals of Plato's philosophy to a different method, and this is what Aristotle had to do. The whole story of that re-adaptation is written in Aristotle's formulation of his own philosophical system, of which the science and art of politics was but a single chapter, though an important one. The embedding of constitutional rule in the ideals of the state — the recognition of law, consent, and public opinion as intrinsic parts of a good political life — was an important first step but one which required Aristotle to go farther. He had to go on to analyze the city-state into its political elements, to study the bearing upon these of underlying social and economic forces. And to studies such as these a speculative method was obviously inappropriate. The collection of constitutions was Aristotle's attempt to amass the data needed to deal with these problems, and the more empirical and more realistic theory of Books IV to VI was his solution of them. But a more empirical method carried with it a change in the conception of the art which it was to serve. An end outside the political process upon which a state could be modeled would no longer suffice. The statesman of Aristotle's art is, so to speak, seated in the midst of affairs. He cannot model them to his will, but he can take advantage of such possibilities as the posture of events offers. There are necessary consequences which cannot be avoided; there are the chances brought by untoward circumstances which may wreck even a good plan; but there is also art, the intelligent use of available means to bring affairs to a worthy and desirable end.[5]

For Aristotle, then, political science became empirical, though not exclusively descriptive; and the art included the improvement of political life even though this has to be done on a modest scale. It was natural that this advance in his ideas should turn his attention back to first principles and lead him to reconsider the underlying problems from which both he and Plato had started. This he did briefly in the introduction which he wrote for the completed *Politics,* the first book of the present text. Much of this

[5] *Metaph.* 7, 7; 1032 a 12 ff.; Cf. Plato, *Laws,* 709b–c.

book merely enlarged upon the theory of household government, including economics, and recapitulated the distinction between this and political rule. This subject was not very completely worked out, probably because the re-examination of the household brought Aristotle face to face with questions already considered in Book II as part of the criticism of communism. He never undertook the task of rewriting which would have been needed to fuse the two discussions. In the first part of Book I, however, he went back to the fundamental question of nature and convention, since for his theory as for Plato's it was necessary to show that the state has intrinsic moral value and is not merely an imposition of arbitrary force.

In order to deal with this problem Aristotle canvasses more systematically the definition of the state, starting substantially from the same point as Plato at the beginning of the *Republic*. His procedure follows the theory of definition by genus and differentia which is developed in his logical works. The state, he says, is a kind of community. A community is a union of unlike persons who, because of their differences, are able to satisfy their needs by the exchange of goods and services. This is substantially identical with Plato's belief that the state depends upon a division of labor, but Aristotle differs from Plato because he distinguishes several species of community of which the state is only one. The object of this, of course, is to distinguish the rule of a household — over wife, children, or slaves — from political rule. Plato, in other words, had confused the genus with the species. The problem, therefore, is to determine what kind of community a state is. In Book I the discussion is so entirely levelled against Plato that Aristotle seems not quite to have developed his whole thought. Elsewhere [6] he points out that the exchange of goods by buying and selling, or merely contractual relations, makes a community but not a state, because there need be no common ruler. In Book I he stresses communities, so to speak, at the other extreme, where there is a distinction of ruler and ruled but not a constitutional or political ruler. This is illustrated by the relation of master and slave, where the latter exists wholly for the master's good. The state lies then in an intermediate position, distinguished from contract on one side and from ownership on the other. This

[6] 3, 9; 1280 b 17 ff.

method of definition by approximation, the discrimination of what might be called limiting cases, is frequently used by Aristotle in his scientific works. Unfortunately in the *Politics* he does not consider as systematically as might have been expected the differences between household relations other than slavery, for example, the relation between the head of a household and his wife, which he believed to be different in kind both from his relation to a slave and from the relations of a political ruler to his subjects.

He does, however, propose a general principle for defining the state in contrast with the household. This is the reference to growth or historical development. "He who thus considers things in their first growth and origin, whether a state or any thing else, will obtain the clearest view of them."[7] Aristotle thereupon appeals to the traditional history of the Greek city, which Plato had already used in the *Laws* to introduce the construction of the second-best state. Thus history shows that the family is the primitive kind of community, brought into being by such elemental needs as those for shelter, food, and the propagation of the race. So long as men have progressed no farther than to satisfy these needs, they live in detached families under a patriarchal government. A higher stage of development is represented by the village, which is a union of several families, and a still higher by the state, which is a union of villages.

The growth is not, however, merely in size. At a certain point a community arises which is different in kind from the more primitive groups. It becomes what Aristotle calls "self-sufficing." This refers in part to its territory and its means of economic support, and also to its political independence, but not primarily to these. What is distinctive about the state is, for Aristotle, that it first produces the conditions necessary to a really civilized life. It originates, as he says, in the bare needs of life but it continues for the sake of a good life. To this end it is as important that the state should not be too large as that it should not be too small. For Aristotle never contemplates any social unit other than the Greek city-state as fulfilling the needs of a civilized life. It includes the household as one of its necessary elements — and Plato was in error in desiring to abolish the more primitive unit — but it is a more developed and therefore a more perfect kind of com-

[7] 1, 2; 1252 a 24 f.

munity. This is shown by the fact that the needs which the state satisfies are the more typically human needs. Even the family, which in its most primitive form depends on physical needs that man shares with all animals, requires capacities definitely beyond those which unite the gregarious animals. For it requires speech and the power to distinguish right from wrong, which are characteristics only of the rational animal. But the state gives the opportunity for a higher development even of these rational powers. Man is distinctively the political animal, the only being that dwells in cities and subjects himself to law and produces science and art and religion and all the many-sided creations of civilization. These represent the perfection of human development and they are attainable only in civil society. To live without it a being must be either a beast or a god; that is, either below or above the medium plane on which humanity lives. In their highest form, as Aristotle believes — dominated as he is by a belief in the unique human capacity of the Greeks — the arts of civilization are attainable only in the city-state.

NATURE AS DEVELOPMENT

The meaning and value of the state arise from the fact that, as Edmund Burke said, it is a partnership in all the sciences and all the arts, and this is Aristotle's final argument against those who assert that law and morals are matters of convention. The argument as Aristotle uses it represents a careful redefinition of the term " nature," such that it can be adapted to every branch of science and made the general principle of a philosophy. It is a practical rule for the guidance of investigation that the simplest and most primitive comes first in time, while the more complete and perfect comes only later after growth has taken place. The later stage, however, shows more adequately than the earlier what the true " nature " of a thing is. This rule Aristotle had found useful on a large scale in his biological studies. A seed, for example, discloses its nature only as it germinates and as the plant grows. The physical conditions, such as soil and heat and moisture, are necessary, but even though they are identical for two different seeds — like an acorn or a mustard seed — the resulting plants are quite different. Aristotle infers that the effective cause of the difference lies in the seeds; each plant contains its own "nature" which displays itself as it gradually unfolds and becomes explicitly what the seeds are implicitly. The same kind of explanation applies also to the growth of the community. In its primitive form, as the family, it shows its intrinsic nature as a division of labor, but in its higher forms, without failing to satisfy the primitive needs, it shows itself able to give scope for the development of higher capacities which would be dormant if the family only existed. The family, Aristotle says, is prior in time but the state is prior "by nature"; that is, it is the more completely developed and therefore the more indicative of what the community has implicit in it. For the same reason life in the state shows what human nature intrinsically is. No one could even have guessed that the arts of civilization were possible if life had not progressed beyond the kinds of exchange needed to satisfy the primitive needs.

Aristotle's use of the word nature with reference to society has, therefore, a double significance. It is true that men are instinctively sociable because they need each other. The primitive community depends upon impulses embedded in all life, such as sex and the appetite for food. They are indispensable but they are not distinctive of human life, because they are not very different in man and in the lower animals. Human nature is more characteristically displayed in the development of those powers that belong to men alone. And since the state is the only medium in which these can develop, it is "natural" in a sense that is in some respects the opposite of instinctive. Just as it is "natural" for an acorn to grow into an oak, so it is natural for human nature to expand its highest powers in the state. This does not mean that the development must inevitably take place, for the absence of the needed physical conditions will prevent the growth in both cases. Aristotle in fact believes that it is only in the very limited case of the city-state that the higher development takes place and he attributes this to the fact that only Greeks of all men possess the faculty for such a growth. Where it does take place it shows what human nature is capable of, just as a well-watered and well-nourished oak shows what a good acorn really has in it. The state is natural because it contains the possibility of a fully civilized life, but since it requires physical and other conditions for its growth, it presents an arena for the stateman's art. The application of understanding and will does not create it but may very well turn it toward a more perfect unfolding of its innate possibilities.

A theory of nature such as this — derived from biological as well as social studies — appears to Aristotle to provide a logical foundation for his more broadly conceived science and art of politics. Nature is at bottom a system of capacities or forces of growth directed by their inherent nature toward characteristic ends. They require for their unfolding what may be called broadly material conditions, which do not produce the ends at which growth is directed but may aid or hinder growth according as they are favorable or the reverse. The events and changes that go on continually are the processes of appropriation by which the powers of growth take possession of such material conditions as are available. These three factors, called by Aristotle form, matter, and movement, are the fundamental constituents of nature. They offer scope to the arts because within some limits not easy to discover the plans of the artist can serve as forms toward which the available material can be made to converge. Thus in politics the statesman cannot do anything he chooses, but he can wisely choose those courses which tend at least to a better and more desirable development of social institutions and of human life. In order to do this he needs to understand both what is possible and what is actual. He must know what potentialities of growth are present in the situation before him and what material conditions will give these ideal forces the means of working themselves out in the best way. His investigations always combine two purposes. They must be empirical and descriptive, because without the knowledge of the actual he cannot tell what means are at his disposal or how the means will turn out if used. But they must consider also the ideal dimension of the facts, for otherwise the statesman will not know how his means should be used to bring out the best that his material affords.

Aristotle's conception of the science and art of politics represents the type of investigation which offered the greatest scope to his own mature intellectual genius. In originality and boldness of speculative construction he was by no means the equal of Plato, and the underlying principles of his philosophy were all derived from his master. In the power of intellectual organization, especially in the ability to grasp a pattern or a tendency in a vast and complicated mass of details, he was not only superior to Plato but the equal of any thinker in the later history of science. The use of this capacity, in social studies and in biology, shows Aristotle at the top of his bent, after he had freed himself in some measure from Plato and had struck out for himself a line of thought in accordance with his own originality. It was his growth in this direction that caused him to turn aside from the borrowed purpose of sketching an ideal state and to carry his investigation first toward constitutional history and second toward general conclusions about the structure and functioning of states based upon observation and history. Aristotle was the founder of this method, which has been on the whole the soundest and most fruitful that the study of politics has evolved.

SELECTED BIBLIOGRAPHY

The Political Thought of Plato and Aristotle. By Ernest Barker. London, 1906. Chs. 5–11.

The Politics of Aristotle. Eng. trans. by Ernest Barker. Oxford, 1946. Introduction.

"Aristotle's Conception of the State." By A. C. Bradley. In *Hellenica,* ed. by E. Abbott. 2nd ed. London, 1898.

Greek Thinkers: A History of Ancient Philosophy. By Theodor Gomperz. Vol. IV. Eng. trans. by G. G. Berry. New York, 1912. Book VI, chs. 26–34.

Aristotle: Fundamentals of the History of his Development. By Werner Jaeger. Eng. trans. by Richard Robinson. Oxford, 1934. Ch. 10.

"The Philosophy of Aristotle and the Hellenic-Macedonian Policy." By Hans Kelsen. In *Ethics,* Vol. XLVIII (1937–38), p. 1.

The Politics of Aristotle. By W. L. Newman. 4 vols. Oxford, 1887–1902. Vol. I, Introduction; Vol. II, Prefatory Essays.

Aristotle. By W. D. Ross. 3rd ed. rev. London, 1937. Ch. 8.

Aristotle's Constitution of Athens. Ed. by Sir John Edwin Sandys. 2nd ed. rev. and enlarged. London, 1912. Introduction.

The Politics of Aristotle. Ed. by Franz Susemihl and R. D. Hicks. London, 1894. Introduction.

Aristoteles und Athen. By Ulrich von Wilamowitz-Moellendorff. 2 vols. Berlin, 1893.

"Aristotle on Law." By Francis D. Wormuth. In *Essays in Political Theory.* Ed. by Milton R. Konvitz and Arthur E. Murphy. Ithaca, New York, 1948.

CHAPTER VII

THE TWILIGHT OF THE CITY-STATE

The political philosophy of Plato and Aristotle was singularly devoid of immediate influence both of a practical and a theoretical kind. In fact, if it were judged by the part that it played in the two centuries following Aristotle's death, it could only be described as a magnificent failure. The reason for this is that the two philosophers between them had stated more completely and perfectly than any successor could hope to do the ideals and the principles of the type of political institution with which they dealt, the city-state. There was in truth no further progress to be made upon that line. This is not to say that what Plato and Aristotle had written had value only as applying to the city-state. The presumption upon which Plato worked — that human relations may be made the object of rational study and may be subjected to intelligent direction — is a *sine qua non* of any social science whatever. And the more general ethical principles of Aristotle's political theory — the conviction that a state ought to be a relation between free citizens morally equal, conducting itself according to law and resting upon discussion and consent rather than force — have never vanished from European political philosophy. These great qualities explain why later thinkers, even down to the present, have repeatedly gone back to Plato and Aristotle. But though much that they wrote thus had permanent significance, it is a fact that Plato and Aristotle believed it to apply to the city-state and to that alone. They never conceived of these or of any political ideals as capable of being realized in any other form of civil society. Their assumption was justified by the facts as they then were, for it is hard to imagine political philosophy taking its rise in any society that then existed except the Greek cities.

Plato and Aristotle were quite aware, of course, that no city in Greece had realized the ideals which they believed to be implicit in the city-state. Had the need for criticism and correction not been clearly present to their minds, they would never have tried to analyze the society in which they lived or to distinguish its perversions from its successes. But while they criticised — and often sharply — they still believed that the conditions of a good life did measurably exist in the city-state. And while they would gladly have changed many of its practices, they never doubted that the city-state was fundamentally sound and the only ethically sound foundation for the higher forms of civilization. Their criticism was, therefore, basically friendly. They spoke for the class of Greeks that found life in the city-state substantially satisfying, though by no means perfect. But it is an ominous symptom that both men, certainly without intending to be spokesmen for a class, were driven to make citizenship more and more explicitly a privilege and therefore the prerogative of those who had the property and the leisure to enjoy the luxury of political position. The deeper Plato and Aristotle penetrate into the underlying ethical meaning of the city-state, the more they are forced to the conclusion that this meaning exists only for a few and not for the whole mass of artisans and farmers and wage-earners, as the democracy of the Periclean Age had imagined. This in itself suggests — what was the fact — that others less vocal or less favorably situated might see in the city-state a form of society that needed not to be improved but to be superseded; at least they might regard it as a thing to be neglected by men in search of a good life. Such a criticism, of protest or at least of indifference, did exist, somewhat obscurely, in the age of Plato and Aristotle. But the historical circumstances were such that the immediate future lay with it rather than with the more imposing theories of the greater men, and this explains the temporary eclipse of their political philosophy after Aristotle's death. When the city-state had been relegated to history and it was no longer possible to picture political values as realizable only in it, men could return to exploit the infinite fertility of the *Republic*, the *Laws*, and the *Politics*.

The common form taken by these diverse philosophies of protest or indifference — and their startling significance in the fourth and third centuries — can be grasped only by keeping clearly in mind the ethical presumption which lay behind all that Plato and Aristotle wrote about the state. This is the presumption that a good life implies participation in the life of the state. It was this which enabled Plato to start with the proposition that the state is at bottom a division of labor in which men of differing capacity satisfy their needs by mutual exchange. Plato's conception was made merely more complete in Aristotle's analysis of the community. This presumption caused both men to regard participation as a conception ethically more important than either duties or rights, and to see in citizenship a sharing of the common life. From this point of view citizenship stands at the summit of human goods, or at least this would be so if both the city and human nature were developed to the top of their bent. This presumption represents the very genius of the ethics and politics of the city-state. And for this reason the essence of protest is the denial of it. Assert that a man, in order to live a good life, must live outside the city-state, or being in it should at any rate not be of it, and you have set up a scale of values not only foreign to but essentially opposed to that assumed by Plato and Aristotle. Say that the wise man will have as little to do with politics as he can, that he will never willingly take the responsibilities or the honors of public office, but will shun both as a useless cause of anxiety, and you have said that Plato and Aristotle have set up a wholly erroneous notion of wisdom and goodness. For such a good is private, something which a man gains or loses in himself and by himself, and not something that requires a common life. Self-sufficiency, which Plato and Aristotle regarded as an attribute of the state, becomes an attribute of the individual human being. The good becomes something not strictly conceivable within the confines of the city-state — a good of privacy and withdrawal. It is the growth of this kind of ethical theory that marks the twilight of the city-state.

The attitude of Plato and Aristotle toward this ethics of withdrawal is significant. They know its existence but they cannot quite take it seriously. Thus there is perhaps a gibe at the Cynic scheme of life in the "pig-state" of the *Republic*,[1] where living is reduced to the barest and rudest necessaries. There is almost certainly a sneer behind Aristotle's remark that the man who can live without the state is either a beast or a god. The moralist who sets up the ideal of individual self-sufficiency claims the

[1] 372 d.

attributes of a god, but he is likely to live the life of a beast. Only in the introduction to his ideal state does Aristotle propose to argue the relative merits of the statesman's and the philosopher's life, and here he does not really argue. He merely asserts that "happiness is activity" and that "he who does nothing cannot do well."[2] He almost certainly is thinking of the Cynics, and it is not improbable, as Jaeger suggests, that some of Plato's students had enlarged upon the ideal of the contemplative life in the spirit of Plato's own remark that the philosopher might have to be compelled to return to the den. At all events the Academy certainly had moved in this direction a generation later. But for Aristotle the argument has really not got beyond the level of epigram. The whole structure of his political thought assumes that the citizen's activity is the chief good and he never takes any other view seriously.

THE FAILURE OF THE CITY-STATE

Beside the theoretical assumption that only the city-state is morally self-sufficient there is also in the reformist political philosophy of Plato and Aristotle a practical assumption of great importance and one which had the misfortune to be not quite true under existing circumstances. The improvement of the city-state within limits set by that form of government took for granted that its rulers were free agents, able by the choice of wise policies to correct its internal defects. The complete acceptance of it as a moral institution by Plato and Aristotle meant in effect that their political horizon was bounded by it. In consequence neither of them was as keenly aware as he should have been of the part which foreign affairs played even in the internal economy of the city-state. It is true that Aristotle criticised Plato for this omission,[3] but it cannot be said that he did better himself. If Plato had been as closely associated with Macedonia as Aristotle, he would hardly have failed to perceive the epoch-making importance of the career of Alexander. It is interesting to conjecture what might have happened if it had occurred to Aristotle to consider the hypothesis that the city-state needed to be absorbed into some still more self-sufficing political unit, as it had itself absorbed the family and the village. But this was beyond his power of

[2] 7, 3; 1325 a 16 ff.

[3] *Politics,* 2, 6; 1265 a 20.

political imagination. In fact, however, the fate of the city-state depended not upon the wisdom with which it managed its internal affairs but upon its interrelations with the rest of the Greek world and upon the relations of Greece to Asia on the east and to Carthage and Italy on the west. The supposition that the city-state could choose its mode of life regardless of limits fixed by these foreign relations was fundamentally false. Plato and Aristotle might deplore, like many other intelligent Greeks, the contentiousness and belligerency of the relations between the Greek cities, but as the event proved, these vices were ineradicable so long as the cities remained independent.

As Professor W. S. Ferguson has pointed out,[4] the Greek city-state from a date early in its history was confronted by a political dilemma which it never was able to cope with. It could not attain self-sufficiency, either in its economics or its politics, without adopting a policy of isolation, and it could not isolate itself without suffering stagnation in that very culture and civilization which Aristotle regarded as its crown of glory. On the other hand, if it chose not to isolate itself, it was driven by political necessity to seek alliances with other cities, and these alliances could not be successful without impairing the independence of their members. The dilemma ought to be comprehensible to a modern political observer, for it was substantially similar to that in which a more inclusive economy has placed the nation-state. The modern nation can neither isolate itself nor, as yet at least, curb its independence enough to form a more viable political unit. All the modern fictions about complete national sovereignty united with international regulation find their parallel in the Greek alliances of allegedly independent cities. By the middle of the fourth century these federations were the prevailing form of government in the Greek world, but they quite failed to make permanent and stable states. Even as late as the formation of the Panhellenic League by Philip, at Corinth in 338, the cities, had they been able to work together, might have gone far toward influencing and even controlling the policy of Macedonia, but the inherent particularism of the city-state was unable to rise to the opportunity. It is a matter of speculation whether, had the Greek cities been left to themselves, they would ever have succeeded in producing

[4] *Hellenistic Athens* (1911), pp. 1 ff.

a really effective kind of federal government. It was of the essence of the situation that they could never hope to be left to themselves.

Greek particularism and its dangers to Greek political life were an old story even in Plato's day. Especially the orators, from the beginning of the fourth century, had urged the cities to unite against the barbarians either of the east or of the west. Gorgias of Leontini had made it the subject of an oration at the Olympian Games, as had also Lysias a little later in 388. Isocrates had urged unity and lived to see in Philip of Macedon, as he believed, the man of destiny who might bring it about. Yet the treaty of Antalcidas (387–6) had established the suzerainty of Persia over the Greek world in matters of war and peace, and the Persian power persisted until it passed into the hands of Philip by the formation of the League at Corinth. Two centuries later the control of Greece was taken over by the expanding power of Rome. In foreign affairs, therefore, the city-state had failed permanently and more or less obviously from a date quite early in the fourth century. Even if the confederation had succeeded in stabilizing relations among the cities themselves, they would still have had to deal with the great political forces that surrounded the Greek world on the east, north, and west. And this they were doubly incapable of doing.

The failure of the cities to stabilize their relations with one another was not, however, a failure only in a special branch of administration. Foreign and domestic affairs were never really separable in the city-states, for the class-interests which were oligarchic or democratic in internal politics were similar from city to city and continually made common cause. No important aspect of local government could avoid making its peace in some fashion or other with the political and economic ties which ran between cities. And this is as true of the Macedonian intervention as of the relations between cities. The interests of property were in general on the side of Macedonia and this is one important reason why the more prosperous classes tended to look with complaisance upon the rise of Philip's power. For obvious reasons democratic interests had more local patriotism. The inextricable intertwining of foreign and domestic policy is admirably illustrated by the treaties between Alexander and the cities of the League of Corinth. In addition to the control of foreign affairs, Macedonia and the League were given the responsibility of repressing, in the cities of the League, any movement for the abolition of debt, the redivision of land, the confiscation of property, or the liberation of slaves. Later leagues included similar provisions.[5] The old issue between wealth and poverty, which Plato and Aristotle regarded as the essential difference between oligarchy and democracy, was in no way diminished as time went on. If anything it grew sharper; foreign intervention might draw the lines anew but the lines were still there.

The truth is that the social and political problems of the Greek world were not soluble by the city-states. It would be false to imply that they were really solved by the confederations and the monarchies that followed the conquests of Alexander. What became ever clearer was that the politics of the city-state did not even state the problems. The rise of Macedonia forced home the recognition of two facts that had existed but that Plato and Aristotle had for the most part overlooked. The one fact was that the city-state was too small and too contentious to govern even the Greek world and that no perfecting of it would make it commensurable with the economy of the world in which it lived. The other fact was that the assumed political superiority of Greeks over barbarians was not viable in the eastern Mediterranean, in view of the economic and cultural relations which had long existed between the Greek cities and the Asiatic hinterland. When Alexander deliberately adopted the policy of merging his Greek and his oriental subjects — a policy which must have been flatly contradictory of all that Aristotle had taught him about politics — he was at once accepting a fact whose importance his master had missed and also taking a step which made his master's political presumptions definitely obsolete.

WITHDRAWAL OR PROTEST

It is clear, then, that there was nothing accidental about the existence and the spread of a political philosophy much more negative in its attitude toward the values native to the city-state than that of Plato and Aristotle. The city-state of course continued to exist, and most of them continued for a long time to

[5] W. W. Tarn, *Hellenistic Civilisation* (1927), p. 104.

control their local affairs by the old governing bodies. No general statement can be made that will cover all the degrees and kinds of control over them in the Hellenistic Period. But no intelligent observer who had a sense of humor could take them quite so seriously as to suppose that their offices formed the capstone of a very significant career. A negative attitude might arise merely from a perception of the fact that the government of the city was not so important as men had imagined, that the life of any city was not for the most part in its own power, and that the most gifted statesmen could not hope to accomplish much in that arena. The result would be a defeatist attitude, a mood of disillusionment, a disposition to withdraw and to create a private life in which public interests had a small or even a negative part; a public career would be indifferent or even an actual misfortune. This point of view was perhaps best illustrated by the Epicureans or the Skeptics. On the other hand, a much more forthright negation of the city-state and its values might arise in so far as the unfortunate and dispossessed succeeded in making themselves vocal. Here it might be expected that withdrawal would be accompanied by a note of protest or a stress upon the seamy side of the existing social order. Such a protest might well be unable to state an adequate ideal of its own and might therefore run to fantastic or even indecent extremes. This tendency was illustrated best by the Cynic School.

It was characteristic of all these Schools, as has been said, that they did not follow the lines laid down by Plato and Aristotle. Their significance lies in the fact that they branched out in a new direction and began lines of thought to which the future was to give importance. For this reason they stand in some respects upon a much lower level of perfection than the work of the great theorists of the city-state. None of their authors possessed the transcendent genius of Plato and none had Aristotle's incomparable mastery of the history and government of the city-states. Their importance lies in the fact that they present a different point of view, that they raise questions about first principles, and that they make an opening for the restatement of these principles in a situation very different from that which Plato and Aristotle had envisaged. Considered sympathetically the failure of the city-state must be interpreted as a major moral disaster, at least for those classes that were mainly affected. It meant infinitely more than the closing of a political career can possibly mean in an age when in any case the whole scheme of values is largely private and personal. It forced upon men the creation for the first time of ideals of personal character and private happiness such as a Greek, trained in the ideals of the city-state, could scarcely see as other than a makeshift and a renunciation. This may be perceived in the growth of large numbers of private societies for religious or social purposes, such as the classical age had felt no need for, a tendency characteristic of the Hellenistic age.[6] These are manifestly an effort to compensate for the social interests left unsatisfied by the recession of the city from a place of first-rate importance. To Plato and Aristotle the values offered by citizenship still seemed fundamentally satisfying, or at least capable of being made so; to a few of their contemporaries and increasingly to their successors this appeared to be false. It was this profound difference of point of view that made it necessary for the time being to turn aside from the political philosophy which they had left.

All the schools that taught the ideal of individual self-sufficiency professed to arise directly from the teaching of Socrates. How much truth there may have been in any of these claims is impossible to say, and after the generation had passed that had known him in person, his professed followers probably knew little more about it than is known now. Socrates became and remained almost a myth, the ideal wise man and philosophic hero, whom every school set up as the professed example of its teaching. In one sense, however, the philosophical problem really did return to the posture in which it had stood before the work of Plato. It was a recanvassing of the old issue about the meaning of nature and its relation to customary and conventional rules of popular morals. This was of course true for the generation to which Plato belonged, since everyone really did begin where Socrates left off, but it was true at a later date also for those who found themselves unable to accept the elaborate solutions offered by Plato and Aristotle. The more it became doubtful whether the city-state actually did provide the only conditions upon which a civilized life can be lived, the more it was necessary to re-examine the previous ques-

[6] Tarn, *op. cit.*, p. 81.

tion: What are the essential and permanent factors in human nature from which a theory of the good life can be derived? Theories that Plato considered and rejected get a new hearing.

There were, as has been said, two chief forms of political philosophy to be considered in this connection. The one was most fully developed in the Epicurean School, though the differences between Epicureans and Skeptics were not very important, so far as the negations of their political theories were concerned. The second was the very different political philosophy of the Cynic School. It will be convenient to consider the two forms of theory in this order.

THE EPICUREANS

The purpose of Epicureanism [7] was, in general terms, the same as that of all the ethical philosophy of the period after Aristotle, namely, to produce in its students a state of individual self-sufficiency. To this end it taught that a good life consists in the enjoyment of pleasure, but it interpreted this negatively. Happiness consists actually in the avoidance of all pain, worry, and anxiety. The pleasures of congenial friendship, which Epicurus sought to realize within the circle of his pupils, were those which formed the positive content of his doctrine of happiness, and this involved a withdrawal from the useless cares of public life. The wise man, therefore, will have nothing to do with politics unless circumstances compel him to do so. The philosophical basis of this teaching is a system of thoroughgoing materialism adopted from earlier philosophies, and apparently chosen less because it was certainly true than because of the consolations which it was believed to hold out. The secret of its power of consolation lay in the fact that Epicurus counted the anxieties of religion, of divine retribution, and the incomprehensible whims of gods and spirits, as among the most serious to which men are heir. The gods, we may be sure, care nothing about men and do not interfere either for good or ill in the course of their lives. This was in fact the most virile part of the Epicurean teaching. The School was a caustic critic of all sorts of superstitious practice and belief, such

[7] The School was founded by Epicurus at Athens in 306 and remained for centuries one of the four great Athenian Schools. It was connected with Socrates through Aristippus.

as divination and astrology — a really substantial evil — and its record in this respect is in honorable contrast to that of Stoicism, which was only too ready to find adumbrations of truth in popular beliefs that were obviously not true.

So far as the world at large is concerned, then, nature means simply physics, the atoms out of which all things are made. So far as human beings are concerned, nature means self-interest, the desire of every man for his own individual happiness. All other regulation of human action belongs to the class of conventions and is therefore meaningless for the wise man, except in so far as a conventional rule may be serviceable in producing more happiness than men would get without it. There are, therefore, no intrinsic moral virtues and no intrinsic value of any sort except happiness.

> There never was an absolute justice but only a convention made in mutual intercourse, in whatever region, from time to time, providing against the infliction or suffering of harm.[8]

The argument against intrinsic values is the variety of moral rules and practices which have prevailed in different times and places, an argument which was originally exploited by certain of the Sophists and which had been noticed (and in intention refuted) by Plato in the discussion of justice in the *Republic*. At a later date it was vastly elaborated by the Skeptic Carneades against the Stoics.[9] The vital point in the argument is the view that the good is a feeling privately enjoyed and that social arrangements are justified, if at all, only as devices to secure the largest possible private good.

States, then, are formed solely for the sake of obtaining security, especially against the depredations of other men. All men are essentially selfish and seek only their own good. But in this way the good of everyone is jeopardized by the equally selfish action of all other men. Accordingly men enter into a tacit agreement with each other neither to inflict nor to suffer harm. The doing of injustice is not bad in itself, but suffering its consequences without protection is worse than any advantage to be gained. Since the state of affairs resulting from a general prac-

[8] Golden Maxims, 33. See R. D. Hicks, *Stoic and Epicurean* (1910), pp. 177 ff.

[9] Carneades's argument is reviewed at length by Cicero, *Republic*, Bk. III, 5–20.

tice of injustice is intolerable, men adopt as a working compromise the plan of respecting the rights of others for the sake of obtaining an equal forbearance from them. In this way the state and the law come into existence as a contract to facilitate intercourse between men. If no such contract exists, there is no such thing as justice. Law and government exist for the sake of mutual security and they are effective solely because the penalties of the law make injustice unprofitable. The wise man will act justly because the fruits of injustice are not worth the risk of detection and punishment. Morality is identical with expedience.

It follows, of course, that what men regard as right and just conduct will vary with circumstances and with time and place.

> Whatever in conventional law is attested to be expedient in the needs arising out of mutual intercourse is by its nature just, whether the same for all or not, and in case any law is made and does not prove suitable to the expediency of mutual intercourse, then this is no longer just. And should the expediency which is expressed by the law vary and only for a time correspond with the notion of justice, nevertheless, for the time being, it was just, so long as we do not trouble ourselves about empty terms but look broadly at facts.[10]

In general, no doubt, justice is largely the same among all peoples, for human nature is much the same everywhere, but still it is easy to see that at least in its applications the principle of expedience will vary more or less according to the kind of lives men lead. Thus what is wrong for some peoples may be right for others. For similar reasons a law which was perhaps originally just because it facilitated human intercourse may become wrong if the conditions change. In any case the test of law and of political institutions lies solely in expedience; in so far as they meet the need for security and make mutual intercourse safer and easier they are just in the only intelligible sense of the word. It was not unnatural therefore that the Epicureans, while caring little about forms of government, should have had a general preference for the monarchy as being the strongest and therefore the securest of governments. They were drawn no doubt mainly from the propertied classes, for whom security is always a major political good.

The social philosophy of the Epicureans was backed up by a really impressive theory of the origin and development of human

[10] Golden Maxims, 37.

institutions upon purely materialist principles. This has been preserved in the fifth book of Lucretius's poem *De rerum natura* but it presumably originated with Epicurus. All the forms of social life, its political and social institutions, the arts and sciences, in short, all human culture, have come about without the intervention of any intelligence other than man's. Living beings themselves are the result of purely physical causes, and Epicurus borrowed from Empedocles a theory that rather crudely suggests the modern hypothesis of natural selection. Man has no instinctive leaning toward society and no impulsion other than the restless pursuit of his individual happiness. In the beginning he lived a roving and solitary life, seeking shelter in caves, and struggling to maintain himself against wild beasts. The first step toward civilization was the accidental discovery of fire. Gradually he learned to shelter himself in huts and to clothe himself with skins. Language originated from the cries by which instinctively he expressed his emotions. Experience and the more or less intelligent adaptation of action to the conditions of nature in time produced the various useful arts, as well as the institutions and laws of organized society. Civilization is wholly the creation of natural human powers acting within the conditions set by the physical environment. Belief in the gods arises from dreams; the beginning of wisdom lies in the realization that the gods take no part in human affairs.

The full possibilities of such a theory of social evolution, and of a political philosophy based upon pure egoism and contract, could not be exploited until modern times. Then it was revived and the political philosophy of Hobbes — in its underlying materialism, its reduction of all human motives to self-interest, and in its construction of the state upon the need for security — is remarkably like Epicureanism. In the ancient world the drift of thought was against its most vital element — its attack upon religion and superstition — for the importance of religion among human interests was pretty steadily on the increase. It is true, however, that Epicureanism was on the whole a philosophy of escape. The charges of sensualism which gave its very name a bad meaning are mostly groundless, but it probably tended to foster a kind of bloodless aestheticism incapable of influencing, or of wishing to influence, the course of human affairs. For individual men it was a source of peace and consolation, but for the time being it had nothing to do with the progress of political ideas.

THE CYNICS

The Cynics also, perhaps, held a philosophy of escape but of a very different kind. More than any other School they formulated a protest against the city-state and the social classifications upon which it rested, and their escape lay in the renunciation of everything that men commonly called the goods of life, in the levelling of all social distinctions, and in abandoning the amenities and sometimes even the decencies of social conventions. Apparently they were recruited from the ranks of the foreigners and exiles, that is, from those who already stood outside the citizenship of the state. The founder of the School, Antisthenes, had a Thracian mother; its most notorious member, Diogenes of Sinope, was an exile; and its most able representative, Crates, seems to have renounced his fortune to adopt a life of philosophic poverty as a wandering beggar and teacher. His wife, Hipparchia, was a woman of good family who was first his pupil and then the companion of his wanderings. The Cynics formed a somewhat vague and quite unorganized body of roving teachers and popular philosophers who adopted a life of poverty on principle and who suggest somewhat the mendicant friars of the Middle Ages. Their teaching was addressed for the most part to the poor; they taught contempt for all the conventionalities; and in their behavior they often affected a shocking rudeness and disregard for decorum. In so far as the ancient world produced such a phenomenon, the Cynic may be described as the earliest example of the proletarian philosopher.

The philosophical basis of their teaching was the doctrine that the wise man ought to be completely self-sufficing. This the Cynics take to mean that only what is within his power, his own thought and character, is necessary to a good life. Everything except moral character is a matter of indifference. Among things indifferent the Cynic includes property and marriage, family and citizenship, learning and good repute, and in short all the pieties and conventions of a civilized life. All the customary distinctions of Greek social life were thus subjected to an annihilating criticism. Rich and poor, Greek and barbarian, citizen and foreigner, freeman and slave, well-born and base-born are all equal, for they are all reduced to the common level of indifference. The equality of the Cynics, however, was the equality of nihilism. The School never became the medium for a social doctrine either of philanthropy or of amelioration, but leaned always toward the ascetic and puritanical. For poverty and slavery were literally of no consequence in their eyes; true, the freeman was no better than the slave, but neither the one nor the other had any value in himself, nor would the Cynic admit that slavery was an evil or freedom a good. They appear to have been actuated by a real hatred of the social discriminations universal in the ancient world, but this hatred led them to turn their backs on inequality and to seek in philosophy the entrance into a spiritual realm where the abominations would not matter. It was hardly less a philosophy of renunciation than Epicureanism, but it was the renunciation of the ascetic and nihilist rather than of the esthete.

The result was that the political theory of the Cynics was utopian. Both Antisthenes and Diogenes are said to have written books on politics and both seem to have sketched a kind of idealized communism, or perhaps anarchy, in which property, marriage, and government disappeared. The problem was not one that, as the Cynic conceived it, touched the lives of the great majority of men. For most men, of whatever social class, are in any case fools, and the good life is only for the wise man. Equally, a true form of society also is for the wise man only. Philosophy emancipates its votaries from the laws and conventions of the city; the wise man is equally at home everywhere and nowhere. He requires neither home nor country, neither city nor law, because his own virtue is a law to him. All institutions are equally artificial and equally beneath the notice of the philosopher, for between men who have attained moral self-sufficiency these things are all unnecessary. The only true state is that in which wisdom is the requirement for citizenship and this state has neither place nor law. All wise men everywhere form a single community, the city of the world, and the wise man is, as Diogenes said, a "cosmopolitan," a citizen of the world. This conception of world-wide citizenship involved important consequences and had a distinguished history in Stoicism, but this was due chiefly to the positive meaning which the Stoics gave it. What the Cynics emphasized was its negative side: primitivism, the abolition of civic and social ties and of all restrictions except those that arise from the wise man's sense of duty. The protest of the Cynic against social convention was a doctrine of the return to nature in the most nihilist sense of the term.

The chief practical importance of the Cynic School lay in the fact that it was a matrix from which Stoicism emerged. But the Cynics have an interest perhaps out of proportion to their importance. After an interval of more than two thousand years it is not easy to recover the obscurer elements of political thought and those not in accord with the more vocal classes in the state. The rise and spread of Cynicism shows that, even as far back as the time of Socrates, there were some upon whom the institutions of the city-state bore heavily and who saw in it by no means an object to be idealized. With Plato and Aristotle in opposition these men were bound to be minor prophets. Yet what they saw at the beginning of the fourth century of the declining importance of the city-state was only what all men saw by the end of the century.

SELECTED BIBLIOGRAPHY

The Greek Atomists and Epicurus: A Study. By Cyril Bailey. Oxford, 1928. Ch. 10.

Titi Lucreti Cari: De rerum natura. Ed. with Prolegomena, Critical Apparatus, and Commentary by Cyril Bailey. 3 vols. Oxford, 1947. Prolegomena, Section IV.

A History of Cynicism from Diogenes to the 6th Century A.D. By Donald R. Dudley. London, 1937.

Greek Thinkers: A History of Ancient Philosophy. By Theodor Gomperz. Vol. II. Eng. trans. by G. G. Berry. New York, 1905. Book IV, ch. 7.

Stoic and Epicurean. By R. D. Hicks. New York, 1910. Ch. 5.

Diogenes of Sinope: A Study of Greek Cynicism. By Farrand Sayre. Baltimore, 1938.

Lucretius, Poet and Philosopher. By Edward E. Sikes. Cambridge, 1936.

The Stoics, Epicureans, and Sceptics. By Eduard Zeller. Eng. trans. by O. J. Reichel. London, 1880. Ch. 20.

PART II

THE THEORY OF THE UNIVERSAL COMMUNITY

CHAPTER VIII

THE LAW OF NATURE

In the history of political philosophy the death of Aristotle in 322 marks the close of an era, as the life of his great pupil, who died the year before him, marks the beginning of a new era in politics and the history of European civilization. The failure of the city-state is drawn like a sharp line across the history of political thought, whereas from this date forward its continuity is unbroken down to our own day. As Professor A. J. Carlyle has said, if there is any point where the continuity of political philosophy is broken, it is at the death of Aristotle.[1] The rise of Christianity produced, by comparison, only superficial changes in its course, and however great the later changes in political thought, they were at all events continuous, from the appearance of the theory of natural law in the Stoic School down to the Revolutionary doctrine of the rights of man. No other contrast is so dramatic as the magnificent statement of the ideals of the city-state by Plato and Aristotle, seen against the decline of the city and the total inapplicability of this philosophy a generation later.

Man as a political animal, a fraction of the *polis* or self-governing city state, had ended with Aristotle; with Alexander begins man as an individual. This individual needed to consider both the regulation of his own life and also his relations with other individuals who with him composed the " inhabited world "; to meet the former need there arose the philosophies of conduct, to meet the latter certain new ideas of human brotherhood. These originated on the day — one of the critical moments of history — when, at a banquet at Opis, Alexander prayed for a union of hearts (*homonoia*) and a joint commonwealth of Macedonians and Persians.[2]

THE INDIVIDUAL AND HUMANITY

In short, men had to learn to live alone as they had never done, and they had to learn to live together in a new form of social union much larger and much more impersonal than the city-state. How

[1] *History of Mediaeval Political Theory,* Vol. I (1903), p. 2.
[2] W. W. Tarn, *Hellenistic Civilisation* (1927), p. 69.

difficult the first task was may perhaps best be seen by the steady growth throughout the ancient world of forms of religion that held out the hope of personal immortality and provided rites of initiation into some mystic union with a god, often a suffering and dying god, that provided the means of salvation both in this life and in a life after death and, in their more vulgar forms, a magic to coerce fate and secure the aid of spirits.[3] All the philosophies after Aristotle became agencies of ethical instruction and consolation, and, as time passed, took on more and more the characteristics of religion; often philosophy was the only religion that an educated man had, in any sense that implied conviction or feeling. No social tendency is more clearly marked in this period than the increasing part that religion played in men's interests, or the increasing importance of religious institutions, a tendency which culminated in the appearance of Christianity and the formation of the Christian Church. It is impossible not to see in this religious growth an emotional aid for men who, without it, felt that they faced the world alone and found their native powers too feeble for the ordeal. Out of this process there grew a self-consciousness, a sense of personal privacy and internality, such as the Greek of the classical age had never possessed. Men were slowly making souls for themselves.

How difficult was the task of learning to live together in a new form of human brotherhood may perhaps best be seen in the effort of political and ethical philosophy to reinterpret social relations in terms other than those provided by the city-state. The sense of individual privacy and isolation had its reverse side, which was the consciousness of man as a human being, a member of the race, possessing a human nature more or less identical everywhere. For the breaking down of the intimate tie that had held citizens together left him simply a man. There was not in the ancient world any such consciousness of nationality as keeps the modern Frenchman or German a distinct kind of man, in his own estimation at least, even when he lives in a foreign country. With Attic Greek for a language a man in the Hellenistic age could get on comfortably, at least in the cities, from Marseilles to Persia. As time went on even citizenship, once a matter of birth alone, might be held in several cities at once, and indeed cities

[3] See Tarn, *op. cit.*, ch. x

might grant their citizenship to the whole citizen-body of another city. There was little to create a distinct consciousness of kind, setting men off from one another in groups. In so far as a man was not an individual and merely himself, he was a man like other men and a member of the species. At least this came to be more and more the case as the older ties grew progressively weaker and as even the distinction of Greek and barbarian receded before the intermingling in Egypt and Syria.

Political thought had, therefore, two ideas to make clear and to interweave into a common scheme of values: the idea of the individual, a distinct item of humanity with his purely personal and private life, and the idea of universality, a world-wide humanity in which all are endowed with a common human nature. The first could be given ethical meaning on the supposition that the individual person as such had a worth which other individuals were bound to respect. This was an assumption which had played small part in the ethics of the city-state, where the individual appeared as a citizen and where his significance depended upon his status or his function. In the great world an individual could hardly be said to have a function — unless in some religious sense — but he might, so to speak, make a virtue of his very insignificance. He might claim his own unsharable inner life as the origin from which all other values grow. In other words, he could set up the claim of an inherent right, the right to have his personality respected. But this in itself would require a corresponding addition of ethical meaning to the idea of universality. To mere likeness of kind it adds likeness of mind, *homonoia* or *concordia,* a union of hearts which makes the human species a common family or brotherhood. "Now there are diversities of gifts, but the same spirit," said St. Paul, adapting to the purposes of Christianity what was by that time a commonplace, "and there are diversities of operations, but it is the same God which worketh all in all. . . . For as the body is one and hath many members, and all the members of that one body, being many, are one body, so also is Christ."[4]

Great as is the gap between this conception of a world-wide society of autonomous individuals and the moral intimacy of the city-state, the two are not wholly discrepant. It would be

[4] *I. Corinthians,* 12, 4–12.

truer to say that the philosophy of the Hellenistic age tried to project upon a cosmic field ideals which, in their first appearance, were confined within the limits of the city. Aristotle had held that the two essentials of citizenship were that it should be a relation between equals, rendering a voluntary loyalty to a government having lawful rather than despotic authority. But he had inferred that equality could be asserted only of a small and very select body of citizens. The new conception posited equality for all men, even for the slave, the foreigner, and the barbarian. It had therefore to dilute the content of individual personality, either to a somewhat mystical equality of every soul in the eyes of God or to the equality of every man in the eyes of the law, neglecting inequalities of intelligence, character, and property. But though more abstract it could still argue, like Aristotle, that free citizenship implies some sphere of like treatment within which the state should be no respecter of persons. It had also, like Aristotle, to hold that the claim to authority is a claim of right and not of force, a claim to which a man of good will can assent without the loss of his proper moral dignity. This, too, involved a dilution of content. In place of a law embodied in the closely unified tradition of a single city, it had to conceive a law for the whole civilized world, an inclusive law of which the civil law of each city is only a particular instance.

This readjustment of ideas and readaptation of ideals is the tremendous task confronting political philosophy at the breakdown of the city-state. There is perhaps no better evidence of the intellectual vitality of Greek philosophy than the fact that the task was accomplished. What threatened to be a disaster to civilization became a fresh starting-point. The twin conceptions of the rights of man and of a universally binding rule of justice and humanity were built solidly into the moral consciousness of the European peoples. However much they might be disregarded or violated in the letter, they were too deeply rooted to be destroyed, even by the rise of a force so powerful as modern nationalism. The ideal of free citizenship was transformed to meet a situation in which the holding of public office and the performance of political function played a negligible part, and yet the ideal did not wholly vanish, for it persisted as the conception of a legal status and a body of rights in which the individual could claim the protection of the state. Finally, the conception was preserved that use and wont, prescriptive right and privilege, and overmastering power ought to justify themselves at the bar of a higher law, that they were at least subject to rational criticism and inquiry.

CONCORD AND MONARCHY

This work of reinterpretation and readaptation required a long time and received contributions from many sources. Its beginnings especially are obscure but, so far as philosophy was concerned, it came in the long run to be mainly identified with the philosophy of the Stoic School. This was the fourth and last of the great Athenian Schools, founded a little before 300 B.C. by Zeno of Citium. But it was less closely bound to Athens, and indeed to Greece, than any of the other Schools. Its founder was a "Phoenician," which must mean that at least one of his parents was Semitic. After him the heads of the School came usually from outlying parts of the Greek world, especially from Asia Minor, where the mingling of Greeks and Orientals proceeded most rapidly, and it was not until the first century B.C., when the School at Athens had ceased to be the center of Stoicism, that it was headed by an Athenian. Thus Chrysippus, its second founder, came from Cilicia, and Panaetius, who carried Stoicism to Rome, came from Rhodes. Stoicism was, then, from the start a Hellenistic and not a Greek School, and the ancients themselves believed in the relation of its teaching to Hellenistic politics, witness the remark of Plutarch that Alexander had founded the kind of state proposed by Zeno,[5] though this speaks rather for later Stoicism than for Zeno himself. Of special importance was the fact that Stoicism made a strong appeal to educated Romans of the second century and thus became the medium by which Greek philosophy exerted an influence in the formative stage of Roman jurisprudence.

In its beginnings Stoicism was a branch of Cynicism. According to the tradition, which is probably false, Zeno's book on the state was written while he was still a pupil of Crates, and its fragments show that it must have been a utopia much upon the lines of that written by Diogenes. In the ideal state, he said, men

[5] *I. de Alex. virt.*, 6.

would live as a single "herd," without family and presumably without property, with no distinction of race or rank, and without the need of money or courts of law. Zeno broke with the Cynics because of the crudeness and lack of decorum to which their naturalism led, but his early dependence on them remained to plague the new School. An element of doctrinaire utopianism was embedded in Stoicism which it never got rid of, though this was more and more disregarded, especially when the Middle Stoa adapted its teaching to Roman use. So long as its political theory held up an impossible ideal for a hypothetical world of philosophers, it could not really adopt the new idea of concord. To give up the distinction of Greek and barbarian was a gain, but to substitute for it an equally sharp distinction of wise men and fools did not greatly improve matters.

The idea of concord was intimately connected with the Hellenistic theory of kingship. The personal relation of Zeno to Antigonus II, king of Macedon, who was his pupil, and the fact that a member of the School was chosen to educate Antigonus's son, suggest a leaning toward enlightened despotism, but this was not a general characteristic of Stoicism. Mr. Tarn has argued that the plan to produce concord between Greeks and barbarians was Alexander's own, and that the philosophers took it up later. However this may be, the theory of kingship may well have had sources that were not Stoic.[6] It was in the nature of the situation that monarchy should receive the attention of political theorists as it had not in the classical age. Aristotle had treated monarchy as an academic question, but Alexander's empire and the parts into which it divided made a large part of the ancient world subject to kings — the Ptolemies in Egypt, the Selucids in Persia, and the Antigonids in Macedonia — and even the confederations were subject to their influence or control. The new monarchies (other than Macedonia) were predestined to be absolute, since there was no other form of government that could combine Greeks and Orientals. The king was not only the head of the state; he was

[6] W. W. Tarn, *Alexander the Great and the Unity of Mankind* (1933), Proceedings of the British Academy, Vol. XIX. See E. R. Goodenough's "Political Philosophy of Hellenistic Kingship" in *Yale Classical Studies*, Vol. I (1928), pp. 55 ff., which discusses a group of Pythagorean fragments, of uncertain date, preserved in Stobaeus. See also M. H. Fisch, "Alexander and the Stoics," *Am. J. Philology*, Vol. LVIII (1937), pp. 59, 129.

practically identical with it, for there was no other cohesive force to hold it together. Composed as they were of very diverse elements, these kingdoms necessarily left standing a large amount of local custom and local law, subject to such regulations as the unity of the kingdom required. Thus there grew up the distinction of king's law, or common law, and local law. The king became in a peculiar sense the symbol of unity and good government.

At the same time Hellenistic absolutism never wholly lost the Greek sense that government ought to be something more than military despotism. In Asia and Egypt the sanction was found in religion, the divinity of the king, who was worshiped in an official cult after his death or even in his life-time. Beginning with Alexander, Hellenistic kings were enrolled also among the gods of the Greek cities. The deified king became a universal institution in the East and in the end it had to be adopted by the Roman emperors. Thus a belief in "the divinity that doth hedge a king" came into European thought and persisted, in one form or another, down to modern times. The conception argued no special abjectness in subjects. So far as educated Greeks were concerned, the practice certainly involved nothing that was genuinely religious, and in any case there was nothing inherently shocking about a man being elevated to the rank of a god. Many Greek cities had heroes or lawgivers who had enjoyed that honor. Its purpose and its consequences in the cities were political; it gave Alexander and his successors who enjoyed it the authority needed to make their alliance with the cities effective.[7] Even in the monarchies the official cult of the king had a constitutional significance, not altogether unlike that which the theory of divine right had in the monarchy of the sixteenth century. It was the best available means of giving unity and homogeneity to the state and it was a way of saying that the king's authority had some claim of right behind it. Moreover, it gave to the king's law a continuance beyond his life-time which it could not have claimed if it were only the expression of his will. Finally, religious titles, such as Savior and Benefactor, might be real descriptions of what a good king could do; the gratitude of subjects for peace and good government was often genuine.

Consequently there grew up in Hellenistic times a theory of

[7] W. W. Tarn, *Hellenistic Civilisation* (1927), pp. 45 ff.

the deified king which in effect ascribed to his essential nature the beneficial effects which he ought to have. A true king was divine because he brought harmony to his kingdom as God brings harmony into the world. In a phrase widely current, he was an Animate Law, a personalized form of the principles of law and right that govern the whole universe. For this reason he possessed a divinity which the common man did not share and which brought to disaster the unworthy usurper who claimed the high office without the blessing of Heaven. Consequently his authority had a sanction, moral and religious, which his subjects could recognize without loss of their own moral freedom and dignity. For the conviction persisted that kingship and despotism are essentially different.

> Oh, that it were possible to put from human nature all need for obedience! For the fact that as mortal animals we are not exempt from it is the basest trace of our earthiness, inasmuch as a deed of obedience is very close to being one of necessity.[8]

THE CITY OF THE WORLD

This idealization of divinely sanctioned monarchy, however, does not appear in the classic form of Stoicism, perhaps because it was given its systematic statement at Athens at a date when the city had regained at least a qualified independence of Macedonia. In the hands of Chrysippus the Stoa in the last quarter of the third century became the greatest and most honored of the Athenian Schools, and Stoicism assumed the systematic shape which it retained throughout its history. Though he wrote a forbidding style that made him a by-word for dryness and verbalism, he succeeded in giving to the Stoic philosophy a form which made it in antiquity "the intellectual support of men of political, moral, and religious convictions."[9] It gave a positive moral meaning to the idea of a world-wide state and a universal law, which the Cynics had left merely as a negation of the city-state.

The ethical purpose of Stoicism was like that of the other post-Aristotelian philosophies, namely, to produce self-sufficiency and individual well-being. In fact, the School was always a little uncertain whether its ideal was the saint, who stands above

[8] Translated by Goodenough, *loc. cit.*, p. 89.
[9] W. S. Ferguson, *Hellenistic Athens* (1911), p. 261.

worldly interests, or the man of action. A Stoic as well as an Epicurean might teach that the part of wisdom was to withdraw from the world. For two reasons, however, this was not the prevailing bent of the School. First, it sought to teach self-sufficiency by a rigorous training of the will; its virtues were resolution, fortitude, devotion to duty, and indifference to the solicitations of pleasure. And second, the sense of duty was re-enforced by a religious teaching which was not unlike Calvinism. The Stoic had a strong belief in the overruling power of Divine Providence; he felt his own life as a calling, a duty, assigned to him by God, as a soldier is assigned to duty by his commander. Another figure of speech often used was the stage, upon which men are only players. The duty of every man is to play well the part for which he is cast, whether it be conspicuous or trifling, happy or miserable. The fundamental teaching of the Stoics was a religious conviction of the oneness and perfection of nature or a true moral order. A life according to nature meant for them resignation to the will of God, co-operation with all the forces of good, a sense of dependence upon a power above man that makes for righteousness, and the composure of mind that comes from faith in the goodness and reasonableness of the world.

There is, then, a fundamental moral fitness between human nature and nature at large. This the Stoic expressed by saying that man is rational and that God is rational. The same divine fire that animates the world has cast a spark into the souls of men. And this gives to humanity a special position among the creations of the world-soul. The animals are given instinct and the impulses and powers needed for life according to their several kinds, but men have reason; they have speech and the sense of right and wrong; hence they alone of all beings are fitted for a social life and for them such a life is necessary. Men are the sons of God and therefore brothers to one another. The belief in Providence is, for the Stoics, essentially a belief in the value of social purposes and in the duty of good men to bear a share of them. It was this conviction that made Stoicism a moral and a social force. There was nothing intrinsically utopian about it, though it is true that the earlier Stoics were likely to put their philosophic heroes on a pedestal.

Hence there is a world-state. Both gods and men are citizens of it and it has a constitution, which is right reason, teaching men what must be done and what avoided. Right reason is the law of nature, the standard everywhere of what is just and right, unchangeable in its principles, binding on all men whether ruler or subjects, the law of God. Chrysippus expressed it as follows in the opening words of his book *On Law:*

> Law is the ruler over all the acts both of gods and men. It must be the director, the governor and the guide in respect to what is honorable and base and hence the standard of what is just and unjust. For all beings that are social by nature the law directs what must be done and forbids what must not be done.

The conventional social distinctions that prevail in particular localities have no meaning for the world-state. The earlier Stoics continued to deny, after the fashion of the Cynics, that a city of wise men would need any institutions at all. Greek and barbarian, well-born and common, slave and free, rich and poor are all declared to be equal; the only intrinsic difference between men is that between the wise man and the fool, between the man whom God can lead and the one whom he must drag. There can be no doubt that the Stoics used this theory of equality from the start as a ground for moral improvement, though social reform was always with them a secondary consideration. Chrysippus says that no man is a slave " by nature " and that a slave should be treated as a " laborer hired for life," which has a very different tone from Aristotle's description of him as a living implement. Potentially at least citizenship in the world-city was open to all, for it depends on reason, which is a common human trait; in practice the Stoics, like most rigorous moralists, were impressed by the number of fools. Strait is the way and narrow is the gate and few there be that find it, but at all events a man stands here on his merits; externals cannot help him.

If Stoicism diminished the importance of social distinctions between individuals, it tended also to promote harmony between states. There are for every man two laws, the law of his city and the law of the world-city, the law of custom and the law of reason. Of the two the second must have the greater authority and must provide a norm to which the statutes and customs of cities should conform. Customs are various but reason is one, and behind variety of custom there ought to be some unity of purpose. Stoicism tended to conceive of a world-wide system of law having endless local branches. Localities might differ according to circumstances without being unreasonable, while the reasonableness of the whole system tended to keep the variation from becoming opposition. Substantially this is not unlike the harmony or "union of hearts" for which Alexander prayed. Everywhere in the Hellenistic world there were great numbers of cities and other local authorities with more or less autonomy. The kingdoms held these together with a common or king's law. Between the cities arbitration became a recognized and widely practiced way of settling disputes. In internal government the adjudication of private disputes by judicial commissions called in from other cities largely displaced the old popular juries.[10]

Both procedures implied a comparison of customs, an appeal to equity, and ultimately the growth of a common law — the circumstances in which natural law has always exerted its greatest influence. For later history the incidence of the Stoic idea of a higher law on Roman law had a greater importance, but the nature of its influence seems to have been the same from the start. It held up an ideal of reasonableness and equity as a means of criticising law at a time when positive law was likely to be narrowly customary. The point is not merely the assertion that positive law should be equitable; the Greeks had always believed that the law provides a moral code and a general rule of right. What the Stoics added to this was the doctrine of two laws, the customary law of the city and the more perfect law of nature. The use of equity as a principle of criticism requires a clear perception that justice cannot be identified with law as it is. The world-city of the Stoics was already on the way to becoming the City of God of later Christian thought.

THE REVISION OF STOICISM

The general principles of the Stoic philosophy remained always what Chrysippus left them at the close of the third century. But these principles underwent important changes which had the effect of adapting them to popular understanding and acceptance and especially to acceptance at Rome. The difficulty with earlier Stoicism arose largely from the elements of Cynicism that re-

[10] Tarn, *op. cit.*, p. 77.

mained implicit in it — a tendency to think of the wise man as a being quite unlike ordinary mortals and so aloof from ordinary concerns and a corresponding tendency not to bring the law of nature into relation with the actual variety of custom and usage. The cause of the readjustment was largely the incisive negative criticism of the Skeptic Carneades. By the second century Stoicism had attained a place among the Schools which warranted a life-time devoted to its criticism; Carneades is said to have inquired jocularly, "If it were not for Chrysippus, where should I be?" Carneades's criticism attacked Stoicism all along the line, in its theology, its psychology, and of course with respect to the theory of natural justice. So far as it concerned political theory the gist of the criticism appears to have been, first, that the Stoic wise man is a monstrosity, like nothing in nature, and utterly inhuman in his effort to extirpate all feeling and emotion. This criticism was quite justified so far as the theory was concerned, though the Stoics were in general better than their theory. Second, Carneades pointed out the difficulty of believing that there is a universal law of justice in the face of the discrepancies that actually exist in moral belief and practice. Carneades himself asserted that men are in fact governed wholly by self-interest and prudence, for which justice is merely an honorific title.

The answer to these criticisms was not precisely a reconstruction of Stoicism but rather its modification by the inclusion in it of ideas drawn especially from Plato and Aristotle. By the end of the second century a world-wide culture needed, and perhaps tried consciously to create, a world-wide philosophy, which could hardly be made fit for popular adoption except by the inclusion of elements syncretized from many sources. By this time also it was possible to go back to the great philosophers of the fourth century without being repelled by their absorption in the city-state, which had been a dead issue longer than men could remember. This is the first of the many occasions on which a return to the classical tradition in philosophy was the means to a more humane view of life and social relations. So far as Stoicism was concerned, this work was done by Panaetius of Rhodes, who headed the School shortly before the close of the second century. Stoicism lost certainly in logical rigor but it gained enormously in its urbanity and in the appeal which it was able to make to educated men who cared nothing for the technicalities of the Schools. And this was a matter of first-rate importance in respect to the social and political influence that it could exert. The great work of Panaetius was to restate Stoicism in a form such that it could be assimilated by Romans of the aristocratic class, who knew nothing of philosophy and who yet were fired by enthusiasm for the learning of Greece, so different from anything that Rome could produce for herself. No other Greek system was so well qualified as Stoicism to appeal to the native virtues of self-control, devotion to duty, and public spirit in which the Roman took especial pride, and no political conception was so well qualified as the Stoic world-state to introduce some measure of idealism into the too sordid business of Roman conquest. The point of contact at the critical stage — the third quarter of the second century — was in the relation of two Greeks, Panaetius and Polybius, personal friends, to the group of aristocratic Romans that formed the circle about Scipio Aemilianus.

In effect what Panaetius did was to turn Stoicism into a kind of philosophy of humanitarianism, his concessions being of the sort required to meet the objections advanced by Carneades. He admitted the moral justification of the nobler and more public-spirited ambitions and passions and denied that the wise men should strive for complete cessation of feeling. In place of self-sufficiency he set up an ideal of public service, humanity, sympathy, and kindness. What is of even greater importance, he abandoned the opposition between an ideal community of wise men and the everyday social relationships. Reason is a law for all men, not merely for the wise. There is a sense in which all men are equal, even after allowance has been made for the inevitable differences of rank, native endowment, and wealth. They ought all to have at least that minimum of rights without which human dignity is impossible, and justice requires that the law should recognize such rights and protect men in the enjoyment of them. Justice is, therefore, a law for states, the bond that holds them together, not of course in the sense that a state cannot be unjust, but in the sense that, in so far as it becomes so, it loses that ground of harmony which makes it a state. This theory of the state, probably the work of Panaetius, is preserved in Cicero. The humanitarianism of Panaetius's philosophy left its impression strongly upon all the Roman Stoics.

> The unity of the human race, the equality of man and therefore justice in the state, the equal worth of men and women, respect for the rights of wives and children, benevolence, love, purity in the family, tolerance and charity toward our fellows, humanity in all cases, even in the terrible necessity of punishing criminals with death — these are the fundamental ideas which fill the books of the later Stoics.[11]

To Polybius is due the earliest extant history of Rome and the first study of Roman political institutions. His history accepts the world-state under Roman domination as a fact. He tries to follow the course of events from Spain to Asia Minor, and to show " by what means, and thanks to what sort of constitution, the Romans subdued the world in less than fifty-three years." In his sixth book he offers a theory of the Roman constitution, which probably reflects the ideas of Panaetius also, and which certainly commended itself to the Scipionic Circle. There is in history, Polybius believes, an inevitable law of growth and decay. This he explains by the tendency of all the unmixed forms of government to degenerate in characteristic ways: of monarchy to become tyrannous, of aristocracy to become oligarchical, and so on. He uses here the old sixfold classification of constitutions in Plato's *Statesman* and Aristotle's *Politics,* merely supplementing it by a more definite theory of the cycle that causes one form to run into another. The reason which he assigns for the strength of Rome is that it has unconsciously adopted a mixed constitution in which the elements are " accurately adjusted and in exact equilibrium." The consuls form a monarchical factor, the Senate an aristocratic factor, and the popular assemblies a democratic factor; but the true secret of Roman government lies in the fact that the three powers check each other and thus prevent the natural tendency to decay which would result if any one of them became too powerful. Polybius modified the old theory of mixed government, long a commonplace, in two respects. First, he made the tendency of the unmixed governments to degenerate an his-

[11] Jacques Denis, *Histoire des théories et des idées morales dans l'antiquité* (1856), Vol. II, pp. 191 f.; quoted by Janet, *Histoire de la science politique* (1913), Vol. I, p. 249.

torical law, but his cycle is formed on Greek experience and does not fit the development of the Roman constitution at all. Second, his mixed government is not, like Aristotle's, a balance of social classes but of political powers. Here he probably drew upon the Roman legal principle of collegiality by which any magistrate could impose a veto barring action by any other magistrate having an equal or a less *imperium*. Polybius thus gave to mixed government the form of a system of checks and balances, the form in which it passed to Montesquieu and the founders of the American constitution.

So far as historical accuracy is concerned, Polybius's analysis of the Roman constitution was not more penetrating than Montesquieu's analysis of the English constitution. The tribunes of the people — the most important of all the magistracies in later constitutional development — do not fit into his scheme at all. Like Montesquieu he grasped only a passing phase of the constitution he was examining. Indeed, the theory of the mixed government had only temporary importance in the transference of Stoic ideas to Rome. Doubtless Roman aristocrats during the later days of the Republic were flattered to hear that their ancestral constitution had copied by instinct the greatest discovery of Greek political science. Doubtless also the Stoic world-state lent itself easily to a kind of sentimental imperialism which enabled the conquerors to imagine that they were assuming the white man's burden and were bringing the blessings of peace and order to a politically incompetent world. Finally, there was a special historical circumstance at the end of the second century B.C. — the attempted reforms of Tiberius Gracchus in 133 by a frank appeal to the opposed interests of economic classes — which made an appeal to a *concordia ordinum* the appropriate reaction of aristocratic republicans. The theory of the mixed state bulked large in the thought of Cicero, but it was only the forlorn hope of the Republic. The direct line of development under the empire was toward world-wide Roman citizenship, achieved by the Edict of Caracalla in 212 A.D., and the abolition of class-distinctions. The implied egalitarianism of this movement was much more in the spirit of Roman Stoicism than the form which Stoicism temporarily assumed under the influence of Panaetius and Polybius.

THE SCIPIONIC CIRCLE

The permanently significant result of the incidence of Stoicism upon the Scipionic Circle lay in the fact that it affected the men who undertook the earliest studies in Roman jurisprudence. Panaetius's restatement of Stoicism appeared to these Romans of the ruling class to offer the means for preserving the best of the older Roman ideals, enlightened by the cultivation of art and letters and harmonized by a broader sympathy, good will, and gentleness. This the Romans named *humanitas* — a corrective for the crudeness of a society drunk with power and unenlightened by taste or ideas and a means of idealizing conquest. Through the Scipionic Circle, or men intimately associated with its members, this ideal was brought to bear at a critical period upon the study of Roman law. There can be no question that these earliest attempts at systematic jurisprudence were made by men strongly influenced by Stoicism.[12]

The way had been prepared by the history of the law itself before Stoicism came to Rome. The law of Rome, like most systems of ancient law, had been at the start the law of a city, or more precisely, of a very limited body of citizens who were born to it as part of their civic heritage. It combined religious ceremonial and ancestral formularies which made it inapplicable to anyone not by birth a Roman. As Roman political power and wealth grew, there came to be a larger and larger body of alien residents in Rome who had to transact business both among themselves and with Romans. Thus it became practically necessary to take legal cognizance of their doings in some way or other. About the middle of the third century B.C. the Romans met this problem by creating a special judge (the *praetor peregrinus*) to handle this class of business. Since no ceremonial law was applicable, all sorts of informalities in procedure had to be permitted, and, for the same reason, formal law had continually to be pieced out by considerations of equity, fair dealing, and common sense, in short, by taking into consideration what good business practice regarded as honest and fair. In this way an effective body of law grew up, largely stripped of formality and conforming in general to prevailing ideas of honorable dealing and public utility, to

[12] See *Cicero on the Commonwealth,* ed. by Sabine and Smith (1929), Introduction, p. 36.

which the lawyers had already given the name *ius gentium,* the law that is common to all peoples. The process of its formation was in substance not different from that which brought about English Mercantile Law. And just as the latter was finally incorporated into the main body of English Law, so the *ius gentium* affected the development of Roman Law. In fact, because it was more equitable and reasonable and altogether better suited to the times than the old strict law, it co-operated with other factors to enlighten the practice of the whole body of Roman Law.[13]

The *ius gentium* was a legal concept with no particular philosophical meaning, while *ius naturale* was a philosophical term made by translating Stoic Greek into Latin. In effect the two very nearly coalesced. The two concepts were able to interact fruitfully, for general acceptance and practice were properly felt to give some guarantee of substantial justice, at least as compared with local custom, while they in turn gave the rule of reason a point of contact with practice. Thus the ideal law of the Stoics and the positive law of states were brought into co-operation. The effect upon jurisprudence in the end proved to be exceedingly beneficial. The conception of natural law brought enlightened criticism to bear on custom; it helped to destroy the religious and ceremonial character of law; it tended to promote equality before the law; it emphasized the factor of intent; and it mitigated unreasoning harshness. In short, it set before the Roman lawyers the ideal of making their profession an *ars boni et aequi.*

In order to appreciate the full accomplishment of the Stoic political philosophy it is necessary to reflect upon the long road that political society had travelled in the two centuries that elapsed after the death of Aristotle. Compared with Athens in 322 the Mediterranean world of two centuries later was almost modern. It was at all events a society that included the effectively known world, in which wide communication was habitual, and in which local differences had a small and a diminishing importance. Accepting as accomplished fact the wreckage of the city-state and the impossibility of its self-centered provincialism, of its rigid distinction between citizens and foreigners, and of a citizenship limited to those who can actually have a share in governing,

13 See "The Development of Law under the Republic," by F. de Zulueta, *Cambridge Ancient History,* Vol. IX (1932), pp. 866 ff.

Stoicism had boldly undertaken to reinterpret political ideals to fit the Great State. It had outlined the conception of a world-wide human brotherhood united in the bonds of a justice broad enough to include them all. It had proposed the conception that men are by nature equal, despite differences of race, rank, and wealth. It had insisted that even the Great State, no less than the city, is an ethical union which ought to lay a moral claim upon its subjects' loyalty and not merely exact their obedience by overmastering force. However much honored in the breach by political practice, these conceptions of what human relations ought to be could never thereafter be altogether omitted from the political ideals of the European peoples.

SELECTED BIBLIOGRAPHY

"Roman Religion and the Advent of Philosophy." By Cyril Bailey. In the *Cambridge Ancient History,* Vol. VIII (1930), ch. 14.

Chrysippe. By Émile Bréhier. Paris, 1910.

"The Law of Nature." By James Bryce. In *Studies in History and Jurisprudence*. New York, 1901.

Alexander and the Greeks. By Victor Ehrenberg. Eng. trans. by Ruth F. von Velsen. Oxford, 1938.

"Legalized Absolutism en route from Greece to Rome." By W. S. Ferguson. In *Am. Hist. Rev.*, Vol. XVIII (1912–13), p. 29.

Hellenistic Athens: An Historical Essay. By W. S. Ferguson. London, 1911.

"The Leading Ideas of the New Period." By W. S. Ferguson. In the *Cambridge Ancient History,* Vol. VII (1928), ch. 1.

"Polybius." By T. R. Glover. In the *Cambridge Ancient History,* Vol. VIII (1930), ch. 1.

"The Political Philosophy of the Hellenistic Kingship." By Erwin R. Goodenough. In *Yale Classical Studies,* Vol. I. New Haven, Conn., 1928.

The Politics of Philo Judaeus: Practice and Theory. By Erwin R. Goodenough. New Haven, Conn., 1938.

Stoic and Epicurean. By R. D. Hicks. New York, 1910. Chs. 3, 4, 7, 8.

The Greek Sceptics. By Mary Mills Patrick. New York, 1929.

"The History of the Law of Nature." By Sir Frederick Pollock. In *Essays in the Law*. London, 1922.

Die Philosophie der mittleren Stoa in ihrem geschichtlichen Zusammenhange. By August Schmekel. Berlin, 1892.

Hellenistic Civilisation. By W. W. Tarn. London, 1927.

"The Development of Law under the Republic." By F. de Zulueta. In the *Cambridge Ancient History,* Vol. IX (1932), ch. 21.

CHAPTER IX

CICERO AND THE ROMAN LAWYERS

By the beginning of the first century before Christ the political processes which began with Alexander's conquest of the East had in a large measure completed themselves. The whole Mediterranean world had been cast into the melting pot and had become in no small degree a single community. The city-state had ceased to count, and there were no politically self-conscious nations such as the modern era has produced. Already it was apparent that the successor to Macedonia and also to Egypt and the Asiatic Kingdoms would be Rome, and that the known civilized world would be united under a single political rule, as indeed happened in the course of the century following. By the beginning of the first century, also, the Stoic philosophy had spread the ideas of a world-state, of natural justice, and universal citizenship, though these terms had an ethical rather than a legal sense. The stage was set for the further development and clarification of these philosophical ideas. The more negative ethics of the Epicureans and the Skeptics — the identification of " nature " with individual self-interest — continued to exist, but the immediate future, at least, lay with the ideas developed by the Stoics. These had now become so dispersed that they were ready to lose their identification with any philosophic system and become the common property of educated men.

These ideas included a number of convictions having an ethical or a religious import but no very high degree of philosophical precision. With an ever-increasing tendency of the Schools to borrow from one another, they had even lost some of the precision which they had in the Stoicism of Chrysippus, as was to be expected when they became current in a culture that was substantially world-wide. They included the belief that the world is the subject of divine government by a God who is, in some sense, reasonable and good, and who stands therefore in a relation to men that may be compared with that of a father to his children. They included also the belief that men are brothers to one another and members of a common human family, in which their rationality makes them as a race akin to God and in some fundamental way alike, even after allowance has been made for the distinctions which diversity of language and local custom create among them. Hence there are some rules of morality and justice and reasonableness in conduct which are binding upon all men, not because they are laid down in the positive law or because a penalty follows their violation, but because they are intrinsically right and deserving of respect. Finally, and perhaps vaguest of all, men were felt to be fundamentally "social" in their nature. This idea had no such precision as Aristotle's theory that man is an animal who reaches the highest stage of his development in the civilization of the city-state. It suggested merely that respect for the laws of God and man is a native endowment of human nature and that by following the lead of this innate reverence he fulfills his own nature, while he stultifies himself if he elects to do the opposite.

The development of these ideas, in the first century before Christ and in the two or three centuries thereafter, followed two main lines. The one continued in the direction already indicated by the influence of Stoicism upon the beginnings of Roman jurisprudence; it had the effect of embedding natural law in the philosophical apparatus of the Roman Law. The other had to do with the religious implications of the idea that law and government are rooted in the plan of Divine Providence for the guidance of human life. In both cases the development of a political philosophy was incidental. Of the writers to be considered, only Cicero was avowedly a political theorist, yet his effort to deal specifically with the political problems of the Roman Republic was the least important part of his work. But though a political theory was incidental to more general purposes — in the one case to the construction of a system of law and jurisprudence and in the other to the construction of a theology and an ecclesiastical organization — the resulting modes of political thought departed widely from the point of view that had prevailed in Greek political theory and exerted a profound influence upon political reflection in the centuries following. Legalism — the presumption that the state is a creature of law and is to be discussed not in terms of sociological fact or ethical good but in terms of legal competence and rights

—had hardly existed in Greek thought; it has been an intrinsic part of political theory from Roman times to the present. The relation of the state to religious institutions and of political philosophy to theology had scarcely been problems for the Greeks, but they set the chief problems and colored the discussion of every problem throughout the Middle Ages and well down into modern times. In the history of political theory, therefore, the changes wrought in the age just before and not long after the beginning of the Christian era were of momentous importance, though they produced no systematic treatises on political philosophy.

This chapter and the following will deal respectively with these two tendencies, the legal and the theological. In respect to dates they lie nearly parallel to one another. Perhaps a word of explanation is required for allocating Cicero to the first and Seneca to the second, thus violating a chronological arrangement and also, as it may seem, slurring over the break which might be assumed to have occurred with the rise of Christianity. The reason for including Cicero in the same chapter with the lawyers is not, of course, either that he was a great jurist, for he was not, or that only lawyers read him. It is merely that his political ideas seem to have a secular cast and so a relatively close affinity with those of the lawyers. Seneca, on the other hand, gave a definitely religious bias to his philosophy. The reason for including Seneca with the Christian Fathers is to mark the fact that, in the beginning, the rise of Christianity did not carry with it a new political philosophy. Christianity itself and its ultimate establishment as the legal religion of the empire were the consummation of social and intellectual changes that had long been at work and which affected almost equally thinkers who never embraced the new faith. So far as political ideas are concerned, those of the Fathers were for the most part those of Cicero and Seneca. For purposes of historical accuracy there is no reason why the Christian era should be taken as beginning a new period in political thought.

CICERO

The political thought of Cicero is not important because of its originality; his books were frankly compilations, as he himself avows. They had, however, one merit which is far from negligible: everybody read them. An idea once embedded in Cicero was preserved to the reading public for all future time. So far as his political thought is concerned, his philosophy was the form of Stoicism which Panaetius had produced for a Roman public and transmitted to the Scipionic Circle. In fact, nearly all that is known of this philosophy as it stood at the beginning of the first century before Christ has to be gathered from Cicero. His own political treatises, the *Republic* and the *Laws,* were written at about the middle of the century and are the best index of political thought at Rome, especially in conservative and aristocratic circles, during the last days of the Republic.

For the understanding of Cicero and his historical importance it is necessary to distinguish rather sharply between the immediate purpose for which he wrote and the long-time influence that he exerted. His influence was very great, but what he attempted was a total failure, if not actually an anachronism in its own time. The moral purpose for which he wrote was to commend the traditional Roman virtue of public service and the pre-eminence of the statesman's career, enlightening and harmonizing these with a tincture of Greek philosophy. His political object was nothing less than to turn back the clock and restore the republican constitution to the form that it had had before the revolutionary tribunate of Tiberius Gracchus. This explains his adoption in the *Republic* of the younger Scipio and Laelius as the heroes of the dialogue. Needless to say, this object had little reality when Cicero wrote and none at all within a generation after his death.

To this part of his political theory must be assigned two ideas to which he attached great importance but which, in the age under discussion, had hardly more than antiquarian interest: a belief in the excellence of the mixed constitution and the theory of the historical cycle of constitutions. Both these he derived from Polybius, and perhaps also from Panaetius, though he endeavored to modify them in the light of his own understanding of Roman history. In fact, Cicero had a really promising plan, if only he had possessed the philosophical capacity to carry it out. This was to set forth a theory of the perfect state (a mixed constitution), by permitting its principles to be developed in the course of a history of the Roman constitution (according to the theory of the cycle). Contributed by many minds working under diverse circumstances and embodying piecemeal the solutions of political problems as they arose, the constitution of Rome, as Cicero conceives, was the most stable and perfect form of government that political experience had evolved. By tracing its development and analyzing its parts in relation to one another it should be possible to arrive at a theory of the state in which mere speculation is reduced to a minimum. Unfortunately, however, Cicero lacked the originality to strike out a new theory for himself, in line with Roman experience and in defiance of his Greek sources. The Polybian cycle — the orderly alternation of good and bad constitutions, from monarchy to tyranny, from tyranny to aristocracy, from aristocracy to oligarchy, from oligarchy to moderate democracy, and from democracy to mob-rule — had been commendable chiefly for its logical neatness, but such empirical observation as lay behind it was that of the city-states. Cicero was uncomfortably aware that it did not fit his ideas of Roman history, and in the event he did little more than render lip-service to the theory of the cycle while robbing it even of logical neatness. In a somewhat similar way he praised the advantages of a mixed constitution, the type of which he believed to be Rome, without even making clear what Roman institutions he took to represent each element of the composite. His account of the matter justifies Tacitus's gibe that it is easier to praise a mixed constitution than to realize one. The intention to sketch a theory of the state in close relation to Roman institutional history was laudable, but it was not to be realized by a man who took his theory ready-made from Greek sources and grafted it upon an account of Roman history.

Cicero's true importance in the history of political thought lies in the fact that he gave to the Stoic doctrine of natural law a statement in which it was universally known throughout western Europe from his own day down to the nineteenth century. From him it passed to the Roman lawyers and not less to the Fathers of the Church. The most important passages were quoted times without number throughout the Middle Ages. It is a significant fact that, though the text of the *Republic* was lost after the twelfth century and not recovered until the nineteenth, its most striking passages had already been excerpted into the books of Augustine and Lactantius, and so had become matters of common knowledge. The ideas were, of course, in no sense original with Cicero but his statement of them, largely in Latin expressions of his own devising to render the Stoic Greek, became incomparably the most important single literary means for spreading them through western Europe. A few of Cicero's great passages must be kept in mind by anyone who wishes to read political philosophy in the centuries that followed.

First of all, there is a universal law of nature arising equally from the fact of God's providential government of the world and from the rational and social nature of human beings which makes them akin to God. This is, as it were, the constitution of the world-state; it is the same everywhere and is unchangeably binding upon all men and all nations. No legislation that contravenes it is entitled to the name of law, for no ruler and no people can make right wrong:

> There is in fact a true law — namely, right reason — which is in accordance with nature, applies to all men, and is unchangeable and eternal. By its commands this law summons men to the performance of their duties; by its prohibitions it restrains them from doing wrong. Its commands and prohibitions always influence good men, but are without effect upon the bad. To invalidate this law by human legislation is never morally right, nor is it permissible ever to restrict its operation, and to annul it wholly is impossible. Neither the senate nor the people can absolve us from our obligation to obey this law, and it requires no Sextus Aelius to expound and interpret it. It will not lay down one rule at Rome and another at Athens, nor will it be one rule to-day and another to-morrow. But there will be one law, eternal and unchangeable, binding at all times upon all peoples; and there will be, as it were, one common master and ruler of men, namely God, who is the author of this law, its interpreter, and its sponsor. The man who will not obey it will abandon his better self, and, in denying the true nature of a man, will thereby suffer the severest of penalties, though he has escaped all the other consequences which men call punishments.[1]

In the light of this eternal law all men, as Cicero insists in the most unequivocal terms, are equal. They are not equal in learning, and it is not expedient for the state to try to equalize their property, but in the possession of reason, in their underlying psychological make-up, and in their general attitude toward what they believe to be honorable or base, all men are alike. Indeed Cicero goes so far as to suggest that it is nothing but error, bad habits and false opinions, that prevents men from being in fact

[1] *Republic,* III, 22. Trans. by Sabine and Smith.

equal. All men and all races of men possess the same capacity for experience and for the same kinds of experience, and all are equally capable of discriminating between right and wrong.

> Out of all the material of the philosophers' discussions, surely there comes nothing more valuable than the full realization that we are born for Justice, and that right is based, not upon man's opinions, but upon Nature. This fact will immediately be plain if you once get a clear conception of man's fellowship and union with his fellow-men. For no single thing is so like another, so exactly its counterpart, as all of us are to one another. Nay, if bad habits and false beliefs did not twist the weaker minds and turn them in whatever direction they are inclined, no one would be so like his own self as all men would be like all others.[2]

Professor A. J. Carlyle has said that "no change in political theory is so startling in its completeness" as the change from Aristotle to a passage such as this.[3] The process of reasoning is, in truth, the exact opposite of that which Aristotle had used. The relation of free citizenship for Aristotle can hold only between equals, but because men are not equal, he had inferred that citizenship must be restricted to a small and carefully selected group. Cicero on the contrary infers that, because all men are subject to one law and so are fellow-citizens, they must be in some sense equal. For Cicero equality is a moral requirement rather than a fact; in ethical terms it expresses much the same conviction that a Christian might express by saying that God is no respecter of persons. There is no implication of political democracy, though without some such moral conviction democracy would be hard to defend. What is asserted is that some measure of human dignity and respect is due to every man; he is inside and not outside the great human brotherhood. Even if he were a slave he would not be, as Aristotle had said, a living tool, but more nearly as Chrysippus had said, a wage-earner hired for life. Or, as Kant rephrased the old ideal eighteen centuries later, a man must be treated as an end and not as a means. The astonishing fact is that Chrysippus and Cicero are closer to Kant than they are to Aristotle.

The political deduction which Cicero draws from this ethical axiom is, that a state cannot exist permanently, or at least cannot exist in any but a crippled condition, unless it depends upon, and acknowledges, and gives effect to the consciousness of mutual

[2] *Laws,* I, 10, 28–29 (Trans. by C. W. Keyes).

[3] *A History of Mediaeval Political Theory in the West,* Vol. I (1903), p. 8.

obligations and the mutual recognition of rights that bind its citizens together. The state is a moral community, a group of persons who in common possess the state and its law. For this reason he calls the state, in a fine phrase, the *res populi* or the *res publica*, "the affair of the people," which is practically equivalent in meaning to the older English use of the word "commonwealth." This is the ground for Cicero's argument, against the Epicureans and Skeptics, that justice is an intrinsic good. Unless the state is a community for ethical purposes and unless it is held together by moral ties, it is nothing, as Augustine said later, except "highway robbery on a large scale." A state may of course be tyrannous and rule its subjects by brute force — the moral law does not make immorality impossible — but in the measure that it does so, it loses the true character of a state.

The commonwealth, then, is the people's affair; and the people is not every group of men, associated in any manner, but is the coming together of a considerable number of men who are united by a common agreement about law and rights and by the desire to participate in mutual advantages.[4]

The state, then, is a corporate body, membership in which is the common possession of all its citizens; it exists to supply its members with the advantages of mutual aid and just government. Three consequences follow: First, since the state and its law is the common property of the people, its authority arises from the collective power of the people. A people is a self-governing organization which has necessarily the powers required to preserve itself and continue its existence: *Salus populi suprema lex esto*. Second, political power when rightfully and lawfully exercised really is the corporate power of the people. The magistrate who exercises it does so by virtue of his office; his warrant is the law and he is the creature of the law.

For as the laws govern the magistrate, so the magistrate governs the people, and it can truly be said that the magistrate is a speaking law, and the law a silent magistrate.[5]

Third, the state itself and its law is always subject to the law of God, or the moral or natural law — that higher rule of right which transcends human choice and human institution. Force is an

[4] *Republic*, I, 25.

[5] *Laws*, III, 1, 2.

incident in the nature of the state and is justified only because it is required to give effect to the principles of justice and right.

These general principles of government — that authority proceeds from the people, should be exercised only by warrant of law, and is justified only on moral grounds — achieved practically universal acceptance within comparatively a short time after Cicero wrote and remained commonplaces of political philosophy for many centuries. There was substantially no difference of opinion about them on the part of anyone in the whole course of the Middle Ages; they became a part of the common heritage of political ideas. There might, however, be considerable differences of opinion about the application of them, even among men who had not the remotest doubt about the principles themselves. Thus everyone agrees that a tyrant is despicable and his tyranny a bitter wrong against his people, but it is not obvious just what the people are entitled to do about it, or who is to act in their behalf in doing it, or how bad the abuse must be before measures are justified. In particular, the derivation of political authority from the people does not of itself imply any of the democratic consequences which in modern times have been deduced from the consent of the governed. It does not say who speaks for the people, how he becomes entitled so to speak, or exactly who "the people" are for whom he speaks — all questions of the utmost practical importance. The use of the ancient principle that political authority comes from the people to defend the modern forms of representative government was merely the adaptation of an old idea to a new situation.

THE ROMAN LAWYERS

The classical period in the development of Roman jurisprudence fell in the second and third centuries after Christ, and the writings of the great jurists of that age were excerpted and compiled into the *Digest* (or *Pandects*), which the Emperor Justinian caused to be published in 533. The political philosophy which is embedded in this body of legal writing is a repetition and elaboration of the theories found in Cicero.

Political theory forms an insignificant proportion of the whole work, the relevant passages being neither very numerous nor very extensive. The lawyers were jurists, not philosophers. For this reason it is often hard to tell just how seriously a philosophical idea is to be taken when it occurs; one does not know whether the writer himself regarded it as a polite embellishment or whether it really influenced his legal judgment. Obviously it was never part of the lawyers' purpose to formulate a political philosophy or to inject a philosophy into the law. The philosophy of the Roman lawyers was not philosophy in a technical sense but certain general social and ethical conceptions, known to all intelligent men, which were in some way considered to be useful for their own juristic purposes. This makes it the more striking that they uniformly selected philosophical ideas belonging in the Stoic and Ciceronian tradition. The ideas of egoistic individualism, contained in the writings of the Epicureans and the Skeptics, must have been equally at their disposal, but the lawyers found no use for them. The fact that their interest in political theory was desultory and unsystematic does not mean that what they had to say was unimportant. The enormous authority attached to the Roman law throughout western Europe gave weight to any proposition which was a recognized part of it. Moreover, any general conception embedded in the law was certain to be known to all educated men as well as to lawyers, and ultimately by common report to many who were not scholars at all. In the end the Roman law became one of the greatest intellectual forces in the history of European civilization, because it provided principles and categories in terms of which men thought about all sorts of subjects and not least about politics. Legalist argumentation — reasoning in terms of men's rights and of the justifiable powers of rulers — became and remained a generally accepted method of political theorizing.

The lawyers excerpted in the *Digest,* as well as those who formulated Justinian's *Institutes* in the sixth century, recognized three main types of law, the *ius civile,* the *ius gentium,* and the *ius naturale.* The *ius civile* is, of course, the enactments or the customary law of a particular state, what would now be called positive municipal law. The other two classes are not quite so clear, either in respect to the distinction between *ius gentium* and *ius naturale* or in respect to the relation of both to the *ius civile.* Cicero had used both these terms but had apparently made no distinction of meaning between them. In origin, as was said in the preceding chapter, the term *ius gentium* belonged to the lawyers, while *ius naturale* was a rendering of Greek philosophical terminology. In meaning the two apparently coalesced, both for the earlier lawyers and for Cicero. They signified indifferently principles that were generally recognized and therefore common to the law of different peoples and also principles that were inherently reasonable and right without reference to their occurrence in any system of law. The distinction was easy to overlook because common consent was taken as a test of validity. It seemed a fair presumption that what many peoples have arrived at independently is more likely to be right than what is peculiar to any single people.

As time went on the lawyers apparently saw a reason for distinguishing *ius gentium* from *ius naturale.* Gaius, writing in the second century, continued to use the terms synonymously, but Ulpian and later writers in the third century made a distinction, as did also the lawyers who prepared the *Institutes* in the sixth.[6] The distinction added precision to legal definition, but it perhaps signified also a more penetrating ethical criticism of the law; even what is generally practiced may still be unjust and unreasonable. The main point upon which *ius gentium* and *ius naturale* are distinguished is slavery. By nature all men are born free and equal, but slavery is permitted according to the *ius gentium.*[7] It is hard to tell just what this natural liberty meant to the lawyers who asserted its reality so flatly, but in view of the efforts made, not without success, to throw legal safeguards about slaves and other oppressed classes, it seems reasonable to construe it as representing some moral reservation about practices whose legality was unquestionable according to all known codes. Perhaps the idea was, as Professor Carlyle suggests, that in some purer or better form of society slavery had not existed, or would not exist. At all events, such passages would be so understood after Christianity had made the story of the fall of man a common belief.

Whether or not they distinguished between *ius gentium* and *ius naturale,* none of the lawyers doubted that there is a higher law than the enactments of any particular state. Like Cicero they

[6] A. J. Carlyle, *A History of Mediaeval Political Theory,* Vol. I (1903), pp. 38 ff.

[7] *Digest,* 1, 1, 4; 1, 5, 4; 12, 6, 64; *Institutes,* 1, 2, 2.

conceived of the law as ultimately rational, universal, unchangeable, and divine, at least in respect to the main principles of right and justice. The Roman law, like the English common law, was only in small part a product of legislation. Hence the presumption was never made that law expresses nothing but the will of a competent legislative body, which is an idea of quite recent origin. It was assumed that " nature " sets certain norms which the positive law must live up to as best it can and that, as Cicero had believed, an " unlawful " statute simply is not law. Throughout the whole of the Middle Ages and well down into modern times the existence and the validity of such a higher law were taken for granted. As Sir Frederick Pollock says, the central idea of natural law, from the Roman Republic to modern times, was " an ultimate principle of fitness with regard to the nature of man as a rational and social being, which is, or ought to be, the justification of every form of positive law." [8]

In theory, therefore, the positive law is an approximation to perfect justice and right; these represent its objects and form its standards. It is, as Ulpian says, quoting Celsus, *ars boni et aequi.*

> Justice is a fixed and abiding disposition to give to every man his right. The precepts of the law are as follows: to live honorably, to injure no one, to give to every man his own. Jurisprudence is a knowledge of things human and divine, the science of the just and the unjust.[9]

Hence the lawyer is a " priest of justice," " the practitioner of a true philosophy, not a pretender to an imitation." It is not necessary to take Ulpian's rhetoric as a literal statement of fact. But it remains true that the Roman jurists did build up a more enlightened body of law than had ever existed, and though the changes they wrought had their economic and political causes, it is not to be imagined that they came about without reference to the ideals of the profession.

Natural law meant interpretation in the light of such conceptions as equality before the law, faithfulness to engagements, fair dealing or equity, the superior importance of intent to mere words and formularies, the protection of dependents, and the recognition of claims based on blood relationship. Procedure was more and more freed from mere formality; contracts were made to rest on

[8] " The History of the Law of Nature," in *Essays in the Law* (1922), p. 31.

[9] *Digest,* 1, 1, 10.

agreement rather than on words of stipulation; the father's absolute control over the property and persons of his children was broken; married women became the full legal equals of their husbands in the control of their property and children; and finally great progress was made in throwing legal safeguards about slaves, partly by way of protecting them against cruelty, partly by making their manumission as easy as possible. A modern exponent of "just law," Rudolf Stammler, has regarded this belief in justice as the crowning glory of Roman jurisprudence.

> This, in my opinion, is the universal significance of the classical Roman jurists; this, their permanent worth. They had the courage to raise their glance from the ordinary questions of the day to the whole. And in reflecting on the narrow status of the particular case, they directed their thoughts to the guiding star of all law, namely the realization of justice in life.[10]

It should be noted that these reforms in the Roman law, though they were completed after the beginning of the Christian era, were not due to Christianity. The effective humanizing influence was Stoicism and there seems to be no evidence whatever of any effect of the Christian communities upon the great jurists of the second and third centuries. At a later date, in the time of Constantine and after, Christian influence can be seen, but it was not exerted in the directions mentioned above. Its purpose was to secure in one way or another the legal position of the church or of its officials, or to aid in carrying out policies of the church. Typical legal changes which the church secured for the protection of its interests were the right to receive property by will, the establishment of the jurisdiction of bishops' courts, the power to supervise charities, the repeal of the laws against celibacy, and the enactment of laws against heresy and apostasy.

Finally, the Roman law crystallized the theory, already contained in Cicero, that the authority of the ruler is derived from "the people." The theory was summed up in a sentence by Ulpian, repeatedly quoted, and there is no dissent by any of the lawyers either of the *Digest* or the *Institutes:*

> The will of the Emperor has the force of law, because by the passage of the *lex regia* the people transfers to him and vests in him all its own power and authority.[11]

[10] *The Theory of Justice,* Eng. trans. (1925), p. 127.
[11] *Digest,* 1, 4, 1.

The theory is to be understood, of course, in a strictly legal sense and it is couched in terms that had a definitely technical significance. In itself it justifies neither the implication of royal absolutism, which was sometimes derived from the first clause, nor of representative government, which the sovereignty of the people came to signify later. The latter meaning would have been especially absurd in the Roman Empire when Ulpian wrote. The idea behind Ulpian's statement is that expressed by Cicero, that law is the common possession of a people in its corporate capacity. This idea appears in the theory that customary law has the consent of the people, since custom exists only in the common practice. It appears also in the classification of the sources from which law is derived. Thus law might arise by the enactment of a popular assembly (*leges*), or by the vote of some authorized part of the people such as the plebeian assembly (*plebescita*), or by a decree of the Senate (*senatus consulta*), or by a decree of the Emperor (*constitutiones*), or by the edict of an ordinance-issuing official. In all cases, however, the source must be authorized and in the last resort all forms of law go back to the legal activity inherent in a politically organized people. In a sense every established organ of government does " represent " the people in some degree and some capacity, but there is obviously no implication that representation has anything to do with voting and still less that voting is a right inherent in every person. The " people " is an entity quite different from the persons who happen at any given time to be included in it.

At the same time some essence has been preserved from the ancient doctrine that law is an " impersonal reason " and that in consequence there is a broad moral distinction between lawful government and successful tyranny. Even though the former be often bad and the latter sometimes efficient, subjection to law is not incompatible with moral freedom and human dignity, while subjection to even the kindliest master is morally degrading. The Roman law preserved the spirit of Cicero's striking phrase: " We are servants of the law in order that we may be free."[12] And indeed, there is no more astonishing evidence of the strength that this conviction had come to have in European morals than the fact of its preservation in a system of law which reached its ma-

[12] *Pro Cluentio,* 53, 146.

turity at a time when the personal power of the Emperors was often unlimited and when their authority rested frequently on nothing better than force. Yet the fact remains that in the long run the ideal embedded in the law was a permanent factor in European political civilization — a distillation from the old free life of the city-state — which was able to endure through and beyond an age in which all the servility of oriental despotism had apparently been transplanted to Rome.

SELECTED BIBLIOGRAPHY

Roman Stoicism. By E. V. Arnold. Cambridge, 1911. Ch. 12.

A Text-book of Roman Law from Augustus to Justinian. By W. W. Buckland. Cambridge, 1921. Ch. 1.

"Classical Roman Law." By W. W. Buckland. In the *Cambridge Ancient History,* Vol. XI (1936), ch. 21.

A History of Mediaeval Political Theory in the West. By R. W. Carlyle and A. J. Carlyle. 6 vols. London, 1903–1936. Vol. I (1903), Parts I and II.

On the Commonwealth: Marcus Tullius Cicero. Eng. trans. by George H. Sabine and Stanley B. Smith. Columbus, Ohio, 1929. Introduction.

"The 'Higher Law' Background of American Constitutional Law." By Edward S. Corwin. *Harvard Law Review,* Vol. XLII (1928–29), pp. 149, 365.

Rome the Law-giver. By J. Declareuil. Eng. trans. by E. A. Parker. London, 1927. Prolegomena.

Historical Introduction to the Study of Roman Law. By H. F. Jolowicz. Cambridge, 1932. Ch. 24.

"Original Elements in Cicero's Ideal Constitution." By C. W. Keyes. *Am. J. of Philol.,* Vol. XLII (1921), p. 309.

"The Idea of Majesty in Roman Political Thought." By Floyd S. Lear. In *Essays in History and Political Theory in Honor of Charles Howard McIlwain.* Cambridge, Mass., 1936.

The Growth of Political Thought in the West, from the Greeks to the End of the Middle Ages. By C. H. McIlwain. New York, 1932. Ch. 4.

Cicero, a Biography. By Torsten Peterson. Berkeley, California, 1920.

Gai Institutiones, or Institutes of Roman Law by Gaius. Eng. trans. by Edward Poste. 4th ed. rev. and enlarged by E. A. Whittuck. With an Historical Introduction by A. H. J. Greenidge. London, 1904.

Roman Law in the Modern World. By Charles P. Sherman. 3 vols. Boston, 1917. Vol. I. History.

History of Roman Legal Science. By Fritz Schulz. Oxford, 1946.

CHAPTER X

SENECA AND THE FATHERS OF THE CHURCH

In one respect — the belief in human equality — the idea of a common race, as it was developed by the jurists, broke sharply with the scale of values which prevailed in the city-state. In another respect, however, the two were quite continuous. For Cicero as for Plato, to found or to govern states is the labor in which the human hero shows himself most godlike, and a life of political service is the crown of human blessedness. The well-centralized system of authority presented in the Roman law reflects not only the administrative unity of the Empire but also the ancient conviction that the state is supreme among human institutions. In this tradition there was no thought of a divided allegiance in which another loyalty might compete with the claims of civic duty, and no impossible gulf between the "dear City of Cecrops" and the "dear City of God." Yet this contrast between the earthly and the Heavenly City, drawn by a Roman Emperor and the most conscientious ruler of his age, was symptomatic of a cleft that was opening in men's moral experience. The weary loyalty of Marcus Aurelius toward the station to which it had pleased God to call him and his obvious longing for a more satisfying life show how far even the pagan soul had travelled since the days when Cicero, in the Dream of Scipio, envisaged heaven as a reward reserved for distinguished statesmanship. The ripe fruit of Marcus's world-weariness was a church which claimed to be the spokesman for a spiritual life higher than any that earth afforded, but the fruit grew in a soil long prepared for it.

SENECA

The changing valuation placed upon a political career and the diminishing expectation that statesmanship would be able to deal successfully with social problems are clearly perceptible by a comparison of Cicero with Seneca, who wrote about a century later and who therefore reflects Roman opinion in the early days of the Empire, as Cicero reflects it in the closing period of the Republic. The contrast is the more striking because there is little difference of a systematic sort between the philosophical beliefs of the two men; both held an eclectic Stoicism for which nature represents a standard of goodness and reasonableness. Both men, also, look upon the great age of the Republic as the time at which Rome achieved her political maturity whence she has latterly declined. But there is this essential difference: Cicero has the illusion that the great day may be recaptured, but for the minister of Nero the time of illusion has passed. Rome has fallen into senility, corruption is everywhere, and despotism is inevitable. Upon social and political matters Seneca already shows much of the despondency and pessimism that overshadows the Latin literature of the second Christian century.[1] The question is not whether there shall be absolute government but only who shall be the despot. Even dependence upon a despot is preferable to dependence upon the people, since the mass of men is so vicious and corrupt that it is more merciless than a tyrant. Clearly, then, a political career has little to offer the good man except the annihilation of his goodness, and clearly also the good man can do little for his fellows by holding political office. For similar reasons Seneca attached little importance to differences between forms of government; one is as bad or as good as another since none can accomplish much.

Yet it was by no means Seneca's view that the wise man ought merely to withdraw from society. He insisted as strongly as Cicero upon the moral duty of the good man to offer his services in some capacity or other, and he was as decisive as Cicero in rejecting the Epicurean pursuit of private satisfaction sought by the neglect of public interests. Unlike Cicero, however, and indeed unlike all political and social philosophers before his time, Seneca was able to envisage a social service which involved no office in the state and no function of a strictly political sort. This gives a definitely new turn to the ancient Stoic doctrine that every man is a member of two commonwealths, the civil state of which he is a subject and the greater state, composed of all rational beings,

[1] See Samuel Dill, *Roman Society from Nero to Marcus Aurelius* (1904), Bk. III, ch. 1.

to which he belongs by virtue of his humanity. The greater commonwealth is for Seneca a society rather than a state; its ties are moral or religious rather than legal and political. Accordingly the wise and good man renders a service to humanity even though he has no political power. He does this by virtue of his moral relation to his fellows or even through philosophical contemplation alone. The man who, by virtue of his thought, becomes a teacher of mankind fills a place at once nobler and more influential than the political ruler. It would scarcely be forcing Seneca's meaning to say that the worship of God is itself a truly human service, as Christian writers taught.

The significance of Seneca's attitude in this respect would be difficult to exaggerate. Seneca's Stoicism, like that of Marcus Aurelius a century later, was substantially a religious faith which, while offering strength and consolation in this world, turned toward the contemplation of a spiritual life. This drawing apart of worldly and spiritual interests — the sense that the body is but "chains and darkness to the soul," and that "the soul must struggle continually against the burden of the flesh"[2] — was a real characteristic even of the pagan society in which Christianity grew up. The growing need for spiritual consolation gave to religion an ever higher place in men's regard and set it ever more apart from secular interests, as the only means of contact with a higher range of realities. The essentially secular unity of life in the classical age was breaking down, and religion was achieving more and more an independent footing beside or even above the life of the state. It was but a natural sequel to this growing independence when the interests of religion were able to embody themselves in an institution of their own, to represent on earth the rights and the duties which men shared as the members of a Heavenly City. Such an institution, already taking form in the Christian church, must by the very logic of its existence lay hold upon men's loyalty by a claim which it could not permit the state to adjudicate. Seneca's interpretation of the two commonwealths was only one of several surprising parallels between his thought and that of the Christians, parallels which produced in antiquity a body of forged letters supposed to have passed between him and St. Paul.

[2] *Consol. ad Marc.*, 24, 5.

Two other related aspects of Seneca's thought were closely connected with the prevailingly religious tone of his philosophy. On the one hand he was intensely conscious of the inherent sinfulness of human nature and on the other his ethics showed the tendency toward humanitarianism which became continually more marked in later Stoicism. Despite the fact that Seneca repeats the Stoic commonplaces about the self-sufficiency of the wise man, the moral pride and harshness of earlier Stoicism have greatly receded. The sense of human wickedness haunts him and wickedness is ineradicable; no one escapes it and virtue consists rather in an endless struggle for salvation than in its achievement. Probably it is this consciousness of sin and misery as a universal human quality that caused him to place so high a value on human sympathy and gentleness, virtues which had not been very characteristic of Stoicism in its more rigorous versions. Already the fatherhood of God and the brotherhood of man have taken on the connotation of love and good will toward all mankind which came to characterize Christian teaching. As the civic and political virtues dropped back into second place, the virtues of mercy, kindliness, charity, benevolence, tolerance, and love — together with the condemnation on moral grounds of cruelty, hatred, anger, and harshness toward dependents and inferiors — were given a far higher place in the moral scale than they ever had in earlier ethics. The effects of this humanitarianism were apparent in the classical Roman law, especially in placing safeguards about the property and the persons of women and dependent children, in protecting slaves, in a more humane treatment of criminals, and in a common policy of protecting the helpless. It is a curious fact that a strong feeling for the humanitarian virtues should have first appeared as the accompaniment of a growing sense of moral corruption, both being definitely departures from the ethical sentiments of the earlier period of antiquity. Probably both were aspects of a more contemplative attitude toward life, which now replaced the older belief that the supreme virtue was the service of the state.

Seneca's departure from the ancient belief that the state is the highest agency of moral perfection was strikingly marked by his glowing account of the Golden Age which, as he conceived, preceded the sophisticated age of civilization. In his Ninetieth

Letter he described this idyllic state of nature with something approaching the rhetorical enthusiasm which Rousseau expended upon the same subject in the eighteenth century. In the Golden Age, as he believed, men were still happy and innocent; they loved a simple life without the superfluities and luxuries of civilization. They were not, indeed, either wise or morally perfect, for their goodness resulted rather from the innocence of ignorance than from practiced virtue. In particular, in the state of nature as Seneca pictured it, men had not yet acquired that great agency of greed, the institution of private property; in fact, it was the growth of avarice which destroyed the condition of primitive purity. Moreover, so long as men remained pure, they had no need for government or law; they obeyed voluntarily the wisest and best men, who sought no advantage of their own in ruling over their fellows. But when men were smitten with the desire to make things their own, they became self-seeking and rulers became tyrants. The advance of the arts brought luxury and corruption. It was this train of consequences that made law and coercion necessary in order that the vices and corruptions of human nature might be curbed. In short, government is the necessary remedy for wickedness.

The glorification of an idyllic state of nature, already suggested in certain passages of Plato's *Laws* and now elaborated by Seneca, has played a not inconsiderable rôle in utopian political theory. Whether thrown back into the past, as by Seneca and Rousseau, or projected into the future, as by the utopian socialists, it has usually had the same purpose — to bring into high relief the vices and corruptions of mankind and to indict the political or the economic abuses of an age. In the case of Seneca the Golden Age was another expression of his haunting sense of decay in the Roman society of Nero's reign. For reasons that are not hard to understand, his view that private property did not exist in a state of nature would hardly be shared by lawyers, who apparently regarded ownership as strictly in accord with natural law. The closest analogue in the case of the lawyers was perhaps slavery, which, as was said in the preceding chapter, was sometimes regarded as belonging to *ius gentium* but not to *ius naturale*. In general Seneca's conception of the law as a mere cure for sin was wholly at odds with Ulpian's description of it as a "true philosophy" and an *ars boni et aequi.* But Seneca's idea of the state of nature might well commend itself to Christian theologians. The belief in a primitive condition of purity was implied by the story of the fall of man, and certainly it became among Christian writers not uncommon to conceive this condition as one of communism and one in which force would not be needed. Such a view would be almost necessary after it became settled doctrine that poverty was morally superior to riches and monasticism to a secular life.

It is important to note, however, that this doctrine, whether in Seneca or in Christian writers, was in no sense a subversive attack upon property or upon law and government. What is implied is merely that these institutions represent an ethical second-best. In a perfect society, or with a purified human nature, they would not be necessary. But the wickedness of mankind being what it is, private property may well be a useful institution, and law supported by force may well be quite indispensable. It is easy to hold at once that government arises solely from human wickedness and yet that it is the divinely appointed means for ruling mankind in its fallen state and so has an indefeasible claim upon the obedience of all good men. This in fact became common Christian belief.

At the same time Seneca's representation of government as a more or less makeshift remedy for human evil was the index of an enormous shift in moral opinion, not only from the estimate set upon political institutions by the Greek philosophers but even from that supported only a short time before by Cicero. It would be hard to exaggerate the discrepancy between Seneca's view and the ancient conception expressed in Aristotle's belief that the city-state is the necessary condition of a civilized life and the only means for bringing human faculties to their highest form of development. The change implied by Seneca's position on the function of the state is precisely comparable to that implied by Cicero's position on human equality. Taken together the two changes undermine completely the ancient valuation of politics. In place of the supreme value of citizenship there is a common equality shared by all sorts and conditions of men; and in place of the state as a positive agency of human perfection there is a coercive power that struggles ineffectually to make an earthly life tolerable. Though this revolutionary change in the scale of values is as yet only suggested, its implications were destined to be explored and to become more and more firmly embedded in the political philosophy of the Christian Fathers.

CHRISTIAN OBEDIENCE

The rise of the Christian church, as a distinct institution entitled to govern the spiritual concerns of mankind in independence of the state, may not unreasonably be described as the most revolutionary event in the history of western Europe, in respect both to politics and to political philosophy. It by no means follows, however, that the political conceptions of the early Christians were in any way distinctive of them or specifically different from those of other men. The interests that went to the making of Christians were religious, and Christianity was a doctrine of salvation, not a philosophy or a political theory. The ideas of Christians upon the latter subjects were not very different from those of pagans. Thus Christians no less than Stoics could believe in the law of nature, the providential government of the world, the obligation of law and government to do substantial justice, and the equality of all men in the sight of God. Such ideas were widespread before Christianity appeared, and numerous familiar passages in the New Testament show that they were incorporated at once in Christian writings. Thus the author of *The Acts* reports St. Paul's preaching to the men of Athens in terms familiar to anyone who had ever heard a Stoic lecture: "For in him we live, and move, and have our being; as certain also of your own poets have said." [3] Only the new religious teaching about the resurrection of the dead is incomprehensible to the Athenians. Similarly, St. Paul writes to the Galatians, rejecting for the church differences of race or social position:

> There is neither Jew nor Greek, there is neither bond nor free, there is neither male nor female, for ye are all one in Jesus Christ.[4]

And to the Romans, asserting the law inherent in all human nature as contrasted with the Jewish law:

[3] *Acts,* 17, 28. [4] *Galatians,* 3, 28.

For when the Gentiles, which have not the law, do by nature the things contained in the law, these, having not the law, are a law unto themselves.[5]

In general, it may be said that the Fathers of the church, in respect to natural law, human equality, and the necessity of justice in the state, were substantially in agreement with Cicero and Seneca.[6] It is true that the pagan writers knew nothing of a revealed law, such as Christians believed was contained in the Jewish and Christian Scriptures, but the belief in revelation was in no way incompatible with the view that the law of nature also is God's law.

The obligation of Christians to respect constituted authority had been deeply embedded in Christianity even by its founder. When the Pharisees had attempted to entrap Jesus into opposition to the power of Rome, he had uttered the memorable words:

Render therefore unto Caesar the things which are Caesar's, and unto God the things that are God's.[7]

And St. Paul, in his letter to the Romans, had written the most influential political pronouncement in the New Testament:

Let every soul be subject unto the higher powers. For there is no power but of God: the powers that be are ordained of God. Whosoever therefore resisteth the power, resisteth the ordinance of God; and they that resist shall receive to themselves damnation. For rulers are not a terror to good works, but to the evil. Wilt thou then not be afraid of the power? Do that which is good, and thou shalt have praise of the same: For he is the minister of God to thee for good. But if thou do that which is evil, be afraid; for he beareth not the sword in vain: for he is a minister of God, a revenger to execute wrath upon him that doeth evil. Wherefore ye must needs be subject, not only for wrath, but also for conscience sake. For for this cause pay ye tribute also: for they are God's ministers, attending continually upon this very thing. Render therefore to all their dues: tribute to whom tribute is due; custom to whom custom; fear to whom fear; honor to whom honor.[8]

It may well be true, as some historians suppose,[9] that this passage, and others to a similar effect, were written to combat an-

[5] *Romans,* 2, 14.
[6] Carlyle, *op. cit.,* Vol. I (1903), Part III.
[7] *Matt.* 22, 21; cf. *Mark,* 12, 17; *Luke,* 20, 25.
[8] *Rom.* 13, 1–7; cf. *I. Peter,* 2, 13–17.
[9] See Carlyle, *op. cit.,* Vol. I, pp. 93 ff.

archical tendencies existing in the early Christian communities, but if so, they accomplished their purpose. The words of St. Paul became accepted Christian doctrine, and the obligation of civic obedience became an admitted Christian virtue which no responsible leader of the church denied. It is probably true that St. Paul, like Seneca, believed that the magistrate's power was a necessary consequence of human sin; the ruler's work is to repress evil and encourage good. But as has already been said, this does not imply that respect for rulers is any less a binding obligation.

St. Paul and other writers in the New Testament stress the view that obedience is a duty imposed by God, and this fact gives to the Christian teaching a different emphasis from the Roman constitutional theory, stressed by the lawyers, that the ruler's authority is derived from the people. Once the Jewish Scriptures were accepted, this view would naturally be strengthened by the account of the origin of Jewish kingship in the Old Testament.[10] The king of the Jews is habitually spoken of as the Lord's anointed; according to the tradition the kingship was established by God as a result of the rebelliousness of the people; and finally — a point not lost upon later ecclesiastical writers — he was instituted by being anointed at the hands of a prophet. In a sense the Christian conception of rulership always implied a theory of divine right, since the ruler is a minister of God. But modern constitutional controversies have sharpened the contrast between the two views in a way that no one thought of at first, or indeed for centuries afterward. Even though authority were derivative from the people, there was no reason why respect for it might not be a religious duty; or, contrariwise, if the ruler were ordained of God, he might still owe the particular form of his office to the institutions inherent in a people. In fact, the underlying purpose of the two theories might be said to be identical. For St. Paul and for all Christians it was the *office* rather than its holder to which respect was due; the personal virtues or vices of a ruler had nothing to do with the matter. A bad ruler is a punishment for sin and must still be obeyed. For the lawyers the choice of the people signified broadly the constitutional or legal nature of the power exercised. Both views assumed — the one as law or the other as theology — the difference between the au-

[10] See *I. Samuel,* chs. 8–10.

thority inherent in an institution and the merely arbitrary power that an individual might possess. For this reason both views could stand side by side without incompatibility.

DIVIDED LOYALTY

Respect for lawful authority, then, was a duty which no Christian denied. Yet it was a fact of the utmost importance that the Christian was inevitably bound to a twofold duty such as had been quite unknown to the ethics of pagan antiquity. He must not only render unto Caesar the things that are Caesar's but also to God the things that are God's, and if the two came into conflict, there could be no doubt that he must obey God rather than man. The possibility of such a conflict was implicit in any view, such for example as Seneca's, which put civic duties into second place, but there is no evidence that Seneca was aware of the possibility. The Christian, who was a member of a persecuted minority, could hardly avoid being aware of it, nor can it be denied that a conscientious emperor like Marcus Aurelius, in whose reign persecution flourished, was right in his conviction, firm if somewhat vague, that Christianity contained an idea incompatible with the Roman virtue of unlimited obligation to the state. The Christian, who believed that his religion was a truth revealed by God to guide him into a salvation far higher than any destiny that this world afforded, could not but believe that that religion imposed duties from which no emperor could absolve him and in the light of which the admitted duty of civic obedience must be weighed and judged. The principle was in one sense old — that every man is a citizen of two states — but the application was new, since for the Christian the greater state was not merely the human family but a spiritual realm, a true kingdom of God, in which man was the heir to eternal life and to a destiny immeasurably transcending the life which any earthly kingdom could offer him.

It is true that Christianity was not unique in posing a problem of this sort. The properties of Christianity as a "spiritual" religion were shared more or less by other religions which existed in the Roman world. The older native cults of Greece and Rome — though sedulously fostered for political purposes — had substantially yielded, before the end of the second century, to a variety of religions of oriental origin of which Christianity was only one. All these religions were similar in offering salvation and eternal life to a sin-stricken and world-weary generation, and in supporting a class of professionally trained priests skilled in the art of offering spiritual consolation.

> In the heavy atmosphere of a period of oppression and powerlessness, the despondent souls of men aspired with ineffable ardour to the radiant spaces of heaven.[11]

This was a prevailing social characteristic of the age, upon which the spread of Christianity and the other oriental religions depended. With the rising tide of religious and other-worldly interest, and with the rise to independence of religious institutions, a break with the old tradition which made religion an adjunct of the state was inevitable. Christianity — the church beside the state — represented the final breakdown of the old imperial idea and the starting-point of a radically new development.

The world-empire had always been impossible without religious support. A congeries of peoples and tribes and cities, lacking any such strong tie as the modern sentiment of nationality, could find no other practicable bond of union except a common religion. From the beginning Alexander and his successors had been obliged to copy the practice of the East in this respect, and Rome was forced to embark upon the same course. In the eastern provinces the earlier emperors were deified in life as well as after death, but the constitutional restrictions that descended from the Republic to the Empire held back the process in Italy. But constitutionalism grew steadily more shadowy, and with the reorganization of the Empire under Diocletian and the establishment by that emperor of Mithraism as the official religion of the state, Rome was transformed into something comparable with an oriental caliphate. Even this arrangement proved only a temporary expedient. The growth in the power of religion which first made possible, and then necessary, the deification of the emperor ended by making it impossible. For what was required was not an official religion, which could still be regarded as largely an appendage of the state, but rather a religion with its autonomous ecclesiastical organization, standing beside the state as its equal

[11] Franz Cumont, *After Life in Roman Paganism* (1922), p. 40. See also the same author's *The Oriental Religions in Roman Paganism*, Eng. trans., 1911, ch. 2.

and indeed, in respect to the prevailing estimate of the interests it represented, as its superior. The Christian obviously could not admit, consistently with his religion, the claims of the deified emperor to be the court of last resort in spiritual questions. But once this claim of Rome to be the source of religious as well as of political authority was set aside, he could co-operate loyally as either a citizen or soldier of the Empire. The church was in fact well adapted to bring support to secular authority, to teach the virtues of obedience and loyalty, and to train its members in the duties of citizenship.

The novelty of the Christian position lay in its assumption of a dual nature in man and of a dual control over human life corresponding to its twofold destiny. The distinction between spirituals and temporals was of the essence of the Christian point of view, and for this reason the relation between religious and political institutions presented to the Christian a new problem. His convictions on this matter, from the standpoint of the old imperial conception of political obligation, were fundamentally treasonable, just as the imperial ideal was, from a Christian standpoint, fundamentally pagan and irreligious. For the pagan the highest duties of morality and religion met in the state, symbolically in the person of the emperor, who was at once the supreme civil authority and a divinity. For the Christian the duties of religion were a supreme obligation, owed directly to God, and the outgrowth of a relationship between a spiritual deity and the spiritual essence in human nature. The interference of an earthly force in this relationship was something which in principle a Christian could not allow, and for this reason the quite formal ceremony of paying religious honor to the emperor's genius was a requirement which he must refuse. An institution which had in its keeping this higher relationship and which existed to provide a medium for the communication of the soul with God, must claim to be distinguished from, and in some degree to be independent of, those secular institutions which existed to provide the means of bodily and earthly existence. For this reason Christianity raised a problem which the ancient world had not known — the problem of church and state — and implied a diversity of loyalties and an internality of judgment not included in the ancient idea of citizenship. It is hard to imagine that liberty could have played the part it did in European political thought, if ethical and religious institutions had not been conceived to be broadly independent of, and superior in importance to, the state and legal enforcement.

It was of the essence of the situation that the church had first grown strong, both in doctrine and ecclesiastical organization, before its legal establishment; this fact made it a valuable adjunct to the Empire. So long as it was merely a voluntary association, and frequently an unlawful one, its relation to the state called for no special theory. After its establishment, however, the need for insisting upon its autonomy in spiritual matters was more apparent. On the other hand, no ecclesiastical statesman ever supposed that the church and the state could fail to be always in contact with one another, just as soul and body were constantly joined in human life though they were of different essence. The independence of church and state was assumed to include the mutual helpfulness of the two, both being divinely appointed agencies for the government of human life in this world and the world hereafter. The duty of civic obedience was an undoubted Christian virtue as truly imposed upon man by God as any other moral obligation, and yet it was not an absolute obligation. The support which the discipline of the church could give to the state was the real reason for its legal establishment by Constantine. On the other hand, the duty of a Christian prince to nourish and protect the church was equally undoubted, and this duty could not fail to include maintaining at need the purity of its doctrine. This duty was not thought to be in any way contrary to the secular nature of a ruler, nor was it supposed that the prince was thereby made the judge of doctrine. The Christian position implied two classes of duties, spiritual and secular, which might on occasion come into apparent opposition but which could not be ultimately irreconcilable, and similarly it implied two institutional organizations which remained distinct, though each needed, and in all normal cases received, the support and aid of the other.

The possibilities of conflict and ambiguity in such a conception are apparent; indeed, it is hard to imagine any really Christian form of society in which difficulties of this sort might not arise, since they reflect a complication in the moral life itself. Nothing is easier, therefore, than to show that church and state were not really independent, since in the period of its establishment the church must depend largely upon the emperor's support, while at a later date its greater power might threaten the autonomy of secular authority. The difficulties of the problem may be illustrated by the inconsistencies of a thinker like St. Augustine with respect to religious toleration. In principle the acceptance of Christianity could not depend merely on force without a gross invasion of spiritual freedom, and yet the Christian statesman, believing as he sincerely did that heresy was a deadly sin, could not contemplate its spread unopposed by those who were responsible for the earthly as well as the eternal welfare of their subjects. Thus in his earlier life Augustine opposed the use of force against the Manichaeans, while later he argued in his controversy with the Donatists that, for the good of his own soul, the heretic must be compelled to receive instruction. Similarly it was plain historical fact that the influence of Constantine was decisive in bringing about the defeat of the Arians at the Council of Nicaea, but obviously no Christian, without stultifying his faith, could believe that the orthodox doctrine of the Trinity had been settled by an imperial edict. The problem involved an elaborate delimitation of jurisdictions and even to the end of the Middle Ages jurisdictional disputes might arise, though for normal circumstances the lines were drawn with sufficient clearness. In the beginning the primary need was to emphasize the autonomy of the church in spiritual matters.

AMBROSE, AUGUSTINE, AND GREGORY

The views of churchmen in respect to these questions, and also the lack of sharp discrimination in the concepts employed, may be illustrated by reference to three great thinkers of the two centuries following the legal establishment of the church: St. Ambrose of Milan in the second half of the fourth century, St. Augustine in the beginning of the fifth, and St. Gregory in the second half of the sixth. None of these men was concerned to work out a systematic philosophy of the church and its relation to the state; they belonged rather to the formative period of Christian thought and dealt with questions that were immediately pressing. But they all expressed views which formed an essential part of Christian conviction and which became an integral part of Christian thought upon the relations of the two institutions.

St. Ambrose was especially notable for his strong statement of the autonomy of the church in spiritual matters. There is no reason to think that in this respect he differed from other Christians of his time, but his outspoken statement of the principle and his courageous adherence to it in the face of opposition made him an authority to whom Christian writers returned in all later controversies where the point arose. Thus he clearly asserted that in spiritual matters the church has jurisdiction over all Christians, the emperor included, for the emperor like every other Christian is a son of the church; he "is within the church, not above it."[12] He stated boldly in a letter to the Emperor Valentinian that in matters of faith "bishops are wont to judge of Christian emperors, not emperors of bishops." He questioned in no way the duty of obedience to civil authority but he affirmed that it was not only the right but the duty of a priest to reprove secular rulers in a matter of morals, a precept which he not only taught but practiced. On one famous occasion he refused to celebrate the Eucharist in the presence of the Emperor Theodosius because of his guilt in causing a massacre at Thessalonica, and on another he withheld it until the emperor had withdrawn an order which Ambrose regarded as injurious to the privileges of a bishop. In yet another case, he steadfastly refused to surrender a church for the use of Arians upon order of the Emperor Valentinian. "The palaces belong to the Emperor, the Churches to the Bishop." He admitted the authority of the emperor over secular property, including the lands of the church, but church buildings themselves, as being directly dedicated to a spiritual use, he denied the right of the emperor to touch. At the same time, however, he definitely repudiated any right to resist with force the execution of the emperor's orders. He will argue and implore but he will not incite the people to rebel. According to Ambrose, therefore, the secular ruler is subject to the church's instruction in spiritual matters and his authority over some ecclesiastical property, at least, is limited, but the church's right is to be maintained by spiritual means rather than by resistance. The precise limits between the two kinds of property were left vague.

The most important Christian thinker of the age now under

[12] The quotations occur in Carlyle, *op. cit.*, Vol. I, pp. 180 ff., and footnotes.

discussion was Ambrose's great convert and pupil, St. Augustine. His philosophy was only in a slight degree systematic but his mind had encompassed almost all the learning of ancient times, and through him, to a very large extent, it was transmitted to the Middle Ages. His writings were a mine of ideas in which later writers, Catholic and Protestant, have dug. It is not necessary to repeat all the points upon which he was in substantial agreement with Christian thought in general and which have already been mentioned in this chapter. His most characteristic idea is the conception of a Christian commonwealth, together with a philosophy of history which presents such a commonwealth as the culmination of man's spiritual development. Through his authority this conception became an ineradicable part of Christian thought, extending not only through the Middle Ages but far down into modern times. Protestant no less than Roman Catholic thinkers were controlled by Augustine's ideas upon this subject.

His great book, the *City of God,* was written to defend Christianity against the pagan charge that it was responsible for the decline of Roman power and particularly for having caused the sack of the city by Alaric in 410. Incidentally, however, he developed nearly all his philosophical ideas, including his theory of the significance and goal of human history by which he sought to place the history of Rome in its proper perspective. This involved a restatement, from the Christian point of view, of the ancient idea that man is a citizen of two cities, the city of his birth and the City of God. The religious meaning of this distinction already suggested by Seneca and Marcus Aurelius, became explicit in Augustine. Man's nature is twofold: he is spirit and body and therefore at once a citizen of this world and of the Heavenly City. The fundamental fact of human life is the division of human interests, the worldly interests that center about the body and the other-worldly interests that belong specifically to the soul. As has already been said, this distinction lay at the foundation of all Christian thought on ethics and politics.

St. Augustine, however, made the distinction a key to the understanding of human history, which is and always must be dominated by the contest of two societies. On the one side stands the earthly city, the society that is founded on the earthly, appetitive, and possessive impulses of the lower human nature; on the other stands the City of God, the society that is founded in the hope of heavenly peace and spiritual salvation. The first is the kingdom of Satan, beginning its history from the disobedience of the Angels and embodying itself especially in the pagan empires of Assyria and Rome. The other is the kingdom of Christ, which embodied itself first in the Hebrew nation and later in the church and the Christianized empire. History is the dramatic story of the struggle between these two societies and of the ultimate mastery which must fall to the City of God. Only in the Heavenly City is peace possible; only the spiritual kingdom is permanent. This then is Augustine's interpretation of the fall of Rome: all merely earthly kingdoms must pass away, for earthly power is naturally mutable and unstable; it is built upon those aspects of human nature which necessarily issue in war and the greed of domination.

A certain caution is needed, however, in interpreting this theory and especially in applying it to historical fact. It was not Augustine's meaning that either the earthly city or the City of God could be identified precisely with existing human institutions. The church as a visible human organization was not for him the same as the kingdom of God, and still less was secular government identical with the powers of evil. An ecclesiastical statesman who had depended on the imperial power for the suppression of heresy was not likely to attack government as representing the kingdom of the Devil. Like all Christians Augustine believed that "the powers that be are ordained of God," though he also believed that the use of force in government was made necessary by sin and was the divinely appointed remedy for sin. Accordingly, he did not think of the two cities as visibly separate. The earthly city was the kingdom of the Devil and of all wicked men; the Heavenly City was the communion of the redeemed in this world and in the next. Throughout all earthly life the two societies are mingled, only to be separated at the last judgment.

At the same time Augustine did think of the kingdom of evil as at least represented by the pagan empires, though not exactly identified with them. He also thought of the church as representing the City of God, even though the latter cannot be identified with the ecclesiastical organization. One of the most influential phases of his thought was the reality and force which he attached to the conception of the church as an organized institution. His scheme of human salvation and the realization of the heavenly life depended absolutely upon the reality of the church as a social union of all true believers, through which the Grace of God can work in human history.[13] For this reason he regarded the appearance of the Christian church as the turning-point of history; it marked a new era in the struggle between the powers of good and the powers of evil. Henceforth human salvation is bound up with the interests of the church and these interests are consequently paramount over all other interests whatsoever.

The history of the church, therefore, was for Augustine quite literally "the march of God in the world," to use an expression which Hegel applied rather lamely to the state. The human race is indeed a single family, but its final destiny is reached not on earth but in Heaven. And human life is the theatre of a cosmic struggle between the goodness of God and the evil of rebellious spirits. All human history is the majestic unfolding of the plan of divine salvation, in which the appearance of the church marks the decisive moment. Henceforth the unity of the race means the unity of the Christian faith under the leadership of the church. It would be easy to infer from this that the state must logically become merely the "secular arm" of the church, but the inference is not necessary and the circumstances were such that Augustine could not possibly have drawn it. His theory of the relation between secular and ecclesiastical rulers was no more precise than that of other writers of his time and consequently, in the later controversies on the subject, his authority could be invoked by either side. But what he put beyond question for many centuries was the conception that, under the new dispensation, the state must be a Christian state, serving a community which is one by virtue of a common Christian faith, ministering to a life in which spiritual interests admittedly stand above all other interests and contributing to human salvation by preserving the purity of the faith. As James Bryce said, the theory of the Holy Roman Em-

[13] It must be admitted that there is another side to Augustine's thought. His character was always divided between the interests of an ecclesiastical statesman and those of a Christian mystic. In the latter character he might think of Grace as the relation of an individual soul to God, and writers with a Protestant leaning are prone to interpret him so. For historical purposes, however, and especially in the light of his influence in the Middle Ages, the statement in the text is correct.

pire was built upon Augustine's City of God. But the conception by no means disappeared with the decadence of the empire. No idea was harder for a seventeenth-century thinker to grasp than the notion that the state might stand entirely aside from all questions of religious belief. Even in the nineteenth century Gladstone could still argue that the state had a conscience that enabled it to distinguish between religious truth and falsity.

The necessity that a true commonwealth must be Christian is put by Augustine in the strongest possible way. He took exception to the views of Cicero and other pre-Christian writers, that it is the business of a true commonwealth to realize justice, precisely on the ground that no pagan empire could possibly do this. It is a contradiction in terms to say that a state can render to everyone his own, so long as its very constitution withholds from God the worship which is his due.[14] Augustine's philosophy of history required him to admit that the pre-Christian empires had been in some sense states, but he was clear that they could not be so in the full sense of the word which was applicable after the Christian dispensation. A just state must be one in which a belief in the true religion is taught, and perhaps also, though Augustine does not directly say so, one in which it is maintained by law and authority. No state can be just, since the advent of Christianity, unless it is also Christian, and a government considered apart from its relation to the church would be devoid of justice. Thus the Christian character of the state was embedded in the universally admitted principle that its purpose is to realize justice and right. In some fashion or other the state is bound to be also a church, since the ultimate form of social organization was religious, though what form the union should take might still be a subject of controversy.

The account so far given of the political ideas of St. Ambrose and St. Augustine stresses the autonomy of the church in spiritual matters and the conception of government as shared between two orders, the regal and the clerical. This position implied not only the independence of the church but equally that of secular gov-

[14] The meaning of Augustine in questioning Cicero's definition of the state has been the subject of controversy. C. H. McIlwain (*The Growth of Political Thought in the West,* 1932, pp. 154 ff.) has taken exception, I believe rightly, to the interpretation given by A. J. Carlyle and J. N. Figgis.

ernment, so long as the latter acts within its own proper jurisdiction. The duty of civic obedience, of subjection to the powers that be, which St. Paul had expressed so vigorously in the thirteenth chapter of *Romans,* was in no way superseded by the growing power of the church. It is an interesting fact, which illustrates the absence of any intention on the part of churchmen in this age to encroach upon the prerogatives of civil government, that the strongest claims made by any of the Fathers for the sanctity of secular rulers occur in the writings of the great and powerful pope who has been called the father of the medieval papacy. The astonishing success with which St. Gregory secured the defence of Italy against the Lombards, and also his influence in behalf of justice and good government throughout western Europe and North Africa, greatly enhanced the prestige of the Roman See, while the feebleness of the secular power practically forced him to assume the duties of a political ruler. Yet Gregory is the only one of the Fathers who speaks of the sanctity of political rule in language that suggests a duty of passive obedience.

It seems to be Gregory's view that a wicked ruler is entitled not only to obedience — which would probably have been conceded by any Christian writer — but even to silent and passive obedience, an opinion not stated with equal force by any other Father of the church. Thus in his *Pastoral Rule,* which discusses the kind of admonition that bishops should give to their flocks, he asserted most emphatically not only that subjects must obey but also that they must not judge or criticise the lives of their rulers.

> For indeed the acts of rulers are not to be smitten with the sword of the mouth, even though they are rightly judged to be blameworthy. But if ever, even in the least, the tongue slips into censure of them, the heart must needs be bowed down by the affliction of penitence, to the end that it may return to itself, and, when it has offended against the power set over it, may dread the judgment of him by whom the power was set over it.[15]

This conception of the sanctity of government was not unnatural in an age when anarchy had become a greater danger than the control of the church by the emperors. In spite of the fact that Gregory exercised an authority, both secular and ecclesiastical, that was virtually regal, there is a marked difference in tone be-

[15] Quoted by Carlyle, *op. cit.,* Vol. I, p. 152, n. 2.

tween his letters to the emperors and the bold reproofs and protests that came from the pen of St. Ambrose.[16] Gregory protests indeed against acts that he considers uncanonical but he does not refuse to obey. His position seems to be that the emperor has power even to do what is unlawful, provided of course that he is willing to risk damnation. Not only is the ruler's power of God but there is none higher than the emperor except God. The ruler's acts are ultimately between God and his conscience.

THE TWO SWORDS

The characteristic position developed by Christian thinkers in the age of the Fathers implied a dual organization and control of human society in the interest of the two great classes of values which needed to be conserved. Spiritual interests and eternal salvation are in the keeping of the church and form the special province of the teaching conducted by the clergy; temporal or secular interests and the maintenance of peace, order, and justice are in the keeping of civil government and form the ends to be reached by the labors of magistrates. Between the two orders, that of the clergy and that of the civil officials, a spirit of mutual helpfulness ought to prevail. This doctrine of mutual helpfulness left almost no line that might not rightfully be crossed in an emergency which threatened either anarchy in temporals or corruption in spirituals. But despite this vagueness of definition, it was felt that such emergencies did not destroy the principle that the two jurisdictions ought to remain inviolate, each respecting the rights which God had ordained for the other.

This conception is often spoken of as the doctrine of the two swords, or two authorities, which received authoritative statement at the close of the fifth century by Pope Gelasius I. It became the accepted tradition of the early Middle Ages and formed the point of departure for both sides when the rivalry between the pope and the emperor made the relation of spirituals and temporals a matter of controversy. Probably the conception of a society under dual control, presided over by twin hierarchies having distinguishable jurisdictions, remained even in the age of controversy the ideal of most men of moderate views, who were apt to dislike the extreme claims of either of the contesting parties.

[16] See letters quoted by Carlyle, *op. cit.*, Vol. I, pp. 153 ff.

Since Gelasius was writing to an emperor in Constantinople, and always with the object of defending what had now become orthodox doctrine in the west against the heresies that continued, especially in the east, to echo and re-echo from the great trinitarian dispute of the preceding century, he naturally followed the line already laid down by St. Ambrose. In doctrinal matters the emperor must subordinate his will to the clergy and must learn rather than presume to teach. It follows that the church, through its own rulers and officials, must have jurisdiction over all ecclesiastics, for obviously in no other way can it be an independent and self-governing institution.

> The Omnipotent God has willed that the teachers and priests of the Christian religion shall be governed not by the civil law or by secular authorities, but by bishops and priests.[17]

In accord with this principle Gelasius insists that, at least where spiritual matters are involved, ecclesiastics must be tried for their offences in ecclesiastical courts and not by the secular authorities.

The philosophical principle behind this practical deduction was the theory, quite in accord with the teaching of St. Augustine, that the distinction between spirituals and temporals is an essential part of the Christian faith and consequently a rule for every government following the Christian dispensation. The combination of spiritual and secular authority in the same hands is typically a pagan institution, lawful perhaps before the coming of Christ but now quite definitely a wile of the Devil. Because of human weakness and for the curbing of natural arrogance and pride, Christ decreed the separation of the two powers; accordingly Christ was the last who could lawfully wield both royal and sacerdotal power. Under the Christian dispensation it is unlawful for the same man to be at once king and priest. It is true that each power has need of the other:

> Christian emperors need bishops for the sake of eternal life, and bishops make use of imperial regulations to order the course of temporal affairs.[18]

But the responsibility of the priest is heavier than that of the secular ruler, for he is answerable on the Day of Judgment for

[17] Quoted by Carlyle, *op. cit.,* Vol. I, p. 187, n. 2.

[18] Gelasius, *Tractatus,* IV, 11. Quoted by Carlyle, *op. cit.,* Vol. I, pp. 190 f., n. 1.

the souls of all Christians, not excepting those of rulers themselves. In no case is it right for either power to exercise the authority which is proper to the other.

The conception of a universal Christian society which was transmitted from the Fathers of the church to the Middle Ages, therefore, differed fundamentally from the ancient idea of a world-wide community and also from the ideas of church and state that came to prevail in modern times. It differed from the latter because the church, as the Fathers understood it, was not a distinct group of persons joined together by a voluntary acceptance of Christian doctrine. In their conception the church was as universal as the empire, for both included all men. Mankind formed a single society under two governments, each with its own law, its own organs of legislation and administration, and its own proper right. This conception differed, however, from any that prevailed in pre-Christian antiquity, because it divided men's loyalty and obedience between two ideals and two rulerships. By giving to the universal community a religious interpretation as participation in the divine plan of human salvation, Christianity added to the requirement of justice in the earthly state the obligation to maintain a purity of worship which would make this life the gateway to life in another world. Upon the idea of earthly right it superimposed the idea of Christian duty, and beside and above citizenship in the state it placed membership in a heavenly fellowship. Thus it placed the Christian under a twofold law and a twofold government. This double aspect of Christian society produced a unique problem which in the end contributed perhaps more than any other to the specific properties of European political thought. Far beyond the period in which the relation of the two authorities was a chief controversial issue, the belief in spiritual autonomy and the right of spiritual freedom left a residuum without which modern ideas of individual privacy and liberty would be scarcely intelligible.

SELECTED BIBLIOGRAPHY

L'Augustinisme politique: essai sur la formation des théories politiques du moyen-âge. By H. X. Arquillière. Paris, 1934.

"The Conception of Empire." By Ernest Barker. In *The Legacy of Rome*. Ed. by Cyril Bailey. Oxford, 1923. (Reprinted in *Church, State, and Study*. London, 1930.)

The Political Ideas of St. Augustine's de civitate dei. By Norman H. Baynes. Historical Association Pamphlet No. 104. London, 1936.

Grégoire le grand. By Louis Bréhier. Paris, 1938.

A History of Mediaeval Political Theory in the West. By R. W. Carlyle and A. J. Carlyle. 6 vols. London, 1903–1936. Vol. I (1903), Part III.

Christianity and Classical Culture: A Study of Thought and Action from Augustus to Augustine. By Charles N. Cochrane. Oxford, 1940.

Roman Society from Nero to Marcus Aurelius. By Samuel Dill. London, 1904.

Roman Society in the Last Century of the Western Empire. By Samuel Dill. London, 1898.

The Life and Times of St. Ambrose. By F. Homes Dudden. 2 vols. Oxford, 1935.

The Political Aspects of St. Augustine's City of God. By John Neville Figgis. London, 1921.

Introduction à l'étude de Saint Augustine. By Étienne Gilson. Paris, 1931. Ch. 4.

" Gregory the Great." By W. H. Hutton. In the *Cambridge Medieval History,* Vol. II (1913), ch. 8 (B).

Paganism to Christianity in the Roman Empire. By Walter W. Hyde. Philadelphia, 1946.

" The Triumph of Christianity." By T. M. Lindsay. In the *Cambridge Medieval History,* Vol. I (1911), ch. 4.

The Growth of Political Thought in the West, from the Greeks to the End of the Middle Ages. By C. H. McIlwain. New York, 1932. Ch. 5.

The Mind of Latin Christendom. By Edward M. Pickman. London, 1937. Ch. 2.

The Church in the Roman Empire. By Sir William M. Ramsay. 2nd ed. rev. London, 1893. Ch. 15.

Die Staats- und Soziallehre des hl. Augustinus. By Otto Schilling. Freiburg i. B., 1910.

" Thoughts and Ideas of the Period " [The Christian Roman Empire]. By H. F. Stewart. In the *Cambridge Medieval History,* Vol. I (1911), ch. 20.

CHAPTER XI

THE FOLK AND ITS LAW

The period of the church Fathers, extending down to the sixth or seventh century, still belongs to antiquity. Despite the vast changes — social, economic, and political — which occurred in the first six Christian centuries, Seneca and St. Gregory were still both Romans. Both men lived within the circle of Roman political ideas; for both the Empire was the only significant political entity; both agreed substantially in their main conceptions of the state and of law. Even the rise of the church into an autonomous social institution, and even the necessity which in Gregory's time forced it to step into the place left vacant by the fall of the Empire, had not as yet been sufficient to break the continuity of the ancient world. Between the sixth and the ninth centuries, however, the political fortunes of western Europe passed once for all into the hands of the Germanic invaders whose impact upon the old imperial structure had at last broken it. Charlemagne might adopt the titles of Emperor and Augustus, writers both lay and clerical might picture his kingdom as a reincarnation of Rome, yet by no stretch of the imagination were Charlemagne and the men who conducted his government Romans. The Roman Empire, withdrawn into the East, had left Rome itself, to say nothing of the western provinces, without even the shadow of the imperial power; the Roman Church, divided from the Church of Constantinople on the orthodoxy of image-worship, had become the church of western Europe; and because of the heretical Lombard power, the Bishop of Rome had cemented an alliance with the Frankish Kingdom which made the pope himself effectively the temporal ruler of central Italy. The barbarian conquest itself, with its attendant social and economic changes, had made government on a large scale impossible. Both politically and intellectually western Europe was beginning to revolve around a center of its own, instead of being merely the hinterland of a world whose center was the Mediterranean basin.

From the sixth to the ninth century the state of Europe was not such as to permit much philosophical or theoretical activity, nor were the Germanic barbarians as yet capable of grasping — not to say extending — the remains of ancient learning at their disposal. The comparative orderliness of the age of Charlemagne, with its brief revival of scholarship, was an episode. New barbarian invasions in the tenth and eleventh centuries — the Norsemen in the north and the Huns in the east — again threatened to reduce Europe to a state of anarchy. Not until the latter part of the eleventh century, when the great controversy between the spiritual and temporal authorities began, was there again an active canvassing of political ideas. Yet with this great and violent break in social and political history which divides the ancient from the medieval period, there was no conscious or intentional departure from the political conceptions which bore the sanction of Christian antiquity. Reverence for Scripture, for the authority of the Fathers and the tradition of the church, even for ancient pagan writers like Cicero, remained unbounded. The validity of natural law and its binding authority over rulers and subjects, the obligation of kings to govern justly and in accordance with law, the sanctity of constituted authority both in church and state, and the unity of Christendom under the parallel powers of *imperium* and *sacerdotium* were matters of complete and universal agreement.

Nevertheless, allowance must be made for the appearance in the early Middle Ages of ideas about law and government which had not existed in antiquity and which yet, by their gradual incorporation into common modes of thought, had an important influence upon the political philosophy of western Europe. Some of these ideas may have been in some peculiar sense Germanic; at least they belonged to the Germanic peoples. But it is not necessary to adopt the myth that Germanic thought had an aura of its own. The ideas of the Germanic peoples about law were broadly similar to those of other barbarous peoples with a tribal organization and a semi-nomadic habit of life. They developed in contact with the vestiges of Roman law and under the stress of political and economic circumstances which were much alike in all parts of western Europe. It is the purpose of this chapter to describe briefly some of these new conceptions that made their way into political thought in the early Middle Ages and which, like the ancient tradition that came through the Fathers of the church, became matters of common acceptance.

THE OMNIPRESENT LAW

The most significant of the new ideas about law may be summed up by saying that the Germanic peoples conceived the law as belonging to the folk, or the people, or the tribe, almost as if it were an attribute of the group or a common possession by which the group was held together. Each member lived within the people's "peace," and the law provided especially the regulations necessary to prevent that peace from being broken. Outlawry, the primitive punishment for crime, put a man outside the people's peace; and injury to a particular person or family, the primitive equivalent of tort, put him outside the peace of the injured party, and the law provided the composition by which feud could be prevented and the peace restored. Germanic law in this early state was never written but consisted of customs perpetuated by word of mouth and constituting, as it were, the wisdom by which the peaceful life of the tribe was carried on. The law was, of course, "in every case the law of the tribe or folk which it rules, and attaches to every member of the tribe by virtue of his membership."[1] This was a natural consequence of the fact that the people to whom the law belonged were as yet but lightly attached to the soil, a nomadic habit of life being not far in the past and agriculture being as yet of comparatively minor importance.

Thus it happened that the barbarian peoples who made their way into the Roman Empire brought their law with them and it remained the personal possession of each member, even though he might settle down among persons governed by Roman law. This is the state of affairs which existed when the Germanic laws were first committed to writing, in Latin and not in the Germanic tongues, between the sixth and the eighth centuries. Such "barbarian codes" were formulated in the kingdoms of the Ostrogoths, the Lombards, the Burgundians, the Visigoths, and for various branches of the Franks, and contained not only an attempt to reduce Germanic custom to writing for their Germanic inhabitants, but frequently a formulation of Roman law for the Roman

[1] Munroe Smith, *The Development of European Law* (1928), p. 67.

inhabitants. Between Romans some remnant of Roman law was still administered; between persons of Germanic origin the appropriate form of Germanic law was still binding. In the course of time, since in many localities there were frequent conflicts of law, elaborate rules were developed for dealing with cases in which the parties were of different laws, much as modern law includes rules for dealing with transactions that in one way or another involve the law of several states.[2] The idea that law is an incident to membership in a folk or a tribe persisted long after the folk had ceased to be a unified group distinct from other groups and occupying a place of its own.

As the amalgamation of Roman and Germanic peoples progressed, however, this conception that law is a personal attribute gradually gave way to the conception that law follows the locality or the territory. The advantages of the latter conception for orderly and unified administration are obvious, and the speed with which the idea gained ground probably depended upon the success of the kings in gathering administration into their own hands. Relatively early, about the middle of the seventh century, there was a code of common law for both Roman and Gothic subjects of the Visigothic kingdom in Spain. In the Frankish empire, where the diversity of laws was great, the process was slower and very irregular. The king's law was always territorial (though not always uniform for the whole territory) and no doubt, on the whole, it was better law than the older (personal) folk-law, and also better administered. By the beginning of the ninth century the punishment of crimes by the law of the locality where they were committed had begun, in some parts of the Frankish empire, to displace the personal law. In some divisions of the law in which the church was especially interested, such for instance as that of marriage, the influence of the church also was against the diversity of laws. The processes by which the change took place are often impossible to trace, but in the course of time law was transformed, as it always tends to be in a settled community, into local custom, the principle of its applicability being territorial rather than tribal. Such local custom, however, was not identical with the king's law or with common law for a

[2] For a brief historical account of the barbarian codes, see Munroe Smith, *op. cit.*, Book II.

whole kingdom. The diversity of law, and especially of private law, persisted more or less everywhere, depending again upon the king's success in extending the jurisdiction of his own courts. In France, for example, private law remained largely local until after the Revolution, though the administrative law had long been unified; in England on the other hand, largely by reason of the greater strength of the Norman kings, the law had become substantially common by the end of the twelfth century.

Throughout the changes which transformed law from tribal practice to personal attribute, and from the latter to local custom, the conception in some way persisted that the law belongs essentially to a people or a folk. This idea did not connote, however, that law was the creature of a people, dependent upon their will and capable of being made or changed by their volition. The order of ideas was rather reversed: the folk as a communal body was perhaps more truly conceived to be made by their law, much as a living body might be identified with its principle of organization. The law, indeed, was not supposed to be made by anyone, either an individual or a people. It was imagined to be as permanent and as unchangeable as anything in nature, a "brooding omnipresence in the sky," as Justice Holmes said in one of his celebrated opinions. Only, the law as it was popularly conceived in the Middle Ages was by no means in the sky alone. It was rather like a circumambient atmosphere which extended from the sky to the earth and penetrated every nook and cranny of human relationship. It is true, as was said above, that everyone in the Middle Ages, whether a professional lawyer or a layman, believed in the reality of natural law, but this belief by no means exhausted the extraordinary reverence in which law was held. Literally all law was felt to be eternally valid and in some degree sacred, as the providence of God was conceived to be a universally present force which touched men's lives even in their most trifling details. The custom which was rooted in the folkways was in no sense set off from natural law but rather was felt to be a twig of the great tree of the law, which grew from earth to heaven and in whose shade all human life was lived. It was true both of the civilians and the canonists, when there came to be again a legal profession, that law was identified with right and equity and that human and divine law were conceived to be all of a piece.[3] But the theory was only a learned restatement of what everyone unquestioningly took for granted.

FINDING AND DECLARING LAW

This ramification of law through all the relations of life, as if it were a permanent structure within which all human affairs go on, is a conception not easy to recapture in an age when legislation takes place daily and by processes which the most optimistic would hesitate to identify with the providence of God. Nevertheless it was not unnatural in a society where legislation in the sense of enactment could hardly be said to take place at all. A society simple in its social and economic structure changes comparatively slowly, and it appears to its members to change more slowly than it often does. Immemorial custom is conceived to cover all questions that need to be adjudicated, and over considerable periods of time this may be almost true. When it ceases to be true, the natural explanation is not that new law needs to be made but rather that it is necessary to find out what the old law really means. Reciprocally, the fact that any state of affairs has existed for a considerable time creates the presumption that it is lawful and right. This, as Professor Munroe Smith [4] has pointed out, was the underlying assumption of the whole procedure of inquest which was so largely used in Frankish and Norman law and which in time produced the English jury. From this point of view it is appropriate to say that law is " found " rather than made, while it would be definitely inappropriate to say that any body of men exists whose business it is to make law. When by inquest or otherwise it has been found out what the law is on an important point, the king or some other appropriate authority may set forth the discovery in a " statute " or an " assize," in order that it may be known and generally followed, but this would not imply, for a person whose mind moved in this circle of ideas, that the statute enacted something which had not previously been valid. The powerful hold of custom upon legal ideas in the Middle Ages is shown by the fact that, even after the revival of the study of the Roman law, some lawyers believed that custom " founds, abro-

[3] Many citations will be found in Carlyle, *op. cit.*, Vol. II (1909), Part I, chs. 2–6; Part II, chs. 2–6.

[4] *Op. cit.*, p. 143.

gates, and interprets" the written law, though others of course held the contrary.[5] The decrees or capitularies of the Frankish kings, therefore, were not legislation in any modern sense of the word. They might instruct the king's commissioners how to deal with certain classes of cases, either for the whole kingdom or for some part of it, but they did not, in any contemporary understanding of the matter, enact the law. They told what, in the wisdom of the king's council and in the light of prevailing practice, the law had been found to be.

Such a declaration of the law was naturally made in the name of the whole people, or at least in the name of someone who was felt to be competent to speak for the whole people. Since the law belonged to the folk and had existed time out of mind, the folk were entitled to be consulted when an important statement of its provisions was to be made. Thus the capitularies of the Merovingian kings as early as the sixth century contain, apparently as a matter of course, the assertion that the decree has been issued after consultation with "our chief men," or with the "bishops and nobles," or that the decision has been made "by our whole people."[6] In the ninth century similar assertions are continually found, so frequently in fact that law seems regularly to have been issued in the name of the whole people definitely with the sense that their consent is an important factor in its validity. The term "consent," however, probably referred less to an act of will than to an acknowledgment that the law is really as stated. Thus, to cite a single illustration, Charlemagne used the following enacting formula: "Charles the Emperor . . . together with the bishops, abbots, counts, dukes, and all the faithful subjects of the Christian Church, and with their consent and counsel, has decreed the following . . . in order that each loyal subject, who has himself confirmed these decrees with his own hand, may do justice and in order that all his loyal subjects may desire to uphold the law."[7] In a well-known phrase an edict of 864 states

[5] The views of the civilians in the eleventh and twelfth centuries on this point are analyzed by Carlyle, *op. cit.*, Vol. II, Part I, ch. vi; those of the canonists in the twelfth and thirteenth centuries in Part II, ch. viii.

[6] Many illustrations of decrees containing these or similar expressions will be found in *M.G.H.*, Leg. Sect. II, Vol. I, pp. 8 ff.

[7] *M.G.H.*, Leg. Sect. II, Vol. I, No. 77. Many illustrations are given by Carlyle, Vol. I, ch. xix.

the principle in general terms: "Because the law is made with the consent of the people and by the declaration (*constitutione*) of the king. . . ." The following is a random illustration from English history in the twelfth century: "This is the assize of lord Henry the King, the son of Matilda, in England, concerning the forest and his venison, by the advice and assent of the archbishops, bishops and barons, earls and nobles of England, at Woodstock." [8]

A practically unlimited number of illustrations might be given, drawn from either the earlier or the later Middle Ages, of this conviction that the law belongs to the people whom it governs and is evidenced by their observance of it or, in case of doubt, by the statement of some body properly constituted to determine what the law is. Two illustrations, however, will suffice. One is the story which John of Ibelin, writing in the thirteenth century, tells of the making of the Assizes of Jerusalem some two centuries before. He says that Duke Godfrey caused "wise men to inquire from the people of different countries who were there [in Jerusalem] the customs of their countries." Then, with the advice and consent of the Patriarch and of the princes and barons, "he selected the practices that seemed good to him and made assizes and customs to be observed and followed in the Kingdom of Jerusalem." [9] As history this is no doubt worthless, but it shows admirably what the author believed to be the process of formulating a body of law. After the prevailing practice has been ascertained by consulting those who know, and after the men learned in the law have found the practices that ought to be binding, the result is reduced to writing and promulgated by the king, in order that there may be no further doubt about it. There was no thought in John's mind of Godfrey's having made the law or indeed of anyone having made it. And in order to ascertain the law, those who have it must of course be consulted.

The second illustration comes from England and has a certain interest because it belongs to a date when the medieval constitution was upon the eve of taking shape. After the Battle of Lewes (1264), which led directly to the calling of the Model Parliament,

[8] Henry II's Assize of Woodstock, 1184, Stubbs, *Select Charters,* ninth ed. (1913), p. 188; translation in Adams and Stephens, *Select Documents of English Constitutional History* (1901), No. 18.

[9] Carlyle, *op. cit.,* Vol. III (1915), p. 43, n. 2.

a follower of Simon de Montfort celebrated the victory in a curious poem wherein the rebels' view of law was stated:

> Therefore let the community of the kingdom advise, and let it be known what the generality thinks, to whom their own laws are best known. Nor are all those of the country so ignorant that they do not know better than strangers the customs of their own kingdom which have been handed down to them by their ancestors.[10]

The custom of the country is assumed to be binding, and the purpose of the parliament was to make certain what this custom really was and to give it effect.

The belief that law belongs to the people and is applied or modified with their approval and consent was therefore universally accepted. The belief was, however, very vague, so far as concerned the procedure of government. It implied no definite apparatus of representation and was in fact centuries old before medieval constitutionalism took form in such bodies as the parliaments that appeared in the twelfth and thirteenth centuries. There was, and indeed is, nothing essentially incongruous in the idea that a locality, a borough, or even a whole people, might make decisions, present their grievances, be called to account for their negligence, and give their approval to policies for which they had to provide money or soldiers. It is a modern convention that all this is done by elected representatives, but everyone knows that the convention often is not true. Effectively a community expresses its "mind" through a few persons who, for one reason or another, really count in crystallizing the vague thing called public opinion. So long as a community is so organized that these few persons are pretty clearly designated, and so long as the issues are relatively few and not subject to too rapid change, representation may be effective enough without much apparatus. Historically the apparatus was later than the idea that the people was a corporate body which expressed its corporate mind through its magistrates and natural leaders. Just who these leaders were or how they were designated leaders, or indeed who exactly "the people" severally were whom they represented, only became matters of primary importance when the making of devices to implement representation was undertaken. The older

[10] Translated in S. R. Gardiner, *Students' History of England,* Vol. I (1899), p. 202.

idea, in the form of a legal fiction, may perhaps still be seen in Blackstone's theory that English laws are not promulgated because every Englishman is conceived to be present in Parliament.[11]

THE KING UNDER THE LAW

The belief that the law belongs to the folk, and that their recognition of it has an important part in determining what it is, implies that the king is only one factor in making or declaring it. For this reason it was commonly believed that the king himself is obliged to obey the law quite as his subjects are. It was of course obvious that kings, like all other mortals, are subject to the laws of God and of nature, but this was not all that was meant nor the really important point. As has already been said, the discrimination of the several kinds of law, divine and human, did not mean that they were radically distinct. The law, conceived as a pervasive medium, penetrated and controlled all kinds of human relationship, and that of subject and ruler among others. Accordingly the king was felt to be obliged not only to rule justly rather than tyrannously, but also to administer the law of the kingdom as it actually was and as it could be ascertained to be by consulting immemorial practice. The king could not lawfully set aside rights which custom guaranteed to his subjects or which his predecessors had declared to be the law of the land. Thus a ninth-century writer, Archbishop Hincmar of Rheims, says:

> Kings and ministers of state have their laws by which they ought to govern those who live in every province; they have the capitularies of Christian Kings and of their ancestors, which they have lawfully promulgated with the general consent of their loyal subjects.[12]

And the capitularies abound in promises made by kings to give to their "loyal subjects" such law "as your ancestors had in the time of our ancestors,"[13] and not to oppress any of them "contrary to law and justice." The latter phrase was certainly not intended to mean justice in the abstract but justice as defined by the expectations created in settled practice. Such promises were often given by a king at his coronation and embodied in

[11] *Commentaries,* I, 185.

[12] Quoted by Carlyle, *op. cit.,* Vol. I, p. 234, n. 1.

[13] In a declaration of the Frankish king Lewis at Coblenz in 860 (*M.G.H.,* Leg. Sect. II, Vol. II, No. 242, 5).

his oath. Not infrequently they were extorted by the forcible measures of his "loyal subjects" when, without having the requisite power, the king showed himself too disregardful of their established rights and privileges. That such measures were justifiable upon suitable provocation was a settled belief, in spite of the strong statements of Gregory about passive obedience mentioned in the preceding chapter. For none in principle doubted that a man was entitled, by the law both of God and man, to the treatment and the status which he and his ancestors had long enjoyed or which had been guaranteed to him by the act of some previous ruler. The law created a tie binding upon the whole people and upon every man in the station to which he had been called; reciprocally it guaranteed to every man the privileges and rights and immunities proper to that station. The king was no exception to this general rule. Since he ruled by the law he was subject to it.

But while the king was thought to be subject to the law, it would not be accurate to say that he was subject in precisely the same way as other men. The point of the conception was not equality before the law. It was rather that every man was entitled to enjoy the law according to his rank and order. The firmly fixed idea of status made almost any amount of inequality justifiable. No one denied that the king's position was in many important respects unique. By virtue of his office he had a large responsibility for the well-being of his people, a considerable discretion in adopting measures to foster it, and indefeasible rights within the sphere of duties imposed by his position.[14] In accordance with what has already been said about the vagueness of constitutional conceptions, it is not to be expected that the modes in which the king could exercise unique powers within the law would be accurately defined. Even with modern constitutional devices the powers of government can be almost indefinitely stretched to meet an emergency by methods which the courts will hold to be lawful. And in the Middle Ages there was almost no means of defining accurately any constitutional authority. Thus it could be held at once that the king was bound by law and yet that no writ would run against him. No one doubted that there were limits somewhere which he could not exceed without violat-

[14] C. H. McIlwain, *op. cit.,* ch. 7.

ing both law and morals; on the other hand no one doubted that he ought to have powers not equalled by those of any subject. The king was *singulis maior universis minor.*

Consequently there was a fundamental difference between the conception of the king implied in the capitularies and that embodied in the Roman law. It is true that the constitutional theory of the Roman lawyers regarded the emperor's legal authority as derived from the Roman people. In the famous dictum of Ulpian this was given as the ground for the emperor's legislative power. But the lawyer's theory regarded the cession of power as made once for all; after the emperor has been invested with his authority, *quod principi placuit legis habet vigorem.* The medieval theory, on the other hand, assumes a continuous co-operation between the king and his subjects, both being, so to speak, organs of the realm to which the law belongs. The difference is in part explainable by the enormous differences between the societies in which the two conceptions of law grew up. The tradition of the Roman law was that of a highly centralized administration in which conscious legislation by imperial edicts, senatorial decrees, and the opinions of expert jurisconsults was a matter of common experience, and in which also the law itself had been brought to a high level of scientific systematization. A medieval kingdom was not centralized either in theory or in practice, and nothing perhaps is more recalcitrant to logical systematization than local custom. The realm or the folk was vaguely felt as a unit organized under its law and including the king along with other officials and persons who were its appropriate spokesmen and agents, but there was as yet no precise definition of the powers and duties of these agencies and no consciousness that they needed to be strictly co-ordinated in such a way that authority flowed from a single source. The conception of delegated power was continually crossed by the conception that authority resides also in position or status and is therefore inherent in persons who, in other respects, might be regarded as agents of the king. Even in the seventeenth century Sir Edward Coke could still think of the crown, the parliament, and the courts of common law as enjoying inherent powers under the law of the realm. The king was not the " head " of the state, as he became in the era of absolute monarchy at the opening of the modern period. Still less were men aware of the state as "an artificial person," such as analytic jurists have consciously created in order to give unity of operation to the functions of government.[15]

THE CHOICE OF A KING

The relation of king and people under the law of the folk, and the political conceptions which this relation engendered, are further clarified by considering how the king was believed to be invested with his authority and what constituted the lawful claim to his office. Medieval ideas on the subject throw light upon the prevailing notions both of the people's consent and of the king's subjection to law, and also illustrate excellently the lack of precise legal ideas about the title to authority. According to the political ideas of the present day a ruler may be elected or he may inherit his office but he can hardly do both at once. The striking fact about many medieval kings is that, according to the prevailing ideas of their time, they not only inherited and were elected but ruled also "by the grace of God," the three titles being not alternative but expressing three facts about the same state of affairs.

This vague state of mind can best be made clear by taking an actual case. When Louis the Pious in the year 817 wished to provide for the succession of his sons, he set forth his decision and the grounds for it as follows.[16] He first recited how the "holy assembly and totality of our people" had met according to custom, and how "suddenly by divine inspiration" his loyal subjects advised him that the succession of the kingdom should be settled while God granted peace. After three days of fasting and prayer, it was brought about,

> by the will of Almighty God, as we believe, that our own wishes and those of our whole people agreed in the election of our beloved Lothair, our eldest son. Therefore it seemed good to us and to all our people that he, being thus indicated by divine direction, after being solemnly crowned with the imperial diadem, should by the common desire be made our consort and successor in the empire, if God shall so will.

[15] See the definition of the state in John Chipman Gray's *Nature and Sources of the Law,* 2nd edition (1921), p. 65.

[16] *M.G.H.,* Leg. Sect. II, Vol. I, No. 136. Translated in E. F. Henderson, *Select Historical Documents of the Middle Ages* (1892), p. 201.

Certain provisions were then made for the younger sons and the decisions reached were " written down and confirmed with our hands, so that, with the help of God, as they were made by the common will of all, they might be kept inviolate through the common devotion of all."

In this choice of a ruler it will be noted that three grounds were assigned for the validity of the choice. First, Lothair was in fact the emperor's eldest son, though this was not emphasized. Second, he was elected and this election was said to be an act of the whole people done " by the common will of all." And third, the choice was believed to be made under the direct inspiration of God. Lothair's claim to the crown evidently rested, in the mind of Louis, upon all three facts in combination. The idea doubtless was that, subject to the will of God, the king's son was a normal candidate to succeed him, but the actual choice required some sort of ratification or acceptance of the candidate in the name of the people.

These factors were exactly similar to those supposed to conspire in the issuing of an assize: the validity of the law was ultimately divine but it was enunciated by the king and it had behind it the consent of the people expressed through the magnates of the realm. It is of course true that the machinery of such an election was as vague as that for enunciating law; no one could possibly have told what exactly were the qualifications of electors. The conjunction of the three factors in everyone's mind, moreover, helps to explain the idea that the king, once elected, was still subject to law. Inheritance was not the king's indefeasible right, while the suffrage of the magnates who chose him was cast by virtue of the rights inherent in their stations rather than because they were electors in a strict constitutional sense. This view was expressed in a highly characteristic way in a letter written in 879 to Lewis III by Archbishop Hincmar:

> You have not chosen me to be a prelate of the Church, but I and my colleagues, with the other loyal subjects of God and your ancestors, have chosen you to rule the kingdom on the condition that you shall keep the law.[17]

In the earlier Middle Ages, then, three sorts of claim to royal power were combined: the king inherited his throne; he was

[17] Quoted by Carlyle, *op. cit.,* Vol. I, p. 244, n. 2.

elected by his people; and he ruled of course by the grace of God. Election and hereditary right became more clearly distinguished as constitutional practices became more regular and more clearly defined. The two most characteristic medieval monarchies, the empire and the papacy, though efforts were made more than once to make them perquisites of a family, became definitely elective. In constitution-making the papacy led the way by the establishment in the second half of the eleventh century of an orderly process of election by the clergy, to replace the older informal kind of election which often made a papal election the plaything of the petty Roman nobility or of imperial politics. It was not until 1356 that the Golden Bull of Charles IV crystallized the practice of imperial elections, thus giving to the empire a constitutional document which fixed the number and identity of the electors and established majority rule. In the kingdoms of France and England, on the other hand, the principle of primogeniture prevailed, perhaps on the analogy of the usual rule of feudal succession. There is no doubt that under feudalism hereditary monarchy had the better chance of becoming strong. But even in the kingdoms the feeling that the king was in some sense the choice of the people persisted for a long time. Thus the succession of King John in 1199, which was not in fact strictly in accord with primogeniture, was described by the chronicler Matthew of Paris, in a speech attributed to Archbishop Hubert of Canterbury, as the result of an election.[18] Perhaps the idea of election never wholly disappeared from popular feeling, even after the legal right of inheritance was settled. Thus in France in the sixteenth century, when it became important to fix responsibility in the king, men could argue that monarchy is always in principle elective.

Whether the king succeeded to his office by election or by heredity, he still ruled by the grace of God. That secular rule was of divine origin, that the king was the vicar of God, and that those who resisted him unlawfully were "subjects of the Devil

[18] Stubbs, *Select Charters,* ninth ed. (1913), p. 265; translated in Adams and Stephens, *Select Documents of English Constitutional History* (1901), No. 22. The fact that Hubert probably did not speak as reported is unimportant, so far as showing a popular sentiment is concerned, since Matthew wrote only about fifty years after the event. His account gives a good idea of the vagueness of the idea of election.

and the enemies of God" was doubted by no one. At the same time expressions such as these had no such precise meaning as divine right came to have in the sixteenth century. In particular, they were not thought to imply an obligation on the subject's part to render passive obedience irrespective of the justice or the tyranny of the king's commands. In the absence of strict hereditary succession the conception that the king's authority was divine could not issue in a theory of dynastic legitimacy such as the expression "divine right" implied between the sixteenth and the eighteenth centuries; and in the absence of a strongly coordinated monarchy with the king at its head the duty of passive obedience could not take on the ethical importance which it attained in later political philosophy. Since the king was himself conceived to be bound by the law of the land, the propriety of resistance under some not very strictly defined circumstances, when the fundamental law was believed to have been invaded, was looked upon as both a moral and a legal right. But this was not regarded as violating the Christian duty of subjection to constituted authority, and St. Gregory's pronouncements in favor of passive obedience were sure to be quoted against fomentors of disorder.

LORD AND VASSAL

The idea that law belongs to the folk and regulates all the relations of men with one another from the top to the bottom of society carried with it the germs of certain constitutional conceptions, such as the corporate nature of the realm, representation, and the legal authority of the crown. In the early Middle Ages, however, these ideas lacked precise definition and also any definite institutional embodiment in a constitutional apparatus. The latter was developed from the social and economic arrangements and the rather vague mass of ideas known as feudalism. As Vinogradoff has said, feudal institutions dominated the Middle Ages as completely as the city-state dominated antiquity. Unfortunately it is impossible to define feudalism, both because it connotes a great variety of institutions and also because it was very unequally developed in different times and places. For the latter reason dates are notoriously independable. In some places characteristic feudal arrangements, like serfdom, existed as early as the fifth century, but feudalism was most fully developed after the breaking up of the Frankish empire, and produced its fullest effects on social and political institutions in the eleventh and twelfth centuries. No general description that can be given will fit the facts, though behind this variety there were certain arrangements and certain ideas that were pretty well exemplified in most parts of western Europe. Some of these had important theoretical implications and for this reason must be examined, though their history in different countries is too complicated even to be mentioned.

The key to feudal arrangements lay in the fact that, in a period of disorder often approaching anarchy, large political and economic units were impossible. Governments tended, therefore, to be restricted to a size, small by modern or Roman standards, which was viable in the circumstances. The essential economic fact was a condition of agriculture which made the village community, with its dependent farm lands, an almost self-sufficing unit. The end of the era began with the rise of the trading cities in the twelfth century, though many of the most important political effects of feudalism appeared after that date. Since land was the only important form of wealth, every class, from king to fighting man, was dependent directly upon the products of the soil. The control of land was in the hands of this small community with its customary regulations, and minor police functions were the duty of the village.[19] The organization of society and of government was fundamentally local. Upon this foundation the typical feudal organization was built. In a state of continual disorder and with the most primitive means of communication, a central government could not perform even such elementary duties as safeguarding life and property. In such a situation the small landowner or the man of small power had but one recourse: he must become the dependent of someone strong enough to aid him. The relation thus formed had two sides; it was at once a personal relation and a property relation. The small man obligated himself to render services to the great man in return for protection, and he surrendered the ownership of his land and became a tenant upon the condition of paying a rent in services or

[19] For a description of an English manor see W. J. Ashley, *The Economic Organization of England* (1914), Lecture I.

goods. The property and power of the great man were thus augmented, while the small man had behind him a powerful patron whose interest as well as duty it was to protect him. A similar result was reached when the process worked from the top down. A king or an abbot could put his land to use only by granting it to a tenant who would make a return in services or rent.

The whole system may be regarded as a system by which all the land of the realm was drawn into the service of the realm, or as a system by which those who render service to the community receive, in the form of the yield or produce of land, payment or salary for their services.[20]

Feudalism, then, in its legal principles, was a system of land-tenure in which ownership was displaced by something like leasehold. Or as a modern jurist has expressed it:

Practical ownership consists of a life interest, inalienable in most cases, and of a reversion or remainder which again, when vested, is simply another life interest.[21]

Now this system of vested interests must be conceived to run through the community from top to bottom and to touch all the principal functions of government. Thus, if the land-system were logically worked out, the king would be the sole landowner. His barons would be tenants upon lands granted to them for specified services, and the barons would in turn have tenants under them, until the bottom is reached in the serfs, upon whose labor the whole system rests. Since military service was the typical form of return for a barony, the army of the kingdom would be a feudal army. That is, each tenant would be obligated to produce a specified number of men, armed in specified ways, and each baron would command his own men. The revenues of the kingdom (aside from those coming directly to the king from his own domain) would arise less from general taxation than from dues or reliefs, which the king's tenants were obligated to pay upon fixed occasions. Last and most important of all, the grant to the tenant might carry with it the right to administer justice in his own barony with an immunity from interference by the king's officers. The theory of feudal law is expressed in the saying that "the man's man is not the lord's man." For obvious reasons kings were slow to grant such immunities if they could

[20] Munroe Smith, *op. cit.*, p. 165.
[21] Munroe Smith, *op. cit.*, p. 172.

avoid it. Thus the relatively powerful Norman kings of England required the insertion into oaths of fealty of the qualifying clause, " saving the faith that I owe to our lord the King."

Consequently feudalism affected in the most important way the three great instruments of political power, the army, the revenues, and the courts. In all three cases, the king might be able to deal with the great mass of his subjects only at second or third hand. The feudal relation of lord and vassal was fundamentally different from that conceived to hold between sovereign and subject in a modern state. The personal side of the relationship, with its stress upon the loyalty and reverence which a vassal invariably owed to his superior, had elements not unlike those of political subordination, though it often operated to withdraw the loyalty of men in the lower ranks from the king to their more immediate overlords. On the other hand, the property relation was more like a contract in which the two parties retained each his private interest and co-operated because it was mutually advantageous to do so, though the king's ownership of the land might work in the long run to increase his power. The greatest prudence needs to be used in drawing conclusions as to the way in which the system actually worked, for it had in fact diverse tendencies.

In the first place, the obligation between a lord and his vassals was always mutual. It was not exactly equal, since the vassal owed general duties of loyalty and obedience which the lord did not share. He owed also more specific duties, such as military service, attendance upon the lord's court, and various payments to be made on stated occasions, such as the succession of an heir into the tenancy. It was characteristic of these specific duties that they were limited. The amount and kind of military service, for instance, was fixed, and beyond this the vassal's obligation strictly speaking did not go. On the other hand, the lord was obligated to give aid and protection to his vassals and also to abide by the customs or the charter which defined the vassal's rights and immunities. In theory, at least, the vassal could always surrender his tenancy and renounce his subjection — in practice a rather speculative remedy — or he might keep his land and disavow his obligations if the lord denied him the rights to which he was entitled. Consequently the promise of a king to give his subjects the law which their ancestors enjoyed in the time of his ancestors was merely a recognition of an arrangement conceived as existing and as having a right to exist. In this feudal arrangement there was an aspect of mutuality, of voluntary performance, and of implied contract which has almost wholly vanished from modern political relationships. It was somewhat as if a citizen might refuse to pay taxes beyond a certain amount, decline military service beyond a stipulated period, or perhaps refuse both until his liberties were recognized. In this respect the position of the king was weak in theory and often doubly weak in practice, and the feudal monarchy appears by comparison with a modern state to be highly decentralized. On the other hand, however, the feudal system of land-tenure, sometimes permitted a king, or more particularly a family, to increase its power by lawful feudal means, such for instance as escheat. The early growth of the power of the Capetian dynasty in France took place largely by the operation of feudal law itself.

In the second place, the relation of lord and vassal differed from that of sovereign and subject because it tended to obscure the distinction between private rights and public duties. Though a feudal holding was typically land, it was not necessarily so. Any object of value might be so held: the right to operate a mill, to collect a toll, or hold an office of government. The whole system of public administration tended to follow the prevailing form of land-tenure and public office tended to become, like land, a heritable interest. In this way office became vested in perpetuity in a man and his heirs. The vassal's right to his property implied a public service of some specified kind but, on the other hand, the obligation to public service was incidental to the property right. This led to the result that a public official held his place not as an agent of the king but because he had a prescriptive right to be there. His authority was not delegated but owned; obviously the king's power depended largely upon his ability to limit this tendency. But the tendency goes far to explain the apparently informal character of feudal institutions. The men about the king owe him court-service as part of their feudal duty. So long as their status was sufficiently clear, questions as to whom precisely they represent or who is entitled to be consulted need not arise. They are not so much public servants as men discharging a contractual obligation.

THE FEUDAL COURT

The court of a lord and his vassals was the typical feudal institution.[22] It was essentially a council of the lord and his men for the settlement of disputes arising among them relative to the arrangements on which their feudal relations depend. The striking fact is that both the lord and the vassal had precisely the same remedy in case either believed that his right had been invaded: he could appeal to the decision of the other members of the court. The notion that the king or lord should decide out of his own plenary power and according to his own will was quite foreign at least to the theory of the proceedings. The charters or customary rights of the parties were supposed to be strictly maintained. A decision of Henry II of England in a trial before his court (c. 1154) will illustrate the point. The trial concerned the title to lands claimed alike by the Abbot of St. Martin and Gilbert de Balliol. The Abbot offered a charter to prove his claim and Gilbert, whose claim was weak, introduced a quibble about its lacking a seal. "By the eyes of God," said King Henry, "if you can prove this charter false, it will be worth a thousand pounds to me in England." But Gilbert had no evidence. Whereupon the king decided the case:

> If the monks by means of a similar charter and confirmation were able to show that they had a right of this sort to the present place, to wit, Clarendon, which I chiefly love, there would be no just reply for me to make to save me from entirely surrendering it to them.[23]

In theory, then, the feudal court guaranteed to every vassal a trial by his peers, in accordance with the law of the land and the specific agreements or charters at issue. The court's decision was enforceable by the united power of its members, and in the extreme case enforcement was conceived to run even against the king. The sixty-first section of Magna Charta, empowering a

[22] For an example of a feudal court see the account of the Haute Cour of the Latin Kingdom of Jerusalem, John L. LaMonte, *Feudal Monarchy in the Latin Kingdom of Jerusalem, 1100–1291* (1932), ch. iv. The Latin Kingdom is perhaps an especially good illustration of feudal *ideas*, because the accounts of it, written some two centuries after its founding, embody prevailing theories, legal and other, of what a government ought to be and also because transplanted institutions usually embody theories better than those of native growth.

[23] Adams and Stephens, *op. cit.*, No. 12.

committee of twenty-five of King John's barons to enforce the charter, was an effort thus to legalize constraint applied to the king.

> Those twenty-five barons, with the whole land in common, shall distrain and oppress us in every way in their power . . . until amends shall have been made according to their judgment.

Similarly the right of vassals to coerce the lord in defense of their just liberties as determined by the court was secured by the Assizes of Jerusalem. Under a typical feudal organization the king was *primus inter pares,* and the court itself, or the king and the court together, exercised a joint rule, which included all that, in a modern state, would be distinguished as legislative, executive, and judicial functions of government. At the same time the essentially contractual relation between the members of the court, including the king, tended to prevent the concentration of authority anywhere. The probability that such a system would issue, pretty frequently, in something like legalized rebellion is too obvious to need comment.

FEUDALISM AND THE COMMONWEALTH

While a state of affairs such as has been described often existed, it probably did not represent, either in theory or in practice, quite the whole truth about a medieval monarchy. Aside from the intolerable inconvenience of legalized rebellion, a definitely contractual relation between the king and his vassals by no means exhausted the medieval theory of kingship. Both theory and practice united with this conception ideas of a quite different sort. The reverence and obedience which a vassal owed to his lord were elements of feudal homage itself that conceded to the king a unique position in his realm. Moreover, no one doubted that the king was the anointed of God and that resistance, except in unusual cases, was unlawful. The authority of St. Paul in the thirteenth chapter of *Romans* and the strong statements of St. Gregory on the duty of obedience would never have been denied in principle. Finally, the tendency of feudalism to subvert public authority and to substitute for it a network of private relations never wholly swallowed up the ancient tradition of the *res publica* which came to the Middle Ages through Cicero, the Roman law, and the Fathers of the church. The conception that a people makes up a commonwealth, organized under its law and capable of exerting through its rulers a public authority, crossed and mingled with the feudal bent toward particularism. Between the ninth and the twelfth centuries this ancient tradition was perpetuated mainly through ecclesiastical writers. Its existence in the ninth century is witnessed by Hincmar of Rheims, and its perpetuation is witnessed by the fact that, in the twelfth century, it produced in the *Policraticus* of John of Salisbury the first elaborate medieval treatise on politics. The latter work, though produced at a time when feudalism was perhaps at its height, was in its main outlines distinctively in the ancient mode.[24] In the long run the king was very definitely the beneficiary of this conception of a commonwealth, since he remained the titular representative of the public interest and in some degree the repository of public authority. It was this fact that made the feudal king the starting-point for the development of national monarchy.[25]

The mingling of two ideas — that which conceived the king as party to a contractual relation with his vassals and that which regarded him as the head of the commonwealth — may be illustrated from the theories of the feudal lawyers about the royal power. The king was universally regarded as created by the law and subject to it, and yet, on the other hand, it was commonly admitted that "no writ will run against the king" and that accordingly he cannot be coerced by the ordinary processes of his own courts. The passages so often quoted from Bracton's *De legibus et consuetudinibus Angliae* show the crossing of the two ideas:

> The king ought to have no equal in his realm, because this would nullify the rule that an equal cannot have authority over his equals. Still less ought he to have a superior or anyone more powerful than he, for he would then be below his own subjects, and it is impossible that inferiors should be equal to those who have greater powers. But the king himself ought not to be subject to any man, but he ought to be subject to God and the law, since law makes the king. Therefore let the king

[24] See the Introduction by John Dickinson to his translation of a part of the work; *The Statesman's Book of John of Salisbury* (1927), pp. xviii ff.

[25] The importance of the ecclesiastical tradition in the theory of the Capetian monarchy and the contrast with feudal authority has been emphasized by Luchaire, *Institutions monarchiques de la France sous les premiers Capétiens,* 2nd ed. (1891), Bk. I, ch. 1.

render to the law what the law has rendered to the king, viz., dominion and power, for there is no king where will rules and not the law.[26]

As the vicar of God, the king ought to do justice and accept the ruling of the law in his own cases, even as the least in his kingdom; if he will not, he becomes the minister of the Devil, but his subjects have no recourse except to leave him to the judgment of God. Yet Bracton was willing to entertain the idea that the *universitas regni et baronagium* perhaps can and ought to correct the evil in the king's court.[27] And in a remarkable passage, now agreed to be a contemporary interpolation, the propriety of coercing an "unbridled" king is flatly asserted.

But the king has a superior, namely God. Likewise the law, by which he was made king. And likewise his court, to wit, the counts and barons, for the counts are called, as it were, the king's associates, and he who has an associate has a master. Thus if the king should be without a bridle, that is, without the law, they ought to put a bridle on him.[28]

In these passages both the king and the court evidently appear in a twofold capacity. In the one the king is the chief landowner of the realm and the court comprises his tenants; as an institution the court exists to dispose of the difficulties which arise between them in this contractual relation. In the other the king stands as the chief bearer of a public authority inherent in the realm or the folk, which however he shares in some not very definite way with his court. In the first relationship the king may be proceeded against like others of the court; in the second capacity no writ will run against him and his responsibility to the law rests ultimately on his own conscience. The one view represents a typical tendency of feudalism to submerge public authority in private relationships; the other represents the continuing tradi-

[26] F. 5b. Quoted, with similar examples from other feudal lawyers, in Carlyle, *op. cit.,* Vol. III, Part I, ch. iv.

[27] F. 171b; Carlyle, *op. cit.,* Vol. III, p. 71, n. 2.

[28] F. 34; Carlyle, *op. cit.,* Vol. III, p. 72, n. 1. On this passage see G. E. Woodbine's edition of *De legibus,* Vol. I (1915), pp. 332 f.; F. W. Maitland, *Bracton's Note Book,* Vol. I (1887), pp. 29 ff.; Ludwik Ehrlich, "Proceedings against the Crown (1216–1377)," *Oxford Studies in Social and Legal History,* Vol. VI (1921), pp. 48 ff., 202 ff. On Bracton's extraordinary treatment of the dictum *quod principi placuit* in F. 107, see McIlwain, *op. cit.,* pp. 195 ff.

tion of a commonwealth in which the king is the chief magistrate. Perhaps it was just the meeting and mingling of the two conceptions which made the feudal court the matrix from which the constitutional principles and institutions of the later Middle Ages developed. By a process of differentiation a variety of governing bodies — such as the king's councils, law-courts taking cognizance of differing kinds of cases, and finally parliament — came to carry on distinct branches of public business. As late as the civil wars of the seventeenth century, as Professor McIlwain has amply shown, Englishmen still thought of parliament as a court rather than as a legislature. Through this development the conception of public authority emerged into greater clearness, but that authority never centered itself exclusively in the person of the king. When the king became absolute, this was a development of modern rather than of medieval states. The medieval king had still to act through his council, and the court or some of its branches retained some vestiges of its feudal right to be consulted. From this beginning constitutional ideas, such as representation, taxation and legislation by assemblies, supervision of expenditures, and petition for the redress of grievances, could emerge. In England, at least, the right to legislate could be settled ultimately not in the king, but in the king in parliament.

SELECTED BIBLIOGRAPHY

Civilization during the Middle Ages. By G. B. Adams. Revised edition. New York, 1922. Ch. 9.

The King's Council in England during the Middle Ages. By J. F. Baldwin. Oxford, 1913. Ch. 1.

A History of Mediaeval Political Theory in the West. By R. W. Carlyle and A. J. Carlyle. 6 vols. New York and London, 1903–1936. Vol. I, Part IV, The Political Theory of the Ninth Century; Vol. III, Part I, The Influence of Feudalism on Political Theory.

"Proceedings against the Crown (1216–1377)." By Ludwik Ehrlich. In *Oxford Studies in Social and Legal History*, Vol. VI. Oxford, 1921.

Law and Politics in the Middle Ages. By Edward Jenks. New York, 1898.

The Growth of Political Thought in the West. By C. H. McIlwain. New York, 1932. Ch. 5.

Constitutional History of England. By F. W. Maitland. Cambridge, 1911. Period I.

" Roman Law." By H. J. Roby. In *Cambridge Medieval History,* Vol. II (1913), ch. 3.

The Development of European Law. By Munroe Smith. New York, 1928.

" Foundations of Society (Origins of Feudalism)." By Paul Vinogradoff. In *Cambridge Medieval History,* Vol. II (1913), ch. 20.

" Feudalism." By Paul Vinogradoff. In *ibid.* Vol. III (1922) ch. 18.

The Growth of the Manor. By Paul Vinogradoff. 2nd edition. London, 1911.

" Customary Law." By Paul Vinogradoff. In *The Legacy of the Middle Ages.* Ed. by G. C. Crump and E. F. Jacob. Oxford, 1926.

CHAPTER XII

THE INVESTITURE CONTROVERSY

The latter part of the eleventh century brought a resumption of intellectual labor upon the body of political and social ideas that had been preserved from antiquity in the tradition of the Christian Fathers and began a development which produced in the centuries following an astonishingly brilliant and virile culture. Order emerged once more from chaos and especially in the Norman states began to promise administrative efficiency and political stability such as Europe had not known since Roman times. Feudalism began to settle itself into a more definite system from which were to arise constitutional principles that carried over from the Middle Ages into modern Europe. The cities, first in Italy and a little later in the north, began to build up trade and industry which were to supply the basis for an original and humane art and literature. Philosophy and scholarship made a beginning soon to be fructified by the recovery of important masses of ancient learning. The study of jurisprudence, in southern France and the Italian cities of Ravenna and Bologna, began to restore a knowledge of Roman law and to apply it to contemporary legal and political problems. In this general rise of the intellectual level, affecting every branch of thought, it was natural that political philosophy should share.

In the eleventh and twelfth centuries political writing was in the main controversial, centering about the contest between the popes and the emperors over the boundaries of the secular and ecclesiastical authorities. Its extent, however, is astonishing. Probably the whole extant body of political philosophy written between the death of Aristotle and the eleventh century would occupy fewer pages than the great collection of political tracts that grew out of the struggle over the lay investiture of bishops. As a subject of systematic scholarly investigation political theory emerged more slowly than other branches of philosophical interest. In the thirteenth century it was still overshadowed by the great systems of theology and metaphysics which were the typical creations of the scholastic philosophers. In the fourteenth century treatises on political philosophy became more common, as they continued to be from that time to the present. Yet the preservation of great numbers of tracts from the earlier centuries speaks for a continuous interest in the subject. And even in the eleventh century certain main issues began to be drawn and certain fundamental problems began to emerge which evolved continuously in the centuries following.

THE MEDIEVAL CHURCH-STATE

The starting-point for the eleventh-century controversialists, in respect to the relations of the secular and spiritual authorities, was the Gelasian theory of the two swords already described, in which the teaching of the Christian Fathers had been summed up. The distinction between spirituals and seculars, between the interests of soul and body, was part of the warp and woof of Christianity itself. According to the view universally accepted in the eleventh century — and indeed not overtly denied for centuries thereafter — human society is divinely ordained to be governed by two authorities, the spiritual and the temporal, the one wielded by priests and the other by secular rulers, both in accordance with divine and natural law. No man, under the Christian dispensation, can possess both *sacerdotium* and *imperium*. Neither authority was conceived to exercise an arbitrary power, for both were believed to be subject to law and to fill a necessary office in the divine government of nature and of man. Between the two, accordingly, there could be in principle no conflict, though sinful pride or greed of power might lead the human agents of either to overstep the boundaries allotted by the law. As parts of a divinely unified plan, each authority owed aid and support to the other.

Within this circle of ideas, there was, properly speaking, neither church nor state in the modern meaning of those terms. There was not one body of men who formed the state and one which formed the church, for all men were included in both. There was only a single Christian society, as St. Augustine had taught in his *City of God,* and it included, at least for the eleventh century, the whole world. Under God this society had two heads, the pope and the emperor, two principles of authority, the spiritual rule of priests and the temporal rule of kings, and two hierarchies of governing officials, but there was no division between two bodies or societies. A controversy between these two hierarchies was in a legal sense jurisdictional, such as might arise between two officials of the same state. The question was one of the proper boundaries of authority and of what the one or the other might lawfully do within the limits, express or implied, of his office. In this sense, and in this sense only, was there controversy between church and state at the beginning of the dispute. As time went on this original conception was gradually set aside, especially as the legal aspects of the dispute became more clearly defined. But in the beginning the issue was between two groups of officials each invested with an original authority and claiming to act within the limits of that authority.

The theory of the separation of the two authorities had never been very literally carried out; it had not been understood to deny that in their earthly exercise they were in contact, or that each body of officials owed aid to the other in their proper functions. Thus it was possible, when controversy broke out, to point on either side to historical acts which were admitted to be justifiable and which yet might be interpreted as a control of the one hierarchy by the other. In the declining days of Rome Gregory the Great had exercised great temporal power. Both ecclesiastical synods and individual churchmen had followed the precedent of Ambrose in admonishing kings for their misdoings; bishops were regularly counted among the magnates with whose consent laws were enacted; and churchmen had exercised great influence in electing and deposing rulers. Pippin had sought and obtained papal approval for setting aside the Merovingian dynasty in the Frankish kingdom. The famous coronation of Charles the Great in 800 could readily be interpreted as a translation of the empire to the Frankish kings by an authority vested in the church, on the analogy of the institution of Jewish kingship by Samuel. Indeed, the administering of a coronation oath was universally felt to have some religious significance, and like all oaths it might fall within the disciplinary power of the church in moral matters.

On the whole, however, down to the time when the controversy between the ecclesiastical and the imperial jurisdictions broke out in the eleventh century, the control of the emperor over the papacy was more conspicuous and effective than that of the pope over the emperor. This had usually been true as a matter of course in Roman times, and anyone who reads the instructions of Charlemagne to the officers whom he sent on circuit to conduct inquests through his empire will have no doubt that he regarded both churchmen and laymen as his subjects, or that he took full responsibility for the government of the church. In the case of Leo III he had extended his inquisitorial authority to the alleged crimes of the pope himself. In the tenth century, when the papacy fell into exceptional degradation, it was the emperors from Otto I to Henry III who had applied reformatory measures, extending to the deposition, under canonical forms, of Gregory VI and the infamous Benedict IX. In fact, the emperors had exerted a major influence in abolishing the scandals that flowed from a state of affairs in which papal elections were the football of petty patrician politics in the city of Rome. There were, of course, obvious reasons of policy which impelled the emperors to exert their influence in the selection of popes. But this influence, while preferable from a churchman's point of view to local Roman intrigue, was potentially a threat to the autonomy of the church in spiritual affairs.

THE INDEPENDENCE OF THE CHURCH

The controversy of the eleventh century originated in an increased self-consciousness and sense of independence on the part of churchmen and in a desire to make the church an autonomous spiritual power in consonance with the admitted validity of its claims. The tradition of Augustine presented Europe to men's minds as essentially a Christian society, unique in the history of the world because for the first time it brought secular power into the service of divine truth. According to this conception, the ancient ideal of government for the sake of justice reached its consummation in rendering not only to every man his right, but in the more vital duty of rendering to God the worship that was his due. Gelasius, writing against the subordination of ecclesiastical policy to the imperial court at Constantinople, had asserted that the priest's responsibility, being directed toward eternal salvation, was weightier than the king's. Indeed, no other conclusion was logically possible, if spiritual ends had in fact the importance which Christianity imputed to them, and if the church were truly the institution by which alone these ends were to be attained. The rising enlightenment of the eleventh century, growing up within the church and dominated by the teaching which the Augustinian tradition made part of the climate of Christian opinion, could not escape the obligation to make this teaching effective. Earlier the circumstances had been lacking which made such an effort possible, but the first great effort of Christian civilization could hardly have been directed to anything but realizing, under papal auspices, the ideal of a Christian society in which the church should be, in fact as in right, the directing force behind a Christian state.

Already in the ninth century, in the brief revival of scholarship permitted by Charles's empire, churchmen had begun to develop the claims of the church in a Christian society. Thus Archbishop Hincmar of Rheims had written:

> Let them defend themselves, if they will, by earthly laws or by human customs, but let them know, if they are Christians, that at the day of judgment they will be judged not by Roman or Salic or Gundobadian law but by divine apostolic law. In a Christian kingdom even the laws of the state ought to be Christian, that is, in accord with and suitable to Christianity.[1]

The revival of the ninth century was a flash in the pan, but in the meantime changes were taking place in the church itself which gave greater effectiveness to claims for the Christian state when the more permanent revival of the eleventh century occurred. These changes affected in part the centralization of papal authority and of ecclesiastical organization within the church and in part the greater seriousness and militancy of churchmen in the pursuit of the Christian ideal. The first change was connected with the fabrication of the forgeries known as the Pseudo-Isidorian Decretals in the ninth century, and the second with the Cluniac reforms in the tenth.

The False Decretals [2] were evidently produced with the object

[1] Quoted by Carlyle, *op. cit.,* Vol. I, p. 277, n. 3.

[2] They consist of over a hundred spurious letters attributed mostly to the popes of the first three centuries and of numerous spurious reports of councils, inserted into an older body of authentic material. They originated

of strengthening the position of the bishops; in particular, to protect them from deposition and confiscation of property by secular rulers, to consolidate their control over the clergy of the diocese, and to free them from immediate supervision except by their own synods. As means to these ends they aimed to diminish the authority of the archbishops, who were likely to be the agents of secular supervision, and to exalt correspondingly the authority of the popes. They insured to the bishop the right to appeal his case to Rome and to be secure against deposition or loss of property while it was pending. The finality of a decision by the papal court in every sort of ecclesiastical case was asserted in the strongest terms. The False Decretals, therefore, signify a tendency in the ninth century to centralize the church in Frankish territory about the papal see, to make the bishop the unit of church government, to enforce his direct responsibility to the pope, and to reduce the archbishop to an intermediary between the pope and the bishop. In broad outline this was the type of government that came to prevail in the Roman church. There was probably no immediate purpose to exalt papal authority in general and no immediate effect in that direction. In the eleventh century, however, when the False Decretals were universally accepted as genuine, they provided a mine of arguments for the independence of the church from secular control and for the sovereign authority of the pope in ecclesiastical government. The controversy between the pope and the emperor resulted in no small degree from the fact that the former had now become effectively the head of the church and no longer felt himself to be dependent on the emperor for its good government.

The second event which had greatly increased the church's desire for autonomy was the wave of reform which spread with the growth of the congregation of monasteries subject to the abbot of Cluny.[3] Cluny itself was founded in 910. An important peculiarity in its organization was the entire independence which the body enjoyed in the management of its affairs and the choice

in Frankish territory about the year 850. See P. Fournier, "Études sur les fausses décrétales," *Revue d'histoire ecclésiastique de Louvain,* Vol. VII (1906), pp. 33, 301, 543, 761; Vol. VIII (1907), p. 19.

[3] The standard account is given by E. Sackur, *Die Cluniacenser in ihrer kirchlichen und allgemeingeschichtlichen Wirksamkeit,* 2 vols., Halle, 1892–94.

of its heads. A second significant feature of its growth was the fact that, as new monasteries were organized or old ones amalgamated with it, control of these branches continued to be vested in the abbot of the parent body. The Cluniac monasteries were accordingly much more than isolated bodies of monks; they formed virtually an order centralized under the control of a single head. They were thus well qualified to be the instrument for spreading the idea of reform in the church. Moreover, the purposes of the reformers were much the same as those which had motived the growth of the Cluny monasteries themselves. Simony, or the sale of ecclesiastical offices, was a serious evil which much needed reforming, and it was an evil intimately connected with the employment of ecclesiastics in the work of secular government. The evil consisted not only in the actual sale of offices but also in the giving of ecclesiastical preferment as a reward for political services. It was a foregone conclusion, therefore, that a heightened conception of spiritual functions should bring with it a demand for the purification of the church, for permanently raising the papacy from the degradation into which it had too often fallen, and for an autonomous control of the pope over ecclesiastical officers. It was precisely the more conscientious churchmen who felt most keenly the menace to the spiritual office occasioned by the entanglement of the clergy in the business of secular government. The direction which the reform movement must take in respect to the government of the church was foreshadowed at the Lateran Synod of 1059 by the attempt to secure an orderly method of papal election in the College of Cardinals. Reform meant that the church must seek to make itself a self-governing community with ecclesiastical policy and administration in the hands of ecclesiastics. The progress of such a reform necessarily contained latent possibilities of conflict between the pope and the emperor.

The desire for the autonomy of the church was, in fact, an answer to an abuse which was deeply rooted and which had been steadily growing. Long before the ninth century churchmen were already great landowners. Charles Martel had feudalized large amounts of church land to finance his wars against the Saracens, and as feudalism developed churchmen had been more and more drawn into the system by which government had to be carried on.

As an owner of land he owed feudal services and had, in turn, his own vassals who owed services to him, and even though he had to perform the secular duties of his station nominally through lay agents, his interests were largely identical with those of the feudal nobility. The higher clergy, by virtue of their wealth and standing, were deeply concerned with every question of secular politics; they were magnates whose power and influence no king could overlook. Indeed, feudalism apart, their superior education, at least on the average, had made them the most eligible class from which a king could draw the higher officials of his kingdom. It is probably true, as was said in the previous chapter, that the church had been, all through the centuries which had intervened since the fall of Rome, the main repository of the ancient ideals of public authority and civic order, and that churchmen were likely to be the best agents for carrying out any royal policy which required a degree of royal control. In the eleventh century, therefore, both for reasons that inhered in feudalism itself and for reasons of policy that went beyond feudalism, churchmen were deeply involved in secular politics. In the persons of the higher clergy the organizations of the church and of the state met and overlapped. So completely was this true that a radical separation of the two hierarchies, on the basis of a surrender of political functions by the clergy, was obviously impossible.

The story of the great controversy is told in every medieval history; there is no need to mention here more than a few of the principal moves. It began with the accession to the papal throne of Gregory VII in 1073. In its first phase it concerned especially the lay investiture of bishops, that is, the part of secular rulers in the choice of the higher clergy. Lay investiture was prohibited by Gregory in 1075. The following year Emperor Henry IV tried to secure the deposition of Gregory, who replied by excommunicating Henry and absolving his vassals from their feudal oaths. In 1080 Henry attempted to set up an antipope to replace Gregory, and Gregory supported the pretensions of Rudolf of Swabia to Henry's crown. After the death of the two chief actors the outstanding event was the attempted settlement between Henry V and Paschal II on the basis of a surrender by churchmen of all political functions or *regalia,* which proved wholly impracticable.

The first phase of the controversy closed with the Concordat of Worms in 1122, a compromise by which the emperor gave up the technical right of investiture with the ring and staff, the symbols of spiritual authority, but retained the right to bestow the *regalia* and to have a voice in the choice of the bishops. After this date, however, the controversy continued at intervals on much the same lines down to the end of the twelfth century, which makes a convenient stopping place for an exposition of the opposed views of the two contending parties.

GREGORY VII AND THE PAPALISTS

In the position taken by Gregory, it is important to bear in mind his conception of his own office in the church, though this was not strictly at issue. At the same time the issue with the empire could hardly have taken the form it did had he not conceived the papal office as he did. From Gregory's point of view the pope was nothing less than the sovereign head of the whole church. He alone could create and depose bishops; his legate was to take precedence of bishops and all other officers of the church; he alone could call a general council and give effect to its decrees. Papal decrees, on the other hand, could be annulled by no one, and a case once called into the papal court was not subject to judgment by any other authority. In short, Gregory's theory of government in the church was monarchical, not in the sense of a feudal monarchy but more nearly in the sense of the imperial Roman tradition; under God and the divine law the pope was absolute. This Petrine theory of the papacy, though it ultimately gained acceptance, was a novelty by no means universally admitted in the eleventh century and sometimes it embroiled Gregory with his bishops. As the church had kept alive the conception of public authority in the face of the decentralizing influences of feudalism, so it was the first power to apply the conception in its own political reconstruction.

It is difficult if not impossible to bring the two sides in the investiture controversy to a clear-cut issue. The reason for this was that both sides professed to accept the long-established principle of the two swords, each supreme in its own province. Yet both sides were obliged to advance arguments which by implication set it aside. This was true of the imperialists because what they really desired was the continuation of a state of affairs which, in fact if not in theory, had given the empire a preponderating voice in papal affairs. Their case was weak theoretically but strong in respect to precedents, and as they were forced into a defensive position, they were obliged to make the Gelasian theory the corner stone of their argument for secular independence. The claims of the church, on the other hand, were virtually unanswerable in the light of the whole scheme of accepted Christian values. But the theory could be made good only if the church could assume a position of leadership and direction which it had not had and which must carry it far away from the admission of coordinate authority, under God, to the secular power. Probably neither side intended to usurp authority that properly belonged to the other. The claims on both sides are hard to evaluate because in the eleventh century the legal concepts used had no such exact meaning as they came to have with the development of the Roman and the canon law.

The position taken by Gregory in opposition to Henry IV was a natural, if extreme, development of the church's admitted jurisdiction over questions of morals. In respect to the crime of simony Gregory proposed to proceed not only against the offending ecclesiastic but directly against the secular ruler, who was equally guilty. After forbidding the lay investiture of bishops and finding the emperor contumacious, he undertook to enforce his decree with an excommunication. This in itself was not a novel proceeding, but to it Gregory added the corollary that an excommunicated king, being an outcast from the body of Christians, could not retain the services and fealty of his subjects. He did not claim that oaths could be dissolved by the church at will, but only that it was within its jurisdiction as a court of conscience when it pronounced that a bad oath was lawfully void. The ground upon which Gregory defended his action was the right and the duty of a spiritual authority to exercise moral discipline over every member of a Christian community. He argued, like St. Ambrose, that a secular ruler is himself a Christian and therefore, in moral and spiritual matters, subject to the church. In effect, however, this amounted to the claim that the right to excommunicate carried with it the right to depose, of course for adequate cause, and to absolve subjects from their allegiance.

By implication the co-ordinate authority of a secular ruler disappeared, not in the sense that the church would itself take over the functions of secular government, but in the sense that the pope would become a court of last resort on whose judgment a ruler's legitimacy would depend.

It is not easy to tell how far Gregory was clear in his own mind about the implications of the policy which he followed and the argument by which he defended it. There seems to be a fair presumption that he thought of the whole issue as concerning the church's claim to exercise a moral discipline and not as involving a claim of legal supremacy. He professed, and there is no reason to doubt his sincerity, that his object was to protect the independence of the church within the twofold system contemplated by the Gelasian theory. Hence there is probably no reason to believe that he meant to assert in principle a power over temporal rulers in temporal matters.[4] It would be manifestly unfair to assume that his argument had the same precise legal meaning that it would have had in the hands of a canonist like Innocent IV, after two centuries of advance in the precision of juristic definition. On the other hand there can be no doubt what Gregory's claims really implied.

It is true also that in controversy he was addicted to an unbridled use of language which sometimes put his case with startling violence. This is illustrated by the famous passage, so often quoted, in his letter to Hermann of Metz in 1081.[5] Here he speaks of political rule as if it were literally "highway robbery on a large scale," a passage often compared with that in which John of Salisbury named the hangman as the type of secular government.

> Who does not know [said Gregory] that kings and rulers took their beginning from those who, being ignorant of God, have assumed, because of blind greed and intolerable presumption, to make themselves masters of their equals, namely men, by means of pride, violence, bad faith, murder, and nearly every kind of crime, being incited thereto by the prince of this world, the Devil?

[4] Carlyle, *op. cit.*, Vol. IV (1922), pp. 389 ff.

[5] Quoted by Carlyle, *op. cit.*, Vol. III (1915), p. 94. Cf. also Vol. IV, Part III, ch. 1. Gregory's writings are in *Bibliotheca rerum Germanicarum*, ed. P. Jaffé, Vol. II, Monumenta Gregoriana; see p. 457.

This passage was bitterly resented when it was written and has since been quoted, times without number, as an example of clerical arrogance. Certainly it was a violent overstatement of the common belief that government originates in sin, yet it is clear from other passages that Gregory had no intention whatever of attacking the kingly office as such. He claimed merely the same right of discipline over an emperor that as pope he had over every Christian. But he was clear that discipline included the right of the church to be the arbiter of European morals, and that spiritual and moral control must not be stopped by a recalcitrant ruler. His conception of the rôle which churchmen ought to play in directing the affairs of Europe appears in his words to a council at Rome in 1080:

> So act, I beg you, holy fathers and princes, that all the world may know that, if you have power to bind and loose in Heaven, you have power on earth to take away or to grant empires, kingdoms, principalities, dukedoms, marches, counties, and the possessions of all men according to their merits. . . . Let kings and all the princes of the world learn how great you are and what power you have and let these small men fear to disobey the command of your church.[6]

Gregory's argument obviously assumed the superiority of spiritual to temporal power. If Peter has been given power to bind and loose in Heaven, must he not even more have power to bind and loose on earth? This premise to the argument was not really a point at issue, since in general terms no one would have denied it. In itself, however, the superior importance of spiritual matters would not prove that secular rulers derive their authority from the church. Gelasius had never drawn such a conclusion and neither does Gregory. Evidently, however, it would not be difficult to amend the argument into this form, thus leaving the traditional theory of the two swords definitely behind. This step was taken by ecclesiastical writers in the twelfth century and the argument was greatly elaborated in the thirteenth and fourteenth. This was probably an effect of the controversy itself in clarifying the issues, and also a mark of greater definiteness about constitutional and juristic relationships. Perhaps also a more systematic conception of feudalism contributed to the same end, as well as

[6] Quoted by Carlyle, *op. cit.,* Vol. IV, pp. 201, n. 1; Jaffé, *op. cit.,* p. 404.

the tendency of the papacy to assume a relation of feudal suzerainty toward southern Italy and other parts of Europe.[7] At a later date, after the reception of Aristotle, the superior importance of spiritual power would in itself constitute an argument for the dependence of the lower authority upon it, since Aristotelianism conceived it to be a general law of nature that the lower exists for, and is governed by, the higher.

The derivation of temporal from spiritual authority appears to have been first definitely maintained by Honorius of Augsburg in his *Summa gloria*,[8] which was written about 1123. His principal proof was drawn from an interpretation of Jewish history, namely, that there was no royal power until Saul was crowned, that Saul was anointed by Samuel who was a priest, the Jews having been governed by priests from the time of Moses. In a similar fashion he argued that Christ instituted the priestly power in the church and that there was no Christian king until the conversion of Constantine. It was the church, therefore, which instituted Christian kingship to protect it from its enemies. Coupled with this theory was an interpretation (or rather a misinterpretation) of the Donation of Constantine as a surrender of all political power to the pope.[9] According to Honorius the emperors from Constantine on held all their imperial authority by papal concession. In line with this contention he held that emperors ought to be chosen by the pope, with the consent of the princes.

But having been radical in principle, Honorius was willing to be conservative in application, for he concluded that, in strictly secular matters, kings should be honored and obeyed even by priests. Even thinkers who were logically cutting the ground from under the old doctrine of the two swords were not willing to abolish it root and branch. Honorius showed also an uncertainty of juristic analysis. His argument from the Donation of Constan-

[7] See Carlyle, *op. cit.*, Vol. IV, Part iii, ch. 4.

[8] *M.G.H.*, *Libelli de lite*, Vol. III, pp. 3 ff. See Carlyle, *op. cit.*, Vol. IV, pp. 286 ff.

[9] The Donation was forged in the papal chancellery some time in the third quarter of the eighth century, and its purpose was apparently to support the papal claims in Italy at that time. Honorius's interpretation of it as applying to the whole imperial power was novel and must have been either a misunderstanding of its intent or a deliberate extension of its meaning, as this had previously been understood. See *Cambridge Medieval History*, Vol. II, p. 586; Carlyle, *op. cit.*, Vol. IV, p. 289.

tine was in the highest degree perilous, for if the pope's authority were delegated, it would seem that the emperor might resume what he had granted. Presumably Honorius thought of Constantine as merely recognizing a right inherent in the church under a Christian dispensation. A stronger position was taken by John of Salisbury in his *Policraticus* some thirty years later. John depended upon the inherent superiority of spiritual power to prove that both swords belong of right to the church and that the church conferred the power of coercion on the prince.

For every office existing under, and concerned with the execution of, the sacred laws is really a religious office, but that is inferior which consists in punishing crimes, and which therefore seems to be typified in the person of the hangman.[10]

Hence John could defend the power of deposition by quoting the *Digest* to the effect that "he who can lawfully bestow can lawfully take away." The secular ruler has a *ius utendi* but not strictly ownership. It was true, of course, that John did not regard this theory as derogating from the worth of political power in its proper employment or from the sanctity of the political office.

HENRY IV AND THE IMPERIALISTS

The position taken by the imperialist parties to the investiture controversy was, on the whole, more defensive than that of the papalists. Essentially they were arguing for what had been the *status quo,* in which the choice of bishops, and also papal elections, had been largely subject to imperial influence. They could appeal, against the practically novel claim of ecclesiastical independence, to the generally admitted theory of two independent spheres of authority. The corner stone of the imperial position, therefore, was the accepted doctrine that all power is of God, the emperor's as well as the pope's. This was the note struck by Henry himself in the letter which he addressed to Gregory in March, 1076.[11] Since his power was derived from God directly and not through the church, he was responsible for its exercise solely to God. Hence he was to be judged by God alone and could not be deposed, unless for heresy.

10 *Policraticus,* 4, 3; Dickinson's trans., p. 9.
11 *M.G.H., Constitutiones,* Vol. I, No. 62.

> You have laid hands upon me also who, though unworthy among Christians, am anointed to kingship, and who, as the tradition of the Holy Fathers teaches, am to be judged by God alone and not to be deposed for any crime, unless I should wander from the faith, which God forbid.[12]

The "tradition of the Holy Fathers" upon which Henry depended was undoubtedly in the main the strong statements of Gregory the Great upon the duty of passive obedience. This conception of the indefeasibility of royal authority had never died out. Hincmar of Rheims had commented in the ninth century on the opinion, which he says was held by certain scholars, that kings are "subject to the laws and judgments of no one except God alone,"[13] though he qualified the view as being "full of the spirit of the Devil." From the eleventh century on this theory was an important part of the imperialist position. It fitted well, of course, with the Gelasian theory that the two swords can never be united in the same hands. What God has given none but God can take away. The argument was undoubtedly strong for it turned the tables on the papal party of reform. The head and front of Gregory's offense, as Henry presented it, was precisely that he had attempted to wield both powers and so had conspired against the divinely appointed order of human society. To confound spirituals and temporals would defeat the very purpose which formed the chief moral defense for Gregory's action. Under a pretense of making the church independent he would have entangled it still further in secular affairs. Such an argument might well appeal to the more moderate of Gregory's followers. Moreover, Henry's position provided the proper theological answer to be given in all cases where undue clerical ambition could be alleged, namely, the sanctity of secular authority itself. In its own province, therefore, political power could claim to be what King James called "free monarchy." It was this fact which made the divine right of the king a standard argument under all political circumstances which could be construed to threaten ecclesiastical interference.

The theological defense of the emperor, though repeated times without number, did not offer much chance for logical develop-

[12] Quoted by Carlyle, *op. cit.,* Vol. IV, p. 186, n. 1.

[13] Quoted by Carlyle, *op. cit.,* Vol. I, p. 278, n. 2; see also Vol. III, Part II, ch. 4.

ment. This was not true, however, of the juristic arguments, and in the long run the lawyers were the ablest and most effective defenders of secular power. In the beginning, however, this form of argumentation was not so well developed as in later controversies, such as that between Boniface VIII and Philip the Fair of France. Nevertheless, there were interesting beginnings. The earliest of these was the *Defensio Henrici IV regis*[14] (1084) of Peter Crassus, who is said to have been a teacher of Roman law at Ravenna. Peter professed to argue the case between Henry and Gregory on legal grounds. The gist of his argument lay in his insistence upon the indefeasibility of the right of hereditary succession. He urged that the pope or Henry's rebellious subjects had no more right to interfere with his possession of his kingdom, which he had received as heir to his father and his grandfather, than they had to take away any person's private property. For this theory Peter claimed the authority of Roman law as well as of divine law and *ius gentium*. This argument bore no relation to the constitutional theory of imperial authority in the Roman law, as stated by the lawyers either of antiquity or of the Middle Ages, and it was definitely inappropriate to an elective monarch. Peter's theory suggested, however, the characteristic connection of divine right with indefeasible hereditary right. On the whole the theory was less important for its intrinsic merits than for its indication of a tendency to support the secular power by using legal conceptions.

A more important form of the anti-papal argument is to be found in the York Tracts,[15] produced about 1100 in the controversy over investiture between Anselm and Henry I of England. On the issue of investiture the author's argument is hard to evaluate. He asserted sweepingly that the authority of a king is of a higher kind than that of a bishop, that the king ought to rule over bishops, and that he is competent to call a council of the church and to preside over it. Yet at the same time he denied the king's right to invest bishops with their spiritual authority. More interesting, and probably more important, was this author's attack

[14] *M.G.H., Libelli de lite,* Vol. I, pp. 432 ff. See Carlyle, *op. cit.,* Vol IV, pp. 222 ff.

[15] *M.G.H., Libelli de lite,* Vol. III, pp. 642 ff., especially Tract IV. See Carlyle, *op. cit.,* Vol. IV, pp. 273 ff.

upon the sovereign authority which Gregory had claimed to exercise in the church, since a critical examination of the nature of spiritual authority, and of the pope's share in it, was to form an important part of the later debates. In an earlier tract, written in defense of the deposed Archbishop of Rouen, he flatly denied the right of the pope to discipline other bishops, arguing that in spiritual matters all bishops are equal, that all enjoy the same authority from God, and are all equally exempt from judgment save by God. The actual power wielded by the Bishop of Rome he called usurpation and explained it as an historical accident depending on the fact that Rome had been the capital of the empire.[16] In yet another of the tracts[17] he asserted that obedience was owed not to Rome but solely to the church; "only the elect and the sons of God can rightly be called the Church of God." The York Tracts appear to contain the germ of the argument which was elaborated two centuries later by Marsilio of Padua in the *Defensor pacis,* where it formed an important part of a tendency to construe spiritual authority not as a power but as a right to teach and preach. The more completely spiritual authority could be given exclusively an other-worldly significance, the more completely it must leave secular authority untrammeled in the fields of law and politics, however great its moral value might be held to be. The argument of the York Tracts was apparently the first somewhat uncertain step on this line of argument.

The controversy, even in the eleventh century, tended to encourage an examination of the foundation of secular authority too. The problem was clearly involved in Gregory's attempt to depose the emperor. As this called out the claim of indefeasible right from the emperor's defenders, so it produced the argument on the papal side that his authority is conditional and that accordingly his subjects' obligations are less than absolute. The conditional or contractual nature of political obligation was implied not only by the practice of feudalism but was suggested also in the ancient tradition transmitted by the Fathers of the church, especially by the principle that law and government ought always to be contributory to justice. There is, therefore, a fundamental difference between a true king and a tyrant, which implies that there are conditions under which it is justifiable to resist a tyrant.

16 Tract III.

17 Tract VI.

In the eleventh century this position was most clearly stated by Manegold of Lautenbach,[18] and in the twelfth by John of Salisbury, who developed in the eighth book of his *Policraticus* the revolting theory of tyrannicide. In neither case does the argument imply a low estimate of political authority; rather the reverse, since the evil of tyranny is greater just in proportion as true kingship is more august. But the essence of kingship is the office and not the person; hence the individual's right to the office cannot be indefeasible. Manegold used this principle to show that deposition could be justified when a king has destroyed those goods which the office was instituted to preserve. He thus arrived at a comparatively definite theory of contract (*pactum*) between the king and his people.

> No man can make himself emperor or king; a people sets a man over it to the end that he may rule justly, giving to every man his own, aiding good men and coercing bad, in short, that he may give justice to all men. If then he violates the agreement according to which he was chosen, disturbing and confounding the very things which he was meant to put in order, reason dictates that he absolves the people from their obedience, especially when he has himself first broken the faith which bound him and the people together.[19]

A people's allegiance to its ruler is therefore a pledge to support him in his lawful undertakings and is *ipso facto* void in the case of a tyrant. So far as the pope's power to depose a king was concerned, Manegold conceived this as the right of a court of conscience to pronounce upon the reality of a *fait accompli;* Gregory's action was defended on the ground that he had "publicly annulled what was inherently invalid." The theory that the king stands in a contractual relation to his people in no way contradicted the view that the kingly office itself was of divine origin.

Manegold's theory of a contract was not, therefore, an out-and-out defense of a papal right of deposition. In fact, the dependence of the royal power upon the people could, with equal propriety, be construed as implying its independence of the church. This position had the great advantage of agreeing with the constitutional theory of Roman law, as well as with the imperialist

[18] *Ad Gebehardum* (written between 1080 and 1085), *M.G.H.*, *Libelli de lite,* Vol. I, pp. 300 ff.; see Carlyle, *op. cit.*, Vol. III, pp. 160 ff.

[19] Quoted by Carlyle, *op. cit.*, Vol. III, p. 164, n. 1.

emphasis upon the distinction of the two swords. Its development led to a more critical examination of the historical precedents, such as the deposition of the Merovingian dynasty and the crowning of Pippin, alleged in favor of the Pope's power to depose.[20] The conclusion drawn was that the deposition and the choice of a new king were done " by the common suffrage of the princes," and merely with the approval of the pope. The position thus taken was historically sound and pierced a weak spot in Gregory's argument. It was especially interesting, moreover, in illustrating a marshalling of secular history in defense of the emperor's independence, and in claiming the decision of secular princes as a sufficient constitutional authority for the deposition or coronation of a king.

The controversy in the eleventh and twelfth centuries served to show the instability and vagueness of the relation between the temporal and spiritual powers in the Gelasian tradition. The two sides stressed different aspects of the tradition, both of which were equally well established. The papalists emphasized the moral superiority of the spiritual power and the imperialists the independence of the two powers from one another. Both positions continued to be an intrinsic part of the argument as the debate was continued into the thirteenth and fourteenth centuries. The earlier controversy suggested also the lines that would be followed as the argument on either side was developed. It needed only that more definite juristic and constitutional ideas should prevail in order that the church's claim of moral superiority should be transformed into a claim of legal suzerainty. And this position had only to be stated to call out a counter argument designed to limit spiritual duties to non-coercive instruction and exhortation. On the side of the temporal power also two developing lines of argument were suggested, that which stressed the responsibility of secular rulers directly to God with no earthly intermediary, and that which stressed the right of secular society, under God, to provide for its own government.

[20] See especially the tract *De unitate ecclesiae conservanda* written by an unknown author between 1090 and 1093. The tract was an answer to Gregory's second letter to Hermann of Metz, mentioned above. *M.G.H., Libelli de lite,* Vol. II, pp. 173 ff. See Carlyle, *op. cit.,* Vol. IV, pp. 242 ff.

SELECTED BIBLIOGRAPHY

Saint Grégoire VII: essai sur sa conception du pouvoir pontifical. By H. X. Arquillière. Paris, 1934.

"Gregory VII and the First Contest between Empire and Papacy." By Z. N. Brooke. In the *Cambridge Medieval History,* Vol. V (1926), ch. 2.

A History of Mediaeval Political Theory in the West. By R. W. Carlyle and A. J. Carlyle. 6 vols. London, 1903–1936. Vol. IV (1922). The Theories of the Relation of the Papacy and the Empire from the Tenth Century to the Twelfth.

"Respublica Christiana." By John Neville Figgis. In *Transactions of the Royal Historical Society,* 3rd Series, Vol. V (1911), p. 63. (Reprinted in *Churches in the Modern State,* London, 1913, Appendix I).

The Medieval Empire. By H. A. L. Fisher. 2 vols. London, 1898. Ch. 10.

Political Theories of the Middle Age. By Otto Gierke. Eng. trans. by F. W. Maitland. Cambridge, 1900. (From *Das deutsche Genossenschaftsrecht,* Vol. III.)

"Roman and Canon Law in the Middle Ages." By Harold Dexter Hazeltine. In the *Cambridge Medieval History,* Vol. V (1926), ch. 21.

"Political Thought." By E. F. Jacob. In *The Legacy of the Middle Ages.* Ed. by C. G. Crump and E. F. Jacob. Oxford, 1926.

"The Investiture Contest and the German Constitution." By Paul Joachimsen. In *Mediaeval Germany, 911–1250: Essays by German Historians.* Eng. trans. by Geoffrey Barraclough. 2 vols. Oxford, 1938. Vol. II, ch. 4.

Die Publizistik im Zeitalter Gregors VII. By Carl Mirbt. Leipzig, 1894.

Church, State, and Christian Society at the Time of the Investiture Contest. By Gerd Tellenbach. Eng. trans. by R. F. Bennett. Oxford, 1940.

"The Monastic Orders." By Alexander Hamilton Thompson. In the *Cambridge Medieval History,* Vol. V (1926), ch. 20.

Feudal Germany. By James Westfall Thompson. Chicago, 1928. Ch. 7.

Roman Law in Mediaeval Europe. By Paul Vinogradoff. London, 1909.

"Pope Gregory VII and the Hildebrandine Ideal." By J. P. Whitney. In *Church Quarterly Review,* Vol. LXX (1910), p. 414.

"Gregory VII." By J. P. Whitney. In *Eng. Hist. Rev.,* Vol. XXXIV (1919), p. 129.

"The Reform of the Church." By J. P. Whitney. In the *Cambridge Medieval History,* Vol. V (1926), ch. 1.

CHAPTER XIII

UNIVERSITAS HOMINUM

As scholarly performances the controversial tracts described in the preceding chapter were quickly outmoded in the extraordinary intellectual rebirth that began in the latter years of the twelfth century and which made the thirteenth one of the most brilliant in the history of Europe. This new scholarly activity, in so far as it depended on institutions, was due chiefly to the new universities, especially Paris and Oxford, and to the two great Mendicant Orders in the church, the Dominicans and the Franciscans. The universities rapidly became centers of an astonishingly active intellectual life. They attracted great numbers of students and counted among their teachers the most active intelligences of the age, who set themselves to study systematically the sciences and especially philosophy and theology. With the universities should be mentioned also the great Law Schools in which an accurate knowledge of Roman law was recovered in the course of the twelfth and thirteenth centuries. The Mendicant Orders almost from the beginning played a large part in the development of the universities, setting up courses of study for the training of their members and providing an important part of the faculties. In the thirteenth century a large proportion of the most original scholars were included in their membership — Albert the Great and Thomas Aquinas among the Dominicans, Duns Scotus and Roger Bacon among the Franciscans.

The universities and the Orders were the agencies through which the new enlightenment spread, but its content was supplied in the first instance by the recovery of ancient works of science, especially the works of Aristotle, together with a large body of commentary upon them by Arabic and Jewish scholars. In the earlier Middle Ages nothing had been known of Aristotle beyond his works on logic. Early in the thirteenth century his scientific works began to be known, at first in parts and often in Latin translations of Arabic versions, but finally in complete translations direct from the Greek original. Besides Italy, the main channel for these books was Spain; the Bishop of Toledo fostered great collective enterprises in translating, because contact with the Moors made Arabic texts available. In the history of political thought the translation of the *Politics* from the Greek text by William of Moerbeke about 1260 was of great importance. This translation formed part of a general effort, under the auspices of Thomas, to secure a reliable report of Aristotle's philosophy. The ultimate effect of this revival of Aristotle upon the intellectual development of western Europe would be impossible to exaggerate. Not only was a great fund of information made available, such as the earlier Middle Ages could scarcely imagine, but this was already ordered and arranged in sciences, such as physics, zoology, psychology, ethics, and politics, and these sciences were co-ordinated as parts of a systematic conception of nature, whose first principles were drawn out in the form of metaphysics. Most important of all, Aristotle brought to the Middle Ages a new vision of the intellectual life of Greece and the belief that reason is the key which must unlock the door to a knowledge of the natural world. From the thirteenth century to the present, this stimulus has never been wholly lost. At the start it produced an intense intellectual effort to master Aristotle, to adapt and harmonize him with the system of Christian belief, and to construct an all-embracing system of natural and theological knowledge.

While it would be impossible to overstate the importance in the long run of the recovery of Aristotle, its immediate effects upon political philosophy can easily be exaggerated. What the study of the *Politics* produced at once was an improvement in the technique of presenting the subject, such as a standard list of subjects to be treated, a body of technical terms and conceptions, and a plan for the arrangement of material. Until the sixteenth century it was scarcely possible to write a treatise on politics which in these respects did not owe a debt to the *Politics*. Clearly, however, the adoption of Aristotelian arguments need not imply a change in fundamental political convictions or in the nature of the concrete problems that political philosophers were thinking about. In any case conceptions framed by Aristotle relative to the city-state could have no literal application to medieval society but required a considerable revision for the purposes in hand.

Moreover, Thomas at least had no desire to depart from the great body of political and social tradition that had descended to the thirteenth century from the Fathers of the church; so far as this inheritance was concerned, as in the case of the whole body of Christian belief, he valued Aristotelianism less as a means of making innovations than as a better philosophical support for well-founded beliefs. In the thirteenth century, also, the chief attention of the new scholarship was given rather to theology and metaphysics than to political theory. In the fourteenth, the writing of political treatises was much more frequent.

JOHN OF SALISBURY

This conclusion, that the recovery of Aristotle did not at once change the main lines of political philosophy, is supported by a consideration of the *Policraticus*,[1] written by John of Salisbury in 1159. This book has the great interest of being at once the first attempt in the Middle Ages at an extended and systematic treatment of political philosophy and the only such book written before the recovery of Aristotle. It is a compendium of the ancient tradition which had descended to the twelfth century from Cicero and Seneca through the Fathers of the church and the Roman lawyers. In most respects it tried to set forth with a fair degree of order what everyone believed and, so far as was known in the twelfth century, had always believed. Those who have studied the book most carefully have agreed that there is surprisingly little in it that depends consciously on the feudal organization of society which actually prevailed when John wrote. His ideal was rather that of the commonwealth, the *res publica*, conceived after the manner of Cicero as a society " united by a common agreement about law and rights." In spite of the centrifugal influences of feudalism the essential idea in John's political thought was still that of a people ruled by a public authority which acts for the general good and is morally justified by the fact that it is lawful.

The law in John's conception forms an omnipresent tie running through all human relationships including that between the ruler

[1] The standard edition is edited by C. C. J. Webb, Oxford, 1909. Parts are translated by John Dickinson under the title, *The Statesman's Book of John of Salisbury*, New York, 1927. Dickinson has added an excellent introduction.

and the ruled. Consequently it is binding mutually on king and subject. So true is this that the distinction between a true king and a tyrant was of major importance for John. His book had the doubtful honor of presenting the first explicit defense of tyrannicide in medieval political literature. " He who usurps the sword is worthy to die by the sword."

> Between a tyrant and a prince there is this single or chief difference, that the latter obeys the law and rules the people by its dictates, accounting himself as but their servant. It is by virtue of the law that he makes good his claim to the foremost and chief place in the management of the affairs of the commonwealth.[2]
>
> Now there are certain precepts of the law which have a perpetual necessity, having the force of law among all nations, and which absolutely cannot be broken with impunity. . . . Let the white-washers of rulers . . . trumpet abroad that the prince is not subject to the law, and that whatsoever is his will and pleasure, not merely in establishing law according to the model of equity, but absolutely and free from all restrictions, has the force of law. . . . Still I will maintain . . . that kings are bound by this law.[3]

Except the defense of tyrannicide, there was nothing in John's conception of law and its universal validity which Thomas did not share. John expressed the idea in terms drawn largely from Cicero while Thomas elaborated it by adapting Aristotle's technical terms. In both men the universality of law was a fundamental conception.

ST. THOMAS: NATURE AND SOCIETY

Coming first to Christian Europe through Jewish and Arabic sources, the works of Aristotle bore the stigma of infidelity. The earliest inclination of the church was to ban them, and their use at the University of Paris was forbidden in 1210 and later, though the prohibition seems never to have been very effective. The church wisely relied less on prohibition than on reconstruction, and there is no better evidence of the intellectual virility of medieval Christianity than the rapidity with which Aristotle was not merely received but made the corner stone of Roman Catholic philosophy. In less than a century what had been feared as a source of anti-Christian innovation was turned into a new and, it

[2] Bk. IV, ch. i; Dickinson's trans., p. 3.
[3] Bk. IV, ch. vii; *ibid.*, pp. 33 f.

was hoped, a permanent system of Christianized philosophy. This work was accomplished by the teachers of the Mendicant Orders, especially by the two Dominicans, Albert the Great and his still greater pupil, Thomas Aquinas. It is true that the completeness and the permanence of the victory were overestimated. Beside the Christianized Aristotle of Thomas there was, from the thirteenth century on, the anti-Christian Aristotle of the Averroist tradition. And even within the limits of orthodox scholasticism Franciscan thinkers, such as Duns Scotus and William of Occam, had always a doubt about the close synthesis of faith and reason that Thomas attempted. In the fourteenth century these divergences of thought appeared in political theory no less than in general philosophy.

It was of the essence of Thomas's philosophy that it essayed a universal synthesis, an all-embracing system, the keynote of which was harmony and consilience. God and nature are large enough and opulent enough to afford a niche for all the endless diversity that makes up finite existence. The whole of human knowledge forms a single piece. Broadest in extent but least highly generalized are the particular sciences each with its special subject-matter; above these is philosophy, a rational discipline which seeks to formulate the universal principles of all the sciences; above reason and depending upon divine revelation is Christian theology, the consummation of the whole system. But though revelation is above reason, it is in no way contrary to reason; theology completes the system of which science and philosophy form the beginning, but never destroys its continuity. Faith is the fulfillment of reason. Together they build the temple of knowledge but nowhere do they conflict or work at cross purposes.

The picture which Thomas drew of nature conformed exactly to his plan of knowledge. The universe forms a hierarchy reaching from God at its summit down to the lowest being. Every being acts under the internal urge of its own nature, seeking the good or form of perfection natural to its kind, and finding its place in the ascending order according to its degree of perfection. The higher in all cases rules over and makes use of the lower, as God rules over the world or the soul over the body. No matter how lowly it may be, no being is wholly lacking in value, for it has its station, its duties and its rights, through which it contributes to the perfection of the whole. The essence of the scheme is purpose, subordination to an end. In such a structure human nature has a unique place among created beings, since man possesses not only a bodily nature but also a rational and spiritual soul by virtue of which he is akin to God. He alone of all beings is at once body and soul, and on this fundamental fact rest the institutions and the laws by which his life is directed.

Thomas's conception of social and political life falls directly into his larger plan of nature as a whole, and the most important passages in which he treated the subject were a part of his great systematic work on philosophy and theology.[4] Like all nature society is a system of ends and purposes in which the lower serves the higher and the higher directs and guides the lower. Following Aristotle, Thomas described society as a mutual exchange of services for the sake of a good life to which many callings contribute, the farmer and artisan by supplying material goods, the priest by prayer and religious observance, and each class by doing its own proper work. The common good requires that such a system shall have a ruling part, just as the soul rules the body or any higher nature rules the lower. Thomas compares the founding and ruling of states, the planning of cities, the building of castles, the establishment of markets, and the fostering of education to the providence whereby God creates and rules the world.

Hence rulership is an office or a trust for the whole community. Like his lowest subject, the ruler is justified in all that he does solely because he contributes to the common good. His power, because it is derived from God for the happy ordering of human life, is a ministry or service owed to the community of which he is the head. He cannot rightfully exercise power or take property by taxation beyond what is needed. The moral purpose of government is therefore paramount. Broadly speaking, it is the duty

[4] *Summa theologica,* 1a, 2ae, qq. 90–108 (Eng. trans. by the Fathers of the English Dominican Province, London, 1911–22). Two other works were left unfinished at his death: *De regimine principum* (Eng. trans. by Gerard P. Phelan, Toronto, 1935), of which Book I and Book II, chs. 1–4 are by Thomas, the rest probably by Ptolemy of Lucca; the commentary on Aristotle's *Politics,* of which Books I and II and Book III, chs. 1–6 are by Thomas, the rest probably by Peter of Auvergne. See M. Grabmann, *Die echten Schriften des hl. Thomas von Aquin* in C. Baeumker's *Beiträge zur Gesch. d. Phil. d. Mittelalters,* Vol. XXII.

of the ruler so to direct the action of every class in the state that men may live a happy and virtuous life, which is the true end of man in society. Ultimately, of course, this must lead to a good beyond earthly society, to a heavenly life, but this is beyond human power and is in the keeping of priests rather than of rulers. But it is characteristic of Thomas that he should regard an orderly political life as a contributing cause even to this ultimate end. More specifically it is the function of the earthly ruler to lay the foundations of human happiness by maintaining peace and order, to preserve it by seeing that all the needful services of public administration, of judicature, and of defense are performed, and to improve it by correcting abuses wherever they occur and by removing all possible hindrances to the good life.

The moral purpose for which political rule exists implies that authority ought to be limited and that it ought to be exercised only in accordance with law. Thomas's dislike of tyranny was as great as that displayed by John of Salisbury, though he explicitly disavowed the latter's defense of tyrannicide. Justifiable resistance is a public act of a whole people, and the right is safeguarded by the moral condition that those who resist are responsible for seeing that their action is less injurious to the general good than the abuse which they are trying to remove. Sedition he regarded as a deadly sin, but justifiable resistance to tyranny he denied to be sedition. In respect to tyranny the harmonizing of the older medieval tradition with Aristotle presented no difficulties, for both were versions of the same Greek detestation of unlawful force and both proceeded from the principle that power is justified only in so far as it serves the common good. It cannot be said that Thomas derived anything important from Aristotle to add to existing opinion on this subject. His interest was essentially in the moral limitations laid upon rulers, and the legal or constitutional phases of the subject seem not to have concerned him. Thus he had little to say about forms of government beyond what he got from Aristotle, and his defense of monarchy, which he regarded as the best form, followed the rather academic lines pursued in the *Politics*. He was explicit on the point that a king's power should be " limited " (*temperetur*), though he nowhere explained exactly what this meant. It is probably safe to assume that he had in mind a sharing of power between the king and the magnates of the realm, who are his natural advisers and electors.

Thomas was explicit also on the point that true government, as distinguished from tyranny, is "lawful," but he was curiously unconscious of the need to define precisely what lawful authority means in this connection. Though he was acquainted with the Roman law, he was evidently unaware of any tendency in this study to exalt the power of a sovereign ruler over the law itself. He must have known also the great controversial literature dealing with the papal and the imperial authorities, but this failed to stimulate him to a precise examination of the principles upon which political authority is based. In connection with his treatment of tyranny he referred to two remedies which are available against tyrants. There are, he assumed, governments in which the ruler's power is derived from the people, and in this case it is lawful for the people to enforce the conditions upon which authority has been granted. The other remedy mentioned is in the case of a ruler who has a political superior, and here the redress of grievances is by an appeal to that superior.[5] But he clearly regarded these as two distinct types of government, which seems to show that he had no general theory of the derivation of political authority.

THE NATURE OF LAW

The reason why Thomas could thus pass over what seems an essential point in political philosophy probably lay in the fact that he was so deeply immersed in the medieval tradition of the sanctity of law. His reverence for law was such that he assumed its authority to be inherent and not dependent upon any human origin. His constant attempt was to relate human law as closely as possible to divine law. To this he was led not only by his own inclination to harmonize but also by the assumption that law is something much broader in its scope than a means of regulating human relationships. Human law was for him part and parcel of the whole system of divine government whereby everything both in heaven and earth is ruled. Such a system Thomas regarded as quite literally an emanation from the reason of God, regulating the relationships between all creatures, animate and inanimate,

[5] *De reg. princ.*, 1, 6.

animal and human. Law in the narrower human sense was therefore merely one aspect, important indeed but still an aspect, of a cosmic fact. This was the point which seemed to him important and accordingly he developed his general theory of law more carefully than any part of his political theory. His classification of law was therefore one of the most characteristic parts of his philosophy. But it had the effect of reducing a specifically legal or institutional definition of lawful authority to the status of a subordinate question. An unlawful ruler was not primarily a violator of human rights and institutions, though he was that, but a rebel against the whole divine system by which God rules the world.

In Thomas's fourfold classification of law only one of the four is human. It was significant of his point of view that he was thus able to find a conception of law which he conceived to be applicable to a range of phenomena so wide and to modern thought so diverse. This was not, as might be imagined, because he thought of nature as miraculously governed by the will of God, but for an almost contrary reason. It was because he thought of human society and its institutions as a typical level of the cosmic order, in which the same principles obtain that manifest themselves in different forms on the other levels. Arbitrary will had very little to do with the matter, either in nature or society. Both are governed by reasons or ends, more than by forces; certainly Thomas had no conception of a will, divine or human, that made law by fiat, either for nature or for society. His four kinds of law are four forms of reason, manifesting themselves at four levels of cosmic reality, but remaining one reason throughout. The names which he gave to them were the Eternal Law, the Natural Law, the Divine Law, and Human Law.

The first of these, the Eternal Law, is practically identical with the reason of God. It is the eternal plan of divine wisdom by which the whole creation is ordered. In itself this law is above the physical nature of man and in its entirety beyond human comprehension, though it is not for this reason foreign or contrary to human reason. So far as his finite nature permits, man really participates in the wisdom and goodness of God; these are reflected in him, though his nature reproduces only a distorted image of divine perfection. The second, Natural Law, may perhaps be described as a reflection of divine reason in created things. It is manifest in the inclination which nature implants in all beings to seek good and avoid evil, to preserve themselves, and to live as perfectly as possible the kind of life suitable to their natural endowments. In the case of mankind this means, as Aristotle had taught, the desire for a life in which the rational nature may be realized. Thomas mentioned as examples of this the inherent inclination in men to live in society, to preserve their lives, to beget and educate children, to seek the truth and develop intelligence. Natural Law enjoins all that is implied to give these human inclinations their widest scope.

Thomas's treatment of Divine Law was interesting because here he reached the borders of what might be called natural reason, and the position which he took was very characteristic. By Divine Law he meant substantially revelation. An example would be the special code of laws which God gave to the Jews as the chosen people or the special rules of Christian morals or legislation, given through Scripture or the church. Divine Law is a gift of God's grace rather than a discovery of natural reason. Thomas was little likely to underestimate the importance of Christian revelation, but what must be noticed is the care that he took not to open too wide a cleft between this and reason. Revelation adds to reason but never destroys it. The structure of Thomas's system is built of reason and faith but he never doubted that it was one structure. His applications even on the political level were interesting and important. Natural Law, because it is produced by the unaided reason, is common to all men, both Christian and pagan; hence morals and government do not in general depend upon Christianity. The obligation to civic obedience is not weakened, but rather strengthened, by it, and the Christian subjects of a pagan prince are not justified in refusing him obedience. Heresy, indeed, he regarded as one of the worst of crimes, since it falsifies the truth on which salvation depends, and the church may rightly absolve the subjects of an apostate or heretic ruler. But even the church ought not to depose a ruler merely because he is an infidel. Thomas's very moderate and reasonable position on this question perhaps reflects the influence of Aristotle's natural community upon him. It is diametrically opposed to that taken by extreme papalists of the following century, such as Egidius Colonna, upon whom the Aristotelian influence was less marked.

The Eternal, the Natural, and the Divine Laws all set standards of behavior which, though sometimes applicable to human beings, are not exclusively applicable to them or specifically derived from human nature. The law especially designed for human beings Thomas called the Human Law, which he subdivided into *ius gentium* and *ius civile*. This law he regarded as in one sense specific, since it regulates the lives of a single kind of creature and so must be applicable especially to the distinguishing properties of that kind. In another sense Human Law might be said to introduce no new principles; it merely applies to human kind the greater principles of order that prevail throughout the world. Any law sets a standard according to which a being of some sort is moved to act or restrained from acting. In the case of human beings, since man is distinguished from other beings by rationality, the standard is set by reason; and since reasonableness in man implies sociability, the law sets a standard for the general good, rather than for the advantage of an individual or a particular class. For this reason also the law has behind it a general authority rather than an individual will: it is a product of the whole people acting for their joint good, either by legislation or by the less tangible means of creating custom, or it has the sanction of a public personage to whom the care of the community has been delegated. Finally, Thomas regarded promulgation as an essential quality of law. His completed definition therefore describes law as " an ordinance of reason for the common good, made by him who has care of the community, and promulgated."[6] Thomas thus translated the ancient belief in " true law," embedded from the beginning in the Christian tradition, back into the terminology of Aristotle and freed the latter from any specific reference to the city-state. The tradition was changed in no essential respect, but Aristotle provided a more systematic mode of statement.

Though the definition just given has a special reference to Human Law, probably the weight of Thomas's argument falls on the point that Human Law is derivative from Natural Law.

[6] *Summa theol.*, 1a, 2ae, q. 90, 4.

The justification for human regulation, and for the coercion by which it is made effective, he conceived always to lie in the nature of human beings; power merely gives force to that which is inherently reasonable and right. As a whole, then, Human Law might be called a corollary of Natural Law, which merely needs to be made definite and effective in order to provide for the exigencies of human life or of special circumstances in human life. Thus, for example, murder is contrary to nature, since it is incompatible with peace and order, but Natural Law does not provide a precise definition of murder as distinct from other kinds of homicide, nor does it provide a specific penalty. In other words, the act is wrong because it violates a general principle of conduct in society; because it is wrong it must be prevented or punished; but the best way to prevent or punish it is partly a question of policy and may vary with time, place, and circumstance. The principle is the same always and everywhere, since the fundamental inclinations of men remain the same; the precise way in which this underlying human nature develops can vary endlessly from nation to nation, and from time to time. Government is therefore a kaleidoscope of changing patterns, and yet there is one right, one law, and one justice behind all. Life has a single end but many means.

It speaks volumes for the persistence and the pervasiveness of this moral conception of law and government that John Locke, writing four centuries later, could still find no argument more convincing with which to defend the fundamental right of a people to depose a tyrannous ruler. The underlying moral relations between Natural and Human Law are still for Locke substantially what they were for Thomas. For both men the ruler is as definitely bound by reason and justice as his subjects, and his power over the positive law arises from the need of keeping it in agreement with Natural Law. Enactment is less an act of will than an adjustment to time and circumstance; the granting of dispensations or pardons is a way of meeting cases where the literal interpretation of Human Law would be inequitable, but the ruler's power is only such as is implied by his guardianship of the common good. Thus, according to Thomas, he may not take private property beyond what public need requires, though strictly speaking property is an institution of Human rather than Natural Law.

Above all, the rulership of one man over another must not take away the free moral agency of the subject. No man is bound to obedience in all respects and even the soul of a slave is free (a doctrine which Aristotle would hardly have understood). It is for this reason that the resistance of tyranny is not only a right but a duty.

It is probable that Thomas's Christian Aristotelianism explains the fact that he took so temperate a stand on the controversy between the spiritual and the secular authorities. His position may be described as that of a moderate papalist. He was convinced that there are circumstances in which it is lawful for the church to depose a ruler and absolve his subjects from their allegiance,[7] and as a matter of course he regarded the *sacerdotium* as a higher kind of authority than the *imperium*.[8] But he still felt himself to be within the Gelasian tradition. The fact that the church represented to him the fullest embodiment of the unity of human kind was not thought to imply either an abridgement of secular power in respect to seculars or any serious obscurity in the distinction between the two authorities. Thomas was little touched by the tendency already apparent in the canon lawyers to transform the church's admitted spiritual superiority into legal supremacy and he was probably restrained by his Aristotelianism from developing the theological arguments used by extreme papalists who were less influenced by Aristotle. On the other hand, he was of course quite untouched by the Averroist or naturalistic Aristotelianism which he was mainly instrumental in defeating and which drew a sharp line between reason and revelation.[9] This separation, best illustrated by Marsilio of Padua, played a decisive part in producing a purely secular theory of the state. The conception of a Christian society, as it had been transmitted in the Christian tradition, Thomas took to be eternal. Controversies might come and go but they could not make essential

[7] *Summa theol.*, 2a, 2ae, q. 12, 2.

[8] *De reg. princ.*, 1, 14.

[9] Martin Grabmann has correlated Thomas's Christianized Aristotelianism with the sixteenth-century theory of "indirect" papal power, Averroist Aristotelianism with the theory which separated church and state, and the anti-Aristotelian or Augustinian tradition with the theory of "direct" power. See his "Studien über den Einfluss der aristotelischen Philosophie auf die mittelalterlichen Theorien über das Verhältnis von Kirche und Staat," *Sitzungsberichte der Bayerischen Akademie der Wissenschaften*, Philosophisch-historische Abtl., 1934, Heft 2.

changes there. His philosophy sought to find the reasons for it as it was believed to be; to construct a rational scheme of God, nature, and man within which society and civil authority find their due place. In this sense Thomas's philosophy expresses most maturely the convictions, moral and religious, upon which medieval civilization was founded.

DANTE: THE IDEALIZED EMPIRE

Thomas's philosophy may be considered as an authoritative statement of the ideal of a Christianized Europe from the point of view of the church. Beside it may be placed for purposes of comparison, though with a slight violation of chronological order, the theory of the universal monarchy set forth by the poet Dante.[10] Dante's book was, to be sure, a defense of imperial independence against papal control and hence, on the controversial issue, on the opposite side to that taken by Thomas and John of Salisbury. Yet there is substantial agreement in respect to general principles, despite the controversial differences. All three men conceived Europe as a unified Christian community governed by the two divinely appointed authorities, the *sacerdotium* and the *imperium,* which are vested in the two great medieval institutions, the church and the empire. All three look at political and social questions from the point of view of the religious and ethical tradition of the earlier Middle Ages, and Thomas and Dante are still under the control of this tradition, though they have adopted Aristotle as the best technical medium in which to express their ideas. Of the two Dante, though he wrote a half century later, is the more bound by the tradition, since the empire which he defends never existed outside the realms of imagination.

It is true that Dante's political philosophy was related both to his exile from Florence as a result of factional political quarrels and to the endless dissension between the papal and imperial parties in Italy during his lifetime. In this situation he saw no hope for peace except in the unity of the empire and under the all-embracing authority of the emperor. Neither by birth nor breeding was Dante a partisan of the imperial cause. His im-

[10] *De monarchia* was probably written on the occasion of the Emperor Henry's Italian expedition, 1310–13. There are several English translations, the most accessible being those by P. H. Wicksteed (in the Temple Classics) and by A. Henry (Boston, 1904).

perialism was purely an idealization of universal peace. His opposition to the papacy was of the sort that, again and again, inspired Italian patriots. He saw that papal policy was a source of never-ending dissension, with France always ready to "mediate" at the invitation of one faction or the other. But he was no nationalist in politics, though his writings did so much to create an Italian vernacular. At the very time when a nationalist note was making its appearance in France, in the controversy between the pope and Philip the Fair, Dante looked back to an already obsolete imperial policy which had ruined the Hohenstaufen.

The purpose of his treatise was identical with that of all defenders of the empire since the controversy with the church began in the days of Henry IV and Gregory VII, to show that the emperor's power is derived directly from God and is therefore independent of the church. The spiritual power of the pope he fully admitted, but like the imperialists generally he clung to the Gelasian theory that the two powers are united only in God and consequently that the emperor has no human superior. The main line of proof which Dante developed was perhaps first suggested by the renewed study of Roman law, the theory that the medieval empire, being continuous with the Roman Empire, was the heir to the universal authority which had rightfully belonged to Rome. But his way of presenting this argument was theological rather than legal. Like Thomas, he placed his theory of the universal community within a framework of principles derived from Aristotle.

In the first book of his treatise Dante discussed the question "whether the temporal monarchy is necessary to the well-being of the world." The "temporal monarchy" he defined as the government of the whole body of temporal beings. Every association of human beings is formed for the sake of an end, and by a line of argument roughly analogous to that used by Aristotle to prove the superiority of the city-state to the family and village, Dante assigned the highest place among communities to the universal empire. Since the special character of man is reason, the end or function of the race is to realize a rational life, and this is possible only if there is universal peace, which is the best of things for human happiness and a necessary means to the ultimate end of man. Every co-operative enterprise requires direction, and hence every community must have a ruler. In this way Dante proved that the whole race forms one community under a single ruler. The government of this ruler he compared to the government of God over nature. As the latter is perfect because of its unity, so the former to be perfect must embrace all men under a single authority. That which has the most reality has the greatest unity, and that which has the greatest unity is best. Moreover, the existence of peace among men is impossible unless there is a highest judge altogether above greed and partiality, who can adjudicate quarrels between kings and princes. Similarly, freedom is impossible unless there is in the world a power raised altogether above tyranny and oppression. The argument combines curiously the traditional idealization of the empire with the new Aristotelian categories of explanation.

Dante approached his conclusion more closely in his second book, which answered the question "whether the Roman people were justified in assuming the dignity of empire." The main contention was that God's will is manifested in history, and that the history of Rome showed the marks of providential guidance in her rise to a position of supreme power. This Dante proved by pointing to the miraculous interventions of providence which protected the Roman state and also to the nobility of the Roman character. The Romans sought empire not from greed but for the sake of the common good of the conquered as well as the conquerors.

> Putting aside all greed, which is always contrary to the public interest, and choosing universal peace with liberty, this holy people, pious and renowned, is seen to have neglected its own advantage to care for the public safety of the human race.[11]

Finally, the will of God is manifested in contests and battles. The Roman Empire, in Dante's conception, was the fifth of the historic attempts at world empire and it alone succeeded. By distancing all other contestants, as well as by actually conquering its rivals, Rome proved that it was destined in the providence of God to rule the world. Dante clinched the argument by deducing the same conclusion from the principles of Christianity itself. Unless the death of Christ were decreed by a lawful authority he

[11] *De monarchia,* Bk. II, ch. 5.

would not truly have been "punished" for the sins of men and would not have redeemed the race. Hence the authority of Pilate, and equally that of Augustus, must have been lawful and right. In these arguments also there is a strange combination of the new and the old — enthusiasm for pagan antiquity defended by the arguments of Christian theology.

The last book was more controversial; it sought to show that imperial authority was derived immediately from God and to refute the arguments of the papalists, who held that it is derived mediately through the pope. Here Dante showed a strong animus against the canon lawyers and the tendency to make papal decretals into foundations of faith. Only the Scriptures, he held, have a supreme authority over the church; next in weight are acts of the principal councils, while the decretals are merely traditions which it is within the power of the church to change. Having thus cleared the ground, Dante examined the principal passages of Scripture alleged as authorities for the power of the church over temporal rulers, and the two critical precedents from secular history, the Donation of Constantine and the translation of the empire to Charlemagne. The former of these he regarded as unlawful, since the emperor had no legal power to alienate the empire, a common view among lawyers long before the historical authenticity of the document was attacked. This argument disposed also of the second alleged precedent, for if the pope could not legally have imperial power he could not bestow it on Charles. Finally, Dante concluded with a general argument to show that the possession of temporal power is in principle contrary to the nature of the church, whose kingdom is not of this world.

Though Thomas and Dante stood thus on opposite sides of the controversy between pope and emperor, they were wholly at one in their fundamental convictions. Nor has the acceptance of Aristotle by the two later thinkers made a profound difference between them and John of Salisbury, who preceded the Aristotelian revival. For all three the race forms a single community whose existence implies a single head. All agree that the distinguishing mark of human nature is its combination of a spiritual and a physical principle, each requiring an appropriate kind of authority. The government of the world is therefore shared between a spiritual and a temporal power, each having its proper jurisdiction and marked off from the other by a line not too hard to trace. This single world-wide society may be called, with only a difference of emphasis, either a commonwealth or a church. Whether in church or state, power is justified ultimately as a factor in the moral or religious government of the world, and yet as equally a factor in the life of a self-sufficing human community. Authority is derived at once from God and from the people. The king is at once the head of the legal system and subject to the law. His power exceeds that of his subjects and yet is less than that of the whole society. His authority is the voice of reason and yet his coercive power is needed to give force to the rules which reason imposes. The controlling social conception is that of an organic community in which the various classes are functioning parts, and of which law forms the organizing principle. The rightfully controlling force is the well-being of the community itself, which includes the eternal salvation of its members. In this vast system of cosmic morals all men, and indeed all beings, are included. From God at the summit down to the meanest of His creatures all act their part in the divine drama that leads to eternal life.

This supreme synthesis was the first reaction of the new Aristotelianism upon the long tradition of Christendom from the age of the Fathers down to the thirteenth century. In Thomas and Dante the intellectual stimulus of Aristotle has resulted mainly in a firmer systematization of the tradition, which concealed its inherent difficulties rather than removed them. Scarcely was Thomas's system complete before the seams of his great structure began to open. The difficulty of applying Aristotle's conception of a self-sufficing society to the empire was obviously insuperable: this was apparent in Dante and would have been so in Thomas, had the nature of the empire been a major concern with him. Scarcely less was the difficulty of bringing the church, with its claim of supernatural origin and theocratic authority, into a system so profoundly naturalistic in its implications as Aristotle's philosophy. The root of political Aristotelianism is the belief that society grows from natural human impulses which, human nature being what it is, are unescapable and that the human community thus formed provides all that a perfected human nature requires. The well-being of spirit as distinct from body, the destiny of the soul beyond an earthly life, an institution with an other-worldly claim of right, and a truth revealed from sources beyond reason were all out of harmony with the temper of Aristotle's philosophy and out of place in his conception of society. For the essence of his political theory is the presumption that the state is an outgrowth of the natural evolution of society and is justified by the moral values it sustains, without any explicitly religious sanction. In Thomas himself this phase of Aristotelianism accounted for the extreme moderation with which he treated the right of the church to intervene in secular affairs. The following century produced the works of William of Occam and Marsilio of Padua, not less Aristotelian than Thomas, but vastly farther from the Christian tradition which he tried to rationalize and from the synthesis of philosophy and revealed truth which he tried to frame. There was as yet no thought of a frontal attack on the church or on revelation. The first sign of decadence was the sharper discrimination of reason and faith, of spiritual and secular, to be followed by a long process of limitation and restriction which ultimately would immure the spiritual power innocuously in the supersensible world and the inner life.

SELECTED BIBLIOGRAPHY

"The Unity of Mediaeval Civilization." By Ernest Barker. In *Church, State, and Study*. London, 1930. Ch. 2.

A History of Mediaeval Political Theory in the West. By R. W. Carlyle and A. J. Carlyle. 6 vols. London, 1903–1936. Vol. V (1928), Part I, chs. 4, 5; Vol. VI (1936), Part I, ch. 7.

The Statesman's Book of John of Salisbury, being the Fourth, Fifth, and Sixth Books, and Selections from the Seventh and Eighth Books of the *Policraticus*. Eng. trans. by John Dickinson. New York, 1927. Introduction.

A History of Political Theories, Ancient and Mediaeval. By W. A. Dunning. New York, 1902. Ch. 8.

Réformateurs et publicistes de l'Europe: Moyen âge, Renaissance. By Adolphe Franck. Paris, 1864.

Dante et la philosophie. By Étienne Gilson. Paris, 1939. Ch. 3.

Thomas Aquinas: His Personality and Thought. By Martin Grabmann. Eng. trans. by Virgil Michel. New York, 1928. Chs. 11, 12.

The Social and Political Ideas of some Great Mediaeval Thinkers. Ed. by F. J. C. Hearnshaw. London, 1923. Chs. 3, 4, 5.

Social Theories of the Middle Ages, 1200–1500. By Bede Jarrett. London, 1926.

Die Staatslehre des Dante Alighieri. By Hans Kelsen. Vienna, 1905.

" Organic Tendencies in Medieval Political Thought." By Ewart Lewis. In *Am. Pol. Sci. Rev.*, Vol. XXXII (1938), p. 849.

" Natural Law and Expediency in Medieval Political Theory." By Ewart Lewis. In *Ethics,* Vol. L (1939–40), p. 144.

The Growth of Political Thought in the West, from the Greeks to the End of the Middle Ages. By C. H. McIlwain. New York, 1932. Ch. 6.

Illustrations of the History of Medieval Thought and Learning. By R. L. Poole. 2nd ed. rev. London, 1920. Ch. 8.

" Political Thought to *c.* 1300." By W. H. V. Reade. In the *Cambridge Medieval History,* Vol. VI (1929), ch. 18.

" The Political Theory of Dante." By W. H. V. Reade. In *Dante: De monarchia,* Oxford, 1916. Introduction.

La doctrine politique de Saint Thomas d'Aquin. By B. Roland-Gosselin. Paris, 1928.

The Social Teaching of the Christian Churches. By Ernst Troeltsch. Eng. trans. by Olive Wyon. 2 vols. London, 1931. Ch. 2.

John of Salisbury. By Clement C. J. Webb. London, 1932.

" Dante and United Italy." By Karl Witte. In *Essays on Dante.* Eng. trans. by C. M. Lawrence and P. H. Wicksteed. London, 1898.

L'idée de l'état dans Saint Thomas d'Aquin. By J. Zeiller. Paris, 1910.

CHAPTER XIV

PHILIP THE FAIR AND BONIFACE VIII

St. Thomas and Dante stood so completely within the tradition of a single European society that they failed to realize how insecure were the foundations of this tradition or how imminent were the changes that would destroy the system which they took to be eternal. Dante failed to see how hollow were the pretensions of the fourteenth-century empire to exert any real control over European politics, and how completely the nascent differences of nationality divided the peoples that such an empire would have to rule. Both Dante and Thomas failed to appreciate the effect of legal studies in the thirteenth century, both in the civil and canon law, on the old vague comity which the Gelasian theory assumed between the two powers. Aristotle here was a bad guide, and the growing legalism of political discussion influenced philosophers and theologians more slowly than men of affairs. The canon lawyers had already created a theory of the papacy which changed the church's right of spiritual discipline into a claim of legal supervision. In the fourteenth century this claim could hardly be met, as it was in the sixteenth, by a sweeping denial of the validity of canon law. What was first needed was a more precise analysis of the spiritual and secular authorities and especially a more exact delimitation of the spiritual, if the papal jurisdiction was to be hedged within tolerable limits. Finally, both men failed to appreciate at its full weight the dangerous secularism that might lurk in Aristotle's *Politics,* especially in the theory that civil society is itself perfect and self-sufficing, not requiring sanctification by any supernatural agency. All these tendencies of disintegration made their appearances in the fourteenth and fifteenth centuries.

The process took place in three great waves which form the subjects of this and the following two chapters. In the first, the controversy between the papacy and the kingdom of France in 1296–1303, the theory of papal imperialism, already well settled in the canon law, was brought to completion. At the same time it was decisively defeated by the national cohesion of the French kingdom, and the opposition to it began to take definite form and direction, in hedging about the spiritual power and in laying claim to independence for the kingdoms as independent political societies. In the second, the controversy between John XXII and Lewis the Bavarian some twenty-five years later, the opposition to papal sovereignty crystallized. William of Occam, speaking for the intransigent spiritual Franciscans, marshaled against it all the latent elements of opposition in the Christian tradition itself, and Marsilio of Padua developed the self-sufficiency of the civil community into a form of virtual secularism and Erastianism. In the course of this controversy the process of limiting and driving back the spiritual power to purely other-worldly functions was carried as far as it could go while the church as an institution remained intact. In the third controversy, this time in the church itself, the opposition to papal absolution took a new form: no longer an issue between spiritual and secular authority, it became the first instance in which the subjects of an absolute sovereign tried to force on him, as a measure of reform, the limitations of constitutional and representative government. In the church this effort by the conciliar party was, to be sure, a failure, but it developed the main lines of political theory upon which similar controversies, between secular rulers and their subjects, would be waged.

THE PUBLICISTS

In the controversy between Boniface VIII and Philip the Fair, the debate on both sides, for the papacy and for the king, was conducted on a significantly higher level of precision in respect to the issues than any part of the earlier controversy. All the old arguments, to be sure, reappeared and were canvassed afresh. The same passages of Scripture were re-analyzed; the same historical precedents were re-examined; the same landmarks, such as the Donation of Constantine and the translation of the empire, were reinterpreted. Superficially it might seem as if nothing were changed, but in reality political theory had turned over a new page. In the first place, the theory of papal imperialism reached a definite systematic conclusion in which the argument for the sovereign power of the pope over all forms of secular authority was accurately stated. The older Gelasian theory of the two powers was not expressly abandoned but it was explained away or reinterpreted out of all semblance to its older meaning. It is significant that this systematic statement of the theory of a papal empire was exactly coincident with its disastrous failure as a practical policy. The effort of Boniface to revive policies successfully pursued by Innocent III a century earlier not only proved their impracticability but ended in the disgrace of the "Babylonish captivity," which made the papacy for three-quarters of a century a tool of the French monarchy. This failure showed the appearance in European politics of a new force of national sentiment, but it had also a theoretical importance. It produced the conception of the kingdom as a political power not dependent upon the tradition of the empire. Instead of two worldwide jurisdictions, the *sacerdotium* and the *imperium*, the issue was between the independent king of France as one power and the papacy as another.

The controversy produced a large mass of controversial and occasional literature.[1] Particularly in the works written in defense of Philip, this literature had a tone very different from that of the earlier controversy between the pope and the emperor. It would be misleading to say that the writers were less interested in theological arguments, but certainly many of them have a more definitely secular interest; perhaps it would not be extreme to speak of a middle-class point of view in much of it. Most of the king's defenders were lawyers, men professionally trained and professionally employed in the royal courts or the royal council, prepared to bring the resources of the Roman law to the aid of the hereditary monarchy. It is natural that their writings speak with the voice of political realism and show a concern for the problems of administration. The relations of government to trade, to the coinage, to secular education, to judicial procedure, and to colonies all come in for consideration. A new type in European intellectual life, the educated and professionally trained

[1] There is no collection corresponding to the *Libelli de lite,* but the whole literature is analyzed by R. Scholz in *Die Publizistik zur Zeit Philipps des Schönen und Bonifaz' VIII,* Stuttgart, 1903. This is the authoritative work on the subject. Much of the literature is summarized by Carlyle, *op. cit.,* Vol. V (London, 1928), Part II, chs. 8–10.

layman, has definitely made its appearance. No political literature produced earlier in the Middle Ages had been equally critical or equally free from the shackles of authority.

This quality, which was typical of much of the writing on the royalist side of the controversy, will here be indicated by a single example. For this purpose the interesting figure of Pierre Dubois may be chosen. If he was not precisely a political theorist, he was at least one of the greatest medieval pamphleteers. A lawyer by profession,[2] he wrote overtly to offer a plan for renewing the crusades, though it is hard to believe that he took this part of his projects very seriously. His plan was that France should step into the international position assigned by medieval thought to the empire and left vacant by its weakness. Substantially the proposal was a European alliance for the abolition of war, with France at its head, and having a representative council and a standing court to adjudicate disputes between the allied powers. To this end he desired a drastic reform of the church, including the abolition of clerical celibacy, the transference of ecclesiastical jurisdiction to the king's courts, and the surrender of the papal territory in return for an annual pension. Dubois suggested also the complete reorganizing, and to a large extent the secularizing, of education, with provision for the instruction of women, and with the inclusion in the curriculum of Greek, Hebrew, Arabic, and modern languages; law, medicine, and the sciences; as well as philosophy and theology. There could be no better sign of the place the universities had assumed in the intellectual life of Europe. Finally, he sketched a thoroughgoing plan for the internal reform of France, including a reorganization of the army, an improvement of the courts to make the administration of justice speedier, cheaper, and more equal, the standardizing of the coinage and the fostering of trade. The plan was grandiose and as a whole utopian, but parts of it had already been discussed, and where Dubois was at home, as in his proposal to reform the judiciary, it was far from doctrinaire.

[2] He was the author of many pamphlets, the best known of which is his *De recuperatione terre sancte,* written c. 1306; edited by Ch. V. Langlois, Paris, 1891. The first part only, addressed to the King of England, was published, but the book was certainly intended for Philip the Fair and the second part included a grandiose plan for extending French influence over practically all Europe and the Near East. See Scholz, *op. cit.*, pp. 375 ff.

THE RELATIVE POSITION OF THE TWO PARTIES

The nature of the issue between Philip and Boniface had much to do with developing the theories advanced on either side. The most important questions arose from Philip's efforts to raise money by imposing taxes on the French clergy, an attempt met by the Bull *Clericis laicos* in 1296, in which Boniface declared such taxation to be illegal and forbade the clergy to pay without papal permission. From this position he was forced to recede a few years later because he discovered, to his surprise, that even the French clergy would stand with the French king on a question which, in modern terminology, would be called national. So far as practical politics is concerned the quarrel was notable because of the failure of the traditional tactics on which papal power in the past had rested: it proved impossible for Boniface to coerce the king by inciting factional disturbances among the feudal nobility. Obviously a new force of political cohesion was at work. On the other hand, the taxation of ecclesiastical property was a matter of life and death for the monarchy. If Boniface had made good what seemed to be the literal meaning of *Clericis laicos,* no monarchy in Europe could have existed except on sufferance of the pope. Even feudal monarchy could not have survived if all the land held by churchmen had been exempt from feudal rents. Moreover, the king would have been prevented from pursuing the only policies by which feudal kings could become strong, that of drawing business into the royal courts and of placing administration in the hands of officers dependent upon themselves. The outstanding success of Philip's reign was the organization of the great French law-court, the Parlement of Paris.

The fact that the issue concerned the rights of ecclesiastical property obliged the defenders of the pope to take a much more advanced position relative to the papal powers than had been the case previously. The investiture struggle really had involved the independence of the church in spiritual matters, but it could hardly be held that this independence made it necessary that the property of churchmen should be free from all civic obligations. The question inevitably arose whether the papal claim on behalf of property was not contrary to the profession of clerical poverty which Christianity had always made. In any event the issue made it practically necessary to draw a more exact line between spirituals and temporals and this involved a more searching inquiry into the nature of both powers. Property as such was certainly to be counted among temporals, though it was impracticable for the church to do its work without property in some form. If this implied that the spiritual power extended to everything that might be a means to spiritual ends, then the church must be the court of last resort even in temporals. On the other hand, if spirituals were limited to functions for which no material means were required, then there could be very little point in describing the spiritual as a power, whatever dignity or worth might be abstractly imputed to it. There were, therefore, two directions in which theory could go. The papal theory was forced logically toward the claim of an ultimate power of supervision and direction in which the church and its courts, without superseding secular government, became the powers of last resort in any issue which it was worth while to dispute. The royalist theory was forced to hedge in and limit the spiritual power as much as possible, restricting it to questions of conscience and making it dependent on the secular arm for coercive power.

In the French controversy the tactical positions of the two contestants were reversed: the ecclesiastical and not the secular power was on the defensive. For this reason it was not only the authority of the king that was on trial but equally the papal power itself. The extent of the pope's power in the church, the possibility of supporting a charge of heresy against him, his control of ecclesiastical property, his authority in doctrinal questions — in short, the whole question of church government and of the pope's part in it — were subjected to searching criticism. The opening up of this question was of the greatest importance in the progress of the discussion. During the century that followed, the subjection of the papacy to the influence of France and the scandal of the Great Schism, which was a direct consequence, made the question of government in the church the most interesting and important subject of political debate in Europe. Not only was the nature of spiritual authority analyzed, but in the long run the opposition to the papacy as the supreme power of the church was developed and spread broadcast, with consequences that were made fully apparent in the Protestant Reformation. Moreover, the question of absolute as against representative power in the church had important oblique influences when the same issue came to be discussed in states.

The number of books which appeared on either side was large. Barely to mention them would be unprofitable and to describe them all would be impossible. The best plan seems to be to state in general the positions taken by the papalists on the one side and by the defenders of the secular power on the other, emphasizing in each case the newer factors which were appearing in the argument. But in order to give a clearer idea of the manner in which the case was presented, it will be well to choose a representative writer from each side for fuller treatment. For this purpose the choice on the papal side is obvious: the book on the *Power of the Church* by Egidius Colonna (Giles of Rome) was probably the strongest statement of papal imperialism produced at any time. On the side of the king the book which probably, in the long run, carried the greatest weight was that of the Dominican John of Paris. In this chapter, then, the theory of the papal power will first be described and especially the case as presented by Egidius; and second, the theory of the antipapalists with a more extended account of the argument by John of Paris.

THE PAPAL CLAIMS

The position which Boniface attempted to make good against the kingdom of France and the policy which he undertook to follow were derivative from the course previously taken by the great popes of the thirteenth century, especially Innocent III and Innocent IV, and from the theory of the papal power already developed by the canonists, of whom Innocent IV himself was not the least.[3] The difference between this theory and that held by Gregory VII lay not so much in a claim to greater power. Perhaps it would have been difficult to formulate a more august conception of the papal office than that held by Gregory. The difference is essentially legal; it consists in a greater precision in the conception of the pope's authority, resulting from a thorough exploration of the relations between the pope and his subordinates

[3] These are treated at length by Carlyle, *op. cit.*, Vol. V (1928): for Innocent III, see Part II, chs. 1 and 2; for Innocent IV, *ibid.*, ch. 5; see also Vol. II, Part II.

in the church and between the spiritual and temporal powers. Broadly speaking the difference is between a general but somewhat vague claim to spiritual superiority with a right of moral discipline and a systematic theory of jurisdictional rights and powers. The writings of Thomas show that the importance of this advance was largely unperceived by students of political philosophy in the thirteenth century. The controversy of Boniface with France shows that it was very accurately perceived by lawyers and publicists at the end of the century. The revival of legal studies, both in Roman and ecclesiastical law, renewed the elements of legalism which had always been an important part of the Roman heritage and confirmed it as a permanent part of political thought.

The formidable list of powers which the canon lawyers had come to claim, and which greater popes like Innocent III had exercised, did not overtly carry with it a rejection of the ancient distinction between the two powers or even the denial that the two were distinct in purpose and in their exercise. They clearly implied, however, that the supposed independence and separation of *sacerdotium* and *imperium* was in process of being explained away. It was this process of explaining away that reached its culmination in the controversy with France. In respect to imperial elections Innocent III had claimed in his famous Bull *Venerabilem* (1202) the right to pass upon the fitness of the elected candidate and also to review disputed or irregular elections. In his dealings with other rulers he had sought to establish papal jurisdiction in special questions or over special classes of persons. Thus he had claimed the power to confirm and adjudicate treaties and agreements between rulers, on the theory that the church has special jurisdiction over oaths; in effect this amounted to a general guardianship over war and peace and the right to oblige contesting parties to submit to arbitration. He had claimed also a special guardianship over widows and minors, and special powers for the suppression of heresy, including the right to confiscate heretics' property, to exclude them from office, and to discipline rulers who failed to enforce the church's authority in such matters. He had sought also to set up a general right of supervision over the administration of justice, including the privilege of taking cases into his own courts where the secular courts had permitted a miscarriage of justice. Obviously, in such cases the pope himself, or the ecclesiastical courts, must necessarily have the last word in deciding where jurisdiction lay. Doubtless Innocent intended that the secular authorities should retain their powers and should continue to function in the great majority of cases; he did not assert that his power superseded that of temporal rulers or even that they derived their power from him. But he conceived the papacy as having a general power of review which could be extended at need to practically any sort of question, the ecclesiastical authority itself being the judge of the need.

The essence of the theory was that it claimed for the papacy a unique power, both in the church itself and in the relations of the church to secular powers, superior and different in kind from that exercised by any other authority. The pope had *plenitudo potestatis,* an expression hard to render except with the word sovereignty. This theory was stated with great precision by Innocent IV. He took the papal power quite out of the categories of feudal dependence by asserting that the right to intervene or to supersede a negligent king was in no way dependent upon the king's being a vassal of the pope; it depended solely on the pope's *plenitudo potestatis,* "which he has because he is the vicar of Christ." Such a power is a peculiar consequence of the Christian dispensation:

> Jesus Christ himself made Peter and Peter's successors his vicars when he gave them the keys of the heavenly kingdom and said, "Feed my sheep." Though there are many offices and governments in the world, there can always be an appeal to the pope when necessary, whether the need arises from the law, because the judge is uncertain what decision he ought legally to give, or from fact, because there is no higher judge, or because inferior judges cannot execute their judgments, or are not willing to do justice as they ought.[4]

This unique power possessed by the pope alone is therefore in a special sense a "divine right"; it confers a peculiar superiority, a power of revision and supervision over all the other forms of authority, whether ecclesiastical or secular. In this sense all power both temporal and spiritual resides in the church and is vested in the pope. In substance the theory amounts to a claim

[4] Quoted by Carlyle, *op. cit.,* Vol. V, p. 323, n. 1.

of universal sovereignty which makes the pope the head of the entire legal system, not indeed as a universal executive but as a court of final authority and as the fountain-head of legal power.

The papal writers in the controversy with France had behind them the actual exercise of power by Innocent III and the theory of papal power formulated by Innocent IV and other canonists. The papal position was stated by Boniface himself in the bull *Unam sanctam* in 1302, which took the most advanced ground on papal imperialism that was ever written into an official document.[5] The bull asserted two main principles essential to the papal position: first, the pope is supreme in the church and subjection to him is a doctrine necessary to salvation, and second, both swords belong to the church. The distinction of function between them is still admitted; the temporal sword is not to be actually used by the clergy, but it is to be used by kings "at the command and with the permission of priests." For the spiritual power is the higher, and it is a general law of nature that order requires the subjection of the lower to the higher. Hence earthly authority is set up and judged by spiritual, while spiritual authority is judged only by God. The authority of the church flows from the fact that the pope is the successor of Peter and the vicar of Christ. The bull was little more than a sweeping statement in general terms of what had been asserted in detail by Innocent IV.

EGIDIUS COLONNA

As was said above, the most thorough-going presentation of the argument for papal imperialism was contained in the *De ecclesiastica potestate,* which was written about the year 1302 by Egidius Colonna.[6] The book claimed to present the papal case

[5] The writings of Boniface are published in *Les registres de Boniface VIII,* Bibliothèque des Écoles Françaises d'Athènes et de Rome, 2e série. An English translation of *Clericis laicos* and *Unam sanctam* is given in E. F. Henderson's *Select Historical Documents of the Middle Ages* (1892), pp. 432 ff.

[6] The book was unprinted until the edition by G. Boffito and G. U. Oxilia, Florence, 1908. There is now a better edition by R. Scholz, *Aegidius Romanus, De ecclesiastica potestate,* Weimar, 1929. Egidius was the author also of a popular textbook on government, *De regimine principum,* written in 1285 for Philip the Fair, whose tutor he was. This was frequently printed in early modern times and an old French version, entitled *Li livres du gouvernement des rois,* was edited by S. P. Molenaer, New York, 1899.

not as a legal argument but from the point of view of a philosophy uniting the newer Aristotelianism with the older Augustinian tradition which made the state, under a Christian dispensation, necessarily Christian. Indeed, Egidius showed in his earlier work what Professor Carlyle calls a "curious and somewhat laughable contempt for the lawyers,"[7] which makes only the more striking the dependence of his theory upon the legalism which had now become an essential part of the papal position. The book is decidedly repetitious and somewhat lacking in formal organization, but its principles are perfectly clear. The case is presented in three main divisions: the general argument for papal sovereignty, or *plenitudo potestatis;* the deductions from this principle relative to property and government; and answers to objections, especially those based on the decretals of the popes themselves.

The similarity between the argument in the first part and the bull *Unam sanctam* is very close, extending even to forms of expression; since the book was probably written first, the intimacy between Boniface and its author must have been considerable. The spiritual power vested in the pope, Egidius argues, is unique and supreme. This authority is inherent in the office, and is therefore not dependent upon the personal qualities of the man who holds it. Spiritual authority has the power to set up temporal authority and judge it. All the older arguments, such as the Donation of Constantine, the translation of the empire, and the Scriptural texts and historical precedents reappear in Egidius, but they do not form the kernel of his argument. This depends upon the intrinsic superiority of the spiritual and upon the argument that the higher everywhere governs and controls the lower by a law of nature. For order in nature depends upon such subordination, and it cannot be supposed that there is less order in a Christian society than in nature generally.

> As in the universe itself corporeal substance is ruled by spiritual — for the heavens themselves, which are the highest among corporeal beings and have control over all bodies, are ruled by spiritual substances as moving intelligences — so among Christians all temporal lords and all earthly power ought to be governed and ruled by spiritual and ecclesiastical authority, and especially by the pope, who holds the summit and the highest rank among spiritual powers and in the church.[8]

[7] *Op. cit.,* Vol. V, p. 71.

[8] I, 5; ed. by Scholz, p. 17.

The argument as Egidius develops it appears to be a conflation of St. Augustine with the Aristotelian doctrine of form and matter.

The second part of the treatise, in which the author applied his philosophy specifically to the questions in hand, sets forth his essential conclusions. The argument turns upon the conception of *dominium*, which includes the ownership and use of property and also political authority. Now *dominium* is a means, and the authority of Aristotle is quoted to prove that the value and legitimacy of a means depend upon the end it serves. The ownership of goods and the possession of political power are only good when they serve human ends, and human ends are, in their highest form, spiritual ends. Unless a man subordinates his power and his property to spiritual ends, such things are not goods for him, for they lead not to salvation but to the damnation of his soul. But the church is the sole avenue of salvation, and from this it follows that all *dominium* requires the sanctification of the church in order to be just and lawful. It is an error to suppose that the inheritance of *dominium* is justified by carnal generation only; it is justified far more by the spiritual regeneration which comes through the church. There is no lawful ownership or use of property and no lawful exercise of civil authority unless he who has it is subject to God, and he cannot be subject to God unless he is subject to the church.

> It follows therefore that you ought to admit that you have your inheritance, and all your property, and all your possessions, rather from the Church and through the Church and because you are a son of the Church, than from your father after the flesh and through him and because you are his son.[9]

Baptism and penitence for sin can alone make a man worthy to possess goods and power, and an infidel can have no just claim to either, for his possession is mere usurpation. Excommunication annuls law, contracts, property-rights, and marriage, in short, the whole legal machinery on which society depends. Despite Aristotelian terminology the conclusion was a tremendous generalization from Augustine's argument[10] that a just state must necessarily be Christian, and in its application it was much less enlightened than Thomas's opinion that infidelity is no bar to

[9] II, 7; *ibid.*, p. 75.

[10] *City of God*, 19, 21.

the exercise of political power. In fact, Egidius's use of Aristotelianism was superficial, a mere argument in the prevailing academic mode, with no such appreciation of the moral claims of secular government as Thomas showed. In substance his book harked back to the theocratic tradition which antedated both the revival of legal studies and the rediscovery of Aristotle.

The remainder of Egidius's book was mainly devoted to explaining away the intrinsic opposition between his own theory of universal papal sovereignty and the many admissions, in the decretals and elsewhere, regarding the independence of the two powers. He protests that he does not mean to deny that they are distinct or that in general they should be kept so in their exercise. The rights of the temporal power are not taken away but confirmed, for the church has no desire that the powers should be confounded. It does not supersede the temporal power but intervenes only for adequate cause and to preserve spiritual values. But his protestations are less impressive than the enormous list of special cases in which he justifies papal intervention. The spiritual authority can intervene in any case where temporal goods or power are put to a use that involves mortal sin. This power, as Egidius remarks a little naively, is " so broad and ample that it includes all temporal cases whatsoever." Moreover, the church has a special jurisdiction in maintaining peace between rulers and in securing the observance of treaties, and it can intervene where rulers show negligence or where the civil law is ambiguous or insufficient. The whole list purports to enumerate special powers rather than powers to be ordinarily exercised, but clearly the pope is competent to take jurisdiction in any case at his own discretion. It is true that he ought not to act arbitrarily; he ought not to be " without a bridle," but he must be trusted to bridle himself with the law.

Egidius concluded his book with a few chapters in which he tried to explain a little more definitely what is meant by the *plenitudo potestatis* attributed to the pope. This sovereignty he defines as independent or self-motivating power; an agent has it, " when he can do without a cooperating cause anything that he can do with one." Egidius in fact knows only two such powers, God and the pope. The supremacy of the pope in spiritual matters is absolute under God. Substantially he *is* the church, in the sense that he can neither be removed nor held responsible and has ultimate authority over ecclesiastical law and over the rest of the hierarchy. Thus Egidius asserts that he has full power to create bishops and could do so without any of the customary forms of election, though he is under obligation to retain the forms of law. The argument, it will be observed, is substantially similar to that used in the sixteenth century to support monarchy by divine right; the divine right of a king is a replica, *mutatis mutandis,* of the divine right of the pope. But Egidius regards *plenitudo potestatis* as a property peculiar to papal authority. When he wrote, the argument could not have been applied to a secular ruler who was in no sense the successor of St. Peter. But where the purpose was to defend the independence of kings from clerical interference, always an important part of the royalist argument, the claim for the secular power had to advance parallel to that for the pope. The divine right of kings was, as John Neville Figgis held, an anomalous, but intelligible, use of theology to detach secular institutions from theology. But it was also an instrument ready to the hand of royalists when the political controversy was between kings and their subjects.

ROMAN LAW AND ROYAL POWER

In the system advanced by Egidius papal imperialism has reached its fullest form. The word imperialism may be used advisedly, for though the theory still depended upon the claim of the church to a power of spiritual discipline, its developed form depended also upon the position ascribed to the emperor in Roman law. There was truth in Hobbes's malicious description of the papacy as " the ghost of the deceased Roman Empire sitting crowned upon the grave thereof." Papal sovereignty, as the sole principle upon which *dominium* can lawfully rest, has become the arbiter of private and public rights everywhere. The Gelasian theory of the two independent powers has become merely a tradition to which conventional respect must be given but which effectively means little or nothing. Assuming that spiritual authority was to be clothed in legal powers, no other conclusion could follow from the development of the forces which Gregory VII had set in motion. The alternative was to deny that a spiritual force needs, or can have, a legal structure. The spiritual must be restricted so far as possible to the duty of moral and religious instruction, with the result in the end that civil government on its side becomes purely a secular institution. The beginnings of this process also can be traced to the French controversy at the opening of the fourteenth century.

Roman law, with its conception of legal authority centralized in the emperor, was no less important for the argument in behalf of the king of France than for that in behalf of the pope. In the thirteenth century there appeared the conception, wholly novel so far as the earlier medieval tradition is concerned, that law is dependent upon the enactment of the prince, and this was almost certainly due to the study of Roman law.[11] The theory of the lawyers was, of course, that of the *Digest:* the emperor's will has the force of law, though he derives this power from the act of the people which invests him with it. In the thirteenth century there was a difference of opinion among lawyers on the question whether this act had wholly divested the people of the power to make law, some holding that it had and others that a residual authority remained with the Roman people. In any event, however, the conception had gained a footing among certain jurists, that law requires enactment and expresses the will of a chief magistrate, and this imported a new element into a situation where law had been regarded as the custom of a people. It brought with it also a distinction between governments in which law comes from the people and those in which it comes from a king, roughly the distinction between constitutional and absolute governments.

The power which Roman law imputed to the emperor, however, was an anachronism so far as the empire of the thirteenth century was concerned, and the letter of the law had no application to kings and other actually independent powers. A long process of interpretation was required to detach the law from its literal reference to the emperor, so that any ruler who was *de facto* independent could figure as a *princeps* within the meaning of the law.[12] This step was essential in forming the conception both of an independent political power, invested with the imperial attribute

[11] Carlyle, *op. cit.*, Vol. V, Part I, ch. 6.

[12] The historical process is discussed by Cecil N. Sidney Woolf in his *Bartolus of Sassoferrato,* Cambridge, 1913; especially ch. 3.

of sovereignty, and of a power mainly secular and legal in its nature. The formation of the latter idea required much time and its completion belonged to the history rather of modern than of medieval states, but the controversy between the French king and the pope at the beginning of the fourteenth century had a critical part in settling the national sovereignty of the French monarchy. Even the French clergy stood by the king in asserting the independence of France both from the papacy and the empire. The legal formula which emerged, about the middle of the fourteenth century, was that the king has the same power in his kingdom that the emperor has in the empire. *Rex in regno suo est imperator regni sui.*[13] Philip required his sons to take an oath that they would never acknowledge a superior under God.

If the royalist literature be taken as a whole, the influence of legal studies upon the argument is obvious. Distinctions which had been vague are by way of being given greater precision. This is true particularly of the fundamental distinction between spirituals and temporals, which the lawyers attacked as essentially a problem of defining the limits of two jurisdictions. Certain classes of cases are allocated to the ecclesiastical courts; others belong wholly to the secular courts; while there are still others in which both jurisdictions have an interest. The clarifying of this legal question tended also to make clearer the distinction between legal questions, in which the coercive power of the king could be invoked, and moral questions, which belong to the teaching of the church. On the whole the tendency, on the side of the royalist lawyers, was to define the spiritual authority as ethical or religious instruction and hence to divest it of coercive force, except as this was applied from the side of the secular power. In other words, the tendency is in a direction which culminated a generation later in Marsilio's conclusion that spiritual authority is merely the right to teach. This more limited conception of spiritual authority had an important application to the claims of papal absolutism within the church, because all priests, or at least all bishops, could properly be regarded as equal in respect to the performance of purely spiritual duties, and the power of the hierarchy could therefore be conceived as merely a convenient administrative arrangement. The importance of property in the

[13] On the origin of this dictum see Woolf, *op. cit.*, pp. **370** ff.

controversy tended to a similar result. From the point of view of the church's spiritual duties, the control of property was only a means, and as the distinction between spirituals and temporals was sharpened, it was natural that the control of property as such, even though it were devoted to ecclesiastical purposes, should fall within the province of the king. At the same time this analysis of property tended to clarify the distinction between a public right to control or tax property and the private right of ownership.

JOHN OF PARIS

Of the many works written in defense of the king probably none was more characteristic or historically more important than the *De potestate regia et papali* (1302–3) of John of Paris.[14] The book is the more significant because its author was a Dominican; but he was also a Frenchman. John hardly undertook to present a systematic political philosophy; his book is more notable for its details than for its general structure, and though couched in general terms, it was written definitely with the events of the preceding half dozen years in mind. At the same time, the Aristotelianism which he shared with St. Thomas was an important factor in determining his point of view and set him off quite clearly from the mock Aristotelianism of Egidius. For one thing, John felt no need, as a lawyer would do, to attach special pre-eminence to the empire. He argues in his opening chapters that the church requires universality but that political authority does not. Civil society arises by a natural instinct and men are diverse in their inclinations and interests. The natural political division is the province or kingdom, and there is no need that these should be subordinated to a single head. It is true that he sometimes attributes to the emperor a somewhat shadowy universal authority, but he is perfectly definite in asserting the independence of France. The self-sufficing community which he adopts from Aristotle is for him the kingdom, and he sees no difficulty in admitting as many such autonomous units as there actually are. In the second place, and perhaps most important, John's Aris-

[14] It was printed in M. Goldast's *Monarchia sancti Romani imperii*, Hanover and Frankfort, 1612–14, Vol. II, p. 108, and in S. Schard's *De jurisdictione, autoritate, et praeeminentia imperiali, ac potestate ecclesiastica* (Basel, 1566), p. 142. There is an abstract in R. Scholz, *op. cit.*, pp. 298 ff. and in Carlyle, *op. cit.*, Vol. V, Part II, ch. 10.

totelianism enables him to refute the view of Egidius, that secular power requires the sanctification of the church in order to be legitimate. Secular power is older in time than true priesthood and not derivative from it. Moreover, it is false to regard secular power as corporeal only in its nature. He adopts from Aristotle, as St. Thomas had done, the view that civil government is necessary in itself to a good life and is therefore justified by its ethical benefits even apart from its sanction by Christianity. Hence it is a misuse of the Aristotelian rule that the higher controls the lower to argue that the spiritual in all respects is higher than the temporal. He does not, of course, regard this as denying the greater intrinsic worth of spiritual authority. But he uses the naturalness of secular government to support the traditional defense of the independence of temporals.

John wrote, as he states in his preface, especially to solve the problem of ecclesiastical property and with the purpose of marking out a middle course between two opposed errors. There are those, he says, who assert that the clergy should have no property at all and he calls these Waldensians, and there are those who argue that the spiritual power of priests gives them indirectly a control over all property and all secular power. The latter error he identifies with that of Herod, who thought that the kingdom of Christ was of this world; but his argument is obviously aimed at the extreme partisans of papal imperialism like Egidius. John's book was written against the second error, and his middle position consists in arguing that it is lawful for the clergy to have property, as a means to doing their spiritual work, but that the legal control of property vests in the secular authority. It is totally false to argue that, because property is needed for spiritual purposes, therefore the spiritual authority extends to an indirect control over property. With this general position John unites several interesting and important supplementary points. He denies, first, that the ownership of ecclesiastical property vests in the pope; it belongs to no individual but to the community as a corporate body, and the pope's control of it is that of an executive (*dispensator*). The pope can be held responsible for a misuse of the church's property. Second, he makes a clear distinction in the case of secular rulers between ownership, which in the case of laymen vests in individuals, and the political or public regulation of the uses of property which the ruler has as the head of a civil society. The king is to respect the rights of private property, regulating it only as public need directs.

In the same spirit of clarifying issues John deals with the distinction of spirituals and temporals. The argument still depends, as did the earlier defense of the empire against Gregory, upon the separateness of the two authorities, each derived directly from God. But John covers the whole argument systematically. He distinguishes forty-two reasons which have been assigned for the subordination of secular to spiritual authority and refutes them one by one. What is more important, he analyzes the spiritual authority inherent in priests and inquires what control, if any, this implies over temporal goods and secular power. The consecration and administration of the sacraments and the right to preach and teach he finds to be purely spiritual, requiring no material means. The clerical right of judging and correcting evil doers is the main source of confusion, and here he finds that the spiritual authority extends only to excommunication, which has intrinsically no material consequences. Coercion belongs to the secular arm. Excommunication, as applied for instance to a heretical ruler, may lead his people to refuse obedience, but this is incidental and implies no right in the spiritual power to coerce rulers. John points out that a protest by secular authorities against an abuse in the church may have similar incidental effects in bringing a pope to terms. In law the right of a pope to depose a king is no greater than that of a king to depose a pope. Both can protest and the protest may have weight; both may lawfully be deposed, but only by the properly constituted authority that elects them. The remaining two powers implied by the spiritual authority — that of regulating the clergy and of owning the property required for spiritual uses — imply no power over the secular authority. Coming from a churchman this precise analysis and, in effect, limitation of the church's spiritual authority is very striking.

John's general argument on the relation between the two powers is supplemented by his treatment of the relation between the pope and the king of France. This part of his case was largely historical, and because it turned upon the Donation of Constantine, involved also the relation of France to the empire. His purpose was to show that, whatever the relations between the papacy and the empire, there was no ground for holding the king of France subject to the pope. The conclusion is somewhat complicated because he seemingly set himself to pulverize the Donation. He first shows, on historical ground, that it was in any case applicable only to certain parts of Italy. He then attacked its legal validity on the ground that the emperor could not lawfully have alienated part of the empire. Next, he argued that, even if these points were waived, it could not have applied to France, because the Franks had never been subject to the empire. And finally, even if they had been, they might well have gained their independence by prescription. There could hardly be a greater contrast than between John's treatment of the empire and Dante's fanciful idealization of it. It was always, he says, filled with disorder and corruption; it had usurped its power from earlier peoples; why, then, should not later peoples make good a claim to independence against it? For Frenchmen at least the empire had ceased to possess a mythical charm.[15]

The concluding chapters of John's book deal with the powers of the pope from another angle. By implication what he does, though not in set terms, is to deny completely the papal claim to a unique type of authority, a *plenitudo potestatis,* in the church. The primacy of the pope he treated as mainly a matter of administrative organization, since in spiritual authority all bishops are equal. The papal office, to be sure, is unique and is from God, but the choice of an incumbent requires human cooperation. This formed the weakest point in Egidius's argument, for seemingly in the interval when a papal election was taking place, the papal power must reside somewhere, and there seemed no good reason why, if a pope could be invested with it, he might not also be divested of it by some legal process. John argues accordingly that a pope may resign and also may be deposed for incorrigible misconduct. Following the line already marked out by his treatment of ecclesiastical property, he regards the spiritual authority as residing in the church itself as a corporation. He has no doubt whatever that a General Council can depose a pope, and he states it as his own opinion that the College of Cardinals can lawfully

[15] Cf. the plans for reconstructing the empire after the fall of the Hohenstaufen discussed by C. N. S. Woolf, *op. cit.*, pp. 209 ff.

do it. It is evident that he conceives the College as standing in the same relation to the pope as the feudal parliaments of the estates to the king.

> Certainly it would be the best government for the church if, under one pope, representatives were chosen by and from each province, so that in the government of the church all should have their share.[16]

Accordingly he justifies resistance to the pope on the same general principles that many medieval writers used to justify resistance to a king. It is true that no legal process will run against the pope, but if he causes rebellion and cannot be persuaded to stop,

> I think that in this case the church ought to be moved to act against the pope; the prince may repel the violence of the papal sword with his own sword, within measure, and in so doing he would not be acting against the pope but against his enemy and the enemy of society.[17]

These passages show how repugnant, even to churchmen, the claim of papal sovereignty was. They point very clearly to the effort, abortive to be sure, which the Great Schism produced to constitutionalize the government of the church on the lines of a medieval system of representation.

John has little to say, except incidentally, about the organization of the secular state. In general, it is clear that he envisages government under the form of the medieval constitutional monarchy. Thus he denies that the pope deposed the Merovingians and put Pippin in their place; Pippin was chosen "by election of the barons." In all temporal matters it is the barons who check or discipline the king. Here again John brings Aristotle to his aid by identifying constitutional monarchy with the polity, which is a mixture of democracy and aristocracy. It was of course the fact that medieval constitutionalism was taking form everywhere at the time when John wrote. The first meeting of the States General was held in France in 1302; and similar representative bodies composed of the estates of the realm had been held in the course of the thirteenth century in England, Italy, Germany, and Spain. The political views represented by John were therefore characteristic of his age, much more characteristic than the tendency toward absolutism represented by Egidius or some of the civilians.

Without presenting a systematic political theory, the work of

[16] C. 20; Schard (1566), p. 202b.

[17] C. 23; *ibid.*, p. 215a.

John of Paris was highly significant both for its own time and for the future. A Frenchman as well as a cleric, he made a strong case on both historical and legal grounds for the independence of the French monarchy. He drew a clear distinction between the ownership of property, whether by the church or by lay individuals, and the political control of it by the king or the administration of it for the church by the pope. He restated the argument for the independence of spiritual and secular authority, supplementing it with a penetrating analysis of the nature and purposes of spiritual power. On the whole, this analysis leans toward the view that spiritual authority is not properly a legal power at all. It either does not require coercion, or if it does, this must be sought from the side of the secular arm. The moral and religious character of the spiritual is strongly stressed. Substantially his argument is a protest against the invasion of religion by law and against investing the pope with a sovereign power modeled on the legal position of the emperor. And finally he suggests, as against the absolutism of the pope, the advisability of tempering monarchy with representation. In every case these arguments had an important part in the political discussion of the future. As compared with the argument of Egidius, John's position is a striking example of the secularizing and rationalizing influence which Aristotle had already exerted, even within the limits of thought undoubtedly orthodox.

The controversy between Boniface and Philip was of great importance in the development of political theory. It produced a clear-cut claim to unique, sovereign power, vested in the pope and exercised directly in the church and indirectly as between the pope and secular rulers, and it defended this claim upon the principle of divine right. The appearance of this claim, a theological offshoot of legalism, was the signal for a concerted attack upon it. Even in the French controversy this attack began to develop on two main lines. Objection was made to papal sovereignty on the presumption that it was a case of clerical pretension, peculiar to an ecclesiastical power, and hence to be met by hedging it in to a proper moral and religious exercise. On the other hand, objection was made to sovereign power as such, on the ground that it was intrinsically tyrannous wherever it existed and needed to be tempered and limited by representation and consent. The first of these two objections, that of hedging in the spiritual power and setting it apart from secular powers, was carried forward by William of Occam and reached almost logical completeness in Marsilio of Padua. The case for representation as an intrinsic part of all good government was first elaborately stated in the conciliar theory of church government.

SELECTED BIBLIOGRAPHY

Boniface VIII. By J. S. R. Boase. London, 1933.

A History of Mediaeval Political Theory in the West. By R. W. Carlyle and A. J. Carlyle. 6 vols. London, 1903–1936. Vol. V (1928), Part II, chs. 1–2, 8–10.

The Decline of the Medieval Church. By Alexander C. Flick. 2 vols. London, 1930. Chs. 1, 2.

Argument from Roman Law in Political Thought, 1200–1600. By Myron P. Gilmore. Cambridge, Mass., 1941.

Social and Political Ideas of Some Great Mediaeval Thinkers. Ed. by F. J. C. Hearnshaw. London, 1923. Ch. 6.

"Innocent III." By E. F. Jacob. In the *Cambridge Medieval History,* Vol. VI (1929), ch. 1.

"France: The Last Capetians." By Hilda Johnstone. In the *Cambridge Medieval History,* Vol. VII (1932), ch. 11.

"Saint Louis. Philippe le Bel. Les derniers Capétians directs (1226–1328)." By C. V. Langlois. In *Histoire de France.* Ed. by E. Lavisse. Paris, 1900—. Vol. III, Part II.

"Pope Boniface VIII." By F. M. Powicke. In *The Christian Life in the Middle Ages.* Oxford, 1935. Ch. 3.

Die Publizistik zur Zeit Philipps des Schönen und Bonifaz' VIII: Ein Beitrag zur Geschichte der politischen Anschauungen des Mittelalters. By Richard Scholz. Stuttgart, 1903.

Bartolus of Sassoferrato: His Position in the History of Medieval Political Thought. By Cecil N. Sidney Woolf. Cambridge, 1913.

CHAPTER XV

MARSILIO OF PADUA AND WILLIAM OF OCCAM

Hostility to the theory of papal sovereignty, already evidenced by the criticism of John of Paris, was enhanced by the failure of Boniface's grandiose claims in France and more particularly by the seventy-five years' residence of the popes at Avignon under the influence of the French monarchy. For if secular rulers had little wish to be subjects of the Church of Rome, they were still less willing to be subjects of what William of Occam derisively called the Church of Avignon. The "Babylonish Captivity" gave great offense to those who were not of French nationality. Even in the *Divine Comedy* Dante paid his respects to the French popes, "ravening wolves in garb of shepherds," and Petrarch with his invective blackened their characters much beyond their deserts. Quite apart from its implication of clerical interference in secular affairs, also, the Petrine theory of the papacy was deeply repugnant to many loyal Catholics because it violated their convictions about spiritual freedom within the church. Finally, the question of ecclesiastical property involved the pope, early in the fourteenth century, in a violent controversy with an influential part of the Franciscan Order on the subject of clerical poverty.[1] All these facts conspired, therefore, to make the nature of spiritual power, and especially the relation of papal absolutism to it, the chief subject of political theory.

The immediate occasion of the next controversy between the pope and a secular ruler was the attempt of John XXII to intervene from Avignon in a disputed imperial election. The quarrel

[1] Following what they believed to be the principles of St. Francis, a considerable part of the Order held that renunciation of property beyond the bare needs of subsistence was necessary to the proper performance of spiritual offices. John XXII declared the position heretical, deposed and excommunicated the General of the Order, and altered its rules. Three chief figures in this controversy — Michael of Cesena, Bonagratia of Bergamo, and William of Occam — became supporters of the emperor.

which thus began in 1323 continued through the pontificates of John XXII and Clement VI and was not settled until after the death of Lewis the Bavarian in 1347. It produced another large body of occasional literature[2] and two figures of lasting importance in the history of political philosophy, Marsilio of Padua and William of Occam. The outcome was another repudiation of the papacy's effort to set itself up as an international arbitral power. In 1338 the Imperial Electors, acting for the first time as a corporation in a capacity not purely electoral, asserted in the Declaration of Rense that an election required no papal confirmation, thus embodying in constitutional law the independence which the emperors since Henry IV had claimed. The Golden Bull, which in 1356 enacted a procedure for imperial elections, omitted all reference to confirmation by the pope, and Innocent VI had no alternative but to concede the point. The powers which Innocent III had claimed in his Bull *Venerabilem* were thus finally lost. The political forces which brought about this result were substantially similar to those that defeated Boniface in his quarrel with the king of France. A rudimentary sentiment of German nationality prevented the pope from finding support among disaffected vassals of the emperor. In Germany the dependence of the pope upon the king of France was bitter even to his defenders, and the desire for reforms in the church was by no means confined to the imperial party.

On the whole, however, the national aspects of the quarrel were less obvious than in the earlier French quarrel, and while systematic writing about German constitutional law is sometimes dated from this period,[3] the most generally interesting point did not arise, because the legal standing of a kingdom, not subject to the empire, was not involved. Of the two most important writers in the emperor's cause, one was by birth an Italian and the other an Englishman, men who owed their training respectively to the Universities of Padua and Oxford, and neither of whom had any real concern for Germany or for the tradition of the empire. For these writers the overt issue — settled by establishing the in-

[2] A list comprising sixty titles is given by R. Scholz, *Unbekannte kirchenpolitischen Streitschriften aus der Zeit Ludwigs des Bayern (1327–1354)*, *Bibliothek des Kgl. preussischen historischen Instituts in Rom,* Vol. X (1914), pp. 576 ff.

[3] See C. H. McIlwain, *op. cit.*, pp. 288 ff., with references there given.

dependence of the Imperial Electors — was almost incidental. Their argument on the principles of political authority had no special application to Germany whatever. Its application was far more to the government of the church and to the Petrine theory of papal power. Already an issue in the work of John of Paris, this problem of papal government and of ecclesiastical reform became the chief question a half century later.

The controversy between John XXII and Lewis the Bavarian permanently changed the center of political discussion. In its course the independence of the temporal from the spiritual authority was settled, except as this question might arise as an incident of national politics in connection with other issues, and the question of absolute monarchy as against representative or constitutional monarchy was definitely raised. The problem was shifted to the relation between a sovereign and the corporate body which he ruled. It is true that this issue concerned as yet only the pope and the subjects of a sovereign power claimed as a special attribute of spiritual authority, and it is also true that as a practical movement the attempt to constitutionalize the church failed. But so far as the theory of political authority is concerned this was not so important as the fact that the center of discussion was changed. Moreover, the failure to reform the church by constitutional means was historically connected with the revolutionary attack upon it in the sixteenth century.

Because the results of the debate were of this sort, the writings of the papal party may be neglected. They dealt largely with the right of the pope to confirm or annul imperial elections and therefore fought a battle already lost. In defense of the absolute power of the pope in the church, there was not much to say that had not already been said by writers like Egidius Colonna. This chapter may therefore be confined to the two great writers who took up the case in behalf of Lewis, Marsilio of Padua and William of Occam. Marsilio's theory is one of the most remarkable creations of medieval political thought and showed for the first time the subversive consequences to which a completely naturalistic interpretation of Aristotle might logically lead. The theory reaches a high level of logical consistency and includes many elements which attained their full importance only much later, but in respect to the state of affairs which existed in 1324, it is often doctrinaire. The theories of William of Occam were less systematic, probably because political questions were for him after all a side issue, but they were on the whole much more closely in touch with contemporary fact than Marsilio's. For this reason they were probably more influential in directing the course which political theory followed in the later fourteenth and fifteenth centuries.

MARSILIO: AVERROIST ARISTOTELIANISM

Marsilio's book, the *Defensor pacis*,[4] was addressed to Lewis the Bavarian and after its publication Marsilio obtained protection in Germany, where he lived during the greater part of his later life, but neither Germany nor the empire is in any distinctive way related to the theory of the book. Indeed, it may well have been begun before the quarrel started between Lewis and the pope, and it might have been nearly the same if that quarrel had never occurred. Mr. Previté-Orton has pointed out that Marsilio's theory of secular government was based directly upon the practice and conceptions of the Italian city-states, and that his discussions of practical questions usually refer to the problems of that form of government. As a patriotic Italian his enmity for the papacy needed no more stimulus from Germany than Dante's, and as a citizen of Padua he need feel no more friendship for the empire than the interests of his city dictated. His bitterness toward the papacy as a cause of disunion in Italy suggests that of Machiavelli two centuries later.[5] He wrote not to defend the empire but to destroy the whole system of papal imperialism that had developed in the practice of Innocent III and the theory of the canon law. His object was to define and limit in the most dras-

[4] Completed in 1324. There are two recent editions: *The Defensor Pacis of Marsilius of Padua,* edited by C. W. Previté-Orton, Cambridge, 1928, and *Marsilius von Padua Defensor Pacis,* Herausgegeben von Richard Scholz (Fontes iuris Germanici antiqui), Hannover, 1933. About 1342 Marsilio wrote a shorter work, called *Defensor minor,* first edited by C. K. Brampton, Birmingham, 1922. The papal condemnation of the *Defensor pacis* named John of Jandun, a professor at Paris and the author of several commentaries on Aristotle from the Averroist point of view, as co-author with Marsilio. There have been numerous efforts to distinguish parts written by John, but both the recent editors (without denying that the two men collaborated) are emphatic in asserting unity of authorship, both on stylistic grounds and because of the well-knit structure of the book.

[5] See, for example, *Defensor pacis,* I, i, 2 and 3.

tic manner the pretensions of the spiritual authority to control, either directly or indirectly, the action of secular governments, and to this end he went farther than any other medieval writer in placing the church under the power of the state. Marsilio might be not inaptly described as the first Erastian.

The philosophical basis for the theory was derived from Aristotle. Marsilio in his introduction evidently thought of his work as a supplement to that part of the *Politics* which discussed the causes of revolution and civil discord. For there was one cause necessarily unknown to Aristotle, he said, namely, the claims of the pope to a supreme power over rulers, and especially those of recent popes, which have filled all Europe, and more particularly Italy, with strife. It is the remedy for this cause of disorder that Marsilio proposes to seek. The Aristotelian principle which he followed most closely was that of the self-sufficing community capable of supplying both its physical and its moral needs. But he brought this to a conclusion fundamentally different from that reached by any other medieval Aristotelian, and it seems probable that this was connected with the influence of Latin Averroism, though it is not as yet known whether any of the earlier Averroists had anticipated the conclusions of the *Defensor pacis*.[6]

The essential characteristics of Latin Averroism were its thoroughgoing naturalism and rationalism. It admitted, indeed, the absolute truth of Christian revelation but it divorced this entirely from philosophy, and unlike St. Thomas, held that the rational conclusions of the latter might be quite contrary to the

[6] Since John of Jandun was the chief representative of the Averroist tradition at Paris in the first quarter of the fourteenth century, there has been a tendency to trace to him passages having this tone, and indeed the part of the work dealing directly with Aristotle. But as Scholz remarks, there is no reason why Marsilio should not have been as much an Averroist as John. Besides Paris, Padua was the chief center of Averroist teaching, and Marsilio had certainly studied there. See Scholz's edition, p. liii. The authoritative work on Latin Averroism is P. Mandonnet's *Siger de Brabant,* 2 vols., 2nd ed., Louvain, 1911. Siger certainly lectured on the *Politics,* for Pierre Dubois heard him (*De recuperatione terre sancte,* sect. 132), but no Averroist commentaries on the work are known. The connection between Averroism and the denial of secular power to the pope is stressed by Martin Grabmann, "Studien über den Einfluss der Aristotelischen Philosophie auf die mittelalterlichen Theorien über das Verhältnis von Kirche und Staat," *Sitzungsberichte der Bayerischen Akademie der Wissenschaften,* Philosophisch-historische Abtl., 1934, Heft 2.

truths of faith. It was responsible therefore for the doctrine of a twofold truth. With this tendency the separation in the *Defensor pacis* of reason and revelation, "which we believe by pure faith without reason,"[7] is quite in accord. On the side of ethics also the Averroists leaned toward a secularism quite at variance with the ecclesiastical tradition, holding — again like the *Defensor pacis* — that "not all the philosophers in the world could prove immortality by demonstration,"[8] that theology contributes nothing to rational knowledge, that happiness is attained in this life without the aid of God, and that moral living according to Aristotle's *Ethics* suffices for salvation.[9] From the point of view of reason, then, and Marsilio is careful to say that this is all that concerns him, human societies are self-sufficing in the fullest sense. Religion has social consequences apart from its truth and may therefore be regulated by society; whatever effects it has in a life to come may be left to the future. From the point of view of Marsilio's naturalistic Aristotelianism spiritual interests are identical with other-worldly interests and they are logically irrelevant. On the other hand, moral or religious concerns that do affect the present life all without exception fall within the control of the human community.

THE STATE

The *Defensor pacis* is divided into two main parts. The first is a statement of Aristotelian principles, though hardly a complete and systematic discussion of all phases of political philosophy. Its purpose is to supply the foundation for the second part in which Marsilio draws his conclusions regarding the church, the functions of priests, their relation to civil authority, and the evils which arise from a misunderstanding of these matters. There is also a short third part in which are stated forty-two theses or conclusions drawn from the theories developed in the first two parts.

Following Aristotle, Marsilio defines the state as a kind of

[7] I, ix, 2.

[8] I, iv, 3.

[9] See Martin Grabmann, "Der lateinische Averroismus des 13. Jahrhunderts und seine Stellung zur christlichen Weltanschauung," *Sitzungsberichte der Bayerischen Akademie der Wissenschaften*, Philosophisch-historische Abtl., 1931, Heft 2.

" living being " composed of parts which perform the functions necessary to its life. Its " health," or peace, consists in the orderly working of each of its parts, and strife arises when one part does its work badly or interferes with another part. He follows also the derivation of the city from the family, the city being a " perfect community " or one able to supply all that is needed for a good life. But the expression, " a good life," has a double meaning: it means good in this life and also in the life to come. The first is the proper study of philosophy by means of reason; knowledge of the second depends on revelation and comes only from faith. Reason shows the need for civil government as a means of peace and order, but there is a need for religion also, which has its uses in this life and is the means of salvation in the life to come. Still following Aristotle, Marsilio then enumerates the classes or parts which cooperate to form a society. There are farmers and artisans who supply material goods and the revenue needed for government; and there are soldiers, officials, and priests who make up the state in a stricter sense. The last class, the clergy, causes special difficulty and its place in society has been especially subject to differences of opinion, because of the twofold purpose of religion and because its other-worldly purpose cannot be comprehended by reason. Nevertheless, all men, Christian and heathen alike, have agreed that there must be a special class devoted to worship. The difference between the Christian clergy and the other priesthoods is simply that, as a matter of faith, Christianity is true while the other religions are not, but from the point of view of philosophy, this extra-rational truth hardly affects the matter. Thus Marsilio reaches a definition of the function of the Christian clergy:

> The function of the clergy is to know and teach those things which, according to Scripture, it is necessary to believe, to do, or to avoid, in order to obtain eternal salvation and escape woe.[10]

It can hardly be denied that Marsilio does follow Aristotle pretty closely, but he arrived at a conclusion widely different from that of any other medieval Aristotelian. So far as Aristotle is concerned, he availed himself of the implicit naturalism of Greek philosophy and supplemented the *Politics,* as he in-

[10] I, vi, 8.

tended, by bringing into the picture a religion which claimed a supernatural sanction. As compared with any other medieval Aristotelian, he has walled off Christianity as, in its essence, supernatural and beyond rational discussion. The contrast with St. Thomas's tendency to harmonize reason and faith is as sharp as possible, and Marsilio has gone far beyond the tendency in John of Paris to limit spiritual powers and duties. The practical importance of Marsilio's conclusion can hardly be exaggerated. Whatever reverence faith may deserve as a means of eternal salvation, it has become from a secular point of view simply irrelevant. Being irrational it cannot be brought into a consideration of rational means and ends, which is exactly the same thing as to say that secular questions have to be decided on their own rational merits without reference to faith.

For political purposes the essential point of Marsilio's conclusion is that, in all secular relations, the clergy is merely one class in society along with all other classes. From a rational point of view he obviously considers the Christian clergy as precisely like any other priesthood, since the truth of what it teaches is beyond reason and applies only to a future life. It follows that in all temporal concerns the control of the clergy by the state is in principle exactly like the control of agriculture or trade. Stated in modern terminology, religion is a social phenomenon; it uses material agencies and produces social consequences. In these respects it is subject to social regulation at need like other human interests. As for its truth, in the sense in which it claims truth, that is a matter about which reasonable men cannot dispute. Such a separation of reason and faith is the direct ancestor of religious skepticism, and in its consequences amounts to a secularism which is both anti-Christian and anti-religious. There is, to be sure, no frontal attack on the spiritual interests which the church professes to serve and which Christians believe to be the ultimate interests of mankind. One may say, if he wishes, that such things are too sacred for reason to touch. But practically there is little difference between too sacred and too trivial. The church is a part of the secular state in every respect in which it affects temporal matters.

LAW AND THE LEGISLATOR

Marsilio next proceeds to carry forward the radical distinction of spirituals and temporals into his definition of law. In the *Defensor pacis* he distinguishes four kinds of law, though the important point is rather a twofold distinction between divine law and human law. In the *Defensor minor,* written later, he presented the argument more pointedly, though to the same effect. Law is of two sorts, either divine or human:

> Divine law is a command of God directly, without human deliberation, about voluntary acts of human beings to be done or avoided in this world but for the sake of attaining the best end, or some condition desirable for man, in the world to come.[11]
>
> Human law is a command of the whole body of citizens, or of its prevailing part, arising directly from the deliberation of those empowered to make law, about voluntary acts of human beings to be done or avoided in this world, for the sake of attaining the best end, or some condition desirable for man, in this world. I mean a command the transgression of which is enforced in this world by a penalty or punishment imposed on the transgressor.[12]

In these definitions the two kinds of law are distinguished by the kind of penalties entailed. Divine law is sanctioned by the rewards or punishments which will be meted out by God in a future life. It follows that there is no earthly penalty for its violation but only a penalty beyond the grave. Human law, therefore, is not derived from divine law but is contrasted with it. Any rule that involves an earthly penalty belongs *ipso facto* to human law and has its authority from human enactment. This is a point of vital importance for the later argument because from it results the conclusion that the spiritual teaching of priests is not properly a power or authority, since it lacks coercive force in this life, unless, of course, a human legislator delegates such a power to priests. Marsilio's definitions of law are extraordinary also because of the weight which they give to the elements of command and sanction, the will of the legislator and his power to impose his will. He notes, indeed, that the word law is used to mean a rule of reason or of intrinsic justice, but he clearly regards law, at least in its juristic sense, as characterized by its emanating

[11] *Defensor minor,* i, 2.

[12] *Ibid.,* i, 4.

from a constituted authority and carrying a penalty for its violation. Marsilio's treatment of law is in the sharpest contrast with that of Thomas, which presented divine and human law as all of a piece and stressed the rational derivation of human law from the law of nature.

Law then implies a legislator and Marsilio next inquires who the human legislator is. The answer brings him to the heart of his political theory:

> The legislator, or first and proper efficient cause of law, is the people or whole body of citizens, or a prevailing part of it, commanding and deciding by its own choice or will in a general assembly and in set terms that something among the civil acts of human beings be done or omitted, on pain of a penalty or temporal punishment.[13]

Human law arises by the corporate action of a people setting up rules to govern the acts of its members, or conversely, a state is the body of men who owe obedience to a given body of law.[14] The result is the same whether law be used to define the state, or the state to define law, since either implies a corporate body competent to control the behavior of its members. The source of legal authority is always the people or its prevailing part, even though it act in a particular case through a commission (or, in the case of the empire, through the emperor) to which it has delegated its authority. There can be little doubt that Marsilio was thinking primarily of government in a city-state, though apparently he saw no difficulty in applying his definition to any state.

In the definition just given, two expressions call for explanation. The word legislator has a deceptively modern suggestion which it could hardly have had for Marsilio. What he presumably means is that the whole people makes its law in the sense that all authority is to be conceived as the act of the people and is to be exercised in their name. Thus he expressly provides for the case in which a commission acts with derivative authority. The conception was common in city-states, as when an Athenian jury was addressed simply as "Athenians," and it was carried over to explain the legislative power of the Roman emperor. Also it was not very different from the medieval fiction by which the whole

[13] *Defensor pacis,* I, xii, 3. [14] *Defensor minor,* xii, 1.

realm was supposed to be consulted in a parliament. Presumably Marsilio thought of a people's legislation as including custom, which he elsewhere names as a part of law. The other expression which might be misleading is the "prevailing part" (*pars valentior*) by which the legislator decides. This is emphatically not a numerical majority, as some commentators have imagined. For Marsilio enlarged his definition with the words, "I say the prevailing part, both their number and quality in the community being taken into account."[15] He meant literally the part which carries the greatest weight, with not the least thought that everybody should count for one. The magnates would naturally carry a greater weight than the commonalty, though numbers properly count for something. The idea is essentially Aristotelian as well as medieval.

The executive and judicial part of government (*principatus* or *pars principans*) Marsilio regards as set up or elected by the body of citizens (*legislator*). The manner of election follows the custom of each state, but in all cases the authority of the executive is derived from the legislative act of the whole body. Hence it is essential that this authority should be exercised in accordance with law and that its duties and powers should be such as the people determine. It is the duty of the executive to see that every part of the state performs its proper function for the good of the whole, and if it fails it may be removed by the same power which elected it, namely, the people. Marsilio's preference for an elective as compared with an hereditary monarchy is explicit, but even here he is thinking of city-states rather than the empire, of which he speaks rather slightingly. But above all, the executive, however it may be organized, must be unified and supreme, so that its power may exceed that of any faction, but particularly so that it may proceed as a unit in administering the law. Such unity is absolutely necessary to the state as an organized body and without it strife and disorder are sure to result. This part of Marsilio's theory has reference to the lack of unity prevalent in medieval government and probably especially to the difficulties arising from the twofold jurisdiction of secular and ecclesiastical courts.

[15] The words *et qualitate* were omitted from the earlier printed editions. On the meaning of the two expressions discussed in this paragraph see McIlwain, *op. cit.*, pp. 300 ff.

The unity of the state is a necessary premise for his own treatment of spiritual authority in the second part of his book.

This completes Marsilio's outline of the natural or self-sufficing political community. It is an organic whole composed of classes, including everything within itself, both physical and ethical, that is needed for its continued existence and the good life, in a secular sense, of its citizens. Its power of legislation is the inevitable right of such a corporation to regulate its own parts for the well-being of the whole. Its executive power is the agent of the corporation to put into effect whatever the unity of the state requires; and because of this unity there is no room for differences of jurisdiction or dispersion of power. From a secular point of view the community is absolutely self-sufficient and absolutely omnipotent. It is the guardian of its own life and its own civilization, in every sense in which civilization has any meaning or consequences on earth. If its citizens have a "spiritual" well-being, this belongs in another world and another life, beyond the life of the state, indeed, but also powerless to touch that life. With this conception of human society and its government Marsilio turns to the real purpose of his book, to consider the spiritual life as he believed it to be misconceived by the church. With it he proposes to check the incursions of the spiritual authority into the concerns of the self-sufficient community and to lay bare the greatest of all the causes of civic strife and disorder, which had been unknown to the master philosopher.

THE CHURCH AND THE CLERGY

Since every official of the corporate community possesses his authority only by the mandate, mediate or immediate, of the people, it follows that the clergy, as such, have no coercive power whatever. If they are permitted to exercise such power — and when Marsilio wrote many important relationships were regulated by ecclesiastical law — they are acting as delegates of the civil power. The clergy, being themselves merely a class set apart to perform religious service, are subject to regulation like any other class, and like laymen they are amenable to the civil courts for violations of human law. Within the meaning of human law there is, strictly speaking, no such thing as a spiritual offence. Such offences are judged by God only in a future life and the penalties are incurred beyond the grave. If spiritual offenses incur an earthly penalty, and of course they may do so by human legislation, they become *ipso facto* offenses against human law. Heresy, therefore, if it is punished in this world, is a civil offense; its spiritual penalty is damnation but this is beyond the power of the clergy or any human judge. Similarly Marsilio argues that excommunication belongs wholly to the civil power. In short, his theory makes a clean sweep of the canon law as a distinct jurisdiction. In so far as it is really a divine law, its penalties are otherworldly; in so far as it assesses earthly penalties, it is a part of human law and so within the power of the secular community. The duty which the clergy has to perform Marsilio compares to the advice of a physician. Apart from the celebration of religious rites, the clergy can merely advise and instruct; they can admonish the wicked and point out the future consequences of sin, but they cannot compel men to do penance. No other writer in the Middle Ages went so far as Marsilio in thus setting apart the spiritual and religious from the legal.

Marsilio is equally sweeping in his destruction of the church's temporal establishment. The church can hardly be said to own property at all. Ecclesiastical property is of the nature of a grant or subsidy made by the community to support public worship. Thus a project put forward by Pierre Dubois to be accomplished by agreement between the pope and the king of France is deduced by Marsilio from his theory of the self-sufficing community. It is obvious of course that, from Marsilio's point of view, the clergy have no right to tithes, or any right of exemption from taxation, except as it is granted by the community. Ecclesiastical office, like ecclesiastical property, is within the gift of civil officers. He holds also that the clergy can be legally compelled to perform the offices of religion, so long as they receive their benefices, and every ecclesiastical officer, from the pope down, can be deposed by civil action. It was not without reason that the ill-judged and ill-starred attack of Lewis on the church during his Roman expedition in 1327–30, including his effort to secure the election of an antipope with the suffrages of a Roman mob, was attributed to Marsilio's advice and regarded as a doctrinaire attempt to put the *Defensor pacis* into practice. The notion that Marsilio's political philosophy was a defense of religious liberty is wholly fallacious. The national despots of the Reformation period, lawless as they were, rarely went to the lengths that his theory would warrant. Its upshot would be to subject religion to a thorough-going regimentation by civil power.

It is not quite true to say, however, that Marsilio proposed to treat the church merely as a branch of the state, for this would imply as many churches as there are states. In 1324 a national church would have seemed a strange anomaly even to a skeptic like Marsilio, to say nothing of a church for every independent city. His theory is a root-and-branch attack upon the ecclesiastical hierarchy and especially upon a papal *plenitudo potestatis*, but he recognized that, even for spiritual purposes and to resolve spiritual questions, the church requires some organization distinct from the civil community. The problem causes some difficulties, both practical and theoretical, because a universal church consorts ill with a congeries of self-sufficing communities, typically city-states, such as Marsilio envisaged. It is hard to see how the church is to be organized, without an independent hierarchy and with its spiritual judgments wholly dependent upon distinct civil powers for their effect. Like many Protestants after him, Marsilio was really in a position where he ought to have remitted all religious questions to private judgment and regarded the church as a purely voluntary organization, but it is hardly surprising that he did not draw in the fourteenth century a conclusion which Protestants refused to draw in the sixteenth. He lived in a day when only the discontented were looking even as far as a General Council of the church to cure the evils which they attributed to the hierarchy.

The ecclesiastical hierarchy, from Marsilio's point of view, is obviously of human origin and has its authority from human law. As an arrangement of earthly ranks and powers it is drawn completely within the sphere of civil control. Hence the hierarchy, or even the priesthood, is not the church. The church is composed of the whole body of Christian believers both lay and clerical. Thus Marsilio continued in some sense the Christian tradition of two organizations of the same society, though he stripped the church of its coercive power. Even the laity, Marsilio says, are churchmen (*viri ecclesiastici*), an expression which suggests Martin Luther's phrase, "the priesthood of the Christian man." But since all distinctions of rank among the clergy arise by human institution, in respect to their strictly spiritual character all priests are equal. Neither a bishop nor a pope has any spiritual quality that a simple priest does not have. The "priestly character" which authorizes them to celebrate the rites of religion is a purely mystical stigma, proceeding directly from God or Christ, having no earthly origin and carrying with it no earthly power or ecclesiastical rank. Marsilio thus generalized an argument which John of Paris had already used to reduce the pope to spiritual equality with other bishops, and by so doing he eliminated from the spiritual all reference to ecclesiastical rank. *A fortiori* he eliminated papal sovereignty from the organization of the church. He denied absolutely that the pope has any authority as the successor of Peter, or that Peter had any preeminence over the other Apostles. In a rather remarkable bit of historical analysis he denied that there is any reliable evidence that Peter ever was in Rome and still less that he was bishop. The preeminence of the church at Rome he attributes to its situation in the capital of the empire.

With this complete rejection of the spiritual powers of the hierarchy and the pope there went also, very naturally, a low estimate of the sacerdotal aspect of religion and a tendency to treat it as if the inner experience itself were sufficient. It is hard to tell, however, whether this corresponds to a strong conviction on Marsilio's part or whether it represents merely the tendency of a rationalist to confine religion as narrowly as possible. In treating the confessional, penance, indulgence, absolution, and excommunication he stressed the view that repentance for sin and forgiveness by God are the only essentials. Without these the ceremony is powerless, and if a sinner has made his peace with God, absolution is complete without the ceremony. Similarly he showed somewhat the same enmity for the canon law as his two contemporaries, Dante and William of Occam, and as Luther after him. The Bible, or perhaps more narrowly the New Testament, he regarded as the only source of revelation and hence as the only text of divine law; papal decretals would either not be law at all or, if given the sanction of the community, would be a part of human law. Accordingly only beliefs contained in Scripture, or clearly implied by it, are necessary to salvation.

These opinions, so suggestive of later Protestant belief, show how fully the Reformation was prepared in the two preceding centuries of the Middle Ages.

THE GENERAL COUNCIL

There is then for Marsilio still a core of Christian belief upon which the church must be able to speak authoritatively, and for which his theory must provide a human institution. For this purpose, like others of the fourteenth and fifteenth centuries who were convinced of the shortcomings of the hierarchy, he chose a General Council, which he regarded as the organ of the church for deciding such disputes. He is unwilling that the pope and the hierarchy, being merely human agents, should be permitted to pass on disputed articles of faith. To the church itself as a corporate body, or more narrowly to a General Council, he is willing to concede — a little naively, it must be admitted, if this part of his theory is to be taken seriously — a mystical infallibility, the one point of contact between reason and faith which the prevailing rationalism of his system permitted. In a General Council, he chose to assume, inspiration would join hands with reason to supply an authoritative version of the divine law contained in Scripture and a satisfactory answer to the reasonable differences of opinion that might arise about such matters. On this point William of Occam was more acute than Marsilio, for William perceived that in matters of faith a council, being itself a human institution, could no more be counted infallible than the pope.

Marsilio's theory of the church is therefore a bit of patchwork in his system. He transfers to the church an element of his political theory, assuming that the whole body of Christian believers, like the whole body of citizens in a state, is a corporation (*universitas*) and that the General Council, like the political executive, is its delegate. The difficulty is that this transference requires citizens to figure as the members of two corporations, their respective states and the universal church, and there is really nothing in his theory of society to account for this kind of dual citizenship. It is a concession to the fact that Marsilio's theory was more purely secular than the prevailing conception of the society to which he had to apply it. In respect to organization the important difference which he makes between the church and the state is that the council is a representative body. He proposes that all the main territorial divisions (*provinciae*) of Christendom shall choose representatives, as their rulers shall direct, and in proportion to the numbers and quality of their Christian population. These representatives shall include both churchmen and laymen and shall be men of approved life and learned in the divine law. They are to meet in a convenient place, as their rulers shall direct, and shall decide in the light of Scripture any dubious matters of belief or religious practice likely to cause strife among Christians, and their decisions shall be binding on all, and more particularly on priests. But Marsilio's General Council, perhaps as he himself intended, is really dependent upon secular governments, for it is called by their cooperation, and its decisions, if they need to be enforced, depend upon coercion supplied by the states. The authority of a General Council is as nebulous as the corporation of all Christian believers of which it was the organ. The truth is that Marsilio's conception of European society provided no real basis for an international organization like the church. In this respect, in providing a theory for a General Council, he provided also the reasons why, when the theory was tried, it proved to be merely a paper constitution, impractical because of the national jealousies and particularism which it lacked the force to unite. Effective as a destructive attack on the spiritual authority of the hierarchy, it was ineffective as a means of restoring the unity of the Christian commonwealth of the Middle Ages.

Few theorists in any age, and none in the Middle Ages, cared to go as far as Marsilio in whittling down the spiritual freedom which formed the permanently important claim fostered by Christianity. Not until the Erastian theories of the seventeenth century, such for instance as that of Hobbes, was there an equally consistent attempt to reduce religion to an ineffectual private faith, with overt action wholly in the control of secular government. Essentially his political philosophy was a recrudescence of the theory of a city-state, competent to regulate every branch of its civilization. In this respect it represented the purest form of a naturalistic Aristotelianism that medieval philosophy produced, and it suggested the revived paganism of the Italian renaissance, which appeared full grown in Machiavelli two centuries later. It is true that his theory as a whole is something of a compromise. His citizens still appear as members of two corporations, the state and the church. The latter, however, has wholly lost its authority, though the idea is still preserved that a common belief and a universal ecclesiastical discipline can be maintained. Marsilio's state is therefore not quite a separate secular institution, obligated to keep its hands off religious faith, as his church is certainly not a purely voluntary association with no need for coercive power. His self-sufficing human community is in the dangerous position of having to act as an agent of a supernatural church. That this was an impossible position experience was to reveal. Papal absolutism might be disposed of as a fictitious spiritual claim, but only on the condition that secular governments would grant to their subjects a much larger measure of religious freedom than Marsilio ever contemplated.

WILLIAM: THE FREEDOM OF THE CHURCH

The nature of the struggle against the papal *plenitudo potestatis* in the fourteenth century is more apparent in the works of Marsilio's great contemporary, William of Occam,[16] than in the *Defensor pacis*. William's theory is less complete and less consistently worked out than Marsilio's, and it is more difficult to get at, spread as it is through controversial works of enormous size. A political philosophy was never a primary object with William, since he was first and foremost a dialectician and a theologian. But perhaps because he did not try to make a systematic

[16] There is no collected edition of the works of William of Occam but his political writings are in process of being published: *Guillelmi de Ockham opera politica,* ed. by J. G. Sikes, Vol. I, Manchester, 1940. Several of his tracts, not previously published, were printed with analyses by Richard Scholz in *Unbekannte kirchenpolitische Streitschriften aus der Zeit Ludwigs des Bayern (1327–1354), Bibliothek des kgl. preuss. historischen Instituts in Rom,* Vols. IX (1911), X (1914). One of these, *De imperatorum et pontificum potestate,* was edited also by C. Kenneth Brampton, Oxford, 1926; re-issued 1930. Both editions of this work lacked the final chapter, which was separately printed in *Archivum Franciscanum Historicum,* anno XVII, fasc. 1, p. 72. A tract of which the last part is lacking, *Breviloquium de potestate papae,* was edited by L. Baudry in *Études de philosophie médiévale,* Vol. XXIV (1937). The largest collection of William's controversial tracts is contained in the second volume of Melchior Goldast's *Monarchia Sancti Imperii Romani,* 3 vols., Hanau and Frankfort, 1611–14; re-issued 1621 and 1668.

theory of the state, his views were less doctrinaire than Marsilio's sometimes are. Probably he represented more typically than Marsilio the reaction of a large body of Christian opinion to the papal imperialism which, as he conceived, had ended so disastrously for the church and for Europe. Specifically William spoke for the part of the Franciscan Order, the so-called "Spirituals," who defended clerical poverty and who had been excommunicated by John XXII. He was therefore the spokesman of a type which figured largely in the political writing of later centuries: a minority persecuted, as they believed, for conscience' sake and appealing in the name of liberty to enlightened public opinion against constituted authority. His question, therefore, was essentially the rights of subjects against their rulers, the limitation of sovereign papal authority in matters of faith, and the right of a minority to resist coercion. For William papal sovereignty is, from the standpoint of Christianity, a heresy, and from the standpoint of policy, a disastrous innovation that has filled all Europe with strife, has destroyed Christian freedom, and has led to an invasion of the rights of secular rulers. The last point, however, is not the most important. His primary purpose was to assert the independence of the whole body of Christian believers against the pretensions of an heretical pope. The issue is between the universal and apostolic church and the "Church of Avignon."

In this connection William's general philosophical position is not without importance. The breaking down of Thomas's closely knit structure of reason and faith, of science, philosophy, and theology, was not in the first instance due to an effort to liberate reason but rather to an effort to liberate faith. Even in Thomas's lifetime his ambitious plan of synthesis failed to win the assent of many contemporaries, chief among them the great philosopher of the Franciscan Order, Duns Scotus. William continued in the tradition that Scotus began. As compared with Thomas both men greatly sharpened the distinction between reason and faith. The contrast depended upon the fact that they thought of theology as having to do mainly with supernatural things, known only to faith through revelation and having mainly moral uses, while they confined philosophy more definitely to theoretical truths which are within the power of unaided natural reason. The tendency was similar to that which reached a climax in Latin

Averroism, already mentioned as having influenced the Aristotelianism of Marsilio, but the Occamists managed to remain somewhat precariously within the bounds of orthodoxy. Though they held that important dogmas like God and immortality were indemonstrable, they at least stopped short of the Averroist doctrine of a twofold truth. But the total effect was none the less destructive of Thomas's system: Reason gained its freedom by vindicating for faith the large but shadowy realm of the unknownable. Closely connected with this separation of reason and faith was a sharper distinction between reason and will, both in psychology and in theology. In man and in God William regarded the will as a force and spontaneous power of action not determined by any reasons whatever and in consequence he referred the moral difference between good and evil to the will of God. The implications of this for legal theory were important, since it seems to identify law with legislative fiat, but there is a question how far William actually carried his metaphysics over into his theory of law.[17]

Despite the subversive tendency of William's philosophy as a whole, his political theory was essentially conservative in intention. In his effort to vindicate Christian freedom against the pope he moved within a circle of ideas well known to his time. He argued against papal absolutism as an innovation and a heresy, and he marshalled against it views for which he claimed, not without truth, a common acceptance. William's argument stood upon the ancient distinction and independence of the spiritual and temporal authorities, and on the assumption that independence was feasible while each power was granted a large and ill-defined discretion for correcting the faults of the other. Mutual support and comity between the two powers, provided each acted within the limits set by divine and natural law, still seemed to him possible. The circumstances under which he wrote caused him to argue for a representative check upon what he regarded as the arbitrary exercise of papal power, but he had no real objection to a large discretionary power even in the pope, provided only it

[17] See O. Gierke, *Political Theories of the Middle Age,* trans. by F. W. Maitland, pp. 172, n. 256. M. A. Shepard, " William of Occam and the Higher Law," *American Political Science Review,* Vol. XXVI (1932), p. 1009, takes issue with Gierke.

were exercised by one whom he could admit to be a true pope. In other words, the legal definition of the two jurisdictions seems not to have interested him greatly. The essential questions were for him theological rather than juristic.

A similar indefiniteness may be noticed in his treatment of the empire. He denied of course that the emperor's power was in any sense derivative from the pope, that the ceremony of coronation added to his lawful authority, and that papal confirmation of an election was necessary. In other words, he derived the emperor's power from the election itself, the College of Electors standing in the place of the " people " and speaking for them. In this general sense he conceived of the imperial power — indeed any royal power — as arising from the consent of a corporate body of subjects, expressed through their magnates. Because of his standing controversy with the pope, William attributed very great powers to the emperor to intervene for the sake of reforming the church, but he evidently regarded these as exceptional and for use in an emergency, such as he believed the existing situation to be. On the whole he stood upon the traditional distinction of the two powers, leaving the question of definition very much where it had always been. In the same way he had practically nothing definite to say about the relation between the emperor and the national kingdoms of France and England. He attributed a vague precedence to the emperor over other kings but as an Englishman he certainly had no sentiment for Germany. His writing lacked the traces of national feeling apparent in much that had been written by Frenchmen in defense of Philip the Fair, and also the enthusiasm for the city-state, which may often be felt in Marsilio. In this respect also William stood definitely in the older medieval tradition.

The basis of his political ideas was the rooted and almost universal medieval dislike of arbitrary power, or of force exercised outside the framework of what was felt to be law. In this respect his principles were substantially identical with those of St. Thomas. The whole body of the law included, for William as for Thomas, both the revealed will of God and the principles of natural reason, the dictates of natural equity and the common practices of civilized nations, as well as the special customs and positive law of particular peoples. Together it all formed a single system, flexible in its details, allowing for changes of time and circumstance but without felt violations of the underlying principles. The law of a single people falls within this great system; it can never justly establish a rule contrary to natural law, though it may provide in the spirit of reason and equity for new conditions as they arise. The law therefore provides potentially for every contingency, and all exercise of authority must be justified by the common good and by its consonance with natural justice and sound morals. Without this sanction force is arbitrary and government becomes, to use St. Augustine's telling phrase, " highway robbery on a large scale." This is the conception, characteristic of all medieval political thought, that underlies William's opposition to the acts of the pope. John has exceeded his power; he has set up dogmas in defiance of Scripture and has invaded the eternal rights of secular rulers and of Christians everywhere.[18] The pope, who styles himself " the servant of the servants of God," has become a mere tyrant.

THE CONCILIAR THEORY

In his belief in the omnipotence of law William represented a conviction almost universal in the fourteenth century. He was important mainly because of his determined opposition to what he held to be tyranny in the church, because of the latitude of Christian freedom which he was led to assert, and incidentally because of his desire to provide the church with a government which could less arbitrarily decide moot points of Christian belief and practice. Here too he was more concerned with doctrinal questions than with forms of government. Essentially his position was a defense of critical scholarship and of the enlightened judgment of Christendom against the fiat of constituted authority. He was confronted by a dilemma: a pope who claimed to be infallible and who was widely held to be so but who was, in William's judgment, a heretic. It followed that papal judgments are not always valid. Like most men in the fourteenth century who were dissatisfied with the religion of the church, he could see

[18] See the account of William's theory of the higher law by M. A. Shepard. cited above, in the *Am. Pol. Sci. Rev.,* Vol. XXVI (1932), pp. 1005 ff., and Vol. XXVII (1933), pp. 24 ff. I am unable to see that William added materially to the prevailing belief of his time in respect to the sanctity of law.

no expedient more practical than a General Council to check and, as it were, to constitutionalize, the power of the hierarchy. With the beginning of the Great Schism in 1378 this became the great issue in ecclesiastical politics, for which William's theories, like those of John of Paris and Marsilio, prepared the way. But William was too acute to suppose that any practical expedient could solve a logical difficulty. He was no more ready to grant the infallibility of a council than of the pope, for even a council might err, though in so far as it represented the wisdom of Christendom, it would be less likely to do so. William was really posing a larger question: How can human beings ever be sure that they have reached the absolute truth?

On this point, however, he had really no doubts. Like all scholastic philosophers he had an implicit belief in reason, and also an abiding trust that Christian faith could establish its validity by its own inherent authority. The final judgment in a moot point of doctrine he conceived to lie in the living body of the church, continuous throughout its whole history, and the recipient of a divine revelation. The unique source from which this revelation can be learned is Scripture, in comparison with which the decretals of the popes or even the decisions of councils have only secondary value. Like all the earlier Protestants he assumed unquestioningly that sound scholarship and honest research would bring to light religious truth which would commend itself to all men of good will. Inquiry is not only a right but a duty, and the decision belongs to the wisest, not to any constituted power. There was, of course, for William no question of a literal freedom of belief, for he assumed that with proper search what must be believed would be apparent. But there must be freedom to search and by implication freedom to judge. Hence for him the great political problem of the age was the curbing of papal absolutism. Only if clergy and laymen could unite to lay down just limits to papal power could peace be restored between the pope and Christendom. For this end the best expedient that he could see was a constitutionalized form of church government by means of a General Council representing the sound body of Christian scholarship and belief.

The council William proposed to make broadly representative. He said explicitly that it must include laymen as well as the clergy, and he has no objection even to including women. The basis of representation should be the great number of corporations, such as parishes or monasteries or cathedral chapters, into which the membership of the church falls. Certainly William had no thought of representing Christians individually, as so many discrete units, or territorially, as the inhabitants of such and such districts. A corporate body (*communitas*), he says, can act as a whole and also through its chosen representatives. What he proposed, therefore, was a rough plan of what might be called indirect representation: the religious corporations of some convenient district, such as a diocese or kingdom, should choose representatives to a provincial synod, which in turn should choose representatives in a General Council. Unorganized as the plan seems in comparison with modern electoral machinery, it might be feasible so long as the constituent corporations were sufficiently well marked and well unified. William was, in fact, drawing upon contemporary experience both in the church and in the state. Medieval parliaments represented essentially the communes of the realm, such as boroughs and counties, not as territorial districts but as corporate bodies. But William's plan for a General Council was probably based even more directly upon the government of the two great Mendicant Orders. The houses of the Dominican Order were organized by provinces and by the middle of the thirteenth century there was already a well developed electoral system for choosing representatives to the various assemblies. The Franciscan Order, to which William himself belonged, adopted a similar plan, and in the course of the thirteenth century some such plan of representation was widely used by various monastic orders.[19] The conciliar plan was therefore a scheme for extending in the church generally a device already widely in use and one quite in accord with the prevailing idea that corporate bodies could act and speak as units. Unfortunately there were special obstacles that made it unsuccessful when applied to the whole church, though it was a very natural device for ecclesiastical reformers to adopt.

The political philosophy of William of Occam was characteristic

[19] Ernest Barker, *The Dominican Order and Convocation* (1913), Part I. On the growth of representative institutions see C. H. McIlwain, "Medieval Estates," in *Cambridge Medieval History*, Vol. VII (1932), ch. 23.

of the state of political thought in the mid-fourteenth century, both for what it saw and for what it failed to see. It still moved within the limits of the old discussion about the relation between *imperium* and *sacerdotium,* though anything approaching a general control by the papacy over the secular kingdoms was already a thing of the past. Yet it brought into the center of political discussion the relationship between a sovereign and his subjects and the right of the latter to resist on grounds of conscience and in defense of what they held to be Christian truth. It was in the nature of the case that this issue should first have been drawn within the church. For the theory of papal *plenitudo potestatis* was the first definite claim in the Middle Ages to a power that was absolute, indefeasible, and sovereign. As such it was repugnant both to medieval conviction and practice, and the controversy with the spiritual Franciscans marshalled against it the weight of ancient tradition and current belief. The Great Schism which followed produced in the church the first great controversy between the claims of sovereignty and the principle of constitutional and representative government.

SELECTED BIBLIOGRAPHY

The Dominican Order and Convocation: A Study of the Growth of Representation in the Church during the Thirteenth Century. By Ernest Barker. Oxford, 1913.

"Marsiglio of Padua. Part I. Life." By C. Kenneth Brampton. In the *Eng. Hist. Rev.,* Vol. XXXVII (1922), p. 501.

The De imperatorum et pontificum potestate of William of Ockham. Ed. by C. Kenneth Brampton. Oxford, 1927. Introduction.

A History of Mediaeval Political Theory in the West. By R. W. Carlyle and A. J. Carlyle. 6 vols. London, 1903–1936. Vol. VI, Part I.

Marsilio da Padova: studi raccolti nel VI centenario della morte. Ed. by Aldo Checchini and Norberto Bobbio. Padua, 1942.

The Defensor Pacis of Marsiglio of Padua: A Critical Study. By Ephraim Emerton. Cambridge, Mass., 1920.

Reason and Revelation in the Middle Ages. By Étienne Gilson. New York, 1938.

The Social and Political Ideas of some Great Mediaeval Thinkers. Ed. by F. J. C. Hearnshaw. London, 1923. Ch. 7.

La renaissance de l'esprit laïque au déclin du moyen âge. By Georges de Lagarde. 6 vols. Vienna and Paris, 1934–1946. Vol. II. Marsile de Padoue; ou, Le premier théoricien de l'état laïque; Vols. IV–VI. L'individualisme ockhamiste.

The Medieval Contribution to Political Thought: Thomas Aquinas, Marsilius of Padua, Richard Hooker. By Alexander Passerin d'Entrèves. Oxford, 1939. Chs. 3, 4.

Illustrations of the History of Medieval Thought and Learning. By R. L. Poole. 2nd ed. rev. London, 1920. Ch. 9.

"Marsiglio of Padua. Part II. Doctrines." By C. W. Previté-Orton. In the *Eng. Hist. Rev.*, Vol. XXXVIII (1923), p. 1.

Die literarischen Widersacher der Päpste zur Zeit Ludwig des Baiers: Ein Beitrag zur Geschichte der Kämpfe zwischen Staat und Kirche. By S. Riezler. Leipzig, 1874.

Unbekannte kirchenpolitische Streitschriften aus der Zeit Ludwigs des Bayern (1327–1354). By Richard Scholz. 2 vols. Rome, 1911–14.

"William of Occam and the Higher Law." By Max A. Shepard. In *Am. Pol. Sci. Rev.*, Vol XXVI (1932), p. 1005; Vol. XXVII (1933), p. 24.

Die Staatstheorie des Marsilius von Padua: Ein Beitrag zur Erkenntnis der Staatslehre im Mittelalter. By L. Stieglitz. Leipzig, 1914.

"Marsiglio of Padua and William of Ockham." By James Sullivan. In *Am. Hist. Rev.*, Vol. II (1896–97), pp. 409, 593.

"Germany: Lewis the Bavarian." By W. T. Waugh. In the *Cambridge Medieval History,* Vol. VII (1932), ch. 4.

CHAPTER XVI

THE CONCILIAR THEORY OF CHURCH GOVERNMENT

In the century which followed the writings of William of Occam the controversy over absolute papal authority in the church was spread far and wide through Europe, so that it became the subject of a vast and popular debate. The absolute power of the pope in the church was no academic question, touching merely the abstract rights of his ecclesiastical subjects. It meant the tightening up of the whole process of government, including papal control over the giving of benefices, the drawing of ecclesiastical cases into the papal courts, the diversion of great sums of money into the papal revenues, and the systematic exercise of irritating forms of papal taxation. Thus the luxury of the papal court and the venality of papal government became the ground of bitter criticism, as they continued to be down to the Reformation. The Great Schism, which lasted from 1378 to 1417, made matters worse; it would be hard to exaggerate its effects on popular thought everywhere in Europe. The spectacle of two and sometimes three rival popes, often no more than appendages to dynastic and national ambitions, using all the arts of theological invective and political chicanery against each other, must have gone far to destroy the respect in which the papal office had traditionally been held. Moreover, the whole ecclesiastical organization became infected with corruptions and abuses, partly the result of the Schism itself, which tended to bring the clergy generally into disrepute. Chaucer's Pardoner and Summoner are examples of the disreputable hangers-on of the church as they appeared to a fourteenth-century literary man.

THE REFORM OF THE CHURCH

Here then was a problem of government — in the church rather than the state, to be sure — which was certain to be debated from one end of Europe to the other, and by men of all social classes and all degrees of learning. "The reform of the church in head and members" was a popular question. The discussion of it may not unreasonably be called the first great movement of popular political education. Wycliffe (c. 1320–1384) in England and John Hus (c. 1373–1415) in Bohemia attracted great popular followings, and their teaching was by no means confined to those who could read their crabbed scholastic philosophy. Yet there was a direct transference of ideas from the polemical writings of the days of Lewis the Bavarian to Wycliffe and through him to Hus. The papal Bull of 1377, which condemned Wycliffe's conclusions, traced his opinions to Marsilio "of damned memory," and he himself acknowledged indebtedness to William of Occam and the spiritual Franciscans. National questions, peculiar to England or Bohemia, traversed each reformer's purposes, but behind these lay common problems, such as the ownership and taxation of church property and the exactions of papal taxation. And with both reformers the animus of their thought was opposition to ceremonialism, to the monopoly of spiritual authority by the hierarchy, and to the absolute power of the pope. Without having any definite theory of church government, both Wycliffe and Hus united in identifying the church with the whole body of Christians, lay as well as clerical. It is the church and not the hierarchy that is the recipient of divine law and spiritual power. The spiritual bond of this society, the direct relation of the believer to God, expressed in faith and good works, is all that gives weight to religious observance, not the ceremonial or the sacrament. "Crown and cloth make no priest . . . but the power that Christ giveth." The church as a perfect society must include the powers needed for its own regeneration, and for this reason it must be right for laymen to reform evil manners in the clergy.

The independence and self-sufficiency of the church in spiritual matters was therefore a ground for anti-clericalism. By an even stranger paradox it was made a ground for strengthening secular power. The mechanics of this result was simple: the reformer discovered that he was dependent on royal support to coerce the pope and the hierarchy, even in the interest of reform. It was thus that Martin Luther was thrown into the arms of the German princes, and that the divine right of the king became almost an official philosophy for Lutherans and Anglicans. Even in the fourteenth century Wycliffe was pressed in the same direction, though for more than a century men would still pin their hope of reform to a General Council within the church. The king, he argued,[1] is the vicar of God and to resist him is wicked. Even bishops derive their power from him, and so far as this world is concerned, the royal power is of greater dignity than that of priests, for a spiritual power requires neither earthly power nor property. Hence it is the right and the duty of the king to remedy abuses in the government of the church. This language is at once reminiscent of the *York Tracts* and suggestive of the argument which ultimately made the king the temporal head of a national church. In the long run the political beneficiary of a spiritualized religion was the secular power itself, and the first result of freeing the church from the control of the hierarchy was to place it more completely in the power of the king.

The reform movements led by Wycliffe and Hus thus had the effect of transferring the question of papal power, and all its innumerable ramifications, to the forum of popular discussion. For this reason it is not irrelevant to mention in this connection the appearance, below the level of respectable political philosophy, of a sort of proletarian doctrine of equality, connected with the religious issue but going far beyond it in the direction of an attack upon social and economic distinctions. Such ideas appeared in the peasant revolts of the fourteenth century, in France in 1351 and in England in 1381. These revolts, the result of bitter economic pressure and of unjust taxation and labor legislation, had always their obscure sense of the opposition between class-interests:

> When Adam delved and Evé span,
> Who was then the gentleman?

Even earlier in date the moralist continuator of the *Romance of the Rose* could assert:

> Naked and impotent are all,
> High-born or peasant, great and small:
> That human nature is throughout
> The whole world equal, none can doubt.[2]

[1] *De officio regis* (1378–9), ed. by A. W. Pollard and Charles Sayle, London, 1887.

[2] Ll. 19411–14; trans. by F. S. Ellis.

But in the mass such ideas had always a strong religious coloring; they were the thoughts of simple-minded folk who believed with pathetic literalness in the Christian ideals of brotherhood and equality. It was just in the submerged classes that the more obscure heretical sects flourished, the Lollards in England and the extremists among Hus's followers in Bohemia. In the Bohemian sects especially the idea is found that the law of the Gospel is a kind of communism, in which Christians dwell together in freedom and equality, with no distinctions of rank or privilege such as are imposed by human law and institutions. The belief that the ideas of Wycliffe and Hus implied these extremes caused their opinions to be condemned by many who sincerely desired reform in the church. Such obscure ideas of social equality were of no practical importance in the fourteenth century, but they show how the movement for reform was becoming — what it had not previously been — a mass-movement among men who had little knowledge of scholastic philosophy.

THE SELF-SUFFICING COMMUNITY

The party which stood for a conciliar reform of church government at the Councils of Constance (1414–1418) and Basel (1431–1449) had no sympathy with popular agitation, even in the more moderate form represented by Wycliffe and Hus. Its leaders were among the most active in the condemnation of Hus at Constance. The conciliar theory was in the main the creation of a group of scholars [3] connected with the University of Paris, men thoroughly conversant with the scholarly writings of predecessors like John of Paris and William of Occam. Its deficiency as a popular movement is proved by the rapidity of its subsidence,

[3] The conciliarists included a considerable number of writers, of whom the chief were Henry of Langenstein, Conrad of Gelnhausen, Francisco Zabarella, Peter d'Ailly, John Gerson, and Nicholas of Cusa. Their writings on the subject are listed in Otto Gierke, *Political Theories of the Middle Age,* trans. by F. W. Maitland, pp. LXX ff. The most considerable collection is in the edition of Gerson's works published in 5 vols. at Antwerp, 1706, which includes tracts by Henry of Langenstein, Peter d'Ailly, and others, as well as the writings of Gerson. S. Schard, *De jurisdictione, autoritate, et praeeminentia imperiali, ac potestate ecclesiastica,* prints Zabarella's tract and Nicholas's *De concordantia catholica.* A new edition of the works of Nicholas of Cusa under the auspices of the Heidelberg Academy contains a critical text of Book I of this work; Vol. XIV (1939).

once the Council of Constance had succeeded in removing the scandal of the Schism. The general sentiment of Christendom was agreed about the need of restoring unity in the church; it was not equally determined to change the whole principle of church government by abolishing the supremacy of the pope. Indeed, it was quite unable to do this, for Christendom was in fact no longer sufficiently a unit to produce a system of representative government on a European scale. The effort of the Councils of Constance and Basel to draw up a workable plan of constitutional government failed completely, and from the point of view of practical politics, the movement seems, at least after the event, to be somewhat academic. The conciliarists could pass resolutions but they could not make a government. After the curing of the Schism the project of reforming the church by a General Council, though it could still be talked about even as late as the sixteenth and seventeenth centuries, was definitely not within the region of practical politics. The importance of the conciliar movement in political thought lay in the fact that it was the first great debate of constitutionalism against absolutism, and it prepared and spread ideas which were used in the later struggles.

The principle which the conciliarists developed had already been clearly stated by the opponents of the papacy from John of Paris to William of Occam. The church, being a complete and self-sufficing society, must possess all the powers needed to insure its continuance, its orderly government, and the removal of abuses as they occur. Consequently the spiritual power with which it is endowed is vested in the church itself, in the whole body of the faithful as a corporate body, and the clergy, including the pope, are merely the ministers or organs by which the society acts.

> Therefore when it is said that the pope has sovereign power, this should be understood not of the pope by himself but as he is in the whole body, so that the power is in the whole body as its foundation and in the pope as its chief minister, by whom the power is exercised.[4]

In this conception several ideas were combined. Most explicit, at least in Zabarella, is the legal analogy of the corporation which acts through its authorized agents but which itself provides the authority that its agents exercise; it is the whole body which

[4] Zabarella, *De schismate,* in Schard, *op. cit.* (1566), p. 703 a.

speaks and acts through its organs. There is also, of course, obliquely a reference to Aristotle's theory of the self-sufficing community which is capable of doing all that its life requires and whose well-being is the justification for what is done in its name. But perhaps more important than either of these is the rooted belief, already very ancient in the fifteenth century, that a people or a community has an inherent power to make its own law and set up its own rulers, and that it is by virtue of this consent or acceptance that lawful government differs from tyranny. The right of a council or other representative body depends upon the fact that it stands in the place of the community and speaks for it, witnessing to the fact that a rule really has the consent which gives it binding force. At the start this had been the guiding idea of the inquest or jury: competent representatives declared what the valid practice was. Unlike modern ideas of legislation it looked to the past rather than to the future; not the will but the custom of the community was binding.

HARMONY AND CONSENT

The defense of the General Council was very carefully developed by Nicholas of Cusa in his *De concordantia catholica,* which was presented to the Council of Basel in 1433. The keynote of the work is harmony rather than authority, and it leaves the question in doubt whether ultimately power is vested in the pope or in the council. The superiority of the council lies in the fact that it represents, better than any individual can, the agreement or consent of the whole church. Nicholas argues, evidently on the authority of the canonists, that approval or acceptance by the community is an essential ingredient of law. Such approval is shown by usage or custom (*approbatio per usum*) and the council, which stands for the whole body, speaks with more authority on this point than an individual. Papal decretals have often failed to attain the force of law because they have not been "accepted," and similarly a law which drops out of use loses its force. Acceptance even by a "province" is necessary to make a rule locally binding, because "all law ought to fit the country, place, and time."[5] In this general sense, therefore, all government depends upon consent:

[5] II, x–xi.

> Accordingly, since by nature all men are free, any authority by which subjects are prevented from doing evil and their freedom is restrained to doing good through fear of penalties, comes solely from harmony and from the consent of the subjects, whether the authority reside in written law or in the living law which is in the ruler. For if by nature men are equally strong and equally free, the true and settled power of one over the others, the ruler having equal natural power, could be set up only by the choice and consent of the others, just as a law also is set up by consent.[6]

Kings are therefore to be regulated by "the general pact of human society," for it is to this that kings owe their existence. The thought is obviously the same as that quoted in an earlier chapter from Bracton, that the king ought to obey the law because law makes the king.

The verbal identity of this quotation from Nicholas with the revolutionary arguments of the sixteenth to the eighteenth centuries is sufficiently obvious, but unless taken with proper qualifications it is also somewhat misleading. That the conceptions of natural law and the rights of subjects expressed by Nicholas were the direct ancestors of the later revolutionary theories is not open to question. These ideas had long been part of the heritage of European society. The important point is that the conciliarists, along with the earlier antipapal controversialists, turned them against constituted authority, making of custom itself a defense of what they chose to believe an ancient liberty, against a power that they regarded as arbitrary. This element remained, more or less, in the later revolutionary argument, as may be seen from the facile way in which seventeenth-century radicals confounded the natural rights of man with the traditional rights of Englishmen. But there is still a fundamental difference between the context, at least, of Nicholas's argument and that of the revolutionary era. By consent the later argument meant, or tended to mean, individual acceptance by each and every human being acting as a unit. In the fifteenth century such a meaning was hardly possible, for the right of private conscience and inward conviction had not the force that it had after the unity of the church was broken. Nor had the breaking-up of traditional social and economic institutions produced the "masterless man" who can be conceived to act only from his own internal motive-power. With Nicholas

[6] II, xiv.

the emphasis was all on the natural freedom of the community, the society that by its own spontaneous approval generates binding practices for its members, that makes law half-consciously and gives its assent through the voice of its natural magnates.

The substance of the conciliar theory, then, was that the whole body of the church, the congregation of the faithful, is the source of its own law and that the pope and the hierarchy are its organs or servants. It exists by virtue of divine and natural law; its rulers are subject to natural law and also to the law of the church's own organization or being. It is right and proper that they should be restrained within the limits of this law and that they should be checked and limited by the other organs of the ecclesiastical body. The pope ought to submit his decretals to consultation and approval by a representative body in order that they may be "accepted" by the church. If he does not do so, and especially if he tries to usurp an authority beyond that which is proper to his office, he may be justly deposed. The precise grounds for deposition were vague. The strongest ground, and the one which the conciliarists were most likely to try to fasten upon a contumacious pope, was heresy. Some writers held, however, that other offenses would suffice. There was common agreement that a General Council could depose, though some held, following John of Paris, that the College of Cardinals also was competent to do this. The model of government which guided the conciliarists was the medieval constitutional monarchy with its assembly of estates, or perhaps more definitely, the organization of the monastic orders, in which lesser corporations were combined through their representatives in a synod representing the whole body. If the conciliar theory had become a workable form of government, it would have had either to create the General Council as a regularly functioning body or to transform the College of Cardinals into something like a medieval parliament. Neither plan was in fact feasible.

Looking at a controversy such as this after the event, it is easy to say that the issue was whether the ultimate right of decision lay in the pope or in the council, but this way of putting the point is not accurately historical, for the issue developed only in the course of the controversy. In the case of the conciliarist controversy it never clearly evolved, as it did later in the similar issue in England between the king and parliament. Everyone, it should be remembered, entered controversies of this kind with the presumption that they were dealing with a temporary emergency, which could be removed without altering fundamentally the existing form of government. So far as the conciliarist movement was concerned, its popular power grew out of the admitted need to abolish the scandal of the Schism and it subsided when this was accomplished, with no result except to confirm by its failure the sovereign power of the pope. The reason why the issue was not clearly drawn between the authority of the pope and that of the council was that, in contemporary opinion, ultimate power did not reside in either the one or the other, or in fact in any organ of ecclesiastical government. The essential principle of the conciliar theory, like that of the medieval monarchy, was that the church or the community or the people was self-governing and that its power was resident in the whole body. Obviously, however, the whole body had no political existence and could become vocal only through some one or more of its organs. The conciliar theory, moreover, was opposed to the idea that some single organ must be chosen as having the last word. Precisely because ultimate power lay in the whole church, each of its organs — pope, council, or college — was less than final; they were in a sense coordinate as the creatures of the whole church, or if they were not strictly coordinate, each had at least an underived right to perform its own function. In no case was the power of one clearly delegated by another. All had an inherent power as compared with the others, though all derived their power from the whole community. Government, therefore, was properly a cooperative enterprise, a harmony or *concordantia,* as Nicholas called it, and not a delegation of power from a sovereign head.

Evidently, however, the whole trouble was that harmony among the governing organs of the church had ceased to exist. Consequently the conciliarists faced a difficulty which could hardly be settled in terms of existing law. A council might be, in an emergency, a better organ for determining the consensus of the whole church than the pope. But legally a council could hardly exist and certainly could not function without the cooperation of the pope, and if there were two or three popes the problem was insoluble. The argument so often used in defense of the council, that necessity overrides all law and that in an emergency the emperor might call a council and secure the election of a canonical pope, was logically an evasion and practically a makeshift. The only practicable outcome of the conciliarist position would have been for the council to establish itself as the source of papal authority by reducing the pope to the position of its own executive, and this solution equally would have been extra-legal. Such a result would have entailed a thorough-going alteration in the idea that government is a cooperation of the organs of a self-governing community. The whole situation prefigures surprisingly that in which the English Parliament found itself in its struggle with Charles I. Here, too, the inherent power both of the crown and of parliament was, at the start, an accepted proposition. Parliament could exist only at the king's call and legislate only with the king's approval, though parliament itself had an inherent right to be consulted. King and parliament together formed what Nicholas of Cusa would have called the *concordantia* of the realm. In the end, of course, parliament asserted a power over the crown which violated the initial conception of harmony quite as much as the absolute power of the king would have done.

THE POWER OF THE COUNCIL

In general the conciliarists aimed to erect the council into an integral part of church government, able to correct abuses and check what they believed to be the arbitrary power of the pope. Their practical purpose was to remedy and prevent disasters such as the Schism in which unrestrained papal power had resulted. Possibly a few extremists really faced the idea that papal authority might be made merely derivative from that of the council, but as a rule they conceived the power of the church as jointly shared between the pope and the council, with no serious intention of destroying, for ordinary purposes, the monarchical power inherent in the papal office. In short, they stood on much the same ground as the feudal lawyers. Strictly speaking, a writ would not run against the pope and yet, in extraordinary cases, he might be cited to appear before a council and might be condemned for contumacy if he did not do so. An abuse due to papal usurpation might be corrected by a council, as Bracton had said a king might be called to account by the *baronagium* of the realm. The council, as most truly representing the whole church, was first among its organs of government. But the council's functions were primarily regulatory and it was hardly intended that it should either supersede the other organs or reduce them to the status of its agents. The idea was a monarchy tempered by aristocracy in which the authority conceived to lie in the whole church was shared concurrently among its representative organs. Each organ had the right and the duty to keep the other organs in their places, while all were subject to the organic law of the whole body.

The measures which the Councils of Constance and Basel enacted illustrate this theory. Early in its proceedings the Council of Constance stated the principle in a famous decree:

> This synod, lawfully assembled in the Holy Ghost, and forming a general council representing the Catholic Church, has its power directly from Christ, and everyone, of whatever rank and office, even the Pope, is obliged to obey it in matters touching the faith, in the removal of the Schism, and in the reformation of the church in head and members.[7]

This decree was re-enacted at Basel in 1432, an action far more radical, since by that time there was only a single pope, who was generally recognized as canonical. The Council of Basel further declared the principle to be an article of faith whose denial was heresy. Both councils, like the Long Parliament after them, enacted that they were not to be dissolved without their own consent. The Council of Basel cited Eugenius IV to appear and declared him contumacious for failing to do so and finally deposed him, though without practical effect. Both councils tried to secure the convocation of future councils at regular intervals. The Council of Basel tried to revive diocesan and provincial synods throughout the church and to regulate papal elections in such a way as to insure obedience to conciliar decrees. There was, moreover, an effort to place the College of Cardinals on a footing more representative of the church and more independent of the pope, perhaps with the idea that it might become a third, or aristocratic, element in the government of the church, between the pope and the General Council, or a standing council to act as a permanent check on the monarchical power of the pope. In this the conception of a mixed constitution was clearly the guiding idea.

[7] Mansi, *conciliorum coll.,* Vol. XXVII, col. 585.

Since Nicholas of Cusa has already been quoted to illustrate a rather strong statement of the doctrine of government by consent, it will perhaps be well to refer briefly to his theory as a whole, in order to show that the conciliarist theory, in combating the absolute power of the pope, had no intention of substituting for it the sovereign power of the council. It is true that Nicholas wrote after the healing of the Schism, and that a few years after the Council of Basel he left the conciliar party and became the most important of the ecclesiastical statesmen who tried to foster reform as the servants of an absolute pope. He was, perhaps, more truly a diplomat than a political theorist, but at least, in 1433, he had the advantage of having the conciliar theory completely before him. If the *De concordantia catholica* be judged as a theory of coordinated legal authority, it is conspicuous for its logical difficulties. The author holds at once that a general council must be called by the pope in order to be œcumenical and yet that, once it is in existence, it may for good reasons depose the pope that called it. He treats the papal power as at once administrative and yet as derived from Christ and St. Peter. The pope represents the unity of the church but the council represents it better. The pope's adhesion is necessary to make a council and yet the council is superior to the pope. The pope is a member of the church and subject to its law; his election presumes his utility to the church, and his failure in this duty absolves churchmen from their obedience. But no legal process, strictly understood, will reach him. The purpose of citing these contrarieties is not to show that Nicholas was confused but to illustrate the fact that it is an anachronism to regard his *concordantia* as a theory of powers delegated by a supreme authority. His point is that the church itself is a unity and that it alone is supreme and infallible, but neither the pope nor a council is the sole spokesman of this infallibility. With good reason he distrusted them both, though he unquestionably believed in reform and hoped that a representative system, by bringing the hierarchy more closely into relation with the various parts of the church, would tend in that direction. But the problem as he saw it was one of cooperation rather than of legal subordination.

THE IMPORTANCE OF THE CONCILIAR THEORY

The conciliar movement neither reformed the church nor changed its form of government. A council which was itself a prey to every form of national jealousy was ill qualified to attack the stupendous mass of vested interests that made up ecclesiastical patronage. Everyone believed in reform but preferred to have it begin somewhere else, with the result that reform had to be postponed until rulers of the stripe of Henry VIII were prepared to reform most of the church's perquisites out of existence. In picturing a general representative form of government for the church, the conciliarists were imagining the impossible. They failed to realize that even the feudal constitutional monarchy depended upon a political cohesiveness which, in realms like France and England, provided something for an assemblage of estates to represent. Whatever unity the church had in the fifteenth century was not of this kind. Unity of belief there still was, at least to a degree, and some unity of moral and religious ideals, but not a sense of political oneness which could cope with divergences of local or national interest and make the council a functioning organ of government. Even so, however, the fate which the conciliarist theory met in the church was not far different from that which befell the medieval parliaments before the advancing power of the king. Everywhere in the sixteenth century medieval constitutional institutions fell under the sway of royal absolutism. In states, unlike the church, national unity provided a force of coherence which permitted representative institutions in the long run to revive, though it was only in England that the continuity with medieval constitutionalism was preserved.

The Council of Basel had not yet dissolved when the reaction began in the church which established the sovereign power of the pope, to remain unquestioned until the Reformation, and indeed until the present time in the Roman Church. This conception was a reversion to the theory of the papal power developed in the canon law in the days of Innocent III, now fixed and defined by the failure of a definite effort to displace it. Conciliarism might occasionally reappear for controversial purposes even in writers whose orthodoxy was not open to attack, but both as a movement for ecclesiastical reform and as an amendment to ecclesiastical law, it was a dead issue. The leader of this reaction was John of Torquemada, whom John Neville Figgis has called "the first modern exponent of the divine right of kings,"[8] though John still regarded the power of secular rulers as limited by law. In the present-day Catholic theory of the papacy, the pope is indubitably sovereign. His power is conceived to be limited only by divine and natural law; a council cannot exist without him; the decrees of a council require papal confirmation; and the pope is competent to revise decrees which a council has passed.[9] Thus the pope in the fifteenth century established himself as the first of the absolute monarchs, and the theory of papal absolutism became the archetype of the theory of monarchical absolutism. The main argument for papal divine right was that it is impossible to invest the community itself, rather than its head, with the supreme authority by which it is governed.

The conciliar theory was not important, then, for any practical results that it brought about, but it was none the less important. The controversy in the church first drew the lines upon which the issue between absolute and constitutional government was drawn, and it spread the type of political philosophy by which in the main absolutism was to be contested. Both the divine right of the sovereign and the sovereign power of the community were transferred to the field of secular government. This transfer was easy and in the fifteenth century it was easier than it would be today. The distinction between the church and secular government was still pictured as a distinction not between two societies but between two organizations of the same society. Any argument about the nature of authority in either church or state must therefore go back to the fundamental nature of society itself. The conciliarist argument depended throughout upon the premise that any complete community must be capable of governing itself and that its consent is vital to any kind of lawful authority. The argument might apply indifferently to a church or a state, when the two came to be thought of as two societies. Under God both secular and spiritual powers must equally be latent in the people

[8] *From Gerson to Grotius* (1907), p. 234, n. 15.

[9] L. Pastor, *History of the Popes* (Ed. by F. I. Antrobus), Vol. I (1906), pp. 179 ff.

or community, and in itself this belief was in no way contrary to the accepted belief that all power is of God. But when the theory of divine right became definitely a theory of royal supremacy, the theory that power inheres ultimately in the people became the normal way to contradict it. The conciliar controversy in the church was the first occasion on which the issue between the two theories was drawn in this form, and in this form it continued to be drawn when the controversy lay between a king and his subjects.

The conciliar theory in the fifteenth century, like the theory of representative or constitutional government, stood curiously balanced between past and present. It was born partly of the ancient belief in the eternal validity of natural law, partly of the conception that any community consists of necessary services and interests in a condition of mutual dependence. Hence it conceived of government as an exchange, a give-and-take, a balance between powers all of which are in their own nature indefeasible. The unity of government was thus a reflection of the unity of the community. If the word sovereign could be appropriately used at all, it would be of the whole community and not of any political institution in it, but the ancient word *res publica,* commonwealth, was far more descriptive. Thus the conciliarists opposed the papal argument that authority must somewhere come to a head as a dangerous and subversive innovation, setting against it the ideal of a harmony of powers cooperating by free and mutual consent. In a sense this constitutional ideal, which was typical of medieval theory and practice, fought a losing battle in the state, for the forces that made for the centralization of power were generally on the increase. With this tendency toward a more rigid type of political organization, in which the parts were related by the delegation of authority from a single head, the ideal of government by consent must make its peace as best it could. But in the end centralized power also must make its peace with the consent of the governed. From the conciliar theory of the fifteenth century there is a directly developing line of thought to the liberal and constitutional movements of the seventeenth and eighteenth centuries. Running through this development and connecting it with the Middle Ages was the conviction that lawful authority is a moral force while despotism is not, and that society itself embodies a force of moral criticism to which even legally constituted power is rightly subject.

SELECTED BIBLIOGRAPHY

Nicholas of Cusa. By Henry Bett. London, 1932.

A History of Mediaeval Political Theory in the West. By R. W. Carlyle and A. J. Carlyle. 6 vols. London, 1903–1936. Vol. VI (1936), Part II, chs. 1, 3.

A History of the Papacy during the Period of the Reformation. By M. Creighton. 5 vols. Boston, 1882–1894. Vols. I and II.

Studies of Political Thought from Gerson to Grotius, 1414–1625. By John Neville Figgis. 2nd ed. Cambridge, 1923. Ch. 2.

The Decline of the Medieval Church. By Alexander C. Flick. 2 vols. London, 1930. Chs. 11–19.

The Social and Political Ideas of some Great Thinkers of the Renaissance and the Reformation. Ed. by F. J. C. Hearnshaw. London, 1925. Ch. 2.

The Life and Times of Master John Hus. By F. H. von Lützow. London, 1909.

"Medieval Estates." By C. H. McIlwain. In the *Cambridge Medieval History,* Vol. VII (1932), ch. 23.

"Wyclif." By Bernard L. Manning. In the *Cambridge Medieval History,* Vol. VII (1932), ch. 16.

"The Popes of Avignon and the Great Schism." By Guillaume Mollat. In the *Cambridge Medieval History,* Vol. VII (1932), ch. 10.

The History of the Popes from the Close of the Middle Ages. By Ludwig Pastor. Ed. by F. I. Antrobus. 16 vols. London, 1899–1928. Vol. I, Bks. 1, 2.

Wycliffe and Movements for Reform. By R. L. Poole. London, 1896.

England in the Age of Wycliffe. By G. M. Trevelyan. New ed. London, 1909.

The Social Teaching of the Christian Churches. By Ernst Troeltsch. Eng. trans. by Olive Wyon. 2 vols. London, 1931. Ch. 2, Section 9.

La crise religieuse du XVe *siècle: Le pape et le concile (1418–1450)*. By Noël Valois. 2 vols. Paris, 1909.

Le cardinal Nicolas de Cues (1401–1464), l'action, la pensée. By E. Vansteenberghe. Paris, 1920.

PART III

THE THEORY OF THE NATIONAL STATE

CHAPTER XVII

MACHIAVELLI

The failure of the conciliar party to carry the principles and practice of medieval constitutionalism into the church anticipated by only a generation or two a general recession of representative institutions in the state. And the revival of papal absolutism in the middle of the fifteenth century, astonishingly rapid in view of the degradation which the papal office had suffered for more than a century, was paralleled by a tremendous growth of monarchical power in almost every part of western Europe. In all the kingdoms royal power grew at the expense of the competing institutions, whether nobility, parliaments, free cities, or clergy, and almost everywhere the eclipse of the medieval representative system was permanent. Only in England the comparatively brief duration of Tudor absolutism permitted the continuity of parliamentary history to be preserved. The change, both in government and in ideas about government, was enormous. Political power, which had been largely dispersed among feudatories and corporations, was rapidly gathered into the hands of the king, who for the time being was the main beneficiary of increasing national unity. The conception of a sovereign who is the fountain-head of all political power, which had been the possession of a few jurists under the influence of Roman imperial law and of the extreme papalists, who had transformed the same conception into a theory of papal divine right, became in the sixteenth century a common form of political thought.

These changes of political thought and practice reflected changes in the whole fabric of European society, which were everywhere similar though with innumerable local differences. By the end of the fifteenth century economic changes which had been going on for years produced an accumulation of effects that amounted to a revolutionary remodeling of medieval institutions. These institutions, despite theories about the universal church and the universal empire, had depended on the fact that medieval society, in its effective economic and political organization, was almost wholly local. This was an inevitable consequence of limitations on the means of communication. A large political territory was not governable except by a kind of federalism that left to local units a large amount of independence. Trade also was mainly local, or where it was more than that, it consisted of specified commodities that moved in fixed routes, to monopolized ports and markets. Such a trade could be controlled by producers' guilds, which were municipal institutions; the unit of the medieval trading organization was the city. Neither freedom of movement nor the use of money was very general in the fourteenth century.

Any considerable extension of the ease of communication was totally incompatible with the continuance of a trade thus locally monopolized and controlled. Economic advantage passed to the side of freedom from fixed routes and monopolized markets. The greatest profits went to the "merchant adventurer," who was prepared to take advantage of every market, who had capital to put into his business, and who could trade in any commodity that offered large returns. Such a merchant, having the command of the markets, could more and more gain control over production also, and he was quite beyond the power of the guilds and the cities. In so far as trade was to be controlled, the quality of goods standardized, or prices and conditions of employment regulated, this had to be done by governments of larger size than the medieval municipality. All the royal governments of Europe undertook regulation of this sort. Moreover, in so far as extended trade was to be protected and encouraged, this also became a task wholly out of the power of local government. By the sixteenth century all the royal governments had adopted a conscious policy of exploiting national resources, of encouraging trade both at home and abroad, and of developing national power.

These economic changes had profound social and political consequences. For the first time since the Roman Empire European society included a considerable class of men who had both money and enterprise. For obvious reasons this class was the natural enemy of the nobility and of all the divisions and disorders which they fostered. Their interests were on the side of "strong" government both at home and abroad, and hence their natural political alliance was with the king. For the time being they were content to see his power increase at the expense of all the checks and limitations which had surrounded medieval monarchy. Parliament they could not yet aspire to control against the influence of the nobility; hence they were willing to subordinate representative institutions to the monarchy. The nobility they were glad to see prevented from maintaining disorderly bands of hangers-on, who intimidated the courts and officers of the law and recruited the ranks of brigands. From every point of view the bourgeoisie saw its advantage in concentrating military power and the administration of justice as much as possible in the hands of the king. On the whole the gain in orderly and efficient government was probably considerable. The king's power, to be sure, became arbitrary and often oppressive, but royal government was better than any that the feudal nobility could give.

MODERN ABSOLUTISM

By the opening years of the sixteenth century, therefore, absolute monarchy either had become, or was rapidly becoming, the prevailing type of government in western Europe. Everywhere there was an enormous wreckage of medieval institutions, for the absolute monarchy was a thing of blood and iron which rested in large part quite frankly on force. How destructive it was is concealed only by the fact that, after the event, men were more prone to take pride in the national monarchies which it helped to found than to grieve for the medieval institutions which it destroyed. Absolute monarchy overturned feudal constitutionalism and the free city-states, on which medieval civilization had largely depended, just as nationalism later overturned the dynastic legitimacy to which absolute monarchy gave rise. The church itself, the most characteristic of all medieval institutions, fell a prey to it, or to social forces upon which it depended. Weak and rich — a fatal combination in an age of blood and iron — the monasteries were expropriated by Protestant and Catholic monarchies alike, to provide the wealth of a new middle class which was the main strength of the monarchy. Ecclesiastical rulers were everywhere subjected more and more to royal control, and in the end the church's legal authority disappeared. The *sacerdotium* vanished as a power, and the church became — what it had never before been for Christian thought — either a voluntary association or a partner of national government.

The growth of absolute monarchy, like that of the feudal constitutional monarchy, took place in almost every part of western Europe. In Spain the uniting of Aragon and Castile by the marriage of Ferdinand and Isabella began the formation of an absolute monarchy which made that country the greatest of European powers throughout the larger part of the sixteenth century. In England the conclusion of the Wars of the Roses and the reign of Henry VII (1485–1509) began the period of Tudor absolutism, which extended through the reign of Henry VIII and much of that of Elizabeth. Though Henry VII owed his throne — to which he had hardly a shadow of hereditary title — to a combination of the nobility, his policy in general ran true to the forms of the period. He could not succeed without attracting the support of the middle class; he was obliged to put down with all his strength the disorderly followers of the nobility who threatened the crown and the middle class alike; he established order and thus promoted trade; he encouraged maritime ventures; and his royal power quite eclipsed the House of Commons, in which the influence of the nobility upon elections was still too strong to be safe. Germany, it is true, formed an apparent exception to the rule, for here the weakness of the empire both permitted anarchy and discouraged the growth of that national sentiment which had been the main support of Lewis the Bavarian in his controversy with the popes. But even in Germany the prevailing tendency was delayed rather than stopped, for the rise to sovereign power of Prussia and Austria was not unlike the change which took place earlier in Spain and England and France.

It is France, however, that furnishes the most typical example of the growth of highly centralized royal power.[1] The beginnings of French national unity, already mentioned in connection with Philip the Fair, were largely lost during the Hundred Years' War. But though this period of foreign and civil war was injurious to the monarchy, it was fatal to all the other medieval institutions — communal, feudal, and representative — which had threatened to

[1] See "France," by Stanley Leathes, in the *Cambridge Modern History*, Vol. I (1903), ch. 12, and G. B. Adams, *Civilization during the Middle Ages* (1914), ch. 13.

overshadow the monarchy. The second half of the fifteenth century brought a rapid consolidation of royal power which made France the most united, compact, and harmonious nation in Europe. The Ordinance of 1439 gathered the entire military force of the nation into the king's hands and made his authority effective by granting him a national tax with which to support it. The success of the measure was startling and shows clearly enough why the rising nations were willing to support royal absolutism. Within a few years a well-trained and well-equipped citizen-army had been created and had expelled the English from the country. Before the end of the century the great feudatories — Burgundy, Brittany, and Anjou — had been reduced to subjection. In the meantime the Estates had lost forever their control over taxation and with it their power to influence the king, and the latter had made good his power over the French church. From the early years of the sixteenth century down to the age of the Revolution, the king became almost the sole spokesman for the nation.

Catastrophic changes such as these, occurring throughout Europe, produced as a matter of course an equal change in political theory. And in the opening years of the sixteenth century this change was summed up in the difficult — almost the contradictory — figure of Machiavelli. No man of his age saw so clearly the direction that political evolution was taking throughout Europe. No man knew better than he the archaism of the institutions that were being displaced or accepted more readily the part that naked force was playing in the process. Yet no one in that age appreciated more highly the inchoate sense of national unity on which this force was obscurely based. No one was more clearly aware of the moral and political corruption that went with the decay of long-accustomed loyalties and pieties, yet no one, perhaps, felt a keener nostalgia for a healthier social life, such as was typified in his mind by ancient Rome. Certainly no one knew Italy as Machiavelli did. And yet, writing on the eve of the Protestant Reformation, he was almost blind to the part that religion was to play in the politics of the next two centuries. Indoctrinated as he was in the pagan revival in Italy, he was unable both by training and temperament to grasp the constitutional and the moral ideals that European politics would carry over from the Middle Ages. Clear and broad as his vision of politics was, Machiavelli was still in a peculiar sense an Italian of the first quarter of the sixteenth century. Had he written in any other time and place, his conception of politics must have been significantly different.

ITALY AND THE POPE

In Italy the forces of a new commercial and industrial system had been especially destructive of older institutions, but for reasons implicit in the political situation, the constructive forces were peculiarly neutralized and retarded. The free cities of northern Italy, upon which the imperial projects of the Hohenstaufen had been wrecked, had become political and economic anachronisms, unable to cope with a situation which required concentrated power, a citizen-soldiery, and a larger and more vigorous foreign policy. When Machiavelli wrote, Italy was divided among five larger states: the kingdom of Naples in the south, the duchy of Milan in the northwest, the aristocratic republic of Venice in the northeast, and the republic of Florence and the Papal State in the center. The downfall of the Florentine republic in 1512 — which produced in Machiavelli's life the enforced period of idleness responsible for his political writing — illustrated the fate awaiting a form of government which was incapable of coping with the political forces of its day. The tendency toward concentration was illustrated also in the recreating of the Papal State after its decay during the Schism. The popes of Machiavelli's time, scoundrels and profligates though they often were, succeeded in making their state the best consolidated and the most permanent in Italy. Nothing perhaps is more significant of the change in European politics than this, which transformed the pope into one Italian ruler among others. The old ambition to stand as arbiter of all the quarrels of Christendom had dwindled to the more practicable, but more worldly, ambition to retain the sovereignty of central Italy.

But though consolidation had begun, it could not be completed, and this left Italy, as Machiavelli saw it, in a state of arrested political development. In Italy no power appeared great enough to unite the whole peninsula. Italians suffered all the degradation and oppression of tyranny with few of its compensations, and divisions among the tyrants left the land a prey to the French, the Spanish, and the Germans. Like most Italians of his day, Machiavelli held the church to be peculiarly responsible for this state of affairs. Too weak to unite Italy himself, the pope was still strong enough to prevent any other ruler from doing so, while his international relationships made him a leader in the vicious policy of inviting foreign intervention. This is the reason for the bitter irony with which Machiavelli so frequently assails the church.

> We Italians then owe to the Church of Rome and to her priests our having become irreligious and bad; but we owe her a still greater debt, and one that will be the cause of our ruin, namely, that the Church has kept and still keeps our country divided. And certainly a country can never be united and happy, except when it obeys wholly one government, whether a republic or a monarchy, as is the case in France and in Spain; and the sole cause why Italy is not in the same condition, and is not governed by either one republic or one sovereign, is the Church. . . . The Church, then, not having been powerful enough to be able to master all Italy, nor having permitted any other power to do so, has been the cause why Italy has never been able to unite under one head, but has always remained under a number of princes and lords, which occasioned her so many dissensions and so much weakness that she became a prey not only to the powerful barbarians, but of whoever chose to assail her.[2]

Italian society and politics, as Machiavelli conceived them and as historians have for the most part agreed to picture them, were peculiarly illustrative of a state of institutional decay. It was a society intellectually brilliant and artistically creative, more emancipated than any in Europe from the trammels of authority, and prepared to face the world in a coolly rational and empirical spirit, yet it was a prey to the worst political corruption and moral degradation. The older civic institutions were dead; medieval ideas like the church and the empire which, in Dante's day, could still awaken a noble enthusiasm, were no longer even memories. Cruelty and murder had become normal agencies of government; good faith and truthfulness had become childish scruples to which an enlightened man would hardly give lip-service; force and craft had become the keys to success; profligacy and debauchery had become too frequent to need comment: and selfishness, naked and unadorned, need only succeed in order to supply its own justi-

[2] *Discourses on the First Ten Books of Titus Livius,* I, 12; trans. by C. E. Detmold, *The Historical, Political, and Diplomatic Writings of Niccolo Machiavelli,* 4 vols., Boston and New York, 1891.

fication. It was a period truly called the age of "bastards and adventurers," a society created as if to illustrate Aristotle's saying that "man, when separated from law and justice, is the worst of all animals." Machiavelli is, therefore, in a peculiar sense, the political theorist of the "masterless man," of a society in which the individual stands alone, with no motives and no interests except those supplied by his own egoism. In this he represents a phase of all modern society, but he represents it in the exaggerated form appropriate to Italy in the sixteenth century.

MACHIAVELLI'S INTEREST

His most important political works were the *Prince* and the *Discourses on the First Ten Books of Titus Livius,* both begun and largely finished in 1513. The treatment of government in the two books is significantly different; some writers, following Rousseau, have believed them to be inconsistent with each other. In fact, this seems not to be the case, especially if the circumstances attending the composition of the *Prince* be taken into account, but it is unfortunate that most readers have known Machiavelli through this work. Both books present aspects of the same subject — the causes of the rise and decline of states and the means by which statesmen can make them permanent. The *Prince* deals with monarchies or absolute governments, and the *Discourses* mainly with the expansion of the Roman Republic. This corresponds to the twofold classification of states which Machiavelli makes at the beginning of the *Prince.* The *Prince* was a selection of the author's views for a special purpose and was occasioned, it is true, by a desire to obtain employment under the Medici, but the latter fact did not produce the opinions expressed in it. As Villari says, anyone acquainted with the *Discourses* and knowing the author's special purpose could have forecast nearly everything in the *Prince.* Both books show equally the qualities for which Machiavelli has been especially known, such as indifference to the use of immoral means for political purposes and the belief that government depends largely on force and craft. What does not appear in the *Prince* is his genuine enthusiasm for popular government of the sort exemplified in the Roman Republic, but which he believed to be impracticable in Italy when he wrote.

Machiavelli's political writings belong less to political theory than to the class of diplomatic literature, of which a great volume was produced by Italian writers of his age. Never has the game of diplomacy been played more fiercely than in the relations between the Italian states of Machiavelli's day. Never have the shifts and turns of negotiations counted for more than between these rulers — adventurers all — who relied for their success about equally upon skillful gambling and the crassest force. Diplomatic writing, and Machiavelli's works as well, has characteristic merits and defects. There is the shrewdest insight into points of weakness and strength in a political situation, the clearest and coolest judgment of the resources and temperament of an opponent, the most objective estimate of the limitations of a policy, the soundest common sense in forecasting the logic of events and the outcome of a course of action. It is such qualities as these, possessed in a superlative degree, that made Machiavelli a favorite writer for diplomats from his own day to the present. But diplomatic writing is peculiarly likely to exaggerate the importance of the game for its own sake and to minimize the purposes for which the game is presumably played. It naturally assumes that politics is an end in itself.

This is Machiavelli's most conspicuous quality. He writes almost wholly of the mechanics of government, of the means by which states may be made strong, of the policies by which they can expand their power, and of the errors that lead to their decay or overthrow. Political and military measures are almost the sole objects of his interest, and he divorces these almost wholly from religious, moral, and social considerations, except as the latter affect political expedients. The purpose of politics is to preserve and increase political power itself, and the standard by which he judges it is its success in doing this. Whether a policy is cruel or faithless or lawless he treats for the most part as a matter of indifference, though he is well aware that such qualities may react upon its political success. He often discusses the advantages of immorality skillfully used to gain a ruler's ends, and it is this which is mainly responsible for his evil repute. But for the most part he is not so much immoral as non-moral. He simply abstracts politics from other considerations and writes of it as if it were an end in itself.

MORAL INDIFFERENCE

The closest analogue to Machiavelli's separation of political expedience from morality is probably to be found in some parts of Aristotle's *Politics,* where Aristotle considers the preservation of states without reference to their goodness or badness. It is not at all certain, however, that Machiavelli took these passages as his model. It is not likely that he was conscious of following anyone, though there may possibly have been a connection between his secularism and the naturalistic Aristotelianism that produced the *Defensor pacis* two centuries before. Apart from a common hatred of the papacy as the cause of Italian disunion, which Machiavelli shared with Marsilio, the two men had substantially similar ideas about the political utility which religion ought to have as its secular consequence.[3] Machiavelli's secularism, however, goes much beyond Marsilio's and is free from all the sophistications imposed by the twofold truth. Marsilio defended the autonomy of reason by making Christian morals otherworldly; Machiavelli condemns them because they are otherworldly. The Christian virtues he believed to be servile in their effects on character and he contrasted Christianity unfavorably in this respect with the more virile religions of antiquity.

> Our religion places the supreme happiness in humility, lowliness, and a contempt for worldly objects, whilst the other, on the contrary, places the supreme good in grandeur of soul, strength of body, and all such other qualities as render men formidable. . . . These principles seem to me to have made men feeble, and caused them to become an easy prey to evil-minded men, who can control them more securely, seeing that the great body of men, for the sake of gaining Paradise, are more disposed to endure injuries than to avenge them.[4]

As this passage suggests, Machiavelli was not indifferent to the effects which morals and religion, in the masses of mankind, have upon social and political life. He sanctioned the use of immoral means by rulers to gain an end, but he never doubted that moral corruption in a people makes good government impossible. He

[3] Previté-Orton has noted several important parallels in his notes; see his edition of the *Defensor*, Index B, *s.v.* Machiavelli. Cf. the passage about Italy in II, xxvi, 20, and *Prince,* ch. 26.

[4] *Discourses,* II, 2.

had nothing but admiration for the civic virtues of the ancient Romans and of the Swiss in his own day, and he believed that these grew out of purity in the family, independence and sturdiness in private life, simplicity and frugality of manners, and loyalty and trustworthiness in performing public duties. But this does not mean that the ruler must believe in the religion of his subjects or practice their virtues. Machiavelli was by no means blind to imponderable forces in politics, but the imponderables were still for him merely forces. An army fights with morale as truly as with guns, and the wise ruler sees that both are of the best quality. Machiavelli offers an extreme example of a double standard of morals, one for the ruler and another for the private citizen. The first is judged by success in keeping and increasing his power; the second, by the strength which his conduct imparts to the social group. Since the ruler is outside the group, or at least in a very special relation to it, he is above the morality to be enforced within the group.

Machiavelli's indifference to morality has sometimes been described as an example of scientific detachment,[5] but this account of the matter seems far-fetched. Machiavelli was not detached; he was merely interested in a single end, political power, and indifferent to all others. He never hesitated to express sweeping judgments of rulers who allowed their states to grow weak. Moreover, he was in no definite sense scientific, though his judgment was formed empirically, by the observation of rulers that he had himself known or by studying historical examples. But his empiricism was that of common sense or of shrewd practical foresight rather than an inductive empiricism controlled by the wish to test theories or general principles. In the same way it is misleading to say, as has been done, that Machiavelli followed an "historical" method, because his examples were often drawn from the past. He used history exactly as he used his own observation to illustrate or support a conclusion that he had reached quite without reference to history. In one sense he was very unhistorical. He asserted explicitly that human nature is always and everywhere the same, and for this reason he took examples where he found them. His method, in so far as he had one, was observation guided by shrewdness and common sense. The most

[5] Sir Frederick Pollock, *History of the Science of Politics* (1911), p. 43.

telling description of his accomplishment is that given by Janet, that he translated politics into the vernacular.

Machiavelli's political theories were not developed in a systematic manner, but in the form of remarks upon particular situations. Behind them, or implicit in them, however, there often was a consistent point of view, which might be developed into a political theory and in fact was so developed after his time. Machiavelli was not much interested in philosophy and not much inclined to generalize beyond maxims useful to a statesman. He sometimes merely stated his principles, often merely took them for granted; practically never did he try to give any proof of them. At the risk of giving a more unified impression than his works warrant, it will be useful to draw his scattered generalizations together, especially since later thinkers did erect into a systematic theory suggestions drawn from him.

UNIVERSAL EGOISM

Behind nearly everything that Machiavelli said about political policy was the assumption that human nature is essentially selfish, and that the effective motives on which a statesman must rely are egoistic, such as the desire for security in the masses and the desire for power in rulers. Government is really founded upon the weakness and insufficiency of the individual, who is unable to protect himself against the aggression of other individuals unless supported by the power of the state. Human nature, moreover, is profoundly aggressive and acquisitive; men aim to keep what they have and to acquire more. Neither in power nor in possessions is there any normal limit to human desires, while both power and possessions are always in fact limited by natural scarcity. Accordingly, men are always in a condition of strife and competition which threatens open anarchy unless restrained by the force behind the law, while the power of the ruler is built upon the very imminence of anarchy and the fact that security is possible only when government is strong. Machiavelli constantly takes this conception of government for granted, though he nowhere develops it into a general psychological theory of behavior. He frequently remarks, however, that men are in general bad and that the wise ruler will construct his policies on this assumption. In particular he insists that successful government must aim at security of property and of life before everything else, since these are the most universal desires in human nature. Hence his cynical remark that a man more readily forgives the murder of his father than the confiscation of his patrimony. The prudent ruler may kill but he will not plunder. When completed by a systematic psychology to explain and justify it, this phase of Machiavelli became the political philosophy of Hobbes.

Machiavelli, however, is not so much concerned with badness or egoism as a general human motive as with its prevalence in Italy as a symptom of social decadence. Italy stands to him as the example of a corrupt society, with no such partial mitigation as the monarchy brings in France and Spain.

> In fact it is vain to look for anything good from those countries which we see nowadays so corrupt, as is the case above all others with Italy. France and Spain also have their share of corruption, and if we do not see so many disorders and troubles in those countries as is the case daily in Italy, it is not so much owing to the goodness of their people . . . as to the fact that they have each a king who keeps them united. . .[6]

The problem in Italy, then, is to found a state in a corrupt society, and Machiavelli was convinced that, in such circumstances, no effective government was possible except absolute monarchy. This explains why he was at once an enthusiastic admirer of the Roman Republic and an advocate of despotism. By corruption Machiavelli means in general that decay of private virtue and civic probity and devotion that renders popular government impossible. It includes all sorts of licence and violence, great inequalities of wealth and power, the destruction of peace and justice, the growth of disorderly ambition, disunion, lawlessness, dishonesty, and contempt for religion. A republican form of government he believed still to be possible in Switzerland and some parts of Germany, where a vigorous civic life had been preserved, but not in Italy. When the necessary virtues have decayed, there is no possibility either of restoring them or of carrying on orderly government without them, except by despotic power.

Apart from moral corruption, however, the natural aggressiveness of human nature makes struggle and competition a normal feature of every society. This explains, on the one hand, the defeat that dogs the steps of every government: " Men always com-

[6] *Discourses,* I, 55.

mit the error of not knowing when to limit their hopes." But on the other hand, it explains also the stability of a healthy society in which opposing interests are held in equilibrium. The rivalry of patricians and plebeians in Rome Machiavelli regarded as the secret of Roman strength. From it was born the independence and sturdiness of character that supported the greatness of Rome. When directed by wise rulers, having great but lawful authority, the virility that made turbulence possible became a chief reason why the Romans were a war-like, conquering people. For this reason Machiavelli stated again the ancient theory of the mixed or balanced constitution. Not very appropriately, it must be confessed, he reproduced at the beginning of the *Discourses* almost word for word the theory of the constitutional cycle from the sixth book of Polybius's *Histories*. The balance which he had in mind, however, was not political but social or economic — an equilibrium of competing interests held in check by a powerful sovereign. In this respect also a systematic statement of Machiavelli's philosophy needed the conception of sovereign power which Bodin and Hobbes added to it.

THE OMNIPOTENT LEGISLATOR

A second general principle that is continually assumed by Machiavelli is the supreme importance in society of the lawgiver. A successful state must be founded by a single man, and the laws and government which he creates determine the national character of his people. Moral and civic virtue grows out of law, and when a society has become corrupt, it can never reform itself but must be taken in hand by one lawgiver, who can restore it to the healthy principles set up by its founder.

> But we must assume, as a general rule, that it never or rarely happens that a republic or monarchy is well constituted, or its old institutions entirely reformed, unless it is done by only one individual; it is even necessary that he whose mind has conceived such a constitution should be alone in carrying it into effect.[7]

Machiavelli was not thinking only, or even mainly, of political organization, but of the whole moral and social constitution of a people, which he conceived to grow out of the law and from the wisdom and foresight of the lawgiver. There is practically no

[7] *Discourses*, I. 9.

limit to what a statesman can do, provided he understands the rules of his art. He can tear down old states and build new, change forms of government, transplant populations, and build new virtues into the characters of his subjects. If a ruler lacks soldiers, he says, he need blame no one but himself, for he should have adopted measures to correct the cowardice and effeminacy of his people. The lawgiver is the architect not only of the state but of society as well, with all its moral, religious, and economic institutions.

This exaggerated notion of what a ruler and a state can do had several causes. In part it merely reproduced the ancient myth of the lawgiver which Machiavelli found in writers like Cicero and Polybius. In part it reflected his understanding of the problem that confronted a ruler amid the corruption of sixteenth-century Italy. By sheer political genius a successful ruler had to create a military power strong enough to overcome the disorderly little cities and principalities and in the end to evolve a new public spirit and civic loyalty. All the circumstances of his time conspired to make him see in an absolute ruler the arbiter of a nation's fate. But beside these historical circumstances, the logic of his own political philosophy weighed heavily in the same direction. For if human individuals are by nature radically egoistic, the state and the force behind the law must be the only power that holds society together; moral obligations must in the end be derived from law and government. In this respect also it was Hobbes who gave a systematic statement of what Machiavelli suggested.

From this point of view it is easier to understand the double standard of conduct for the statesman and the private citizen which forms the main connotation of what is called "Machiavellism." The ruler, as the creator of the state, is not only outside the law, but if law enacts morals, he is outside morality as well. There is no standard to judge his acts except the success of his political expedients for enlarging and perpetuating the power of his state. The frankness with which Machiavelli accepted this conclusion and included it in his advice to rulers is the chief reason for the evil reputation of the *Prince,* though the *Discourses* were really no better. He openly sanctioned the use of cruelty, perfidy, murder, or any other means, provided only they are used with sufficient intelligence and secrecy to reach their ends.

> It is well that, when the act accuses him, the result should excuse him; and when the result is good, as in the case of Romulus [his murder of his brother], it will always absolve him from blame. For he is to be reprehended who commits violence for the purpose of destroying, and not he who employs it for beneficent purposes.[8]
>
> For the manner in which men live is so different from the way in which they ought to live, that he who leaves the common course for that which he ought to follow will find that it leads him to ruin rather than to safety. . . . A prince therefore who desires to maintain himself must learn to be not always good, but to be so or not as necessity may require. . . . Nor need he care about incurring censure for such vices, without which the preservation of his state may be difficult. For, all things considered, it will be found that some things that seem like virtue will lead you to ruin if you follow them; whilst others, that apparently are vices, will, if followed, result in your safety and well-being.[9]

Machiavelli's prince, the perfect embodiment of shrewdness and self-control, who makes capital alike of his virtues and his vices, was little more than an idealized picture of the Italian tyrant of the sixteenth century. He is a true, if exaggerated, picture of the kind of man that the age of the despots threw into the forefront of political life. Though the most extreme examples occurred in Italy, Ferdinand of Spain, Louis XI of France, and Henry VIII of England were of the same type. There is no doubt that Machiavelli had a temperamental admiration for the resourceful, if unscrupulous, type of ruler and a deep distrust of half-way measures in politics, which he rightly believed to be due to weakness more often than to scruple. His admiration for this type sometimes betrayed him into serious superficialities of judgment, as when he held up the unspeakable Cesare Borgia as the model of a wise prince and asserted that his political failure was due to nothing but unavoidable accident.

Machiavelli never erected his belief in the omnipotent lawgiver into a general theory of political absolutism, as Hobbes did later. His judgment was swayed by two admirations — for the resourceful despot and for the free, self-governing people — which were not consistent. He patched the two together, rather precariously, as the theories respectively of founding a state and

[8] *Discourses,* I, 9.

[9] *Prince,* ch. 15.

of preserving it after it is founded. In more modern terms it might be said that he had one theory for revolutions and another for government. Hence he recommended despotism only in two somewhat special cases, the making of a state and the reforming of a corrupt state. Once founded, a state can be made permanent only if the people are admitted to some share in the government and if the prince conducts the ordinary business of the state in accordance with law and with a due regard for the property and rights of his subjects. Despotic violence is a powerful political medicine, needed in corrupt states and for special contingencies in all states, but still a poison which must be used with the greatest caution.

REPUBLICANISM AND NATIONALISM

There was nothing in Machiavelli's account of the absolute monarchy corresponding to his obviously sincere enthusiasm for the liberty and self-government of the Roman Republic. The preservation of the state, as distinct from its founding, depends upon the excellence of its law, for this is the source of all the civic virtues of its citizens. Even in a monarchy the prime condition of stable government is that it should be regulated by law. Thus Machiavelli insisted upon the need for legal remedies against official abuses in order to prevent illegal violence and pointed out the political dangers of lawlessness in rulers and the folly of vexatious and harassing policies. In particular, the prudent ruler will abstain from the property and the women of his subjects, since these are the matters on which men are most easily stirred to resistance. He favored a gentle rule wherever possible and the use of severity only in moderation. He said explicitly that government is more stable where it is shared by the many and he preferred election to heredity as a mode of choosing rulers. He spoke for a general freedom to propose measures for the public good and for liberty of discussion, in order that both sides of every question may be heard before a decision is reached. He believed that the people must be independent and strong, because there is no way to make them warlike without giving them the means of rebellion. Finally, he had a high opinion both of the virtue and the judgment of an uncorrupted people as compared with those of the prince. They are unfitted to take a long view of intricate policies, but in matters that fall within their understanding, such as estimating the character of a magistrate, they are both more prudent and more sound in their judgment than a prince. Despite the cynicism of Machiavelli's political judgments, there is no mistaking his esteem for liberal and lawful government. It is this which explains the admiration for him felt by a constitutionalist like Harrington.

Closely related to his favorable judgment of popular government where possible, and of monarchy where necessary, is his exceedingly low opinion of aristocracy and the nobility. More than any other thinker of his time he perceived that the interests of the nobility are antagonistic both to those of the monarchy and of the middle class, and that orderly government required their suppression or extirpation. These " gentlemen," who live idly on the proceeds of their wealth without giving any useful service, are " everywhere enemies of all civil government."

> The only way to establish any kind of order there is to found a monarchical government; for where the body of the people is so thoroughly corrupt that the laws are powerless for restraint, it becomes necessary to establish some superior power which, with a royal hand, and with full and absolute powers, may put a curb upon the excessive ambition and corruption of the powerful.[10]

The only thing which gave plausibility to Machiavelli's admiration for Cesare Borgia is the fact that, despite all his crimes, Cesare did give better government to the Romagna than the horde of robber barons whom he displaced. Machiavelli set his prince the task of fighting the devil with fire, but there was at least a largeness of aim and breadth of political conception in the prince's villainy which were lacking in the equal villainy of the prince's opponents.

Side by side with Machiavelli's dislike of the nobility stands his hatred of mercenary soldiers. Here again he had in view one of the most serious causes of lawlessness in Italy, the bands of hired ruffians who were ready to fight for whosoever would offer the largest pay, who were faithful to no one, and who were often more dangerous to their employer than to his enemies. Such professional soldiers had almost wholly displaced the older

[10] *Discourses,* I, 55.

citizen-soldiers of the free cities, and while they were able to terrorize Italy, they had proved their incompetence against better organized and more loyal troops from France. Machiavelli had a clear perception of the advantage which France gained from nationalizing her army and consequently he was never tired of urging that the training and equipment of a citizen-army is the first need of a state. As he knew from his own observation, mercenary troops and foreign auxiliaries are alike ruinous to the ruler who must depend upon them. They exhaust his treasury and almost invariably fail him in a pinch. The art of war is therefore the primary concern of a ruler, the condition of success in all his ventures. Before everything else he must aim to possess a strong force of his own citizens, well equipped and well disciplined, and attached to his interests by ties of loyalty to the state. Machiavelli would have all able-bodied citizens between the ages of seventeen and forty subject to military training. With such a force the ruler can maintain his power and extend the limits of the state; without it he becomes a prey to civil strife within and to the ambition of neighboring princes.

Behind Machiavelli's belief in a citizen-army and his hatred of the nobility stood the one sentiment which mitigated the cynicism of his political opinions. This was national patriotism and a desire for the unification of Italy and her preservation from internal disorders and foreign invaders. He was perfectly frank in asserting that duty to one's country overrides all other duties and all scruples.

> For where the very safety of the country depends upon the resolution to be taken, no considerations of justice or injustice, humanity or cruelty, nor of glory or of shame, should be allowed to prevail. But putting all other considerations aside, the only question should be, What course will save the life and liberty of the country? [11]

This was the sentiment behind his idealization of absolute and ruthless power, as appears in the eloquent chapter which concludes the *Prince*. Machiavelli hoped that somewhere among the tyrants of Italy, perhaps in the house of Medici, there might arise a prince with a vision broad enough to see a united Italy and bold enough to make the vision real.

[11] *Discourses,* III, 41.

> And if . . . it was necessary for the purpose of displaying the virtue of Moses that the people of Israel should be held in bondage in Egypt; and that the Persians should be oppressed by the Medes, so as to bring to light the greatness and courage of Cyrus; and that the Athenians should be dispersed for the purpose of illustrating the excellence of Theseus; so at present, for the purpose of making manifest the virtues of one Italian spirit, it was necessary that Italy should have been brought to her present condition of being in a worse bondage than that of the Jews, more enslaved than the Persians, more scattered than the Athenians, without a head, without order, vanquished and despoiled, lacerated, overrun by her enemies, and subjected to every kind of devastation.[12]

But while the hope of peace and unity for Italy was a real motive of Machiavelli's thought, it was with him rather a sentiment than a definite plan. Aside from the belief that it must come under the leadership of an absolute monarch, as he saw national unity being achieved in France and Spain, he had nothing that could be called a policy for Italian unification. He thought of it rather as a distant hope, without which the happiness and prosperity of the country could never be attained; he never really conceived government on a national scale. The government which evoked his sincerest enthusiasm was an expanding city-state such as Rome, a city-state which, to be sure, should follow a far-sighted policy in attracting and retaining the support of its allies, but which in Machiavelli's conception never rose to the height of establishing a nation-wide citizenship. Thus it happens that the concluding chapter of the *Prince,* though doubtless sincere, is the exception rather than the rule in his usually sordid advice to princes.

INSIGHT AND DEFICIENCIES

The character of Machiavelli and the true meaning of his philosophy have been one of the enigmas of modern history. He has been represented as an utter cynic, an impassioned patriot, an ardent nationalist, a political Jesuit, a convinced democrat, and an unscrupulous seeker after the favor of despots. In each of these views, incompatible as they are, there is probably an element of truth. What is emphatically not true is that any one of them gives a complete picture either of Machiavelli or his thought. His thought was that of a true empiric, the result of a wide range

[12] *Prince,* ch. 26.

of political observation and a still wider range of reading in political history; it has in it no general system to which he tried to relate all his observations. In the same way his character must have been complex. His writings show, it is true, a surprising concentration of interest. He writes about nothing and thinks about nothing except politics, statecraft, and the art of war. For deeper-lying social questions, economic or religious, he had no interest except as they bore upon politics. He was perhaps too practical to be philosophically profound, but in politics pure and simple he had of all his contemporaries the greatest breadth of view and the clearest insight into the general tendency of European evolution.

> Living at a time when the old political order in Europe was collapsing and new problems both in state and in society were arising with dazzling rapidity, he endeavoured to interpret the logical meaning of events, to forecast the inevitable issues, and to elicit and formulate the rules which, destined henceforth to dominate political action, were then taking shape among the fresh-forming conditions of national life.[13]

Machiavelli more than any other political thinker created the meaning that has been attached to the state in modern political usage. Even the word itself, as the name of a sovereign political body, appears to have been made current in the modern languages largely by his writings. The state as an organized force, supreme in its own territory and pursuing a conscious policy of aggrandizement in its relations with other states, became not only the typical modern political institution but increasingly the most powerful institution in modern society. To it more and more fell the right and the obligation to regulate and control all the other institutions of society, and to direct them on lines overtly set by the interests of the state itself. The part that the state, thus conceived, has played in modern politics is an index of the clearness with which Machiavelli grasped the drift of political evolution.

Yet it would be hard to say whether the intense brilliance that his genius cast on the statecraft of the despots and of the national states which followed them did not hide as much as it revealed. A philosophy which attributes the successes and failures of politics chiefly to the astuteness or the ineptitude of statesmen is

[13] L. A. Burd, in the *Cambridge Modern History*, Vol. I (1903), p. 200.

bound to be superficial. Machiavelli thought of moral, religious, and economic factors in society as forces which a clever politician can turn to the advantage of the state, or which he can even produce for the sake of the state, and this not only reverses a sane order of values but also the usual order of causal efficacy. At all events it is certain that Machiavelli misrepresented completely the state of European thought at the beginning of the sixteenth century, except among a few disillusioned Italians. His two books were written within ten years of the day on which Martin Luther nailed his theses to the door of the church in Wittenberg, and it was the effect of the Protestant Reformation to involve politics and political thought more closely with religion and with differences of religious faith than had been the case during most of the Middle Ages. Machiavelli's indifference to the truth of religion became in the end a common characteristic of modern thought, but it was emphatically not true of the two centuries after he wrote. In this sense his philosophy was both narrowly local and narrowly dated. Had he written in any country except Italy, or had he written in Italy after the beginning of the Reformation, and still more after the beginning of the Counter Reformation in the Roman church, it is impossible to suppose that he would have treated religion as he did.

SELECTED BIBLIOGRAPHY

A History of Political Thought in the Sixteenth Century. By J. W. Allen. London, 1928. Part IV, ch. 2.

Il principe. Ed. by L. A. Burd. Oxford, 1891. (Introduction by Lord Acton; reprinted in the *History of Freedom and other Essays.* London, 1907.)

"Florence (II): Machiavelli." By L. A. Burd. In the *Cambridge Modern History,* Vol. I (1903), ch. 6.

The Statecraft of Machiavelli. By H. Butterfield. London, 1940.

"Economic Change." By William Cunningham. In the *Cambridge Modern History,* Vol. I (1903), ch. 15.

A History of Political Theories, Ancient and Mediaeval. By W. A. Dunning. New York, 1902. Ch. 11.

"Machiavelli's Political Philosophy." By C. R. Fay. In *Youth and Power.* London, 1931.

Studies of Political Thought from Gerson to Grotius, 1414–1625. By John Neville Figgis. 2nd ed. Cambridge, 1923. Ch. 3.

Machiavelli's Prince and its Forerunners: The Prince as a Typical Book de regimine principum. By Allan H. Gilbert. Durham, N. C., 1938.

The Social and Political Ideas of some Great Thinkers of the Renaissance and the Reformation. Ed. by F. J. C. Hearnshaw. London, 1925. Ch. 4.

Histoire de la science politique. By P. Janet. 2 vols. 4th ed. Paris, 1913. Vol. I, pp. 491–602.

" Machiavelli and the Present Time." By H. J. Laski. In *The Dangers of Obedience and other Essays.* New York, 1930.

Machiavelli. The Romanes Lecture, 1897. By John Morley. London, 1897.

Machiavelli and his Times. By D. Erskine Muir. London, 1936.

Nicolo Machiavelli, the Florentine. By Giuseppe Prezzolini. Eng. trans. by Ralph Roeder. New York, 1928.

Machiavelli: The Man, his Work, and his Times. By Jeffrey Pulver. London, 1937.

The Life and Times of Niccolo Machiavelli. By P. Villari. Eng. trans. by Linda Villari. 2 vols. Rev. ed. London, 1892.

CHAPTER XVIII

THE EARLY PROTESTANT REFORMERS

The Protestant Reformation mixed political theory with differences of religious belief and with questions of theological dogma more closely than had been the case even in the Middle Ages. There is, however, no simple formula for this relationship. Everywhere political theories were defended with theological arguments and political alliances were made in the name of religious truth. Nowhere was there any religious party, Protestant or Catholic, that really related its political convictions with the theology which it professed. The reasons for this are evident. Catholics and Protestants alike, and every subdivision of Protestants, drew upon the same Christian heritage and the same body of European political experience. The scholars of all churches had the same stock of ideas, a rich and varied body of thought extending continuously back to the eleventh century and embodying a tradition which carried it back to antiquity. The logical dependence of any part of this political tradition upon any particular theological system was loose, as it had always been in the Middle Ages. Protestants could select from it, as Catholics had always done, according to their purposes and circumstances. Consequently the Reformation produced no such thing as a Protestant political theory, any more than the Middle Ages produced a Catholic one, nor for that matter did it produce even an Anglican or a Presbyterian or a Lutheran theory that had any close dependence upon the theologies of these Protestant churches. Given time and a stable relationship to government, any group could select a more or less coherent political doctrine, suitable to its situation and fairly characteristic of its members' beliefs (though always with individual exceptions). But similarity of political conviction depended more on circumstances than on theology, and political differences resulted rather from the varying situations in which the churches found themselves than from theological differences. Thus an Anglican, a Lutheran, and a Gallican Catholic might agree much better about the divine right of kings than about their theology, and also they might agree to regard both Calvinists and Jesuits as public enemies. A classification of political theories would never correspond with a classification of religious denominations, though it is true that religious groups did form typical bodies of theory.

In no case did the mere breaking of relations with the Roman Church solve for Protestants any of the intrinsic difficulties that had arisen in the Middle Ages over clerical interference in politics or secular interference in religion. It changed their form but at the same time it intensified them, because, for the time being, religion was more dependent upon and involved with politics than ever before. Moreover, the relation of church and state varied with the political and religious situation in each country. Current conceptions of the church and of religion changed much more slowly than the facts warranted, and the results achieved were never in any great degree like those intended. Thus the unity of the church was permanently broken, so that instead of one church there was a growing number of churches, but it was a century before even liberal Protestants could contemplate this as a fact. The conception of a church as the guardian of the only revealed truth remained, and the fact that Protestantism replaced the authority of the hierarchy with the infallibility of Scripture made it no less authoritarian. Everyone assumed, with what now seems incredible naiveté, that agreement about religious truth was possible or even certain, if only the blindness, or more usually the wickedness, of their opponents could be removed. Except in the case of a mere handful of writers there was no question of religious toleration. The belief was general on the side of churchmen that pure doctrine ought to be maintained by public authority, and on the side of statesmen that unity of religion was an indispensable condition of public order. Where the government of the Roman Church was broken the maintenance of the faith became a charge on the civil authorities, because no one else could do it. In effect the decision as to what is pure doctrine passed largely to secular rulers. When this was honestly attempted, government became charged with the impossible task of deciding what religious truth is, and when it was not honestly done, politicians were given an infinity of troubled water to fish in.

PASSIVE OBEDIENCE AND THE RIGHT TO RESIST

On the whole, therefore, the Reformation, together with the sectarian controversies to which it gave rise, accelerated the tendency, already in existence, to increase and consolidate the power of the monarchies. The failure of the church to reform itself by a General Council meant that no successful reform was possible unless it could enlist the support, or even the force, of secular rulers. Martin Luther early discovered that the success of reform in Germany depended upon obtaining the help of the princes. In England the Reformation was carried through by the already well-nigh absolute power of Henry VIII, and its immediate consequence was to strengthen royal power still farther. In Europe generally, as controversies spread, the king was the one point around which national unity could rally. This was notably true in France in the latter part of the sixteenth century. Without much exaggeration it may be said that everywhere success went to the religious party that happened to be allied with a strong internal policy. In England and northern Germany Protestantism was on the side of the princes. In France and Spain it became allied with particularist movements of the nobility, the provinces, or the cities, with the result that the national religion remained Catholic. Thus, whoever lost, the kings won, and the absolute monarchy, which the Reformation did not originate and which was no more naturally related to one form of religious belief than another, was in the first instance its chief political beneficiary.

This effect was increased by the fact that the more powerful reforming groups continually felt obliged to fight their war on two fronts. They had, of course, to contend against the pope, and for this purpose they used all the principles and arguments that had become common property in the two centuries since William of Occam. But leading Protestant reformers, even more than Catholics, felt compelled to distinguish themselves sharply from the obscurer and more radical movements of religious and social reform which composed the "lunatic fringe" of Protestantism. Movements of this sort, which had no doubt been simmering under the surface for centuries, immediately came to light when the stable order began to be agitated. Anabaptism and the peasant revolts were feared and hated by the rising bourgoisie of the sixteenth century more fiercely and more nervously than similar proletarian disturbances of a later day. They were suppressed with savage cruelty, which received the blessing of both Luther and Calvin. Not for nothing did monarchy receive the support of the growing middle class, but for this reason also the religious reformers were thrown bodily into the arms of the princes. Thus the Reformation joined with economic forces already in existence to make royal government, invested with absolute power at home and with a free hand abroad, the typical form of European state.

At the same time, however, Protestantism produced another result which, in the long run, tended to work in an opposite direction. In most parts of northern Europe it produced relatively strong religious minorities, bodies too numerous to be coerced without endangering public order and quite as determined as the party in power to gain for its own faith the benefits of legal establishment. Every such body was, for obvious reasons, a potential source of disorder, and every religious difference was at the same time a political issue. Only slowly and under the compulsion of circumstances that permitted no other solution did a policy of religious toleration emerge, as it was discovered that a common political loyalty was possible to people of different religions. In the meantime the amalgamation of religion and politics was complete. The upholding of rulers became a primary article of religious faith, while defense of a religious creed was felt to be, and often in fact was, an attack upon a ruler of a different belief. The cause of religious reform, at least on the part of a dissenting and disestablished group, involved not only a right to disagree with the government in power but possibly also the right to resist in the interests of what the dissenters honestly believed to be true religion. In the fourteenth and fifteenth centuries reformers had claimed the right to resist an heretical pope. In the sixteenth century they had to claim the right to resist heretical kings, who now, rather than the pope, were " laying waste the church." The issue was still religious reform, but it was a political at least as much as a religious issue.

For this reason the most controverted point in political philosophy became the question whether subjects have the right to resist their rulers — of course for supposedly good reasons, usually concerned with the maintenance of sound Christian doctrine —

or whether they owe a duty of passive obedience such that resistance is in all cases wrong. The latter view became the modernized theory of monarchical divine right, since passive obedience to any form of government except a monarchy was an academic question. The right to resist, on the other hand, could best be defended on the hypothesis that kings derive their power from the people and may be called to account, for sufficient cause, by them. These two types of theory therefore came to prevail in the sixteenth century and they came to be regarded as antithetical to one another, as indeed they were in the consequences that each was now held to entail. Both were for the time being equally theological, though it proved possible to detach the theory of popular rights from theology more easily than divine right.

Obviously neither theory was in itself new, though both were more or less new in respect to the uses to which they were put. The belief that civic obedience was a Christian virtue enjoined by God was as old as St. Paul. No Christian had ever doubted that in some sense the powers that be are of God, and in itself this implied no denial of the view that in some sense power comes also from the people. An occasional medieval writer, following the tradition of Gregory the Great, could approximate the doctrine of passive obedience, though it was not a common belief, as it came to be in the sixteenth and seventeenth centuries. On the other hand, the general theory that political authority comes from the people had not been in any specific sense a defense of the right to resist. The specialization of the two theories, and the setting up of one as monarchical and the other as anti-monarchical, came about in the course of the sixteenth century.

MARTIN LUTHER

The interesting point to be observed about the first reformers is that both Luther and Calvin stood on substantially identical ground relative to the fundamental moral issue. That is to say, they both held the view that resistance to rulers is in all circumstances wicked. This fact is striking in view of the contrast between the later history of the Lutheran and Calvinist churches. Both in Scotland and France the Calvinists were largely responsible for developing and spreading the theory that political resistance is justified as a means of religious reform. It was John

Knox in Scotland, the leader of a reform which must succeed by popular force against a court-party that was immovably Catholic, who was in the first instance responsible for this important departure from the teaching of Calvin himself. The circumstances in which French Calvinists found themselves contributed to a similar end. On the other hand, the state of affairs in northern Germany tended to make passive obedience a permanent part of the teaching of the Lutheran Church.

This result has in it an element of historical irony. On the ground of temperament Luther was much better fitted to sympathize with the cause of personal liberty than Calvin. By inclination he disliked coercion in matters of belief, and this was in fact the only view consistent with his idea of religious experience.

> Heresy can never be kept off by force. For that another tool is needed, and it is another quarrel and conflict than that of the sword. God's word must contend here. If that avail nothing, temporal power will never settle the matter, though it fill the world with blood.[1]

For the substance of religion lay for Luther in an inner experience, essentially mystical and incommunicable, while its outward forms and the ministrations of the clergy are merely an aid or a hindrance to attaining this goal. This was the meaning of his doctrines of justification by faith and "the priesthood of the Christian man." Obviously force is a wholly unsuitable means to foster religion so understood.

The antecedents of all Luther's ideas both about church and state had been current since the fourteenth century. The charges which he brought against the Roman Church — the luxury and evil living of the Roman court, the draining of German ecclesiastical revenues to Rome, the advancement of foreign prelates to preferment in German churches, the corruption of the papal judiciary, and the sale of indulgences — all referred to ancient grievances. The basis of his argument against the pope and the hierarchy was precisely the principle made current by the conciliar controversy, that the church is "the assembly of all believers in Christ upon earth." His attack upon the special privileges and immunities of the clergy followed the lines of the older antipapal argument: differences of rank are merely administrative conven-

[1] "On Secular Authority," 1523; *Werke*, Weimar ed., Vol. XI, p. 268.

iences, and all classes of men, laymen as well as clergy, have callings useful to the community. Hence there is no reason why the clergy should not be answerable in temporal matters just as a layman is.

> It is indeed past bearing that the spiritual law should esteem so highly the liberty, life, and property of the clergy, as if laymen were not as good spiritual Christians, or not equally members of the Church.[2]

Nevertheless, though Luther was temperamentally averse to religious coercion and though he knew how to muster the priesthood of the Christian man against the Canon Law and against sacerdotalism, he wholly failed to envisage religion as able to dispense altogether with ecclesiastical discipline and authority. Reluctantly but none the less surely he was led to the conclusion that heresy must be suppressed and that heretical teaching must be prevented. This conclusion, in spite of his inclination, led straight to coercion, and since the church had itself failed to correct its shortcomings, the hope for a purified church lay necessarily with secular rulers.

> But this would be the best, and also the only remedy remaining, if kings, princes, nobility, cities and communities themselves began and opened a way for reformation, so that the bishops and clergy, who now are afraid, would have reason to follow.[3]

Luther still adhered, it is true, to the ancient subterfuge that this is a temporary device to meet an emergency. Kings and princes, he says, are " bishops by necessity." But the practical upshot of his break with Rome was that secular government itself became the agent of reform and the effective arbiter of what reform should be. Nothing certainly was farther from his intention than to make government the judge of heresy, but in effect the power that enforces also defines. In the event, therefore, Luther helped to create a national church, something which he would certainly have regarded as a religious monstrosity.

Being thus dependent upon the princes for the success of reform, it became a foregone conclusion that he would adhere to the

[2] " To the Nobility of the German Nation," 1520 (trans. by Wace and Buchheim); *Werke*, Vol. VI, p. 410.

[3] " On Good Works," 1520 (trans. by W. A. Lambert); *Werke*, Vol. VI, p. 258.

view that subjects owe their rulers a duty of passive obedience. Despite his own independence of judgment and his genuine love of religious liberty, the adoption of this point of view probably cost him little or nothing in respect to political convictions. He had in fact very little interest in politics except as events forced it on his attention, and by temperament he had great respect for civil authority; he was always markedly opposed to political pressure exerted through sedition and violence. Luther was no respecter of persons — he once said that rulers were "generally the biggest fools and worst knaves on earth" — but he had great respect for office as such and he had no confidence whatever in the masses of mankind.

> The princes of this world are gods, the common people are Satan, through whom God sometimes does what at other times he does directly through Satan, that is, makes rebellion as a punishment for the people's sins.
>
> I would rather suffer a prince doing wrong than a people doing right.[4]

As might be expected, his assertion of the duty of passive obedience was as strong as it could possibly be made:

> It is in no wise proper for anyone who would be a Christian to set himself up against his government, whether it act justly or unjustly.[4]
>
> There are no better works than to obey and serve all those who are set over us as superiors. For this reason also disobedience is a greater sin than murder, unchastity, theft, and dishonesty, and all that these may include.[5]

It is true that in this respect, as in others, Luther was not very consistent; his political opinions were too much governed by circumstances, and passive obedience was not without its difficulties. The very princes upon whom he depended were, in law at least, the subjects of the emperor. In this contingency he was driven to concede that the emperor might be resisted when he exceeded his imperial authority, which was clearly inconsistent with the general principle of passive obedience. However, the emperor's actual power over the princes was sufficiently shadowy so that the discrepancy had little practical importance. The weight of Lu-

[4] Quoted by Preserved Smith, *The Age of the Reformation* (1920), pp. 594 f.

[5] "On Good Works" (trans. by W. A. Lambert); *Werke,* Vol. VI, p. 250

ther's authority was quite definitely on the side of the doctrine that resistance to civil authority is in all circumstances morally wrong.

The result of Lutheranism was on the whole quite different from what Luther intended. Religiously more liberal, at least by inclination, than Calvin, he instituted the Lutheran state churches, dominated by political forces and almost, it might be said, branches of the state. The disruption of the universal church, the suppression of its monastic institutions and ecclesiastical corporations, and the abrogation of the Canon Law, removed the strongest checks upon secular power that had existed in the Middle Ages. Luther's stress upon the pure inwardness of religious experience inculcated an attitude of quietism and acquiescence toward worldly power. Religion perhaps gained in spirituality but the state certainly gained in power. The submissiveness of the Lutheran churches, with a suggestion of mysticism, is sharply in contrast with the type of religion that developed in the Calvinist churches, where worldly activity and even worldly success figured as Christian duties.

CALVINISM AND THE POWER OF THE CHURCH

The Calvinist churches, in Holland, Scotland, and America, were the chief medium through which the justification of resistance was spread through western Europe. The difference depended in no way upon the primary intention of Calvin himself; in fact, he believed as emphatically in the duty of passive obedience as Luther, and in character he was far more legalist and authoritarian than the German reformer. In so far as the difference depended upon anything in Calvinist theology, the relation was indirect and might, under different circumstances, have had quite a different history. The crucial fact was that Calvinism, especially in France and Scotland, was in opposition to governments which it had practically no chance to convert or capture. For this reason chiefly Calvin's strong statements about the wickedness of resistance — natural enough in Geneva or so long as there was any hope of successful reform in France — were permitted by his followers to lapse and were supplanted by teaching to exactly the opposite effect. John Knox's first steps in this direction took advantage of certain minor features of Calvin's teaching, but in themselves these features need never have led to any such change of position.

In its initial form Calvinism not only included a condemnation of resistance but it lacked all leaning toward liberalism, constitutionalism, or representative principles. Where it had free range it developed characteristically into a theocracy, a kind of oligarchy maintained by an alliance of the clergy and the gentry from which the mass of the people was excluded and which was, in general, illiberal, oppressive, and reactionary. This was the nature of Calvin's own government in Geneva and of Puritan government in Massachusetts. It is true that Calvin objected on principle to a combination of state and church. It was on this ground that he broke with the reform of Zwingli at Zürich; and Calvinists generally, in England for example, continued to oppose such a union as resulted from admitting the king to be the head of a national church. The reason for this, however, was not a desire that the state should be free from clerical influence but exactly the opposite. The church must be free to set its own standards of doctrine and morals and must have the full support of secular power in enforcing its discipline upon the recalcitrant. In Geneva excommunication deprived a citizen of the right to hold office, and in Massachusetts civic rights were limited to church-members. In this respect Calvin's theory of the church was more in the spirit of extreme medieval ecclesiasticism than that held by nationalist Catholics. This is the reason why, to members of the national churches, Calvinist and Jesuit seemed to be two names for the same thing. Both stood for the primacy and independence of spiritual authority and the use of secular power to give effect to its judgments about orthodoxy and moral discipline. In practice, wherever possible, Calvinist government placed the two swords of Christian tradition in the church, and gave the direction of secular authority to the clergy rather than to secular rulers. The result was likely to be an intolerable rule of the saints: a meticulous regulation of the most private concerns founded upon universal espionage, with only a shadowy distinction between the maintenance of public order, the control of private morals, and the preservation of pure doctrine and worship.

With these practical results the characteristic doctrines of

Calvinist theology — election and foreordination — were not unconnected. The belief that men are saved not by their own merit but by the free act of God's grace might seem, on its face, to take the heart out of human effort. In fact it had exactly the opposite effect. Calvinism lacked almost all trace of the mysticism and quietism which colored Luther's idea of religious experience. Calvinist ethics was essentially an ethics of action. And indeed, what better motive can there be to relentless activity — to steel the will and, if need be, to harden the heart — than a whole-souled conviction that a man is the chosen instrument of God's will? The Calvinist theory of predestination had nothing in common with the modern conception of universal causality. It was rather a belief in a cosmic system of quasi-military discipline. Thus Calvin exhausted the vocabulary of the Roman law to describe the sovereignty of God over the world and man. His morals taught not so much love of one's fellows as self-control, discipline, and respect for one's comrades in the battle of life, and these became indeed the sovereign moral virtues of Puritanism. It was this ethics which made the Calvinist churches the peculiarly militant parts of Protestantism. The dogma of election was ideally suited to the autocratic temper of the moral reformer who set himself to do battle against the unregenerate mass of mankind.

The doctrine of foreordination was the saints' mandate to rule. Lacking Luther's inclination toward mystical religious experience, Calvin in one sense put a higher value on secular institutions, which for Luther had only a worldly importance. This did not imply their independence of the church but the opposite; they are among the "external means of salvation." Hence the first duty of government is to maintain the pure worship of God and to uproot idolatry, sacrilege, blasphemy, and heresy. The emphasis in Calvin's enumeration of the objects for which secular power exists is enlightening.

> It is the purpose of temporal rule, so long as we live among men, to foster and support the external worship of God, to defend pure doctrine and the standing of the church, to conform our lives to human society, to mold our conduct to civil justice, to harmonize us with each other, and to preserve the common peace and tranquility.[6]

[6] *Institutes,* IV, xx, 2.

It is true that Calvin reiterated the ancient Christian view that genuine belief cannot be compelled, but he put practically no limit upon the duty of the state to enforce outward conformity.

Calvinism, then, aimed primarily at censorship in morals and discipline in doctrine; it was notable for the power and influence which it gave to the clergy. The fact is the more striking because it went beyond other Protestant bodies in its opposition to ceremonialism and also because the Calvinist form of church government included representation of the congregation by lay elders. The latter practice was an efficient means for applying censorship; it was not intended to introduce democracy into the church or to curb the influence of the clergy, nor did it do so in the earlier forms of Calvinism. In theory the power of the church was supposed to lie in the whole Christian body, and at Geneva this power was exercised by a consistory which included the clergy and twelve lay elders chosen nominally by the town council. In reality the power of the clergy was practically unlimited, and the system was representative only in the vague sense that the consistory was supposed to exercise an authority belonging to the whole church. At the start the elders were in no specific sense representative of the congregation, as they later came to be when the Presbyterian churches adopted a plan of election, and there was no self-government in church-meeting such as appeared later in the Congregational bodies.

It is quite true, however, that Calvinism in Scotland did embody the principle of representation in a way that was politically important. The general assembly of the Scottish Church, together with its presbyteries and provincial synods, was far more representative of the nation generally than the Scottish parliament, which had remained feudal in its make-up. The reformation in Scotland was substantially a popular and national movement directed against a Catholic court and nobility closely allied with France, but this was not because Calvinism in its original form stood either for popular rights or representation. Politically it had no such general implication, and in church government lay eldership came to have these qualities only when circumstances brought the result about.

In so far as Calvinism had any leaning away from monarchical power, this resulted from a negative rather than from a positive quality. It was probably true — certainly the later sixteenth century believed it to be true — that Calvinism was not a form of church government which could commend itself to a national church of which the king was the temporal head. The essential reason for this was the fact, already noted, that Calvinism stood on the Hildebrandine principle that spiritual authority is superior to secular, and so tended to make the clergy independent of the temporal head of a state church. The difference between Calvinism and Catholicism in this respect lay in the fact that the former made the church generally, including both clergy and laity, autonomous, instead of concentrating spiritual power in the bishops. In the national churches the bishops, having been detached from Rome, became the most eligible agencies for conducting royal government in the church, and in consequence episcopalianism became the natural form of government to be adopted by the national churches. This was the reason for the pregnant aphorism of King James, "no bishop, no king," which was based upon a long and poignant experience of Calvinist presbyteries. In this sense, then, Calvinism was predestined to be the form of church government for opposition parties. It was not intrinsically popular and certainly not in intention anti-monarchical, but it was non-monarchical in the sense that the monarchy always had more favorable forms of church government to choose from.

CALVIN AND PASSIVE OBEDIENCE

Of Calvin's specifically political views, by far the most important, at least as concerns his own time and place, is his strong and on the whole consistent assertion of the duty of passive obedience, in respect to which he was quite in agreement with Luther. Since secular power is the external means to salvation, the estate of the magistrate is, he says, most honorable; he is the vicar of God and resistance to him is resistance to God. It is a vain business for the private man, who has no duty to govern, to dispute what is the best condition for the state. If anything needs correction, let him show it to his superior and not put his own hand to the work. Let him do nothing without the command of his superior. The bad ruler, who is a visitation on the people for their sins, deserves the unconditional submission of his subjects no less than the good, for submission is due not to the person but to the office, and the office has inviolable majesty. It is true that Calvin, like practically all sixteenth-century advocates of the divine right of kings, expressed strong views on the duty of rulers to their subjects. The immutable law of God is binding on kings as well as on subjects, and the evil ruler is guilty of sedition against God. Like Locke later he held that civil law merely fixes a penalty for what is intrinsically wrong. But the punishment of a derelict magistrate belongs to God and not to his subjects. This was a natural position for Calvin to take, both in view of his own power in Geneva and because of the hope that Calvinist protestantism might yet become the religion of the kings of France.

There was one phase of Calvin's theory of political resistance, of minor importance in his own writing, which was greatly developed by some of his followers. He pointed out that there are constitutions in which certain " inferior magistrates " are charged with a duty to resist tyranny in the head of the state and to protect the people against him.[7] He was clearly thinking of officials like the plebeian tribunes in ancient Rome. In case a constitution does include such inferior magistrates, the right to resist is itself derived from God; it is in no sense a general right of the people to resist. The sovereign power is held jointly, and one sharer has the duty to prevent aggression by another. This theory of the inferior magistrate got an importance among certain Calvinists out of all proportion to the place given it by Calvin. Once the doctrine of passive obedience was dropped, as it was first in Scotland and later in France, the right to resist was usually lodged not in private persons but in the inferior magistrates or " natural leaders " of the people. The theory formed an aristocratic mitigation of a general theory of natural rights inherent in the people. In Calvin himself, however, there was no theory of popular rights. The ruler's obligation to govern lawfully is owed to God and not to the people; his power is limited by the law of God and not by the rights of the people; and if there is in a particular constitution a right to resist the chief magistrate, this also comes from God and not from the people.

It is a point of minor importance that Calvin's own political convictions were aristocratic rather than monarchical. There was room in his system for only one king, namely, God himself. Thus

[7] *Institutes,* IV, xx, 31.

he described the selection of one man or one family for political power as *lese majesté* against the divine kingship. This opinion was probably reenforced by an intellectual preference, based upon humanistic studies, for the ancient aristocratic republic. This preference can be seen clearly in the *Institutes.* He reproduced from Polybius the ancient argument for mixed government. His criticism of hereditary monarchy recalls Cicero, and his strictures on democracy are as bitter as Plato's. Nothing could surpass the contempt expressed in his description of the Anabaptists as "those who live pell mell like rats in the straw." The bias of Calvin's own political and social opinions was markedly aristocratic, and this remained in general the bias of Calvinism, except as it was transformed in certain of the left-wing sects.

In its main aspects Calvin's political theory was a somewhat unstable structure, not precisely because it was illogical but because it could readily become the prey of circumstances. On the one hand it stressed the wickedness of all resistance to constituted authority, but on the other its fundamental principle was the right of the church to declare pure doctrine and to exercise universal censorship with the support of secular power. It was practically a foregone conclusion, therefore, that a Calvinist church, existing in a state whose rulers refused to admit the truth of its doctrine and to enforce its discipline, would drop the duty to obey and assert the right to resist. At least, such a result might be expected where there was little chance of converting the government and a good chance of gaining by resistance. This was the situation in which Calvinists found themselves in the later sixteenth century in both Scotland and France.

JOHN KNOX

The reversal of position was first made by John Knox, not because of any special originality on his part but because of the situation in which Scottish Protestantism was placed. In 1558 Knox found himself in exile and under sentence of death by the Catholic hierarchy in Scotland but still the leader of a strong Protestant following. The crown, because of its alliance with France, was irretrievably Catholic. Thus he could hope much from a policy of resistance and nothing from any other policy, and in fact by this means he accomplished the Scottish reformation only two years later. It was in this situation that he wrote his *Appellation* to the nobility, estates, and commonalty of Scotland, asserting the duty of every man in his station to see that true religion is taught and that those are punished with death who deprive the people of "the food of their souls, I mean God's lively Word."

In essentials Knox did not depart from Calvin's principles. He assumed the incontestable truth of Calvin's version of Christian doctrine and also the duty of the church to enforce its discipline against all who do not willingly accept it. Every Christian is obliged to bring it about that this doctrine and this discipline shall have the weight to which their truth entitles them. So far Knox is merely Calvin over again. But in Scotland there is a Catholic regent for a Catholic queen who not only refuses the true faith but actively upholds idolatry (that is, Catholicism). What, then, ought a true believer to do? Knox boldly asserted that it was their duty to correct and repress whatever a king does contrary to God's word, honor, and glory, and thereby he rejected Calvin's doctrine of passive obedience.

> For now the common song of all men is, We must obey our kings, be they good or be they bad; for God hath so commanded. But horrible shall the vengeance be, that shall be poured forth upon such blasphemers of God his holy name and ordinance. For it is no less blasphemy to say that God hath commanded kings to be obeyed when they command impiety, than to say that God by his precept is author and maintainer of all iniquity.
>
> The punishment of such crimes as are idolatry, blasphemy, and others that touch the majesty of God, doth not appertain to kings and chief rulers only, but also to the whole body of that people and to every member of the same, according to the vocation of every man and according to that possibility and occasion, which God doth minister to revenge the injury done against his glory, what time that impiety is manifestly known.[8]

Behind some of Knox's statements there appears to lie the presumption that kings owe their power to election and hence are

[8] *Appellation; Works* (ed. by Laing), Vol. IV, pp. 496, 501. Strangely enough, this was written in Geneva. Views similar to Knox's were published in the same year by Christopher Goodman in his *How Superior Powers ought to be Obeyed*. The two men had evidently collaborated. See J. W. Allen, *Political Thought in the Sixteenth Century* (1928), p. 110.

responsible to the people for its exercise,[9] but this is quite vague and undeveloped. The essential points are, first, that he abandoned Calvin's belief that resistance is always wrong and, second, that he defended resistance as part of the duty to sustain religious reform. His stand was taken upon the ground of religious duty, not of popular rights, but it put one great wing of the Calvinist churches in opposition to royalist power and boldly justified the use of rebellion. The next step was taken in France, where the outbreak of the religious wars again put a Calvinist party in opposition to a Catholic monarchy. Here the theory that royal power is derived from and responsible to the people received a much fuller development than Knox gave it, though still with a very definite reference to the religious question. The fuller development of Knox's revolutionary or anti-monarchical Calvinism may therefore be sought in such a work as the *Vindiciae contra tyrannos*.

SELECTED BIBLIOGRAPHY

A History of Political Thought in the Sixteenth Century. By J. W. Allen. London, 1928. Part I.

Calvins Staatsanschauung und das konfessionelle Zeitalter. By Hans Baron. Berlin, 1924.

"Calvin and the Reformed Church." By A. M. Fairbairn. In the *Cambridge Modern History*, Vol. II (1903), ch. 11.

Das Naturrecht bei Luther und Calvin: Eine politische Untersuchung. By Alfred Grobmann. Harburg-Wilhelmsburg, 1935.

Der Staat in Calvins Gedankenwelt. By Hans Haussherr. Leipzig, 1923.

The Social and Political Ideas of some Great Thinkers of the Renaissance and the Reformation. Ed. by F. J. C. Hearnshaw. London, 1925. Chs. 7, 8.

John Ponet (1516?–1556): Advocate of Limited Monarchy. By Winthrop S. Hudson. Chicago, 1942.

"Luther." By T. M. Lindsay. In the *Cambridge Modern History*, Vol. II (1903), ch. 4.

Calvin and the Reformation. By James Mackinnon. London, 1936.

"The Anglican Settlement and the Scottish Reformation." By F. W. Maitland. In the *Cambridge Modern History*, Vol. II (1903), ch. 16.

The Political Consequences of the Reformation: Studies in Sixteenth-century Political Thought. By Robert H. Murray. London, 1926.

[9] *The Second Blast of the Trumpet* (1558).

The Life and Letters of Martin Luther. By Preserved Smith. 2nd ed. Boston, 1914.

The Age of the Reformation. By Preserved Smith. New York, 1920.

The Social Teaching of the Christian Churches. By Ernst Troeltsch. Eng. trans. by Olive Wyon. 2 vols. London, 1931. Ch. 3.

The Political Theories of Martin Luther. By L. H. Waring. New York, 1910.

The Protestant Ethic and the Spirit of Capitalism. By Max Weber. Eng. trans. by Talcott Parsons. London, 1930.

CHAPTER XIX

ROYALIST AND ANTI-ROYALIST THEORIES

When Calvin died in 1564 the lines were already drawn for the religious wars which, as Luther had said, were to "fill the world with blood." In Germany divisions of territory made it a struggle between princes, with the result that the fundamental issue of religious liberty need not be pressed. In the Netherlands it took the form of a revolt against a foreign master. In England, as also in Spain, the supremacy of royal power prevented the outbreak of civil war during the sixteenth century. But in France and Scotland a factional struggle arose which threatened the stability of the nations. Thus in France between 1562 and 1598 there were no fewer than eight civil wars, marked by such atrocities as the St. Bartholomew Massacre and the reckless use of assassination on both sides. Not only was orderly government interrupted but civilization itself was jeopardized. In the sixteenth century, therefore, it was in France that the most significant chapter in political philosophy was written. Here appeared the main oppositions of thought which were elaborated in the English civil wars of the next century. The theory of the people's right as a defense of the right to resist and the theory of the divine right of kings as a bulwark of national unity both began their history as modern political theories in France.

THE RELIGIOUS WARS IN FRANCE

In the most general respects political development in France and England was similar, though there were important differences. In both it was the new monarchy which first formed an organ of national unity and the source of modern, centralized government. The task of the monarchy was easier in England, for the tradition of provincial and municipal independence was on the whole weaker than in France, where royal power prevailed only after a period of civil war. On the other hand, there was in France no such parliamentary tradition as there was in England.

Though the power of parliament was temporarily eclipsed by Tudor absolutism, in the end it prevailed and established itself as a national government. In France differences of provincial privilege made a parliamentary constitution on a national scale impossible. Characteristic differences of political thought followed from the different ways in which national unification came about in the two countries. In England, because the king's power was not seriously threatened in the sixteenth century, the theory of royal absolutism, or complete sovereignty vested in the king, did not develop, whereas in France this theory came to prevail by the end of the century. When opposition to royal power did develop in England in the seventeenth century, the issue was between the king and a national parliament, a form it could not possibly take in France. On the other hand, opposition to royal absolutism in France failed largely because it was allied with a medieval particularism that was incompatible with centralized national government.

In France, and indeed everywhere, differences of religion were inextricably interwoven with political and economic forces. The centralized system of French monarchy, which Machiavelli had admired as the best type of royal government, had by the middle of the sixteenth century proved to be subject to abuses so serious that for the moment they threatened to cost the crown the support of the higher middle classes, upon which its power really depended. Abuses of taxation, the delay and withholding of justice, and the venality of royal executives permitted something which might be called a reaction. The privileges of provinces, of nobility, of more or less self-governing cities, and of medieval institutions generally, all threatened to weaken the more distinctly modern institutions of centralized royal government. None of these issues was specifically Protestant or Catholic but both religious parties used them as their interests dictated. It was the great weakness of the Huguenots, however, that they were in general on the side of local privilege and against the king. The permanent drift of political evolution is shown by the fact that, despite the personal weakness of kings, the crown emerged from the civil wars strengthened rather than weakened. In the long run it defeated both reaction and revolution, and effective centralization became possible toward the close of the sixteenth century under a prevailing theory of royal absolutism. In religion this meant the triumph of what may be called national Catholicism, as against both the ultramontane claims of the papacy, defended by Jesuits, and the forces of particularism represented by Calvinists.

Accordingly the controversial political literature of France after the outbreak of the civil wars was divided into two main types. There were, on the one hand, writings which defended the sanctity of the kingly office; by the end of the sixteenth century this tendency had crystallized in the theory of divine right, asserting the indefeasible right of the king to his throne, derived directly from God and descending to him by legitimate inheritance. The importance of this theory lay chiefly in the practical consequences deduced from it: first, the duty of passive obedience owed by subjects to their sovereigns in spite of doctrinal differences and, second, the impossibility that a king should be deposed by an external power like the papacy. On the other hand, there were various "anti-royalist" theories, as they came to be called,[1] which derived the king's power in some fashion from the "people" or community and defended a right to resist him under certain circumstances. These anti-royalist theories were first developed by Huguenot writers, but there was in fact nothing specifically Protestant about them. The whole literature was essentially controversial and the various parties had a disconcerting fashion of shifting their ground as circumstances dictated.[2]

Since the theory of the divine right of the king was first fully stated in reply to the argument justifying resistance, the latter may be stated first. The most interesting works were those of the French Protestants, which appeared chiefly after the St. Bartholomew Massacre in 1572, though it will be convenient to men-

[1] The name "monarchomach" was apparently invented by William Barclay in his *De regno et regali potestate* (1600) to describe any writer who justified the right to resist. It did not imply an objection to monarchy as such.

[2] When the failure of the Valois line made it apparent that the Protestant Henry of Navarre would probably come to the throne, a group of Catholic anti-royalist writers adopted the argument earlier used by the Protestants. The principal works were Boucher's *De justa Henrici III abdicatione*, 1589; and *De justa reipublicae Christianae in reges impios et haereticos authoritate*, 1592, by an author who uses the pseudonym Rossaeus; probably William Rainolds.

tion here a few other works of similar import produced by Protestant writers outside France. The Jesuit works were for the most part not French and depended in varying degrees on the specifically Jesuit argument for the indirect power of the papacy, but they can conveniently be grouped together. In conclusion the theory of divine right will be stated as representing the upshot of the debate, at least so far as the situation in France was concerned.

THE PROTESTANT ATTACK ON ABSOLUTISM

The Huguenot writers developed two main lines of argument which remained typical of the opposition to absolute royal power and which later reappeared in England. In the first place, there was a constitutional argument alleged to be founded on historical fact. This argument harked back to medieval practice as against the more recent tendency toward royal absolutism. To some extent it was a real appeal to fact, since it could be shown without much trouble that absolute monarchy was an innovation. Unfortunately, however, medieval government had not been constitutional either, in any sense that fitted the sixteenth century. For this reason historical arguments were likely to be inconsequential or specious; they served better to put an opponent in the unwelcome position of defending usurpation than to settle anything. In the second place, an opponent of royal power might turn to the philosophical foundations of political power and seek to show that absolute monarchy was contrary to universal rules of right supposed to underlie all government. At the same time the two lines of argument were not wholly disconnected and both were medieval in origin. The belief in natural law was part of a universally accepted tradition which had come down to the sixteenth century through every channel of political thought and which gained an added importance from the lawlessness of the new monarchy. The historical argument tacitly assumed that immemorial customs had the sanction of natural right.

Constitutional theory was, of course, not the special possession of the Huguenot party. The powers of the king of France had long been subjects of debate, and the view that these powers were limited by natural law or by customary privileges had been frequently stated. Prior to the period of civil war anything resembling a modern theory of sovereignty, investing the king with a universal power to make law, had hardly existed. This theory was the outcome of the threat to orderly and centralized government which the civil wars produced. In particular, it had been frequently held that the king's power was limited by the judicial machinery of the realm — by the supposed right of the Parlements to refuse to register and enforce a royal edict — or by the less definite right of the States General, as representing the whole kingdom, to be consulted in matters of legislation and taxation. Of these two the former was in practice the more serious check upon royal power. The limitation of the king by ancient or local privilege was generally admitted.

Of Huguenot writers on constitutional theory the best known was Francis Hotman, whose *Franco-Gallia* was published in 1573, one of the large number of tracts called out by the Massacre of St. Bartholomew in the preceding year. The book purported to be a constitutional history of France, showing that the kingdom had never been an absolute monarchy. Even hereditary succession Hotman held to be a custom of comparatively recent origin, dependent merely upon the tacit consent of the people. More specifically he held that the king was elective and his power limited by the States General which represents the entire kingdom, supporting this thesis by an array of precedents of more than doubtful authenticity. The argument depended upon the principle of medieval constitutionalism, that political institutions derive their right from immemorial practices inherent in the community itself. In this sense, the consent of the people, expressed in such practices, is the rightful basis of political power, and the crown itself derives its authority from its legal position as an agent of the community. Hotman's main positive contention, however, that the king's power in France had always been shared by the States General, was not true historically, nor had it any practical value in the circumstances, since the development of the States General into a national parliament was not within the region of possibility. Neither the Huguenots nor any other party had any real interest in tying up their fortunes with the States General.

The philosophical type of theory, which inferred the limitation of royal power from general principles, was both more interesting and more important. In the years following the St. Bartholomew Massacre French Protestants produced many works of this kind, all taking the position that kings are instituted by human society to serve the purposes of that society and that their power is therefore limited. The weight of this influence upon French Calvinism is shown by the fact that one of these pamphlets, though published anonymously, was probably the work of Calvin's friend and biographer, Theodore Beza, who was at that time his successor at the head of the government in Geneva.[3] The stress of circumstances drove Beza, as it had driven Knox, to reverse not only Calvin's teaching but his own previous convictions in favor of passive obedience. Somewhat reluctantly but quite clearly he urged the right of inferior magistrates, though not of private citizens, to resist a tyrant, particularly in defense of true religion. Of all this rather numerous class of works, however, the most famous was the *Vindiciae contra tyrannos,* published in 1579,[4] which systematized the argument presented in the preceding few years. The *Vindiciae* became one of the landmarks of revolutionary literature. It was republished again and again, in England and elsewhere, when opposition between king and people came to a crisis. It must therefore be examined with some care, both for what it represents in the France of its own day, and to see just how closely it approximates the later doctrine of popular rights.

[3] *De jure magistratuum in subditos;* also in French under the title *Du droit des magistrats sur les sujets,* probably 1574. The authorship is discussed by A. Elkan, *Die Publizistik der Batholomäusnacht* (1905), pp. 46 ff.

[4] There was a French edition in 1581 and an English translation in 1648 and often thereafter. This was reprinted with an introduction by H. J. Laski: *A Defence of Liberty against Tyrants,* London, 1924. The book was published under the pseudonym Stephen Junius Brutus, and the authorship has been debated since the sixteenth century. As a result of an article in Bayle's *Dictionary,* it was formerly attributed to Hubert Languet. but since Max Lossen's paper in the Proceedings of the Royal Academy of Bavaria in 1887, it has usually been attributed to Philippe du Plessis-Mornay. Ernest Barker in "The Authorship of the *Vindiciae contra tyrannos,*" *Cambridge Historical Journal,* Vol. III (1930), pp. 164 ff., has recently revived the claim of Languet, and J. W. Allen in his *History of Political Thought in the Sixteenth Century* (1928), p. 319, n. 2, has expressed doubt in both cases. On the whole class of French works, see Allen, *op. cit.,* pp. 312 ff.

VINDICIAE CONTRA TYRANNOS

The *Vindiciae* was divided into four parts, each intended to answer a fundamental question of contemporary politics. First, are subjects obliged to obey princes if they command anything against the law of God? Second, is it lawful to resist a prince who desires to nullify the law of God or who lays waste the church, and if so, to whom, by what means, and to what extent? Third, how far is it lawful to resist a prince who is oppressing or destroying the state, and to whom, by what means, and with what right is such resistance allowable? Fourth, can neighboring princes lawfully aid the subjects of other princes, or are they obliged to do so, when such subjects are afflicted for the sake of true religion or are oppressed by open tyranny?

The mere enumeration of these questions is enough to show the author's major interest. He was concerned not with government on its own account but with the relation between government and religion. Only in the third part did he approach a general theory of the state, and even there it cannot be said that politics got into the foreground. The whole book contemplated a situation in which the prince was of one religion and a substantial number of his subjects were of another. Moreover, the author never even imagined what would now seem the obvious solution, that a difference of religious faith should be treated as having nothing to do with political duties. He assumed that rulers must uphold pure doctrine. At the same time the substance of his argument depended little upon Calvin; no such theocracy as the government of Geneva was in sight for French Huguenots, nor did they want it. The political philosophy of the *Vindiciae* really went back to the argument of antipapal writers, like William of Occam or the Conciliarists, against an heretical pope. The ruler is the servant of the community and the community can do whatever its own life requires.

In its main outline the theory of the *Vindiciae* took the form of a twofold covenant or contract. There is, first, a contract to which God is one party and the king and people jointly the other party. By this contract the community becomes a church, a people chosen of God, and obligated to offer true and acceptable worship. This covenant with God stood closest to the revised form of Calvinism as Knox had stated it. Secondly, there is a contract in which the people appear as one party and the king as the other. This is specifically the political contract by which a people becomes a state; the king is bound by this agreement to rule well and justly, and the people to obey so long as he does. The double covenant was required because the author thought always of religious duty as the most important reason for rebellion. His main purpose was to prove the right to coerce an heretical king. From a purely political point of view — which of course could only have been taken if the religious question were divorced from politics — the covenant with God was an encumbrance upon the theory. If this were eliminated there would be left merely the political contract between the king and the community, setting forth the principle that government exists for the sake of the community and that political obligation is therefore limited and conditional. The omission would have required a degree of political rationalism which the author of the *Vindiciae* did not possess.

In another respect also the contract theory of the *Vindiciae* differed from the contract theory of later date. The author saw no discrepancy between the theory that the king's power comes from God and the theory that it arose by a contract with his people. In other words, the theory of divine right had not yet joined hands with the belief in passive obedience, so that, by stressing the king's responsibility to God, an author would be taken to imply that he was not responsible to his people. Accordingly the author of the *Vindiciae* did not hesitate to say also that the king's power was derived from God. The divine right of the kingly office was left standing beside the rights which a particular king derived by covenant from his people. Similarly the duty to obey the king's lawful commands is a religious duty as well as a duty which arises under contract. In no sense therefore was the *Vindiciae* an attempt to base government wholly upon secular principles; like the theory of divine right it was theological through and through.

The method of argument followed was a curious mixture of legalism and Scriptural authority. The forms of contract sanctioned by the civil law are treated as if they were part of the order of nature and as such had universal validity. In order to secure worship according to forms pleasing to him, God adopts a device used by creditors to secure a debt. In the first of the two contracts, the king and the people are jointly bound, as if the people had become surety for the king. Hence they become liable for the purity of worship in case the king defaults. On the side of Scriptural authority, the author uses the analogy of the covenant by which the Jews are supposed to become the chosen people of God.[5] In the Christian era all Christian peoples stand in the place of the Jews and hence are "chosen," that is, committed to right worship and true doctrine. Another form of argument repeatedly used is the analogy of the feudal relation between lord and vassal. In both contracts the power of the king is represented as delegated, in the first by God and in the second by the people. Power is granted for certain purposes and its retention is conditional upon their fulfillment. God and the people are therefore superiors; the king is bound to their service and the obligation owed to him is limited and conditional.

> Then therefore all kings are the vassals of the King of Kings, invested into their office by the sword, which is the cognizance of their royal authority, to the end that with the sword they maintain the law of God, defend the good, and punish the evil. Even as we commonly see, that he who is a sovereign lord puts his vassals into possession of their fee by girding them with a sword, and delivering them a buckler and a standard, with condition that they shall fight for them with those arms if occasion shall serve.[6]

Such passages are numerous and striking. In them the *Vindiciae* joins hands with the historical argument of Hotman and others. They show that the case for the limited sovereignty of the king depended upon the prevalence of medieval modes of thought and was in substance a reaction toward older political conceptions and against the more typically modern position of the absolutists.

From this description of the main lines of argument followed in the *Vindiciae* it is easy to see the grounds upon which the author holds that the king's power may rightfully be resisted. Every Christian must agree that his duty is to obey God rather than the king, in case the king commands anything against God's law. Furthermore, since the king's power arises from a covenant to support true worship, it is clearly lawful to resist him if he violates the law of God or lays waste the church. Indeed, it is more than

[5] *II. Kings*, 11, 17; 23, 3; *II. Chronicles*, 23, 16.
[6] Ed. by Laski, pp. 70 f.

lawful; it is a positive duty. The people are jointly liable with the king for preserving the purity of doctrine and worship; the king's default puts the whole burden upon the people and if they fail to resist him, they lay themselves liable to the full punishment which his sin merits.

The second contract, between king and people, justifies resistance to tyranny in secular government. Though kings are instituted by God, God acts in this matter through the people. Here again the *Vindiciae* took for granted all the forms of a contract at civil law. The people lay down the conditions which the king is bound to fulfill. Hence they are bound to obedience only conditionally, namely, upon receiving the protection of just and lawful government. The king, however, is bound unconditionally to perform the duties of his office; unless he does so, the compact is void. It follows that the power of the ruler is delegated by the people and continues only with their consent. All kings are really elective, even though a custom has grown up in favor of hereditary succession, for prescription does not run against the people's right. Abstracted from its context the argument here closely resembled the contract theory as it occurred later in Locke and in the popular theories of the American and French Revolutions, but in the *Vindiciae* the context of religious strife dominated.

Behind the form of the contract the author of the *Vindiciae*, like the later contract theorists, appealed largely to utilitarian argument. Kingship, he urged, was obviously sanctioned by the people because they considered the king's services worth what they cost. It must be assumed, therefore, that governments exist to further the interests of subjects, for the latter would be mad to accept the burden of obedience without receiving the benefits of protection to their lives and property.

> In the first place every one consents, that men by nature loving liberty, and hating servitude, born rather to command, than obey, have not willingly admitted to be governed by another, and renounced as it were the privilege of nature, by submitting themselves to the commands of others, but for some special and great profit that they expected from it. . . . Neither let us imagine, that kings were chosen to apply to their own proper use the goods that are gotten by the sweat of their subjects; for every man loves and cherishes his own.[7]

[7] Pp. 139 f.

In the main, however, the argument of the *Vindiciae* was not utilitarian. The chief ground for limiting the king's power is his subjection to law, both the law of nature and the law of the land; he depends on the law, not the law on him. The author has all the medieval reverence for law, and he reproduces all the commonplaces in eulogy of it that had accumulated since the times of the Stoics.

> The law is reason and wisdom itself, free from all perturbation, not subject to be moved with choler, ambition, hate, or acceptances of persons. . . . To come to our purpose, the law is an understanding mind, or rather an obstacle of many understandings: the mind being the seal of all the intelligent faculties, is (if I may so term it) a parcel of divinity; in so much as he who obeys the law, seems to obey God, and receive Him for arbitrator of the matters in controversy.[8]

Law comes from the people, not from the king, and hence can be changed only with the consent of the people's representatives. The king can dispose of the lives and property of his subjects only in such ways as the law permits, and he is accountable under the law for his every act.

It is of the essence of the contractual theory that the ruler may be held to account by the people for the justice and legality of his rule. The king who becomes a tyrant thereby loses his title to power. It remains to be shown, therefore, by whom this right shall be exercised. Here the author falls back upon the ancient distinction between a tyrant who is a usurper and has no claim to the kingship, and a lawful king who has become tyrannous. Only the first may be resisted or killed by a private citizen. In the second case, the right of resistance belongs solely to the people as a corporate body and not to " the many-headed multitude " of private individuals. So far as individuals are concerned, the duty of passive obedience was asserted in the *Vindiciae* as strongly as it had been by Calvin. If the whole people resists collectively, they must act through their natural leaders, the inferior magistrates, the nobles, the estates, or local and municipal officials, each in his own territory. Only the magistrate, or one whose position makes him a natural guardian of the community, may resist the king.

This phase of the right to resist throws considerable light upon

[8] Pp. 145 f.

the true purposes of the *Vindiciae*. It was in no sense a claim of popular rights inhering in every individual, nor did the Huguenot party from which it emanated stand for popular rights. It stood rather for the rights (or ancient privileges) of towns and provinces and classes against the leveling effect of royal power. The spirit of the *Vindiciae* was not democratic but aristocratic. Its rights were the rights of corporate bodies and not of individuals, and its theory of representation contemplated the representation of corporations and not of men. No very clear statement of the circumstances justifying resistance was given or probably could have been given. But the point of view implicit in the theory was that of a state composed of parts or classes balanced against each other and governed by mutual agreement rather than by a political sovereign. In this respect the *Vindiciae* might easily have led to something like a federal conception of government. Such a theory, picturing the state as a federation of lesser corporate bodies, actually was formulated a few years later by Althusius in the Netherlands, where the form of government was more suitable to such a view.

The political theory of the *Vindiciae*, taken in its entirety, was a strange mixture. Not unnaturally, in view of the later development of the contract-theory, this element of the book has been chiefly stressed, but at the expense of historical accuracy. It restated the old conception that political power exists for the moral good of the community, is to be exercised responsibly, and is subject to natural right and justice. These ideas were the common heritage of modern Europe from the Middle Ages. It brought the theory of the contract definitely into the service of the right to resist, but it was, on the whole, less in touch with the prevailing modern tendency in government than the theory of absolutism which it opposed. The *Vindiciae* was not in the first instance a theory of secular government at all; that it owed its origin to the religious struggle and was the pronouncement of a religious minority is the clearest thing about it. The author had no conception of a state which could abstain from making itself responsible for religious truth and purity of worship. In particular, its defense of the right to resist was not in the least an argument for popular government and the rights of man. Individual human rights had no part in it, and its practical bias was aristocratic or even in a sense feudal. In spirit, therefore, it was wholly at odds with the doctrines of liberty and equality which were later poured into the mold of the contract-theory.

OTHER PROTESTANT ATTACKS ON ABSOLUTISM

In countries other than France but more or less affected by French thought there appeared works by Protestant writers setting forth theories much like that of the *Vindiciae contra tyrannos*. In the same year in which the *Vindiciae* was published the Scottish poet and scholar, George Buchanan, published his *De jure regni apud Scotos,* which rivaled the French work in fame as a revolutionary document and surpassed it in literary merit. Buchanan lived much of his life in France and might reasonably be classed as a French thinker, though his associations were not especially with Huguenots. His personal interests made him rather a humanist than a sectarian, and perhaps for this reason his book was less dominated by theological motives than the *Vindiciae*. Thus he omitted the peculiar twofold contract and so gave his theory a more definite application to secular government. Power is derived from the community and must therefore be exercised in accordance with the law of the community; obligation is necessarily conditional upon the performance by the king of the duties of his office. Buchanan stated rather clearly the ancient Stoic view that the government originates in the social propensities of men and is therefore natural, and in this respect also he tended to minimize the dependence of politics upon theology. The right to resist was, of course, his main point of emphasis; here his argument was substantially like that of the *Vindiciae,* except that he was more outspoken in justifying tyrannicide and substituted a vague notion that the people act through a majority for the view that they depend upon the natural leadership of subordinate magistrates. To this extent he was less bound by the feudal aspects of Huguenot theory. It is curious to think that Buchanan's book was written for the instruction of his royal pupil, the future James I of England. James's whole-hearted Anglicanism was due to a clear apprehension, gained in his youth, both of the theory and practice of Presbyterianism.

In the Netherlands, also, the same type of political philosophy was used to justify resistance to tyranny. In that country occurred both its most overt popular use and later, in Althusius and Grotius, a systematic and scholarly development that took it beyond merely controversial use. In 1581 the States-General, in the Act of Abjuration,[9] renounced their allegiance to Philip II with the assertion:

> All mankind know that a prince is appointed by God to cherish his subjects, even as a shepherd to guard his sheep. When, therefore, the prince does not fulfill his duty as protector; when he oppresses his subjects, destroys their ancient liberties, and treats them as slaves, he is to be considered, not a prince, but a tyrant. As such, the estates of the land may lawfully and reasonably depose him, and elect another in his room.

The act was in no sense a philosophical disquisition, but analysis shows that it assumed the same two points which appeared in all the anti-royalist arguments, the law of nature and the defense of ancient liberties. It showed how deeply rooted in popular consciousness was the notion that political power ought to depend on moral forces inherent in the community and ought to be used in the service of the community, as the Mayflower Pact a few years later (1620) showed how readily men thought of civil society in terms of common assent or contract.

THE JESUITS AND THE INDIRECT POWER OF THE POPE

While an anti-royalist political philosophy of the type just described, which traced the king's power to the consent of the people and defended the right to resist, was developing among Calvinist Protestants, a similar kind of theory was sponsored by Catholic writers and particularly by the Jesuits. The motives behind this philosophy were mixed, as in the case of the Calvinists. Catholics were, of course, influenced by the same constitutional traditions which caused Protestants to defend representative government against absolutism, and in this respect the difference of religion or the special purposes of the Jesuit Order counted for nothing. On the other hand, the Jesuits had special reasons for espousing anti-royalist views of the kind mentioned above; like the Calvinists they were opposed to a too powerful national monarchy. Unlike the Calvinists, however, they utilized their theory to support a revised form of the old doctrine of papal supremacy in moral and

[9] Analyzed in Motley's *Rise of the Dutch Republic,* Pt. 6, ch. 4.

religious questions. This purpose was specifically Jesuit and was by no means shared by Catholics who were more responsive to national and dynastic interests.

So far as anti-royalist theory was thus specifically Jesuit, it was quite as directly a result of the religious differences of the sixteenth century as Calvinist theory. It grew out of the part that the Order played in the remarkable counter-movement of reform in the Roman church, which within two generations corrected some of the worst abuses that had caused Protestant defection, gave greater precision to many definitions of doctrine, brought a new type of ruler to the papal throne, and produced a more rigid discipline of the reformed papacy over the lower clergy. This counter-reform succeeded amazingly. It not only stopped once for all the spread of Protestantism but it created the hope, or the fear, that the church might win back its lost provinces. In this militant revival there was no greater single force than that ideal missionary organization, the Jesuit Order. Founded in 1534 and bound by the strictest oath of obedience and self-abnegation, the Order drew to itself in the sixteenth century not only men of zeal and administrative power but also some of the ablest minds in the Roman church. The Jesuit schools and the Jesuit scholars were among the best in Europe; the extraordinary fear with which its opponents regarded it was justified by its capacity. Even though its political philosophy was obviously influenced by propagandist motives, the Jesuit statement of the anti-royalist theory was probably, on the whole, on a higher intellectual level than Protestant statements of the same position.

The special purpose of the Jesuits was to reformulate a moderate theory of papal superiority, upon lines suggested by St. Thomas, in the light of political conditions that had come to prevail in the sixteenth century. The conception of the emperor as the temporal head of Christendom, which was hardly alive in the fourteenth century, had ceased to appeal even to the imagination. Europe had become in feeling as in fact a group of national states, effectively self-governing in secular affairs but still in some sense Christian, though no longer acknowledging allegiance to a single church. It was the dream of the Jesuits to win back the seceders and, by conceding the fact of independence in secular matters, to save for the pope some sort of spiritual leadership over a society of Christian states. The latter policy, which as the event proved was quite illusory, was largely the reason for the detestation in which the Jesuits were held by nationalist Catholics no less than by Protestants.

The Jesuit theory of the papacy was given definite form by Robert Bellarmine,[10] the most effective of all the Catholic controversialists of the sixteenth century. Conceding that the pope has no authority in secular matters, Bellarmine argued that he is nevertheless the spiritual head of the church and as such has an indirect power over temporal matters, exclusively for spiritual ends. The power of secular rulers does not come directly from God, as the royalists asserted, nor from the pope, as the extreme papalists had held. It arises from the community itself for the sake of its own secular ends. The king's power is secular in kind and in origin; only the pope among human rulers has his power directly from God. It follows that secular government ought not to be able to exact an absolute obedience from its subjects, and also that spiritual authority, for spiritual purposes, has the right to direct and control secular. There are circumstances, then, in which the pope is justified in deposing an heretical ruler and absolving his subjects from their allegiance. Except for a stronger emphasis on the secular origin of royal power, Bellarmine's theory of church and state was not substantially different from St. Thomas's. Except for its reference to the papacy, it was not substantially different from that of the Calvinists. Both stood for the independence of the church in doctrinal decisions and neither could admit royal supremacy in a national church or the indefeasible divine right of an heretical king. This explains the bracketing of Jesuit and Calvinist in the royalist literature. James I's epigram, that "Jesuits are nothing but Puritan-papists," was typical and on the whole true.

It is one of the ironies of history that both the Jesuit and the Calvinist contributed to a theory of church and state which they abhorred, in so far as they ever thought of it. In the sixteenth century every controversialist assumed, with surprising simplicity of mind, that his own theology was manifestly true and wholesome for everyone. The possibility that no religious system could be

[10] In the first volume of his *Disputationes* (1581): *De summo pontifice*; elaborated in his *De potestate summi pontificis*, 1610.

made universally acceptable simply was not faced. When it became apparent that this was the fact, and that no important religious group could be suppressed without the greatest political danger, there was nothing for government to do except to withdraw altogether from theological controversy and leave each church to teach its own doctrine to such as cared to hear. The whole Christian tradition was against making a political official overtly the arbiter of religious truth, even if the national churches had in fact included the whole nation in their membership. Hence the claim that the church must be independent was unescapable, but independence had to be purchased at the cost of making church and state two distinct societies, and this was just what neither the Jesuit nor the Calvinist contemplated. The Jesuit theory in particular was an approximation to this hated conclusion. The theory that the state is a national society, purely secular in origin and purpose, while the church is world-wide in scope and of divine origin, implied that the church is one social body and the state another, membership in one being independent of membership in the other. The outcome was therefore quite contrary to the revived medievalism that both Jesuits and Calvinists intended.

There was therefore a sound reason why, despite theological differences, the political theories of Calvinists in France or Scotland should have had certain similarities with those of the Jesuits. Both were in a situation where it was necessary to urge that political obligation is not absolute and that a right of rebellion exists against an heretical ruler. Both depended upon a common heritage of medieval thought and argued that the community itself creates its own officials and can regulate them for its own purposes. Both held, therefore, that political power inheres in the people, is derived from them by contract, and may be revoked if the king becomes a tyrant. Without being markedly original, the Jesuit writers were in general clearer in stating the principles of the argument than the Calvinists.

THE JESUITS AND THE RIGHT TO RESIST

The early Jesuit writers were chiefly Spanish and their theory was more influenced by their nationality than by the specific Jesuit purpose just mentioned. This was particularly true of Juan de Mariana,[11] whose theory was mainly governed by constitutional considerations. Like Hotman he admired medieval institutions, especially those represented by the Estates of Aragon. The Estates he regarded as the guardians of the law of the land, to which the king is fully subject. The power of the king he derived from a contract with the people, who are represented by the Estates, and to them the power to change the law is reserved. Hence the king may be removed for violating the fundamental law. This constitutional theory Mariana built upon an account of the origin of civil society from a state of nature preceding government, in which men live a kind of animal existence, lacking both the virtues and the vices of civilized life. Like Rousseau later, he regarded the origin of private property as the crucial step toward law and government. The most important feature of Mariana's theory was that he treated the origin and evolution of government as a natural process, taking place under the impulsion of human needs, and on this ground he based the contention that a community must always be able to control or depose the rulers whom its needs have created. He came much closer than the author of the *Vindiciae contra tyrannos* to a non-theological view of civil society and its functions.

His book has been famous, or rather infamous, for its frank acceptance of tyrannicide as a remedy for political oppression. Actually he was not in principle very different from other writers of his time. The right of private citizens to kill a usurper was very widely recognized, and Buchanan had defended the right to kill an oppressor even though his title were lawful. The greater infamy of Mariana was probably due to his open defense of the murder of Henry III of France, which caused his book to be burnt by the Parlement of Paris. Mariana put little stress upon the spiritual power of the pope and in that respect was not a typical Jesuit.

The most important representative of Jesuit political theory was the Spanish scholastic philosopher and jurist Francisco Suarez,[12] though his politics was incidental to a philosophical system of jurisprudence, which in turn was only one part of a complete structure of philosophy on the model of St. Thomas.

[11] *De rege et regis institutione*, 1599.

[12] *Tractatus de legibus ac deo legislatore*, 1612.

Like Bellarmine, Suarez conceived of the pope as the spiritual leader of a family of Christian nations and consequently as spokesman of the moral unity of humanity. The church is a universal and divine institution; the state is national and particular. On this ground he defended the indirect power of the pope to regulate secular rulers for spiritual ends. The state is specifically a human institution, depending upon human needs, and originating in a voluntary union of the heads of families. By this voluntary act each assumes the obligation of doing whatever the general good requires, while the civil society thus formed has a natural and necessary power to control its members for the general good and to do whatever its life and needs require. In this way he established the principle that the power of society to rule itself and its members is an inherent property of a social group. It has no dependence on the will of God, except as everything in the world depends on His will, but is purely a natural phenomenon, belonging to the physical world and having to do with man's social needs. Aside from the indirect power of the pope, Suarez's view of society was in no special sense theological. From the view that political power is an inherent property of the community, he concluded, as might be expected, that no form of political obligation is absolute. Political arrangements are in a sense superficial: a state may be ruled by a king or in some other way; the government's power may be more or less. In any case political power is derived from the community; it exists for the welfare of the community; and when it does not work well it can be changed. The intent of this theory was no doubt to exalt the divine right of the pope above the merely secular and human power of the king, but the effect was really to set politics more completely apart from theology.

Suarez's political theory was incidental to his jurisprudence. His purpose was to present an encyclopedic philosophy of law in all its divisions, and, as was usual in his writings, he presented a summary and systematization of all phases of medieval legal philosophy. In Suarez and the other members of what is sometimes called the Spanish School of jurisprudence the legal philosophy of the Middle Ages was digested and arranged, and was thus passed on to the seventeenth century. In particular these jurists gave a systematic presentation of the whole doctrine of natural law and so contributed in no small degree to the fact that, for the seventeenth century, this appeared to be the only scientific way to approach problems of political theory. The influence of Hugo Grotius was perhaps decisive in this matter, but behind Grotius was the systematic jurisprudence of the Spaniards. Indeed, in Suarez natural law connoted many of the conclusions to which Grotius was led. If there are in nature and in human nature certain qualities which inevitably make some ways of behaving right and others wrong, then the difference of good and bad is not due to the arbitrary will either of God or man but is a rational distinction. The nature of human relations and the consequences which naturally flow from human conduct constitute a test to which the rules and practices of the positive law may be submitted. No human legislator — as Grotius later said, not even God Himself — can make wrong right; as Suarez argued, not even the pope can change natural law. Behind the special provisions of the law there are rational provisions of general validity. Thus it follows that states, like individuals, are subject to the law of nature, a principle which implies the rule of law within the state and also legal relations between states. Even in Suarez it is possible to see the suggestion of a system in which the law of nature becomes the basis of both constitutional and international law.

THE DIVINE RIGHT OF KINGS

The controversial theory that political power belongs to the people and that rulers may be resisted for valid reasons bred its own answer, and this naturally took the form of a revision of the long-standing belief in the divinity of civil authority. In the sixteenth century such a revision led naturally to the divine right of kings. This theory, like its opponent theory, depended on the struggle for power between religious sects. As a defense of the right to resist came naturally from a party in opposition to what it regarded as an heretical government, so the indefeasible right of the king was defended by those who were on the side of a national establishment and against a threatening opposition. In the beginning the issue was only secondarily absolutism against constitutionalism, and it was not at all autocracy against democracy. Divine right was a defense of order and political stability against a view widely believed to augment the danger implicit in religious civil war. The vital practical question was whether heresy in a ruler is a valid ground for civic disobedience.

In its modern form the theory of the divine right of the king was a development slightly later than the theories of limited royal power and was an answer to them. It crystallized in the disorders of the civil wars themselves and it corresponded accurately to the actual increase of power in the French crown, which emerged at the end of the century stronger than it was when the wars began. By the end of the century it was ready to begin the final course of centralization which ended in the absolute monarchy of Louis XIV. This was the only solution consistent with the maintenance of effective national government in France. As the wars continued it became ever clearer that neither Protestant nor Catholic could gain an unqualified victory, though the contest might easily destroy both French government and French civilization. To set up the king as the head of the nation, the object of loyalty to men of all parties though they remained Protestant or Catholic, was the only feasible course. The political principles involved in this movement were stated at a far higher philosophical level in Jean Bodin's theory of sovereignty, but the doctrine of divine right was a popular version of substantially similar ideas. It represented a national reaction to the disunion at home and the weakness abroad felt to be implicit both in Huguenot provincialism and ultramontane Catholicism.

The theory of divine right, like that of popular right which it was set up to oppose, was a modification of a very ancient and generally accepted idea, namely, that authority has a religious origin and sanction. No Christian, from the time when St. Paul wrote the thirteenth chapter of *Romans,* had ever doubted this. But since literally *all* power was of God, *ius divinum* had no necessary application to a king more than any other kind of ruler. Moreover, though power as such was divine, it might still be right, under proper circumstances, to resist an unlawful exercise of power. For these reasons no incompatibility was felt, before the end of the sixteenth century, between the theories that power comes from God and that it comes from the people. What made the two views incompatible was, first, the development of popular right to mean specifically a right to resist and, second, the counter-development of divine right to imply that subjects owe their rulers a duty of passive obedience. The ancient phrases, almost meaningless in themselves, such as that kings are the vicars of God, thus got a new meaning: rebellion even in the cause of religion is sacrilege. The duty of passive obedience, preached by both Luther and Calvin, was sharpened by investing the king with a special sanctity.

The divine right of kings in this new form was essentially a popular theory. It never received, and indeed was incapable of receiving, a philosophical formulation. But if the importance of a political doctrine depends partly on the number who hold it, the theory compares favorably with any political idea that ever existed, for it was believed with religious intensity by men of all social ranks and all forms of theological belief. The stock arguments for it were the familiar passages of Scripture, such as the thirteenth chapter of *Romans,* which had been quoted by writers time out of mind. What gave these old arguments new force in the sixteenth century were the dangers of disunion and instability inherent in sectarian partisanship, the chance of clerical control over secular government, either from the side of the Calvinists or the Jesuits, and a rising sense of national independence and unity. In the mass, therefore, the theory served mainly as a focus for patriotic sentiment and as a religious rationalization of civic duty. On the side of intellectual construction it was hopelessly weak. Some of its abler proponents, however, did provide an active, and at times not ineffective, criticism of the opponent theory that political power resides in the people.[13]

The logical difficulty with the theory of divine right was not that it was theological — it was scarcely more so than the theory which it opposed — but that the peculiar legitimacy attributed to royal power defied analysis or rational defense. The imposition of divine authority upon the king is essentially miraculous and must be accepted by faith and not by reason. The office of king is, as James I said, a " mystery " into which neither lawyers nor philosophers may inquire. Hence the theory could hardly survive after the quotation of Scriptural texts ceased to be a reputable method of political argumentation. In this respect it differed

[13] The most elaborate statement of the theory of divine right was made by William Barclay, a Scot long resident in France, in his *De regno et regali potestate*, 1600.

from the theory of a political contract, which despite its earlier theological form could be stated in a way that any rationalist might accept and hence could offer the opportunity for a philosophical analysis of political obligation.

In so far as royal legitimacy was presented in terms of natural processes, it meant that the king's power was hereditary, presumably on the ground that God's choice was manifested in the fact of birth. From this point on, however, the argument usually became an elaborate and not very convincing analogy between political power and the "natural" authority of a father, or between the reverence due to a king and the respect which children owe to their parents. This analogy was obviously open to the ridicule with which John Locke treated it. Despite its antiquity it probably never convinced anyone who was not ready to be convinced for other reasons. Analogy apart, the argument for royal legitimacy simply erected the feudal rule of primogeniture into a general law of nature. But this argument was open to the objection that, however natural the facts of birth and heredity may be, the inheritance of land and power is a legal rule which differs from country to country. In France the Salic Law excluded succession in the female lines, which was legal in England. Thus the argument was in the strange position of implying that God changed his mode of imposing the divine right to rule according to the constitutional practice of each country.

The moral doctrine that rebellion is never justified, even though a ruler be a heretic, was a normal part of the modernized theory of divine right. It supplied, however, no logical relation between the two propositions, which had always been regarded as independent. Passive obedience could be, and often was, defended on utilitarian grounds which had nothing whatever to do with divine right. An unusually lively sense of the dangers of disorder might be all that was needed to make the duty of subjection seem paramount. Moreover, some writers who defended the divine right of kings might admit, like William Barclay, that a special crime on the king's part, such as conspiring to overthrow the state, could be treated as a constructive abdication. But this was conceived as a quite exceptional possibility. In general, divine right came to mean that the subject's duty of submission was absolute, unless perhaps in some altogether monstrous circumstance.

The duty of passive obedience did not mean that the king was wholly irresponsible and could do whatever he chose. It was usually argued that the king, being more highly placed than other men, was responsible in a higher degree. The law of God and the law of nature were assumed, as they always had been, to be binding on him, and his general duty to respect the law of the land was commonly asserted. But this obligation is owed to God and the king cannot be held to human judgment either within or without the processes of law. A bad king will be judged by God but he must not be judged by his subjects or by any human agency for enforcing the law, such as the estates or the courts. The law resides ultimately " in the breast of the king." This became the ultimate political issue between the theory of divine right and that of popular or parliamentary right, wherever the lines were drawn for a constitutional struggle between the king and a representative body.

JAMES I

Though the modernized version of divine right was native to France, it appeared also in Scotland at about the same time. Here it was stated by no less person than the king himself, the prince who afterward became James I of England, whose *Trew Law of Free Monarchies* was published in 1598.[14] This book reflected the unhappy experiences of James's family and his own youth with the Scottish Calvinists, as well as his reading of the controversial works produced by the religious wars in France. By " free monarchy " he meant royal government which is independent of coercion both by foreign princes and by sectaries or feudatories within the kingdom. The long struggle between the House of Stuart and the turbulent Scottish nobility, and the more recent humiliations which James and his mother suffered at the hands of the Presbyterians, offer an ample explanation of the importance which he attached to this conception. A Scottish presbytery, he once said, " agreeth as well with monarchy as God and the devil." It is of the essence of free monarchy that it should have supreme legal power over all its subjects.

Kings, therefore, James wrote, " are breathing images of God upon earth."

[14] *The Political Works of James I.* Introduction by C. H. McIlwain. Cambridge, Mass., 1918.

The state of monarchy is the supremest thing upon earth: for kings are not only God's lieutenants upon earth, and sit upon God's throne, but even by God himself they are called Gods.[15]

He is like a father as compared with his children, or like the head as compared with the body. Without him there can be no civil society, for the people is a mere "headless multitude," incapable of making law, which proceeds from the king as the divinely instituted lawgiver of his people. The only choice, therefore, is between submission to the king and complete anarchy. Applying his theory to Scotland, James asserted that kings existed before there were estates or ranks of men, before parliaments were held or laws made, and that even property in land existed only by the grant of the king.

And so it follows of necessity, that kings were the authors and makers of the laws, and not the laws of the kings.[16]

The assertion was supported by much dubious history; what it seems to mean is that originally the king's power depended upon the right of conquest.

Once established the king's right descends to his heirs by inheritance. It is always unlawful to dispossess the rightful heir. Since James's claim to the Scottish throne, and later to the throne of England, was strictly hereditary, it was natural for him to cling to this principle, which expressed merely the inalienable and indefeasible right of the heir in feudal law. The essential legal quality in monarchy is therefore legitimacy as evidenced by lawful descent from the previous legitimate monarch. This became the distinctive position of the Stuart Family in the English Civil Wars. No considerations of utility can set aside a valid hereditary claim; even an accomplished revolution does not invalidate it; and no law of prescription runs against the legitimate heir. In short, the quality of a king is a supernatural stigma, not to be explained and not to be debated. In 1616, James charged his judges in Star Chamber:

That which concerns the mystery of the king's power is not lawful to be disputed; for that is to wade into the weakness of princes, and to take away the mystical reverence that belongs unto them that sit in the throne of God.[17]

[15] *Works*, p. 307. [16] *Ibid.*, p. 62. [17] *Ibid.*, p. 333.

James always admitted that he was responsible in the highest degree, but responsible to God and not to his subjects. In all ordinary matters he acknowledged that a king ought to give the same respect to the law of the land that he demanded of his subjects, but this is a voluntary submission which cannot be enforced.

The true nature of the theory of divine right, as a defense of national stability against threatened disunion, was perhaps best illustrated by the fact that it had little currency in England in Tudor times. Despite differences between Calvinists and Anglicans about the propriety of royal supremacy in the national church, there was at no time prior to the death of Elizabeth any serious threat to the internal peace and order of the kingdom. In the sixteenth century the English Calvinists did not adopt the anti-royalist philosophy characteristic of the French and Scottish Calvinists. On the other side, Anglicans had as yet no special motive for bolstering up passive obedience with the doctrine of indefeasible royal right. The horrible example of the civil wars in France gave ample ground for defending passive obedience on sober utilitarian grounds. The actual stability and the unquestioned power of the Tudor monarchs made the theory of divine right unnecessary. The situation changed in the seventeenth century when the outbreak of civil war required both a defense of resistance on the ground of popular right and a refutation of that position. The divine right of the king then became a common position among clerical apologists for the Stuarts. However, the situations in France and in England were essentially different, because national sentiment in England was at least as well represented by the judges of the common law or by parliament as by the king. The question was not national unity against disunion, but what constitutional agent should stand for national unity. There was no reason why a special divinity should hedge an English king, and in fact the theory of divine right had little importance in English political theory.

SELECTED BIBLIOGRAPHY

A History of Political Thought in the Sixteenth Century. By J. W. Allen. London, 1928. Pt. III.

"The Political Theory of the Huguenots." By E. Armstrong. In the *Eng. Hist. Rev.*, Vol. IV (1889), p. 13.

The French Wars of Religion: Their Political Aspects. By E. Armstrong. 2nd ed. London, 1904.

Die Staatslehre des Kardinals Bellarmin. By Franz X. Arnold. Munich, 1934.

"*God and the Secular Power.*" By Summerfield Baldwin. In *Essays in History and Political Theory in Honor of Charles Howard McIlwain.* Cambridge, Mass., 1936.

"A Huguenot Theory of Politics: The Vindiciae contra tyrannos." By Ernest Barker. In *Church, State, and Study,* London, 1930.

Political Liberty: A History of the Conception in the Middle Ages and Modern Times. By A. J. Carlyle. Oxford, 1941.

The Political Theory of the Huguenots of the Dispersion, with Special Reference to the Thought and Influence of Pierre Jurieu. By Guy Howard Dodge. New York, 1947.

Die Publizistik der Bartholomäusnacht und Mornays Vindiciae contra tyrannos. By Albert Elkan. Heidelberg, 1905.

Studies of Political Thought from Gerson to Grotius, 1414–1625. By John Neville Figgis. 2nd ed. Cambridge, 1923. Chs. 5, 6.

"Political Thought in the Sixteenth Century." By John Neville Figgis. In the *Cambridge Modern History,* Vol. III (1904), ch. 22.

The Divine Right of Kings. By John Neville Figgis. 2nd ed. Cambridge, 1914.

Natural Law and the Theory of Society, 1500–1800. By Otto Gierke. Eng. trans. by Ernest Barker. 2 vols. Cambridge, 1934. (From *Das deutsche Genossenschaftsrecht,* Vol. IV.) Ch. 1.

The Social and Political Ideas of some Great Thinkers of the Sixteenth and Seventeenth Centuries. Ed. by F. J. C. Hearnshaw. London, 1926. Chs. 1, 4, 5.

A Defence of Liberty against Tyrants: A Translation of the Vindiciae contra tyrannos. Introduction by H. J. Laski. London, 1924.

The Political Works of James I. Ed. by C. H. McIlwain. Cambridge, Mass., 1918. Introduction.

The Wars of Religion in France, 1559–1576. By James W. Thompson. Chicago, 1909.

"The Reformation in France." By A. A. Tilley. In the *Cambridge Modern History,* Vol. II (1903), ch. 9.

Studies in the French Renaissance. By Arthur Tilley. Cambridge, 1922. Ch. 11.

Die Monarchomachen: Eine Darstellung der revolutionären Staatslehren des XVI. Jahrhunderts (1573–1599). By R. Treumann. Leipzig, 1895.

Les théories sur le pouvoir royal en France pendant les guerres de religion. By Georges Weill. Paris, 1891.

Franz Suarez. By Karl Werner. 2 vols. Regensburg, 1889. Ch. 12.

CHAPTER XX

JEAN BODIN

Most of the books on politics produced in France in the last quarter of the sixteenth century were controversial tracts, without detachment and without philosophical originality. There was one work, however, the *Six livres de la république,* published by Jean Bodin in 1576,[1] of less ephemeral nature. This book also was occasioned by the civil wars and was written with the avowed purpose of strengthening the king. But Bodin achieved an unusual aloofness from religious partisanship, and he strove for a philosophical system of political ideas which, however confused he may have been, at least put his book out of the class of controversial literature. In the *Republic* Bodin set himself no less ambitious task than to do for modern politics what Aristotle had done for ancient, and while the comparison cannot be seriously sustained, the book achieved a great reputation in its day and has been given by all scholars an important place in the history of political thought. Its importance was less due to its elaborate effort to revive the system of Aristotle than to the fact that it took the idea of sovereign power out of the limbo of theology in which the theory of divine right left it. By so doing it led both to an analysis of sovereignty and to its inclusion in constitutional theory.

RELIGIOUS TOLERATION

The *Republic* might be described as a defense of politics against parties. Published only four years after the Massacre of St. Bartholomew, it formed the main intellectual production of an already growing body of moderate thinkers, known as the Politiques, who saw in the royal power the mainstay of peace and order and who therefore sought to raise the king, as a center of national unity, above all religious sects and political parties. In part they represented the swing toward strong government which always comes

[1] Bodin published an enlarged Latin edition in 1586. There was an English translation by Richard Knolles in 1606.

in a time of disorder, but their position in the sixteenth century was more significant than that. They were among the first who envisaged the possibility of tolerating several religions within a single state. Though mostly Catholic themselves, they were before everything nationalist, and in their political thinking they were prepared to face the solidest political fact of the age, namely, that the division of Christianity was irreparable and that no single sect could either convince or coerce the others. The policy which they advocated, accordingly, was to save what might still be saved from the wreck; to permit religious differences which could not be healed and to hold together French nationality even though unity of religion was lost. Such had been the policy of Catherine de' Medici's chancellor L'Hôpital at the very opening of the civil wars and such was the general policy of settlement which prevailed under Henry IV. Sane as this policy was, it seemed irreligious to most men in the sixteenth century; the Politiques were described by one of their enemies as "those who preferred the repose of the kingdom or their own homes to the salvation of their souls; who would rather that the kingdom remained at peace without God than at war with Him." There was an element of truth in this gibe. The Politiques certainly commended religious toleration as a policy rather than as a moral principle. They never denied the right of the state to persecute or questioned the advantages of a single religion. But they perceived that religious persecution was in fact ruinous and they condemned it on this utilitarian ground. In a general way Bodin was related to this group, and he intended by his book to support their policy of toleration and also to supply a reasoned basis for enlightened policy in respect to many practical questions that arose in a distracted age. But he was emphatically no opportunist. His *Republic* was intended to supply the principles of order and unity upon which any well-ordered state must rest.

Bodin's political philosophy was a singular mixture of the old and the new, as all philosophical thought in the sixteenth century was. He had ceased to be medieval without becoming modern. A lawyer by profession, he won the enmity of his fellow lawyers by advocating an historical and comparative study of law, in place of an exclusive devotion to the texts of Roman law. Both law and politics, he insisted, need to be studied not only in the light of history, but also in the light of men's physical environment, of climate and topography and race. And yet, mingled with this very modern-sounding suggestion was a firm belief that environment includes the influence of the stars and can be understood in its relation to the history of states by the study of astrology. A forthright advocate of religious toleration and of liberal and enlightened administration, Bodin was likewise the author of a handbook on sorcery intended to be used by magistrates in the detection and trial of witches. Often critical and incredulous in his analysis of historical sources, he was ready to accept every folk-tale about the diabolical plots of those who have sold themselves to the Devil. An advocate of policies aimed at the material and economic welfare of the nation and the author of a book that has been called the first modern work on economics, he could still people the physical world with spirits and demons on whose acts the lives of men depend at every turn. A critic of all religious sects so balanced in judgment that no man knew whether he was Protestant or Catholic, and some suspected that he was a Jew or an infidel, he was yet profoundly religious both by temperament and conviction.[2] Bodin's thought was an amalgamation of superstition, rationalism, mysticism, utilitarianism, and antiquarianism.

A similar confusion exists in his political philosophy. It seems clear that he himself believed that he was following a new method, the secret of which consisted in combining philosophy and history. " Philosophy," he says, " dies of inanition in the midst of its precepts when it is not vivified by history." He criticised Machiavelli for the omission of philosophy and attributed to this the immoral tendency of his writings. On the other hand, Bodin had no patience with such utopian politics as he found in Sir Thomas More and in Plato. His ideal was an empirical subject-matter held in a framework of general principles; fact was to give solidity and reason meaning. This conception of political philosophy he derived from Aristotle, and it must be admitted that Bodin con-

[2] Bodin's project for combining the study of law and history is in his *Methodus ad facilem historiarum cognitionem,* 1566; the dependence of history on environment is treated here and also in Book V of the *République.* His work on economics is the *Réponse aux paradoxes de M. de Malestroict,* 1568; also chs. 2 and 3 of Book VI of the *République.* The work on sorcery is the *Démonomanie,* 1580. That on religion is the *Heptaplomeres,* not completely printed until 1857.

ceived the task more broadly than any other writer of his time. Unfortunately his accomplishment was not equal to his designs. He had no clearly conceived system by which to order his historical material. The *Republic,* and indeed his books generally, are unorganized and ill-arranged, repetitious and disconnected, though in parts he was capable of being clear and cogent. Moreover, he deluged his reader with historical illustrations, statistics, citations, and expositions of law and institutions drawn from an appalling erudition. The neglect into which his books fell within a century of his death was mainly due to their being intolerably formless and tedious. Bodin's power of literary presentation was practically non-existent; his systematic capacity was rather a facility in formal definition than a real power of philosophical construction; and despite a genuine insight into the history and working of institutions, he was an antiquarian rather than a philosophical historian.

THE STATE AND THE FAMILY

Such arrangement as the *Republic* has was borrowed from Aristotle, though the outline was obscured by almost endless digressions. Bodin first considered the end of the state and then the family, together with marriage, the relation of father and children, private property, and slavery, all of which he regarded as aspects of the family. The opening part, however, revealed at once his weakness in forming a systematic political philosophy. He had no clear theory of the end of the state. He defined it as "a lawful government of several households, and of their common possessions, with sovereign power." The word lawful is said to signify just, or in accordance with the law of nature, and to distinguish the state from a lawless association like a band of robbers. With respect to the end which sovereign power should seek for its subjects, however, Bodin was very indefinite. He saw that Aristotle was not a safe guide here, the ends sought by the city-state being impossible in a modern kingdom. Hence, he said, the happiness or goodness of citizens is not a practicable end. Yet he was unwilling to restrict the state to the pursuit of merely material and utilitarian advantages, such as peace and the security of property. The state has a soul as well as a body and the soul is higher, though the needs of the body are more immediately pressing. In reality

Bodin never gave a clear account of these higher ends of the state. The result was a serious deficiency in his system, since he never succeeded in explaining precisely the reasons for the citizen's obligation to obey the sovereign.

Bodin's theory of the family is a distinctive part of his work, but it too is hard to relate to the theory of sovereignty. The family — consisting of father, mother, children, and servants, with the common property — he regarded as a natural community from which all other societies arise. Following the Roman conception that the state's jurisdiction ends at the threshold of the house, he seriously proposed reviving the most extreme powers of the *pater familias* over his dependents, with complete control over the persons, the property, and even the lives of his children. At the same time he added to this an excellent refutation both of the right and the utility of slavery. The family forms a natural unit, in which the right of private property inheres, and from it the state and all other communities are formed. The state he defined as a government of households; it is the *pater familias* who becomes a citizen, when he steps outside the house and acts in concert with other heads of families. Many associations of families arise for common defense and for the pursuit of mutual advantages — villages, cities, and corporations of various kinds — and when these are united by a sovereign authority, a state is formed. The actual formation of this last combination Bodin attributed as a rule to force, though it was certainly not his opinion that sovereignty, or lawful rule, is justified merely by its power.

In this derivation of the state Bodin's motive is easier to understand than his logic. He had in his make-up a large measure of Puritanical censoriousness, and the power of the father was meant to be a means of social purification. More important than this, however, was his desire to build an impregnable bulwark to protect private property. Communism, both in the theories of Plato and More and in the supposed practices of the Anabaptists, was an object of repeated criticism with him, and property he regarded as an attribute of the family. The family is the sphere of the private; the state is that of the public or common. Hence he aimed at a radical separation of the two. Sovereignty he believed to be different in kind from ownership; the prince is in no sense the proprietor of the public domain and cannot alienate it. Property belongs to the family, sovereignty to the prince and his magistrates. As the theory develops, the right of property inherent in the family puts a definite limit even to the power of the sovereign. Unfortunately for the clarity of the theory, it is impossible to see on what this inviolable right of the family is based. Bodin's argument for the power of the father was largely authoritarian, consisting of citations from Scripture and Roman law. For the rest he merely followed Aristotle in arguing that men are the embodiment of reason, as against the more passionate nature of women and the immaturity of children. The right of property he of course considered to be rooted in the law of nature. Without much exaggeration Bodin might be said to make the possession of property simply a natural right, somewhat after the fashion of Locke, except that it inheres in the family rather than the individual. But to combine an inalienable right in the family with an absolute power in the state made an insuperable logical difficulty.

If it really was Bodin's purpose to distinguish clearly between the political power of the sovereign and the private rights and powers of the heads of families, he ought to have considered carefully the transition from those spontaneous groupings of families where sovereign power is lacking to the state where it is present. In point of fact he had no clear theory of this transition, just as he had no clear theory of the ends which the state ought to secure. The family and such groups of families as the village or the city he attributed to the natural needs and desires of men — sexual impulse, the care of offspring, defense, and innate sociability. The origin of the state he usually attributed to conquest, and yet he was as far as possible from believing that force is self-justifying or that it forms the primary attribute of the state after it is founded. Superior force may make a band of robbers but not a state. Just what natural needs give rise to the state over and above those supplied by the family and other groups, or why the citizen ought to render obedience to his sovereign, or precisely the nature of the change which transforms a group of families into a true state, he left obscure. The only points that are perfectly clear are that a well-ordered state cannot exist until a sovereign power is recognized and that the units of which it is composed are families. This was a major defect of theoretical construction, because his theory of sovereignty was left standing merely as a definition of something which sometimes exists but for which he has no explanation. He eliminated the mandate of God, which the theory of divine right offered as a foundation for the king's authority, but he did not fill the gap with a natural explanation.

SOVEREIGNTY

Bodin's statement of the principle of sovereignty is generally agreed to be the most important part of his political philosophy. The presence of sovereign power is taken by him to be the mark which distinguishes the state from all the other groupings into which families fall. Accordingly he began by defining citizenship as subjection to a sovereign. The defining conceptions of the state are sovereign and subject, a view which logically places social, ethical, and religious relationships outside the bounds of political theory. As Bodin urged, innumerable other relations may subsist between citizens besides subjection to a common sovereign, but it is subjection which makes them citizens. They may or may not have a common language and religion. Various groups of them may have peculiar laws or local customs which are countenanced by the sovereign. The burghers of a city may have recognized privileges or immunities, and a corporate body may be permitted to make and enforce its own rules for certain purposes. A grouping of this kind, where law, language, religion, and custom are identical, Bodin called a *cité,* a term which corresponds roughly to the idea of a nation, at least in the sense that it suggests a social union rather than a formal political bond. The *cité* is not a state (*république*) ; the latter exists only where the citizens are subject to the rule of a common sovereign. The relation of this conception to the political problems of Bodin's own time is manifest. He is urging, in the manner of the Politiques, that the political bond may be self-sufficient even though the political community be divided by differences of religion and by the survival of local, customary, and class immunities. The essential element of the political community is the presence of a common sovereign.

Bodin's next step was to define sovereignty as " supreme power over citizens and subjects, unrestrained by law " and to analyze the conception of supreme power. It is, in the first place, perpetual as distinguished from any grant of power that is limited to a specific period of time. It is undelegated, or delegated without limit or condition. It is inalienable and not subject to prescription. It is unrestrained by law because the sovereign is the source of law. The sovereign cannot bind himself or his successors and he cannot be made legally accountable to his subjects, though Bodin had no doubt that the sovereign was answerable to God and subject to natural law. The law of the land is simply the sovereign's command and accordingly any limitation on the power to command must be extra-legal. The primary attribute of sovereignty is the power to give laws to citizens collectively and severally, without the consent of a superior, an equal, or an inferior. The other attributes — the power to declare war and treat for peace, to commission magistrates, to act as a court of last resort, to grant dispensations, to coin money, and to tax — are all consequences of the sovereign's position as legal head of the state. As Bodin was careful to explain, this implies also the sovereign's control over customary law, which he sanctions by permitting it to exist. Enactment, Bodin holds, can change custom, but not custom enactment.

This principle of a unified legal headship as the mark of a true state was applied with great clearness by Bodin to the ancient theory of forms of government. From his point of view every government which is not to be a prey to anarchy, every "well-ordered state," must have in it somewhere this indivisible source of authority. Hence different forms of government can vary only in the location of this power. There are no forms of *state,* though there are forms of government. In a monarchy sovereignty resides in the king and therefore the function of the estates is advisory only, as Bodin believed was the case in France and England. It is expedient for monarchs to consult their advisers but it cannot be mandatory, and the monarch cannot be legally bound by the advice given. If a king, so-called, is bound by an act of the estates, then sovereignty really resides in the assembly and the government is an aristocracy. This is the case, according to Bodin, in the empire of his day. Again, if the final power of decision and review rests with some sort of popular body, then the government is democratic. In short, there is no such thing as a mixed state. Either there is no undivided sovereign power, and in that case there is no well-ordered state, or this power resides in some one place, whether it be king, assembly, or populace. Bodin's treatment of forms of government implies a clear-cut distinction between state and government. The state consists in the possession of sovereign power; government consists in the apparatus through which such power is exercised. A monarch may delegate his powei widely and therefore govern popularly, while a democracy may govern despotically.

The theory of sovereignty was applied by Bodin also in his discussion of the subordinate parts of the state. In a monarchy the functions of parliament must be advisory. Similarly the power exercised by magistrates is delegated by the sovereign. Again, all the corporate bodies which exist within the state — religious bodies, municipalities, and commercial companies — owe their powers and privileges to the will of the sovereign. Bodin took for granted the existence of great numbers of such bodies, as was natural in his time, and also their possession of considerable powers of self-direction. He was even favorable to such a policy of practical decentralization. What he was most concerned to urge was that all corporate bodies exist only by the sovereign's permission and that all their powers are derived from his consent. As in the case of customary law, the powers of corporations are constructively derived from the state, even though they may rest upon ancient usage and not upon charter or statute. It was a prime object of the *Republic* to represent the king of France as the head of the entire political organization, though Bodin had no desire for a radical destruction of ancient corporations such as actually took place at the time of the French Revolution. His purpose was to make a foothold for the rights of the monarchy against all the survivors of the feudal age. It is significant that he treated the estates as merely one of the corporations which the sovereign permits, along with trading companies and ecclesiastical bodies.

LIMITATIONS ON SOVEREIGNTY

The preceding account of Bodin's theory of sovereign power takes account only of the parts of his argument which are straightforward and free from difficulties. In its entirety, however, the argument was by no means so simple, but contained serious confusions which must be noted in order to complete the picture. In general, sovereignty meant for Bodin a perpetual, humanly unlimited, and unconditional right to make, interpret, and execute law. The existence of such a right he believed to be necessary to any well-ordered state, forming the characteristic difference between a developed political body and more primitive groups. But the exercise of sovereign power which he regarded as justifiable was by no means so unlimited as his definitions imply, and the result is a series of restrictions that introduce a great amount of confusion into the finished theory.

In the first place, Bodin never doubted that the sovereign was bound by the law of God and of nature. Though he defined law as a sheer act of the sovereign's will, he never supposed that the sovereign could make right by mere fiat. For him as for all his contemporaries, the law of nature stands above human law and sets certain unchangeable standards of right; it is the observance of this law that distinguishes the true state from mere effective violence. There is, of course, no way to make the sovereign legally liable for violating the law of nature. Still, natural law does impose some real disabilities on him. In particular, it requires the keeping of agreements and respect for private property. The sovereign's agreements may involve political obligations toward his subjects or toward other sovereigns, and in such cases Bodin had no doubt that he was bound. It was difficult if not impossible for him to keep these obligations of the sovereign exclusively on a moral plane and so apart from legal and political obligations. What, for example, would be the duty of a magistrate if the sovereign were to command something contrary to natural law? Bodin had no doubt that there might be cases so flagrant that the sovereign ought to be disobeyed. He did all he could to reduce such cases to the narrowest limits, but the confusion was none the less there. Law is at once the will of the sovereign and an expression of eternal justice; yet the two may be in conflict.

A second confusion in Bodin's theory of sovereignty arose from his fidelity to the constitutional law of France. All his natural inclinations, both as a lawyer and a moralist, were on the side of constitutional government and respect for the ancient usages and practices of the realm. In common with the prevailing legal opinion of his time, he recognized that there were certain things which the king of France could not lawfully do. Specifically, he could not modify the succession and he could not alienate any part of the public domain; yet he was convinced that the king of France was sovereign in the full sense of the word, in fact, was the example *par excellence* of a sovereign. He admitted the existence of a peculiar class of laws which are necessarily connected with the exercise of sovereignty itself and which even the sovereign cannot change. These he called *leges imperii,* implying apparently that sovereignty itself would vanish with their violation. The confusion here is manifest; the sovereign is at once the source of law and the subject of certain constitutional laws which he has not made and cannot change.

The fact is that Bodin had two purposes which were united rather by circumstances than by logic. He was seeking to increase and consolidate the powers of the crown, because this was necessary in the circumstances, but he was also a convinced constitutionalist bent on saving and perpetuating the ancient institutions of the realm. Neither on logical nor historical grounds could the realm be identified with the crown. The idea behind the *leges imperii* was that, except as an element of the realm, the crown would have neither existence nor power; the idea behind the definition of sovereignty was that the crown is the chief legislative and executive organ in the realm. These two propositions are not incompatible, but there is room for endless confusion when they are both loosely combined in the conception of sovereignty. To make a really systematic theory, Bodin would have had to make up his mind which of the two was fundamental. For if sovereignty means essentially the supremacy of the prince, then the political community has no existence except by virtue of the relation between the prince and his subjects, and it is impossible that the realm should have laws of its own which the prince cannot change. Substantially this is the line of thought which Hobbes, starting partly from Bodin, later developed. On the other hand, if the state is a political community having laws and a constitution of its own, it is impossible that the sovereign should be identified with the prince.

Bodin's confusion on this point was due partly, no doubt, to his immediate purpose: he could hardly have combated revolution by inculcating loyalty to a juristic abstraction. For this purpose a visible and tangible king, the vicar of God on earth, was altogether the more appealing idea, at least until national sentiment had given the nation itself solidity enough to make the king dispensable. On the other hand, a visible king is not easy to insert into a system of juristic concepts. In part, however, the confusion was deeply involved in the method of political philosophy which Bodin was trying to follow. This method contemplated the combination of history and philosophy, of factual evolution and logical analysis. From the point of view of history the realm of France, the political community, would almost necessarily be taken as a single social being, continuous and self-identical through an indefinitely long series of gradual changes. From the point of view of analysis it would be almost equally necessary to make a cross-section through the historical stream and consider the formal relations between the parts of the legal constitution. No analysis would fit all stages of the history, and for this reason the history would violate the canons of any formal analysis. Bodin was undertaking something that was difficult perhaps to the point of impossibility. His confusions about the *leges imperii* make a starting-point for the long controversy between an analytic and an historical method in jurisprudence.

There was still a third confusion in Bodin's theory of sovereignty more immediately serious than the two already mentioned. This concerned his very strong convictions about the inviolability of private property. This right is guaranteed by the law of nature but it constituted for Bodin more than a moral limitation on the power of the sovereign. So sacred is property that the sovereign cannot touch it without the owner's consent. Accordingly he asserted that taxation requires the assent of the estates. But there is nothing whatever about taxation to justify Bodin in thus setting it apart from other legislation, and he had denied in the most explicit fashion that the estates can act in any but an advisory capacity in the making of law. Indeed, the very existence of the estates depended upon the delegation by the sovereign of a qualified authority to a subordinate corporation.

In this case the confusion amounts to a flat contradiction, arising from the defective organization of his theory already referred to. The right of property he considered to be an indefeasible attribute of the family, and the family is an independently existing unit out of which the state is constructed. A well-ordered state, however, requires a sovereign whose legal power is unlimited. Thus Bodin's state contained two absolutes: the indefeasible rights of the family and the unlimited legislative power of the sovereign.

Of the two the rights of property were more fundamental to his thought, at least in the sense that they formed standing convictions about which he hardly felt the need for argument. The unlimited power of the sovereign had a more occasional origin in the dangers produced by the religious wars.[3] If Bodin ever tried seriously to justify to himself the discrepancy between the two positions, he probably followed a line of thought similar to that used in the treatment of the *leges imperii*. The rights of property are essential to the family and the family is essential to the state; but the power to tax is the power to destroy; and the state cannot possess the power to destroy its own members. At all events he was perfectly explicit in asserting that taxation requires assent and in treating it as an inherent limitation on sovereignty, like the *leges imperii*. Logically his thought breaks in two at the point where the theory of the family ought to be joined to the theory of the state.

THE WELL-ORDERED STATE

The remainder of the *Republic* discussed a multitude of subjects but added nothing to the outlines of the theory. It examined exhaustively the causes and prevention of revolutions, again following the lead of Aristotle. In accord with his general theory, Bodin defined revolution as a displacement of sovereignty. No matter how much laws may change, a revolution does not take place so long as sovereignty resides in the same place. He enumerated many causes of revolution, of various degrees of importance. In general there is little order in this part of the book, though many of Bodin's observations were judicious. His discussion of the prevision of revolutions was a curious excursion into the uses of astrology for this purpose, while his analysis of the means for preventing them led him to cover every branch of administration and permitted him to display a really great fund of political acumen and wisdom. Broadly speaking, this part of the work was an exposition of the policy of the Politiques. The king, he holds, should not ally himself with any faction but should follow a policy

[3] R. Chauviré in his *Jean Bodin* (pp. 271 ff.) holds that there is a significant difference between the *Methodus,* written in 1566, and the *République,* written in 1576. The former was preoccupied with limitations on royal power, the latter with removing them. The difference he attributes to the circumstances that arose in the intervening ten years.

of conciliation, using repression cautiously and only where there is a strong probability of success. The most significant aspect of the argument was his firm defense of religious toleration, which however he here treated rather as a policy than a principle. He later dealt more philosophically with the subject in the extraordinary dialogue called the *Heptaplomeres,* a work which for obvious reasons it was impossible to publish in the sixteenth century.[4]

The examination of revolutions led to the more general subject of the relation of physical environment to national characteristics. Here also Bodin started from Aristotle but greatly elaborated the whole subject. Northern peoples, he believed, are large and physically vigorous but slow of movement and of mind. Southerners are slight of build, vivacious in manner, and surpass in acuteness and ingenuity. For political purposes the middle region, where the two sets of qualities are mingled, is superior, as is shown by the fact that the great states, as well as the science of politics, have originated there. This portion of Bodin's work formed an integral part of his whole political philosophy and suggested the later speculations of Montesquieu on the subject, but he made no attempt to bring it into logical relation with his theory of sovereignty. Its presence in his system, however, marks the vast difference between Bodin and the theological controversialists who wrote most of the political theory of the time.

After this excursus Bodin passed on to consider the obligation of the sovereign to keep faith in treaties and alliances. Here he deplored the growing belief that princes are not bound by promises to their own disadvantage, the argument being aimed at Machiavelli. It showed a growing sense of the need for restraining absolute sovereigns in their international dealings, a need which eventuated some fifty years later in the effort of Grotius to formulate an international law. Finally, Bodin considered at length the financial policies of the state, its sources of revenue, and the desirability of various forms of taxation. Incidentally he argued at length for the revival of the Roman censorship, partly as a means for obtaining exact information about the resources of the kingdom but largely as a means of moral purification.

[4] See "The Colloquium Heptaplomeres of Jean Bodin," by George H. Sabine, in *Persecution and Liberty,* New York, 1931.

The *Republic* was brought to a close with a chapter which in some measure may be regarded as containing the nerve of the whole book. Bodin compared the three forms of state in order to show the superiority of monarchy. Here, and indeed throughout, it is evident that he regarded a monarchy of the French type, or what he took to be the French type, as the only form of well-ordered state. Heredity and even the Salic Law, he tried to prove, were founded not only in custom but in reason. In spite of his previous admission that sovereignty may be vested in an aristocracy or in the people, he was convinced that in practice this leads to anarchy and to the ruin of subjects as well as rulers. The only really "well-ordered state" is one in which sovereignty is undivided because it resides in a single person. This distinction of possible states and the one well-ordered state runs all through Bodin's work, but it is a source of unclearness because it is not steadily maintained. He was never quite certain whether sovereignty is a quality which it is desirable for the state to possess but which actual states sometimes lack, or whether it was a quality which every state must of necessity possess. In general, he preferred to defend the theory as if it were a universal logical necessity, and yet he really believed that many or perhaps most states do not rise to the level of a well-ordered monarchy, in which alone undivided sovereignty is possible. The confusion of the necessary with the desirable is a fault to which the project for uniting philosophy and history was peculiarly prone. Like many later philosophers who had a similar aim, Bodin stated what was really a program of reform under the guise of a pronouncement of eternal truth.

Despite the many confusions in his thought, Bodin's political philosophy was a work of no slight importance. Compared with any other work of the second half of the sixteenth century it was broadly conceived and impressively executed. The neglect into which the *Republic* soon fell was due more to its manner than its substance and many books of less weight survived longer. At the same time, Bodin's system was not a philosophical construction of the first rank. Its two sides — constitutionalism and centralized power — were not really drawn together. Natural law, upon which the structure everywhere rested, was accepted as a tradition and was never analyzed or solidly based. The theory of sovereignty, though Bodin's statement of it was the clearest given in the sixteenth century, floats in the air, a feat of definition rather than of explanation. The ends of a well-ordered state, the nature of the subject's obligation to obey, and the relation between the state and its constituent families all require further analysis. But from this unclearness two problems emerged which largely occupied the attention of political philosophy in the century after Bodin. One was the theory of sovereignty in terms of power — the definition of the state as a relation between political inferiors and a political superior and of law as a command. This conception was systematically developed by Hobbes. The other was a modernizing and secularizing of the ancient theory of natural law, in order to find if possible an ethical and yet a not merely authoritarian foundation for political power. This revision was chiefly the work of Grotius and Locke. So successful was it that natural law became, in the estimation of the seventeenth and eighteenth centuries, the valid scientific form of political theory.

SELECTED BIBLIOGRAPHY

Political Thought in the Sixteenth Century. By J. W. Allen. London, 1928. Part III, ch. 8.

Jean Bodin et son temps. By Henri Baudrillart. Paris, 1853.

Aus Mittelalter und Renaissance. By Friedrich von Bezold. Munich, 1918. Ch. 10.

Jean Bodin, auteur de la République. By Roger Chauviré. Paris, 1914.

Constitutional Thought in Sixteenth-century France: A Study in the Evolution of Ideas. By William F. Church. Cambridge, Mass., 1941.

Weltbild und Staatsidee bei Jean Bodin. By Elizabeth Feist. Halle, 1930.

Réformateurs et publicistes de l'Europe: Moyen âge, Renaissance. By Adolphe Franck. Paris, 1864.

The Social and Political Ideas of some Great Thinkers of the Sixteenth and Seventeenth Centuries. Ed. by F. J. C. Hearnshaw. London, 1926. Ch. 2.

The Growth of Political Thought in the West, from the Greeks to the End of the Middle Ages. By C. H. McIlwain. New York, 1932. Ch. 7.

"The Colloquium Heptaplomeres of Jean Bodin." By George H. Sabine. In *Persecution and Liberty: Essays in Honor of George Lincoln Burr.* New York, 1931.

"Sovereignty at the Crossroads: A Study of Bodin." By Max A. Shepard. In *Pol. Sci. Quar.*, Vol. XLV (1930), p. 580.

CHAPTER XXI

THE MODERNIZED THEORY OF NATURAL LAW

The opening decades of the seventeenth century began a gradual process of releasing political philosophy from the association with theology which had been characteristic of its earlier history throughout the Christian era. The release which came in the seventeenth century was made possible by a gradual recession of religious controversy and by a gradual secularizing of the issues with which political theory had to deal. It was furthered also by a secularizing of intellectual interests which was inherent in the return of scholarship to antiquity and the spread through northern Europe of the admiration for Greece and Rome already so conspicuous in the Italian scholars of Machiavelli's generation. Stoicism, Platonism, and a modernized understanding of Aristotle brought into being a degree of naturalism and rationalism such as the study of Aristotle in the fourteenth century had not been able to produce. Finally, an indirect effect in the same direction was produced by epoch-making progress in the mathematical and physical sciences. Social phenomena generally, and political relationships in particular, began to be conceived as natural occurrences, open to study by observation and more especially by logical analysis and deduction, in which revelation or any other supernatural element had no important place.

This tendency to set political and social theory free from theology was already perceptible in the later Jesuit writers, even though their purpose was in part to support the indirect power of the papacy over secular governments. Their argument stressed the secular and human origin of government, in order that the divine right of the pope might be given a unique place in the category of authorities. Thus the political theory and the jurisprudence of Suarez, though parts of a scholastic philosophy, could be detached from theology without suffering serious mutilation. In the Calvinist writers of the early seventeenth century a similar secularization of interest occurred, though Calvinism probably retarded rather than aided the process. The doctrine of predestination, in its original Calvinist meaning, tied up all moral and social questions with the free grace of God and made every natural phenomenon an incident in a personal and voluntary government of the world. Whatever affinity Calvinist theology may have had with Puritan middle-class morality, it had none at all with a rational explanation of moral phenomena, but the contrary. On the other hand, the expunging of the Canon Law from Protestant systems made necessary a more radical break with the Middle Ages than was required of the Jesuits. Suarez could produce a somewhat modernized form of medieval jurisprudence but the Calvinists, once the strict ties of Calvinism were relaxed, could more easily revert to pre-Christian conceptions of natural law. The critical event in the history of Calvinist theology, so far as political theory was concerned, was the controversy aroused by Arminius and the Remonstrants in Holland, which set Hugo Grotius free from the bondage of strict Calvinism and fortified him in the humanist tradition of Erasmus.[1]

ALTHUSIUS

Even before Grotius, however, the relationship of natural law to theology had begun to wear thin for some writers with Calvinist affiliations. This was notably true of Johannes Althusius, who continued and elaborated the anti-royalist theory of the French Calvinists.[2] His book on politics was in no sense a controversial tract but, as the name signifies, a systematic treatise on all forms of human association including the state. Like Grotius, Althusius objected to the mixture of jurisprudence and politics in Bodin and therefore made a point of separating them. His separation, however, affected somewhat unfortunately his theory of politics. Though his position depended upon the conception of natural law, he never followed this to a thoroughgoing revision of its principles. Like other Calvinist writers he identified natural

[1] Cf. Ernst Cassirer, *Die Philosophie der Aufklärung* (1932), p. 320.

[2] His *Politica methodice digesta* was first published in 1603, and in an extended form in 1610. A modern edition, with some omissions, was edited by C. J. Friedrich, Cambridge, Mass., 1932.

law with the second table of the Decalogue,[3] but thereby he did less than justice to his own thought, because in fact his theory of society depended in no essential respect upon this implied religious authority. The truth is, as Gierke says, that Althusius was more clear than profound and devoted himself rather to formal definition than to a philosophical analysis of principles.[4]

Within these limits he developed a political theory which was both interesting and important, because it depended logically upon the single idea of contract and owed substantially nothing to religious authority. In effect, therefore, it was a naturalistic theory, in so far as contract may be called a natural relationship. Althusius's contract was in fact very much like the innate social propensity which had figured in Stoic theory and which played an even clearer part in the philosophy of Grotius. The important point was that Althusius raised it to the level of a sufficient explanation of human social groupings, thus leaving nothing to be explained by an appeal to theological sanctions. The effect was to produce a theory much closer to the actual spirit of Aristotle than the more explicitly Aristotelian theories of the scholastics. Althusius was not very far from saying that the association of men in groups is simply a natural fact, as much an intrinsic part of human nature as anything else, and accordingly that a society was not, in Hobbes's phrase, " an artificial body " to be explained by extraneous causes. The idea of contract was not very well suited to express this thought but was quite in accord with the individualism which marked all theories of natural law, especially after the writings of Hobbes.

The contract figured in two ways in Althusius's theory: it had a more specifically political rôle in explaining the relations between a ruler and his people and a general sociological rôle in explaining the existence of any group whatever. The first corresponded to a contract of government, the second to a social contract in a broader sense. In the latter use a tacit agreement underlies any association or *consociatio,* a word which corresponds to Aristotle's use of community. By this agreement persons become " dwellers to-

[3] In another field, this tendency to identify natural law with the law of Moses occurs in Bodin's curious association of natural religion with primitive Judaism.

[4] Otto von Gierke, *Johannes Althusius* (1913), pp. 16 f.

gether" (*symbiotici*) and sharers in the goods, services, or laws which the association creates and sustains. Any association has therefore its twofold "law" which defines on the one hand the kind of community existing between the members and on the other creates and limits an authority for administering its common affairs. Althusius offers an elaborate dichotomous classification of associations, but in brief he may be said to distinguish five chief kinds, each more complex sort arising as a combination of the preceding simpler ones: the family, the voluntary corporation (*collegium*), the local community, the province, and the state. In the more advanced groups, the underlying associations rather than individual persons are the contracting parties, and in each case the new group assumes the regulation only of such acts as are necessary to its purposes, leaving the rest in the control of the more primitive groups. There occurs, therefore, a series of social contracts by which various social groups, some political and some not, come into being. This is the basis for Althusius's theory of the state.

The state forms one of this series. It arises by the association of provinces or local communities and its differentia, as compared with any other group, is sovereign power (*majestas*). Here the influence of Bodin upon Althusius was evident, as well as his purpose to avoid some of the confusions in Bodin's theory. The most important aspect of Althusius's theory was that he made sovereignty reside necessarily in the people as a corporate body. They are incapable of parting with it because it is a characteristic of that specific kind of association. Consequently it is never alienated and never passes into the possession of a ruling class or family. Power is bestowed upon the administrative officers of a state by the law of the state. This forms the second of Althusius's two kinds of contract, an agreement by which the corporate body imparts power to its administrators to make the purposes of the corporation effective. It follows that this power reverts to the people if the holder of it should for any reason forfeit it. This theory was the clearest statement of popular sovereignty that had so far appeared. It avoided the difficulties in Bodin's theory, which had arisen because of his confusion between the sovereign and the monarch, and which had led him to describe sovereignty as at once unlimited and yet incapable of changing certain provisions of the historical constitution. It is clearer also than the account of sovereignty later given by Grotius, since it does not confuse public authority with a patrimonial power inherent in the ownership of land.

Althusius's defense of the right to resist tyranny followed pretty closely in the track of the earlier Calvinist theories. This right does not belong to individuals but must be exercised through a special class of magistrates, called "ephors," who are the appointed guardians of the community's rights. The ephors correspond to the inferior magistrates of Calvin and the *Vindiciae contra tyrannos*. Althusius's theory, however, was better based, because the whole structure of his state was federal. The contracting parties which produce the state are not individuals but communities, which, though not sovereign, have the inherent capacity for giving effect to their own ends which all corporate bodies possess. It has been pointed out in a preceding chapter that an approximation to federalism occurred in the *Vindiciae contra tyrannos,* which, in the circumstances prevailing in France, could hardly be anything except a reversion to feudal privileges and exemptions. The case was different in the Netherlands, where central government really was founded upon a confederation of provinces diverse in religion, language, and national sentiment. Althusius's description of the state as a community in which several cities and provinces have bound themselves by a common law offered a better principle for limiting the power of a chief magistrate than a theory which contemplated a union of individuals under a sovereign ruler. Unfortunately it had little application in France and England, where the political thinking of the sixteenth and seventeenth centuries mainly took place. This fact was perhaps one of the reasons why Althusius's work fell into oblivion.

The political theory of Althusius, so far as it went, was remarkably clear and consistent. It reduced the whole range of political and social relationships to the one principle of consent or contract. The compact, express or tacit, was made to account for society itself, or rather for a whole series of societies, of which the state was one. It offered a logical basis for the element of authority inherent in any group, which appears in the state specifically as the sovereign public authority of the group itself, and it afforded a plausible ground for the legal limitation of executives and for a right to resist a tyrannous exercise of executive power. The great virtue of the theory was its clearness. In substance Althusius had made himself independent of any religious sanction for authority, since he treated associations as self-sufficing, at least within the limits set by the purposes which each kind of association was meant to serve. For the principle of consent itself, the contractual obligation upon which he made the right of every association depend, he offered no philosophical foundation at all. Doubtless he regarded the sanctity of contract as a principle of natural law, and he was content to refer natural law for its validity to the Decalogue. To be sure, he made no use of this reference and his theory would be just as strong without it, but at the crucial point his thought had no foundation except a Scriptural authority. In part this was due to an element of superficiality in his own thinking, but in part also it was probably due to the fact that he had not made himself independent of Calvinism. His conception of nature was tied to the essentially supernatural principle of predestination. The final step in detaching natural law altogether from its entanglement with religious authority was made not by Althusius but by the more philosophically minded Grotius.[5]

GROTIUS: NATURAL LAW

It must be admitted, however, that Grotius was less clear than Althusius in his treatment specifically of sovereignty and the state. The subject had only incidental importance for him, and its bearing on international relations made the constitutional powers of rulers more significant than the theoretical principles of sovereignty itself. Consequently Grotius, more than Althusius, was hampered in his thinking about philosophical principles by his fidelity to the letter of positive law. After defining sovereignty as a power not subject to the legal control of another, he distinguished between a common and a special possessor, or subject, of the power. The common subject of sovereignty is the state itself; the special subject is one or more persons, according to the constitutional law of each state. The sovereign is therefore either the political body

[5] The *De jure belli ac pacis* was first published in 1625. The edition of 1646 has been photographically reproduced (Washington, 1913), with an English translation by Francis W. Kelsey and others (Oxford, 1925), as No. 3 of "The Classics of International Law."

itself (Althusius's state) or the government, a use of terms which hardly made for clearness. He reverted also to the view of the Civilians that a people can wholly divest itself of its sovereign power, and to the feudal identification of public authority with a patrimonial power over land, which can be acquired by conquest, transferred, or devised. The result was that sovereignty as a specific property of the state itself was lost to sight in a flood of details that have to do not with a general theory but only with the constitutional powers of specific rulers.

Grotius's importance in the history of jurisprudence rests not upon a theory of the state or upon anything that he had to say about constitutional law, but upon his conception of a law regulating the relations between sovereign states. The practical urgency of the problem in the seventeenth century need hardly be stressed. Always a fertile field for disorder, the relations between independent political powers had become ever more chaotic with the breakdown of such feeble restraints as the medieval church had occasionally applied. The rise of the absolute monarchies and the more or less frank acceptance of a Machiavellian conception of the relations between them made force the arbiter in the dealings of states with states. To this must be added the effects of the religious wars which followed the Reformation, bringing to international relations the intrinsic bitterness of religious hatred and affording the color of good conscience to the most barefaced schemes of dynastic aggrandizement. And behind overt political ambitions lay the economic baits which led the western European nations along the road of expansion, colonization, commercial aggrandizement, and the exploitation of newly discovered territory. There were ample reasons why Grotius should have believed that the welfare of mankind required a comprehensive and systematic treatment of the rules governing the mutual relations among states.

> Such a work is all the more necessary because in our day, as in former times, there is no lack of men who view this branch of law with contempt as having no reality outside of an empty name.[6]

Grotius's contribution to the special subject of international law is beyond the limits of a history of political theory. In re-

[6] Prolegomena, sect. 3 (Kelsey's translation).

spect to the latter his importance lay in the philosophical principles upon which he sought to found his special subject and which he set out especially in the Prolegomena to his great work. In the seventeenth century it was a foregone conclusion that he should appeal to the generally admitted idea of a fundamental law, or law of nature, lying behind the civil law of every nation, and binding, because of its intrinsic justice, upon all peoples and upon subjects and rulers alike. In the long tradition of Christian political thought no writer had denied, or even doubted, the validity of such a law. To the fact of validity Grotius need hardly address himself. But with the breaking up of Christian unity and the decline of Christian authority the grounds of this validity called urgently for reexamination. Neither the authority of the church nor the authority of Scripture, in fact, no form of religious revelation, could establish the foundation of a law binding alike on Protestant and Catholic peoples, and governing the relations between Christian and non-Christian rulers. It was natural that Grotius, with his background of humanistic training, should turn back to the even older, pre-Christian, tradition of natural law which he found in the writers of classical antiquity. Thus he chose, as Cicero had done before him, to put his examination of the grounds of natural law into the form of a debate with the skeptical critic of the Stoic philosophy, Carneades.[7]

The point of Carneades's refutation of natural justice lay in the argument that all human conduct is motived by self-interest and that law is, in consequence, merely a social convention generally beneficial and supported not by a sense of justice but by prudence. Grotius's answer was, in brief, that such an appeal to utility is essentially ambiguous since men are inherently sociable beings. As a result the maintenance of society itself is a major utility which is not measured by any private benefits (other than the satisfaction of their sociable impulses) accruing to individuals.

> Man is, to be sure, an animal, but an animal of a superior kind, much farther removed from all other animals than the different kinds of animals are from one another. . . . But among the traits characteristic of

[7] The account of the debate in Cicero's *Republic* was preserved largely in Books V and VI of Lactantius's *Institutes,* whence Grotius doubtless took it. The relevant passages are now given as testimonia in any edition of the *Republic.*

man is an impelling desire for society, that is, for the social life — not of any and every sort, but peaceful, and organized according to the measure of his intelligence, with those who are of his own kind; this social trend the Stoics called "sociableness."[8]

Hence the preservation of a peaceful social order is itself an intrinsic good, and the conditions required for that purpose are as binding as those which serve more strictly private ends.

This maintenance of the social order, which we have roughly sketched, and which is consonant with human intelligence, is the source of law properly so called. To this sphere of law belong the abstaining from that which is another's, the restoration to another of anything of his which we may have, together with any gain which we may have received from it; the obligation to fulfil promises, the making good of a loss incurred through our fault, and the inflicting of penalties upon men according to their deserts.[9]

There are, then, certain minimal conditions or values which must be realized, human nature being what it is, if an orderly society is to persist. Specifically these are, in the main, the security of property, good faith, fair dealing, and a general agreement between the consequences of men's conduct and their deserts. These conditions are not the result of voluntary choice or the product of convention but rather the reverse; choice and convention follow the necessities of the case.

For the very nature of man, which even if we had no lack of anything would lead us into the mutual relations of society, is the mother of the law of nature.[10]

At one further remove, however, this natural law gives rise to the positive law of states; the latter depends for its validity upon the underlying grounds of all social obligation and especially upon that of good faith in keeping covenants.

For those who had associated themselves with some group, or had subjected themselves to a man or to men, had either expressly promised, or from the nature of the transaction must be understood impliedly to have promised, that they would conform to that which should have been determined, in the one case by the majority, in the other by those upon whom authority had been conferred.[11]

[8] Prolegomena, sect. 6.

[9] *Ibid.*, sect. 8.

[10] *Ibid.*, sect. 16.

[11] *Ibid.*, sect. 15.

Within this framework of natural law Grotius believed that there was ample room for considerations of utility, which may well vary from people to people, and which also may dictate practices looking to the advantage of all nations in their international dealings. But certain broad principles of justice are natural — that is, universal and unchangeable — and upon these principles are erected the varying systems of municipal law, all depending upon the sanctity of covenants, and also international law, which depends upon the sanctity of covenants between rulers.

Grotius accordingly gave the following definition of natural law:

> The law of nature is a dictate of right reason, which points out that an act, according as it is or is not in conformity with rational nature, has in it a quality of moral baseness or moral necessity; and that, in consequence, such an act is either forbidden or enjoined by the author of nature, God.[12]

The precise meaning of this reference to the command of God is important. In point of fact, as Grotius was at pains to make clear, it added nothing to the definition and implied nothing in the way of a religious sanction. For the law of nature would enjoin exactly the same if, by hypothesis, there were no God. Moreover, it cannot be changed by the will of God. The reason for this is that God's power does not extend to making true a proposition that is inherently self-contradictory; such a power would be not strength but weakness.

> Just as even God, then, cannot cause that two times two should not make four, so He cannot cause that that which is intrinsically evil be not evil.[13]

Hence there is nothing arbitrary in natural law more than there is in arithmetic. The dictates of right reason are whatever human nature and the nature of things imply that they must be. Will enters as one factor into the situation but the *sic volo, sic iubeo* of God or man does not create the obligatory nature of the law. Referring to the authority of the Old Testament, Grotius distin-

[12] Bk. I, ch. i, sect. x, 1.

[13] Bk. I, ch. i, sect. x, 5; cf. Prolegomena, sect. 11. A few expressions of similar import occur in writers before Grotius; see Gierke, *Althusius* (1913), p. 74, n. 45.

guished carefully between commands which God gave to the Jews as a chosen people and which therefore depended merely upon divine will, and the evidence which it, along with other important documents, affords of natural human relationships. Nothing could show more clearly his independence of the system of divine sovereignty implicit in Calvinism.

MORAL AXIOMS AND DEMONSTRATION

The surpassing importance of this theory of natural law was not due to the content which Grotius attributed to it, for in this respect he followed the well-worn trails of the ancient lawyers. Good faith, substantial justice, and the sanctity of covenants had been at all times the rules to which a natural origin was attributed. The importance was methodological. It provided a rational, and what the seventeenth century could regard as a scientific, method for arriving at a body of propositions underlying political arrangements and the provisions of the positive law. It was essentially an appeal to reason, as the ancient versions of natural law had always been, but it gave a precision to the meaning of reason such as it had not had in an equal degree in antiquity. The references which Grotius frequently makes to mathematics are significant. Certain propositions in the law, like the proposition two times two equals four, are axiomatic; they are guaranteed by their clearness, simplicity, and self-evidence. No reasonable mind can doubt them, once they are accurately understood and clearly conceived; they form the elements of a rational insight into the fundamental nature of reality. Once grasped they form the principles by means of which systematic inference can construct a completely rational system of theorems. The identity of this method with what was supposed to be the procedure of geometry is obvious.

This quality was exactly what commended it to Grotius. He stated specifically that, like a mathematician, he proposed to withdraw his mind from every particular fact. In short, he intended to do for the law just what, as he understood the matter, was being done with success in mathematics or what Galileo was doing for physics.

I have made it my concern to refer the proofs of things touching the law of nature to certain fundamental conceptions which are beyond question, so that no one can deny them without doing violence to himself. For the principles of that law, if only you pay strict heed to them, are in themselves manifest and clear, almost as evident as are those things which we perceive by the external senses.[14]

Because of the prevalence of this idea of good method, the seventeenth century became the era of "demonstrative" systems of law and politics, the purpose being to assimilate all sciences, the social as well as the physical, as much as possible to a form which was believed to account for the certainty of geometry. Of the English philosophers of the generation following Grotius, Thomas Hobbes followed this plan most consistently. In Holland Spinoza undertook to present his ethics in the form of a geometrical demonstration, with all the paraphernalia of axioms, theorems, scholia, and corollaries, and his *Political Treatise,* though lacking the form, was scarcely less rigorous in its procedure.[15] Samuel Pufendorf, in his great systematic treatise on natural and international law,[16] began by taking exception to Grotius's opinion that morals and mathematics are not equally certain. Nor was this ideal of demonstration confined to law and politics. It was extended to all branches of social study, producing the systems of natural religion and rational ethics that prevailed throughout the seventeenth and eighteenth centuries. Finally, it produced the systems of natural economy that continued to pass as economic science well into the nineteenth century. It would be impossible to exaggerate the importance that these conceptions had in the early modern development of social studies. Everywhere the system of natural law was believed to offer the valid scientific line of approach to social disciplines and the scientific guide to social practice.

The reason for the authority which this method acquired lay largely in the fact that it was believed to parallel the processes by which the physical sciences made dazzling progress in the interval between Galileo and Newton. These processes in turn were believed to depend upon the use of a method already well tried in

[14] Prolegomena, sect. 39.

[15] The *Ethics* and the *Political Treatise* were published posthumously in 1677; Eng. trans. by R. H. M. Elwes, 2 vols., in Bohn's Philosophical Library.

[16] *De jure naturae et gentium,* Lund, 1672; Eng. trans. by Basil Kennet, London, 1710.

geometry. A few years after Grotius wrote Descartes gave the method its classical philosophical statement in the *Discours de la méthode:* resolve every problem into its simplest elements; proceed only by the smallest steps so that each advance may be apparent and compelling; take nothing for granted that is not perfectly clear and distinct. It is evident that Descartes believed himself to be merely generalizing the process by which he had discovered the analytic geometry, and the remarks on method by a great experimental scientist like Galileo, interspersed in his dialogues on the new science of mechanics, were often to substantially the same effect. In the seventeenth century no sharp line was drawn, as would be done now, between mathematics and the physical sciences of experiment and observation, probably because the experimental data required in mechanics were not very great, while the mathematical apparatus was considerable. The method commended itself to scholars generally, and to students of law and politics in particular, not because they expected, like the physicists, to make any use of mathematics, but because the logical ideals of analysis, simplicity, and self-evident clarity appeared to be equally applicable to all subject-matters. They were, moreover, the perfect solvents for authority and mere customary belief. The appeal to reason in the early rationalists was directed against dogmatism and the blind following of tradition.

It was the development of the deductive technique itself that gradually brought to light an ambiguity inherent in the system of natural law, namely, the twofold use of the word truth to mean sometimes the logical dependence of a conclusion on its premises and sometimes the factual existence of the things or events referred to. This formalizing of deductive procedure led in time to a contrast between rational truth and factual data, but among the earlier rationalists, whether in science or law, the appeal to reason was not intended to exclude observation and the accumulation of fact. They believed that reason itself provided an unshakable framework of axiomatic principles and necessary deductions, but within this system they accepted as a matter of course great bodies of empirical fact that had to be learned by observation. Thus Grotius never doubted that much law was due to what he called "free will," that is, enactment, and might perfectly well be changed without violating reason. Some relationships, however, are "necessary"; neither will nor authority can change them. While they leave a considerable range within which positive law may vary, they definitely rule out certain combinations. Some such conception as this with respect to natural and positive law was generally accepted. More than a century later it was still a commonplace, witness the words with which Montesquieu opened the *Spirit of the Laws:*

> Laws, in their most general signification, are the necessary relations arising from the nature of things.

The practical utility of the theory of natural law depended largely upon the fact that it introduced a normative element into law and politics, a body of transcendent values, such as justice, good faith, and fair dealing, by which the performance of positive law could be judged. It was, therefore, the antecedent of all later efforts to moralize the law, such as Rudolf Stammler's theory of "just" law, and even of utilitarian theories such as those of Ihering and Bentham, which retained elements of natural law even while rejecting it in principle. Broadly speaking, the whole point of view, like that of most seventeenth-century science, was Platonic; the Platonism of Grotius's Prolegomena is unmistakable. The law of nature was an "idea," a type or model like the perfect geometrical figure, to which existence approximates but which does not derive its validity from agreement with fact. It was for this reason that *ius gentium,* in the old sense of common practice, could be redefined as international law, since common practice was at most only an indication, and not necessarily a very good indication, of what was reasonable.[17] The rational was supposed to fix its own standard of value to which rulers ought to make the positive law conform. It was a standard of *good* practice to be set against the frequent unreasonableness of customary or conventional practice.

Consequently, the appeal to reason and natural law contained another possible ambiguity, in addition to that already mentioned between factual truth and logical implication. This is the ambiguity between logical and moral necessity. The system of natural law always assumed that its self-evident propositions were,

[17] Cf. Grotius's division of law into natural and volitional (*i.e.,* positive); Bk. I, ch. i, sects. 10–17.

at least in some cases, normative, setting up an ideal standard not only of what is but of what ought to be. Yet the necessity of an axiom in geometry and the necessity that law should be just are pretty clearly two different kinds of necessity, since the latter refers to the realizing of human ends and purposes. Even though it were true, as Grotius argued, that justice consists in a conformity of the law to underlying principles of human nature, the latter forms a highly complicated and changeable body of facts; the proposition that any values hold good eternally is still far from self-evident. The system of natural law tended to prejudge the question whether values have any standing in nature. The only philosopher who seriously tried to face this problem in the seventeenth century was Spinoza. His ethics was intended to have no more reference to ends than mathematics and physics have, but it cannot be claimed that he avoided double meanings in his use of terms. In his political theory he tried consistently to reduce rights to natural forces and to show that strong government in the long run must be good government. Here again he hardly did all that he undertook. Hobbes too had a metaphysical system in which transcendent values had no place, and his effort to square his materialism with the prevalent connotations of natural law proves nothing except that by the middle of the century this terminology had become mandatory. All his most important conclusions were taken over by the Benthamites, who denied natural law on principle. The critical analysis of the system of natural law and the discrimination of the double meanings contained in it were the work of David Hume about the middle of the eighteenth century.

CONTRACT AND INDIVIDUAL CONSENT

What gave unity to the system of natural law in politics was not the self-evidence of its principles but the circumstance that, for the time being, there was general agreement about what it was important to insist upon. What seemed to nearly all thinkers axiomatic was that an obligation, to be really binding, must be freely assumed by the parties bound. The choices, wisely considered, may be inevitable when human nature is taken into account, but the compulsion is an inward one, flowing from the interests and the motives of the man himself. In the final analysis obligation cannot be imposed by force but is always self-imposed. It was this conviction which made all obligation appear under the guise of a promise; what a man promises he may reasonably be held to, since he has himself created the obligation by his own act. In the larger question of a man's obligation to the community in which he lives, it was common to say that there was *no* rational way to conceive the obligation except by attributing it to a promise. Whether such a covenant were historical or a methodological fiction, as Kant afterward said, made little difference; in either case all binding obligation had to be represented as self-imposed. A sentence from Pufendorf, the equivalent of which could be found in a host of writers, will illustrate this:

> On the whole, to join a multitude, or many men, into one Compound Person, to which one general act may be ascribed, and to which certain rights belong, as 'tis opposed to particular members, and such rights as no particular member can claim separately from the rest; 'tis necessary, that they shall have first united their wills and powers by the intervention of covenants; without which, how a number of men, who are all naturally equal, should be link'd together, is impossible to be understood.[18]

As a consequence a political theory based on natural law contained two necessary elements: the contract by which a society or a government (or both) came into being and the state of nature which existed apart from the contract. The latter applied to two important cases: the relations of private individuals to one another and the relations between sovereign states. The agreements of these two kinds of contracting parties gave rise in the one case to municipal law and in the other to international law, both subject to the general principles of the law of nature. Both municipal and international law arise by covenant; both are binding because they are self-imposed. Theories of the form and nature of the contract might vary almost indefinitely. The idea that government depended upon a pact between ruler and people was much older than the modern theories of natural law, being implicit in the relation of a feudal lord to his vassals. In this older conception the people or the community figured as a corporate body. As the theory of natural law was developed it became apparent that this capacity of a people to contract needed

[18] *Op. cit.*, Bk. VII, ch, ii, sect. 6 (Kennet's translation).

explanation. The simplest explanation was to suppose two contracts, one by which the community itself was produced and binding its members to one another and one between the community thus formed and its governing officials. By this means the idea of contract was made into a universal theory covering all forms of obligation and all forms of social grouping. This is the form which the theory took in Althusius and which was continued in Pufendorf.[19] English writers did not develop the theory so far: Hobbes suppressed the contract of government for his own purposes and Locke used both forms of contract without taking the trouble to distinguish them clearly. This was probably due to the fact that natural law never played the part in English jurisprudence that it did on the Continent.

The theory of contract, taken in the large, need not be used as a means of limiting the power of government or of defending resistance, though of course it frequently was so used. Hobbes and Spinoza bent it, or perhaps distorted it, to a defense of absolute power. Althusius and Locke used it to defend the thesis that political power is necessarily limited, and the latter made it the defense of a successful revolution. Perhaps most writers, like Grotius and Pufendorf, followed a middle course: without justifying resistance they stressed moral limitations on rulers. The real emphasis of the theory was that law and government fall within the general field of morals; they are not merely expressions of force but are properly subject to ethical criticism. On the whole, therefore, the theory had a general bias toward political liberalism.

The question whether the obligation of contract is really the most obvious of moral truths has long ceased to be of moment in political theory. What needs to be explained is why so many men, and on the whole the most enlightened, in the seventeenth century thought it self-evident. Probably in no century before or since was there so self-conscious a break with the past or so resolute an effort to win freedom from the dead hand of custom and tradition. In the seventeenth century thinkers were conscious, as they had not been since the classic age of Greek philosophy, of the whimsicality of unsupported habit, of the insignificance of mere inherited position, and of the uncouthness of force without intelligence. By common agreement the agent of human well-

[19] *Op. cit.*, Bk. VII, ch. ii, sects. 7–8.

being was coming to be sought in the enlightened intelligence, and the great enemy of enlightenment seemed to be the blind acceptance of that which has no better credentials than its mere existence. To a self-confidence justifiably bred of successes in mathematical physics that made the century intellectually the most eminent of the modern age it seemed possible to begin construction from the very bottom, with only reason for a guide. Far in advance of any tangible accomplishment by modern science, the more enlightened already sensed, as Francis Bacon said, that knowledge is power. Moreover, the philosophy of the seventeenth century was, for the first time, a philosophy of the middle class. For the time being the middle class was, generally speaking, on the side of liberalism, cosmopolitanism, enlightenment, and individualism.

Looking at its world with these preconceptions and convinced that it must start from what was self-evident, modern philosophy could find nothing apparently so solid and indubitable as individual human nature. The individual human being, with his interests, his enterprise, his desire for happiness and advancement, above all with his reason, which seemed the condition for a successful use of all his other faculties, appeared to be the foundation on which a stable society must be built. Traditional differences of status already began to seem precarious. Not man as a priest or a soldier, as the member of a guild or an estate, but man as a bare human being, a "masterless man," appeared to be the solid fact. Already it was possible to conceive a psychology which would lay bare the springs of action concealed in man as such. Some unity of nature he must have, some natural force distinctive of the kind, which might be stated with the precision now first becoming possible for the bodies that make up the world of matter. If this were true the local and temporal and individual peculiarities in his nature might be explained as deviations from a norm which on the whole remained constant. If there were such an unchangeable core in human nature, there must surely be some minimal conditions required to make possible man's stable combination in social groups and therefore some fundamental laws of good conduct and good government which no ruler could defy with impunity. The philosophy of natural law, of natural religion, of natural economy was rooted in both the intellectual and the social presumptions of the seventeenth century.

One outstanding fact, it seemed, required special explanation. Man the individual is also man the citizen or subject. This the theory of natural law believed to be deducible from his individual nature; it was certain but it was not self-evident. The assumed order of certainty was significant. Under other circumstances man as a member of an organized community might have figured as the axiom, as in general it did for Plato and Aristotle, and man as an individual as the derivative. For the theories of natural law, and more especially after Hobbes, it was membership that required explanation. Society is made for man, not man for society; it is humanity, as Kant said, that must always be treated as an end and not a means. The individual is both logically and ethically prior. To the philosophy of the seventeenth century relations always appeared thinner than substances; man was the substance, society the relation. It was this assumed priority of the individual which became the most marked and the most persistent quality of the theory of natural law, and the clearest differentia of the modern from the medieval theory. Developed especially by Hobbes and Locke, it became a universal characteristic of social theory down to the French Revolution and maintained itself far beyond that date. It persisted, moreover, as a presumption in Bentham's School long after David Hume had destroyed the methodology of natural rights.

SELECTED BIBLIOGRAPHY

"The Law of Nature." By James Bryce. In *Studies in History and Jurisprudence*. New York, 1901.

"The 'Higher Law' Background of American Constitutional Law." By Edward S. Corwin. *Harvard Law Rev.*, Vol. XLII (1928–29), pp. 149, 365.

Studies of Political Thought from Gerson to Grotius. By John Neville Figgis. 2nd ed. Cambridge, 1923. Ch. 7.

National and International Stability: Althusius, Grotius, Van Vollenhoven. By P. S. Gerbrandy. London, 1944.

The Development of Political Theory. By Otto von Gierke. Eng. trans. by Bernard Freyd. New York, 1939. (*Johannes Althusius und die Entwickelung der naturrechtlichen Staatstheorien*).

Natural Law and the Theory of Society, 1500–1800. By Otto Gierke. With a lecture on the Ideas of Natural Law and Humanity by Ernst Troeltsch. Eng. trans. by Ernest Barker. 2 vols. Cambridge, 1934. (From *Das deutsche Genossenschaftsrecht,* Vol. IV).

The Revival of Natural Law Concepts. By Charles Grove Haines. Cambridge, Mass., 1930. Chs. 1–3.

The Life and Works of Hugo Grotius. By W. S. M. Knight. London, 1925.

"The History of the Law of Nature." By Sir Frederick Pollock. In *Essays in the Law,* London, 1922.

Natural Rights. By D. G. Ritchie. 3rd ed. London, 1916. Ch. 2.

Justice and World Society. By Laurence Stapleton. Chapel Hill, N. C., 1944. Ch. 2.

Hugo Grotius. By Hamilton Vreeland. New York, 1917.

CHAPTER XXII

ENGLAND: PREPARATION FOR CIVIL WAR

Before the outbreak of the civil wars in England in the 1640's the lines between rival political ideas were much less clearly drawn than they had become in France in the last quarter of the sixteenth century. In the latter country the right to resist had become definitely attached to the ancient idea that political power resides in the people, the duty of passive obedience was definitely attached to the theory of monarchical divine right, while Bodin's *Republic* had given a fair approximation to a theory of constitutional unity under the crown. In England, where no serious threat of civil disorder occurred until after the first quarter of the seventeenth century, these ideas remained in the inchoate state in which they existed in the medieval tradition. The Tudor monarchs were virtually absolute, but their power rested on the acquiescence of a substantial middle class which they were too prudent to alienate. Hence there was no faction that had any serious interest in supporting royal absolutism with a theory of divine right, and none that had to seek a theoretical defense for the right to resist. No one had as yet been forced to contemplate the consequences of a break between the powers of the constitution, such as the king and parliament or the king and his courts. The older assumption of comity and harmony between these powers under the fundamental law of the realm could still be made, without considering the ultimate legal supremacy of any of them. The traditional rights and limitations which fixed, vaguely but with sufficient precision, the status of all parts of the constitution had not yet been strained to the breaking point.

MORE'S *UTOPIA*

As the sixteenth century advanced, in England as everywhere else in Europe, all other considerations were overshadowed by political problems arising from the Protestant Reformation. The political ambitions of the various churches obscured and concealed the serious economic dislocation that attended the rise of modern trade and the destruction of the older economy. The older stratum of thought may be seen in such a pre-Reformation work as Sir Thomas More's political satire, the *Utopia*.[1] Though modeled externally on Plato's *Republic*, the *Utopia* really expressed its author's dislike of an acquisitive society in which it was becoming good morals to " buy abroad very cheap and sell again exceeding dear." The satire follows a pattern which might serve for any period of economic maladjustment: crime is alarmingly common and is met by corresponding savagery in the criminal law, yet severity avails nothing, for crime is the only means of livelihood open to great numbers of persons. " What other thing do you do than make thieves and then punish them? " Men trained for soldiers are thrown, by the cessation of war, upon the community with no possibility of being absorbed into industry. Industry, especially agriculture, cannot even support those already in it, since wool, the most profitable crop, requires the turning of arable land into pasture and the dispossessing of peasant occupiers. Sheep " consume, destroy, and devour whole fields, houses, and cities," and while peasants starve, or rob to live, the rich affect a " strange and proud new fangledness in their apparel and too much prodigal riot and sumptuous fare at their table." Government, instead of attacking this social disease, is engaged in legal chicanery to extort taxes and in pernicious schemes of war and conquest. More's sharpest shafts of irony were reserved for the perfidy of international diplomacy.

This attack upon the economics of business enterprise, however, was really motived by a longing for the past. It went back to the ideal, though hardly the actuality, of a cooperative commonwealth, which the new economy was displacing. More's conception of what was socially right was derived professedly from Plato's analysis of society into a system of cooperating classes, but perhaps more truly from the assumed validity of this conception in

[1] First published in 1516. A less well-known example of the ideal of a cooperative commonwealth is Thomas Starkey's *England*, a dialogue between Cardinal Pole and Thomas Lupset, written in 1536–38 and first published by the Early English Text Society in 1871. See the chapter on " The Very and True Commonweal " in J. W. Allen's *Political Thought in the Sixteenth Century* (1928), p. 134.

most of the social theory of the Middle Ages. According to this view, current at any time after St. Thomas, a community consists of classes, each entrusted with some task necessary to the common good, each performing its proper function and receiving its due reward without encroaching upon the equal right of others. In such a scheme individual enterprise has practically no place. Perhaps an English manor may have formed an economic unit, and ideally a moral unit, not too remote from such a conception. The moral purpose of a community, as More idealized it, was to produce good citizens and men of intellectual and moral freedom, to do away with idleness, to supply the physical needs of all without excessive labor, to abolish luxury and waste, to mitigate both poverty and wealth, and to minimize greed and extortion; in short, to reach its consummation in "free liberty of the mind and the garnishing of the same."

If a worthy moral idea can ever be pitiable surely this of More, appearing on the threshold of the religious wars and the expansion of modern trade, might be called so. It expressed, as More's life did, the reasonableness and open-mindedness of humanism, and withal the futility of a moral aspiration that cannot make its account with brute fact. Even the effort to give prominence to social and economic problems with their human consequences, failed before the rising tide of theological strife and the problems of political organization which it involved. For this reason the *Utopia* remained comparatively an isolated and unimportant episode in the political philosophy of its time. It illustrated rather the dying utterance of an old ideal than an authentic voice of the age that was coming into being.

HOOKER: THE NATIONAL CHURCH

The conception of a cooperative commonwealth, present in More and in all the English writers of the sixteenth century, formed a matrix from which the sharper issues of the mid-seventeenth century emerged. By the end of the sixteenth century the old conception had become strikingly incoherent; all parties were inclined to rely upon untenable compromises which had to be given up when various claims, really incompatible, were pushed. The main regions of stress were two. There was, in the first place, the old question of the church and secular government, in no way solved by the secession from Rome, but transformed into an internal problem involving national relations with the English church and the other branches of Protestant dissent, Presbyterian, Independent, and sectarian. In all these ecclesiastical and theological positions there were, and continued to be, political implications which could not be avoided. Hence it is necessary to take account of the political differences between the religious parties into which Englishmen were divided. In the second place, there was the question of the centralization of power and its incidence upon the supposedly co-operative relation between the various parts of government. Specifically this concerned the king and his control over his courts, first over the courts of common law and, more seriously in the end, over parliament. This chapter will describe, first, the political positions characteristic of the main religious bodies, and especially the bearing of these positions on the theory of the relation between church and state. Second, it will describe the growing tension between the crown and other elements of the constitution which was gradually breaking down the old belief in the harmony of powers.

For reasons that were quite unavoidable under the circumstances the independence of the English church from Rome could only mean that the king became its temporal head, but the temporal head of a church was a new and incomprehensible idea. Ecclesiastical government must include the power to decide what doctrines were to be believed by its members, yet no Christian could seriously think that the king of England was able to say what was true doctrine. A lawyer who knew little about theology and cared less might content himself with the practical conclusion that heresy was defined in the king's courts like other offenses. A man who earnestly believed that the doctrine of the church was eternal truth might well feel some misgiving at seeing this truth put into the keeping of the bishops, who were appointed by the king to govern the church. The truth is that the temporal headship was plausible just in so far as it was not necessary to understand it. It meant in effect not a theory but a practicable compromise which was unavoidable and on the whole conducive to public order. The religious wars in France presented an alternative that prudent Englishmen willingly took to heart. One essential fact in the situation was that everyone still lived in the shadow of a supposedly universal Christianity, believing that the divisions between the churches were temporary and would presently disappear, restoring the normal condition of a common belief. No one touched with Calvin's strong views on the independence of the church could contemplate the temporal headship as a permanence.

The controversy about the royal headship of the church produced one treatise of lasting importance, *The Laws of Ecclesiastical Polity* by Richard Hooker.[2] In purpose it was controversial, being intended to refute Puritan criticism of the established church, but in temper and breadth of learning it was at the opposite pole from the usual controversial tract. Though dealing explicitly with church government, the book was really an examination of the philosophy of law and government at large, since Hooker conceived church government to be only one aspect of all civil society. Taken as representing the thought of its own day, the *Ecclesiastical Polity* was notable because it was the last great statement of what might be called the medieval tradition, before that tradition was snapped by the stresses and strains of civil war. The striking thing about it was the variety of issues which it could conciliate, instead of making them irreconcilable conflicts as they became a generation later. In the long run, however, the importance of the book lay in providing a means by which this medieval tradition could carry over, with some necessary changes, into the modern political philosophy of the era after the civil wars. John Locke was glad to acknowledge his indebtedness to "the judicious Hooker," and in fact the conservative character of his summing up of the results of the Revolution depended in no small degree upon the continuity of his ideas with those of the earlier thinker.

The main object of Hooker's argument was to show that the Puritans, in refusing obedience to the established church, were implicitly denying the foundations of all political obligation: Englishmen are bound by reason to obey the ecclesiastical law of England, while Puritans are not bound, either by reason or religion, to disobey it. The defense of this thesis took him first into a philosophical examination of all law and the basis of political obligation, and here he followed the lead of Thomas. There are various types of law: the eternal law, or the law of God's own nature, the natural law, or the ordinances which God has laid down

[2] Books I–IV were published in 1594 and Book V in 1597. Books VI–VIII were added in a somewhat mutilated form after Hooker's death.

for governing things after their various kinds, and the law of reason, which man as a rational being is especially obligated to follow. Reason enables a man to perceive the good and his will leads him to follow it. Hence the rule of men's lives is the "sentence that reason giveth concerning the goodness of those things which they are to do." And the sign by which such rules of reason may be known is the general assent of mankind. "That which all men have at all times learned, nature herself must needs have taught."[3] The most fundamental rules of reason are therefore universally accepted as soon as they are understood, and rules of less generality may be deduced from them. So far Hooker hardly went beyond the commonplaces of all medieval political thought, since it was his purpose to argue from principles generally accepted. He restated the theory of law from which Grotius started a generation later, and nothing is lacking except the more rationalist form of argument which Grotius added to the inherited theory.

Manifestly the law of reason is binding upon all men absolutely, even if society and government did not exist. Men are led to form societies, according to Hooker, because they have a native sociability and are unable to satisfy their needs in a life of isolation. A society is impossible without government, and government in turn is impossible without human or positive law. To take away the mutual grievances which inevitably arise when men associate together there is no way but "by growing into composition and agreement amongst themselves, by ordaining some kind of government public, and by yielding themselves subject thereunto." Hooker did not enlarge upon the notion of a contract, though the idea was implied in what he said. The rules by which men elect to live together are agreed upon either expressly or tacitly, and the order thus established is law for the commonwealth, "the very soul of a politic body, the parts whereof are by law animated, held together, and set on work in such actions as the common good requireth."[4] The ground of political obligation is therefore the common consent by which men agree to be ordered by someone. As Hooker says, in words that recall Nicholas of Cusa, without this consent there is no reason why one man should take upon him to be lord or judge of another. He expressly held, however, that consent may be given through representatives and that, a commonwealth

[3] Book I, sect. 8.

[4] Book I, sect. 10.

once existing, its laws are binding upon its members for all time, for " corporations are immortal." Accordingly, though he says that, " Laws they are not which public approbation have not made so," and though he holds that to govern without consent is tyranny, he claimed no right of rebellion. There is no way in which a society can withdraw its consent from an authority it has set up.

The noteworthy fact about this system so far is its substantial agreement with Thomas: the human law of the community is derivative, in a series of descending steps, from the eternal law of God and has behind it all the authority of its origin. The positive law gives effect to what nature requires in general, and the community, as a natural unit, has an inherent capacity to bind its members under the organic law of its own being. When Hooker begins to deal with Puritan attacks on the English church, however, the resemblance to Thomas stops. In brief he argued that the ecclesiastical law of England is not contrary to reason or Christian faith and hence is binding, like the rest of English law, upon all Englishmen. The fostering of religion is a first charge on every body politic, and any society which has a true religion is at once a church and a state. The English church and the English nation are exactly identical in membership, for every Englishman is a Christian and every Christian in England is an Englishman. Ecclesiastical law, therefore, has the same kind of authority as any other law, and disobedience to it undermines all social order. For Hooker the offense of Puritanism is that it makes church and state two distinct societies, as he thinks Roman Catholicism does. In practice, as he pretty clearly implies, this is covertly a way of making the church supreme over the state. Consequently both papalism and presbyterianism are causes of confusion and disorder in the state and ultimately in the church.

This argument is a truly extraordinary combination of medievalism and nationalism. It assumes, first, that the English nation is a commonwealth or a community, a self-sufficing corporate entity whose laws bind its members not only in their individual capacity but as organs of the community. Hence the law prescribes what both princes and prelates may do, and their power belongs not to their personal will but to their offices. On the constitutional side Hooker's theory is still that of the cooperative commonwealth. With respect to religion it assumes, quite in the medieval fashion, that any complete society must be at once church and state, including an ecclesiastical as well as a secular constitution. It takes for granted that Christianity is true — presumably not truer for Englishmen than for others — and yet, it assumes also, what would certainly have amazed Thomas, that this universal truth needs no universal institution of its own but can be put into the keeping of a national government and a national church. Finally, and this forms its fatal weakness from a Puritan point of view, it assumes that the indubitable truth of Christianity leaves the form of church government — the choice between episcopalianism and presbyterianism — a matter of indifference so far as faith is concerned. Obviously no Calvinist could admit this, any more than a Catholic could admit that the spiritual authority of the pope had nothing to do with faith.

If Hooker's theory be taken as representing the state of political thought in England at the end of the sixteenth century, it is as notable for what it omits as for what it includes. His version of the theory of consent was not at all a defense of the right to resist, but equally he made nothing of passive obedience. The ethical belief that rebellion is wrong was stated strongly enough by other English writers in the sixteenth century, and by Puritans as much as by others, but the grounds for the belief were utilitarian and it implied no theory of royal absolutism.[5] In particular, though Hooker wrote as an Anglican, his theory is at the opposite pole from any doctrine of monarchical divine right. The popularity of divine right among Anglicans was strictly a phenomenon of the civil wars and after. It was a clerical theory, most violently held in the universities,[6] and after the execution of Charles I, a peg on which to hang sentimentality about the "royal martyr." It never affected any constitutional issue and probably played a negligible part in the realistic thinking even of royalists. Certainly it had no spokesman in parliament during the reigns of James I and Charles I. Later it received lip-service, but it probably never played a significant part in English political philosophy.

[5] See J. W. Allen, *op. cit.,* Part II, ch. 2.

[6] The strongest statements of it were (1) Constitutions and Canons Ecclesiastical: Concerning Royal Power, adopted by Convocation in 1640; *Synodalia,* ed. by E. Cardwell, Vol. I, p. 389; also in D. Wilkins, *Concilia,* Vol. IV, p. 545. (2) Judgment and Decree of the University of Oxford, adopted in 1683, in *Somers' Tracts* (1812), Vol. VIII, p. 420; also in Wilkins, *ibid.,* p. 610.

CATHOLIC AND PRESBYTERIAN OPPOSITION

On the other hand, Hooker's defense of the royal headship of the national church was intolerable to two classes of Englishmen, the Presbyterians and the Catholics. Both agreed that royal supremacy in the church was an invasion of spiritual independence. Behind the newer doctrinal disputes and differences about church government there still lay the ancient questions of clerical dictation and spiritual freedom. Anglicans stressed opposition to the first; Presbyterians and Catholics stood upon the second as an essential article of Christianity.

The fundamental position of Catholics is illustrated by a passage between Sir Thomas More and the King's Solicitor at More's trial. The Solicitor tried to trap More into a denial of the binding force of an act of parliament by asking him if even the election of a pope must not be settled for Englishmen if parliament chose to pass on it. More replied:

> To your first case, the Parliament may well meddle with the state of temporal princes; but to make answer to your second case, I will put you this case. Suppose the Parliament would make a law that God should not be God, would then you, Master Rich, say God were not God? [7]

More's thought was one with which any conscientious Catholic must have agreed. If king and parliament govern religious belief, then there is no universal organization of all Christians. To a Catholic some acknowledgment of papal authority seemed essential to preserve the unity and freedom of the church. He need not believe with the Jesuits that the pope had even an indirect power to depose the king, but he must believe that royal supremacy in the church was inconsistent with any except a mystical meaning for Christian unity.

The earnestness with which Calvinists detested the pope made them no readier to admit a secular head to the church, for they agreed with Catholics in regarding this as an invasion of the church's spiritual independence. The bent of Calvinism whereever it had a free hand was not toward political control of the church but toward clerical control of politics. The moral and doctrinal discipline over the whole community, which was an essen-

[7] Quoted by Allen, *op. cit.*, pp. 200 f.

tial part of the plan, required that the church should have the support of government, but it implied not less that the church should be free to determine for itself what constituted sound doctrine and godly living. The separation of church and state was therefore an essential element of Calvinism, but not in the modern sense that leaves the state a wholly secular institution. The separation that Calvinism contemplated was one that left the church autonomous but also made its decisions compulsory. Hence the Presbyterians, like the Anglicans, held to a substantial part of the medieval Christian tradition but were always in process of being forced to violate both the letter and the spirit of that tradition. The Anglicans brought over from the Middle Ages the conception of a church-state, which resulted in the astonishing innovation of a church conceived on national lines. The Presbyterians brought over the conception of spiritual independence in the church, which resulted in the no less astonishing innovation of a state that was no church at all. In the sixteenth century the separation of church and state was regarded as a novelty fostered by Puritans and Jesuits.

In one important respect, however, the English Presbyterians differed radically from the Calvinists in France and Scotland: they objected to royal supremacy in the church but they never justified rebellion. In this respect they remained closer to Calvin than to Knox or Beza or the author of the *Vindiciae contra tyrannos*. The reason for this was that in the sixteenth century there was never a time in England when they had any chance of gaining a presbyterian form of church government by means of rebellion. Even in the seventeenth century they remained on the whole half-hearted rebels; hence the gibe that the Presbyterians led Charles to the block but the Independents cut off his head. As a group the English Presbyterians hardly had any distinctive political theories. Their views were mainly aristocratic and conservative, certainly monarchical, and directed less toward political change than toward ecclesiastical reform. During the brief ascendency of the Presbyterian party in the early years of the civil wars their writers defended resistance, but on grounds that were open to any parliamentarian. What they mainly desired was presbyterianism in the English church, and this they hoped for, as a rule, by means of the king rather than against him. They remained therefore a party within the English church, until they were excluded by the Act of Uniformity in 1662, rather than a party with any definite political objective.

THE INDEPENDENTS

Of all the English Puritans the Independents or Congregationalists had the greatest importance for politics. Though Calvinist in their theology, they had taken a step in religious reformation which placed them in a different category from the Presbyterians. They had cut the Gordian knot by deciding that reformation in the church was possible, as Robert Browne had said, "without tarrying for any."[8] They believed that a body of Christians could form a congregation which would be a true church, could ordain its clergy, and set up a reformed mode of worship, without authorization either by civil magistrates or ecclesiastical powers. In principle, therefore, the church became a voluntary association of like-minded believers, and it renounced the support of the civil authorities either in reforming itself or extending its practices to persons of a different mind. The church became substantially identical with the congregations, the latter being united only loosely in a sort of federation for consultative purposes. Thus the Independents stepped outside any possible form of national church and were obliged to claim a greater or a less degree of religious toleration for themselves and to defend it for others. Church and state became quite definitely two societies, not only separate but in principle independent, with the power of coercion concentrated in the state but limited to purposes within the province of secular government.

> To compel religion, to plant churches by power, and to force a submission to ecclesiastical government by laws and penalties belongeth not to them [magistrates] . . . neither yet to the church.[9]

It is true that so-called Independents accepted this momentous principle and its implications only in varying degrees. In the first place, none desired and few countenanced a real breaking-up of religious unity. Like every plan of religious reform, Independency began under the presumption that honest inquiry would reveal a

[8] *A Treatise of Reformation without Tarying for Anie,* 1582.
[9] *Ibid.,* ed. by T. G. Crippen, p. 27.

demonstrable body of Christian beliefs and practices and would therefore lead to uniformity. In the second place, few Independents desired the abolition of all synodal influence over the congregations, though they stood for less control than the presbyterian system made possible. The Independents in Massachusetts hotly rejected the epithet " separatist " and practiced anything rather than toleration. Within Independent congregations, moreover, the principle of voluntary adhesion could be accepted in varying degrees; they were by no means uniformly democratic in allowing to every member a voice in settling either doctrinal or disciplinary questions. On the other hand, there was a general connection between the principle of free assent in religion and consent to government, and congregationalism, far more than presbyterianism, was in a position to countenance resistance, not only to the king but to parliament itself, in defense of fundamental liberties.

Finally, though Independents were necessarily committed to some degree of toleration, the degrees were innumerable, and only occasional Independents took the advanced ground that any religious belief should be permitted which did not adversely affect civil order. Like most religious minorities, they were more zealous in claiming toleration for themselves than in vindicating it for others. This was not so hypocritical as it seems, since with most of them toleration was incidental to the primary purpose of religious reform. They never meant to deny that government ought to repress " idolatry." The most advanced position was taken by Roger Williams in Rhode Island, where for the first time a government was set up on a general principle of toleration. In 1644 he defended this principle in his *Bloudy Tenent of Persecution,* which was regarded at the time as one of the most scandalous books in a scandalous literature. In the same year William Walwyn, a merchant of London who himself disclaimed membership in any of the left-wing sects, published his *Compassionate Samaritane,* defending effectively the toleration of Separatists and Anabaptists. Both Williams and Walwyn were exceptional even among writers known as Independents.[10]

[10] Williams's tract is republished in Publications of the Narragansett Club, first series, Vol. III (1867), and also by the Hanserd Knollys Society, 1848. Walwyn's tract is republished in *Tracts on Liberty in the Puritan Revolution, 1638–1647* (1934), ed. by William Haller, Vol. III, p. 59.

Though they had their origin in the sixteenth century, the Independents were not very numerous in England until the 1640's. Then they formed the backbone of resistance to the king, in so far as resistance depended upon religion. Independency came to its greatest power in Cromwell's New Model Army and in the political experiments which followed the second civil war and the execution of the king. By this time, however, the economic and political disadvantages suffered during the war by the less prosperous part of the middle class had produced in the Levellers a genuine political party. The Levellers were no doubt in the main Independents though most Independents were not Levellers. The political philosophy of the Levellers was in some measure a continuation of left-wing Independency, but it deserves and must receive separate treatment.

SECTARIES AND ERASTIANS

Still further toward the left wing of the Protestant Reformation lay the Baptist and Quaker sects, which had effectively disposed of the question of church government by reducing the organization of the church and its relation to secular power practically to a nullity. Since for them the essence of religion lay in an inward illumination or a spiritual experience, the government of the church was a matter of little moment, and they had abandoned even the notion of a national religious establishment. Between the various bodies that were known as Baptist or Quaker there need be no very substantial agreement, and most of the writers who vilified them spent little care in finding out what they believed. In any case there is no reason to suppose that the sectaries as such had any distinctive political opinions or to doubt that their members were for the most part simple, law-abiding folk. The detestation with which they were regarded was partly due to the overwrought nerves of heresy-hunters like Thomas Edwards,[11] but also to the fact that fantastic notions which really had a sporadic existence were imputed wholesale to any sect that was thought to be fanatical. Thus there were persons, commonly called Baptists, who believed that men of true religious illumination had no need of law and could not rightly be held to obedience by magistrates. This belief

[11] His *Gangraena* (1646) was a rather hysterical review of the enormities of the sects.

was usually associated with the idea that the end of the world was at hand and that in the new dispensation the saints would inherit the earth. It might lead to political quietism or to nihilism, and in the latter case it might end in attacks on both property and law. In so far as communism had any part in English political philosophy at this time, it was in the so-called Diggers, whose leader, Gerrard Winstanley, will be discussed later.

Such an enumeration of religious sects as has just been given should mention a strain of English opinion which was bred of opposition to all of them but more especially to the pretensions of presbyterianism. This is usually called (not very correctly) Erastianism and John Selden may be taken as representing it. Selden's opinions both of politics and religion grew from a kind of secularism not very common in the seventeenth century and from a shrewd worldly-wisdom that pricked the pretenses of both politicians and clergy. Constitutional arrangements he regarded as merely agreements for the sake of order and security. The king's power is just what the law gives him, and effectively the law is what the courts can enforce. Similarly the church's establishments and the privileges of the clergy are what civil authority makes them. Pretensions to divine right anywhere he regarded as juggling tricks to extract money and power from the laity, a judgment which he passed impartially on all denominations but more particularly on the Presbyterians. "Presbyters have the greatest power of any clergy in the world, and gull the laity most." The office of a priest is merely a profession like the practice of law. Selden's utilitarianism, secularism, and rationalism were far from typical but they appeared again in his friend Thomas Hobbes and in a sense they had the last word at the Revolution in the thought of Halifax.

CONSTITUTIONAL THEORIES: SMITH AND BACON

The urgency of ecclesiastical questions and the power of the king as temporal head of the church tended to throw the constitution out of its medieval balance but a variety of other causes also, connected with the growing independence of the upper middle class, tended to produce tensions between the king and the courts by which his power was limited. The civil wars occurred when these tensions reached the breaking point. The result, generally speaking, was that the older constitutional conception of a harmony of powers had to be abandoned for the more modern conception of delegation from a sovereign source of power. Prior to the civil wars there was no clear-cut theory that supremacy resided in any part of the constitution. The powers which belonged by immemorial custom to the king, to parliament, and to the other courts were thought to be inherent in them. Within the limits of its proper liberty each acted on its own initiative. If supremacy resided anywhere, it was in the realm itself and not in any of its organs. Despite the great powers enjoyed by the Tudor kings, there was no theory of royal supremacy as clear even as that of Bodin in France. The civil wars forced both royalists and parliamentarians into claims of supremacy for the king or for parliament which went far beyond what either party originally intended. Though both parties claimed the warrant of English history, both ended by breaking radically with the tradition of the sixteenth century, parliamentarians not less than royalists. The difference was that parliament made good its novel claims and the king failed.

Probably the state of English constitutional theory in the sixteenth century is best indicated by Sir Thomas Smith's *De republica Anglorum*.[12] Historians as competent as Frederic Maitland and Sir Frederick Pollock have regarded this book as stating a theory of parliamentary supremacy, but this is almost certainly a misinterpretation.[13] Smith in fact asserted at once that the king was the " authority " for everything that is done in English government and that parliament was " the most high and absolute power of the realm." He clearly believed that there were certain things that could be done by the king without parliament and some that must be done in parliament. In both cases it was the custom of the country which determined. The most striking feature of Smith's book was that it regarded the constitution as consisting mainly of the courts and represented parliament itself as the highest court in the kingdom. It is in this sense that his statement about the absolute power of parliament should probably be understood: no other court will reverse a decision by parliament. He

[12] Published in 1583 but first written in 1565. Ed. by L. Alston, Cambridge, 1906.

[13] Maitland, *Constitutional History* (1911), pp. 255, 298; Pollock, *Science of Politics* (1911), pp. 57 f. Cf. Alston's Introduction; also C. H. McIlwain, *High Court of Parliament* (1910), pp. 124 ff.

was quite aware that parliament differed from other courts in that it did not usually take cognizance of issues between private parties, but he still thought of it as in the main a judicial body. At all events he had no definite idea of it as a legislature, for he drew no line between making and interpreting law, and he never contemplated a conflict between parliament and the crown. Supremacy resides in the realm and its law, which assigns to the king and his various courts their proper powers, and the harmonious cooperation of all these powers was everywhere assumed. Consequently, to Smith's mind there was no incompatibility in the view that the king was the " head " of the whole system while parliament was the chief court.

This conception of the constitution and of parliament persisted long after there was active opposition to the pretensions of James I to something like absolute power. James's first controversy was not with parliament but with the courts of common law and concerned not legislation but the royal prerogative. In this controversy, in which the chief actors, besides James, were Francis Bacon and Sir Edward Coke, the question was not supremacy, either of the crown or of any other part of the government, but the proper balance between the king and his courts. Circumstances made Bacon the spokesman for a strong royal prerogative, in which he sincerely believed, though he certainly never believed in royal absolutism; they made Coke the chief agent in limiting prerogative, though the supremacy of parliament would have been equally repugnant to him. Opposed as they were, both men still stood on the conception of harmony or balance, regulated by the customary law of the land, which provided a place for the king and every other organ of government without the supremacy of any.

Bacon's whole conception of policy tended to emphasize royal power, but he thought always in terms of the Tudor monarchy, in which the king was the trusted leader of the nation and of parliament. When James ascended the throne Bacon tried anxiously to commend himself to the new monarch by advising a policy of vigorous leadership. The union with Scotland, the colonization of Ireland, and an aggressive policy on the Continent seemed to him well calculated to make England the dominant power in northwestern Europe and the leader of the Protestant interest. All his life he seems to have believed that, if James could be persuaded to take this line, his difficulties with his English subjects would vanish in a wave of patriotism. From his *Essays* it is evident that Bacon's political ideal was a strong and warlike people, not overburdened with taxes, with no great concentration of wealth, and with a nobility not too powerful — good Tudor ideals all — led by a king having great resources in crown-lands, a strong prerogative, and a vigorous policy of national expansion. In his mind this did not imply absolutism. James's determination to stand on his prerogative was flatly against Bacon's ideas of good policy, and his attempt to govern without parliament was contrary to Bacon's advice. From Bacon's point of view nothing could have been more injudicious than to force the alternative of king's right or parliament's right.

In the controversy between James and the judges of the courts of common law Bacon was obliged by his official position to take an *ex parte* attitude, but his belief in strong royal prerogative was quite sincere. The king regarded himself as the fountainhead of justice and the judges as his ministers, and hence he claimed the right to instruct them in cases touching his prerogative, to set aside decisions, or to draw cases out of the courts and into special commissions. In his famous essay "Of Judicature" Bacon emphasized, as James did, the propriety of the courts' keeping clear of questions of state and royal prerogative; judges should be lions but "lions under the throne." The essay seems to be full of oblique references to Coke, whom Bacon doubtless regarded as the type of a bad judge.

SIR EDWARD COKE

The head and front of the opposition to James's effort to stretch the royal prerogative was the chief justice, Sir Edward Coke. The root of all Coke's political ideas lay in his reverence for the common law, which he conceived as at once the fundamental law of the realm and the embodiment of reason, though of reason as grasped only by the lawyers' guild. The common law was a "mystery" and Coke esteemed himself as its chief technician. He reported one of his conferences with James as follows:

> Then the king said, that he thought the law was founded upon reason, and that he and others had reason, as well as the judges: to which it was answered by me, that true it was, that God had endowed his Majesty

with excellent science, and great endowments of nature; but his Majesty was not learned in the laws of his realm of England, and causes which concern the life, or inheritance, or goods, or fortunes of his subjects are not to be decided by natural reason but by the artificial reason and judgment of law, which law is an act which requires long study and experience, before that a man can attain to the cognizance of it . . . with which the King was greatly offended, and said, that then he should be under the law, which was treason to affirm, as he said: to which I said, that Bracton saith, *Quod rex non debet esse sub homine, sed sub Deo et lege.*[14]

In Coke's view it was the common law which assigned to the king his powers, to each of the courts of the realm its proper jurisdiction, and indeed to every Englishman the rights and privileges of his station. The common law, therefore, included all that would now be counted as the constitution, both the fundamental structure of government and the fundamental rights of subjects. Certainly he contemplated these fundamentals as substantially unchangeable.

It was this conception of the law which enabled Coke to render his most famous decision in limitation of the prerogative, that "the king cannot create any offense by his prohibition or proclamation, which was not an offense before."[15] It was the ground also of the writs of prohibition by which the courts of common law sought to restrain other courts and of Coke's sturdy opposition to James's attempts to withdraw cases from the courts and to decide them either by himself or by special commissions. Finally, it provided the reasons for Coke's belief that parliament itself is unable to change the underlying principles of justice embodied in the common law. He was not very definite about the nature of these limitations but he was explicit in asserting their existence. Thus in Bonham's case he said,

It appears in our books, that in many cases, the common law will controul acts of Parliament, and sometimes adjudge them to be utterly void: for when an act of Parliament is against common right and reason, or repugnant, or impossible to be performed, the common law will controul it, and adjudge such act to be void.[16]

This opinion, which though extreme was certainly not peculiar to Coke, shows how little hold the idea of parliamentary sovereignty

[14] Coke's *Reports,* Pt. XII, 65.
[15] *Reports,* Pt. XII, 75.
[16] *Reports,* Pt. VIII, 118a.

had on English lawyers in the earlier seventeenth century and also how deeply the American plan of judicial review was rooted in the English legal tradition.

Coke was peculiarly a practitioner of the common law, but aside from this fact, his fundamental beliefs were extraordinarily like those of Sir Thomas Smith and Hooker. Like Smith, he thought of English government as mainly comprised in the courts, of which parliament is the chief; neither for Coke nor for Smith was parliament primarily a legislative body nor was the making of law primarily the purpose for which government existed. None of the three would have felt that there was any intelligible sense in which law could be said to be made, though all would have agreed that specific provisions of law were changed from time to time. For Coke law was an indigenous growth within the realm; for a philosopher like Hooker it was a natural part of the cosmos, but in practice the difference was not great. The law assigned to every man, public or private, his rights and duties, his liberties and his obligations; it fixed the standards of justice by which he was constrained to act or forbear, and no less so if he were the king than if he were a subject. The king's rights were not the same as the subject's, but both had their rights within the law. Consequently, though the law supported innumerable powers, it knew nothing of a sovereign power, for king and parliament and the several courts of common law had each its powers indefeasibly as the law provided. There was none of which all the others were delegates. Consequently Coke's defiance of James grew out of the fact that he was a thoroughgoing conservative, even a reactionary. If circumstances had made him an opponent of parliament, he could have played this rôle with equal consistency. For he represented a conception of law, and of the relation of law to government, more ancient than the absolutist philosophy of the king or the absolutist philosophy to which the parliamentarians were driven.

It was only slowly and under the stress of circumstances that anyone abandoned the familiar idea of harmony and adopted the novel idea of supremacy. The earlier opposition to Charles I's attempts at personal government grew from a dislike of royal absolutism — exhibited in the imposition of taxes without parliamentary approval and in the imprisonment of subjects without legal process — but it implied no counter theory of parliamentary sovereignty. Even in the early months of 1641 Parliament was mainly content to limit the use of the prerogative, to abolish extraordinary courts, and to insure its participation in levying taxes — in short, to lop off what were felt to be excrescences with which Tudor times had marred the ancient perfection of the constitution. As a practical measure Parliament had to claim the right not to be dissolved without its own consent, and by the end of 1641 it had been forced to claim the power to appoint and dismiss ministers, and to control all the military, civil, and religious affairs of the kingdom. These claims were revolutionary, for they were more at variance with constitutional custom as known to Smith or Coke than the king's broad interpretation of his prerogative. In England as in France the stress of civil war produced a government centralized in theory as it had tended to be in fact, but in England the legal headship of the nation passed to a representative assembly.

SELECTED BIBLIOGRAPHY

A History of Political Thought in the Sixteenth Century. By J. W. Allen. London, 1928. Part II.

English Political Thought, 1603–1660. By J. W. Allen. Vol. I, 1603–1644. London, 1938.

The Early Tudor Theory of Kingship. By Franklin L. Baumer. New Haven, Conn., 1940.

More's Utopia and his Social Teaching. By William E. Campbell. London, 1930.

Thomas More. By R. W. Chambers. New York, 1935.

The High Court of Parliament and its Supremacy. By C. H. McIlwain. New Haven, Conn., 1910.

The Political Works of James I. Ed. by C. H. McIlwain. Cambridge, Mass., 1918. Introduction and Appendices.

The Medieval Contribution to Political Thought: Thomas Aquinas, Marsilius of Padua, Richard Hooker. By Alexander Passerin d'Entrèves. Oxford, 1939. Chs. 5, 6.

Archbishop Laud, 1573–1645. By H. R. Trevor-Roper. London, 1940.

The Social Teaching of the Christian Churches. By Ernst Troeltsch. Eng. trans. by Olive Wyon. 2 vols. London, 1931. Ch. 3.

The Reconstruction of the English Church. By Roland G. Usher. 2 vols. New York, 1910.

CHAPTER XXIII

THOMAS HOBBES

It was the logic of local events which drove the leaders of parliament to claim and exercise a sovereign power which was alike contrary to their own preconceived ideas and to the traditions of the English constitution. Neither the desire for logical consistency nor a philosophical perception of the evolution of European politics played any considerable part either in what parliament did or in what parliamentarians thought. Yet general forces were at work, both intellectual and practical, which extended far beyond the local scene and the immediate occasion. The evolution toward centralized government dominated by a single sovereign power depended on social and economic causes not confined to England, as did also the fact that this sovereign power was to express itself mainly in the making and enforcing of law. The political conceptions of Sir Thomas Smith, Hooker, and Coke were on the way to becoming anachronisms even as they were set down. Civil war, in England and in France, forced political thought to come measurably abreast of the facts.

At the same time vast changes in the intellectual outlook of Europe, in philosophy and in science, demanded equally drastic changes in political theory. More than a century before the beginning of the English civil wars, Machiavelli had stated with brutal clearness the fact that European politics rested in the main on force and selfishness, either national or individual, but he had supplied little interpretation of the fact. Some fifty years after Machiavelli Bodin, writing in the midst of the French wars of religion, had stressed the need that a sovereign power to legislate should be taken as the outstanding attribute of a state, but he had neither detached this principle from antiquated preconceptions about the historical constitution nor clearly stated its implications. On the threshold of the civil wars, Grotius had modernized the theory of natural law by bringing it into relation with a conception of science bred of the rising reverence for mathematics, but there was still the question whether Grotius had rightly conceived the meaning of the new science. All these strains of European thought met and crossed in the political philosophy of Thomas Hobbes, developed in a series of works written between 1640 and 1651.[1]

Hobbes's political writings were occasioned by the civil wars and were intended by him to exert influence upon the side of the king. They were designed to support absolute government and in Hobbes's intention this meant absolute monarchy; all his personal interests attached him to the royalist party and he sincerely believed that monarchy was the most stable and orderly kind of government. Yet any immediate influence that Hobbes's books may have exerted in this direction (and it must have been slight) represents a very small fraction of their long-term value. His principles were at least as contrary to the pretensions of the Stuarts whom he meant to support as to those of the revolutionists whom he meant to refute, and more contrary to both than either royalist or parliamentarian was to the other. The friends of the king might well feel that Hobbes's friendship was as dangerous as Cromwell's enmity. What Clarendon in his refutation of the *Leviathan* called "the lewd principles of his institution" were inconsistent both with the Stuart belief in legitimacy and with prevailing theories of popular representation. Clarendon thought that the book had been written to flatter Cromwell. This was not true, though Hobbes had been at pains to point out that his views were consistent with any *de facto* government. His political philosophy had too wide a sweep to make good propaganda, but its drastic logic affected the whole later history of moral and political thought. Its positive influence was not fully developed until the nineteenth century, when his ideas were incorporated in the philosophical radicalism of the Utilitarians and in John Austin's theory of sovereignty. Hobbes's thought thus served the ends of middle-class liberalism, a cause with which the philosopher would have had little sympathy.

[1] Two essays published, perhaps without Hobbes's consent, in 1650 but written in 1640 bore the titles *Human Nature* and *De corpore politico;* the whole work was published from Hobbes's manuscript by F. Tönnies under the title, *Elements of Law Natural and Politic,* 1889; 2nd ed., 1928. *De cive* was published in Latin in 1642; 2nd ed., 1647; English, 1651. *Leviathan,* 1651.

SCIENTIFIC MATERIALISM

The defense of monarchical absolutism formed therefore a very superficial part of his effective political philosophy, and though the civil wars occasioned his thinking and writing, they account only in a small degree for the importance of what he had to say. Hobbes was in fact the first of the great modern philosophers who attempted to bring political theory into intimate relation with a thoroughly modern system of thought, and he strove to make this system broad enough to account, on scientific principles, for all the facts of nature, including human behavior both in its individual and social aspects. Such a project obviously put his thought quite beyond the range of occasional or controversial literature. Nor is Hobbes to be judged exclusively by the correctness of his conclusions. His ideas of what constituted a sound scientific method were those of his time and are long out of date. Yet the fact remains that he had something which can only be described as a science of politics, which was an integral part of his whole conception of the natural world and was carried through with quite extraordinary clearness. For this reason he benefited not least those thinkers who tried to refute him. His philosophy illustrates the saying of Bacon that "Truth emerges more easily from error than from confusion." Because of this clarity and not less because of the pungency of his style Hobbes was probably the greatest writer on political philosophy that the English-speaking peoples have produced.

Political theory was only one part of what he designed to be an all-inclusive system of philosophy formed upon scientific principles. This system would now be described as materialism. Despite the fact that he came to the study of mathematics and physics late in life and never gained an adequate mastery of them, he at least perceived the end toward which the new natural science tended. As Galileo said, it "made a new science out of an old subject," namely, motion. It suggested the revolutionary idea that the physical world is a purely mechanical system in which all that happens may be explained with geometrical precision by the displacement of bodies relative to one another. The great triumph of science upon this principle — Newton's theory of planetary motion — was as yet in the future, but Hobbes grasped the principle and made it the center of his system. At bottom, he held, every event is a motion and all sorts of natural processes must be explained by analysing complex appearances into the underlying motions of which they consist. Or, as Hobbes preferred to think of it, it begins with the simplest motions of bodies — mere changes of place — and goes on to more complex cases, which seem on their face not to be motions but which can be built up from this simple beginning. Thus he conceived the project of a system of philosophy in three parts, the first dealing with body and including what would now be called geometry and mechanics (or physics), the second including the physiology and psychology of individual human beings, and the third concluding with the most complex of all bodies, the "artificial" body called society or the state. In this bold scheme there was in theory no place for any new force or principle beyond the laws of motion found at the beginning; there were merely complex cases of mechanical causation. All were derivative from geometry and mechanics.

Hobbes's philosophy, then, was a plan for assimilating psychology and politics to the exact physical sciences. All knowledge throughout is of a piece and mechanics gives the pattern. It is important to note the method by which Hobbes believed that this system could be proved, because the same method is used in the parts of the system that deal with psychology and politics. The evidence was in no sense empirical nor did he think of his conclusions as the result of systematic observation. No doubt he regarded them as true and accordingly he often illustrated them by reference to fact, but such references were illustrations rather than inductions. All science in the seventeenth century was under the spell of geometry, and Hobbes's was no exception. Good method meant for him the carrying over into other subjects of the mode of thought which, it seemed, had been superlatively successful in geometry; in this belief he differed little from Grotius or Descartes. Now the secret of geometry is that it takes the simplest things first, and when it goes forward to more complicated problems, it uses only what it has previously proved. In this way it builds solidly because it takes nothing for granted and every step is guaranteed by what precedes, all the way back to the self-evident truths from which the construction begins. It was thus that Hobbes conceived his system. Its structure is pyramidal.

Motion is the completely pervasive fact in nature. Human behavior, including sensation, feeling, and thought, is a mode of motion. And social behavior, upon which the art of government rests, is merely that special case of human behavior which arises when men act with reference to one another. The science of politics is therefore built upon psychology, and the mode of procedure is deductive. Hobbes proposed to show not what government in fact is but what it must demonstrably be in order to control successfully beings whose motivation is that of the human machine.

It is hardly necessary to say that Hobbes did not in fact live up to this ideal of his system, for the good reason that it was impossible. It depended upon a confusion — universal in philosophy before Leibniz — of logical or mathematical knowledge with empirical or factual knowledge and therefore failed to see that a straight-line progress from geometry to physics is out of the question. Whether psychology can be reduced to physics is still another question, but certainly Hobbes did not succeed in actually deducing sensations, emotions, and human conduct from the laws of motion. What he did was to make a fresh start when he came to psychology. Substantially he postulated a principle or axiom for human behavior in general and from this he derived the specific cases by showing the operation of the principle under particular circumstances. By this method he was able to advance from psychology to politics. Once he made a beginning with his psychology, he was true to his plan. He exhibited human nature as governed by a single fundamental law and in his politics he exhibited the working of this law in the specific case of social groups. The method was fundamentally deductive.

MATERIALISM AND NATURAL LAW

Though this mode of procedure was in agreement with that by which Grotius had undertaken to modernize jurisprudence, Hobbes's results were quite at odds with those of Grotius. Grotius had freed natural law from its ancient alliance with theology, holding that it might even by hypothesis dispense with God, but he had never contemplated a real mechanization of nature. The law of nature, in Grotius and in nearly all its applications throughout the seventeenth and eighteenth centuries, remained a teleological and not a mechanical principle. Spinoza, following Hobbes, made the only determined effort to bring both ethics and religion into accord with mathematical natural science, but his success was far from complete and in any event his influence was negligible until the beginning of the nineteenth century. The meaning of natural law remained twofold. In physics and astronomy it meant a principle of mechanics like Newton's laws of motion, while in ethics and jurisprudence it meant a rule of right intuitively perceived, a transcendent value or norm by which the worth of positive law or actual moral practice could be judged. But a philosophy like Hobbes's made right or justice in any such cosmic sense absolutely unintelligible. Both nature and human nature were for him nothing but systems of causes and effects.

There remained a somewhat superficial resemblance between Hobbes's procedure and that of the theory of natural law: both professed to derive their basic principles from human nature and to deduce from this certain rules which law and government must follow. But the meaning of the dependence on human nature was quite different in the two cases. In the typical theories of natural law the dependence was, broadly speaking, Aristotelian: that is to say, natural law states the basic moral conditions of a humane and civilized life. Hence these are ends to be approximated, which exert an ethically regulatory control over positive law and human conduct. For Hobbes, on the other hand, that which controls human life is not an end but a cause, the psychological mechanism of the human animal. The societies which arise from the living-together of such animals are resultants of their mutual actions and reactions upon each other. And the conditions of a stable union between them are not justice and fair dealing, or any moral ideals, but merely the causes that will evoke a generally cooperative kind of conduct. Logically this was all that Hobbes was entitled to mean by laws of nature. It cannot be said that he always took this position. Probably it is not humanly possible to do so. But his system was at any rate the first whole-hearted attempt to treat political philosophy as part of a mechanistic body of scientific knowledge.

It would undoubtedly have been easier for Hobbes if he could have abandoned the law of nature altogether, as his more empirical successors, Hume and Bentham, did. He might then have started from human nature simply as a fact, claiming the warrant of observation for whatever qualities, or even ideal purposes, he might have seen fit to attribute to it. But this course would have been contrary to all that was supposed in the seventeenth century to be good scientific method. A deductive system must have its postulates, and there is no evidence for a postulate unless it be self-evidence. Consequently Hobbes not only retained the laws of nature but gave them an important place in his political theory. All his efforts were bent toward interpreting them in accordance with the principles of his own psychology while retaining, it must be admitted, the occasional advantage of talking as if he meant by them something rather like what others meant. In fact they were quite different. The laws of nature really meant for Hobbes a set of rules according to which an ideally reasonable being would pursue his own advantage, if he were perfectly conscious of all the circumstances in which he was acting and was quite unswayed by momentary impulse and prejudice. Since he assumes that in the large men really do act in this way, the laws of nature state hypothetical conditions upon which the fundamental traits of human beings allow a stable government to be founded. They do not state values but they determine causally and rationally what can be given value in legal and moral systems.

THE INSTINCT OF SELF-PRESERVATION

Hobbes's first problem, therefore, was to state the law of human behavior and to formulate the conditions upon which a stable society is possible. In accordance with his materialistic principles reality consists always in the motion of bodies, which is transmitted through the sense-organs to the central nervous system, where it "appears" as sensation. He further assumed, however, that such transmitted motion always aids or retards the "vital motion," the organ for which, as he supposed, was the heart rather than the brain. According as the vital motion is heightened or repressed, two primitive types of feeling appear, desire and aversion, the first being an "endeavor" toward that which is favorable to the vital processes and the second being a retraction from that which has the opposite effect. From these primitive reactions of advance or retreat Hobbes proceeded to derive all the more complex or remote emotions or motives. These depend upon the relation in which the stimulating object stands to the reaction which it produces. For obvious reasons the emotions are always paired, according as they are forms of desire or aversion. Thus the object which is attractive is in general loved, while that which repels is hated; to attain the one gives joy and to suffer the other gives grief; the prospect of the one gives hope and of the other despair. Other appropriate combinations give fear or courage, anger or benevolence, and so on. By this simple psychological device Hobbes believed that he could derive all the emotions which men experience. What are called "mental" pleasures and pains are more involved but in principle they are not different. The will calls for no special treatment, since every emotion is a form of reaction to stimulation, or an active response to external objects and events; the will is simply the "last appetite." The novel element in Hobbes's psychology was not the rather cynical assumption of human selfishness which it implied, for in this respect he did not differ from Machiavelli. It was rather the psychological theory by which he tried to make egoism a scientifically grounded account of behavior.

The details of this theory of motivation need not be stressed but it is important to note the principles of the explanation. First, the mode of derivation was deductive rather than empirical. Hobbes was not cataloging feelings and motives which he found by observing human nature, but showing rather what reactions can occur in various complex situations on the assumption that all human motive arises from the primitive attraction or retraction which every stimulus is supposed to produce. Second, his theory differed in important respects from the pleasure-pain theory of motivation developed later by the English psychologists of the eighteenth century. It is true that all the emotions derived from desire are in general pleasant while those derived from aversion are unpleasant, but it was not Hobbes's theory that pleasure *per se* is desired or pain avoided. The datum is not pleasure or pain but stimulus and response. The organism always responds in some fashion, and for this reason no special explanation of active behavior is required. It follows, third, that Hobbes's theory of value was widely different from that of the later utilitarians, who supposed that value must be measured in units of pleasure. For him the fundamental psychological fact in value is that every stimulation affects vitality either favorably or adversely. If the effect is favorable the organism responds appropriately to secure and continue the favorable influence; if the effect is adverse the organism withdraws or takes other appropriate action to avoid the injurious effect. The rule behind all behavior is that the living body is set instinctively to preserve or to heighten its vitality. In a word, the physiological principle behind all behavior is self-preservation, and self-preservation means just the continuance of individual biological existence. Good is what conduces to this end and evil what has the opposite effect.

It was of course obvious to Hobbes that self-preservation is no such simple, momentary affair as has so far been assumed. Life affords no breathing space or moment of repose in which the end can be once for all achieved, but is a restless pursuit of the means of continued existence. Moreover, the means of security being precarious, no moderation of desire can place a limit to the struggle for existence. The desire for security, the really fundamental need of human nature, is for all practical purposes inseparable from the desire for power, the present means of obtaining apparent future goods, because every degree of security requires to be still further secured.

> I put for a general inclination of all mankind, a perpetual and restless desire of power after power, that ceaseth only in death. And the cause of this, is not always that a man hopes for a more intensive delight, than he has already attained to; or that he cannot be content with a more moderate power: but because he cannot assure the power and means to live well, which he hath present, without the acquisition of more.[2]

The apparently modest need for security is therefore equivalent to an endless need for power of every sort, whether riches, or position, or reputation, or honor — all that may forfend the inevitable destruction which must in the end overtake all men. The means may be tangible — what Hobbes calls " gain " — or intangible — what he calls " glory " — but the value is the same.

From this account of human motives Hobbes's description of the state of man outside society follows as a matter of course. Each human being is actuated only by considerations that touch his own security or power, and other human beings are of consequence to him only as they affect this. Since individuals are roughly equal in strength and cunning, none can be secure, and

[2] *Leviathan,* ch. 11.

their condition, so long as there is no civil power to regulate their behavior, is a "war of every man against every man." Such a condition is inconsistent with any kind of civilization: there is no industry, navigation, cultivation of the soil, building, art, or letters, and the life of man is "solitary, poor, nasty, brutish, and short." Equally there is neither right nor wrong, justice nor injustice, since the rule of life is "only that to be every man's that he can get; and for so long, as he can keep it." Apparently Hobbes believed that life among savages really approximated this condition, but the historical accuracy of the description was of no importance to him. His purpose was not history but analysis.

RATIONAL SELF-PRESERVATION

So far, however, Hobbes has presented only half of his analysis. The momentary heightening of vitality which is the spring of human desire and the lengthening of life on the whole are quite different matters. There are two principles in human nature, he says, desire and reason. The first hurries men on to take for themselves what other men want and so embroils them with each other, while reason teaches them to "fly a contranatural dissolution." What reason adds is not a new motive but a regulative power, or foresight, by which the pursuit of security becomes more effective without ceasing to follow the general rule of self-preservation. There is a hasty acquisitiveness which begets antagonism and a more calculating selfishness which brings a man into society. Hobbes's psychology was not entirely clear about the relation between reason and instinct, or the way in which the former influences the latter. This is shown by his habitual twofold use of the word natural. Sometimes the natural is that which a man spontaneously does to gain security and means sheer acquisitiveness and aggression; sometimes it is that which perfect reason would prompt him to do to make himself as secure as the circumstances permit.

It is because these two meanings are so far apart that Hobbes is able to contrast as he does the pre-social and the social states. Before the institution of society the natural man is represented as almost non-rational; in instituting and conducting the state he shows preternatural powers of calculation. In order to be social he must be the perfect egoist, and egoists of this sort are rare. The result is a paradox. If men were as savage and anti-social as they are at first represented, they would never be able to set up a government. If they were reasonable enough to set up a government, they would never have been without it. The paradox is due to the fact that what figures as the origin of society is a combining of the two parts of an analytic psychology. By a psychological convention Hobbes treats motivation as if it were wholly nonrational, while at the same time he depends upon reason for that regulation of motives which alone makes society possible. The distinction is of course fictitious. Human nature is neither so reasonable nor so unreasonable as he assumed it to be.

The raw material of human nature from which a society must be constructed consists, then, of two contrasted elements: primitive desire and aversion, from which arise all impulses and emotions, and reason, by which action can be diverted intelligently toward the end of self-preservation. Upon this regulative power of reason depends the transition from the savage and solitary to the civilized and social condition. The transition is made by the laws of nature, the "conditions of society or of human peace." These laws state what an ideally reasonable being would do if he considered impartially his relations with other men in all their bearings upon his own security.

> Therefore the law of nature . . . is the dictate of right reason, conversant about those things which are either to be done or omitted for the constant preservation of life and members, as much as in us lies.[3]
>
> A law of nature is a precept, or general rule, found out by reason, by which a man is forbidden to do, that, which is destructive of his life, or taketh away the means of preserving the same; and to omit, that, by which he thinketh it may be best preserved.[4]

The spring to action, therefore, is still self-preservation but enlightened by foresight of all the consequences, and this foresight provides the condition by which men can unite and cooperate. The laws of nature are the postulates by which Hobbes's rational construction of society is to take place. They are at once the principles of perfect prudence and of social morality, and therefore they make possible the step from the psychological motives of indi-

[3] *De cive*, ch. 2, 1; *English Works* (ed. by Molesworth), Vol. II, p. 16.

[4] *Leviathan*, ch. 14.

vidual action to the precepts and values of civilized law and morality.

The listings of the laws of nature in Hobbes's three accounts of them show that he never made any serious effort to reduce his principles to the minimum required for his purpose. In spite of his undoubted logical power, he never mastered the niceties of exact analysis. The three lists (one in each of the works mentioned above) are similar in substance but not identical in details, and all of them contain rules of no great importance, which might have been treated merely as special cases of more general rules. There is no need to examine them exhaustively or to compare the different lists in detail.

In substance all Hobbes's laws amount to this: peace and cooperation have a greater utility for self-preservation than violence and general competition, and peace requires mutual confidence. By the law of a man's nature he must endeavor to gain his own security. If he must make this endeavor by his unaided efforts, he may be said to have a "right" to take or do whatever he supposes to be conducive to the end. This, as Hobbes recognizes, is a wholly figurative use of the word right; what it really means is an entire absence of right in any legal or moral sense. But an intelligent consideration of means and ends shows, "That every man ought to endeavor peace, as far as he has hope of attaining it." The "ought" means merely that any other course is, in the long run and when practiced by all men, destructive of the security desired. Hence it follows that a man should be "willing, when others are so too, as far forth, as for peace, and defense of himself he shall think it necessary, to lay down this right to all things; and be contented with so much liberty against other men, as he would allow other men against himself." For practical purposes the whole weight of this law is borne by the clause, "when others are so too," since it would be ruinous to grant liberty to others if they would not grant the same to you. Thus the prime condition of society is mutual trust and the keeping of covenants, for without it there can be no certainty of performance, but there must be a reasonable presumption that other persons will meet you on the same ground.

This argument has the perversity already noted in the psychology which underlies it. Hobbes first isolates, rather arbitrarily, those competitive and ruthless qualities of human nature which are inconsistent with mutual confidence. He then shows — what is of course obvious — that society is impossible on these terms. The setting up of the laws of nature is a way of redressing the balance. The two factors in combination give as a resultant a human nature capable of forming a society. Behind the psychological construction, however, lies an assumption about the nature of a society of the greatest importance. Since all human behavior is motivated by individual self-interest, society must be regarded merely as a means to this end. Hobbes was at once the complete utilitarian and the complete individualist. The power of the state and the authority of the law are justified only because they contribute to the security of individual human beings, and there is no rational ground of obedience and respect for authority except the anticipation that these will yield a larger individual advantage than their opposites. Social well-being as such disappears entirely and is replaced by a sum of separate self-interests. Society is merely an " artificial " body, a collective term for the fact that human beings find it individually advantageous to exchange goods and services.

It is this clear-cut individualism which makes Hobbes's philosophy the most revolutionary theory of the age. Beside this his defense of monarchy was superficial. Well might Clarendon wish that Hobbes had never been born to defend his royal pupil with this sort of argument. For it is a perfect solvent of all the loyalty and reverence and sentiment upon which the monarchy had rested. With Hobbes the power of tradition is for the first time fully broken by a clear-headed and cold-hearted rationalism. The state is a leviathan, but no man loves or reveres a leviathan. It is reduced to a utility, good for what it does, but merely the servant of private security. In this argument Hobbes summed up a view of human nature which resulted from two centuries of decadence in customary economic and social institutions. Moreover, he caught the spirit which was to animate social thinking for at least two centuries more, the spirit of *laissez faire*.

SOVEREIGNTY AND THE FICTITIOUS CORPORATION

Since society depends on mutual trust, the next step is evidently to explain how this is reasonably possible, and this brings Hobbes to his theory of sovereignty. Because of the unsocial inclination of men, it is hopeless to expect them to agree spontaneously to respect each other's rights, and unless all do so, it is unreasonable for any to forego self-help. The performance of covenants may be reasonably expected only if there is an effective government which will punish non-performance.

> Covenants, without the sword, are but words, and of no strength to secure a man at all.[5]
>
> The bonds of words are too weak to bridle men's ambition, avarice, anger, and other passions, without the fear of some coercive power.[6]

Security depends upon the existence of a government having the power to keep the peace and to apply the sanctions needed to curb man's innately unsocial inclinations. The effective motive by which men are socialized is the fear of punishment, and the authority of law extends only so far as its enforcement is able to reach. Just how this motive stands in relation to the reasonableness of performing covenants is not quite clear. Apparently Hobbes meant that reason provides a sufficient ground for mutual accord but is too weak to offset the avarice of men in the mass. In substance his theory amounted to identifying government with force; at least, the force must always be present in the background whether it has to be applied or not.

To justify force Hobbes retained the ancient device of a contract, though he carefully excluded the implication of a contract binding upon the ruler. He described it as a covenant between individuals by which all resign self-help and subject themselves to a sovereign. He stated it as follows:

> I authorize and give up my right of governing myself, to this man, or to this assembly of men, on this condition, that thou give up thy right to him, and authorize all his actions in like manner. . . . This is the generation of that great Leviathan, or rather (to speak more reverently) of that Mortal God, to which we owe under the Immortal God, our peace and defence.[7]

Since the "right" resigned is merely the use of natural strength and "covenants without the sword are but words," this is a contract only in a manner of speaking. Properly it is a logical fiction to offset the anti-social fiction of his psychology. Undoubtedly it

[5] *Leviathan,* ch. 17. [6] *Ibid.,* ch. 14. [7] *Ibid.,* ch. 17.

helped him to import the notion of moral obligation into social relations, and this added a good deal of plausibility to his argument. Strictly speaking he is saying merely that in order to cooperate men must do what they dislike to do, on pain of consequences which they dislike still more. In no other sense is there logically any obligation whatever in Hobbes's system.

Hobbes's thought on this point can be stated, perhaps more accurately, by using the legal conception of a corporation instead of contract, as he did in *De cive*.[8] A mere multitude, he argues, cannot have rights and cannot act; only individual men can do this, a conclusion which follows from the proposition that any collective body is merely artificial. Consequently, to say that a body of men acts collectively really means that some individual acts in the name of the whole group as its accredited agent or representative. Unless there is such an agent the body has no collective existence whatever. Hence Hobbes argues with perfect logic, if his premises be admitted, that it is not consent but " union " which makes a corporation, and union means the submission of the wills of all to the will of one. A corporation is not really a collective body at all but one person, its head or director, whose will is to be received for the will of all its members. On this analogy it follows, of course, that society is a mere fiction. Tangibly it can mean only the sovereign, for unless there be a sovereign there is no society. This theory is applied consistently by Hobbes to all corporations. Any other theory, he holds, would make them " lesser commonwealths," " like worms in the entrails of a natural man." The state is unique only in having no superior, while other corporations exist by its permission.

DEDUCTIONS FROM THE FICTITIOUS CORPORATION

From this view of the matter follow some of Hobbes's most characteristic conclusions. Any distinction between society and the state is a mere confusion, and the same is true of a distinction between the state and its government. Except there be a tangible government — individuals with the power to enforce their will — there is neither state nor society but a literally " headless " multitude. Few writers have held this opinion as consistently as Hobbes. It follows also that any distinction between law and

[8] Chs. 5, 6.

morals is a confusion. For society has only one voice with which it can speak and one will which it can enforce, that of the sovereign who makes it a society. Very properly does Hobbes call his sovereign a " mortal God " and unite in his hands both the sword and the crozier.

This theory of corporate bodies lies also at the root of Hobbes's absolutism. For him there is no choice except between absolute power and complete anarchy, between an omnipotent sovereign and no society whatever. For a social body has no existence except through its constituted authorities, and its members no rights except by delegation. All social authority must accordingly be concentrated in the sovereign. Law and morals are merely his will, and his authority is unlimited, or is limited only by his power, for the good reason that there is no other authority except by his permission. Evidently, also, sovereignty is indivisible and inalienable, for either his authority is recognized and a state exists or it is not recognized and anarchy exists. All the necessary powers of government are inherent in the sovereign, such as legislation, the administration of justice, the exercise of force, and the organization of inferior magistracies. Hobbes relieved sovereignty completely from the disabilities which Bodin had inconsistently left standing. But his disjunctions have nothing to do with the nuances of actual political power. His theory was pure logical analysis.

There was another side to his theory of sovereign power which Hobbes emphasized less but to which he was by no means blind. For controversial purposes he stressed the fact that resistance to authority can never be justified, since justification would require the approval of authority itself. It followed equally, however, that resistance will in fact occur wherever government fails to produce that security which is the only reason for subjects' submission. The only argument for government is that it does in fact govern. Hence if resistance is successful and the sovereign loses his power, he *ipso facto* ceases to be sovereign and his subjects cease to be subjects. They are then thrown back upon their individual resources for self-protection and may rightly give their obedience to a new sovereign who can protect them. There was no room in Hobbes's theory for any claim of legitimacy without power, and it was this which gave offense to royalists. This consequence of his theory was most clearly stated in *Leviathan,* the only one of his books on politics written after the execution of Charles and when, as Clarendon says, Hobbes had "a mind to go home." But it was at all times a perfectly evident implication of his principles and he had referred to it in *De cive*. On utilitarian grounds government — any government — is better than anarchy. Monarchical government he thought more likely to be effective than any other kind, but the theory is equally good for any government that can preserve peace and order. Later thinkers had no difficulty, therefore, in adapting it to a republican or parliamentary form of government.

Since government consists essentially in the existence of sovereign power, it follows for Hobbes as for Bodin that the difference between forms of government lies solely in the location of sovereignty. There are no perverted forms of government. People impute perversion, with such terms as tyranny or oligarchy, only because they dislike the exercise of a power, just as they use terms of approval, like monarchy or democracy, if they like it. There is certain to be sovereign power somewhere in every government and the only question is who has it. For the same reason there is no mixed government and no limited government, since the sovereign power is indivisible. Someone must have the last decision and whoever has it and can make it good has sovereign power. Probably there is nothing in political literature that more perfectly illustrates the inability of a congenital utilitarian to enter into the spirit of a revolutionary age than these chapters in which Hobbes argues that all governments which keep order come to the same thing in the end. The aspiration for more justice and right seemed to him merely an intellectual confusion. Hatred of tyranny seemed mere dislike of a particular exercise of power, and enthusiasm for liberty seemed either sentimental vaporing or outright hypocrisy. Hobbes's account of the civil wars in his *Behemoth* makes them a strange mixture of villainy and wrong-headedness. The clarity of his political system had nothing to do with understanding human nature in politics.

From the theory of sovereignty it is only a step to that of the civil law. In the proper sense of the word, law is the "command of that person . . . whose precept contains in it the reason of obedience."[9] It is "to every subject, those rules, which the commonwealth hath commanded him, by word, writing, or other sufficient sign of the will, to make use of, for the distinction of right, and wrong."[10] He was careful to point out that this definition sharply distinguishes civil from natural law, for the former is a command sanctioned by enforcement while the latter is a dictate of reason. The law of nature is law only in a figurative sense, for the imperative or coercive aspect of civil law is the essence of it. This, Hobbes explains, is the confusion in the position both of parliamentarians and of common lawyers like Coke. The former imagine that there is some virtue in the consent of a representative body and the latter that there is some validity in custom. In fact it is the enforcing power that makes the precept binding and the law is his who has the power. He may allow custom to persist, but it is his tacit consent which gives it the force of law. Doubly absurd is Coke's superstition that the common law has a reason of its own. Similarly, the sovereign may consult parliament or permit it to frame statutes, but the enforcement is what makes them law. Hobbes assumes that enforcement takes place in the king's name, but there is nothing in his theory contrary to the sovereignty of parliament, provided that body can both make the law and control its administration and execution. Hobbes was wrong in thinking that he could bolster up absolute monarchy but he was not mistaken in believing that centralized authority in some form was to be a chief mark of modern states.

Since the laws of nature merely state the rational principles upon which a state can be constructed, they are not limitations on the authority of the sovereign. Hobbes's argument sounds like a quibble but there was reason behind it. No civil law, he says, ever can be contrary to the law of nature; property may be a natural right but the civil law defines property, and if a particular right is extinguished, it simply ceases to be property and so is no longer included under the law of nature. What limits the sovereign is not the law of nature but the power of his subjects. Hobbes's sovereign is faced by a condition and not a theory, but there can be no limitation of the civil law in its own field. Bodin's

[9] *De cive,* ch. 14, 1.

[10] *Leviathan,* ch. 26.

conception of a constitutional law limiting the competence of the sovereign has disappeared entirely.

THE STATE AND THE CHURCH

Hobbes's theory of sovereignty brings to completion the process of subordinating the church to the civil power which was begun when Marsilio of Padua carried through to its logical conclusion the separation of the spiritual and temporal authorities. For a materialist like Hobbes the spiritual becomes a mere ghost, a figment of the imagination. He does not deny that there is such a thing as revelation or as spiritual truths but he is clear that there is nothing to say about them.

> For it is with the mysteries of our religion, as with wholesome pills for the sick, which swallowed whole, have the virtue to cure; but chewed, are for the most part cast up again without effect.[11]

The very belief in non-material substances he regarded as a cardinal error derived from Aristotle and propagated by the clergy for their own advantage; it is the metaphysical side of that other cardinal error, the belief that the church is the kingdom of God and so endowed with an authority other than that of the state. Hobbes still affects to think that belief cannot be forced, but the profession of belief is an overt act and therefore falls within the province of law. Freedom of belief is completely inoperative so far as external consequences are concerned. All observance and profession, the canon of religious books, the creed, and the government of the church, if they have any authority, are authorized by the sovereign. Since there is no objective standard of religious truth, the establishment of any belief or form of worship must be an act of sovereign will.

A church therefore is for Hobbes merely a corporation. Like any corporation it must have a head and the head is the sovereign. It is a company of men united in the person of one sovereign and therefore quite indistinguishable from the commonwealth itself. Temporal and spiritual government are identical. Hobbes still holds, like Marsilio, that it is the duty of the church to teach, but he adds that no teaching is lawful unless the sovereign authorizes it. Excommunication or any other ecclesiastical penalty is in-

[11] *Ibid.*, ch. 32.

flicted by the authority of the sovereign. Obviously enough, then, as Hobbes concludes, there cannot be any conflict between divine and human law. In every sense that counts religion is completely under the sway of law and government. One easily conjectures that religion was not a matter of vital moment in Hobbes's experience. He attributed less moral weight to it than Machiavelli. The desire for freedom of conscience, like the desire for political freedom, seems to have figured in his mind merely as an evidence of intellectual confusion, and the force of a genuine religious conviction must have been quite unknown to him. At the same time ecclesiastical questions still bulked very large in his political outlook. Nearly half of *Leviathan* is devoted to them. In this respect English thought must have moved rapidly between 1650 and the end of the century. When Locke wrote forty years later he could assume far more actual separation of political and religious questions than Hobbes ever imagined.

HOBBES'S INDIVIDUALISM

Hobbes's political philosophy is beyond all comparison the most imposing structure that the period of the English civil wars produced. It is notable chiefly for the logical clarity of the argument and the consistency with which it carried through the presumptions from which it started. It was in no sense a product of realistic political observation. The actual motives which sway men in civil life were largely opaque to Hobbes, and his interpretation of the characters of his contemporaries was often grotesque. His psychology was not conceived by him to be the product of observation. It was not so much a description of men as they are as a demonstration of what they must be in the light of general principles. This was what science meant to Hobbes — a rational construction of the complex by means of the simple, as exemplified by geometry. The resulting estimate of government was wholly secular and quite coolly utilitarian. Its value consists solely in what it does, but since the alternative is anarchy, there can be no doubt which a utilitarian will choose. The choice has little sentiment behind it. The advantages of government are tangible and they must accrue quite tangibly to individuals, in the form of peace and comfort and security of person and property. This is the only ground upon which government can be justified or even exist. A general or public good, like a public will, is a figment of the imagination; there are merely individuals who desire to live and to enjoy protection for the means of life.

This individualism is the thoroughly modern element in Hobbes and the respect in which he caught most clearly the note of the coming age. For two centuries after him self-interest seemed to most thinkers a more obvious motive than disinterestedness, and enlightened self-interest a more applicable remedy for social ills than any form of collective action. The absolute power of the sovereign — a theory with which Hobbes's name is more generally associated — was really the necessary complement of his individualism. Except as there is a tangible superior to whom men render obedience and who can, if necessary, enforce obedience, there are only individual human beings, each actuated by his private interests. There is no middle ground between humanity as a sand-heap of separate organisms and the state as an outside power holding them precariously together by the sanctions with which it supplements individual motives. All the rich variety of associations disappears, or is admitted suspiciously and grudgingly as carrying a threat to the power of the state. It is a theory natural to an age which saw the wreck of so many of the traditional associations and institutions of economic and religious life and which saw above all the emergence of powerful states in which the making of law became the typical activity. These tendencies — the increase of legal power and the recognition of self-interest as the dominant motive in life — have been among the most pervasive in modern times. That Hobbes made them the premises of his system and followed them through with relentless logic is the true measure of his philosophical insight and of his greatness as a political thinker.

SELECTED BIBLIOGRAPHY

Thomas Hobbes' Mechanical Conception of Nature. By Frithiof Brandt. London, 1928.

Thomas Hobbes as Philosopher, Publicist, and Man of Letters. By George E. G. Catlin. Oxford, 1922.

English Political Philosophy from Hobbes to Maine. By William Graham. London, 1899.

The Social and Political Ideas of some Great Thinkers of the Sixteenth and Seventeenth Centuries. Ed. by F. J. C. Hearnshaw. London, 1926. Ch. 7.

Hobbes und die Staatsphilosophie. By Richard Hönigswald. Munich, 1924.

Hobbes. By John Laird. London, 1934.

"Hobbes and Hobbism." By Sterling Lamprecht. In *Am. Pol. Sci. Rev.*, Vol. XXXIV (1940), p. 31.

Die Grundlagen des ethisch-politischen Systems von Hobbes. By Z. Lubienski. Munich, 1932.

Hobbes. By Sir Leslie Stephen. London, 1904.

The Political Philosophy of Hobbes, its Basis and its Genesis. By Leo Strauss. Eng. trans. from the German manuscript by Elsa M. Sinclair. Oxford, 1936.

Thomas Hobbes, der Mann und der Denker. By Ferdinand Tönnies. 2nd ed. Stuttgart, 1922.

"La pensée et l'influence de Th. Hobbes." *Archives de Philosophie*, Vol. XII, Cahier II. Paris, 1936.

CHAPTER XXIV

RADICALS AND COMMUNISTS

Hobbes's political thought belonged essentially to the realm of scholarship or science. Though intended to influence the course of events in favor of the royalists, it had little or no effect of that kind, and as a solvent of traditional loyalties and a presentation of enlightened egoism, it contributed in the long run to a more radical liberalism than any that was within the bounds of practical politics in the seventeenth century. At the same time something of the radical individualism which Hobbes used as a philosophical postulate can be seen in the left-wing popular democracy that appeared in the course of the civil wars. This was not, of course, because the radicals learned from Hobbes, but because both were concerned with a social and intellectual change which transcended parties and immediate interests. The dissolution of traditional institutions and the economic pressure which it engendered were facts and not theories. Hobbes's logic turned egoism into a postulate for a social philosophy, but the conditions which made individualism an unescapable point of view existed in their own right. The belief that social and political institutions are justified only because they protect individual interests and maintain individual rights emerged under the pressure of circumstances which first became effective in England in the mid-seventeenth century but which also persisted and became more effective during the two centuries following.

Not the least significant aspect of the English civil wars was the part which popular discussion played in them. They mark the first appearance of public opinion as an important factor in politics. The volume of occasional, controversial writing produced was gigantic, far exceeding that of the French wars of religion, though the latter had not been small.[1] Much of this discussion

[1] The collection of tracts made by the bookseller George Thomason between the assembling of the Long Parliament in 1640 and the coronation of Charles II in 1661 (now in the British Museum), though it is not complete,

was, in a broad sense, philosophical. It dealt at least with general ideas — theological, religious, and ethical — and their application to government. It aired abuses, discussed the constitution, argued for and against religious toleration, attacked or defended the government of the church and examined its relation to civil authority, claimed or denied every form of civil liberty, and proposed at one time or another most of the political devices which democratic governments have since tried. This pamphlet-debate was the first great experiment in popular political education using the printing press as the organ of government by discussion. However vague the ideas may have been or lacking in systematic coherence, they were at least being used to bring a measure of intelligent guidance into the political life of men in the mass. Ideas and aspirations spread among considerable numbers of Englishmen were not important exclusively for the results which they were able immediately to achieve.

Among these movements of popular political thought none is more interesting or important than the democratic radicalism which appeared in the group known as Levellers. In religion they belonged among the Independents and, like this sect generally, they favored religious toleration and were opposed to the establishment of either an episcopal or a presbyterian form of church government. Though the group was not very definite in its composition, it formed for a short time, between 1647 and 1650, something like a real political party, having a definite idea of the political aims of the Revolution and a plan for resettling the constitution on liberal lines, depending upon a well-defined body of common political beliefs. It failed in all its purposes but it represented with remarkable distinctness the modes of thought and argument which were to characterize revolutionary liberalism in the eighteenth and early nineteenth centuries. It drew the lines pretty definitely between the liberalism of the less privileged economic classes and the more conservative liberalism, or Whiggism, of the well-to-do.

At the same time there appeared among the revolutionists an-

---

contains more than twenty thousand titles. See the account of this pamphlet-literature in the commentary by William Haller in Volume I of *Tracts on Liberty in the Puritan Revolution, 1638–1647*. 3 vols. New York, 1934.

other group, the Diggers, who sometimes called themselves the True Levellers and who were not at the time very clearly distinguished from the larger group. In numbers they were quite insignificant, all or nearly all of their written pronouncements coming from the pen of one man, Gerrard Winstanley. In purpose and outlook, however, they seem to have been quite different from the larger group. For as the Levellers were an early instance of a radical middle-class democracy with political aims, the Diggers are more easily classified as the beginning of utopian communism, since they regarded political reform as superficial unless it could redress the inequalities of the economic system. The Levellers appear to have been drawn mainly from the less prosperous part of the middle class, while the Diggers were perhaps members of that class whom economic stress had pushed out into the ranks of the propertyless. At any rate, Winstanley says that he had been ruined in business by the "cheating art of buying and selling." The Diggers may be counted as the first appearance of a proletarian social philosophy. The purpose of the present chapter is to examine these two types of early radicalism.

THE LEVELLERS

The Leveller movement ran its course within pretty definite limits of time and was related to a specific phase of the civil wars which helped to define its purposes as a party. The success of Cromwell's campaign against Charles had created, by the end of 1646, a political triangle from which a settlement of the Revolution had to be evolved. The king, defeated but not destroyed, might still hope for much if he could embroil the several factions of his enemies with each other. Parliament, a little dismayed by its success and uncertain what to do with its newly won sovereignty, was under a leadership more interested in establishing presbyterianism than in carrying out any specific plan of political reform. Finally, and most important, Cromwell's army, which had won the victory, had no intention of allowing the fruits to be gathered either by the king or the Presbyterians. In the game of shifty diplomacy which followed, Charles played for a new civil war and parliament played to get rid of the army and leave itself a free hand. The army, which alone had any real power, could have ended the shuffling at any moment, as it did three years later, but the leaders, Cromwell and his son-in-law Ireton, had a sincere dislike for military dictatorship and were deeply in doubt how best to give the Revolution a constitutional form. So hesitant were they that in 1647 they risked a threat of mutiny in the army. For the rank and file of the soldiers, well knowing that neither the king nor parliament could be trusted, became fearful that Cromwell also would barter away the reforms which they hoped from the Revolution. It was in these circumstances that the Levellers appeared, first as a radical party among the common soldiers, dissatisfied with the cautious and conservative plan of reform promulgated by their officers, and advocating their own radical program of the results to be achieved by the Revolution.

Quite spontaneously regimental committees, remarkably like the soviets that appeared in the Russian army in 1917, sprang into existence and demanded a share in formulating the policies to be pursued. Fortunately there has been preserved an almost *verbatim* report of the discussions which followed in the Army Council, between the representatives of the officers, led by Cromwell and Ireton, and the representatives of the regiments who had, apparently, the sympathy and support of a very few of the higher officers.[2] Both before and after this occurrence in the army there appeared a number of pamphlets, chiefly by the leaders of the Leveller Party, John Lilburne and Richard Overton, setting forth both their practical objectives and the political philosophy upon which they acted.[3]

The debates in the Army Council are peculiarly interesting and vivid because they recreate actual conversations almost three centuries dead. They permit a glimpse into the minds of a group of Englishmen in lowly station, the small tradesmen, artisans, and farmers that made up the rank and file of Cromwell's army. They

[2] *The Clarke Papers,* ed. by C. H. Firth, 4 vols. Camden Society Publications, 1891–1901. Re-edited by A. S. P. Woodhouse in *Puritanism and Liberty,* London, 1938.

[3] *Tracts on Liberty in the Puritan Revolution, 1638–1647,* ed. by William Haller, 3 vols., New York, 1934; *The Leveller Tracts, 1647–1653,* ed. by William Haller and Godfrey Davies, New York, 1944; *Leveller Manifestoes in the Puritan Revolution,* ed. by Don M. Wolfe, New York, 1944. Many excerpts from contemporary pamphlets are given in Woodhouse, *op. cit.,* Part III. The platform of the Levellers as a party was called "An Agreement of the People." Four versions of different dates are printed in Wolfe, *op. cit.*

show what these men thought they had been fighting for and the inevitable clash between their ideas and those of the well-to-do classes represented by their officers. The danger of serious mutiny was real. In November, 1647, Cromwell moved swiftly and sternly to restore discipline and soon after he determined on his own account to negotiate no further with Charles. This decision went far to restore the confidence of the main body of the army. In the latter part of 1648 the Levellers reappeared as a civil party, but their importance ended when the officers committed themselves definitely to a policy of coercion in the first half of 1649.

John Lilburne, the principal leader of the Levellers, was the perfect type of radical agitator. Endlessly pugnacious in defending his " rights " and in attacking abuses, he came into conflict at one stage or another of his career with every branch of government: Lords, Commons, Council of the State, and the officers of the army. He was honest and fearless but also quarrelsome and suspicious. Twice in his life, in 1649 and 1653, he was the hero of a spectacular political trial in which he won his acquittal by appealing to popular sentiment over the head of the court. Lilburne's influence was mainly due to his ability to dramatize himself as a symbol of popular liberties: " Where others argued about the respective right of king and parliament, he spoke always of the rights of the people." As a party the Levellers must have been a relatively small group drawn from the more politically minded of the poorer classes. Their projects attracted neither the landed gentry nor the well-to-do citizens of London. Indeed, they failed on all sides, first, in holding the mass of the army after confidence in the officers was restored; second, in carrying the officers for their radical reforms; and third, in gaining enough weight anywhere to influence parliament. The Levellers are interesting not because of anything they were able to do but because their ideas anticipated in so many respects both the ideology and the program of later democratic radicalism.

AN ENGLISHMAN'S BIRTHRIGHT

The name Leveller was obviously an epithet; it was meant to imply that the party sought to destroy differences of social position, of political rank, and even of property, levelling all men down to a condition of equality. An enemy paraphrased their argument as follows:

> Seeing all men are by nature the sons of Adam, and from him have legitimately derived a natural propriety, right, and freedom, therefore England and all other nations, and all particular persons in every nation, notwithstanding the difference of laws and governments, ranks and degrees, ought to be alike free and estated in their natural liberties, and to enjoy the just rights and prerogative of mankind, whereunto they are heirs apparent; and thus the commoners by right, are equal with the lords. For by natural birth all men are equally and alike born to like propriety, liberty, and freedom; and as we are delivered of God by the hand of nature into this world, every one with a natural innate freedom, and propriety, even so are we to live, every one equally and alike to enjoy his birthright and privilege.[4]

The author of this description was notoriously biased. In the party pronouncements of the Levellers there is not the slightest evidence that the " like propriety " which they desired included equalization of property or the levelling of social distinctions. They objected to political privilege on the part of the nobility and to economic advantage through monopolies in trade or the professional monopoly enjoyed by lawyers. The objection seems to have been aimed exclusively at legally supported privilege and not at social or economic inequality as such. The discussions reported in the *Clarke Papers* are filled with protestations, evidently sincere, that no attack on property was intended. The equality sought was equality before the law and equality of political rights, especially for the class of small property owners. Indeed, the Levellers appear to have grasped with remarkable clearness the point of view of radical democratic liberalism, individualist rather than socialist in its philosophy and political rather than economic in its aims.

The basis of this individualism seems to have been a rationalist belief that the fundamental rights of human beings are self-evident. In view of their time and the evident connection of the Levellers with Independency, the argumentation in the *Clarke Papers* and in the pamphlets is surprisingly little dependent upon religious considerations or appeals to Scriptural authority. In fact their

[4] Thomas Edwards, *Gangraena,* Part III, p. 17. Edwards refers to Richard Overton's *Remonstrance* (1646); see *Tracts on Liberty in the Puritan Revolution, 1638–1647,* ed. by W. Haller, Vol. III, p. 351.

opponents sometimes objected that they had too little respect for revelation in religion or for custom in law and government but wished to measure both by what was natural and reasonable.

> As they do in matters of religion and conscience they fly from the Scriptures, and from supernatural truths revealed there, that a man may not be questioned for going against them, but only for errors against the light of nature and right reason; so they do also in civil government and things of this life, they go from the laws and constitutions of kingdoms, and will be governed by rules according to nature and right reason.[5]

The charge might have been supported by many sentences out of Lilburne's pamphlets, especially the later ones. As early as 1646 he asserted that men, merely because they are the children of Adam, are "by nature all equal and alike in power, dignity, authority, and majesty," and that in consequence all civil authority is exercised "merely by institution, or donation, that is to say, by mutual agreement and consent, given . . . for the good benefit and comfort of each other." In short, governments derive their just powers from the consent of the governed, meaning the individual consent of each and every citizen. One of the most picturesque assertions of this principle was made by one of the representatives of the regiments in the conference with the officers:

> Really I think that the poorest he that is in England hath a life to live as the greatest he; and therefore truly, Sir, I think it's clear, that every man that is to live under a government ought first by his own consent to put himself under that government; and I do think that the poorest man in England is not at all bound in a strict sense to that government that he hath not had a voice to put himself under.[6]

It should be granted that the argument of the Levellers was likely to be a little confused in respect to the "birthright" which they claimed. It might consist of the traditional liberties of Englishmen supposed to be embalmed in the common law or Magna Charta, or it might be the universal rights of man. Like any expert agitator, Lilburne appealed to whatever made the strongest case in the circumstances — to the Commons against the Lords, to Magna Charta against the common law, and to reason against them all. So long as a precedent or a traditional right would serve, there was no need to run into abstractions. But on the whole it

[5] *Gangraena,* Pt. III, p. 20.

[6] *Clarke Papers,* Vol. I, p. 301.

was quite impossible for a party of radical reform to stand on custom. William Walwyn in 1645 observed that

Magna Charta (you must observe) is but a part of the people's rights and liberties, being no more but what with much striving and fighting, was by the blood of our ancestors, wrestled out of the paws of those kings, who by force had conquered the Nation, changed the laws and by strong hand held them in bondage.[7]

In 1646 Richard Overton called Magna Charta a "beggarly thing" and took the argument quite out of the region of custom:

Ye [Parliament] were chosen to work our deliverance, and to estate us in natural and just liberty agreeable to reason and common equity, for whatever our forefathers were, or whatever they did or suffered, or were enforced to yield unto, we are the men of the present age, and ought to be absolutely free from all kinds of exorbitancies, molestations or arbitrary power.[8]

The distinction between customary and natural right was a bone of contention between Ireton and the representatives of the regiments. Ireton's legal mind was irritated by the indefiniteness of the claim:

If you will resort only to the law of nature, by the law of nature you have no more right to this land or anything else than I have.[9]

What makes a right mine, "really and civilly, is the law." The Leveller was arguing that an unjust law is no law at all.

The interesting and distinctive feature of the Leveller philosophy is the new form which it gave to the ancient conceptions of natural right and consent. They interpreted the law of nature as endowing human individuals with innate and inalienable rights which legal and political institutions exist only to protect, and they construed consent as an individual act which every man is entitled to perform for himself. Almost as much as Hobbes, though not with his systematic clarity, they argued that the only justification for society is the production of individual advantages. Had they developed the conception of a contract, which is implicit in their idea of consent, it would clearly have been, like that of

[7] *Englands Lamentable Slaverie, Tracts on Liberty in the Puritan Revolution, 1638–1647,* Vol. III, p. 313.

[8] *A Remonstrance, ibid.,* p., 354.

[9] *Clarke Papers,* Vol. I, p. 263.

Hobbes, a social contract, deriving the social group from individuals who combine for mutual benefits, and not the older form of contract between king and community. The individual and his rights form the basis of the whole social structure. As in the characteristic social philosophy of radical liberalism, the only justification for restraint lies in the fact that restraint itself contributes to individual freedom.

MODERATE AND RADICAL REFORM

The plan of political reform which the Levellers sponsored agreed remarkably well with the principles of their political philosophy. They formed, as has been said, the left wing of the revolutionists in Cromwell's army and their position is best defined by their differences from the more conservative plans formed by the officers. In 1647 the revolution was an accomplished fact and some constitutional settlement was obviously necessary. On many points there was substantial agreement between moderates and radicals, or the difference was a matter of detail rather than of principle. Both sides of course desired the removal of the worst abuses that had caused the war between the king and parliament. The essential difference lay in the fact that the officers, as a group, came from the landed gentry and desired a settlement leaving political power mainly with that class, though it is only fair to say that their plan included many democratic reforms which were not brought about in England until the nineteenth century. The Levellers and the men from the regiments, on the other hand, were men of small property, the class most likely to have been ruined by the war, and therefore desired a settlement distinguishing political rights and property rights as completely as possible. In consequence the officers, headed by Cromwell and Ireton, stood for a settlement making as few changes in the historical constitution as possible, consistent with saving the fruits of the war as they understood them. The Levellers wished to seize the opportunity for making sweeping changes, directed toward what they took to be a just and reasonable arrangement, without much regard for tradition.

Ye know, the laws of this nation are unworthy a free people, and deserve from first to last, to be considered, and seriously debated, and reduced to an agreement with common equity, and right reason, which ought to be the form and life of every government.[10]

In the conferences between the officers and the representatives of the regiments, Cromwell was evidently staggered by the greatness and novelty of the changes proposed. Like many successful revolutionists, he was at heart a conservative; moreover, he knew much better than the Levellers how impractical, in the circumstances, it was to try to give effect to a system of abstract principles.

Before the agitation in the ranks began, the council of officers had already drawn up a document called the "Heads of Proposals," [11] which was the outline of a series of acts by which it was proposed that parliament should give effect to the constitutional changes wrought by the Revolution. The Agreement of the People, which was formulated in the ranks and brought by the representatives of the regiments to the Army Council, was a counterproposal sketching the form of government which the Levellers desired. It was agreed by both groups that the freedom of parliament must be secured, that frequent meetings must be made certain, and that there must be a redistribution of seats to give more equal representation. Both agreed, moreover, that parliament must control executive officers, including commanders of the army and navy, though the officers were content to make this a temporary arrangement for ten years, while the Levellers made it a permanent part of their constitution. Both sides agreed to a policy of religious toleration, except for Roman Catholics, and desired the removal of specified abuses in the administration of the law. With the acceptance of these changes, the officers were willing to restore the personal rights and liberty of the king, though this was not with them a main point and a little later they abandoned it. Some of the Levellers at least were definitely republicans and believed that monarchy was "the original of all oppressions," [12] but its abolition seems not to have been a main point in the program of the party. Republicanism was a means rather than an end in their plan of government.

Behind this rather large measure of agreement about means, however, there was a radical difference of political philosophy.

[10] Richard Overton's *Remonstrance, ibid.*, p. 365.
[11] Excerpted in Woodhouse, *op. cit.*, p. 422.
[12] Overton's *Remonstrance, ibid.*, p. 356.

The Levellers desired the independence of parliament not because of its traditional liberties but because it was the representative of the people. There was no doubt in their minds that the people and not parliament was sovereign and that parliament had a purely delegated authority. In line with the marked individualism of their theory of natural rights, also, they conceived parliament as standing for the actual human beings that composed the nation, and not as representing corporations, vested interests, and rights of property or status. These two features of their political philosophy — the delegated power of parliament and the right of every man to consent to law through his representatives — were the grounds upon which they urged the main parts of their radical program.

Accordingly, while both the Levellers and the officers desired equality of representation in parliament, they had fundamentally different notions of what equality meant. The officers proposed a redistribution of seats on the basis of the proportion of taxes paid by constituencies, while the Levellers desired equality according to population. The more conservative view, which certainly was closer to the historical conception of parliament, looked upon that body as representing interests, the ownership of land or membership in a corporation in which trading was permitted. Ireton stated this view with great clearness. No man has a right to vote, he said, unless he has " a permanent fixed interest in this kingdom," an interest which is by nature irremovable and which forms a permanent part of the economic and political structure.[13] Equality of representation meant that even the least of such interests had a voice in choosing representatives; it did not mean that every man must have a voice. To this the Leveller replied that it is the man, not the interest, that is subject to law and hence it is the man and not property that should be represented. He earnestly disclaimed any desire to interfere with the rights of property, which he regarded as included among man's natural rights, but he drew a sharp distinction between ownership and the possession of political rights. Political rights are not property, and even a poor man has his " birthright," which the state is bound to protect no less than the property of the rich.

Consequently the Leveller stood in theory for universal man-

[13] *Clarke Papers,* Vol. I, pp. 302 ff.

hood suffrage, possibly excepting paupers, or as a practical expedient for the lowest property qualification obtainable, while Ireton's theory meant in practice the restriction of suffrage to landowners. The officers undoubtedly believed that universal suffrage would endanger property and result in sheer anarchy. As Ireton said, if a man has a right to vote merely because he breathes, he may have a natural right even against the legal rights of property. Natural right is no right at all, since both political rights and the rights of property arise from law. But the exactions of the law, the Leveller answered, are just what need to be explained and justified. Unless the law is made with the people's consent, and unless a man has been represented in the body which made it, how can he be justly obliged to obey it? And how can a man be represented unless he has a voice in choosing his representatives? The two points of view are opposed with remarkable vividness: on the one hand, the theory that the community is an organization of permanent interests, particularly the landed interest, held together by customary privileges and exactions; on the other, the new conception of the nation as a mass of free individuals, cooperating from motives of self-interest, and making its law in the interest of individual freedom.

THE CURB ON THE LEGISLATURE

From the Leveller's point of view there was no more merit in parliament's claim to sovereign power than in the king's. Like the king, parliament has merely a delegated power, and it is as important to protect individual rights against a legislature as against an executive. The record then being made by the Presbyterian leaders of the Long Parliament was well calculated to convince a group of Independents that the bridling of a sovereign legislative body was not an academic question. Consequently the Levellers desired a constitutional device that would protect the individual in his fundamental rights even against his own representatives. The plan struck out was substantially that of a written constitution with its bill of fundamental rights. In recognizing the supremacy of parliament over other branches of government, the Agreement of the People expressly laid down the rule that there are certain rights of citizens which even parliament must not touch and it attempts to enumerate some of them. Parliament must not repudiate debts, make arbitrary exceptions to the operation of law, or destroy the rights of property and of personal liberty. Particularly it must not take away or modify any of the rights set down in the instrument itself. In short, the Agreement is to stand as unchangeable constitutional law, a device actually adopted in the Instrument of Government which set up the Protectorate in 1653. In 1648 the Levellers tried to secure what in the United States would be called a constitutional convention, a special representative body "not to exercise any legislative power but only to draw up the foundation for just government." The "agreement" thus made was to stand as a kind of social contract, above the law, fixing the limits of parliament's legislative power; it was to be signed and agreed to by electors and candidates at every election. Like so many later constitutions planned to protect indefeasible human rights, the Agreement of the People undertook to legalize resistance, in case parliament should overstep the bounds set by the Agreement itself.

The Levellers more than any other group in revolutionary England approximated the political philosophy which later became typical of radical democracy. In them the ancient theory of natural law appeared in a new form: the innate right of every man to a minimum of political privilege, the doctrine of consent by participation in the choice of representatives, the justification of law and government as a protection of individual rights, and the limitation of every branch of government under the sovereign power of the people secured by a written list of inalienable rights. The presence of such a body of ideas in mid-seventeenth century England is doubly interesting because of the complete failure of their constitutional projects in that country, compared with their persistence and realization in America. The Instrument of Government in 1653 was the first and the last attempt in England to limit the legislative power of parliament by a written constitution, and the outcome of the Revolution was to settle the legal supremacy of parliament. In America the written constitution with its limitations upon legislatures became the general practice. The difference is not hard to explain. After the Restoration in 1660 the exchange of political ideas between England and America was much restricted, in comparison with what it had been earlier. In consequence the newer idea of parliamentary sovereignty never spread among the English in America, while the older belief in a fundamental law persisted and under favorable circumstances was developed upon lines similar to those suggested by the Levellers. This is not to say that the program of the Levellers was imitated. Constitutional ideas both in England and America had a common root, and the state of affairs in America permitted an immediately more radical effort to give them effect.

THE DIGGERS

The pamphlets of the Levellers are eloquent of the economic distress which the civil wars brought to the small farmers, tradesmen, and artisans in the less prosperous part of the English middle class. For the most part these men either followed the lead of the more prosperous gentry or looked for help to a more radical political equality and the removal of such legal discriminations as monopoly. By a very few persons, however, the political revolution was conceived as an opportunity to bring about economic equality and to lift the burden of poverty from the masses.[14] The name "True Levellers," by which these communists sometimes described themselves, suggests at once that they originated as a left fringe of the radical party and that they were at least vaguely conscious of differing from them. On the other side, Lilburne denied emphatically that he had any connection with the communists. Contemporary confusions aside, the social philosophy of the communists was different in principle from that of the Levellers. The latter were radical democrats with mainly political purposes; the communists were utopian socialists with mainly economic purposes.

The communists sprang into notoriety in 1649 when a small group of them tried to take and cultivate unenclosed common land, with the purpose of distributing the produce to the poor. This gave them the name, Diggers, by which they were known in the

[14] This was first called to the attention of historians by Eduard Bernstein in his *Sozialismus und Demokratie in der grossen Englischen Revolution* (1st ed., 1895), translated by H. J. Stenning as *Cromwell and Communism* (1930). The communist tracts are reprinted in *The Works of Gerrard Winstanley*, ed. by George H. Sabine, Ithaca, New York, 1941. The more important works are contained in *Selections,* ed. by Leonard Hamilton, London, 1944. See D. W. Petegorsky, *Left-wing Democracy in the English Civil War*, London, 1940.

seventeenth century. This action caused a flurry among the landlords concerned but it had no lasting effects. The Diggers, who probably numbered only a few score, kept their experiment going for a year but they were finally dispersed by legal harassment and mob-violence. The only result was a few pamphlets by Gerrard Winstanley, notably a plan for a communist government of England published after the attempt to till the common land had failed. Winstanley's communism unquestionably had its origin in religious mysticism. His religious beliefs were substantially like those of the Quakers a few years later and were quite different from the Calvinism of most of the radical groups.

The common ground between the Leveller and the communist lay in the fact that both claimed the law of nature as their justification, as any radical in the seventeenth century was certain to do. The Leveller turned the law of nature into a doctrine of individual rights, of which the right of property was inevitably one of the most important. The Digger interpreted the law of nature as a communal right to the means of subsistence, of which land was the most important, and gave to the individual only the right to share in the produce of the common land and the common labor. The land is given by God or nature to be "the common treasury" from which all are entitled to draw their sustenance.

> None ought to be lords or landlords over another, but the earth is free for every son and daughter of mankind to live free upon.[15]

The "natural" state of man is therefore one of common ownership, and the communist pictured the English Revolution as nothing less than the occasion for a return to this idyllic condition.

The origins of this conception can only be guessed at. It is natural to suspect that there was some continuity with the ideas of obscure proletarian uprisings which economic distress had produced from time to time both in England and on the Continent, or more specifically with the Peasant Revolt in Germany and the Anabaptist movement. At all events the principle from which the communists started was the Christian belief, widespread through the Middle Ages, that common possession was a more perfect way of life than private ownership, which was commonly held not to be "natural" but the result of human wickedness. The significant

[15] *Works*, ed. by Sabine, p. 289.

part of the Diggers' philosophy was the way in which they reversed the conclusions drawn from this belief. The usual deduction had been that private property, though less perfect than common ownership, is nevertheless the best practicable concession to the fallen nature of man. The Digger inferred that private property itself is the main cause of evil and of all forms of social abuse and corruption. The root of all evil is covetousness and greed, which first produced private property, while the latter causes all supremacy of one man over another, all manner of bloodshed, and the enslaving of the masses of men, who have been reduced to poverty by the wage-system and are forced to support by their labor the very power that enslaves them. Consequently most social ills and most of human vice can be removed by destroying private property, especially in land. The similarity of the Digger argument to Rousseau's essay on " The Origin of Inequality among Men " is striking.

As a matter of course the pamphlets of the Diggers breathe enmity against the landlords.

> O you Adams of the earth, you have rich clothing, full bellies. . . . But know . . . that the day of judgment is begun. . . . The poor people whom thou oppresses shall be the saviors of the land. . . . If thou wilt find mercy . . . disown this oppressing . . . thievery of buying and selling of land, owning of landlords, and paying of rents, and give your free consent to make the earth a common treasury.[16]

But the denunciation was no less bitter of lawyers and the clergy, not so much because the former corrupt the law or the latter teach bad theology, as because both are the main supports of private property. All English history since the Conquest is read in this sense: the Conqueror took the land from the people and gave it to his " colonels " from whom it has descended to the present landlords. England is a prison; the subtleties of the law are its bolts and bars, and the lawyers are its jailors. All the old law books ought to be burned. At the same time the Conqueror hired the clergy with tithes to " preach him up " and to " stop the people's mouths " by teaching them to be submissive. The deduction is evident: since now, by the Revolution, the kingly power has been cast out, the whole system of private landowning must go with it, for unless the people get back the land, they are deprived of the fruits of victory.

[16] *The True Leveller's Standard Advanced* (1649), *Works,* ed. by Sabine, pp. 264 ff.

Fiery as all this sounds, the Diggers disclaimed any intention of inciting to violence or of expropriating the landlords by force. What they might have done if they had been more numerous cannot be known; since they were at most a handful, the preaching of violence would have been suicidal. What they expressly claimed was the right to cultivate common land, leaving the enclosed land to its owners. There is no reason to doubt their sincerity. Like most utopians, they were professed pacifists and they probably believed that the excellence of the new way of life would commend it even to landlords. Perhaps also they counted upon some mysterious softening of hearts, for though they were violently anti-clerical, they were also profoundly religious. "Jesus Christ," they said, "is the head Leveller." Apparently they were simple-minded folk who thought that the Christian doctrine of brotherly love was to be taken as it was written.

WINSTANLEY'S *LAW OF FREEDOM*

Gerrard Winstanley, the only important writer among the Diggers, produced one book, his *Law of Freedom* published in 1652 and addressed to Cromwell, which was more than a pamphlet. It drew the outlines of a Utopian society with some precision, as a "platform of commonwealth's government" according to the rule of righteousness. The fundamental thought behind Winstanley's commonwealth is that the root of all bondage is poverty: "A man had better to have had no body than to have no food for it." True freedom means that all equally have access to the use of the earth and its fruits. In human nature there are two opposed tendencies, the desire for common preservation, which is the root of the family and of all peace and righteousness; and the desire for self-preservation, which is the root of covetousness and tyranny. To the first corresponds commonwealth, in which the weak are protected equally with the strong. To the second corresponds kingly government and the law of the conqueror. The essential difference is that kingly government rules by the "cheating art of buying and selling"; it is the government of the highwayman who has stolen the earth from his younger brother. Hence the essence of reform is the prohibition of buying and selling, especially the land. There can be no equality short of equality of goods, for wealth gives power and power means oppression. Moreover, wealth cannot be honestly earned. No man gains wealth by his own effort but only by withholding a share of what is produced by his helpers.

Real liberty requires, therefore, that land shall be owned in common. The produce of the land should be put into a common store whence all may draw according to his needs. All able-bodied persons must be compelled to work at productive labor, at least until they reach the age of forty. The family, with personal effects and private houses, Winstanley would leave untouched. To perpetuate the commonwealth he provided an elaborate scheme of magistrates and a rigid code of laws, to be kept simple and not interpreted. As political devices he relied mainly upon universal suffrage and the limitation of terms of office to a single year. Not the least interesting part of the plan was his project for reducing the national church to an institution for popular education. Apparently the supernatural had little part in his conception of religion. The clergy, who at present "make sermons to please the sickly minds of ignorant peoples, to preserve their own riches and esteem among a charmed, befooled, and besotted people," are to become schoolmasters, giving instruction on each seventh day in public affairs, history, and the arts and sciences. "To know the secrets of nature is to know the works of God"; what is usually called divinity is the "doctrine of a weak and sickly spirit." "This divining spiritual doctrine is a cheat." Not the least important part of education is training in the useful trades and crafts.

> While men are gazing up to Heaven, imagining after a happiness, or fearing a Hell after they are dead, their eyes are put out, that they see not what is their birthrights.[17]

Winstanley's communism stood quite by itself in the political philosophy of the seventeenth century. It spoke with the authentic voice of proletarian utopianism, giving expression to the first stirring of political aspiration in the inarticulate masses and setting up the well-being of the common man as the goal of a just society. Utopian though it was in its purposes, it rested upon a clear insight into the inevitable dependence of political liberty and equality upon the control of economic causes. Only in Harrington can there be found in the seventeenth century a more definite idea of the dependence of politics upon the distribution of wealth. No-

[17] *Works,* p. 569.

where is there a clearer perception of the incompatibility of economic exploitation with democratic ideals. Winstanley's communism grew directly from his religious experience, but his religion was so free from dogmatism and clericalism that his political and social thought was often quite secular. His ethics, unlike that which attached to Calvinism, made brotherly love rather than individual self-sufficiency the central principle of democracy.

SELECTED BIBLIOGRAPHY

John Wildman, Plotter and Postmaster: A Study of the English Republican Movement in the Seventeenth Century. By Maurice P. Ashley. New Haven, Conn., 1947.

Cromwell and Communism: Socialism and Democracy in the Great English Revolution. By Eduard Bernstein. Eng. trans. by H. J. Stenning. London, 1930. (*Sozialismus und Demokratie in der grossen Englischen Revolution.*)

History of the Great Civil War, 1642–1649. By Samuel R. Gardiner. 3 vols. London, 1886–1891.

The History of English Democratic Ideas in the Seventeenth Century. By G. P. Gooch. 2nd ed. Cambridge, 1927.

Political Thought in England from Bacon to Halifax. By G. P. Gooch. London, 1914.

Tracts on Liberty in the Puritan Revolution, 1638–1647. Ed., with a Commentary, by William Haller. 3 vols. New York, 1934.

The Leveller Tracts, 1647–1653. Ed. by William Haller . . . and Godfrey Davies. New York, 1944.

Mysticism and Democracy in the English Commonwealth. By Rufus M. Jones. Cambridge, Mass., 1932.

The Development of Religious Tolerance in England. By W. K. Jordan. 4 vols. Cambridge, Mass., 1932–40.

The Leveller Movement: A Study in the History and Political Theory of the English Great Civil War. By Theodore C. Pease. Washington, 1916.

Left-wing Democracy in the English Civil War: A Study of the Social Philosophy of Gerrard Winstanley. By David W. Petegorsky. London, 1940.

The Works of Gerrard Winstanley. Ed. by George H. Sabine. Ithaca, New York, 1941. Introduction.

Leveller Manifestoes of the Puritan Revolution. Ed. by Don M. Wolfe. New York, 1944. Introduction.

Puritanism and Liberty, being the Army Debates (1647–9) from the Clarke Manuscripts. With Supplementary Documents Selected and Edited with an Introduction by A. S. P. Woodhouse. London, 1938.

CHAPTER XXV

THE REPUBLICANS: HARRINGTON, MILTON, AND SIDNEY

The issue of republican as against monarchical government does not appear to have played an important part at any stage of the Puritan Revolution. The officers of Cromwell's army were prepared in 1648 to release the king and restore his power, with proper safeguards, after an interval in which the results of the Revolution could be secured. Yet these same officers a few months later were driven to the execution of Charles not by republican principles but by the conviction that no settlement with him could be made permanent. The Levellers, though some of them were convinced republicans, seem not to have regarded the abolition of the monarchy as a chief end. Anti-monarchical principles were therefore of slight practical importance. It is true, however, that there was a small volume of definitely republican theory, though this was somewhat heterogeneous in its nature, perhaps because it never had to organize itself to produce results. John Milton and Algernon Sidney defended republicanism on the abstract ground that it was implied by natural law and the sovereign power of the people. James Harrington, though the creator of a utopia, laid aside more completely than any other writer the familiar legalist argumentation and defended republicanism as a consequence of social and economic evolution. While Harrington was wrong in believing that monarchy had become impossible, he was right about the shifting of economic power which any English government had to take into account.

Harrington was a political thinker of quite unusual power and independence, the only observer of the Puritan Revolution who had any philosophical grasp of the social causes behind it. Though a convinced and outspoken republican, he was by birth and association an aristocrat, an intimate friend who attended King Charles even to the scaffold. He was an admirer of Hobbes, whom he called "the best writer at this day in the world," but his political thought was in method the very antithesis of Hobbes's. What he admired in Hobbes was his belief in universal causation and his attempt to understand scientifically the springs of human conduct. But he must have felt that Hobbes failed to live up to the light that was in him. For his theory of the social contract abandoned causes for a legal analogy, and his theory of sovereign power failed to analyze the social causes which alone give any government real power. It was this analysis which Harrington undertook to supply and in so doing he proved himself to be a political philosopher of first-rate originality, not the equal of Hobbes in the bold sweep of his reasoning but much his superior in the grasp of political realities.

In form Harrington's *Oceana,* published in London in 1656,[1] belongs to the class of political utopias; it described the formation of a new government for the fictitious Commonwealth of Oceana. This government was pictured with a good deal of fanciful detail, yet there was comparatively little in Harrington's thought that was intrinsically utopian. Oceana was obviously England, and there is never any doubt about the real persons or historical events to which he referred. The book was addressed to Oliver Cromwell and was intended as a tract for the times, the elaborate and rather tiresome fiction being perhaps a means of forestalling the censorship. There was nothing imaginative about Harrington's method of political theorizing. He was an ardent admirer of Machiavelli, whom he regarded as the only modern political writer approaching the heights of ancient statesmanship. Like Machiavelli and Bodin, he used a method that was mainly historical and comparative. Every feature of the fictitious government of Oceana was copied from, and defended by reference to, ancient or existing governments, particularly the Jews, Rome, Sparta, and Venice. The study of history and the observation and comparison of existing governments are asserted to be the only means by which one can learn the craft of the statesman.

[1] The only good contemporary edition is by S. B. Liljegren, Heidelberg, 1924. Harrington's *Works* were edited by John Toland, London, 1700, and often.

THE ECONOMIC BASIS OF REPUBLICANISM

Harrington stood alone among the political writers of his time in seeing that government is determined both in its structure and in its working by underlying social and economic forces. In an age when the rancor of parties and sects was intense and when each party explained civil disorder by the stupidity or wickedness of its opponents, Harrington almost achieved scientific detachment, though he was intensely in earnest in offering his imaginary government as a plan for political construction. The underlying thought in Harrington's theory is that the form of government which is permanently possible in a country depends upon the distribution of property, especially property in land. Whatever class owns a preponderating " balance " of the land, say three parts in four, must by sheer economic necessity command the power to control government.

In place of enlarging upon the vices of royalists or parliamentarians, therefore, Harrington offered an economic-historical theory of the civil wars which, so far as it went, was perfectly sound. The explanation, he believed, must be sought far back in the social history of Tudor England. The causes of the demand for popular government began with the destruction of the English nobility in the Wars of the Roses and the consistent policy followed by Henry VII of dividing large estates among relatively small owners and thus of increasing the yeomanry at the expense of the nobility. The second great step in the same direction was the breaking up of the monasteries by Henry VIII, a policy which dispossessed the greatest of English landlords, the church, and put in its place a multitude of small owners. The result in both cases was to distribute wealth among a numerous class of landowners from whom the demand for popular rights was certain sooner or later to arise. With admirable irony Harrington described the political tactics of Elizabeth as " converting her reign through the perpetual love-tricks that passed between her and her people into a kind of romanze." But political play-acting could only put off the day when the realities of popular ownership would have to be recognized.

When a prince, as stiff in disputes as the nerve of monarchy was grown slack, received that unhappy encouragement from his clergy, which became his utter ruin, while trusting more unto their logic, than the rough philosophy of his Parliament, it came unto an irreparable breach.[2]

This theory Harrington derived partly from Aristotle's view that revolutions are caused chiefly by inequalities of property and partly from Machiavelli's belief that a powerful nobility is inconsistent with popular government. The latter, he remarked, had failed to note the economic reason for his observation, but when Machiavelli is supplemented by Aristotle the clue to a correct theory is found. The number of landowners is fundamental; if a large balance of land is held by the nobility, the commoners must be dependent upon them economically and therefore politically. If the land passes into the hands of many commoners, the power of the nobility must be correspondingly curtailed. By this theory Harrington meant also to correct and supplement Hobbes. He went straight to the heart of the latter's superficial explanation of government as mere power resting upon a covenant.

> As he [Hobbes] said of the law, that without this sword it is but paper; so he might have thought of this sword, that without an hand it is but cold iron. The hand which holdeth this sword is the militia of a nation . . . but an army is a beast that hath a great belly and must be fed; wherefore this will come unto what pastures you have, and what pastures you have will come unto the balance of propriety, without which the public sword is but a name or a mere spit-frog.[3]

Power in the legal sense is no self-explanatory term; it presumes social force and this in turn presumes a control of the means of subsistence. The issue between Hobbes and Harrington was that between a legal logician and a social economist.

For Harrington, then, the outcome of the civil wars was a foregone conclusion; it was a question not of abstract right and wrong but of social causes. Control of the land had passed into the hands of the middle class and with it the sources of political power. Temporarily the Tudor monarchy might exercise great power, pending the time when the new class became, so to speak, politically self-conscious, but sooner or later government must conform to the distribution of property. It was upon this ground that Harrington was a republican. He had no theoretical objection to monarchy, though he believed a commonwealth to be superior.

[2] *Oceana*, ed. by Liljegren, p. 49.
[3] *Ibid.*, p. 16.

> The course of England, into a commonwealth, is both certain and natural. The ways of nature require peace: The ways of peace require obedience to the laws: Laws in England cannot be made but by Parliaments: Parliaments in England are come to be mere popular assemblies: The laws made by popular assemblies (though for a time they may be awed, or deceived, in the end) must be popular laws; and the sum of popular laws must amount to a commonwealth.[4]

This sentence was published within a year of the restoration of the monarchy and therefore offered a handle to gibing critics, but few sentences written in the seventeenth century went deeper into the fundamental facts of the change that had taken place in England. For better or worse the landed gentry were in the saddle and no permanent settlement could fail to take account of that fact.

In Harrington's judgment the property which really counts in a political settlement is land. Undoubtedly he exaggerated the political weight of landownership and correspondingly underestimated the influence of manufacture, trade, and finance. He admitted that, in a very small state composed of merchants, such as Florence, money may outweigh land, but he believed this to be impossible in a country the size of England. In this he was right so far as his own time was concerned. But he had the point of view of a landowning class and so failed to see the importance that trade was assuming even in the England that he could observe. Thus his judgment that England would outstrip Holland commercially (which was right as to the fact) was based upon the belief that she would do so because of her ability to produce her own raw materials, which was certainly wrong in the event.

Upon his theory of the balance of landownership Harrington proceeded to make his own classification of the forms of government. He used here the traditional threefold classification into monarchy, aristocracy, and democracy, with the three corresponding perversions derived from Aristotle, but his revision was so original that it completely made over the tradition. His threefold classification consists of absolute monarchy, mixed or feudal monarchy, and the commonwealth, each depending on typical forms of land-tenure. If the king can keep the control of the land in his own hands, letting it out to a large number of small tenants

[4] *Art of Lawgiving, Works,* 1747, p. 432.

who can be forced to give military services to the king, the result is absolute monarchy, a government of the military type exemplified by Rome in the days of the imperial despots and by the Turkish Empire. When the land passes into the hands of a relatively small number of nobles, who control large bodies of their own retainers, a mixed monarchy results. This is inevitably a weak form of monarchy, because the king is dependent upon his great vassals, who tend to be rebellious, though their mutual rivalry prevents them from destroying the kingship outright. Finally, if the great feudal estates are broken up and the nobility are unable to support great troups of retainers, the foundation is laid for a commonwealth or popular form of government.

By means of this theory Harrington was able to sweep away entirely the vague notion of the " corruption " of a people which had bulked large in Machiavelli's thought and which was inherent in the old theory of a cycle of constitutions. The so-called corruption which turns a commonwealth into a monarchy is merely a change in the control of land. " The corruption of one government . . . is the generation of another." If there is moral change at the same time, this too results from a change in the ownership of property. Harrington's classification leaves room for what may be called " perverted " forms of government, but these are merely cases in which, for some temporary reason, a government exists which does not accord with the balance of property. In this sense the monarchy of Elizabeth was a perversion. There are also cases in which the balance of power is not decisive. If the land were about equally divided between nobility and commoners, stable government would be impossible unless one class could " eat out " the other. The plan offered a flexible, and comparatively a realistic, means of classifying governments.

THE EMPIRE OF LAW

Harrington, however, was not an economic materialist. Property is itself a legal institution and hence it is possible by law, not indeed to change radically the distribution of property, but to perpetuate a distribution favorable to a desired form of government. He attributed politics to two principles. The one is force, depending upon the distribution of property and limiting the possibilities of stable government but still leaving some room for choice. The second principle is "authority" which depends, as he says, upon the goods of the mind, such as wisdom, courage, and prudence. Wisdom or reason in an individual looks to the interest of the individual, and similarly wisdom in a commonwealth looks to the good of the whole body. Harrington would perhaps have been more consistent if he had treated authority or prudence as strictly relative to the form of government in which it must work, but he was influenced at this point by his very sincere republicanism. Broadly speaking he made the distinction between force and authority parallel to that between "ancient prudence," or the art of governing by law for the common good, and "modern prudence," or the art of exploiting the community in the interest of an individual or a class. Among modern writers he believed "ancient prudence" to be represented by Machiavelli and "modern prudence" by Hobbes. Since modern prudence begins with the decay of the Roman Republic, the contrast corresponds substantially to that between monarchy, whether absolute or mixed, and the commonwealth. Harrington shared the enthusiasm of the Renaissance for antiquity. His commonwealth was intended to approach as closely as possible to such ancient models as Athens, Sparta, Rome, and the Jewish state, all of which he considered to be popular governments within his meaning of the term.

The distinguishing mark of a commonwealth is that it is "an empire of laws and not of men." Hobbes, Harrington says, was guilty of mere confusion when he argued that, since all governments subject men to some control, the liberty of the subject is equal under every system of law. Harrington's distinction here is practically the same as that drawn by Aristotle between tyranny, which is personal and arbitrary, and constitutional government, which is according to law, in the public interest, and with the participation and consent of its subjects. All forms of government, including the commonwealth, require the coincidence of power with authority. No amount of wisdom can keep a government going smoothly unless political power and economic power fall together, but it is equally true that government does not flow spontaneously from a given economic arrangement. Like Aristotle and Machiavelli Harrington assumed that politics is an art. But the commonwealth, properly organized, is more truly a government of laws than monarchy and is also more stable. For absolute monarchy is essentially a government of men and feudal monarchy is a theater for the rivalry of king and the nobility. The commonwealth alone permits liberty under law and gives adequate scope for true statesmanship and public spirit. Harrington believed that men are intrinsically sociable and not selfish, but he was willing to put as little strain as possible upon unselfishness. True statecraft aims to make self-interest and public interest agree, and popular government most readily does this. Such a state Harrington called an " equal commonwealth." In this form of government those who have any interest in being seditious lack the power, and those who have the power lack the interest. Such a government ought to be permanent, so far as internal causes of decay are concerned.

The remainder of Harrington's political philosophy was devoted to an analysis of the means by which this end could be achieved. Logically the corner stone of the system must be the prevention of serious changes in the distribution of land, or in the case of a commonwealth, the prevention of its being concentrated in a few hands. Hence the importance attached by Harrington to his " agrarian law," which amounted merely to a rule requiring the division of large estates among several heirs in parts having not more than £2000 annual income. The law by which an estate was entailed upon the eldest male heir appeared to him both to endanger political equality and to violate every principle of justice.

> I marvel much how it comes to pass, that we should use our children, as we do our puppies; take one, lay it in the lap, feed it with every good bit, and drown five! [5]

However, he aimed not at the abstract injustice but at the social danger. Under the agrarian law which he proposed, if only one heir exists he may take the whole estate whatever its size, and if the estate is below the maximum it may be devised to a single heir. It is only the large estate to which there are several male heirs that must be divided. Harrington was not concerned to extend the popular ownership of land in England but to keep the *status quo*.

[5] *Oceana,* p. 94

> We do not now argue for that which we would have, but for that which we are already possessed of.[6]

He estimated that five thousand owners were enough to make England safely a commonwealth.

It is difficult to say how broadly based Harrington's popular government was intended to be. Citizenship he restricted to such as "live of their own," which excluded servants and wage-earners, and yet the figures which he used in his outline of government apparently assumed something like half a million citizens above the age of thirty. Accordingly, if he had any accurate conception of the population of England in his time, the excluded classes would have been negligibly small. At all events it was no part of his plan to limit political rights to landowners. His property qualification for the senate was low and he defended the payment of members in order to open it to poor men. On the other hand he took for granted an aristocratic leadership for the commonwealth.

> If any man have founded a commonwealth, he was first a gentleman.[7]

So long as the gentry are too numerous to form a nobility, they are not a threat to a commonwealth but its very life-blood. The choice of magistrates by election commended itself to Harrington because he supposed that it would draw upon the "natural aristocracy" of ability which belongs mainly to the gentry. He scouted the idea that popular government would be used as a means of levelling economic differences.

THE STRUCTURE OF THE COMMONWEALTH

When the foundation of a commonwealth has been laid in an agrarian law, there are three devices of statecraft for keeping government responsive to the popular will. The first is rotation in office, which Harrington compares to the circulation of the blood. Magistrates ought to be elected to office for short terms, usually a year, and ought to be ineligible to immediate reelection. Second, to secure a free choice by electors, election ought to be by ballot. Harrington devoted much space to elaborating a plan for secret voting, following devices which he says he had seen used in Venice. Third, in constructing a free government he thought it essential to secure a separation of powers. Harrington's division of political

[6] *Ibid.*, p. 93.

[7] *Ibid.*, p. 35.

powers, however, did not correspond precisely to that later made familiar by Montesquieu but followed a line suggested by his study of the city-state. The deliberative or policy-forming function he regarded as necessarily aristocratic, in the sense that it must be performed by a few persons who have experience and expert knowledge. The acceptance or rejection of a proposed policy he regarded as a popular function which ought to be performed by a large body elected for that purpose and having no power to deliberate. Rather curiously, in view of English experience just prior to the civil wars, he had nothing to say about the independence of the judiciary.

An agrarian law, rotation in office, the ballot, and the separation of powers are the structural principles of what Harrington called an "equal commonwealth," in which he believed that the interest and the power for sedition could never be united. He defined it as follows:

> An equal commonwealth . . . is a government established upon an equal Agrarian, arising into the superstructure or three orders, the senate debating and proposing, the people resolving, and the magistracy executing by an equal rotation through the suffrage of the people given by the ballot.[8]

Not content with principles, however, he proceeded to work out a constitution for Great Britain, giving his principles detailed application. This elaboration was chiefly responsible for his reputation as a utopian. He took a childish pleasure in drawing the details of the picture, even down to the dates and hours when his assemblies should meet and the clothes which his officials should wear. In fact these fanciful details had little to do with the principles of his philosophy. The doctrinaire part of his thought was his faith in the efficacy of political machinery, and in this respect he did not differ much from his contemporaries. It is strange that a man who saw as far as he did into the economic causes of political power should still have placed so much reliance upon apparatus.

Harrington's constitution begins by dividing the whole people into freemen, who are citizens, and servants. The citizens are then divided on the basis of age into the active military class, who are under thirty, and the elders, who form a military reserve

[8] *Ibid.*, p. 33.

and also the civil " orb " of the commonwealth. They are further divided according to wealth into cavalry and infantry, corresponding roughly to gentry and common people. The plan of government is an elaborate scheme of indirect representation. The smallest local unit is the parish, in which all the elders elect one-fifth of their number to be deputies to the next larger unit, a group of parishes totaling about a hundred deputies. Twenty hundreds combine to form a tribe. The parishes, the hundreds, and the tribes all elect their local magistrates, and in addition each tribe elects two knights each year to the senate and seven representatives (three knights and four commoners) to the " Prerogative Tribe," which functions as the people in enacting legislation. The terms are three years, and since there are fifty tribes, the senate consists of three hundred members, one hundred retiring each year, and the people of ten hundred and fifty, three hundred and fifty retiring each year. The senate elects the chief magistrates and also four councils — on state, war, religion, and trade — in which business mainly originates. In accordance with the division of powers, the function of the senate is debate. After it has formulated legislation or policy, its proposals are printed and transmitted to the people or prerogative tribe, which decides, either by enacting or rejecting or returning the measure to the council for further consideration, but cannot itself debate or amend.

Implicit in Harrington's scheme of government but not clearly stated were the constitutional ideas, already familiar in the seventeenth century, of a written instrument of government, an extraordinary legislative body for constitution-making, and the distinction between statutory and constitutional law. Writing in 1656, he necessarily addressed his plan to Cromwell, whom he clothed in the glamor of a mythical lawgiver. What he wished Cromwell to do was to set up a council of statesmen and scholars to formulate a new government, everyone being free to carry their proposals to the council. Once formulated the constitution was to be promulgated by articles each dealing with some important element of the structure. Harrington nowhere discussed the amendment of this constitution, but it seems clear that he meant to distinguish between its provisions and ordinary acts of the legislature.

In dealing with the thorny problem of religious freedom Harrington tried to effect a compromise between congregationalism and a national church. Some form of national religious establishment he believed to be necessary, both to provide decent stipends for the clergy and to maintain forms of worship in accord with the national conscience. He was opposed, however, to any form of coercion, which he regarded as the cause of "that execrable custom, never known in the world before, of fighting for religion and denying the magistrate to have any jurisdiction of it."[9] Hence he believed that each congregation might be left free to choose its own clergyman and that other forms of worship besides those established by law might be permitted, except in the case of Jews and Catholics. He desired also a national system of schools, supported at public expense and free to indigent students, at which attendance should be compulsory between the ages of nine and fifteen.

Despite the fanciful form of Harrington's republic, he combined in it a surprising number of the devices that later came to be thought typical of liberal government. The written constitution, the election of magistrates, the use of the ballot, short terms and rotation, the separation of powers, guarantees of religious freedom, and popular education at public expense are illustrations of the point. Yet Harrington was emphatically not a democrat either in purpose or theory. The leadership of the commonwealth he believed to be safely in the hands of the landed gentry, and the superiority of this class, both in power and capacity, he treated as axiomatic. His theory of economic causation excluded a democratic ideal such as that of the Levellers, which presumed a separation of political rights from the rights of property. Harrington's political ideal was the ancient republic under aristocratic auspices and in this respect he agreed with all republicans of his time. He stood alone, however, in emphasizing the dependence of forms of government on the distribution of wealth, and his explanation of the origin of the civil wars was probably the most realistic piece of social theorizing that was produced. Harrington was right in believing that the rise to power of the landed gentry was the fundamental social fact of the age, but a better understanding of English trade might have suggested to him that the

[9] *Ibid.*, p. 38.

equalizing of landholdings was no adequate means of perpetuating their power. The extension of trade was quite incompatible with anything like economic equality. Had he seen this, he would have been logically obliged either to look for more drastic kinds of political control over wealth or to alter his whole conception of popular government.

JOHN MILTON

The republicanism of John Milton and Algernon Sidney was less original and less important than that of Harrington. The connecting link between the three men was their admiration for antiquity and their idealization of the aristocratic republic. Milton and Sidney had no such knowledge of political history and comparative institutions as Harrington and no such grasp of the social causes of political change. With them republicanism was a moral ideal based on the abstract ground of natural right and justice. Neither made any significant addition to political ideas generally familiar in the seventeenth century. Milton's tracts are chiefly memorable for the magnificence of the literary form in which he clothed ideas already known to everyone and for the eloquence in which he embodied a noble political ideal. Sidney's rather rambling and ill-constructed book would perhaps hardly have been noticed, had it not been written in a peculiarly lean period of English political thought and had it not become the occasion of one of Jeffrey's most celebrated judicial atrocities.

Of all Milton's tracts the most memorable is the *Areopagitica* (1644), his defense of freedom of publication. Though it apparently received little notice when it was written,[10] it has become, together with John Stuart Mill's essay *On Liberty*, the classic argument for free speech in the English language. Milton stated once for all the faith of intellectual liberalism, that truth will prevail over error when both may be freely tested by investigation and discussion:

> And though all the winds of doctrine were let loose to play upon the earth, so truth be in the field, we do injuriously by licensing and prohibiting to misdoubt her strength. Let her and falsehood grapple; who ever knew truth put to the worse, in a free and open encounter. . . . For who

[10] See *Tracts on Liberty in the Puritan Revolution, 1638–1647,* ed. by William Haller, Vol. I, Appendix B.

knows not that truth is strong next to the Almighty; she needs no policies, nor stratagems, nor licensings to make her victorious, those are the shifts and defenses that error uses against her power.[11]

Hence Milton could do what few men of his age could do: he could look with equanimity on the multiplication of sects and parties as experiments in the search for new truth and new freedom. His defense of religious toleration was limited by the prejudices of his age and his party. It did not extend to Roman Catholics, partly because he thought them idolaters and partly because he thought them incapable of loyalty to any ruler save the pope. But even with this limitation the *Areopagitica* is the finest argument ever written against the stupidities and futilities of censorship.

Milton's fame as a publicist came mainly after his appointment in 1649 to the secretaryship of the Council of State for the Commonwealth. Already in his *Tenure of Kings and Magistrates* he had defended the execution of Charles, especially against the Presbyterians, who had begun to repent the lengths to which the Revolution had gone. This was followed in 1649 by the *Eikonoklastes* and in 1651 by the *Defensio pro populo Anglicano,* written in reply to Salmasius of Leyden, who had been employed by the royalists to write a defense of the king. These works contain an outspoken defense of the death penalty for a tyrannous king, proved from natural law, from Scripture, and from the law of England. He presented his case so powerfully that the *Defensio* was compared with Cromwell's army as a bulwark of the Commonwealth. No writer was better qualified to express the enthusiastic idealism of the Revolution:

And here I cannot but congratulate myself upon our ancestors, who founded this state with no less prudence and liberty than did the most excellent of the ancient Romans or Grecians; and they likewise, if they have any knowledge of our affairs, cannot but congratulate themselves upon their posterity, who, when almost reduced to slavery, yet with such wisdom and courage reclaimed that state, so wisely founded upon so much liberty, from a king's outrageous despotism.[12]

Milton's argument in substance does nothing more than assert the ancient principle that resistance to a tyrant is a natural right.

[11] *Works,* ed. by F. A. Patterson, Vol. IV. pp. 347 f.

[12] *Defensio prima,* ch. VIII, Eng. trans. by Wolff; *Works,* Vol. VII, p. 451.

In the *Tenure* he argued that men are born free and set up governments for the sake of mutual defense. Public authority takes the place of each man's right to protect himself and the law is set up to limit and control public authority. The magistrate's power is derived from the people for the public good, and hence the right to protect the common good against a tyrant must always reside in the people.

> The power of kings and magistrates is nothing else, but what is only derivative, transferred and committed to them in trust from the people, to the common good of them all, in whom the power yet remains fundamentally, and cannot be taken from them, without a violation of their natural birthright.[13]

The king has no indefeasible right but may be deposed as often as the people see fit. It is perfectly lawful to kill a tyrant, whether a usurper or a legitimate ruler. The argument is supported by the usual citations to the Protestant reformers, especially Knox and Buchanan.

In respect to the religious question Milton's views were those of the most advanced Independents.[14] Constraint in matters of belief and the support of the clergy from public revenues he regarded as the chief causes of religious corruption. He not only accepted the Protestant principle that Scripture is the rule of faith but he gave it the broadest interpretation: every man must interpret Scripture for himself. No man can know that he is perfectly right, and hence neither a magistrate nor a church should enforce belief in a particular interpretation. Individual conscience is the court of last resort and no sincere believer is a heretic. The church is concerned only with the spiritual man, who cannot be enlightened by force, while the state is concerned only with outward acts. The two institutions are distinct in nature and purpose and therefore ought to be severed. Nothing but corruption follows if the clergy look to government for their support and not to the voluntary contributions of those who profit by their teaching. Church and state are therefore two distinct societies, with no community of membership or purpose. Such a

[13] *Works,* Vol. V, p. 10.

[14] *A Treatise of Civil Power in Ecclesiastical Causes* and *Considerations touching the Likeliest Means to Remove Hirelings out of the Church,* both published in 1659.

separation, operating equally in both directions, was quite different both in theory and practice from that for which Hooker had criticised Presbyterians and Catholics. Milton's conclusion was practically the same as that to which Independency had brought Roger Williams some twenty years before in his controversy with the theocracy in Massachusetts. On the eve of the Restoration it was far from realizable in England.

Behind Milton's republicanism lay a vague Platonic principle that the real justification of authority is moral and intellectual superiority. "Nature appoints that wise men should govern fools." Hereditary power is therefore unnatural. In his last political pamphlet, *The Ready and Easy Way to Establish a Free Commonwealth,* published in 1660 immediately before the Restoration, he even expressed a doubt whether Jesus himself had not put "the brand of Gentilism upon kingship." This tract was a last despairing cry against monarchy, written when Milton must have known that the Restoration was inevitable. In it he faces the wreck of all the noble aspirations for which he had believed the Revolution stood.

> That a nation should be so valorous and courageous to win their liberty in the field, and when they have won it, should be so heartless and unwise in their counsels, as not to know how to use it, value it, what to do with it, or with themselves; but after ten or twelve years prosperous war and contestation with tyranny, basely and besottedly to run their necks again into the yoke which they have broken . . . will be an ignominy if it befall us, that never yet befell any nation possessed of their liberty.[15]

Yet nothing illustrates so well as this pamphlet — Milton's chief effort in constructive politics — the failure of his ideals to articulate with reality. His "ready and easy way" was in fact a fantastic impossibility. All he had to propose was that the people should lay aside their prejudices and selfish interests and elect the "best men" of the nation to a perpetual council in which the members shall hold office for life. The pamphlet is a curious mixture of doctrinaire faith in the "best men" and of distrust for the electorate which must choose any council, permanent or periodic. Milton merely assumed that the one election which he desired would work well but that all others, which he did not desire, would work badly. With a real passion for individual liberty

[15] *Works,* ed. by Mitford, Vol. V., p. 431.

he united contempt for the intelligence and good will of men in the mass. A native fastidiousness of mind made him instinctively an aristocrat, and he despised parliaments as much as he despised kings. He wholly failed to see that individual liberty is an impracticable ideal if men are unfit to be trusted with a voice in government. Like all who idealize the early stages of a revolution as a new birth of civilization, he was ill-prepared to face the realities of its last stage.

FILMER AND SIDNEY

Algernon Sidney's republicanism was in all important respects like that of Milton. With the Restoration in 1660 the active discussion of politics in England died down, after producing in the preceding two decades two great classics, the *Leviathan* of Hobbes and the *Oceana* of Harrington, besides a host of controversial tracts covering every phase of political philosophy and constitutional theory. It was not until the approaching death of Charles II made imminent a Catholic succession that the old issue of hereditary right against the right of parliament reappeared. James's hereditary claim was sound and quite in accord with royalist principles, but his succession without proper safeguards for Protestantism filled most Englishmen with apprehension. When the issue began to be apparent, the royalists put forward the strangely antiquated figure of Sir Robert Filmer, who had died in 1653 after writing a number of royalist pamphlets almost unnoticed at the time. A volume of these was reprinted in 1679, and the next year his best-known work, *Patriarcha or the Natural Power of Kings,* was printed for the first time. This work has enjoyed a posthumous fame because it was refuted in detail by Sidney and Locke. Sidney's *Discourses Concerning Government* was written between 1680 and 1683 but was not published until 1698, a belated act of piety like parliament's repeal of his attainder in 1689. Sidney was executed in 1683 for complicity in the Rye House Plot, his papers, including the *Discourses,* being used against him. The indictment cited sentences saying that the king is subject to law, is responsible to the people, and may be deposed, as a " false, seditious, and traitorous libel."

Certainly nothing in Filmer's *Patriarcha* was so significant as the fact that it was first published in 1680. That the case for indefeasible hereditary right had to be presented in a book that had lain forgotten in manuscript for nearly thirty years, and a book so easily made to appear absurd, shows how little vitality the issue had. In truth Filmer's book was an anachronism even when it was written. It was a polemic against the two enemies of royal power, the Jesuits and the Calvinists, by whom "Monarchy hath been crucified between two thieves, the pope and the people," and it attempted to restate the two royalist principles, divine right and the duty of passive obedience. But Filmer adopted the dangerous tactics of carrying the war into the enemy's country. Instead of relying on Scriptural authority, he tried to prove that the king's power is "natural," and to do this he derived it from the natural authority of parents. In short, Adam was the first king and "present kings are, or are to be reputed, next heir to him." The feebleness of this "are to be reputed" was lost on none of Filmer's critics. Since there can be by primogeniture only one present heir to Adam and since no one knows who he is, the conclusion ought to be that every king's power is unlawful. The tiresome persistence with which Sidney and Locke follow this obvious argument merely shows that an absurd conclusion is a godsend which no controversialist has the heart to overlook.

It is mere justice to Filmer, however, to say that, had he not been whipping a dead horse, his critics would not have had all the advantage on their side. They were committed to the theory that political power resides in "the people" and that governments arise only by their consent. Filmer easily showed that these statements, if supposed to be literally true, are as absurd as any ever uttered. For who are the people? If they are the whole population, when did they enter into a contract and how can they consent to anything? And if consent be taken literally, how can there be any limits to faction? In these arguments, curiously enough, Filmer borrowed a good deal from Hobbes whom he esteemed highly. The people, he insisted, are a "headless multitude," so many units of population, while conceptions like representation, election, and majority-rule are meaningless except in a legal community. To form a community there must be a sovereign. Had Filmer not discredited himself with his absurd argument about the royal power of Adam, he might have been a rather formidable critic. He had quite as good a grasp of English constitutional history as Sidney or Locke,[16] and like most men who are known only by what their critics say of them, he was by no means so foolish as he has been made to appear.

Apparently Sidney never intended to publish the *Discourses* and despite the esteem in which it was later held, for example by Thomas Jefferson, it is not in fact an effective book. It follows Filmer, expanding every objection into a short discourse until all sense of direction is lost. It might have made an effective pamphlet of a tenth its size. There is not an original idea in it. The argument against Filmer merely recited the familiar propositions: all peoples have a natural right to govern themselves; they can choose their rulers as they see fit; government derives its power from the people; it exists for their safety and well-being and may be held accountable for these ends. In England, Sidney held, " Parliament and people have the power of making kings," but he also believed that the power of parliament is delegated and may be revoked in some unspecified way.

According to Bishop Burnet, Sidney was " stiff to all republican principles," and presumably he was so in the days of the Commonwealth, but there is nothing in the *Discourses* really incompatible with constitutional monarchy. Certainly he believed that elected representatives were less likely to be corrupt than the favorites of a prince. Like Milton, whom he greatly resembled, he admired the aristocratic republic and imagined that election is a way of selecting the " best men " to govern. Like Milton also he idealized the Commonwealth and looked back to it as an age of noble achievement in which for a moment English liberty reached a height equal to the great days of Greece and Rome. Perhaps in 1680, after twenty years of the Stuart Restoration, Sidney had an excuse which Milton lacked in 1660 for seeing Cromwell's thinly veiled dictatorship through a rosy mist. He was most effective when he loosed his righteous indignation on the systematized bribery and disreputable intrigues which, as a republican, he believed the monarchy had brought from France " since His Majesty's happy restoration." Let men examine, he says,

16 See his *Freeholders Grand Inquest touching Our Sovereign Lord the King and his Parliament.*

whether bawds, whores, thieves, buffoons, parasites, and such vile wretches as are naturally mercenary, have not more power at Whitehall, Versailles, the Vatican, and the Escurial, than in Venice, Amsterdam, and Switzerland: whether Hide, Arlington, Danby, their graces of Cleveland and Portsmouth, Sunderland, Jenkins, or Chiffinch, could probably have attained such power as they have had amongst us, if it had been disposed of by the suffrages of the parliament and people.[17]

The importance of English republicanism in the seventeenth century is not easy to sum up. On one side it was hopelessly doctrinaire, since the abolition of the monarchy was never a real issue, was temporarily forced only by circumstances, and by its association with Cromwell's dictatorship was soon discredited. In Milton and Sidney it reflected mainly a mood of enthusiastic idealism but without the rugged force possessed by the abstractly similar philosophy of the Levellers. Republicanism in the seventeenth century was essentially an aristocratic doctrine and not at all a general proclamation of the rights of man such as the political program of the Levellers suggested. For Milton and Sidney "the people" was still a community led by a natural élite, not at all a mass of equal individuals endowed with innate rights. It is true that the actual settlement of the Revolution, by placing the country gentry in a position of power, was far more aristocratic than democratic, but this settlement was in no way related to republicanism. The gentry made their peace easily enough with the monarchy after the latter became dependent on parliament. For this reason republicanism as such was never a live issue. Harrington's economic analysis was not doctrinaire but it had no close logical relation to his republicanism. Had he not happened to write during the Commonwealth, he could easily have adapted it to a constitutional monarchy.

SELECTED BIBLIOGRAPHY

Milton and the Puritan Dilemma, 1641–1660. By Arthur Barker. Toronto, 1942.

"Harrington and his Influence upon American Political Institutions and Political Thought." By Theodore W. Dwight. In *Pol. Sci. Quar.*, Vol. II (1887), p. 1.

[17] *Discourses*, ed. by J. Toland, 1763, p. 205.

The Life and Times of the Hon. Algernon Sydney, 1622–1683. By A. C. Ewald. 2 vols. London, 1873.

The Classical Republicans: An Essay in the Recovery of a Pattern of Thought in Seventeenth-century England. By Zera S. Fink. Northwestern University Studies in the Humanities. Evanston, Illinois, 1945.

Political Thought in England from Bacon to Halifax. By G. P. Gooch. London, 1914. Ch. 5.

The History of English Democratic Ideas in the Seventeenth Century. By G. P. Gooch. 2nd ed. Cambridge, 1927.

Milton and Wordsworth, Poets and Prophets: A Study of their Reactions to Political Events. By Sir Herbert J. C. Grierson. Cambridge, 1937.

The Rise of Puritanism: or, The Way to the New Jerusalem as set forth in Pulpit and Press from Thomas Cartwright to John Lilburne and John Milton, 1570–1643. By William Haller. New York, 1938.

The Social and Political Ideas of some Great Thinkers of the Sixteenth and Seventeenth Centuries. Ed. by F. J. C. Hearnshaw. London, 1926. Ch. 8.

The Social and Political Ideas of some English Thinkers of the Augustan Age, A.D. 1650–1750. Ed. by F. J. C. Hearnshaw. London, 1928. Ch. 2.

"A Historical Sketch of Liberty and Equality as Ideals of English Political Philosophy from the Time of Hobbes to the Time of Coleridge." By F. W. Maitland. In *Collected Papers.* 3 vols. Cambridge, 1911. Vol. I, p. 1.

Milton's Contemporary Reputation. By William R. Parker. Columbus, Ohio, 1940.

Milton in the Puritan Revolution. By Don M. Wolfe. New York, 1941.

CHAPTER XXVI

HALIFAX AND LOCKE

The final act in the drama of English politics in the seventeenth century came with climactic suddenness in the bloodless Revolution of 1688. The ill-judged efforts of James II to foster catholicism touched Protestant opinion in England as the stupidities and degradation of Restoration government had not, for this question was settled. The bulk of Englishmen were unchangeably Protestant and after a brief experience with James were ready to decide that Protestant supremacy was essential. The speed and ease with which the " Glorious Revolution " was accomplished, though helped along by the incomparable fatuity of James, showed that more than Protestantism was settled. It laid the ghost of republicanism, if indeed that ghost was still able to walk, for no one worth mentioning wished to try again the sad experiment of the Commonwealth. England was to be a monarchy, but a monarchy controlled by parliament upon lines fixed by the results of the civil wars. After the settlement of the succession in William and Mary there could never again be a doubt that the crown was in the keeping of parliament, if it chose to exert itself. English government thus settled into the form which it kept for upwards of a hundred years, and without the reforms of representation which seemed inevitable in 1650. It was, indeed, a crass form of class-government, which in the course of the eighteenth century developed some of the worst abuses of class-government, but still it was after its fashion representative, and in comparison with any other European government it might be called liberal. The principles of this settlement were summed up by the two most enlightened Englishmen of their generation, the statesman George Savile, First Marquis of Halifax, and the philosopher John Locke.

Though the threat of a Catholic dynasty probably occasioned the Revolution, the settlement closed a chapter in the relations of religion and politics. Never again would the two be united as they had been since the Protestant Reformation. The Toleration Act was the only practicable basis for permanent peace between the churches, and though the Test Act survived to become a curiosity of English legislation, the injustice to Catholics and Dissenters was far different from persecution. Nothing is clearer in the political thought of Halifax and Locke than the recession of doctrinal and ecclesiastical questions from the position of dominant interest which they had held. Locke as a young man had hoped for a policy of "comprehension" in the English church itself, and when this hope was defeated he turned to a theory of almost universal toleration and of practical separation between church and state. Something not too remote from this was achieved in England by the Revolution, and more and more it became the accepted solution everywhere of this ancient problem. The whole intellectual temper of both Locke and Halifax was secular to a degree that would have been practically impossible fifty years before. The contrast even with Hobbes was striking. Though he had been perhaps as nearly non-religious as any man that ever lived, he had devoted half of *Leviathan* to the problem of *imperium* and *sacerdotium*. Locke, whose personal life was a distillation of the best qualities of Puritanism, was able to pass the whole question over except as it affected his argument for toleration. Both Halifax and Locke belonged in this respect to the eighteenth rather than the seventeenth century: they could meet theological dispute with the deadliest weapon, indifference. Personally religious and ethically Christian, Locke was profoundly reasonable and anti-dogmatic.

The same qualities of mind are discernible in the political theories of both Halifax and Locke. In both, common sense counts for more than logic. Both were cautious and willing to remain conservative where circumstances permitted. Both were in a marked degree pragmatic and compromising, not inclined to argue over much with what they took to be accomplished fact but inclined rather to accept and make the best of it. Halifax perhaps came nearer than any man in the seventeenth century to making this frame of mind a working political hypothesis. No man had a greater distrust of large generalizations or a prettier wit for pricking bubbles. With characteristic irony and perhaps with a shade of gentlemanly indifference to careful thinking, he let himself off the hard task of making a positive theory; he was enlightened and penetrating in the highest degree, but he was essentially an empiric and a skeptic. To a philosopher like Locke this easy-going distrust of generalization was not possible. He too was an empiricist but with a large residue of philosophic rationalism and a firm belief in self-evident principles of right and wrong. Unfortunately common sense is a poor organ for synthetizing really opposed philosophical positions. The result in Locke was a series of compromises which always left the first principles unclear. It is true that his compromises satisfied nearly everyone for upwards of a half century and that by common sense he grasped firmly the fundamental ethical ideal of the English settlement, that of individual rights. Yet his compromises went far to conceal the insufficiencies both of the ideal itself and of its realization in eighteenth-century England. As a consequence later political thought was related to Locke in a highly complex fashion.

HALIFAX

What chiefly impressed Halifax's [1] inquiring and skeptical mind is the fact that there are few if any general principles that hold good of government. It is, as he says, a "coarse thing," made up mostly of expedients and compromises, with hardly a proposition in it that is "not deceitful." A loud profession of principles is usually a pretense to cloak the pursuit of private or partisan advantage. What men choose to call "fundamentals," he says, is

> a nail everybody would use to fix that which is good for them; for all men would have that principle to be immovable that serves their use at the time.[2]
>
> Fundamental is a word used by the laity, as the word sacred is by the clergy, to fix everything to themselves they have a mind to keep, that nobody else may touch it.[3]

[1] Halifax's works have been edited by Walter Raleigh, Oxford, 1912; they are printed also in H. C. Foxcroft's *Life and Letters of Sir George Savile, Bart., First Marquis of Halifax,* 2 vols., London, 1898. His most important essays are "The Character of a Trimmer," written in 1684 and first printed in 1688; "A Rough Draught of a New Model at Sea," published in 1694 from an essay first written much earlier; and "The Anatomy of an Equivalent," 1688. All were occasional pieces.

[2] Foxcroft, Vol. II, p. 492.

[3] *Ibid.*, p. 497.

Nothing is more certain than that every human institution will change and the so-called fundamentals of government with them. The divine right of kings, the indefeasible rights of property or persons, and laws which may not be repealed or modified are all attempts to bind the future; they neither can nor ought to be effective. Laws and constitutions, he says, are made not once but a hundred times. In themselves they can do little and in the end they mean just what those who interpret and administer and enforce them intend them to mean. The common law, he says, with evident reference to Coke, " hovers in the clouds," except as it is set in motion by a court or an executive, and then it becomes whatever the execution of the court's judgment makes of it. In the last resort law and government depend upon the intelligence and good will of the persons who conduct them. Abstractions count for something, but concrete interests and forces for much. Government as Halifax envisaged it was mainly the business of a ruling class, but of an intelligent and public spirited class. Its chief virtue is to be a practicable compromise between power and liberty, capable of expanding to meet an emergency, adaptable to changing circumstances, strong enough to keep the peace but liberal enough to avoid repression.

Despite this emphasis on the personnel of government, Halifax had too much experience of affairs to imagine that a government could do as it liked. Behind the government is the nation, and nations make governments, not contrariwise. A people who loses its king is still a people, but a king who loses his people is no longer a king. There is in every nation a supreme power that alters the constitution as often as the good of the people requires. Some such principle of national life and self-preservation — which Halifax frankly admits he cannot define or forecast — is the nearest thing to a fundamental known to politics.

> There is a natural reason of state, an undefinable thing, grounded upon the common good of mankind, which is immortal, and in all changes and revolutions, still preserveth its original right of saving a nation, when the letter of the law perhaps would destroy it.[4]

This inherent power of self-development in a people will not and ought not to be curbed. The real power of a government depends upon its responsiveness to this internal drive. Without

[4] *Trimmer* (ed. by Raleigh), p. 60.

it neither constitutions nor force can long prevail. In this very general sense all government depends upon consent. A representative body is the best practicable device for giving voice to a nation's aspirations, but Halifax clearly regarded it as only a device. For practical purposes there must be room also for an indefinable power of leadership, a kind of omnipotence for great occasions, by which "a nation may at some critical times be secured from ruin."

It is upon this basis of expediency and national history that Halifax constructed his estimate of the crisis in England. Abstractly, he says in his *New Model at Sea,* there are three possibilities. One would be absolute monarchy — he was thinking of France — which, he admits, has some advantages in unity and speed of execution. But it destroys the "competent state of freedom" in which men ought to live, and in any event it is impossible in England both because of the national tradition and because England's greatness must lie in trade, which is "the creature of liberty." A second possibility, which might be theoretically preferable to monarchy, would be a commonwealth, but the invincible objection is that Englishmen do not like it. Monarchy is perhaps a thing of "bells and tinsel," but the fact remains that England's one experiment with a commonwealth ended in military dictatorship. The one remaining and the only real possibility, therefore, is a "mixed monarchy," a constitutional government divided between king and parliament. Halifax was well content with the choice, for such government, he thought, gives the best compromise between power and liberty. It is a mean between absolute monarchy and commonwealth:

> We take from one the too great power of doing hurt, and yet leave enough to govern and protect us; we take from the other, the confusion, the parity, the animosities, and the license, and yet reserve a due care of such a liberty, as may consist with men's allegiance.[5]

Parliaments may be troublesome but they give great strength to a wise administration.

In two respects, however, Halifax failed to understand the machinery of the new government. He did not see that ministers must become dependent on parliament and responsible to it, instead of being the personal choice of the monarch. Probably no

[5] *Ibid.,* p. 54.

one could have seen this until the course of parliamentary history made it plain, and Halifax died before the evidence was fairly in. Very naturally, therefore, he failed to see also that political parties had become an inherent part of parliamentary government. His judgment of parties was markedly hostile, an attitude due in part to his experience with the disreputable cabals of the Restoration and the intransigent factions of the revolutionary period, but also to a fastidiousness of temper that made it hard for him to cooperate when he could not control. A party he judged to be at the best a kind of conspiracy against the rest of the nation, and party-discipline he felt to be incompatible with liberty of private opinion. This low estimate of political parties was typical until the publication of Burke's *Present Discontents* in 1770.

Halifax's political acumen surpassed that of every other English statesman of his age. Probably most historians would now agree with Macaulay's assertion that "through frequent and violent revolutions of public feeling, he almost invariably took that view of the great questions of his time which history has finally adopted." He had, to be sure, almost no political theory; almost he said that no political theory was possible. Certainly none was possible for him in terms of the absolute rights and obligations — the strong blacks and whites with no grays — that the seventeenth century characteristically loved. In this qualifying temper, this willingness to compromise, this readiness to judge in terms of expedience, lay the note of the eighteenth century. His onslaught on "fundamentals," side by side with Locke's attack on innate ideas, was the antecedent to Hume's empirical criticism of the theory of natural rights. His emphasis upon expedience as an ever-present factor in political adjustment was introductory to ethical and political utilitarianism, which was the only live social philosophy in England throughout most of the eighteenth century and which attained its mature influence only in the philosophical radicalism of Bentham and the Mills. Thus Halifax, though he would not have been flattered by being called a philosopher, displayed an intellectual temper which became an integral part of philosophy.

LOCKE: THE INDIVIDUAL AND THE COMMUNITY

The political philosophy of John Locke wore the guise of an occasional performance. It was contained in two essays published in 1690 with the avowed purpose of defending the Revolution,[6] and of these essays the first, which was devoted to the refutation of Filmer, had no permanent importance. In fact, however, the second treatise was far from being merely a tract for the times; it reached back into the past, right across the whole period of the civil wars, and joined hands with Hooker's *Ecclesiastical Polity,* which had summed up the political thought of England at the close of the Reformation and before the break between parliament and the king. Through Hooker Locke was joined with the long tradition of medieval political thought, back to St. Thomas, in which the reality of moral restraints on power, the responsibility of rulers to the communities which they ruled, and the subordination of government to law were axiomatic. It was not that Locke was in any sense an antiquarian. The chief mark of his genius was neither learning nor logic but an incomparable common sense by which he gathered together the chief convictions, in philosophy, politics, morals, and education, that the experience of the past had generated in the more enlightened minds of his generation. By giving to these a simple and sober yet persuasive statement, he passed them on to the eighteenth century, where they became the matrix from which grew the later political philosophy both of England and the Continent. The medieval tradition, which Locke tapped through Hooker, was an indispensable part of the constitutional ideals of the Revolution of 1688. The years of the civil wars had changed but had not destroyed it. Locke's problem, therefore, was not to reproduce historically the thought of Hooker but to gather together anew the abiding elements of that thought and to restate them in the light of what had happened in the intervening century.

Of all the figures in this intervening century incomparably the most important for the development of a consistent political theory had been Thomas Hobbes. Hobbes, with his clear-cut proof

[6] *Two Treatises of Government.* His *Letter concerning Toleration* was published in 1689, the *Second Letter* in 1690, and the *Third Letter* in 1692. But Locke had written (not published) on toleration as early as 1667; see H. R. Fox Bourne's *Life of John Locke,* Vol. I, p. 174.

of the logical necessity of political absolutism, was the opponent whom Locke must refute if he was to set up an equally clear theory of constitutional government, and in fact the second treatise *Of Civil Government* was meant to refute Hobbes upon lines suggested by Hooker. It is most unfortunate that Locke did not assume the full obligation thus laid upon him. Had he done so, he would have been compelled to go much deeper into the principles of society and government than he ever did, and this would have tended to save him from the confusions which abound below the surface of his superficially simple theory. For the sake of the immediate effect it was more advantageous to flog poor Filmer, who had the merit of being absurd and of appearing more absurd than he was. Locke quite failed to discriminate Filmer's absurdities from his solid arguments, which for the most part were derived from Hobbes. The greatest weakness of Locke's philosophy in all its branches was that he never got back to first principles. His common sense saved him perhaps from many dialectical quibbles, but in the end it meant that he took much for granted on inadequate analysis and combined propositions that analysis showed to be incompatible.

So far as concerns his political philosophy, the gist of the issue may be stated as follows. The medieval tradition that reached Locke through Hooker, and the constitutional ideals followed in the settlement of 1688, held that government — the king specifically but not less parliament itself and every political agency — is responsible to the people or the community which it governs; its power is limited both by moral law and by the constitutional traditions and conventions inherent in the history of the realm. Government is indispensable and its right is therefore in a sense indefeasible, but it is also derivative in the sense that it exists for the well-being of the nation. This argument clearly presumes the corporate or social reality of the community, not a difficult assumption in an age when society was regulated by custom and in any event a settled principle of the medieval Aristotelianism which inspired Hooker. The main result of Hobbes's analysis, however, had been to show that a community as such is a pure fiction, that it has no existence except in the cooperation of its members, that this cooperation is always due to advantages enjoyed by its members individually, and that it becomes a community only because some individual is able to exercise sovereign power. Upon this analysis Hobbes had based his conclusion that subjection is unavoidable in any form of government, and that ideas such as contract, representation, and responsibility are meaningless unless backed by a sovereign's power. Hence they are valid within the state but not for the state.

The logical opposition between these two points of view is extreme. The first is stated in terms of functions. It conceives both individuals and institutions as doing a socially valuable work, regulated by government for the good of all, and within the framework of the law which makes the group a community. The second is stated in terms of individual self-satisfaction. It conceives society as composed of persons actuated by selfish motives, looking to law and government for security against their equally selfish fellows, and seeking the largest amount of private good consistent with keeping the peace. If Locke could have adopted either point of view and rejected the other, he would have been more consistent than he was. The circumstances under which he wrote required him to adopt both, and this ought to have entailed an examination of principles and a synthesis of the highest order. It was in fact a task that exceeded Locke's powers. His defense of the Revolution was practically upon the lines marked out by Hooker and already adopted in substance by Halifax. It assumes that the English people forms a social group persisting continuously through the changes of government required by its political evolution and setting moral standards which its rulers must respect. On the other hand, there were urgent reasons why Locke had to adopt into his social philosophy a large part of Hobbes's premises. With or without Hobbes's systematically egoistic psychology a theory of society in terms of individual interests was in Locke's day a foregone conclusion. The whole drift of the theory of natural law was in this direction and to this tendency Locke made no small contribution. For he interpreted natural law as a claim to innate, indefeasible rights inherent in each individual. Of such rights that of private property is the typical case. Consequently his theory was by implication as egoistic as that of Hobbes. Both government and society exist to preserve the individual's rights, and the indefeasibility of such rights is a limitation on the authority of both. In one part of

Locke's theory, therefore, the individual and his rights figure as ultimate principles; in another society itself plays this part. There is nothing which adequately explains how both can be absolute.

THE NATURAL RIGHT TO PROPERTY

The portion of Hobbes's political theory which Locke selected for explicit attack was the description of the state of nature as a war of every man against every man. He held on the contrary that the state of nature is one of "peace, good will, mutual assistance and preservation." This is defended on the ground that the law of nature provides a complete equipment of human rights and duties. The defect of the state of nature lies merely in the fact that it has no organization, such as magistrates, written law, and fixed penalties, to give effect to the rules of right. Everything that is ever right or wrong is so eternally; positive law adds nothing to the ethical quality of different kinds of conduct but merely provides an apparatus for effective enforcement. In the state of nature every man must protect his own as best he can, but his right to his own and his duty to respect what is another's are as complete as ever they can become under government. It will be noted that this is exactly the ground that Thomas had taken centuries before Locke. Locke was merely repeating Hooker and through him the medieval tradition about the relation between law and morals. If the fiction about a state of nature be laid aside, this can mean only one thing, namely, that moral rules are broader in their application than the rules of positive law and are valid whether governments observe them or not. Just what gives morality its force remains a question. It might depend upon divine will, or it might be rationally self-evident, or it might depend on the fact that society is more deeply ingrained in human nature than government and so sets standards that governments cannot defy. Against Hobbes, however, Locke set up the proposition that moral rights and duties are intrinsic, that morality makes law and not law morality, and that governments have to give effect to what is naturally right prior to its enactment.

It is evident, then, that Locke's whole theory depended upon explaining exactly what was meant by the law of nature upon which his pre-political condition of mutual assistance rested and in accordance with which political society arose. At least it was incumbent on him to show why it was binding even without administration or enforcement. In fact he never gave any careful analysis of it at all, his most explicit treatment of it being merely incidental to his discrimination — following Aristotle and directed against Filmer — of paternal from political power. Because it was traditional to discuss property in connection with the family, this had the effect of uniting his treatment of natural law with his theory of the origin of private property. Before discussing the general question of the validity which Locke attributed to natural law, therefore, it will be better to present his theory of the right to private property, for he constantly assumes that this is the type to which all natural rights are analogous.

In the state of nature, Locke believed, property was common in the sense that everyone had a right to draw subsistence from whatever nature offers. Here again he was bringing ideas from a far distant past. In the Middle Ages it had been not uncommon to suppose that common ownership is a more perfect and hence a more "natural" state than private ownership, the latter being attributed to the effects of sin upon human nature after the fall of man. In the Roman law also there existed the very different theory that private property begins with the appropriation of things which before had a common use though no communal ownership. Locke departed from both theories by asserting that a man has a natural right to that with which he has "mixed" the labor of his body, as for example by enclosing and tilling land. Apparently he was generalizing from the example of colonists in a new land like America, but it is probable that he was influenced also by a strong sense of the superior productivity of private agricultural economy as compared with the communal tillage of a more primitive system. Locke believed that greater production would raise the standard of living throughout the community. In the eighteenth century the enclosure of land did in fact increase the yield, but the capitalist landlord took advantage of his strategic position to sequestrate the benefits. Whatever the origin of Locke's theory may have been, his argument was that the right to private property arises because by labor a man extends, so to speak, his own personality into the objects produced.

By expending his internal energy upon them he makes them a part of himself. In general their utility depends upon the labor expended upon them, and thus Locke's theory led to the later labor-theories of value in classical and socialist economics.

From Locke's theory of the origin of private property it follows that the right is prior even to the primitive society which he described as the state of nature. As he himself said, property is "without any express compact of all the commoners."[7] It is a right which each individual brings to society in his own person, just as he brings the physical energy of his body. Hence society does not create the right and except within limits cannot justly regulate it, for both society and government exist, in part at least, to protect the prior private right of property. This account of property, though introduced almost casually, had a profound effect on Locke's whole social philosophy. He never said, and almost certainly did not believe, that there was no natural right except property. The expression which he most commonly used to enumerate natural rights was "life, liberty, and estate." Frequently, however, he used "property" where he seems to have meant any right, and since property was the only natural right which he examined at length, it was inevitable that it should stand out as the typical and important right. In any case, he conceived all natural rights on the same lines as property, that is to say, as attributes of the individual person born with him, and hence as indefeasible claims upon both society and government. Such claims can never justly be set aside, since society itself exists to protect them; they can be regulated only to the extent that is necessary to give them effective protection. In other words, the "life, liberty, and estate" of one person can be limited only to make effective the equally valid claims of another person to the same rights.

PHILOSOPHICAL AMBIGUITIES

This theory, in all its social and political implications, was as egoistic as that of Hobbes. It is true that Locke drew a different picture of the state of nature. The war of all against all no doubt seemed to his common sense to be overdrawn, but like Hobbes he was saying in substance that society exists to protect property

[7] *Of Civil Government* (Book II), sect. 25.

and other private rights which society does not create. As a result the psychology which in the eighteenth century grew out of Locke's theory of mind was fundamentally egoistic in its explanation of human behavior. It ran in terms of pleasure and pain, and not like Hobbes's in terms of self-preservation — a doubtful improvement — but the calculation of pleasure was exactly as self-centered as the calculation of security. Hobbes's better logic had its way in spite of Locke's better feeling. By a strange and undesigned cooperation the two men fastened on social theory the presumption that individual self-interest is clear and compelling, while a public or a social interest is thin and unsubstantial. Perhaps the influence of Locke, precisely because it was less aware of its principles, was the more insidious. He left standing the old theory of natural law with all its emotional connotations and almost religious compulsions, but he completely changed, without knowing it, the meaning which the term had in writers like Hooker. Instead of a law enjoining the common good of a society, Locke set up a body of innate, indefeasible, individual rights which limit the competence of the community and stand as bars to prevent interference with the liberty and property of private persons. Like later liberals he assumed that the two things — preservation of the common good and protection of private rights — come to the same thing. In the existing state of politics and industry perhaps this was measurably true, but there was no logical ground for it except the vague assumption that in the harmony of nature "somehow good will be the final goal of ill." This sentimental trust in nature, quite unwarranted by anything that modern science or modern philosophy knew about it, ran right across the history of political and economic theory in the eighteenth century.

It is exceedingly difficult to understand exactly what Locke believed to be the philosophical justification for his theory of natural rights, or in other words to see how he meant to unite his political theory with his general philosophical position. That all individuals are endowed by their creator with a right to life, liberty, and estate, aside from all reference to their social and political associations, is certainly not a proposition for which any empirical proof can be given. There seems to be no way whatever to prove it; it must stand, as Thomas Jefferson said, simply as self-evident, an axiom from which social and moral theorems can be deduced but which in itself is more obvious than any other ethical principle. Probably this is what Locke believed. The tendency to regard natural law in moral and legal science as analogous to axioms in geometry was well settled in seventeenth-century thought after Grotius. But even if some moral values are admitted to be self-evident, it is far from obvious that they must take the form of innate individual rights. Probably Locke never really faced this question, since he seems not to have been aware how greatly his own theory of natural rights differed from the older versions of the theory.

If this latter question be put aside, however, it is still hard to see how Locke's philosophical position warranted him in believing that an apparently self-evident proposition, in ethics or any other subject, is for that reason true. The first book of the *Essay concerning Human Understanding* was devoted to showing that no idea is innate, that is, so fundamentally a part of the mind that belief in it is warranted apart from evidence. For practical purposes this is the same as saying that self-evidence is not reliable, since even a false proposition, because of custom or habit, may appear to be obvious. Undoubtedly Locke meant his attack on innate ideas to be a solvent for all kinds of prejudice, in morals and religion as well as in science. His own belief, that ideas come from the senses, he regarded as affording a basis for knowledge quite different from the spurious test of innateness.

The truth is, however, that he never perceived how far this empiricism, logically developed, would carry him. His conception of knowledge was colored by the prevailing reverence for mathematics, and after explaining the origin of ideas empirically he denied the certainty of practically all empirical knowledge, namely, the report of the senses about physical existences. In ethics particularly he retained the belief — by virtue of never trying to act on it — that a demonstrative science of morals analogous to geometry could be constructed. His political theory, or at least the ethical foundations of it, retained the impress of this belief. Thus Locke's philosophy as a whole presented the anomaly of a theory of the mind and a procedure in describing it which was generally empirical, joined to a theory of the sciences and a procedure in political science which was rationalist. The curious result in his social philosophy was a theory markedly tolerant and critical in defending religious freedom and capable of being highly dogmatic in defending rights of property.

In philosophy the weight of Locke's influence was on the side of empiricism, that is, on the side of a psychology in which human knowledge and behavior are explained from the senses and in which the rules of conduct claim the validity of generalizations from experience. It was manifest that natural rights — indefeasible claims to liberty of action inherent in human beings whatever their social relationships or without social relationships — could not be verified in this way, nor could they pass unchallenged as axioms after his refutation of innate ideas. Thus it happened that his English successors in the first half of the eighteenth century (following suggestions in the *Essay*) rapidly developed a theory of behavior in terms of pleasure and pain, the first operating as a force of attraction and the second as one of repulsion, and a theory of value in which the greatest net sum of pleasures, after deducting the pains as negative quantities, was set up as the socially valuable end of conduct. At first a mainly academic psychology allied to a theological ethics, this theory passed through a French medium into the hands of Bentham and the philosophical radicals. Logically, as Hume showed, it eliminated altogether Locke's natural rights and fictions about the state of nature and a contract. It remained egoistic, however, both in its psychological explanation of behavior and in its theory of value — ethical, political, and economic — and merely assumed the coincidence of individual freedom with the greatest public good. The individualism of all social theory between Locke and John Stuart Mill depended less on logic than on its agreement with the interests of the class that mainly produced it.

THE CONTRACT

Having described the state of nature as a condition of peace and mutual aid and having defined natural rights, on the analogy of property, as prior even to society, Locke next proceeded to derive civil society from the consent of its members. This part of his theory suffered inevitably from the inherent contrariety of what he took from Hooker and what he took from Hobbes. Civil power he had defined as "the right of making laws with penalties . . . for the regulating and preserving of property, and of employing the force of the community, in the execution of such laws . . . all this only for the public good."[8] Such a power can arise only by consent, and though this may be tacitly given, it must be the consent of each individual for himself. For civil power can have no right except as this is derived from the individual right of each man to protect himself and his property. The legislative and executive power used by government to protect property is nothing except the natural power of each man resigned "into the hands of the community," or "resigned to the public," and it is justified merely because it is a better way of protecting natural rights than the self-help to which each man is naturally entitled. This is "the original compact" by which men "incorporate into one society"; it is a bare agreement "to unite into one political society, which is all the compact that is, or needs be, between the individuals, that enter into, or make up a commonwealth."[9]

The difficulty with this theory is that Locke is nowhere clear as to what precisely does arise by the "original compact." Is it society itself or only government? That the two are different he emphatically asserted at a later point in the second *Treatise*, where he argued that a political revolution which dissolves a government does not as a rule dissolve the community which that government rules. Moreover, the individual resigns his natural right to the community or the public, which presumably must be some kind of entity if it can receive a grant of power. On the other hand, right is lodged, necessarily according to Locke's theory, only in the hands of individuals until they resign it. Yet he regarded this surrender of individual right as conditional against both society and government, for individual power is resigned "only with an intention in everyone the better to preserve himself his liberty and property," and society itself is "obliged to secure everyone's property."[10] To clarify this problem those Continental writers, like Althusius and Pufendorf, who had elaborated the theory of compact most carefully, had postulated two contracts, the one between individuals giving rise to a community and the other between the community and its government. Some such position Locke tacitly assumes, though he nowhere states

[8] *Ibid.*, sect. 3. [9] *Ibid.*, sect. 99. [10] *Ibid.*, sect. 131.

it. The twofold contract, of course, explains nothing, since the propriety of using the same concept to cover the two cases is really the doubtful point, but it does give formal clarity to the theory. Formal clarity was not a quality which Locke greatly valued and hence he contented himself with a conflation of two points of view. The older theory which he got from Hooker assumed a community capable of holding its magistrates morally responsible; this he mainly followed in his defense of the Revolution as a justifiable effort to make English government serve the needs of English society. The newer theory, most clearly stated by Hobbes, assumed only individuals and their private interests, and this also Locke followed in so far as he made both society and government agencies for protecting life, liberty, and estate.

The two phases of Locke's theory are united — very precariously, it must be admitted — by the hypothesis that an act of the community is constituted by the agreement of a majority of its members. The consent by which each person agrees with others to form a body politic obligates him to submit to the majority; as Pufendorf had argued, the fiction of a social contract must be helped out with the further fiction of unanimous consent. And the agreement of a majority is identical with an act of the whole society.

> That which acts any community, being only the consent of the individuals of it, and it being necessary to that which is one body to move one way; it is necessary the body should move that way whither the greater force carries it, which is the consent of the majority.[11]

This way of solving the difficulty, however, is open to objection from both sides. If an individual's rights are really indefeasible, it is no better for him to be deprived of them by a majority than by a single tyrant; apparently it did not occur to Locke that a majority could be tyrannous. Nor is there any good reason why an individualist should resign his private judgment merely because those who disagree with him are numerous. On the other hand, if the "public" or the "community" really has a unitary quality of its own, there is no *a priori* reason why its decision must always be made by a numerical majority. Older theories of popular sovereignty, such as Marsilio's, had commonly held that the

[11] *Ibid.*, sect. 96.

"prevailing part" of a community may be weighted for quality as well as for quantity. In general it cannot be said that the principle of majority-rule has any such obvious validity as Locke imputed to it.

SOCIETY AND GOVERNMENT

On the whole Locke regarded the setting up of a government as a much less important event than the original compact that makes a civil society. Once a majority has agreed to form a government, "the whole power of the community is naturally in them." The form of the government depends upon what disposition the majority, or otherwise the community, makes of its power. It may be retained or it may be delegated to a legislative body of one form or another. Following the experience of the English Revolution, Locke assumed that the legislative power is supreme in government, though he admitted the possibility that the executive may share in lawmaking. Both powers, however, are limited. Legislative power can never be arbitrary, for even the people who set it up had no such power; it cannot rule by extemporary decrees, since men unite to have known law and judges; it cannot take property without consent, which Locke interprets to mean by majority-vote; and it cannot delegate its legislative power, since this is unalterably in the hands where the community has placed it. In general, its power is fiduciary, since the people have supreme power to alter the legislature when it acts contrary to the trust reposed in it. The executive is further limited by a general dependence on the legislature and also because the prerogative is limited by law. For the sake of freedom it is important that legislative and executive power should not be in the same hands. Every detail of Locke's account of the relation between legislatures and executives reflects some phase of the controversy between the king and parliament.

The power of the people over government, however, is still not quite as complete in Locke as it came to be in later and more democratic theories. Though he called the power of the legislature fiduciary and a delegation from the majority that acts for the community, he retained the older view that the grant of the community divests the people of power so long as the government is faithful to its duties. In this respect his theory was logically somewhat arbitrary, as Rousseau later pointed out. For if government is merely the trustee of the people, it is hard to see why the principal should have bound his hands by executing the trust. The people's legislative power is in effect limited to a single act (though Locke admits that a democracy is conceivable), namely, that of setting up a supreme legislature. Even if the community resumes its power for good cause, it cannot do so "till the government be dissolved." A democrat like Rousseau naturally considered this to be an unwarranted limitation on the perpetual power of the people to govern itself as it saw fit. Probably several causes united to fix Locke in his opinion. He was a cautious and sober-minded man, in no wise willing to encourage licence even though he had to defend a revolution. Besides, he rightly regarded democratic government, at least in England, as an academic question. More important than these reasons, probably, was the persistence in his mind of the tradition which he derived from Hooker and which had governed the thought of Coke and Sir Thomas Smith. The right of a community to govern itself had not been thought inconsistent with a kind of indefeasibility in the right of its king and other governing organs, which after all had a status or a vested interest in their places. This phase of Locke's theory persisted in the Whig liberalism of the eighteenth century, which regarded government, while responsible for the common well-being, as a balance between the great interests of the realm, such as crown, nobility, church, and commonalty. With Edmund Burke this conception became a starting-point for the theory of modern conservatism. The English Revolution did not break violently the tradition of English government, and similarly Locke, its philosophical exponent, was the most conservative of revolutionists. Locke's ideas in France in the eighteenth century had quite a different history.

Since Locke's purpose was to defend the moral validity of the Revolution of 1688, he devoted the latter part of the second treatise to discussing the right to resist tyranny. The most effective part of this argument is that which he drew from the principles of Hooker. In substance it amounts to this: English society and English government are two different things. The second exists for the well-being of the first, and a government which seriously jeopardizes social interests is rightly changed. This argument is supported by a rather lengthy examination of the right which can be gained by conquest. Locke here distinguished between just and unjust warfare. A mere aggressor gains no right, and even a conqueror in a just war can never establish a right which contravenes the liberty and property of the conquered. The argument is evidently directed against Hobbes in particular and in general against any theory that governments derive a just power from the successful use of force. The principle of Locke's argument is essentially the same as that later developed by Rousseau, that moral validity and force are two distinct things, the latter being incapable of giving rise to the former. Consequently a government which begins in force can be justified, as all governments are justified, only by its recognition and support of the moral rights inherent in persons and communities. In other words, the moral order is permanent and self-perpetuating, and governments are only factors in the moral order. In this sense natural law meant for Locke substantially what it had meant for Cicero and Seneca and the whole of the Middle Ages.

A government, as distinct from a society, is dissolved either by a change in the location of legislative power or by a violation of the trust which the people have reposed in it. Locke contemplated two cases, both drawn from English experience in the preceding fifty years. He wished to show that the king had been the real author of the Revolution by attempting to stretch the prerogative and to rule without parliament; this was a dislocation of the supreme legislative power vested by the people in their representatives. He had also a retentive memory for the misbehavior of the Long Parliament and accordingly he had no thought of leaving the legislature unfettered. Any invasion of the life, liberty, or property of subjects is *ipso facto* void, and a legislature which attempts these wrongs forfeits its power. In this case power reverts to the people, who must provide by a new act of constitutional legislation for a new legislature. As in all such arguments, Locke created a considerable, and perhaps needless, confusion by his use of the word "lawful." He continually speaks of unlawful acts of the executive or legislature when he well knows that there is no legal remedy, and of lawful resistance to tyranny when he means resort to an extra-legal but morally defensible remedy. Broadly speaking he used lawful as synonymous with just or right and made no distinction between what is morally just and what is legally actionable. This usage grew from and perpetuated the traditional belief that law — natural, positive, and moral — is all of a piece, and that there are therefore "fundamental" laws not made even by the supreme legislature. The reality of such rules in English law disappeared with the very Revolution which Locke was defending, though the belief in moral limitations on parliament persisted. Perhaps the American practice of discriminating between constitutional and statutory law, and between ordinary legislation and extraordinary legislation by referendum, was closer to Locke's ideas.

THE COMPLEXITY OF LOCKE'S THEORY

Locke's political philosophy can hardly be represented in a simple and straightforward exposition because of the logical difficulties which it reveals when it is subjected to analysis. In spite of the simplicity which it seems on the surface to possess and which made it the most popular of political philosophies, it is in reality involved. This was due to the fact that Locke saw with great clarity a multitude of issues involved in the politics of the seventeenth century and tried conscientiously to combine them all. But his theory had no logical structure elaborate enough to contain so complicated a subject-matter. Though circumstances made him the defender of a revolution, he was by no means a radical, and in intellectual temperament he was the least doctrinaire of philosophers. Perhaps something is explained by the fact that his mature life fell in a generation when the results of civil war were accomplished but not acknowledged. His principles he mainly inherited and he never examined them very thoroughly. But he was extraordinarily sensitive to realities and absolutely candid in trying to face them. The mid-period of the seventeenth century had changed enormously both English politics and English thought, and yet it had not broken continuity with the days before the civil wars. Locke's political philosophy was an effort to combine past and present and also to find a nucleus of agreement for reasonable men of all parties, but he did not synthetize all that he combined. As he combined diverse elements from the past, so from his political philosophy emerged diverse theories in the century following him.

The defects of logical structure in Locke's political theory arose from the fact that he never made up his mind what exactly was fundamental and what was derivative. There are in fact no less than four levels in his account of civil society, and the last three are represented as successively derivative from the first. Yet Locke never hesitated, if it was convenient, to impute a kind of absoluteness to each of the four. The foundation of the whole system was represented as being the individual and his rights, especially that of property. On the whole this must be regarded as the most significant phase of his political theory, which made it primarily a defense of individual liberty against political oppression. Second, men are also members of a community, and though Locke described society as depending on tacit consent and as meaning effectively a majority, he constantly spoke of the community as a definite unit and the trustee of the individual's rights. Third, beyond society there is government, which is trustee for the community, somewhat as the latter is for the individual. Finally, within government the executive is less important and less authoritative than the legislature. Yet Locke certainly did not regard the king and his ministers as merely a committee of parliament. In the defense of liberty and property the legislature controls the executive, and the community controls government. Only in the remote event that society itself is dissolved, a contingency which Locke never seriously contemplated, does the defense of liberty revert to self-help. Society, the legislature, and even the king were all treated as having a kind of vested right, or permanent authority, only to be forfeited for cause, though the individual rights of property and liberty were the only rights which Locke declared to be absolutely indefeasible. The plausibility of Locke's theory was greatly increased by not trying to show too precisely how the actual power of institutions is derived from the equal and inalienable rights of individuals.

The actual complexity of Locke's political thought, concealed beneath its apparent simplicity of statement, makes difficult an estimate of its relations to later theories. What was immediately grasped included its most obvious but also its least important consequences. The enormous vogue which he enjoyed during the earlier part of the eighteenth century was probably due precisely to the deceptive simplicity of his thought, which has always commended his philosophy to common sense. Such liberal thought as survived the success of the Revolution carried on the spirit of Locke's philosophy most truly in respect to religious toleration, which had real vitality in eighteenth-century England despite the political disqualification of Catholics and Dissenters by the continuation of the Test Act. The supremacy of parliament was no longer a controversial issue and party differences about the power of the crown had little importance. With some lip-service to Locke, Whiggism in the eighteenth century represented quite subsidiary elements of his *Treatise:* that the powers of government remain indefeasibly in the organs where they have once been placed, unless one tries to invade the province of another, and that government is at bottom a balance of the vested interests of the realm: crown, landed aristocracy, and corporations.[12] In this almost nothing of Locke's theory of individual rights remained but much of what Ireton, in his dispute with the Levellers, had called the "permanent fixed interests" of the kingdom. This made it possible for the myth of a separation of powers to persist to the end of the century. As Blackstone said,

> Every branch of our civil polity supports and is supported, regulates and is regulated, by the rest: for the two houses naturally drawing in two directions of opposite interest, and the prerogative in another still different from them both, they mutually keep each other from exceeding their proper limits; while the whole is prevented from separation, and artificially connected together by the mixed nature of the crown, which is a part of the legislative, and the sole executive magistrate.[13]

The monopoly of power by the landowning class was contrary not only to Locke's theory of individual rights but also to his theory of the importance of property in general.

The greatest importance of Locke's philosophy, therefore, lay beyond the contemporary English settlement in the political thought of America and France which culminated in the great revolutions at the end of the eighteenth century. Here Locke's defense of resistance in the name of inalienable rights of personal liberty, consent, and freedom to acquire and enjoy property had their full effect. Because all these conceptions were in germ

[12] See the account of Whig principles in Burke's *Appeal from the New to the Old Whigs.*

[13] *Commentaries,* Bk. I, ch. 2, sect. 2.

much older than Locke and had been the birthright of all European peoples since the sixteenth century, it is impossible to attribute their existence in America and in France to him alone, but he was known to everyone who gave any attention to political philosophy. His sincerity, his profound moral conviction, his genuine belief in liberty, in human rights, and in the dignity of human nature, united with his moderation and good sense, made him the ideal spokesman of a middle-class revolution. As a force in propagating the ideals of liberal but not violent reform Locke probably stands before all other writers whatsoever. Even his more doubtful ideas, such as the separation of powers and the inevitable wisdom of majority-decisions, remained a part of the democratic creed.

In the course of the eighteenth century the system of natural law, which provided the logical basis for Locke's political philosophy, receded gradually from the dominating position which it held in the scientific thought of the seventeenth century. This was due in part to a general progress of empirical method both in the natural sciences and in social studies, but in no small degree to the development of those parts of Locke's philosophy which stressed the importance of a natural history of human understanding. This development followed lines already suggested by Locke himself. It greatly expanded the psychological explanation of behavior, making it depend upon the pursuit of pleasure and the avoidance of pain as its sole motives. In place of the rational standard of inherent good sought by the theory of natural law it put a utilitarian theory of moral, political, and economic value. About the middle of the century Hume showed that this development, if logically carried through, made it possible to dispense with the theory of natural law altogether. The internal structure of Locke's political philosophy was thus completely destroyed. Yet most of its practical purposes and much of its inward spirit passed over to utilitarianism. Though less explicitly a defense of revolution, it continued Locke's spirit of cautious but radical reform. Its program continued the same idealization of individual rights, the same belief in liberalism as a panacea for political ills, the same tenderness for the rights of property, and the same conviction that public interests must be conceived in terms of private well-being.

SELECTED BIBLIOGRAPHY

John Locke: Ses théories politiques et leur influence en Angleterre. By Charles Bastide. Paris, 1907.

Life and Letters of Sir George Savile, Bart., First Marquis of Halifax. By H. C. Foxcroft. 2 vols. London, 1898.

A Character of the Trimmer: Being a Short Life of the First Marquis of Halifax. By H. C. Foxcroft. Cambridge, 1946.

"Religious Toleration in England." By H. M. Gwatkin. In the *Cambridge Modern History,* Vol. V (1908), ch. 11.

The Social and Political Ideas of some English Thinkers of the Augustan Age, A.D. 1650–1750. Ed. by F. J. C. Hearnshaw. London, 1928. Chs. 3, 4.

John Locke and the Doctrine of Majority-rule. By Willmoore Kendall. Urbana, Illinois, 1941.

The Moral and Political Philosophy of John Locke. By Sterling P. Lamprecht. New York, 1918.

Property in the Eighteenth Century, with Special Reference to England and Locke. By Paschal Larkin. London, 1930.

Political Thought in England from Locke to Bentham. By Harold J. Laski. London, 1920.

"Locke's Theory of the State." By Sir Frederick Pollock. In *Essays in the Law.* London, 1922. Ch. 3.

Darwin and Hegel, with other Philosophical Studies. By D. G. Ritchie. London, 1893. Chs. 6, 7.

"English Political Philosophy in the Seventeenth and Eighteenth Centuries." By Arthur Lionel Smith. In the *Cambridge Modern History,* Vol. VI (1909), ch. 23.

Studies in the History of Political Philosophy before and after Rousseau. By C. E. Vaughan. 2 vols. Manchester, 1925. Vol. I, ch. 4.

CHAPTER XXVII

FRANCE: THE DECADENCE OF NATURAL LAW

The Revolution of 1688 and the publication of Locke's tracts brought to a close the astonishing half-century of creative political philosophy which accompanied the civil wars in England. There followed, as often happens, a period of quiescence or even of stagnation. The need of the moment was that the new government should consolidate its gains; until the middle of the eighteenth century a Stuart restoration, bringing a Roman Catholic succession under the influence of France, seemed a real threat. The temper of English thought became conservative, even complacent, and not without reason, for though English government was oligarchical and corrupt, in comparison with the rest of Europe it was liberal. At least it offered a large measure of civil liberty to all and political liberty to the classes which alone were politically self-conscious. The growth of a party-system and of ministerial responsibility was a matter of experiment and adjustment rather than of conscious theorizing. Not until David Hume in the middle of the century and Edmund Burke toward its close did British thinkers add materially to social philosophy, and the later years of Burke's thought were controlled by political events in France.

THE REVIVAL OF POLITICAL PHILOSOPHY IN FRANCE

In the eighteenth century, therefore, political theory had its center in France. This fact was in itself a revolution, for though French philosophy in the age of Descartes had led the scientific emancipation of Europe, as French literature had led the arts, it had nothing to say on politics or social questions. Its domain had been rather in mathematics, metaphysics, and theology. There was little that social philosophy could say to an era of personal or bureaucratic autocracy such as began in France under Henry IV, developed in the age of Richelieu and Mazarin, and culminated in the monarchy of Louis XIV. The English civil wars, it is true, did not pass unnoticed at the time of the Fronde,[1] but such attention as they received served only to show that political ideas are powerless except as they respond to political occasions. The only response consonant with Louis's autocracy was that of Bossuet: "The royal throne is not the throne of a man but of God himself."[2] In form it was the old theory of monarchical divine right; in substance, so far as it had any philosophical substance, it depended on Hobbes's argument that there can be no third position between absolutism and anarchy. The last thirty years of Louis's long reign, however, from about 1685 until his death in 1715, were years of increasing decadence. Louis, after a period of military glory that hypnotized France, committed the cardinal sin of failing. His ambition arrayed all Europe against him; his grandiose schemes of conquest ended in humiliation; the cost of his campaigns brought the country to the edge of bankruptcy; oppressive and unequal taxation spread poverty broadcast. His hand was as heavy on the church as on the state, and yet by a Jesuit ultramontane policy he alienated the sympathy of Gallican Catholics. The persecution of Protestants, culminating in the revocation of the Edict of Nantes, not only horrified all men of humane mind but added substantially to the impoverishment of the country.

The decadence of absolute government turned French philosophy once more in the direction of political and social theory. Beginning somewhat doubtfully in the last years of the seventeenth century, the interest in politics grew steadily. In the first half of the eighteenth century there was an amazing output of books on all phases of the subject — historical works on the ancient institutions of France, descriptive works on European government and especially that of England, books of travel describing the morals and institutions of American or Asiatic peoples usually with an oblique reference to France, plans for the reform of taxation and the improvement of agriculture or trade, and philosophical theories of the end and justification of government.

[1] The only writer of any consequence was Claude Joly; see J. B. Brissaud, *Un libéral au xviie siècle: Claude Joly (1607–1700)*, Paris, 1898.

[2] *Politique tirée des propres paroles de l'Écriture Sainte* (written about 1670; first published, 1709), III, ii, 1.

Between 1750 and the Revolution the discussion of such subjects became an obsession. Every branch of literature — poetry, the drama, and the novel — became a vehicle of social discussion. All philosophy, indeed all scholarship, was bent in this direction, and even books on science might include the rudiments of a social philosophy. A poet like Voltaire or a novelist like Rousseau, a scientist like Diderot or D'Alembert, a civil servant like Turgot, and a metaphysician like Holbach produced political theory as naturally as a sociologist like Montesquieu wrote satire.

In this welter of ideas, repeated endlessly with varying applications, it is difficult to produce order without reducing philosophies to formulas that obscure their meaning and doubly difficult to evaluate the new meaning that was continually put into old formulas. Considered merely as abstract theory this French philosophy contained little that was new. For the most part discussion popularized rather than created, and on the score of originality the eighteenth century in philosophy compared badly with the seventeenth. Yet an old idea in a new setting is not quite the same idea. In the course of the century theories that had been reasonably clear-cut tended to become blurred and to take on the eclectic quality characteristic of popular thinking. The self-evidence of natural rights was asserted and reasserted, yet the rationalism essential to a system of self-evident principles became continually more remote from the growing empiricism of social studies. An ethical and political utilitarianism, essentially empirical in its implications, was repeatedly crossed with the theory of natural rights in spite of the logical incompatibility of the two positions. A more serious incompatibility was involved in the growth of a philosophical romanticism that was hostile to empiricism and rationalism alike, though it was still expressed in the old terminology. This new tendency was the most original factor that appeared in the philosophy of the eighteenth century, but its disruptive force was not fully manifest until after the Revolution.

A really satisfactory arrangement of this complex material is probably impossible but on the whole it seems clear that one figure in the French eighteenth century stands apart, Jean Jacques Rousseau. He himself felt it and suffered from it; his acquaintances felt it and detested him for it; all discerning critics have tried to take account of it. Lytton Strachey has said, " He possessed one quality which cut him off from his contemporaries, which set an immense gulf betwixt him and them: he was modern." The word "modern" means nothing, but it suggests an important fact. However much he might use the current catchwords, Rousseau's political philosophy was different, both in its quality and its effects, from anything else written in the eighteenth century; it was differently related both to the Revolution and to the period that followed the Revolution. It seems best, therefore, to reserve Rousseau for a separate chapter and to give a fuller exposition of his vague but significant political philosophy. The present chapter will present summarily the more typical French thought of the age before the Revolution. In the main this philosophy grew from that of Locke but it developed important differences which need to be especially noted.

THE RECEPTION OF LOCKE

The criticism of Louis XIV's government which began at the end of the seventeenth century was not at first the product of any political philosophy but merely the reaction of conscientious men to the shocking effects of bad government. It came from the observations of an engineer like Vauban on the effects of unequal taxation on agriculture or of a magistrate like Boisguillebert on the wasteful effect of oppressive restrictions on trade,[3] and it asked only a more enlightened form of autocracy. Criticism of autocracy itself came in the first instance in the name of the ancient institutions of France which the crown had crushed. This idea was developed speculatively by Fénelon in the romance *Télémaque* and more positively in his occasional writings.[4] Independent local governments and provincial assemblies, the restoration of the States General, the revival of the power and influence of the nobility, and the independence of the parlements were sought as correctives of absolutism and defended as a return to the ancient constitution of the country.[5] Such a dream persisted, especially among the nobility, even down to the Revolution; traces of it may be seen in the *Spirit of the Laws*. But it was only a dream. From

[3] Vauban, *Projet d'une dixme royale,* 1707; Boisguillebert, *Le détail de la France,* 1695.

[4] See his letter to Louis XIV (1694), *Oeuvres* (Paris, 1870), Vol. III, p. 425.

[5] Boulainvilliers, *Histoire de l'ancien gouvernement de la France,* 1727.

time to time the Parlement of Paris might resist the registering of an edict and gain popular favor by so doing, a kind of obstruction which suggests the controversies between Coke and James I. The latter, however, were effective only as preliminary to the struggle between Charles and parliament, and in France there was no parliament to take up the controversy. The parlements in fact represented nothing, and the suppression of their privileges in 1770 was really a reform. Absolutism had left France no traditional constitution which a reforming party could pretend to restore.

Criticism of the absolute monarchy urgently needed a philosophy — needed it doubly since the roots of a constitutional tradition had been so thoroughly grubbed out — and the philosophy of the English Revolution was ready to hand. In the seventeenth century French philosophy and science had been relatively self-contained; in the eighteenth, as Cartesianism hardened into a kind of scholasticism, it was deliberately supplanted by the philosophy of Locke and the science of Newton. In political thought such a result was a foregone conclusion after the revocation of the Edict of Nantes made religious toleration a major part of any reforming philosophy. With the residence of Voltaire in England between 1726 and 1729, and of Montesquieu ten years later, the philosophy of Locke became the foundation of French enlightenment, and the admiration of English government became the keynote of French liberalism. Henceforth the "new way of ideas" was the rule of philosophical and psychological speculation, and the principles of the *Treatises of Government* (supplemented of course by other English works) became axioms of political and social criticism. These principles were very simple and very general. The law of nature, or of reason, was supposed to provide an adequate rule of life without the addition of any revealed or supernatural truth and was believed to be imprinted in essentially the same form upon the minds of all men. As a result of Hobbes and Locke, the content of the law of nature had become substantially enlightened self-interest, but because of the harmony inherent in nature a truly enlightened self-interest was thought to be conducive to the good of all. In accord with these general ethical principles, governments were held to exist only to further liberty, security, the enjoyment of property, and other individual goods. Hence political reform must aim to secure responsible government, to make it representative, to limit abuses and tyranny, to abolish monopoly and privilege — in short, to create a society in which individual energy and capacity are the keys to power and wealth. Upon the validity of these general principles there was no substantial difference among French writers nor between them and Locke, but in France a changed environment gave to the abstractions a coloring quite different from that which they had in England.

THE CHANGED ENVIRONMENT

Reference has already been made to the fact that the autocracy had done its work so thoroughly that no effective reform in France could attach itself to the idea of reviving the traditional constitution. The ancient ideal of a fundamental law, which sixteenth-century France had shared with all Europe and which had still vitality enough to hold an almost equal footing with sovereignty in Bodin's philosophy, had lost all concrete meaning in the monarchy of Louis XIV. In England it was little more than a difference of terminology if a Leveller called his " birthright " the right of a man or the right of an Englishman; in either case it meant something concrete in the tradition of the common law. The rights of Frenchmen — unless one meant the privileges of the nobility — would have been a practically meaningless phrase. In consequence, the rights of man, and there was nothing else that a French liberal could appeal to, were necessarily more abstract, more detached from usage and concrete applicability, more open to speculative interpretation. In importing Locke into France, the French must omit precisely the most characteristic — at all events the most English — quality of Locke's political rationalism. They could not import Richard Hooker or the gradual transition of ideas and institutions which made it possible for Locke to attach his philosophy to a tradition continuous with St. Thomas and the Middle Ages, nor could they tie back the new philosophy to any French thinker of the sixteenth century. The historical and with it the relatively conservative quality of the English Revolution — in fact as well as in idea — was bound to be lost. The effect of this upon French political philosophy was profound. Reason was placed in stark opposition to custom and fact as it had never been in Locke. Probably no English politician would ever have said, as a speaker said before the National Convention,

> In dealing with matters so weighty I have sought the truth in the natural order of things and nowhere else. I have desired, so to speak, to preserve the virginity of my thought.[6]

The *a priori,* dogmatic, and hence radical quality of French political thought, in contrast with its English model, was heightened also by the circumstances under which it was produced. Though a doctrine of liberty it was written under a despotism, mostly by men with no experience of government and no possibility of such experience. Outside the ranks of the civil service no one in France had experience, and bureaucrats (allowing for the exception of Turgot) produced little political philosophy. The autocracy had made government a mystery conducted in secret, never divulging, even if it knew, the information, financial or other, on which an intelligent judgment of policy might be formed. Criticism and discussion, in public assemblies or in the press, were out of the question. Local government, always the school of English politics, had been completely subjected to central control, with the normal accompaniments of delay, friction, and red tape. Neither was there in France any such body of common ideas, tested in continual application, as the English common law. Before the Napoleonic Code France had some three hundred and sixty systems of local private law, left standing by the merely administrative unification of the monarchy. Of necessity French political philosophy in the eighteenth century, far more than English, was a literary philosophy, in a sense a bookish though not a scholarly philosophy, written for the salons and the educated bourgeoisie, the only public to which an author could address himself. It abounds in formulas and sweeping generalizations; it strives after brilliant effects; and it moves largely in an atmosphere of vague but familiar ideas. It is often effective propaganda, more frequently negative than positive, but relatively seldom responsible. It is only fair to add that one knows today as little as in the eighteenth century what criticism of existing French government might have been really constructive.

[6] *Moniteur universel,* May 15, 1793.

There were social causes as well as political that gave to French political philosophy a tone of bitterness that had no counterpart in Locke. French society was a tissue of privilege which made the cleavage between classes more conscious and more irritating, if not more real, than in England. The clergy were still in possession of perhaps a fifth of the soil of France, with an enormous revenue and substantial exemptions and privileges, but with no moral or intellectual preeminence to justify their position. Similarly, the nobility had privilege without political power or leadership. French agriculture offered them no such chance for capitalist development as the English landlord enjoyed, and French politics no such chance for leadership. The feudal rents of the nobility were an economic drain for which no return was made, either economic or political. To the middle class both clergy and nobility seemed parasites decked out with social privilege and with substantial exemptions from the burdens of taxation. Moreover, the French middle class was itself different from the English. There was nothing in France corresponding to the English yeomanry, and French agriculture was notable even before the Revolution for a large number of peasant proprietors. The middle class was typically an urban bourgeoisie, owning nearly all the capital and forming the main creditor of the insolvent state. In French political writing there was a class-consciousness and a sense of exploitation such as had appeared only sporadically in English political writing. And in fact the French Revolution was a social revolution as the English Revolution was not; it compressed into three or four years an expropriation of church lands, crown lands, and lands of *émigré* nobles comparable to that spread through the reigns of Henry VII and Henry VIII. It is hardly an exaggeration to say that Locke's philosophy in France before the Revolution was an attack on vested interests and in England after the Reformation a defense of them.

The foregoing divergences refer to the category of space but equally important ones refer to that of time. The fact that Locke in England belonged to the seventeenth century while Locke in France belonged to the eighteenth was itself a significant difference. In the days of Grotius and Descartes, and even in the days of Locke, the appeal to reason had been a high intellectual adventure, a new exploration on the frontiers of philosophy and science, and a deliverance from authority. In the eighteenth century it ran the risk of becoming a *cliché*. The farther it got from its source, the more assured it became, the more dogmatic, and the more commonplace. For despite the reverence expended on enlightenment, a good deal of what passed for rational ethics or rational politics was an obvious kind of prudential moralizing that was not intellectually penetrating and does not now seem morally stirring. Holbach's materialism proved that the literature of edification can be as flat when written by an atheist as it is when written by the clergy. Yet thousands of Frenchmen, and of Englishmen and Germans too, read such books with passionate interest. They made known to a new and larger public what a series of great philosophers and scientists, from Descartes and Galileo to Locke and Newton, had created. It is inevitable that by comparison the eighteenth century now suffers heavily. A genius of any age is always worth reading, but nothing is so dead as popular philosophy that has ceased to be popular.

There is, however, another and a more important side to this. The assurance of the eighteenth century and its confidence in reason was not bred of familiarity alone but was partly the effect of solid achievement. Until the publication of Newton's *Principia* in 1687, modern science was on trial; a few philosophers had believed passionately in it but no one knew that it would work. After Newton everyone knew, even though he had only the vaguest conception of the new engine. The idea of the new science affected men's imaginations far more than the actuality affected technology. For the reason of Newton seemed to have pierced to the very heart of nature, to have disclosed "that wisdom which we see equally displayed in the exquisite structure and just motions of the greatest and subtilest parts."[7] Nothing was beyond the power of reason; Bacon's saying that knowledge is power had come true and for the first time in history men could cooperate with the benevolent intentions which even atheists like Holbach still attributed to the harmony of nature. Nothing characterizes social thought in the eighteenth century so completely as belief in the possibility of happiness and progress under the guidance of reason. Much of this — the belief in the harmony of nature, for

[7] From Maclaurin's popularization of Newton; quoted by Carl L. Becker, *The Heavenly City of the Eighteenth-Century Philosophers* (1932), p. 62.

example — was sheer confusion in no way warranted by the new science. But on the whole the belief that man's fate was in the keeping of his intelligence was an honorable faith, more humane than the religion of authority that preceded it or the religion of sentimentality that followed it. In the large it did not overestimate the power of scientific reason to control nature, but whether that power extends to human relationships, no one knows today any more than the philosophers knew then. Their superficiality lay in a shocking exaggeration of the simplicity of the problem.

MONTESQUIEU: SOCIOLOGY AND LIBERTY

Of all French political philosophers in the eighteenth century (other than Rousseau) the most important was Montesquieu. Of them all he had perhaps the clearest conception of the complexities of a social philosophy, and yet he too was guilty of extreme oversimplification. He alone undertook what purported to be an empirical study of society and government on a large scale, and yet his supposed inductions were controlled throughout by preconceptions for which he neither had nor sought empirical proof. He attempted a political philosophy avowedly applicable to the widest range of circumstances, and yet nearly all that he wrote was written with an eye upon the state of affairs in France. Consequently Montesquieu presents at once the best scientific aspirations of his age and its unavoidable confusions. Without laying aside the rationalist apparatus, such as the immutable natural law of justice and the contract, in effect he neglected the contract and suggested a sociological relativism quite incompatible with self-evident moral laws. He provided a plan for the study of government in relation to both the physical and the social *milieu* which required the comparison of institutions on a wide scale, but he lacked both the accuracy of knowledge and the detachment needed to make the plan effective. His love of political liberty, the sole enthusiasm of an otherwise chilly temperament, was in the best tradition of the eighteenth century, but he united his theory to a hasty and superficial analysis of the constitutional principles of liberty.

It cannot be said that Montesquieu's *Spirit of the Laws* has any arrangement; it has been saved from the fate suffered by Bodin's *Republic* mainly by superior style. He addressed himself to two main points which had no intrinsic relationship. In the first place, he undertook to develop a sociological theory of government and law by showing that these depend for their structure and functioning upon the circumstances in which a people lives. The circumstances include physical conditions, such as climate and soil, which he supposed to have a direct influence upon national mentality; the state of the arts, trade, and the modes of producing goods; mental and moral temperaments and dispositions; the form of the political constitution; and the customs and habits that have become ingrained in national character. In a word, a form of government, using the expression in its broadest possible sense, is a whole requiring the mutual adjustment of all a people's institutions, if the government is to remain stable and orderly. In the second place, Montesquieu was haunted by the fear that the absolute monarchy had so undermined the traditional constitution of France that liberty had become forever impossible. His detestation of despotism is clearly to be seen even in what purport to be objective statements about governments such as those of Russia and Turkey. His practical object — and much the most influential part of his work — was to analyze the constitutional conditions upon which freedom depends and so to discover the means of restoring the ancient liberties of Frenchmen. In respect to the last point it does not appear that he reached a definite conclusion. His writings gave aid and comfort both to reactionaries who hoped for the restoration of the parlements, the estates, and the provincial assemblies and to liberals who looked to an imitation of English government.

These two aspects of Montesquieu's thought were not definitely separated in his writings, either by place or date. The *Lettres Persanes* (1721) was in the main a social satire on the condition of France, in which the author paid his respects to the church, to Louis XIV, the decline of the parlements, and the decay of the nobility.[8] The thought behind the criticism was the same conception of despotism developed in the *Spirit of the Laws* — a government in which all intermediate powers between the king and the people have been crushed and law has been made identical with the sovereign's will. It was this interpretation of despotism that gave importance to the separation of powers, which he believed

[8] See Letters 24, 37, 92, 98 (ed. by Laboulaye).

he had found in the English constitution. Yet in the *Persian Letters* he already thought that the best government is that which "leads men in the way best suited to their disposition," and his discussion of the causes of depopulation showed a flair for sociological speculation.[9]

The composition of the *Esprit des lois* (1748) extended at least over seventeen years and everyone has recognized that its parts are disparate. The occasional remarks on England in Books I to X by no means suggest the account of the English Constitution in Book XI,[10] and the treatment of the Roman constitution at the end of that book, after he had discovered the separation of powers, is unlike his earlier remarks on the ancient republic.[11] There seems to be no doubt that Montesquieu's travels in Europe between 1728 and 1731, and especially his residence in England, formed the crucial experience in his intellectual history. His love of liberty was in its early phase mainly ethical, bred of his study of the classics and reflecting an admiration for the ancient republic similar to that of Machiavelli, Milton, and Harrington. This phase of his thought remains in the *Spirit of the Laws* in the theory that virtue or public spirit is a precondition of this form of government. But Montesquieu's observation of existing republics, in Italy and in Holland, by no means bore out this preconception, and his residence in England suggested a new idea — that liberty might be the result not of superior civic morality but of a correct organization of the state. His famous eleventh book, on the construction of constitutions in accordance with the separation of powers, was the record of this discovery.

LAW AND ENVIRONMENT

Overtly the general principles of Montesquieu's social philosophy started with the law of nature. A law, he says in the opening sentence of the *Spirit of the Laws*, means "the necessary relations arising from the nature of things." This vague formula covers as always an ambiguity which he does nothing to clear up. In physics a "necessary relation" is merely a uniformity in the

9 Letter 80; 112–122.

10 Cf. Bk. II, ch. 4.

11 On the dates of the various books see J. Dedieu, *Montesquieu* (1913), p. 82.

behavior of bodies. In society a law is a rule or norm of human behavior which presumably ought to be observed but is often violated. Of this fact Montesquieu has two explanations, neither of which explains anything: the freedom of the will and the defective intelligence of men, which prevents them from living up to the perfection displayed by the rest of nature. But he was emphatic in urging, against Hobbes, that nature does provide a standard of absolute justice prior to positive law; to deny it is as absurd as to say that " before describing a circle all the radii were not equal." Evidently he had never considered natural law with any care. His enumeration included factors as disparate as a knowledge of God, the bodily appetites, and the fundamental conditions of society. This was merely a conventional way of getting started. What interested him was the idea that this fundamental natural law in society, which he identified in the usual way with reason, must operate in different environments and so must produce different institutions in different places. Climate, soil, occupation, form of government, commerce, religion, customs are all relevant conditions in determining what in a particular case reason (or law) will set up. This fitness or relation of conditions, physical, mental, and institutional, forms the " spirit of the laws." Obviously what Montesquieu was suggesting was a sociological study, by a comparative method, of institutions and the incidence upon them of other institutions and non-institutional physical conditions. The assumption that all are variants of one " nature " was hardly more than a fiction.

It is not easy to estimate with certainty either the originality or the importance of Montesquieu's project. What was most definitely his was the grandiose scale on which he proposed to carry it out. The idea itself he probably got in the first instance from Aristotle, especially from those books of the *Politics*[12] in which were analyzed the innumerable nuances of democracy and oligarchy in the city-states. That laws must be adapted to a variety of circumstances, physical and institutional, and that good government must be good in this relative sense, had been fully stated by Aristotle, as had the speculation about the relation of national character to climate. Among modern writers Bodin had urged the same conceptions, but neither Aristotle nor Bodin had planned the

[12] Bks. IV–VI in the traditional arrangement.

investigation on what might be called cosmic lines. Montesquieu was intrigued by the great body of travel-literature which had grown up in the seventeenth century, dealing with the aborigines of the Americas and Africa and with the exotic civilizations of Asia. Chardin's *Journal* (1711) had stressed the effects of climate and from this Montesquieu got most of the information used in the *Persian Letters*. What he proposed to do was to show the variability of the main types of government in all the multitude of circumstances to which these types are forced to adapt themselves.

For Montesquieu as for Aristotle the types or species of government were fixed; they are merely modified by the influence of their environment. Since Aristotle limited himself to the Greek cities, this assumption was substantially true; it was much more dangerous in an investigation planned on Montesquieu's scale. Considering the importance of the matter for his project, he devoted surprisingly little effort to determining the forms of government capable of being used in a comparison so wide. He explained his reasons neither for adopting in part the traditional threefold classification nor for departing from it. He merely asserted that governments are of three kinds: republican (a conflation of democracy and aristocracy), monarchical, and despotic. Despotism differs from monarchy in being arbitrary and capricious, while the latter is a constitutional government according to forms of law and requires the continuance of "intermediate powers," such as the nobility or communes, between the monarch and the people. To each of these forms of government he attached a "principle," or motive force in the character of subjects, from which its power is derived and which is necessary to its continuance and functioning. Thus popular government depends on the civil virtue or public spirit of the people, monarchy depends upon the sense of honor of a military class, and despotism depends upon the fear or slavishness of its subjects.

It is impossible to see that Montesquieu's classification followed any principle at all. In respect to the number of rulers, monarchy and despotism fall together; and in respect to constitutionality, a republic can be as lawless as a despotism. Moreover, the idea that despotic governments have no law was a fiction, as was also the idea that his three kinds of government correspond respectively to small, middle-sized, and large states. It cannot be supposed that this classification of forms of government was in any sense produced by observation or comparison. As a venture in political realism it was not comparable with Harrington's theory that governments may be classified according to certain forms of land-tenure. Montesquieu seems to have followed merely a subjective interest motived by his ethical reaction to the political problems of France. His republic, actuated by the sturdy civic virtue of its citizens, was the Roman republic (or his idealization of it), having no relation to modern republics. His despotism was what he feared France had become under the policy of Richelieu and Louis XIV, after local government, the parlements, and the nobility had been deprived of their privileges. His monarchy was what he desired that France should remain, or what he later came to believe that England was. The main outline of Montesquieu's theory, therefore, was determined not by empirical considerations but by his preconceptions about what was desirable in France.

In so far as the *Spirit of the Laws* has any arrangement, it consists in following out the modifications in law and institutions appropriate to each form of government and the variations in each required by circumstances, physical or institutional. But there is not in truth much concatenation of subject-matter, and the amount of irrelevance is extraordinary. Books IV to X deal with educational institutions, criminal law, sumptuary laws and the position of women, the characteristic corruptions of each form, and the type of military organization appropriate to each. Books XI and XII contain the celebrated discussion of political and civil liberty, and Book XIII deals with policies of taxation. Books XIV to XVII have to do with the effects of climate on government and industry, its relation to slavery and to political liberty. Book XVIII covers more briefly the effects of soil. With Book XIX, which reverts incongruously to the influence of custom, even this tenuous outline begins to break down. Books XX to XXII are practically observations at large on commerce and money; Book XXIII on population; and Books XXIV and XXV on religions. The work trails off in Books XXVI to XXXI into remarks on the history of Roman and Feudal Law.

To summarize Montesquieu's conclusions is quite impossible; they are mainly episodic and as a rule they have little dependence on what he alleges to be evidence. With respect to his main purpose it may be said that he oscillates between two tendencies inherent in the confused principles from which he started. On the one hand, he was inclined to assume that human law is rational and that accordingly there is a good reason, under the circumstances, for any usage that is widely and permanently established. Such an attitude agreed with his generally conservative inclination and with the theory that physical causes, such as climate, act directly on mental and moral capacities. Carried to its logical conclusion, however, it would have meant a complete moral relativism, and this was certainly never Montesquieu's position. On the other hand, he perhaps usually thought of climate and certain institutions (like slavery and polygamy) as adverse conditions which have to be compensated by legislation to produce a good moral result. This way of interpreting political evolution implies that the moral ideas at least of legislators are independent of social causation and that the causal influence of climate and the like is effective mainly as it enters into their calculations. Such a view cuts under a sociological theory of politics and repeats the exaggerated ideas about the influence of rulers which Machiavelli had made current. In fact, however, Montesquieu was less guilty on this score than his contemporaries.

It is impossible, therefore, to attach any very precise meaning to Montesquieu's celebrated dictum that laws must be adapted to the circumstances in which a nation lives. Undoubtedly it suggested a corrective for a purely abstract or *a priori* treatment of political justice. Undoubtedly also it suggested a comparative study of law on a wide scale, but it left the plan for such study quite vague. Montesquieu's most positive suggestion — that natural forces like climate act directly on the body and so upon the mind — has shared the fate of the same hypothesis in biology, which seemed so promising to Lamarck. The statement that Montesquieu really envisaged and used an inductive and comparative method of studying social institutions must be taken with extreme qualification. Probably few important political theorists were more addicted to hasty generalizations or less inclined to distinguish between exact inference and the impulsion of prior convictions. He was indeed a man of wide reading but his knowledge was inexact, judged not by the scholarly standards of a later time but in terms of the sources at his disposal. His curious erudition was largely used to illustrate beliefs that would have been exactly the same if he had never heard of Persia. Even of political affairs in Europe, which lay under his eyes, Montesquieu was not so profound an observer as Machiavelli, Bodin, or even Harrington, who made no such pretensions to universal knowledge. What saves him from the charge of being an elegant amateur was not his scientific achievement but his whole-souled enthusiasm for liberty. He was a moralist for whom the eternal verities had begun to wear thin but who lacked the constructive power to get on without them.

THE SEPARATION OF POWERS

On the whole the estimate of Montesquieu's contemporaries — that his importance lay in spreading and strengthening the belief in British institutions as the means of political liberty — was not wrong. His residence in England freed him from the preconception that political liberty depends upon a superior virtue known only to the Romans and realized only in a city-state. It gave substance to his rooted dislike for despotism and suggested a way in which the evil effect of absolutism in France might perhaps be remedied. That Montesquieu himself believed it possible to imitate English government in France is probably not true, but certainly the famous eleventh book of the *Spirit of the Laws,* in which he ascribed liberty in England to the separation of the legislative, executive, and judicial powers, and to the balancing of these powers against each other, set up these doctrines as dogmas of liberal constitution-making. The extent of Montesquieu's influence in this respect is unquestionable and may be read at large in the bills of rights of American and French constitutions.[13]

This idea was, of course, one of the most ancient in political theory. The idea of the mixed state was as old as Plato's *Laws* and had been utilized by Polybius to explain the supposed stability of Roman government. The tempered or mixed monarchy

[13] For example, The Virginia Declaration of Rights (1776), sect. 5; the Massachusetts Constitution of 1780, Preamble, sect. 30; the French Declaration of the Rights of Man and of Citizens (1791), sect. 16. Americans of course were not dependent on Montesquieu alone for the separation of powers.

was a familiar conception throughout the Middle Ages, and medieval constitutionalism had in fact depended on a division of powers, as distinct from the sovereign power claimed by the new monarchy. In England the controversies between the crown and the courts of common law and between the crown and parliament had given concrete importance to the separation of powers. Harrington had considered it to be essential to free government and Locke had given it a subsidiary place in his theory of parliamentary priority. But in truth the idea of mixed government had never had a very definite meaning. It had connoted in part a participation and a balancing of social and economic interests and classes, in part a sharing of power by corporations such as communes or municipalities, and only in a small degree a constitutional organization of legal powers. Perhaps its greatest use had been as a makeweight against extreme centralization and as a reminder that no political organization will work unless it can assume comity and fair dealing between its various parts.

So far as Montesquieu modified the ancient doctrine it was by making the separation of powers into a system of legal checks and balances between the parts of a constitution. He was not in fact very precise. Much of what his eleventh book contained, such for example as the general advantages of representative institutions or the specific advantages of the jury-system or a hereditary nobility, had nothing to do with the separation of powers. The specific form of his theory depended upon the proposition that all political functions must of necessity be classifiable as legislative, executive, or judicial, yet to this crucial point he devoted no discussion whatever. The feasibility of making a radical separation between legislation and the judicial process, or between the making of a policy and control over its execution, would hardly have commended itself in any age to a political realist. Montesquieu, like everyone who used his theory, did not really contemplate an absolute separation of the three powers: the legislative ought to meet at the call of the executive; the executive retains a veto on legislation; and the legislature ought to exercise extraordinary judicial powers. The separation of powers, as Montesquieu described it and as it always remained, was crossed by a contradictory principle — the greater power of the legislature — which in effect made it a dogma supplemented by an undefined privilege of making exceptions.

It is a remarkable fact about Montesquieu's version of the separation of powers that he professed to discover it by a study of the English constitution. In truth the civil wars had destroyed the vestiges of medievalism that made it appropriate to call England a mixed government, and the Revolution of 1688 had settled the supremacy of Parliament. To be sure, when Montesquieu visited England, the status of the ministry was not very clearly fixed, but no man who relied on independent observation would have pitched upon the separation of powers as the distinctive feature of the constitution. But Montesquieu did not rely on observation. Locke and Harrington had taught him what to expect and for the rest he adopted the myth which was current among the English themselves. Thus he may have learned from his friend Bolingbroke:

> It is by this mixture of monarchical, aristocratical, and democratical power, blended together in one system, and by these three estates balancing one another, that our free constitution of government hath been preserved so long inviolate.[14]

This theory of the constitution was preserved, partly under Montesquieu's influence, by Blackstone. Even Burke, though he was the last man to take seriously a rigid separation of legal powers, believed that the Revolution had resulted in the balancing of interests and orders. It was not until Bentham's criticism of Blackstone in the *Fragment on Government* (1776) that the separation of powers was effectively attacked.

VOLTAIRE AND CIVIL LIBERTY

Apart from its analysis of the English constitution, the *Spirit of the Laws* was not in its implications characteristic of political thought in the eighteenth century. The book at least suggested a dependence of political institutions upon physical and social causes, and a consequent relativism of political values, which was contrary to the view that commonly prevailed. In general French writers in the eighteenth century believed as firmly as

[14] *A Dissertation upon Parties.* Letter 13; from the *Craftsman,* written in 1733–34.

those of the seventeenth that reason provides an absolute standard by which human conduct and social institutions can be once for all justified or discredited. The tactical value of this assumption for the criticism of corrupt or oppressive governments is evident. Moreover, the two great triumphs of modern thought — Newton's physics and Locke's psychology — appeared for the time being to lend themselves to such an interpretation. Newton's success in stating the mechanical laws of nature, true without limitation of space or time, gave color to the presumption that political and economic events could be treated in the same highly generalized fashion, while Locke's proposal of a universal natural history of the mind, conceived on lines substantially similar to those of Newton's physics, implied the psychological explanation of social processes without reference to limitations set by history or the evolution of institutions. Newton and Locke were the two writers whose authority stood highest throughout the eighteenth century. To popularize Newton's physics and Locke's philosophy were the two projects that Voltaire brought with him from England when he returned to France in 1729.[15]

Voltaire's admiration for England was directed less toward its representative government than toward the freedom of discussion and publication which it permitted. Hence the first incidence of Locke's philosophy in France was only indirectly political. It came as much from the *Letters on Toleration* as from the *Treatises of Government*, and it coincided both with the tradition of French constitutionalism, which Louis XIV had violated by revoking the Edict of Nantes, and with the effects of Pierre Bayle's genial skepticism, which had urged, even before Locke had published his similar argument, that no religious doctrine is either indubitable or indispensable to morals. The oppressive censorship both of religious and political opinion made the freedom of publication a vital issue in France, and in this cause no publicist labored so tirelessly as Voltaire. His onslaught on persecuting Christianity was probably the greatest contribution to freedom of speech ever made. But he largely divorced this crusade from the cause of popular government, a not very far-sighted policy, since civil liberty was unattainable unless political liberty came with it. He

[15] His *Letters on the English* was published in English in 1733 and in French in 1734.

had little interest in politics on its own account and no interest at all in the masses of men, whom he regarded as cruel and stupid. But he had an intense interest in the freedom of scholars, and he was humane enough to be revolted by the stupidities and brutalities of French criminal law. Best of all, he was endlessly pugnacious and he was gifted with a wit that could always make his enemies ridiculous. Since it was impossible to argue with institutions that had no brains, ridicule was his most effective weapon. Because of the censorship, this sort of attack on the church and also on the state had to be carried on chiefly by innuendo and indirection. Diderot in the *Encyclopaedia* stated the plan upon which that great organ of liberalism was edited:

> In all cases where a national prejudice would seem to deserve respect, the particular article ought to set it respectfully forth, with its whole procession of attractions and probabilities. But the edifice of mud ought to be overthrown and an unprofitable heap of dust scattered to the wind, by references to articles in which solid principles serve as a base for the opposite truths. This way of undeceiving men operates promptly on minds of the right stamp, and it operates infallibly and without any troublesome consequences, secretly and without disturbance, on minds of every description.[16]

The novelty of Voltaire's ideas of religion and toleration consisted not in any quality intrinsic to them. They differed from Locke's only slightly, in a more complete denial of revelation, and not at all from those of many Englishmen. But in France they took on a radical tone which they entirely lacked in England, and the same was true of Locke's political philosophy. This was due less to the ideas themselves than to the environment in which they found themselves. The French government and the French church being what they were, even moderately liberal ideas were subversive. The very same philosophy, abstractly considered, that had a conservative tone in England had a radical tone in France. As John Morley has pointed out, the Englishmen who set the fashions of English thought in the eighteenth century were all on the side of the *status quo,* while any similar group of French writers would include many who were the objects of active and effective persecution.

[16] *S.v.* Encyclopédie; John Morley's translation.

HELVETIUS: FRENCH UTILITARIANISM

The theoretical enlargement of Locke's social philosophy took place on similar lines both in France and England. The *Treatises of Government,* depending substantially on the self-evidence of individual rights, and also the theory of knowledge in the fourth book of the *Essay,* stood in no relation to what was immediately recognized as the most suggestive part of his work — a natural history of the understanding in terms of ideas derived ultimately from the senses, which he had attempted in the second book. The speculative development of Locke's philosophy therefore concerned itself with enlarging what he had called "the new way of ideas" and with eliminating the Cartesianism which still mainly characterized his theory of scientific knowledge. Probably the work which turned the scale was Berkeley's brilliantly successful little essay on a *New Theory of Vision,* published in 1709 and based partly on Malebranche, which showed how effectively the psychological law of association could be used in analyzing and explaining a mental operation (the visual perception of depth) which seemed to be unitary and innate. Moreover, this way of developing Locke's thought seemed to be in line with his own expressed admiration for Newton's physics. Hume in his *Treatise* (1739) compared the association of ideas as an explanatory principle in psychology with the attraction of gravity in the physical world. Henceforth explanations of mental processes meant reducing them to elements of sensation and showing their evolution through the law of association. By the middle of the century Condillac had made this kind of psychology familiar in France.

Locke's ethical and political ideas now needed revision, because these depended upon the intuitive power of reason to grasp manifest truths. He might reject innate ideas but the self-evident rights of individuals were in reality nothing else. There was no great difficulty, however, in constructing a theory of human behavior that would make it, too, explainable by the association of ideas. The simplest hypothesis was to assume two native forces of motivation, the desire for pleasure and the dislike of pain, and to explain all more complicated motives as derivative by the association of pleasure or pain with more or less remote causes of them; substantially conditioned reflexes. The end of human conduct is simply to enjoy as much pleasure and suffer as little pain as possible. Such a theory was developed in England[17] in the 1730's and 1740's and was elaborately presented in France in Helvetius's *De l'esprit* in 1758. Again there was a surprising difference between the tone which this utilitarian ethics had in England and that which it acquired in France. In England it was in origin a theological, even an ecclesiastical, theory preferred by the orthodox because of the importance which they attached to the pleasures or pains of a future life. In France Helvetius made it a program for the reforming legislator, who can utilize the mechanism of human motives to bring private happiness and public welfare into the most complete accord. In short, he made the greatest happiness principle an instrument of reform and passed it on to his two followers, Beccaria and Bentham. Thus it was that the latter learned in France, and in the first instance from Helvetius, an English philosophy which he could bring back to England and use as an agent of radical reform, though its philosophical principles had been bulwarks of English orthodoxy for half a century.

Helvetius says in the Preface of *De l'esprit* that he has tried to treat ethics like any other science and to make it as empirical as physics. Moralists have tended to be hortatory or denunciatory, both equally futile, for morals must start from an understanding of the forces that cause human action. The first principle of conduct is the fact that men must of necessity pursue their own interests; self-interest in the moral sciences has the same place as motion in physics. What any man judges to be good is what he supposes to conduce to his interests, and similarly what any group of men or any nation sets up as moral is what it believes to conduce to the general interest.

> Moralists declaim continually against the badness of men, but this shows how little they understand of the matter. Men are not bad; they are merely subject to their own interests. The lamentations of moralists will certainly not change this motive power of human nature. The thing to complain of is not the badness of men but the ignorance of legislators,

[17] The earliest clear statement of the theory in outline was in John Gay's *Concerning the Fundamental Principle of Virtue or Morality,* 1731; in L. A. Selby-Bigge's *British Moralists,* Vol. II, p. 267. See E. Albee, *English Utilitarianism* (1902), chs. 1–9.

who have always put the interest of individuals into opposition with the general interest.[18]

The only rational standard of conduct on the whole, then, must be the greatest good of the greatest number; what stands opposed to it is the special good of a particular class or group. A group may have an erroneous notion of the causes of its happiness and so may set up a faulty standard, or a small group may exploit a larger group for its own interests. The remedy in either case is a more enlightened understanding of true interest or a more widespread enlightenment. Morality thus becomes the problem of the "legislator," who must make special interests consonant with general and must above all spread the knowledge by which men can see how the public welfare includes their own. Because moral teaching has largely been entrusted to religious fanatics, because tyrannous rulers have not really desired the public good, and because men have been lazy and superstitious and ignorant, ethics has remained backward relative to other sciences. It is idle to tell men to honor virtue and leave them under institutions that put a premium on vice. A proper understanding of human motives places unlimited power in the hands of intelligent rulers and opens an unlimited possibility of progress in human happiness. An ethics thus conceived becomes the key to public policy.

Good laws are the only means of making men virtuous. The whole art of legislation consists in forcing men, by the sentiment of self-love, to be always just to others. To make such laws it is necessary to know the human heart, and first of all to know that men, though concerned about themselves and indifferent to others, are born neither good nor bad but are capable of being the one or the other according as a common interest unites or divides them; that the preference which each man feels for himself — a sentiment on which the continuance of the race depends — is ineffaceably engraved upon him by nature; that physical sensation produces in us the love of pleasure and the dislike of pain; that pleasure and pain have placed the germ of self-love in the hearts of every man, which grows in turn into the passions from which arise all our virtues and vices.[19]

Helvetius supported his conclusion by developing the psychological argument suggested in this quotation. Only the desire for pleasure and the aversion to pain are native impulses. In lan-

18 *De l'esprit,* II. 5; *Oeuvres* (Paris, 1795), Vol. I, p. 208 n.

19 *Ibid.,* II, 24; Vol. I, pp. 394 ff.

guage later borrowed by Bentham he describes these as the two "safeguards" that nature has supplied to men; all other motives are "factices" and come about by the association of pleasure and pain with acts that are more or less remote causes of them. On this foundation he erected what may be called a psychological theory of culture opposed to Montesquieu's theory that it is directly influenced by climate and the like, and implying a denial of the influence of race. Since all mental operations reduce to associations, he concluded that there are no innate differences of intellectual faculty. The forming of associations depends on attention and attention depends upon the motive force supplied by pleasure or pain. In particular there are no innate moral faculties. The ideas of good and evil that men form depend wholly on what circumstance, or in a broad sense education, makes pleasurable or the reverse; the inferiority or superiority of a nation's morals results chiefly from legislation. Despotism brutalizes while good laws make a natural harmony of individual and public interests; on the whole, great and good men appear wherever the skill of legislators has created the proper rewards of talent and virtue. Though difficult, this task is not impossible, and the moral development of any people to any height is at least simple in principle: it consists in creating the necessary incentives to the desired virtues by supplying increments of pleasure or pain at the strategic points.

The associational psychology and the utilitarian ethics appeared to be a great simplification of Locke's political theory because, for an unspecified number of self-evident rights, it substituted a single standard of value, the greatest happiness of the greatest number. In fact, it was much more than a simplification because, thoroughly applied, it destroyed natural right, the contract theory of government, and the whole system of natural law that was supposed to guarantee the harmony of individual interests in society. No writer in the eighteenth century was entirely clear on this point except Hume, and even Bentham, who followed him in setting utility in opposition to natural rights, was far from seeing all the implications of doing so. For if morality and social institutions are justified merely by their utility, rights must be so too, and in consequence any claim to a natural right is either nonsense or merely a confused way of saying that the right really does conduce to the greatest happiness. Helvetius seems to have been quite unaware of this discrepancy.

As the utilitarian ethics was actually worked out it contained assumptions that were in no way justified by the principle of utility but were accepted as in effect self-evident. Thus the presumption that everyone's happiness could be maximized at once was nothing except the old belief in the harmony of nature, which was supposed to prove that realizing all individual rights would produce the most harmonious society. Again, the presumption that one man's happiness ought to be counted as having the same value as another's was identical with the belief in natural equality. It was quite possible that the two principles, utility and natural right, should have led to opposite practical conclusions, and in some degree they really did so. The conclusion that Helvetius drew from the principle of utility was that a wise legislator would use pains and penalties to make men's interests harmonize, which need not imply any great degree of liberty. Natural law, on the contrary, implied that men's interests were naturally harmonious if they were left free, and this argument was used by the economists to prove that the legislator ought to keep his hands off trade. What held the two arguments together was not logic but the fact that those who used them were pretty well agreed about the conclusions they meant to reach. The same political reforms were defended indifferently in the name of utility or of natural law.

THE PHYSIOCRATS

The utilitarianism which Helvetius developed as a theory of morals and legislation was extended simultaneously to economics, Quesnay's *Tableau économique* being published in the same year with *De l'esprit*. Like Helvetius the Physiocrats regarded pleasure and pain as the two springs of human action and enlightened self-interest as the rule for a well-regulated society. But they allowed no such rôle to the legislator; his task is easy, namely, to avoid interfering with the natural operation of economic laws. Since each man is the best judge of his own interests, the surest way to make men happy is to reduce restrictions on individual effort and initiative. Governments ought, therefore, to reduce legislation to the indispensable minimum that will prevent invasions of individual liberty. This argument assumes that there are natural economic laws — what Adam Smith later called "the obvious and simple system of natural liberty" — which produce the greatest prosperity and harmony when they are not interfered with. It was a curious confusion of two quite different meanings of natural law, the older meaning of it as setting up a standard of justice and right reason and the newer meaning of it as giving merely an empirical generalization. From the point of view merely of utility there was no reason to presume that a policy of keeping government out of business would necessarily lead to the greatest good of the greatest number. Economic liberty was not taken to imply political rights; the Physiocrats were content with absolute monarchy if it would follow an enlightened economic policy. In general, all the French philosophers, except Rousseau, were more concerned with civil liberties, such as equality before the law and freedom of action, than they were with popular government.

HOLBACH

The full polemic force of the utilitarian version of natural rights was not felt in France until the 1770's, when Holbach published "the Bible of atheists," his famous *System of Nature,* and also his works on politics.[20] In place of Voltaire's vague deism Holbach put a thoroughgoing atheism or materialism, supposed to depend on physical science, and made it the ground for a drastic attack on religion. The *System of Nature* was the first of a series of books, punctuating philosophy at intervals of about a generation, which have achieved enormous popularity with those who believe that religion is the "opium of the people." Like the others, Holbach's book included a kind of pantheist religion of its own which had no logical dependence on science. Certainly the famous apostrophe to Nature with which he ended was never derived by any intellectual operation from contemplating a mechanical system.

Holbach left Voltaire behind in still another respect; side by side with his attack on religion he placed an equally outspoken attack on government. Governments in general, and the government of France in particular, have been ignorant, incompetent, unjust, rapacious, devoted to the exploitation rather than the well-being of their subjects, indifferent to trade and agriculture

[20] *Système social,* 1773; *La politique naturelle,* 1773.

as well as to education and the arts, mainly interested in war and conquest, and rather the breeders of depopulation and famine than the agents of the general good. Through this indictment ran an intense note of class-consciousness, that of the excluded middle class, acutely aware of its own virtues, bitterly hostile to a government that exploited it in the interest of a class of social parasites, and serenely confident that its own interests were identical with the general good. For Holbach and the English utilitarians the belief that the middle class is in a special sense the representative of social welfare made it appear that class-conflict was merely an evil to be removed by extending political rights. This awareness of class-conflict and of government as an instrument of exploitation was carried to England with utilitarianism, where it lay ready to the hand of Karl Marx.

In its general principles there was little difference between Holbach's political philosophy and that of Helvetius, but Holbach was less interested in psychology and more interested in government. Men are not born bad but are made so by bad government; the essence of bad government is that it has not made the general happiness its main object; the cause of bad government is that it has been in the hands of tyrants and priests whose interest is not to govern but to exploit; and the remedy is to give free scope to the "general will"[21] which implies a harmony of self-interest and natural good. The sovereign is an agent who exercises the authority of society to repress injurious conduct. But society is good only because it gives men freedom to seek their own good, and liberty is an "inalienable right" because prosperity is impossible without it. All nations taken together make up an international society in which war is the counterpart of murder and robbery within a single nation. Despotism is a perversion of sovereignty in which the interests of a governing class usurp the place belonging to the general interest; the division of interests between classes is a chief source of weakness. The remedy, in a word, is education, which by itself Holbach expected to "work the miracle" of a reformation, for men are rational and need only see their true interest

[21] The expression *volonté générale* was used by Diderot in his article on Natural Law and by Rousseau in the article on Political Economy in the *Encyclopaedia* (1755). Which man originated it is uncertain, but Rousseau gave it a special meaning of his own; see the next chapter.

to follow it. Enlighten them, remove the obstacles set up by superstition and tyranny, leave them free to follow the light of reason, convince rulers that their interests are really identical with those of their subjects, and a happy state of society will follow almost automatically. If men see their real interests they will follow them; if they follow their true self-interest, the good of all follows. Nothing is more astonishing than the way in which Holbach can draw an indictment against the stupidity of all history and in the same breath propose to change it by merely pointing out that stupidity does not pay.

In contrast with the violence of Holbach's charges against government is the rather extreme moderation of the liberal remedies that he had to propose. He was in no sense a revolutionist, at least in intention. Again and again he says that reason sheds no blood, that enlightened men are peaceable, that intelligence is slow but sure. Still less was he a democrat. The representatives of the people must be men of property, "bound to the state by their possessions and interested to conserve them as much as to maintain liberty."

> By the word people I do not mean the stupid populace which, being deprived of enlightenment and good sense, may at any moment become the instrument and accomplice of turbulent demagogues who wish to disturb society. Every man who can live respectably from the income of his property and every head of a family who owns land ought to be regarded as a citizen. The artisan, the merchant, and the wage-earner ought to be protected by a state which they serve usefully after their fashion, but they are not true members until by their labor and industry they have acquired land.[22]

Hence for Holbach the true reformer was the sovereign; all that is needed is to convince him that "the absurd right to do wrong" is bad policy. The belief in the omnipotence of enlightenment was not a democratic doctrine because universal education appeared to be impossible. The great democrat of the eighteenth century was Rousseau, and his ideas about education attached least importance to intellectual enlightenment.

[22] *Système social* (1773), Vol. II, p. 52.

PROGRESS: TURGOT AND CONDORCET

Throughout this literature from Helvetius to Holbach runs the idea of human progress. It was implicit in the idea of a natural social order and in the vision of a general science of human nature, in the belief that social well-being is a product of knowledge, and most emphatically in Locke's conception that knowledge results from the accumulation of experience. The idea of progress had never been wholly absent from philosophical empiricism, from the time when Bacon, comparing ancient with modern learning, had asserted that the modern age "is a more advanced age of the world, and stored and stocked with infinite experiments and observations," or when Pascal had suggested that the history of the race, like that of an individual, may be conceived as a continuous process of learning. Voltaire in his histories, by emphasizing the idea that the evolution of the arts and sciences is the key to social development, contributed to the same point of view. Turgot and Condorcet turned the idea of progress into a philosophy of history by enumerating the stages of development through which society has passed.[23] Of the two Turgot's brief essay was philosophically the more important, though Condorcet shows more clearly the aspirations and hopes which inspired the belief in progress. Turgot with profound insight stated the essential difference between those sciences, such as physics, which seek for laws of recurrent phenomena, and history, which follows the ever-growing accumulation of experience that makes up a civilization. In seeking a pattern for this infinitely growing variety he suggested something not very different from Comte's law of the three stages: an animistic, a speculative, and a scientific stage. Condorcet contented himself, after mentioning three hypothetical pre-historical stages, with dividing European history into six stages, two for the ancient, two for the medieval, and two for the modern period. The French Revolution, he thought, marked the beginning of a new and more glorious era. The disasters in which the Revolution involved him and which destroyed him before his book was finally revised could not destroy his confidence in human destiny.

[23] Turgot, *Discours sur les progrès successifs de l'esprit humain,* 1750; Condorcet, *Esquisse d'un tableau historique des progrès de l'esprit humain,* 1794. In England Godwin's *Political Justice* (1793) presented a philosophy similar to Condorcet's.

Condorcet's account of the coming era is more indicative of the meaning which the idea of progress had for him than his division of history. This utopia is to arise from the spread of knowledge and from the power which knowledge gives to men over the obstacles to happiness, physical and mental. Its basis is Locke's empiricism, interpreted after the manner of Helvetius. Progress, Condorcet believed, will probably follow three lines, growing equality between nations, the elimination of class-differences, and a general mental and moral improvement resulting from the first two. It is possible for all nations and all races to become as enlightened as the revolutions have shown the Americans and the French to be. Democracy will do away with the exploitation of backward races and make Europeans the elder brothers rather than the masters of black men. Within each nation it is possible to remove the disadvantages of education, opportunity, and wealth which inequalities of social class have imposed on the less fortunate. Freedom of trade, insurance for the sick and aged, the abolition of war, the elimination of both poverty and luxury, equal rights for women, and above all universal education can give a practically equal chance to all. Finally, Condorcet expected that progress would be cumulative, since the perfecting of social arrangements will improve the mental, moral, and physical powers of the race itself.

> The time will come when the sun will shine only upon a world of free men who recognize no master except their reason, when tyrants and slaves, priests and their stupid or hypocritical tools, will no longer exist except in history or on the stage.[24]

> Bliss was it in that dawn to be alive,
> But to be young was very heaven!

When the philosophy briefly described in this chapter is passed in review, the conclusion cannot be avoided that it was important rather for the extent of the public which it influenced than for the novelty or the profundity of the ideas which it disseminated. It belonged more to the *métier* of popularization than of discovery. The eighteenth century has rightly been called the age of encyclopaedias, an age in which Europe consolidated the gains made by the more original genius of the preceding century. This was true

[24] *Esquisse* (ed. by O. H. Prior), p. 210.

even of a figure as striking as Montesquieu. Its political philosophy remained essentially that of natural rights, inhering in individual personalities and setting the standards of what law and government may rightfully do and the limits beyond which they may not rightfully go. In the nature of the case such rights must be set up as axioms, the products of rational intuition, incapable of proof and still less defensible by empirical generalization. At the worst this was a better dogmatism than that of authority from which it released the seventeenth century, but the appeal to self-evidence was none the less dogmatism. Neither in science nor social studies could it withstand a wide and steady application of empirical methods.

There was a steady though not a completely conscious change in this respect throughout the eighteenth century: social philosophy was empirical as neither Hobbes nor Locke had been. It prosecuted the study of social history as the seventeenth century had never done; it explored the customs and the manners of outlandish folk as no rationalist would have thought worth while; it followed the processes of manufacture and the mechanic arts, of trade and finance and taxation, in a manner shocking to the pundits of the higher learning. Yet this empiricism had, so to speak, all the bias of rationalism; it had the foible of omniscience and the itch for simplicity. It appealed to fact but it insisted that facts should speak a predetermined language. Even the new ethics of utility and the new economics, which were the chief additions made to social theory, were logically incoherent for precisely this reason. They professed to rest on an empirical theory of human motives but they assumed a harmony of nature for which no scientific proof could ever have been given. Thus the popular thought of the eighteenth century reiterated a philosophy which in effect it only half believed and professed a method which it only half practiced. The practical importance of this popular philosophy was very great. It spread through all Europe the belief in science; it fostered the hope that intelligence might make men measurably the masters of their social and political fate; it passionately defended ideals of liberty, opportunity, and humane living, even though it did so mainly in the interest of a single social class. Beyond measure it did not apotheosize its prejudices. But intellectually it was superficial and partly for this reason it fell a prey to an appeal to sentiment, begun by Rousseau, which on the whole lacked its solid virtues.

SELECTED BIBLIOGRAPHY

The Heavenly City of the Eighteenth-century Philosophers. By Carl L. Becker. New Haven, Conn., 1932.

The Idea of Progress: An Inquiry into its Origin and Growth. By J. B. Bury. London, 1920.

Montesquieu. By J. Dedieu. Paris, 1913.

Montesquieu and English Politics (1750–1800). By F. T. H. Fletcher. London, 1939.

Condorcet on the Progress of the Human Mind. By Sir James George Frazer. Oxford, 1933.

Turgot. By C.-J. Gignoux. Paris, 1945.

The Social and Political Ideas of some Great French Thinkers of the Age of Reason. Ed. by F. J. C. Hearnshaw. London, 1930. Chs. 5, 6, 8.

"The Age of Reason." "Diderot." By Harold J. Laski. In *Studies in Law and Politics.* London, 1932.

The Rise of European Liberalism: An Essay in Interpretation. By Harold J. Laski. London, 1936. Ch. 3.

The Political Doctrine of Montesquieu's Esprit des lois. By Lawrence L. Levin. New York, 1936.

French Liberal Thought in the Eighteenth Century: A Study of Political Ideas from Bayle to Condorcet. By Kingsley Martin. Boston, 1929.

"Turgot." "Condorcet." By John Morley. In *Critical Miscellanies.* 4 vols. London, 1898–1908. Vol. II.

Diderot and the Encyclopaedists. By John Morley. 2 vols. London, 1878.

Voltaire. By John Morley. 4th ed. London, 1882.

Essays in the History of Materialism. By G. V. Plekhanov. Eng. trans. by Ralph Fox. London, 1934.

Natural Rights: A Criticism of some Political and Ethical Conceptions. By David G. Ritchie. London, 1895.

The Pioneers of the French Revolution. By Marius Roustan. Eng. trans. by Frederic Whyte. Boston, 1926.

Condorcet and the Rise of Liberalism. By J. Salwyn Schapiro. New York, 1934.

Montesquieu in America, 1760–1801. By Paul M. Spurlin. University, Louisiana, 1940.

Baron d'Holbach: A Prelude to the French Revolution. By W. H. Wickwar. London, 1935.

CHAPTER XXVIII

THE REDISCOVERY OF THE COMMUNITY: ROUSSEAU

Between the writers most characteristic of the French Enlightenment and Jean Jacques Rousseau is fixed a great gulf. Its existence was patent to everyone concerned; its exact nature has never been finally settled. Diderot described it as " the vast chasm between heaven and hell " and said that the very idea of Rousseau disturbed his work " as if I had a damned soul at my side." Rousseau in turn said that any man who could doubt his honesty " deserved the gibbet." All Europe resounded with the quarrel and the bitterness on both sides passes belief. Even the elementary question of personal honesty is still debated, though probably few now believe that Diderot was anything but an upright man or that Rousseau was really a hypocrite. Thomas Carlyle once said that he differed from Sterling only in his " opinions." Rousseau differed from his contemporaries in everything but his opinions; even when he used the same words he meant something different. His character, his outlook on life, his scale of values, his instinctive reactions, all differed essentially from what the Enlightenment regarded as admirable. The twelve years from 1744 to 1756 that he spent in Paris brought him into close association with the circle that wrote the *Encyclopaedia* but they only produced on both sides the conviction that Rousseau did not belong there.

This opposition, and indeed all that Rousseau wrote on philosophy and politics, grew in some devious way from his complex and unhappy personality. His *Confessions* gives a clear picture of a deeply divided personality, in which morbidities both of sex and religion played a large part. " My tastes and thoughts," he says, " always seemed to fluctuate between the noble and the base." His relations with women, both real and imaginary, display a violent sensuality failing alike of animal satisfaction or effective sublimation, but issuing in a riot of sentimental fancy and introspective attitudinizing. For him the discipline, intellectual or moral, characteristic of Calvinism in its more vital forms had never existed. But he continued to be bedevilled by a Puritan conscience, a sense of sin, and the fear of damnation. It had little effect perhaps on what he did but it produced, by way of compensation, a fine crop of moral sentiments. "I easily forget my misfortunes, but I cannot forget my faults, and still less my virtuous sentiments." Rousseau's passionate belief that men are naturally good, which he once said was the fundamental principle of his ethical writings, was less an intellectual conviction than a reversal of his innate fear that he was bad. By throwing the fault on society he was able at once to satisfy his need for condemnation and to shelter himself in a comfortable myth.

This conflict in Rousseau's personality between the noble and the base, the ideal and the real, robbed him of all satisfaction in his work or confidence in its value. The inception of an idea was like a light from heaven, resolving "all the contradictions of our social system." The expression conveyed not one-quarter of the vague but glittering vision. In social relations he labored under a painful sense of inadequacy, stupidity, and self-distrust. He seems never to have been comfortable except with women and in relationships practically devoid of intellectual content. By inclination he was parasitic and during considerable periods he lived in a state of semi-dependence, but he could never accept dependence gracefully. Instead, he built around himself a myth of pseudo-Stoicism and fictitious self-sufficiency, which expressed itself most definitely in suspicion of those who tried to befriend him and in the discovery of elaborate plots, probably imaginary, to ruin and betray him. Before the end of his life these suspicions became well-defined delusions of persecution. Despite his years of not uncongenial vagabondage, he represented in taste and morals the sentimentality of the lower middle class. Essentially he was interested in homely things, was terrified of science and art, distrusted polished manners, sentimentalized commonplace virtues, and enthroned sense above intelligence.

THE REVOLT AGAINST REASON

More than most men Rousseau projected the contradictions and maladjustments of his own nature upon the society about him and sought an anodyne for his own painful sensitivity. For this purpose he adopted the familiar contrast between the natural and the actual, current in all the appeals to reason. But Rousseau did not appeal to reason. On the contrary he turned the contrast into an attack upon reason. Against intelligence, the growth of knowledge, and the progress of science, which the Enlightenment believed to be the only hope of civilization, he set amiable and benevolent sentiments, the good will, and reverence. What gives value to life is the common emotions, perhaps one might say instincts, in respect to which men differ hardly at all and which he imagined to exist in a purer and less perverted form in the simple, uneducated man than in the enlightened and sophisticated. "A thinking man is a depraved animal." All his moral valuations turned upon the worth of these common feelings: the affections of family life, the joy and beauty of motherhood, the satisfactions of the homely arts like tilling the soil, the universal feeling of religious reverence, above all, the sense of a common lot and the sharing of a common life — all that men learned after him to call the "realities" of everyday living. By contrast science is the fruit of idle curiosity; philosophy is mere intellectual frippery; the amenities of polite life are tinsel.

The hero of Rousseau's primitivism was not the noble savage; it was the irritated and bewildered bourgeois, at odds with a society that despised and looked down on him, conscious of his own purity of heart and the greatness of his own deserts, and profoundly shocked at the badness of the philosophers to whom nothing was sacred. By some queer logic of the emotions, therefore, he joined in an equal condemnation both the social order that oppressed him and the philosophy which had attacked the foundations of that society. Against both he set up the pieties and the virtues of the simple heart. The truth is that Rousseau first made vocal a newly awakened fear, the fear that rational criticism, having demolished the more inconvenient pieties like the dogmas and disciplines of the church, might not be made to stop before the pieties which it still seemed judicious to retain.

> These vain and futile declaimers [the philosophers] go forth on all sides, armed with their fatal paradoxes, to sap the foundations of our faith, and nullify virtue. They smile contemptuously at such old names as patriotism and religion, and consecrate their talents and philosophy to the destruction and defamation of all that men hold sacred.[1]

In short, intelligence is dangerous because it undermines reverence; science is destructive because it takes away faith; reason is bad because it sets prudence against moral intuition. Without reverence, faith, and moral intuition there is neither character nor society. This was a note which the Enlightenment could not easily understand — unless it were a covert defense of revelation and the church, as in fact it was not — for the Enlightenment was accustomed to center its faith and its hope in reason and science. The enormous importance of Rousseau lies in the fact that, broadly speaking, he carried philosophy with him against its own tradition. Kant acknowledged that Rousseau had first revealed to him the surpassing value of the moral will as compared with scientific inquiry, and Kant's philosophy, if not the beginning of a new age of faith, at least began a new division between science on the one side and religion and morals on the other. In this new alignment philosophy was less the ally of science than the protector of religion. Science must be carefully confined to the phenomenal world, where it can do no harm to the verities of the heart, to religion and the moral law. To say that science knows only appearances at least suggests that there is some other way of knowing realities. Philosophy, once released from science, did not always walk soberly with the moral law. Sometimes it sought the higher truth by ways nonrational and irrational, by faith, by the light of genius, by metaphysical intuition, or in the will. The distrust of intelligence was written large over the philosophy of the nineteenth century.

A political philosophy which, like Rousseau's, began by magnifying the moral sentiments against reason, might be carried out in a variety of ways but it was bound to be contrary to the traditional liberalism either of natural rights or of utility. Both Rousseau and Kant denied that rational self-interest is a reputable moral motive and excluded prudence from the list of moral virtues. The outcome might be a more radical doctrine of equality than could be

[1] *The Arts and Sciences*, Eng. trans. by G. D. H. Cole, *The Social Contract and Discourses* (Everyman's Library), p. 142.

defended on grounds of reason and individual rights, since Rousseau supposed that the moral virtues exist in the greatest purity among the common people. As he said in *Émile:*

> It is the common people who compose the human race; what is not the people is hardly worth taking into account. Man is the same in all ranks; that being so, the ranks which are most numerous deserve most respect.[2]

A democracy of this sort, however, need imply very little personal liberty because it attaches only slight importance to individual preeminence. An ethics that identifies morality with rational self-interest at least presumes freedom of private judgment, but an ethics of sentiment, especially if it stresses sentiments that are equally native to all men, need not do so. In the end what it is most certain to inculcate is reverence for the authority of tradition and custom. The morality of the plain man, however much of the good will it may embody, is inevitably the morality of his time and place. Its standards are rather those of the group than of the individual, and such a morality always teaches submission to the group and conformity to its customary duties. This being so, there is no assurance that they will turn out in the end to be democratic at all. It was more or less an accident that Rousseau put a high estimate on a simple society with no marked differences of rank. The virtues of loyalty and patriotism, which he chiefly admired, and the glory of finding happiness in the welfare of the group, need have no special reference to democracy. It is hard to say whether Rousseau belonged more truly to Jacobin republicanism or to a conservative reaction.

MAN AS CITIZEN

It is convenient to distinguish between two periods of Rousseau's political writing, a formative period dated about 1754–55, in which he gave shape to his own ideas in opposition to Diderot,[3] and the

[2] Quoted by Morley, *Rousseau* (1886), Vol. II, pp. 226 f.

[3] The chief works were the *Discours sur l'inégalité* (1754), the article in the *Encyclopaedia* on "Économie politique" (1755), a suppressed chapter, "De la société générale du genre humain" (I, ii), of the first draft of the *Contrat social,* and several unpublished fragments. The best edition is C. E. Vaughan's *Political Writings of Jean Jacques Rousseau,* 2 vols., Cambridge, 1915. The published works are translated by G. D. H. Cole, *The Social Contract and Discourses* (Everyman's Library).

period in which the final version of the *Social Contract* was prepared for publication in 1762. Many critics have felt a fundamental logical discrepancy between the works of these two periods, described by Vaughan as " the defiant individualism of the *Discours sur l'inégalité* " and " the equally defiant collectivism of the *Contrat social.*" It is certain that Rousseau himself felt no such opposition; in the *Confessions* he says that " every strong idea in the *Social Contract* had been before published in the *Discourse on Inequality.*" In general Rousseau's opinion was correct, though it is also true that incompatible ideas abound throughout his writings. Much that seems like " defiant individualism " persisted in the *Social Contract,* and none of his works can be reduced to a consistent system. The difference between the earlier works and the *Social Contract* is merely that in the former he was writing himself free from an uncongenial social philosophy and in the latter he was expressing, as clearly as he could, a counter-philosophy of his own.

The social philosophy from which Rousseau had to disentangle himself was the systematic individualism which, by the time he wrote, was attributed to Locke. It held that the value of any social group consists in the happiness or self-satisfaction which it produces for its members, and especially in the protection of their inherent right to own and enjoy property. Human beings are led to cooperate by enlightened self-interest and a nice calculation of individual advantage. A community is essentially utilitarian; in itself it has no value though it protects values; the motive on which it rests is universal selfishness; and it contributes mainly to the comfort and security of its members. Quite rightly Rousseau attributed this philosophy as much to Hobbes as to Locke. Against Hobbes he brought the pertinent objection that the state of war attributed to individual men in a state of nature really belongs to " public persons " or " moral beings called sovereigns." [4] Men fight not as detached individuals but as citizens or subjects.

The writer who did most to release Rousseau from this individualism was Plato. With Rousseau there begins, in fact, a new era of classical influence in political philosophy, which was extended through Hegelianism and which was more genuinely Greek than the pseudo-classicism of the eighteenth century. What

[4] The fragment on *L'état de guerre,* Vaughan, Vol. I, p. 293.

Rousseau got from Plato was a general outlook. It included, first, the conviction that political subjection is essentially ethical and only secondarily a matter of law and power. Second and more important, he took from Plato the presumption, implicit in all the philosophy of the city-state, that the community is itself the chief moralizing agency and therefore represents the highest moral value. The philosophy to which Rousseau stood opposed began with fully formed individuals; to them it imputed a full complement of interests and the power to calculate — a desire for happiness, the idea of ownership, the power to communicate with other men, to bargain with them, to make an agreement, and finally to make a government that will give the agreement force. Plato stimulated Rousseau to ask, Where do individuals get all these capacities except from society? Within a society there may be individuality, freedom, self-interest, respect for covenants; outside it there is nothing moral. From it individuals get their mental and moral faculties and by it they become human; the fundamental moral category is not man but citizen.

To this conclusion Rousseau was led also by his own citizenship in the city-state of Geneva. It is difficult to see in his early life that this ever exerted any tangible influence on him while he was subject to it, but afterward he rationalized and idealized it. This may be seen in the dedication which he placed before the *Discourse on Inequality*, written at a time when he planned to make Geneva his home. This idealization of the city-state was one reason why his political philosophy never articulated closely with contemporary politics. In formulating a theory he never envisaged a state on a national scale, and in writing on concrete questions, his views had little to do with his theories. Rousseau himself was in no sense a nationalist, though his philosophy contributed to nationalism. By reviving the intimacy of feeling and the reverence connoted by citizenship in the city-state, he made it available, at least as an emotional coloring, to citizenship in the national state. The cosmopolitanism implied by natural law he chose to regard as merely a pretext for evading the duties of a citizen.

During the two years in which his political ideas were forming, Rousseau was largely concerned with the meaning of conventional expressions such as the "state of nature" or the "natural man," which were obviously incompatible with his own idea that men have no moral qualities outside a community. A difference of opinion on this subject with Diderot began the life-long quarrel between the two men. The volume of the *Encyclopaedia* published in 1755 contained an article on Natural Law by Diderot and one on Political Economy by Rousseau: about the same time he wrote a criticism of Diderot's article for the *Social Contract* but later excluded it from the final draft.

Diderot's article was a rhetorical flourish with conventional ideas: Man is rational; his rationality subjects him to the law of natural equity; the test of morals and government is the general will of the race, embodied in the law and practices of civilized peoples. Its very conventionality made it the proper object for Rousseau's attack; he dissented from every article of the accepted creed. In the first place, the society of the whole human race is a " veritable chimera "; a race is not a society because mere likeness of kind creates no real union, while a society is a " moral person " arising from a real bond (*liaison*) uniting its members. A society must have common possessions, such as a common language and a common interest and well-being, which is not a sum of private goods but the source of them. The human race as a whole has nothing of this sort in common. In the second place, it is absolutely false that reason by itself would ever bring men together, if they were concerned only with their individual happiness, as the conventional theory supposes. The whole argument is fictitious because all our ideas, even of self-interest, are drawn from the communities in which we live. Self-interest is not more natural or more innate than the social needs that draw men together in communities. Finally, if there is any idea of a general human family, it arises from the little communities in which men live instinctively; an international community is the end and not the beginning.

> We conceive a general society according to our particular societies; the establishment of little states makes us think of large ones; and we begin properly to become men only after we have become citizens. This shows what we should think of those pretended cosmopolitans who, in justifying their love for their country by their love for the human race, make a boast of loving all the world in order to enjoy the privilege of loving no one.[5]

[5] Vaughan, Vol. I, p. 453.

NATURE AND THE SIMPLE LIFE

The argument of the *Discourse on Inequality*, which was published at about the same time, was seriously clouded by the arresting attack on private property for which the work has been mainly known. Obviously if there are no rights of man, property is not one; in his *Plan for a Constitution of Corsica* Rousseau even said that the state ought to be the sole owner. But certainly he was not a communist. In the article on Political Economy he referred to property as " the most sacred of all the rights of citizenship " and even in the *Discourse* itself he treated it as a quite indispensable social right. It is true that the half-century before the Revolution produced in France schemes of utopian communism which bear about the same relation to middle-class radicalism as Winstanley's communism to the political doctrine of the English Levellers. Meslier before Rousseau and Mably and Morelly after him sketched " natural " schemes of society in which goods, especially land, were to be owned in common and the produce shared, and in the revolutionary era itself Maréchal's *Manifesto of Equals* and Babeuf's communist uprising in 1796 carried on the idea that political freedom is a superficial remedy without economic equality. To this body of communist ideas Rousseau's attack on private property in the *Discourse* may be said vaguely to belong. But he had no serious idea of abolishing property and no very definite idea about its place in the community. What Rousseau contributed to socialism, utopian or other, was the much more general idea that all rights, including those of property, are rights within the community and not against it.

As a whole the *Discourse* was meant to deal with the same question as the chapter in criticism of Diderot's article on Natural Law. It was this which Rousseau put into the Preface as the problem of the book: What really is natural and what is artificial in human nature? In general terms his answer is that, over and above self-interest, men have an innate revulsion against suffering in others. The common basis of sociability is not reason but feeling; except to the perverted man suffering anywhere is directly painful. In this sense men are " naturally " good. The calculating egoist of the theories exists not in nature but only in a perverted society. The philosophers " know very well what a citizen of London or Paris is but not what a man is."[6] What then is the truly natural man? The answer cannot be drawn from history because if natural men ever existed, they certainly do not now. If one tries to make a hypothetical picture, the answer is certain: Natural man was an animal whose behavior was purely instinctive; any thought whatever is "depraved." He wholly lacked language, unless in the form of instinctive cries, and without language any general idea is impossible. Consequently the natural man was neither moral nor vicious. He was not unhappy but neither was he happy. Obviously he had no property, for property resulted from ideas, foreseen wants, knowledge, industry, which were not intrinsically natural but implied language, thought, and society. Selfishness, taste, regard for the opinion of others, the arts, war, slavery, vice, conjugal and paternal affection all exist in men only as they are sociable beings who live together in larger or smaller groups.

This argument was quite general: it proved merely that the natural egoist is a fiction, that some kind of community is inevitable, and that no society is purely instinctive. Rousseau intertwined with it, however, another argument that was logically irrelevant. His early writings far more than the *Social Contract* are filled with a kind of pessimism, probably the result of irritation induced by his residence in Paris, which made him believe that existing French society was little more than an instrument of exploitation. Grinding poverty in one class contributes merely to parasitic luxury in another; the arts fling "garlands of flowers over men's chains" because they are beyond the reach of the masses on whose labor they are supported; and economic exploitation issues naturally in political despotism. Against this perverted society Rousseau chose to set an idealized simple society which is in a just mean between primitive indolence and civilized egoism. Evidently the conclusion that existing societies are perverted and should be simplified has nothing to do with the prior conclusion that some kind of society is the only moralizing force in human life. If society as such were a perversion, the conclusion would be that it ought to be abolished: Rousseau has been accused of timidity for not drawing it. In fact this was not his conclusion. The simple society that he chose to admire is

[6] *L'état de guerre,* Vaughan, Vol. I, p. 307.

very far removed, as he was at pains to show, from natural instinct. For this reason it is not very clear just what practical consequences, if any, do flow from his criticism of the state of nature. It all depends on the nature of the society in which the individual is to be imbedded. A national state, a militant working-class, or ultramontane Catholicism might all claim, as easily as the city-state that Rousseau affected, to represent the ultimate value to which men ought to give their loyalty. The implications can be conservative quite as easily as radical.

Of the early works that which stated Rousseau's political theory most clearly is the article on Political Economy in the fifth volume of the *Encyclopaedia*. It was evidently in some sense a companion-piece to Diderot's article on Natural Law in the same volume. Rousseau's most characteristic political idea, the "general will," appeared in both, and it is uncertain whether he or Diderot invented the term. Certainly Rousseau made it his own. His article touched briefly on most of the ideas developed later in the *Social Contract* — the theory that a community has a corporate personality or *moi commun*, the organic analogy for a social group, the doctrine that the general will of the corporate self sets the moral standards valid for its members, and the implied reduction of government to a mere agent of the general will. The general principle behind the argument is that already mentioned, that mere likeness of kind does not make men into a society but only a psychological or spiritual bond — "the reciprocal sensibility and internal correspondence of all the parts" — analogous to the vital principle of a living organism.

> The body politic, therefore, is also a moral being possessed of a will; and this general will, which tends always to the preservation and welfare of the whole and of every part, and is the source of the laws, constitutes for all the members of the state, in their relations to one another and to it, the rule of what is just or unjust.[7]

The tendency to form societies is a universal trait; wherever individuals have a common interest they form a society, permanent or transient, and every society has a general will which regulates the conduct of its members. Larger societies are composed not directly of individuals but of smaller societies, and each more in-

[7] Vaughan, Vol. I, pp. 241 f.; Eng. trans. by G. D. H. Cole, p. 253.

clusive society sets the duties of the smaller societies that compose it. Thus Rousseau still left standing the "great society," the human race, of which natural law is the general will, but as a society rather than as a race. The bonds of this society, however, are obviously weak. In effect Rousseau sets up patriotism as the supreme virtue and the source of all other virtues.

> It is certain that the greatest miracles of virtue have been produced by patriotism: this fine and lively feeling, which gives to the force of self-love all the beauty of virtue, lends it an energy which, without disfiguring it, makes it the most heroic of all passions.[8]

Human beings must be made citizens before they can be made men, but in order that they may be citizens, governments must give liberty under the law, must provide for material welfare and remove gross inequality in the distribution of wealth, and must create a system of public education by which children are "accustomed to regard their individuality only in its relation to the body of the state." The general problem of a political philosophy Rousseau stated almost in the form of the paradox with which he opened the *Social Contract:*

> By what inconceivable art has a means been found of making men free by making them subject? [9]

THE GENERAL WILL

The *Social Contract* was published in 1762. By Rousseau's account it was a part of a much larger work which he had projected but was not able to finish. The plan of this larger work is unknown, but in view of the arrangement of subject-matter in the *Social Contract* itself, he probably began by stating abstractly his theory of the general will and then went on to make observations at large about history and politics. The latter part of the book as published retains traces of the reading of Montesquieu, as did also Rousseau's published plan for a constitution of Corsica and his *Considérations sur le gouvernement de Pologne.* The *Social Contract,* in its theoretical part, is excessively abstract; when Rousseau writes on current questions it is usually difficult to see what the theory has to do with his proposals or the proposals with the

[8] Vaughan, Vol. I, p. 251; Eng. trans. by G. D. H. Cole, p. 263.

[9] Vaughan, Vol. I, p. 245; Eng. trans. by G. D. H. Cole, p. 256.

theory. It is safe to say, therefore, that nothing was lost when he abandoned his more extended work. The general will and the criticism of natural right comprised everything of importance that he had to say. The practical uses to which that theory might be put were various, and Rousseau had neither the knowledge nor the patience to explore them. His belief that a small community like the city-state is the best example of the general will made it impossible for him to discuss contemporary politics with much point.

The development of the theory of the general will in the *Social Contract* was involved in paradoxes, partly because of the cloudiness of Rousseau's ideas but partly, it seems, because he had a rhetorician's liking for paradox. Manifestly, in view of his criticism of the natural man, he ought to have avoided the notion of contract altogether as both meaningless and misleading. Seemingly he retained the phrase because he liked its popular appeal, and in order not to make the inconsistency too glaring, he deleted the criticism of the state of nature which he had written against Diderot. Not content with this complication, after introducing the contract he explained it away, so far as any definite contractual meaning was concerned. In the first place, his contract has nothing to do with the rights and powers of government, since the latter is merely the people's agent and is so devoid of independent power that it cannot be the subject of a contract. In the second place, the imaginary act by which a society is produced is not even remotely like a contract, because the rights and liberties of individuals have no existence at all except as they are already members of the group. Rousseau's whole argument depended upon the fact that a community of citizens is unique and coeval with its members; they neither make it nor have rights against it. It is an " association " not an " aggregation," a moral and collective personality. The word contract was about as misleading as any that Rousseau could have chosen.

The social order is a sacred right which is the basis of all other rights.[10]

The problem is to find a form of association which will defend and protect with the whole common force the person and goods of each associate, and in which each, while uniting himself with all, may still obey himself alone, and remain as free as before.

[10] *Social Contract,* I, i.

> Each of us puts his person and all his power in common under the supreme direction of the general will, and, in our corporate capacity, we receive each member as an indivisible part of the whole.[11]

Another paradox lay in the fact that Rousseau could not persuade himself to give over trying to prove that men individually gain more by being members of society than they would by remaining isolated. This is implied in the famous sentence with which the *Social Contract* opened and in which he proposed to explain what can make the bondage of society " legitimate." This way of putting the question implied that Rousseau was going to show, as Holbach or Helvetius might, that being a member of society is on the whole a good bargain. Of course he was going to do nothing of the sort, if the state of nature was a chimera and all the values by which the bargain might be judged were nonexistent except in a society. Similarly, the assertion that man " is everywhere in chains " implied that society is a burden for which individuals need to be compensated, whereas Rousseau was going to argue that they are not human at all except as members of a community. A bad community might impose chains on its members, but Rousseau was logically bound to hold that it did so because it was bad and not because it was a community. The question, what justifies the existence of communities, should have been treated by him as nonsensical. The question, what makes one community better than another, is of course legitimate; it would involve a comparison of communities in terms of the social and individual interests that each conserves, but not a comparison between a community and its absence. Again, an individual might be better off in one community than in another, but the question whether he would be better or worse off in no community ought to have been ruled out as unmeaning. For it was society, he said, that " substituted justice for instinct and gave men's actions the morality they had formerly lacked." " Instead of a stupid and unimaginative animal, it made him an intelligent being and a man." Apart from society there would be no scale of values in terms of which to judge well-being.

The general will, therefore, represented a unique fact about a community, namely, that it has a collective good which is not the same thing as the private interests of its members. In some sense

[11] *Ibid.*, I, vi.

it lives its own life, fulfills its own destiny, and suffers its own fate. In accordance with the analogy of an organism, which Rousseau had developed at some length in the article on Political Economy, it may be said to have a will of its own, the "general will" (*volonté générale*):

> If the state is a moral person whose life is in the union of its members, and if the most important of its cares is the care for its own preservation, it must have a universal and compelling force, in order to move and dispose each part as may be most advantageous to the whole.[12]

The rights of individuals, such as liberty, equality, and property, which natural law attributed to men as such, are really the rights of citizens. Men become equal, as Rousseau says, "by convention and legal right," not, as Hobbes had said, because their physical power is substantially equal.

> The right which each individual has to his own estate is always subordinate to the right which the community has over all.[13]

In the community men first gain civil liberty, which is a moral right and is not merely the "natural liberty" which by a figure of speech might be attributed to a solitary animal.

THE PARADOX OF FREEDOM

So far this is perfectly true and a fair reply to the extravagances of contemporary speculation about the state of nature. Just what it entails, however, about the rights of men in society is far from obvious, and Rousseau's account of the matter sometimes contradicted itself within the limits of a single page. For example:

> The social compact gives the body politic absolute power over all its members.
>
> Each man alienates, I admit, by the social compact, only such part of his powers, goods and liberty as it is important for the community to control; but it must also be granted that the sovereign is sole judge of what is important.
>
> But the sovereign, for its part, cannot impose upon its subjects any fetters that are useless to the community.
>
> We can see from this that the sovereign power, absolute, sacred, and inviolable as it is, does not and cannot exceed the limits of general conventions, and that every man may dispose at will of such goods and liberty as these conventions leave him.[14]

[12] *Ibid.*, II, iv. [13] *Ibid.*, I, ix. [14] *Ibid.*, II, iv.

In fact, Rousseau moved back and forth at will between his own theory of the general will and the indefeasible individual rights which ostensibly he had abandoned. In itself the mere fact that rights of any sort require social recognition and can be defended only in terms of a common good signifies nothing about what individual rights a well-regulated community will give to its members. Since Rousseau believed as a matter of course that social well-being itself dictates some liberty of individual choice and action, wherever he meets this sort of case he sets it down as a limitation upon the general will. Logically it is nothing of the sort, if liberty itself is one of the things that the general good requires. On the other hand, Rousseau was quite capable of arguing that because there are no indefeasible rights in defiance of the general good, there are no individual rights at all. This again was a logical confusion, unless one argues, as Rousseau certainly did not mean to do, that all liberty is contrary to the social good. The truth is that the general will is so abstract — asserting merely that rights are social — that it justified no inference at all about the extent to which individuals might wisely be left to their own devices within society. At the same time the general position was of course valid against a theory of natural rights that left social well-being entirely out of account.

This confusion in Rousseau's argument gave rise to another paradox which is especially important and especially irritating, the paradox of freedom. He began by assuming a burden that was incumbent on egoistic theories but not upon him, provided he meant really to reject egoism, namely, to prove that in society a man " may still obey himself alone." Consequently he undertook nothing less than to show that real coercion never occurs in society and that what is taken to be coercion is only apparently so, a paradox of the worst sort. Even a criminal wills his own punishment!

> In order then that the social compact may not be an empty formula, it tacitly includes the undertaking . . . that whoever refuses to obey the general will shall be compelled to do so by the whole body. This means nothing less than that he will be forced to be free. . . . This alone legitimizes civil undertakings, which, without it, would be absurd, tyrannical, and liable to the most frightful abuses.[15]

[15] *Ibid.*, I, vii.

In other words, coercion is not really coercion because when a man individually wants something different from what the social order gives him, he is merely capricious and does not rightly know his own good or his own desires.

This kind of argument, in Rousseau and after him in Hegel, was a dangerous experiment in juggling with ambiguities. Liberty had become what Thorstein Veblen called an "honorific" word, the name for a sentiment with which even attacks on liberty wished to be baptized. It was perfectly legitimate to point out that some liberties are not good, that liberty in one direction may entail loss of liberty in another, or that there are other political values which in some circumstances are more highly esteemed than liberty. Straining language to show that restricting liberty is really increasing it, and that coercion is not really coercion, merely made the vague language of politics still vaguer. But this was not the worst of it. What was almost inevitably implied was that a man whose moral convictions are against those commonly held in his community is merely capricious and ought to be suppressed. This was perhaps not a legitimate inference from the abstract theory of the general will, because freedom of conscience really is a social and not merely an individual good. But in every concrete situation the general will has to be identified with some body of actual opinion, and moral intuitionism usually means that morality is identified with standards which are generally accepted. Forcing a man to be free is a euphemism for making him blindly obedient to the mass or the strongest party. Robespierre made the inevitable application when he said of the Jacobins, "Our will is the general will."

> They say that terrorism is the resort of despotic government. Is our government then like despotism? Yes, as the sword that flashes in the hand of the hero of liberty is like that with which the satellites of tyranny are armed. . . . The government of the Revolution is the despotism of liberty against tyranny.[16]

The general will, as Rousseau said over and over again, is always right. This is merely a truism, because the general will stands for the social good, which is itself the standard of right. What is not right is merely not the general will. But how does

[16] To the National Convention, February 5, 1794; *Moniteur universel*, 19 Pluviôse, l'an 2, p. 562.

this absolute right stand in relation to the many and possibly conflicting judgments about it? Who is entitled to decide what is right? Rousseau's attempts to answer these questions produced a variety of contradictions and evasions. Sometimes he said that the general will deals only with general questions and not with particular persons or actions, thus leaving the application to private judgment, but this conflicted with his assertion that the general will itself determines the sphere of private judgment. Sometimes he tried to make the general will equivalent to decision by a majority, but this would imply that the majority is always right, which he certainly did not believe. Sometimes he spoke as if the general will registered itself automatically by making differences of opinion cancel each other. This opinion cannot be refuted but neither can it be proved. It amounted to saying that communities — states or nations — have an inscrutable faculty for discerning their well-being and proper destiny. Rousseau originated the romantic cult of the group, and this was the fundamental difference between his social philosophy and the individualism from which he revolted. The rationalist centered his scheme of values in the culture of the individual, in intellectual enlightenment and independence of judgment and enterprise. Rousseau's philosophy emphasized the aggrandizement of a group, the satisfactions of participation, and the cultivation of the non-rational.

In Rousseau's intention the theory of the general will greatly diminished the importance of government. Sovereignty belongs only to the people as a corporate body, while government is merely an agent having delegated powers which can be withdrawn or modified as the will of the people dictates. Government has no vested right whatever, such as Locke's theory of the contract had left to it, but has merely the status of a committee. Rousseau conceived this to exclude any form of representative government, since the sovereignty of the people cannot be represented. The only free government is therefore a direct democracy in which the citizens can actually be present in town-meeting. Just why the general will should be restricted to this one form of expression is not very clear, apart from Rousseau's admiration for the city-state. Doubtless it was his belief that the theory of popular sovereignty diminished the power of the executive but this was an illusion. For though "the people" have all power and all moral right and wisdom, a corporate body cannot as such express its will or execute it. The more the community is exalted the more authority its spokesmen have, whether they are called representatives or not. Even parties and factions, which Rousseau thoroughly detested, are more likely to be strengthened than weakened by the idea of corporate sovereignty. A well-regimented minority, whose leaders are persuaded of their own inspiration and whose members " think with their blood," has proved an almost perfect organ for the general will.

ROUSSEAU AND NATIONALISM

Rousseau's political philosophy was so vague that it can hardly be said to point in any specific direction. In the age of the Revolution probably Robespierre and the Jacobins owed most to him, for his theory of popular sovereignty and his denial of any vested right in government made, as Gierke said, a kind of doctrine of " permanent revolution " which was very suitable to the purposes of a radical democratic party. Moreover, there was really nothing in the conception of the general will that required it to be shared consciously by the whole people or to be expressed only in a popular assembly. Rousseau's enthusiasm for the democratic city-state was an anachronism. The small community with a prevailingly rural economy, loosely federated with other similar communities, which would perhaps have represented his ideals most literally, had no importance in Europe and only a passing importance in America. Though Rousseau believed that free citizenship was impossible in any form of larger state, it was inevitable under the circumstances that the sentiment which he aroused should result mainly in idealizing national patriotism. Thus in his essay on Poland he might advise a policy of decentralization, but the only effect of the work must lie in its appeal to Polish nationalism. On the other hand, he persistently libelled the humanitarian and cosmopolitan ideals of the Enlightenment as a mere lack of moral principle.

> Today there are no longer Frenchmen, Germans, Spaniards, or even Englishmen; there are only Europeans. . . . They are at home wherever there is money to steal or women to seduce.[17]

[17] *Considérations sur le gouvernement de Pologne,* ch. 3; Vaughan, Vol. II, p. 432.

The net effect was a very uncritical adaptation of the ideal of citizenship as it had been in a city-state to the modern national state, which is an almost wholly different kind of social and political unit. Thus the state was idealized as including all the values of national civilization, much as the Greek city had overlapped nearly all phases of Greek life, though in fact no modern state did anything of the sort. Thus without being himself a nationalist, Rousseau helped to recast the ancient ideal of citizenship in a form such that national sentiment could appropriate it.

Nationalism, however, was not a simple force acting in a single direction or with a single motive. It might mean democracy and the rights of man, as in general it did in the age of the Revolution, but it might mean also an alliance between the landowning gentry and the new middle-class aristocracy of wealth. It might sweep away the remnants of feudal institutions only to build in their place new institutions that would rely no less heavily on traditional loyalties and the subordination of classes. Inevitably nationalism in France and England, where there was no doubt of political union, would be quite different from nationalism in Germany, where the aspiration for a national government commensurate with the unity of German culture would soon overtop all other questions. Rousseau's idealizing of the moral feelings of the plain man found an immediate echo in the ethics of Kant. Its full significance, especially his idealizing of the collective will and of participation in the common life, appeared in German philosophy with the idealism of Hegel. Rousseau's collectivism, however, required a drastic revaluation of custom, tradition, and the accumulating heritage of the national culture, without which the general will was nothing but an empty formula. This, in turn, amounted to a thoroughgoing revolution in philosophical values. Since the time of Descartes custom and reason had by common consent been set in contrast to one another. The proper work of reason had been to release men from the bondage of authority and tradition, in order that they might be free to follow the light of nature. This was the meaning of the whole imposing system of natural law. This the sentimentalism of Rousseau tacitly set aside. The idealism of Hegel tried to weave reason and tradition into a single unit — the expanding culture of a national spirit or consciousness. In effect reason was to be bent to the service of custom, tradition, and authority, with a corresponding emphasis on the values of stability, national unity, and continuity of development.

Hegel's philosophy conceived the general will as the spirit of the nation, expanding and embodying itself in a national culture and creating its organs in an historical constitution. Apart from the incoherence of Rousseau's presentation of it, the obvious defect of the general will as he left it was the extreme abstractness of the conception. It was the mere idea or form of a community, as Kant's categorical imperative was the mere form of a moral will. Nothing but historical accident, so to speak, attached it to the sense of membership in a nation and the idealizing of national citizenship. Rousseau's position as an alien in French national life, his moral incapacity to ally himself with any social cause, and the state of French politics when he wrote, all conspired to prevent him from giving to the general will any concrete embodiment. This want, however, was at once supplied by Edmund Burke. For Burke the conventions of the constitution, the traditional rights and duties of Englishmen, the living presence of a rich national culture growing from generation to generation were not abstractions but real existences, suffused with the warmth of ardent patriotism and the glow of moral sentiment. In the later years of his life the shock and horror of the French Revolution forced him to break the habit of a lifetime and to state in general terms the philosophy upon which he had always acted. The result was at once a contrast and a supplement to Rousseau. In Burke the corporate life of England became a conscious reality. The general will was released from temporary bondage to Jacobinism and made a factor in conservative nationalism.

Throughout the eighteenth century the tradition of philosophical rationalism and the system of natural law which was its most typical creation was in a state of gradual decadence. Rousseau's denial of it was largely a matter of feeling; he lacked the intellectual penetration and the steadiness of intellectual application to criticise the system in place of which he set up the autonomy of sentiment. But this criticism already existed, the work of David Hume. From the time of Locke, the growth of the empirical philosophy and the increasingly empirical practice of social studies had caused a steady infiltration of incongruous ideas into the system of natural law. Perhaps it would be truer to say that the system of natural law itself had included from the start, under the name of reason, a variety of factors which for the sake of clearness needed to be discriminated and which grew steadily more incongruous as social studies advanced. The breaking apart of the old system was due mainly to the analytic genius of Hume. His negative limitation of reason was really a logical precondition both of the value which Rousseau attributed to moral sentiment and of that which Burke attributed to a growing national tradition.

SELECTED BIBLIOGRAPHY

Rousseau and Romanticism. By Irving Babbitt. Boston, 1919.

The Philosophical Theory of the State. By Bernard Bosanquet. London, 1899. Chs. 4, 5.

La politique comparée de Montesquieu, Rousseau et Voltaire. By Émile Faguet. Paris, 1902.

Jean Jacques Rousseau: Discours sur les sciences et les arts. Ed. by George R. Havens. New York, 1946. Introduction.

The Social and Political Ideas of some Great French Thinkers of the Age of Reason. Ed. by F. J. C. Hearnshaw. London, 1930. Ch. 7.

Jean-Jacques Rousseau, Moralist. By Charles W. Hendel. 2 vols. London, 1934.

Du contrat social, précédé d'un essai sur la politique de Rousseau. By Bertrand de Jouvenal. Geneva, 1947.

The Idea of Nationalism: A Study in its Origins and Background. By Hans Kohn. New York, 1944. Ch. 5.

Rousseau. By John Morley. 2 vols. 2nd ed. London, 1883.

Rousseau and Burke: A Study of the Idea of Liberty in Eighteenth-century Political Thought. By Annie M. Osborn. New York, 1940.

La pensée de Jean-Jacques Rousseau: essai d'interpretation nouvelle. By Albert Schinz. Paris, 1929.

The Political Writings of Jean Jacques Rousseau. Ed. by C. E. Vaughan. 2 vols. Cambridge, 1915. Introduction.

The Political Tradition of the West: A Study in the Development of Modern Liberalism. By Frederick M. Watkins. Cambridge, Mass., 1948. Ch. 4.

The Meaning of Rousseau. By Ernest H. Wright. London, 1929. Ch. 3.

CHAPTER XXIX

CONVENTION AND TRADITION: HUME AND BURKE

The philosophy of Rousseau attacked only one limited segment of the system of natural law, the artificiality of seeing in society merely an agent to secure individual goods and in human nature merely a capacity to calculate advantages. Against this he set a single counter-proposition, that the core of healthy personality consists of a few massive feelings which have little to do with intellectual power but which are of a sort to bind men together in communities, so that the well-being of the community makes up the most significant part even of the private good. This proposition he can hardly be said to have defended; he enunciated it rather as a moral intuition, the direct insight of an uncorrupted nature, and attributed to the philosophers as a fault, and to their unmeasured use of intellectual criticism, the selfishness and lack of public spirit which he saw in European society. Had Rousseau stood alone, the imposing system of natural law, elaborated in a century and a half of philosophical development, would hardly have fallen before an attack so ill-directed and leading to a result so uncertain in its applications as the general will. But Rousseau did not stand alone. The acclaim which he won with a body of ideas neither numerous nor well-digested, and which he stated with a sentimentality that was tawdry as often as it was moving, showed that his public was already prepared, emotionally at least, to respond to a new kind of moral appeal. Intellectually, also, the system of natural law was already inadequate, in the sense that it supplied no rational apparatus adequate to the social studies which were being projected and that its dogmatic claim to self-evidence was little better than a boast. It was living in France mainly on its utility as the revolutionary solvent of an antiquated political and social system.

In England this preservative did not exist. The defense of

revolution ended with Locke, until the French Revolution itself produced a reverberation of natural rights, and the temper of English writers throughout the eighteenth century, in respect to both politics and religion, was markedly conservative. In a country where both church and government, though admittedly subject to serious abuses, served well the interests of the classes that were politically vocal, the system of natural law had lost its immediate practical utility. Moreover, English philosophy in the half century after the publication of Locke's *Essay* developed almost exclusively on empirical lines, stressing the natural history of ideas and their derivation from the senses, as Locke himself had suggested. English ethical writing followed the same course. The idea of a deductive ethics starting from self-evident moral laws, which Locke had retained, soon became antiquated. Until Bentham English utilitarianism lacked the radical and reformatory purposes that Helvetius gave the theory in France, but it was systematically clearer because it tried consciously to eliminate incongruous ideas like natural justice and natural right. Even in economics, which remained the stronghold of natural law well into the nineteenth century, Adam Smith was on the whole less devoted to a deductive method than the classical economists after him, probably because the latter were more influenced than Smith by the French Physiocrats. Possibly his economics might have been still more systematically empirical if he had followed more closely the economic essays of his friend Hume.

HUME: REASON, FACT, AND VALUE

This criticism and gradual elimination of the system of natural law culminated in Hume's *Treatise of Human Nature,* published in 1739–40. This work occupies a crucial position in the history of modern philosophy and its importance is not even mainly in the field of political philosophy. At the same time, the general philosophical position that Hume developed had a profound bearing upon all branches of social theory. What Hume supplied was a penetrating logical analysis which, if accepted, destroyed all the pretensions of natural law to scientific validity. In addition he extended this critical result to specific applications of natural law in religion, ethics, and politics. At least the main principles of Hume's analysis must be stated because they affected the whole future course of social theory. The technicalities in which he formulated his argument and which are now obsolete may be neglected.

Hume undertook to analyse the conception of reason, as this term was customarily used in the systems of natural law, to show that under this term there had been uncritically combined and confused three factors or processes which are quite different in their meaning. The effect of this confusion was to describe as necessary truths, or unchangeable laws of nature and of morality, propositions which can make no claim to such absolute certainty. First, Hume undertook to say what can rightly be called reason in this necessary and inevitable sense. There are, he admitted, certain " comparisons of ideas " which yield truths of this kind. They are to be found, he thought, only in limited parts of mathematics and they have definite peculiarities. They are what would now be called formal implications and they state that a conclusion follows if a premise is taken for granted. Nothing need be known about the truth of the premise, because all that is inferred is that if one proposition is true, then another proposition also must be true. As Hume put it, not very accurately, the relationship is merely between ideas; the actual facts do not matter. Because of the direction that his interests took Hume gave less importance than was deserved to this kind of mathematical or formal truth. What he was chiefly concerned to do was to distinguish it from other logical operations with which it was confused, and also to show that this was the precise and proper meaning of rational or necessary truth.

It clearly follows from what has been said that no " comparison of ideas " can prove a matter of fact, and also that relationships between matters of fact are never necessary in the strict logical or rational sense just mentioned. This was the point of Hume's famous analysis of the relation between cause and effect. It is always possible to assume the contrary of any matter of fact, and when two facts or events are found to be related as cause and effect, all that can be really known about them is that they do actually occur together with a certain degree of regularity. Apart from the experience of actually finding them together, it would be impossible to infer the one from the other. Hence the so-called necessary connection between causes and effects is a fictitious idea, provided the term necessary is used in the proper logical sense that it has in mathematics: in cause and effect there is only an empirical correlation. It would follow from this analysis of causal relations and matters of fact that the empirical sciences, which deal with events that actually happen and the correlations that actually occur between them, are fundamentally different from mathematics or from deductive reasoning which merely shows that one proposition follows from another.

In the third place, the word reason or reasonable is applied to human conduct. In particular the law of nature always professed to show that there are rational principles of right or justice or liberty which can be shown to be necessary and unescapable. This, Hume concluded, was still another confusion. For in these cases, where a way of acting is said to be right or good, the reference is not to reason but to some human inclination, or desire, or "propensity." Reason in itself dictates no way of acting. It may show, by adducing knowledge of causes and effects, that the result of acting in a certain way will be so and so; the question will still remain whether, when the reasoning is finished, the result is acceptable to human inclination or not. Reason is the guide of conduct only in the sense that it shows what means will reach a desired end or how a disagreeable result can be avoided; the pleasantness of the result is in itself neither reasonable nor unreasonable. As Hume put it, "reason is and ought only to be the slave of the passions and can never pretend to any other office than to serve and obey them." From this analysis it follows that ethics or politics or any sort of social studies where judgments of value have to be taken into account are different both from deductive and from purely causal or factual sciences.

There are then three fundamentally different operations which have all been confused under the name of reason but which Hume proposed to distinguish: there is, first, deduction or reason in the strict sense; second, there is the discovery of empirical or causal relationships; and third, there is the ascription of a value, as when one speaks of right or justice or utility. If these three operations are carefully distinguished the whole alleged rationality of natural law falls to pieces. Since the two latter are not strictly rational, they both contain factors that cannot be proved. These factors Hume called "conventions," and a large part of his philosophy was devoted to showing the presence of such factors in the empirical and social sciences. These conventions are unescapable, in the sense that both empirical inference and practical common sense require something of the sort. They seem valid because men habitually use them and they are useful in the sense that by means of them more or less stable rules of action are made. But they cannot be shown to be necessary; the contrary could always be assumed. They proceed less from reason than from imagination or from "a propensity to feign," that is, to assume more regularity in nature or society than is certain. In the empirical sciences the law of cause and effect is an example. All the alleged general proofs of it are circular, while its special applications lead at most only to conclusions that are more or less probable. Psychologically, Hume thinks, it is merely a habit, and he can see no reason why nature should conform to human habits, yet without it there is no principle for connecting matters of fact. Similarly, as he proposed to show, social values like justice or liberty also involve conventions which must be referred for their authority to utility, or ultimately to their relation to human motives and propensities to action.

THE DESTRUCTION OF NATURAL LAW

Starting from this general philosophical position, Hume applied his criticism to demolishing various branches of the system of natural law. He did not cover the ground completely, and it was long before the full implications of his argument were seen, but he attacked at least three great branches of the system: natural or rational religion, rational ethics, and the contractual and consensual theory of politics. The very notion of a rational religion, he argued, must be fictitious because, since any deductive proof of a matter of fact is impossible, the existence of God must be indemonstrable. Indeed, the conclusion is more general: a rational metaphysics purporting to show the necessary existence of anything is impossible. The so-called truths of religion, however, lack even the practical reliability of scientific generalizations; they belong purely to the region of feeling. Hence religion may have a "natural history," that is, a psychological or anthropological explanation of its beliefs and practices, but there can be no question of its truth. Similarly, in morals and politics, since values depend upon human propensities to action, it is impossible that reason by itself should create any obligation. Consequently virtue is merely a quality or action of mind that is generally approved. Like religion it can have a natural history but the force of moral obligation depends upon the acceptance of the propensities, the wants, the motives to action that give rise to it. No other validity is possible for it.

Much of Hume's ethical criticism, however, was directed against the prevailing form of utilitarianism which tried to derive all motives from the pursuit of pleasure and the avoidance of pain. His objection to this was empirical; he believed, of course rightly, that it oversimplified motives to the point of falsification. Human nature is not so simple as to have only a single propensity, and many apparently primitive impulses, he thought, have no obvious relation to pleasure. They may be mainly benevolent, as parental affection is within a limited range, or they may be on their face neither selfish nor benevolent. Human nature has to be taken as it is, and the prevailing prejudice that selfish motives are somehow reasonable is part of the same fallacy that made the rationalists think that justice is reasonable. Hume's view of human nature excluded the excessive amount of calculation and foresight that contemporary moralists of all schools were accustomed to impute to it. Men are not, he believed, very calculating in pursuing either their self-interest or anything else. They are only foresighted when their feelings and impulses are not directly engaged, but impulse interferes with self-interest as often as with benevolence. Hume's form of utilitarianism set no special value on egoism and made no undue claims on human intelligence. In this respect it had more in common with that of John Stuart Mill than with that of Bentham, who preferred the simpler but less tenable picture of human nature adopted by the French utilitarians.

Hume's criticism of the theory of consent — that political obligation is binding only because it is accepted voluntarily — was slightly complicated by the fact that he raised no objections to it on historical grounds. On the contrary, he weakened the theory by treating it as nothing but hypothetical history. Like Burke later he was willing to concede that possibly, in the remote past, the first primitive society might have been formed by agreement. Even if this were true it would have nothing to do with present societies. For if the obligation of civic obedience be derived from the obligation to keep an agreement, it is still pertinent to ask why the latter is binding. Empirically the two things are different: no government actually asks its subjects to consent or fails to distinguish between political subjection and the obligation of contract. Among human motives the feeling of loyalty or allegiance to government is as common as the feeling that agreements should be kept. The political world over, absolute governments which do not even do lip-service to the fiction of consent are more common than free governments, and their subjects rarely question their right except when tyranny becomes too oppressive. Finally, the purpose of the two things seems to be different: political allegiance keeps order and preserves peace and security, while the sanctity of contracts mainly creates mutual trust between private persons. Evidently then, Hume argued, the duty of civic obedience and the duty to keep an agreement are different; the one cannot be derived from the other, and even if it could, neither is more obviously binding than the other. Why then should either be binding? Evidently because a stable society in which order is preserved, property protected, and goods exchanged is not possible without them. Both kinds of obligation grow from this single root. If the further question be asked, why men feel obliged to keep order and protect property, the answer is partly that these satisfy motives of tangible self-interest but also partly that allegiance is a habit enforced by education and consequently as much a part of human nature as any other motive. The members of a society do feel a sense of common interest and they admit the obligations that this is seen to impose.

As to its nature, Hume argued that this common interest is more like language than it is like a promise or a rational truth. It is a body of conventions or rough general rules that have been shown by experience to serve human needs in a general way, though particular instances of their application often work a hardship. For the sake of stability men have to know what they can rely on, and hence rules of some sort are necessary. If they become too inconvenient, men will change them, even by violence if there is no other way, but broadly speaking any rules are better than none and the most that can be hoped is that they will work reasonably well. Obviously they are not eternal verities rooted in nature, but merely standard ways of behaving justified by experience of their consequences and fixed by habit. By and large they preserve a stable social life in accord with men's propensities and interests. Hume distinguished two main bodies of such conventions, those that regulate property, which he called the rules of justice, and those that have to do with the legitimacy of political authority. Justice means in general that the possession of property shall be stable, that it may be transferred by consent, and that agreements shall be binding, rules that are justified simply by the fact that they make property into a stable institution and satisfy the needs that create the interests of property. A legitimate government, as distinguished from usurpation, rests on a similar set of conventional rules that serve to discriminate legal authority from mere force. Prescription and formal enactment are the most important of these. Hume illustrated the non-rational character of such rules by pointing out that their effects often extend backward in time. The accession of William in 1688 may have been doubtfully legitimate by any standard then applicable, but he becomes legitimate for present judgment merely because his successors have been accepted as such.

THE LOGIC OF SENTIMENT

If the premises of Hume's argument be granted, it can hardly be denied that he made a clean sweep of the whole rationalist philosophy of natural right, of self-evident truths, and of the laws of eternal and immutable morality which were supposed to guarantee the harmony of nature and the order of human society. In place of indefeasible rights or natural justice and liberty there remains merely utility, conceived in terms either of self-interest or social stability, and issuing in certain conventional standards of conduct which on the whole serve human purposes. Such conventions may, of course, be widespread among men and relatively permanent, because human motives are fairly uniform and in their general outlines change slowly, but in no other sense can they be called universal. They are always contingent upon some state of the facts, upon the causal relations of facts to human inclinations, and upon the formulation of workable rules to give scope to these inclinations. The conventions of society may be explained by history or psychology or anthropology but they cannot claim validity in any but the relative sense of being generally convenient and in accord with men's estimate of utility. All the attempts to find in them an eternal fitness or rightness are merely confused ways of saying that they are useful; granted the principle of utility the whole system of natural right can be dispensed with.

The immediate result of this powerful destructive analysis was not at all what Hume must have anticipated. If the criticism stands, the only possible deduction from it is some form of empirical positivism, without metaphysics or religion and without an ethics that claims validity beyond the circumstances of society and the satisfaction of human needs. What happened proved that metaphysics, religion, and ethics, more or less on traditional lines, were stronger than Hume's criticism. There was, indeed, no disposition on the part of competent philosophers to deny that his conclusions were unescapable if the premises were granted, and there was no special effort to revive the system of natural law with its self-evident truths of reason. On the contrary, after the French Revolution and the conservative reaction against it, the philosophers were more likely to believe that the doctrine of individual rights had suffered only its just fate, as being at once intellectually inept and socially dangerous. But neither had they any desire to stop with Hume's results, which it became the fashion to brand as "merely negative." Consequently there was nothing for it but to go behind Hume's chief premise and to deny that he had been right in making a rigid distinction between reason, fact, and value. If these could be fused into a single operation, or if reason could be interpreted as including them all at once, a new logic, a new metaphysics, and a new defense of absolute values might be produced. This was the course that philosophy, under the guidance of Kant and most completely in Hegel's idealism, elected to follow. Whether it achieved a synthesis or only a new confusion is still subject to debate. In any case Hume's positivism had the paradoxical effect of producing an elaborate metaphysics, a religious revival, and a firmer belief in absolute ethical values.

Though Hegel gave the most systematic statement of this new philosophy, he combined ideas that were everywhere prevalent at the end of the eighteenth century — in a new literary valuation of "sentiment," in romantic pseudo-medievalism, in the revival of folk-poetry and a new interest in the historical roots of national culture, and in the idea that law and institutions express the inner "spirit of the nation." So far as social philosophy is concerned three factors may be mentioned which, it was hoped, might be fused together in a new synthesis. In the first place, there was a tendency either to depreciate logic (or abstract reason) as compared with sentiment, or to hope that the two might be combined in a higher or profounder logic. Carlyle's sneer at Hume's philosophy, as "a flat continuous thrashing-floor for logic, whereon all questions, from the doctrine of rent to the natural history of religion, are thrashed and sifted with the same mechanical impartiality," was typical. In particular, the moral sentiments and the massive feelings of religious reverence and loyalty to the community that Rousseau had glorified were supposed to embody a deeper wisdom than that of mere logical clarity. In the second place, this respect for sentiment and the community carried with it a new estimate of the value of custom and tradition. Instead of regarding them as the antithesis of reason, the new philosophy preferred to see in them the gradual unfolding of a reason implicit in the consciousness of the race or nation. Hence they are no burden which the enlightened individual must shuffle off but a precious heritage to be guarded and into which it is the high privilege of the individual to be inducted. No one expressed this new valuation of the traditional national culture more clearly than Burke. Finally, this change itself implied a new sense of the meaning of history. In the history of civilization it became the custom to see the gradual unfolding of the divine mind and the divine purpose. Hence the values of social life — its morals, its art and religion, and its cultural achievements — were at once absolute and relative, absolute in their ultimate significance though relative in any particular historical embodiment. Reason in man is a manifestation of an underlying cosmic spirit which realizes itself gradually in the history of the nations.

BURKE: THE PRESCRIPTIVE CONSTITUTION

To this imposing but romantic philosophical edifice, which reached completion in the idealism of Hegel and with which the nineteenth century proposed to replace the system of natural law, Burke made an important contribution. He more than any other thinker in the eighteenth century approached the political tradition with a sense of religious reverence. He saw in it an oracle which the statesman must consult and a growing repository of the achievements of the race which must be changed only with a due piety toward its inward meaning. There is, indeed, a certain incongruity in putting Hume and Burke together in a single chapter. The cool and rather sardonic clarity of the Scottish philosopher was the antithesis of the ardent imagination and the innate piety of the Irish statesman. Yet in a sense Burke accepted Hume's negations of reason and the law of nature. There is something almost defiant in his concession that society is artificial and not natural, that it is no product of reason alone, that its standards are conventions, and that it depends on obscure instincts and propensities — even on prejudices. But " art is man's nature." These propensities and the society that grows out of them *are* human nature; without them and without the moral codes and institutions in which they issue a creature might be, as Aristotle said, a beast or a god but not a man. Consequently the traditions of a nation's life have a utility not measured by their contribution merely to private convenience or the enjoyment of individual rights. They are the repository of all civilization, the source of religion and morality, and the arbiter even of reason itself. Burke showed precisely, therefore, the reaction that was to follow upon Hume's destruction of the eternal verities of reason and natural law. Sentiment, tradition, and idealized history stepped in to fill the vacancy left by the removal of self-evident rights, and the cult of the community replaced the cult of the individual.

There has been much discussion about the coherence of Burke's political philosophy, especially about the consistency between his Whig principles and his violent reaction against the French Revolution. This reaction destroyed lifelong political associations and friendships, and to his contemporaries it appeared incompatible with his earlier defense of American liberties, his attacks on the king's control over parliament, and his effort to sweep away the vested rights of the East India Company. In truth this was a misconception. The coherence of Burke's political views was never that of a logically constructed system, but the same conservative principles that actuated his attack on the Revolution ran through everything that he wrote before it. The events in France, it is true, frightened him, unbalanced his judgment, revealed hatreds that had been decently masked, and produced a flood of irresponsible rhetoric in which his impartiality, his judgment of history, and his customary mastery of facts were largely lost. But the Revolution did not produce or even seriously change his ideas. It merely forced him to isolate them from concrete cases and to state them as general propositions. At all times his main political beliefs were the same: that political institutions form a vast and complicated system of prescriptive rights and customary observances, that these practices grow out of the past and adapt themselves in the present with no break in continuity, and that the tradition of the constitution and of society at large ought to be the object of a reverence akin to religion, because it forms the repository of a collective intelligence and civilization. The Revolution made his repudiation of natural rights more violent but not more complete. For convenience in presentation a distinction may be made between Burke's opinions on certain questions specifically English — the nature of the constitution, parliamentary representation, and the value of parties — and generalized statements of theory which were largely called out by the French Revolution.

Burke accepted, as his loyalty to Whig principles required, the theory transmitted from Locke, that the constitution is a balance of crown, lords, and commons. For rhetorical purposes he was not above using the weight of Montesquieu's authority, but in fact his idea of constitutional balance had little to do with the separation of powers which liberals regarded as the bulwark of individual liberties. For Burke the balance is between the great vested interests of the realm and its ground is simply prescription, not at all the inviolability of individual rights. He agreed substantially with Hume that the arrangements of a political society are conventions sanctified by use and wont.

> Our constitution is a prescriptive constitution; it is a constitution whose sole authority is that it has existed time out of mind. . . . Your king, your lords, your judges, your juries, grand and little, all are prescriptive. . . . Prescription is the most solid of all titles, not only to property, but, which is to secure that property, to government. . . . It is a presumption in favor of any settled scheme of government against any untried project, that a nation has long existed and flourished under it. It is a better presumption even of the *choice* of a nation, far better than any sudden and temporary arrangement by actual election. Because a nation is not an idea only of local extent, and individual momentary aggregation; but it is an idea of continuity, which extends in time as well as in numbers and in space. And this is a choice not of one day, or one set of people, not a tumultuary and giddy choice; it is a deliberate election of the ages and of generations; it is a constitution made by what is ten thousand times better than choice, it is made by the peculiar circumstances, occasions, tempers, dispositions, and moral, civil, and social habitudes of the people, which disclose themselves only in a long space of time. . . . The individual is foolish; the multitude, for the moment, is foolish, when they act without deliberation; but the species is wise, and, when time is given to it, as a species it always acts right.[1]

This view of the constitution could, it is true, claim the authority of Locke, but not of those parts of Locke which taught that the rights of individuals are indefeasible and which mainly commended him to revolutionists. It joined rather with the tradition which Locke carried over from Hooker and which went back to a pre-revolutionary idea of the constitution as a comity between powers; all of them have an original authority, because all are organs of the realm, but none of them is legally sovereign. More truly, however, Burke's theory of the constitution and his conception of parliamentary government was based upon the actual settlement of 1688 (as distinguished from Locke's philosophical theory of it) by which effective political control passed into the hands of the Whig nobility. His effort to revivify the Whig Party was already reactionary in 1770, because the great Whig houses no longer had the position of undisputed leadership that they enjoyed after the Revolution. It was his loyalty to this conception of English government that made Burke oppose both the reform of parliament and the growth of George III's influence in it. For he feared, and frankly said that he feared, the patronage of the crown and the money of the East Indian na-

[1] *Reform of Representation in the House of Commons* (1782), *Works*, Vol. VI, pp. 146 f. References are to Bohn's edition, London, 1861.

bobs, which together made up an influence stronger than the Whigs could muster. Burke's conception of parliamentary government accordingly included the independence of the ministry from the court and its leadership in parliament, but it excluded any popularizing of the House of Commons.

PARLIAMENTARY REPRESENTATION AND POLITICAL PARTIES

Consequently his theory of representation also looked back to the seventeenth century. He rejected the idea of a constituency as a numerical or territorial unit and of representation as implying the possession of the ballot by any considerable portion of the population represented. He denied that individual citizens as such are represented and that numerical majorities have any real significance in forming the mature opinion of the country. Virtual representation, that is, representation "in which there is a communion of interests and a sympathy in feelings and desires," he thought had most of the advantages of representation by actual election and was free from many of its disadvantages. In short, Burke visualized parliamentary government as conducted under the leadership of a compact but public-spirited minority, which in general the country was willing to follow, with parliament mainly a place where the leaders of this minority could be criticised and called to account by their party but in the interests of the whole country. At the same time his views permitted some sound criticism of representative government as it then existed. He pointed out effectively difficulties which arose from trying to legislate in parliament in too great detail. He wrote, in his addresses to his constituents at Bristol, the classic defense of a member's independence of judgment and action. Once elected he is responsible for the whole interest of the nation and the empire, and he owes to his constituents his best judgment freely exercised, whether it agrees with theirs or not. As Burke said, a member does not go to school to his constituents to learn the principles of law and government.

Burke's effort to give new life to the Whigs caused him to see, earlier than any other English statesman, the necessary place in parliamentary government held by the political party.[2] This

[2] *Thoughts on the Cause of the Present Discontents* (1770), *Works,* Vol. I, especially pp. 372 ff.

was implied in the Whig conception of the ministry as leaders of the House of Commons. Burke's argument was directed against the prejudice, especially favorable to the pretensions of a "patriot king" like George III, that any combination for a political purpose within the nation is a faction, pursuing only unpatriotic partisan advantages. He formulated the classic definition of a political party:

> Party is a body of men united, for promoting by their joint endeavors the national interest, upon some particular principle in which they are all agreed.

He argued, unanswerably, that any serious statesman must have ideas about what sound public policy requires and, if he is responsible, he must avow the intention to put his policy into effect and seek the means to do it. He must act with others of like views and allow no private considerations to break his loyalty to them. They must hold together as a unit and refuse alliances or leadership incompatible with the principles on which their party is formed. This was unquestionably an idea of great importance for the understanding and operation of constitutional government.

ABSTRACT RIGHTS AND THE POLITIC PERSONALITY

Important though these ideas of English government were, they would hardly entitle Burke to a high place among political philosophers. It was the Revolution in France that forced him, much against his will, to state in general terms the principles upon which he had been accustomed to act. In his earlier writings he had almost ostentatiously eschewed a political philosophy. In the two most celebrated cases in which he played a conspicuous part, the controversy with America and the attack on the privileges of the East India Company, he refused to discuss either the abstract legal powers of parliament or the abstract rights of the colonies or the Company. In the case of America he had proposed to consult the "genius" of the constitution but he had denied that its letter was worth debating. Still more had he been accustomed to speak disparagingly of abstract theories about the rights of citizens, the resort to which he described as "a sure symptom of an ill-conducted state." He had contrasted judgment in the abstract sciences, where it is a merit to consider only one circumstance at a time, with political judgment, which requires consideration of the largest possible number of circumstances. He had denied that moral questions are ever abstract and had asserted that "things are right and wrong, morally speaking, only by their relation and connection with other things." He had described the wisdom of the statesman as prudence, expedience, the knowledge of human nature, and dependence upon opinion. In short, he had conceived politics as an art and a gift of insight, dealing with a subject-matter so "obviously mixed and modified," that human rights "are in a sort of middle, incapable of definition but not impossible to be discerned." It was the militancy of the revolutionary philosophy that forced Burke not, indeed, to state a theory of rights, but to set down in general form his ideas of the social framework in which rights occur.

It is true that he never denied the reality of natural rights. Like Hume he admitted that the social contract may be true merely as a bit of hypothetical history, and much more than Hume he was convinced that some of the conventions of society are inviolable. Just what these immovable principles are he never tried to say — property, religion, and the main outlines of the political constitution would probably have been among them — but he certainly believed in their reality. However, again like Hume, he believed that they were purely conventional. That is to say, they arise not from anything belonging to nature or to the human species at large, but solely from the habitual and prescriptive arrangements that make a particular body of men into a civil society. Burke drew precisely the same contrast between a race and a society that Rousseau had drawn in his criticism of Diderot.

> In a state of *rude* nature there is no such thing as a people. A number of men in themselves have no collective capacity. The idea of a people is the idea of a corporation. It is wholly artificial; and made, like all other legal fictions, by common agreement. What the particular nature of that agreement was, is collected from the form into which the particular society has been cast.[3]

This is the reason why the revolutionary ideal of equality is impossible to realize and destructive in its effects. The rule of

[3] *Appeal from the New to the Old Whigs* (1791), *Works,* Vol. III, p. 82.

majorities is itself merely a social convention, a device of practice settled by general agreement and strengthened by habit; it is quite unknown to "nature." Moreover, natural equality is socially fictitious. The incorporation of men into a politic body requires differences of rank, an "habitual social discipline, in which the wiser, the more expert, and the more opulent conduct, and by conducting enlighten and protect, the weaker, the less knowing, and the less provided with the goods of fortune." In short, a people is an organized group; it has a history and institutions, customary ways of acting, habitual pieties and loyalties and authorities. It is a "true politic personality."

Such a corporate structure depends only in a small degree upon calculation or self-interest or even upon the conscious will. In his ironical attack upon the revolutionists' glorification of reason, Burke was even willing to say that society depends on "prejudice," that is to say, on deep-seated feelings of love and loyalty, beginning with the family and the neighborhood, and spreading out to the country and the nation. At bottom these feelings are instinctive. They make up the massive substructure of human personality in comparison with which reason and self-interest are superficial. At the foundation of society and morals is the need that every man feels to be a part of something larger and more enduring than his own ephemeral existence. Communities are held together not by self-interest cunningly calculated but by the sense of membership and duty, by the feeling that one has a place in the community even though it be but a lowly one, and that one is morally obligated to carry the burden that one's position traditionally imposes. Without such a sense a stable union of men is impossible, for the individual intelligence, unsupported by customary institutions and their duties, is a frail instrument.

> We are afraid to put men to live and trade each on his own private stock of reason; because we suspect that this stock in each man is small, and that the individuals would do better to avail themselves of the general bank and capital of nations and of ages.[4]

It was this sense of the massiveness of the communal life and of the relative impotence of individual reason and will that made

[4] *Reflections on the Revolution in France* (1790), *Works*, Vol. II, p. 359

Burke the enemy of abstract ideas in politics. Such ideas are always too simple to fit the facts. They assume a degree of inventiveness that even the wisest statesman does not possess and a degree of pliability that institutions do not possess. Institutions are not invented or made; they are alive and grow. Hence they must be approached with reverence and touched with caution, for the planning and contriving politician, with venturesome, speculative plans for new institutions, can easily destroy what it passes his wit to rebuild. Old institutions work well because they have ages of habituation and familiarity and respect behind them; no new invention, however logical, will work until it has amassed a similar body of habit and sentiment. Accordingly the pretensions of the revolutionists to make a new constitution and a new government seemed to Burke both mad and tragic. A government may be changed and improved but only a little at a time and always in accordance with the habits of its people and in the spirit of its own history. This was what Burke meant when he spoke of consulting the genius of the constitution. He had an almost mystical reverence for the embodied wisdom of a people. Always, he assumed, a great political tradition contains the clues for its own development, not by the slavish following of precedent but by the adaptation of a customary practice to a new situation. This for him was the art of the statesman, to preserve by changing. It was a faculty of insight as much as reason and as such defied definition.

THE DIVINE TACTIC OF HISTORY

Accordingly, Burke not only cleared away, as Hume had done, the pretense that social institutions depend on reason or nature but far more than Hume he reversed the scheme of values implied by the system of natural law. It is custom, tradition, and membership in a society far more than reason that gives moral quality to human nature. As Rousseau had said, one becomes a man by being a citizen. For it is this "artificial" body that provides everything morally estimable or even genuinely rational in human life; "art is man's nature." The contrast is not between a stupid, repressive authority and the free, rational individual, but between "this beautiful order, this array of truth and nature, as well as of habit and prejudice" and "a disbanded race of deserters and vagabonds." Civilization is the possession not of individuals but of communities; all a man's spiritual possessions come from his membership in an organized society. For society and the social tradition is the guardian of all that the race has created, its moral ideals, its art, its science and learning. Membership means access to all the stores of culture, to all that makes the difference between savagery and civilization. It is not a burden but an open door to human liberation.

> Society is indeed a contract. Subordinate contracts for objects of mere occasional interest may be dissolved at pleasure — but the state ought not to be considered as nothing better than a partnership agreement in a trade of pepper and coffee, calico or tobacco, or some other such low concern, to be taken up for a little temporary interest, and to be dissolved by the fancy of the parties. It is to be looked on with other reverence; because it is not a partnership in things subservient only to the gross animal existence of a temporary and perishable nature. It is a partnership in all science; a partnership in all art; a partnership in every virtue, and in all perfection. As the ends of such a partnership cannot be obtained in many generations, it becomes a partnership not only between those who are living, but between those who are living, those who are dead, and those who are to be born. Each contract of each particular state is but a clause in the great primeval contract of eternal society, linking the lower with the higher natures, connecting the visible and invisible world, according to a fixed compact sanctioned by the inviolable oath which holds all physical and all moral natures, each in their appointed place.[5]

In this eloquent passage, probably the most famous that Burke ever wrote, the peculiar, almost Hegelian, use of the word state ought to be noted. No clear line is drawn between society at large and the state, and the latter is named as in a special sense the guardian of all the higher interests of civilization. Yet the fact is not excluded that the state is also, in one of its lower capacities, the government that fosters "a trade of pepper and coffee." This was, to say the least, a serious confusion of words, since society, the state, and government have certainly very different meanings. Moreover, the interchange served a rhetorical need in Burke's argument. By it he implied that the revolutionary government in France, in overthrowing the monarchy, had become an enemy to French society and was destroying French civilization. Doubtless Burke meant to assert that this was

[5] *Ibid., Works,* Vol. II, p. 368.

true, but he had no right to cast the argument in a form that begged the question. Overthrowing a government and destroying a society are quite different things, and there are many sides of a civilization that depend very little on the state. This tendency to idealize the state by making it the bearer of all that has the highest value for civilization became characteristic of Hegel and of the English idealists.

Burke's reverential attitude toward the state distinguished him absolutely from Hume and the utilitarians; the word expedience was often on his lips but it had hardly the meaning of utility. For he practically united politics with religion. This was true not only in the conventional senses that he was himself a religious man, that he believed good citizenship to be inseparable from religious piety, and that he defended the establishment of the English church as a consecration of the nation. It was rather that he looked upon the social structure, its history, its institutions, its manifold duties and loyalties, with a reverence that was akin to religious awe. He experienced this feeling not only for England but for any ancient, deeply rooted civilization. The vehemence of his attack on the East India Company and of his arraignment of Warren Hastings was in part due to such a feeling toward the ancient civilization of India and to the conviction that the Indians must therefore be governed "upon their own principles and not upon ours," while he believed that the Company had merely exploited and destroyed. He felt a like reverence for the culture of France, even for its monastic institutions, for which as a Protestant he had no strictly religious regard. Burke never could feel that any government or any society was a matter of human concern alone; it was a part of the divine moral order wherewith God governs the world. Nor could he feel that any nation was a law merely to itself. For as every man should have his place in the stable and continuing order of his nation, so every nation has its place in a world-wide civilization unfolding in accord with "a divine tactic." In one pathetic passage, written after Burke had nearly exhausted himself with the violence of his attack on France, this sense of a divine plan in history rose above even his invincible hatred of the Revolution. He said in a spirit of resignation that if indeed a great change is to come, "then they who persist in opposing this mighty current in human affairs will appear rather to resist the decrees of Providence itself, than the mere designs of men." In this feeling for divine immanence in the social order and its historical development Burke was strikingly like Hegel.

> I attest the retiring, I attest the advancing generations, between which, as a link in the great chain of eternal order, we stand.[6]

BURKE, ROUSSEAU, AND HEGEL

Burke is rightly regarded as the founder of self-conscious political conservatism. Nearly all its principles are to be found in his speeches and pamphlets: an appreciation of the complexity of the social system and of the massiveness of its customary arrangements, a respect for the wisdom of established institutions, especially religion and property, a strong sense of continuity in its historical changes and a belief in the relative impotence of individual will and reason to deflect it from its course, and a keen moral satisfaction in the loyalty that attaches its members to their stations in its various ranks. The point is not, of course, that before Burke there was no conservatism, but it is almost true to say that there was no conservative philosophy. He intended indeed to uphold the political privilege of a party that was already losing its control of English government, but his ideas had a much wider application than the defense of the Whig oligarchy. The reaction that he led against the French Revolution was the beginning of a shift which carried the prevailing social philosophy from attack to defense and therefore to a new emphasis on the value of stability and the power of custom on which stability depends. It was not true that this new conservatism stood immovably for the *status quo*. Hegel, whose philosophy embodied systematically all of Burke's scattered principles, was typically the advocate of a new political order in Germany. But the rise to importance of such a philosophy signified an era in which the forces of change were ready to join hands with the forces of stability. Behind it lay a structure of social classes which for the time being was relatively stable and in which even liberals could hope to gain their ends by evolution rather than revolution.

The pervasiveness of this change in the climate of European

[6] *Warren Hastings, Works,* Vol. VIII, p. 439.

opinion is indicated by the astonishing similarity between the basic ideas of Burke and Rousseau. Superficially the two men had nothing in common, and Burke did not fail to record the contempt which a somewhat superficial acquaintance aroused in him for Rousseau's character. Yet Rousseau's nostalgia for the city-state and Burke's reverence for the national tradition were of a piece. Both were phases of the new cult of society which was replacing the old cult of the individual. Not less striking were the differences between Burke and Hume, despite the substantially conservative temper of both men and their agreement about the untenability of the system of natural law. Hume retained the preference for matter-of-fact motives and purposes which always characterizes the utilitarian temperament. If there was anything that aroused downright distrust and dislike in his placid mind it was "enthusiasm." In destroying reverence for the law of nature he felt no need to put a new reverence in its place, and a cult of society would not have appeared to him better than other cults. With Burke the destruction of the pseudo-science of natural law was the occasion, as it was with Kant, for setting up a "rational faith," in which the warmth of reverence did duty for the assurance of truth.

It is perhaps stretching a point to say that Burke had a political philosophy at all. His ideas are scattered through his speeches and pamphlets, all called out by the stress of events, though they have the consistency that is the stamp of a powerful intelligence and settled moral convictions. Certainly he had no philosophy other than his own reaction to the events in which he took part and little knowledge of the history of philosophy. He was therefore unaware of the relation of his own ideas, or of the system of natural law that he opposed, to the whole intellectual history of modern Europe. He could not have given systematic form even to his own reflections on political and social morality; still less could he trace their bearing on the larger questions of religion and science of which they were a part. In the generation after Burke, however, it was just this broader relationship that Hegel tried to show. There is no question of direct influence; Burke seems never to have been mentioned by Hegel, though the influence of Rousseau upon him was important. But what Burke had taken for granted Hegel tried to prove: that the apparently fragmentary social tradition can be placed in a general system of social evolution. And he added what Burke had not thought of: that the rational form of this evolution might be made into a method generally applicable to philosophy and social studies.

SELECTED BIBLIOGRAPHY

A History of English Utilitarianism. By Ernest Albee. London, 1902. Ch. 5.

"Burke and his Bristol Constituency." "Burke and the French Revolution." By Ernest Barker. In *Essays on Government*. Oxford, 1945.

Morals and Politics: Theories of their Relation from Hobbes and Spinoza to Marx and Bosanquet. By Edgar F. Carritt. Oxford, 1935.

Hume's Theory of the Understanding. By Ralph W. Church. Ithaca, New York, 1935.

Edmund Burke and the Revolt against the Eighteenth Century. By Alfred Cobban. London, 1929.

"Europe and the French Revolution." By G. P. Gooch. In the *Cambridge Modern History*, Vol. VIII (1908), ch. 25.

David Hume. By J. Y. T. Greig. London, 1931.

David Hume. By B. M. Laing. London, 1932.

Hume's Philosophy of Human Nature. By John Laird. London, 1932.

Political Thought in England from Locke to Bentham. By Harold J. Laski. London, 1920.

The Political Philosophy of Burke. By John MacCunn. London, 1913.

Edmund Burke, a Life. By Sir Philip Magnus. London, 1939.

Burke. By John Morley. London, 1879.

Edmund Burke, a Biography. By Robert H. Murray. London, 1931.

Edmund Burke. By Bertram Newman. London, 1927.

"Burke's Social Philosophy." By Arthur K. Rogers. In *Am. J. Sociology*, Vol. XVIII (1912–13), p. 51.

The Philosophy of David Hume: A Critical Study of its Origins and Central Doctrines. By Norman Kemp Smith. London, 1941.

History of English Thought in the Eighteenth Century. By Leslie Stephen. 2 vols. 2nd ed. London, 1881. Chs. 6, 10, 11.

Studies in the History of Political Philosophy. By C. E. Vaughan. 2 vols. Manchester, 1925. Vol. I, ch. 6; Vol. II, ch. 1.

Hume and Present-day Problems. The Symposia Read at the Joint Session of the Aristotelian Society, the Scots Philosophical Club, and the Mind Association at Edinburgh, July 7–10, 1939. London, 1939.

CHAPTER XXX

HEGEL: DIALECTIC AND NATIONALISM

The philosophy of Hegel aimed at nothing less than a complete reconstruction of modern thought. Political issues and ideas were an important but still only a secondary factor in it as compared with religion and metaphysics. In a broad sense Hegel's problem was one that had been perennial in modern thought from the beginning and that had grown steadily more acute with the progress of modern science, viz., the opposition between the order of nature as it must be conceived for scientific purposes and the conception of it implicit in the ethical and religious tradition of Christianity. In the half century before Hegel began his philosophical education three important thinkers had sharpened this opposition. Hume had showed the ambiguities concealed in the word " reason " and so had put in doubt the very principle of the system of natural law. Rousseau had set the reasons of the heart against the reasons of the head and had virtually regarded religion and morals as matters of sentiment. And Kant had tried to preserve the autonomy of both science and morals by assigning to each its own sphere and by sharpening to the last degree the contrast between theoretical and practical reason. These three philosophies — the typical conclusions of the Enlightenment — had been constructed upon the analytic principle, divide and conquer. Against them Hegel proposed to set a bolder speculative principle of synthesis. Morals and religion, he believed, could be given a logical justification, but only if a newer and more powerful logic of synthesis could be discovered, transcending the analytic logic of science. What Hegel's philosophy professed to offer, therefore, was an enlarged conception of reason that should overlap and include what had been separated by the analysis of Hume and Kant, and the center of his system was a new logic purporting to systematize a new intellectual method. This he called dialectic. Its virtue, he held, lay in its capacity to demonstrate a necessary logical relationship between the realm of fact and the realm of value. Accordingly it supplied a new and an indispensable tool for understanding the problems of society and of morals and religion. It was to provide a strictly rational standard of value, though rational according to a new definition, to replace the law of nature, the philosophical weakness of which had been proved by Hume and the practical weaknesses of which had been still more glaringly proved by the French Revolution.

In point of fact, however, Hegel's philosophy was not exclusively determined by considerations so formal or by abstractions at so high a level as the preceding statement might suggest. The French Revolution drew a broad line across the intellectual as well as the political history of Europe. Its violence and terrorism, and the imperialist attack on smaller nationalities in which it ended, induced a reaction against it even in the minds of men who at the start had been ardent believers in the rights of man. Among its opponents, such as Burke, they induced the belief that its excesses were the proper fruit of its revolutionary philosophy. The result was to set a new value upon national traditions and the customary pieties which the revolutionists flouted. Moreover, the Napoleonic Wars had left the constitutional systems of all the continental European countries in ruins. Their reconstruction was a major problem and one which, as the event proved, would not be solved by a further appeal to the abstractions, like the rights of man, that had proved so disruptive. More and more the Revolution was felt to be destructive and nihilistic, and its philosophy was pictured as a doctrinaire effort to remake society and human nature according to caprice. Substantially this was the estimation in which Hegel came to hold the Revolution and the individualism of its political philosophy. National reconstruction presented itself to him and to many others in the form of re-establishing the continuity of national institutions, of tapping sources of national solidarity in the past, and of affirming the dependence of the individual upon his heritage of national culture. In the case of Hegel this impulse was not merely reactionary, though it often was so in the romantic medievalism that followed the Revolution. In its purpose it was constructive, but it was profoundly conservative, or if one prefers, counter-revolutionary. His dialectic was in fact a kind of symbol for revolution and recovery. It acknowledged the destruction of obsolete institutions by living social forces but it celebrated the re-establishment of stability by the creative forces of the nation. Neither in tearing down nor in building up did Hegel impute much importance to the volition of individual men. The impersonal forces inherent in society itself work out their own destiny.

Accordingly an outstanding characteristic of Hegel's political philosophy was the high valuation which he set upon the national state. In Hegel's interpretation of history it was the nation, rather than the individual or any other grouping of individuals, that formed the significant unit, and it was the purpose of his philosophy of history to exhibit, through the agency of the dialectic, the achievements of each nation as an element in an evolving world-wide civilization. The genius or spirit of the nation (*Volksgeist*), working through individuals but largely in independence of their conscious will and intention, he regarded as the true creator of art, law, morals, and religion. Hence the history of civilization is a succession of national cultures in which each nation brings its peculiar and timely contribution to the whole human achievement. It is in the national state, and only in the modern history of Western Europe, that this inborn impulse of the nation to create reaches self-conscious and rational expression. The state therefore is the director and the end of national development. It overlaps and includes all that the nation produces that is morally and spiritually significant for civilization. Thus Hegel detached nationalism from the implications of radicalism, egalitarianism, and individualism which it had in the revolutionary era. In this respect he typified correctly the developing nationalism of Germany and the essentially conservative forces that effected German national unification. Indeed, as the nineteenth century advanced, nationalism not only in Germany but elsewhere pretty generally lost the implication of liberalism which it had had so long as it figured as the opponent of dynasticism.

There were, therefore, in Hegel's political philosophy two elements of primary importance, the dialectic, which he put forward as a method capable of yielding new and otherwise indemonstrable conclusions in the social studies, and a theory of the national state as the embodiment of political power. Both proved to be of first class importance in the period after Hegel. No doubt the two, in Hegel's understanding, were inseparably joined, the primacy of the national state being guaranteed by the dialectical reasoning on which his conclusions purported to rest. In fact there was no logical relation between them. Even if the dialectic were the powerful intellectual instrument which he imagined, it provided no valid reason why the nation, of all the possible political or social groupings, must be selected as that in which history has culminated, or why the driving force in modern political history must be the tension between national states. Hegel's concern with nationality was occasioned not by the dialectic but by the same interests that made nationalists of other Germans who did not share his technical philosophy. Conversely the dialectic might be accepted as a method if history were thought to culminate in the classless society and if its dynamics were provided by the antagonism between social classes, as Karl Marx proposed. Reformulated as the materialistic or economic interpretation of history, the dialectic became the intellectual organ of Marxian socialism, which always, by profession at least, was anti-nationalist and the avowed enemy of the state. Thus there were combined in Hegel's philosophy two lines of thought which were later separated and indeed opposed to one another. There was a conservative and in general an anti-liberal theory of the state as national power, and there was the dialectic which provided the starting point for a new proletarian radicalism.

THE HISTORICAL METHOD

Hegel's political and social philosophy centered in the study of history and in the relation of history to the other social studies. Hegel himself was unsurpassed among modern philosophers in his knowledge of the history of western culture. The history of religions, the history of philosophy, and the history of law were created as special subjects of investigation largely under the influence exerted by his philosophy. Such studies assumed so important a place in the nineteenth century that it became the custom to say that the writers of the Enlightenment had been typically "unhistorical" in their treatment of these subjects. This judgment was in fact quite false. The eighteenth century produced Gibbon, Voltaire, and Montesquieu, in intellectual stature certainly the equals of any later historians, and in sheer bulk the Enlightenment probably produced more history than any other type of scholarly performance. What was meant, however, was that the nineteenth century had found a new conception of history and a new way of using it. This was the idea that history provides a specific method that can be applied to the study of social subjects, such as law, politics, economics, religion, and philosophy. When thus applied the historical method was believed to supplant, or at least to supplement, the methods of analysis and generalization. This was certainly an exaggeration, though it is quite true that the nineteenth century greatly extended the scope of historical studies and greatly improved the methods of historical investigation. The historical method, however, as it was conceived in Hegel's philosophy and widely accepted in nineteenth-century social science, was not primarily an improved mode of empirical research. It was rather a mode of deriving from the order of historical evolution standards of valuation, scientific or ethical, by means of which the significance of particular stages in the evolution could be determined. The historical method meant a philosophy of history, or the discovery of a general law or direction of cultural growth, by which it was hoped that a scientifically defensible line could be drawn between advanced and backward peoples, developed and primitive civilizations, progressive and retarded nations. Such a project, strengthened by the really irrelevant idea of organic evolution, became a favorite speculation in the social philosophy of the nineteenth century. In the event it turned out to be almost wholly illusory and often mischievous.

Hegel's philosophy first stated the principles upon which the belief in a historical method, thus conceived, depended. The method assumed that there is in nature a single pattern or a law of development which can be exhibited by a proper arrangement of subject matter. This holds true for the whole evolution of society or for any of the chief phases of civilization, as well as for any subdivision of history. Hence it should be possible to present an orderly evolution of law, of economic institutions, of philosophical or scientific thought, or of government. This order is not imposed on the subject-matter by the investigator but is immanent in the facts themselves once they are seen in a proper perspective. The special work of historical insight consists in bringing to light this pattern, which is of course concealed in a welter of facts, and it is for this reason that historical and theoretical studies are connected. By grasping the general plan or logic of historical development the important can be distinguished from the casual. The purpose, as Hegel conceived it, was not so much to predict the future course of events as to discriminate the main current from the eddies and backwashes in the stream, and thus to arrive at an historically objective standard of values. Such a standard, progressively revealed in the evolution of religion, morals, law, or government, was to fill the place left vacant by the collapse of the philosophy of natural law. Instead of self-evident moral axioms the historical method was to exhibit the necessary stages of moral and social development.

Thus there were thrown into the speculations of nineteenth-century social philosophy three vaguely similar generalizations which tended to coalesce but which were in fact discrepant. There was in the first place the idea of universal human progress which was inherited from the Enlightenment and especially from the thought of Turgot and Condorcet. Second there was the Hegelian idea of a logically necessary order of historical development applying to a progressive succession of national cultures. Finally, after the publication of Darwin's *Origin of Species,* there was the theory of organic evolution. The result was an incredible amount of confusion. Neither the belief in unlimited human progress nor Hegel's belief in a philosophy of history depended in any way upon the variability of biological species or the laws of biological heredity, which Darwin's work proved to be the important factors in organic evolution. Nor do these biological factors imply anything whatever about moral development or social progress. Moreover, Hegel's conception of an inherent law of cultural development differed radically, both in its practical and its theoretical implications, from the idea of progress, which had been part of the faith of the Revolution. On its practical side the historicism of Hegel's philosophy, and indeed historicism in general whether Hegelian or not, usually had a conservative bias quite different from the revolutionary implications of Condorcet's theory of progress. The principal exception to this statement is Marx's readaptation of Hegel's philosophy to make a new type of revolutionary theory. In general, however, Hegelians who were not Marxists stressed the inescapable continuity of history and the impossibility that human volition should make sudden or drastic changes in it. On its theoretical side the distinctive feature of the dialectic, both in the form of Hegel's idealism and of Marx's materialism, was its claim to be a theory of logic rather than of empirical causation. In this respect it differed from both organic evolution and the theory of universal progress. Condorcet, and later Comte, at least supposed that the evidence for progress was empirical and that the reason for it was causal. Progress resulted from the continuous effect of increasing knowledge upon human behavior. It was this empirical or contingent aspect of the theory of progress that led Hegel, and in a lesser degree Marx, to regard it as philosophically superficial. Hegel's purpose was nothing less than the grandiose project of demonstrating the necessary stages by which human reason approximates to the Absolute. And by a converse process he proposed to demonstrate the order of development in which Absolute Reason unfolds in the ideas and institutions of civilization.

The foundation for this speculative venture was Hegel's belief that in the dialectic he had discovered a law of synthesis inherent both in the nature of mind and in the nature of things. It was in this sense that he was an idealist. The laws of thought and the laws of events are ultimately identical, and both include a discernible pattern of growth. This also was Hegel's answer to Hume. For the " necessity " which he imputed to history was a synthesis of logical implication, of causal relationship, and of enlarging purpose. Properly studied, history provides the principles for an objective criticism, immanent in the course of development itself, which distinguishes the true from the false, the significant from the trivial, the permanent from the transient, in short, what Hegel was accustomed to call the "real" from the merely "apparent." Such a study of history called for a special apparatus, and it was this which was to be provided in the dialectic. For the course of development is synthetic, and to grasp it there is required an instrument of synthesis and a higher mental faculty than the power of analysis. The two faculties of analysis and synthesis he distinguished respectively as understanding and reason, terms which he adopted from Kant but to which he gave a new meaning. Kant had contrasted the two, assigning to understanding the causal laws which he regarded as "constitutive" of the empirical world and to reason the "regulative" principles of the ethical world which despite their moral authority lack causal efficiency. Hegel on the contrary conceived the dialectic as an agency by which they are united. His own logic he regarded as a logic of reason, while the deficiencies of social studies in the eighteenth century he attributed to the fact that it employed only a logic of the analytic understanding. The understanding, by analysis, breaks up living organic wholes, such as society, into discrete parts, the human atoms that composed it, and hence is unable to see it as creative and as continuously growing. This Hegel regarded as the philosophical basis for the individualism of the Revolutionary Era, which ends, as he believed, in superficiality of historical understanding, which fosters the illusion that men can remake society according to their own capricious wills, and which thus becomes the stimulus to fanaticism and disorder. Only reason, the faculty of synthesis, can see below the surface of historical detail, can perceive the underlying real forces that control the process, and so can comprehend the necessity that the process should be as it is. This act of synthetic comprehension constitutes for Hegel both intellectual understanding and moral justification. What *is* both must be and ought to be. It is this double rôle that accounts for the frequent identification of might with right in Hegel's political philosophy.

Hegel's conception of the historical method implied to his mind a thoroughgoing intellectual revolution of which his philosophy was to be the exponent. The magisterial tone in which he often enunciated that philosophy was not wholly due to intellectual arrogance. It reflected rather the conviction that his thought employed a method not available to the uninitiated, and also not capable of being formulated in a manner that will commend itself to a logician who has not learned to transcend the limitations of logical analysis.

We cannot by means of predicates, propositions, etc., reach any right estimate of the state, which should be apprehended as an organism. It is much the same with the state as with the nature of God.[1]

The question, of course, is whether this did not really imply a resort to sheer mysticism or authority, even though Hegel did not so regard it. Are the cosmic forces which he supposed that reason could discern behind the facts of history and which he considered to be more real than particular facts and events — forces such as the state — in truth anything but abstractions? And can the dialectic, the logical apparatus for grasping the organic wholes with which social studies are concerned, in truth be brought to any precise methodological formulation, so that its alleged pronouncements can be subjected to critical examination? Finally, if these questions were favorably answered, would it be clear that a synthetic understanding of historical process could effect a combination of causal explanation and moral criticism, which both Hume and Kant had believed to be fundamentally different? Upon the answers to these questions the evaluation of Hegel's philosophical system depends. Upon them depends also the estimate to be placed upon the claim that the dialectic, whether in Hegel or in Marx, is a new logical instrument indispensable for the understanding of social phenomena and for the creation of valid historical science.

THE SPIRIT OF THE NATION

Whatever the validity of Hegel's conclusions, there can be no doubt that the origin of his ideas had very little to do with the parade of logical precision and the formidable terminology in which he finally cast his philosophy. His main ideas were suggested to him by his youthful studies of European culture, especially the history of Christianity, and were only later reduced to the formulas in which he published them.[2] The chief interest of Hegel's youth was not so much politics as religion. His speculations started from Herder and Lessing and from their idea that

[1] *Philosophy of Right,* Section 269, addition. All quotations are from S. W. Dyde's translation.

[2] This point was first suggested by Wilhelm Dilthey in his *Jugendgeschichte Hegels* (1905) and has been developed in great detail by T. L. Haering in *Hegel, sein Wollen und sein Werk,* 2 vols. (1929 and 1938).

the succession of world-religions is a progressive revelation of religious truth and a kind of divine education of the human race. The idea which Hegel elaborated later in his philosophy of history — that process begins with " a potentiality striving to realize itself " which " expands itself actually to what it always was potentially "— was in fact an element of Aristotelianism that had been inherent in German thought since Leibniz. From Herder and Lessing he learned also to think of creeds and ritual as neither wholly true nor wholly superstitious, but as the outward forms in which a spiritual truth symbolically clothes itself. They are at once needful for their time and yet of only passing value. In this mode of criticism and evaluation it is not hard to see the germs of the dialectic. Like the ablest of his contemporaries in Germany, also, Hegel was deeply stirred by a far-reaching renaissance of Greek studies. He early formed the conviction that Western civilization is the product of two great forces, the free intelligence of Greece and the deeper moral and religious insight, as he believed, of Christianity. Intellectually he was forced to estimate Christian theology as decadent when compared with the philosophy of Plato and Aristotle, yet he was convinced also that Christianity brought to western culture a depth of spiritual experience which Greek philosophy lacked. As Hegel reflected upon this problem he came to see, perhaps partly under the guidance of Montesquieu's interpretation of the law of nature, that the philosophy and religion of Athens was an inseparable part of the whole mode of life in the city-state, and that the mysticism, pessimism, and world-weariness of Christianity were correlated with the loss of civic freedom and the travail of bringing to birth the consciousness of a new idea, that of a worldwide humanity.

In this way Hegel's early religious speculation brought to a focus in his mind ideas and a point of view implicit in the thought of the Enlightenment and especially of the German Enlightenment: that all the elements of a culture form a unit in which religion, philosophy, art, and morality mutually affect one another, that these several branches of culture all express the " spirit "— the internal intellectual endowment — of the people which creates them, and that the history of a people is the process in which it realizes and unfolds its unique contribution to the whole of human civilization. As he reflected further on these ideas Hegel came to believe that he could detect in this process a threefold pattern: a period of "natural," happy, youthful, but largely unconscious, spontaneity; a period of painful frustration and self-consciousness in which the spirit is "turned inward" and loses its spontaneous creativeness; and a period in which it "returns to itself" at a higher level, embodying the insights gained from frustration in a new era which unites freedom with authority and self-discipline. These stages, repeated in a thousand contexts, were rationalized by Hegel in the three stages of the dialectic: thesis, antithesis, and synthesis. The total process is what he called "thought." His philosophy of history was an attempt to document this idea on a vast scale from the history of Western Civilization. The Greek city in its creative period represented the first stage, Socrates and Christianity the second, and the period of Protestantism and the Germanic nations beginning with the Reformation the third. The national mind is a manifestation of the world-mind at a particular stage of its historical development.

> Each particular national genius is to be treated as only one individual in the process of universal history.[3]

Its worth is to be estimated according to its contribution to the progress of mankind; not all peoples are to be counted among the *welthistorische Volksgeister*. In general this was already a familiar German speculation. Years before Hegel Herder had said that Germany had always had and would always have "a fixed national spirit," and Hegel's contemporary Schleiermacher said that God "assigns to each nationality its definite task on earth." In no case, and least of all in Hegel, was this belief in the revelatory power of history antiquarian; it was rather the painful search for a national vocation. In popular religion Hegel sought for something less doctrinaire than the Enlightenment's religion of reason and something less stultifying than ecclesiastical orthodoxy. In all branches of social study his thought was guided by the conviction that ideas and institutions must be understood as parts of a total culture and that their history is a clue to their present value and their future rôle in the develop-

[3] See Hegel's account of Philosophical History in his *Philosophy of History*, Introduction, Section 3. Eng. trans. by J. Sibree, Bohn Library, p. 55.

ment of a world-culture. In Schiller's aphorism, *Die Weltgeschichte ist das Weltgericht.*

Hegel's early writings on politics, and more specifically on German politics, show a similar purpose and conception. The frustration of spirit which he regarded as the key to the rise of Christianity he conceived to be also, *mutatis mutandis,* the mark of his own age and the key to great social and spiritual changes which he hoped, or perhaps foresaw, for Germany. Between the spirit of Germany and the actual state of German politics he found a complete discrepancy which he interpreted as at once a cause of pessimism and futility and the ground for new hope and activity. Writing in 1798, doubtless still under the drive of a youthful enthusiasm kindled by the French Revolution, he said:

> The silent acquiescence in things as they are, the hopelessness, the patient endurance of a vast, overmastering fate, has turned to hope, to expectation, to the will for something different. The vision of a better and a juster time has entered alive into the souls of men, and a desire, a longing, for a purer, freer condition has moved every heart and has alienated it from the existing state of affairs . . . Call this, if you like, a fever-paroxysm, but it will end either in death or in eliminating the cause of the disease.[4]

Certainly Hegel was at no time a revolutionist — he believed too fervently in the essential rightness of the institutions in which the national life had embodied itself — yet his political writing was at once a prophecy and an appeal. But it was an appeal rather to the communal will of the nation than to the self-help of its individual members.

> How blind are they who can imagine that institutions, constitutions, and laws can persist after they have ceased to be in accord with the morals, the needs, and the purposes of mankind, and after the meaning has gone out of them; that forms in which understanding and feeling no longer inhere can retain the power to bind a nation!

Such institutions must change or give place to new embodiments of national aspiration. The question was what form these new embodiments must take.

This thought was expanded and particularized, with special reference to the existing condition of Germany, in an essay which

[4] *Uber die neuesten innern Verhältnisse Württembergs* (1798), *Werke* (ed. by Lasson), Vol. VII, pp. 150 f. The quotation next below is on p. 151.

Hegel wrote in 1802 on the *Constitution of Germany*.[5] The work began with the striking assertion, "Germany is no longer a state." Hegel made this good with an exceedingly able analysis of the decline of the empire after the Peace of Westphalia. Germany, he argued, has become merely an anarchical collection of virtually independent units. It is a name which has the connotations of past greatness but as an institution it is wholly out of accord with the realities of European politics. In particular it must be contrasted with the unified national governments which modern monarchy has produced in France, England, and Spain, and which have failed to develop in Italy and Germany. The historical analysis, however, was obviously a means and not an end. Hegel's purpose was to raise the question, How may Germany become a real state?

A GERMAN STATE

Hegel quite properly found the cause of the empire's weakness in the particularism and provincialism which he took to be a national defect of German character. Culturally the Germans are a nation but they have never learned the lesson of subordinating part to whole which is essential for a national government. The empire has no power except what the parts give it, and the existing constitution has in fact no purpose except to keep the state weak. The free cities, the independent princes, the estates, the guilds, and the religious sects go their own way, absorbing the rights of the state and paralyzing its action — all with a good show of legal right in the antiquated feudal law that governs the empire. The motto of Germany, as Hegel said with bitter irony, is *Fiat justitia, pereat Germania.* For there is complete confusion between private and constitutional law. Legislative, judicial, ecclesiastical, and military privileges are bought and sold like private property. In this analysis of the condition of Germany at the beginning of the century there may be seen two characteristic features of Hegel's later political theory. First, he identified German particularism with an anarchical love of "freedom," which misconceives liberty as an absence of discipline and authority. And this he contrasted with "true freedom," which is

[5] *Die Verfassung Deutschlands* (1802), *Werke* (ed. by Lasson), Vol. VII, pp. 1 ff.

to be found only within the bounds of a national state. A nation finds freedom, therefore, in an escape from feudal anarchy and in the creation of a national government. Freedom as Hegel understood it had nothing to do with the individualism of English and French political thought but was rather a quality reflected upon the individual by the national power of self-determination. Second, Hegel assumed a contrast of private with public or constitutional law which was wholly foreign to English political thought. This corresponds to the contrast of the state with civil society, which became a typical property of his finished political theory.

Following his diagnosis of Germany's weakness Hegel defined the state as a group which collectively protects its property; its only essential powers are a civil and military establishment sufficient to this end.[6] In other words a state is *de facto* power, the expression, certainly, of national unity and a national aspiration to self-government, but fundamentally the power to make the national will effective at home and abroad. The existence of a state is consistent with any lack of uniformity which does not prevent effectively unified government. The precise form of government Hegel regarded as a matter of indifference, aside from the fact that he believed monarchy to be indispensable. The existence of a state does not imply, he argued, equality of civil rights or uniformity of law throughout the national domain. There may be privileged classes and wide differences in custom, culture, language, and religion. In fact he branded as "pedantic" the centralized government of republican France, that tried to do everything and that reduced its people to the level of common citizenship. Like Jean Bodin, Hegel regarded the rise of a national, constitutional monarchy as the sole necessary condition for the existence of a state. The experience of France, Spain, and England proved, he thought, that the extinguishing of feudalism and the rise of a national state could be achieved only through monarchy and that this process of itself constituted "freedom."

> From the period when these countries grew to be states dates their power, their wealth, and the free condition of their citizens under the law.[7]

[6] *Ibid.*, p. 17.

[7] *Ibid.*, p. 109. Cf. the remarks on the origin of monarchy in the *Philosophy of History*, Part IV, Section II, ch. 2.

The historical accuracy of Hegel's judgment need not be contested. At the same time he was obviously prescribing for Germany a remedy which an Englishman or a Frenchman would have regarded as politically backward. It is evident also that such an expression as "the free condition of their citizens" never connoted for Hegel anything like the meaning of the French phrase, "the rights of man and citizen."

Believing as he did in the historical rôle of the monarchy, Hegel in 1802 put his hope for the unification and modernizing of Germany upon the appearance of a great military leader, though he considered it essential that such a leader should voluntarily accept constitutional limitations and identify himself with German national unity as a moral cause. Emphatically he did not believe that Germany would ever be unified by common consent or by the peaceful spread of national sentiment. Gangrene, he said bitterly, is not cured with lavender water. It is in war rather than in peace that a state shows its mettle and rises to the height of its potentiality. For Hegel the two heroic figures in modern politics were Machiavelli and Richelieu. The *Prince* he called "the great and true conception of a real political genius with the highest and noblest purpose."[8] For the rules of private morality do not limit the action of states; a state has no higher duty than to preserve and strengthen itself. Richelieu's enemies — the French nobility and the Huguenots — went down not before Richelieu personally but before the principle of French national unity which he represented. Hegel added an aphorism highly characteristic of his philosophy of history: "Political genius consists in identifying yourself with a principle."[9] In 1802 Hegel was already firmly convinced that the modernizing of Germany would require an era of blood and iron but at that time his hopes centered rather in Austria than in Prussia. The shift in loyalty that he later made was one that occurred very often among South Germans after the Napoleonic Wars.

It has seemed worthwhile to refer somewhat at length to this early essay on the *Constitution of Germany* for two reasons. First, Hegel wrote in 1802 as a publicist and quite without that astonishing array of dialectical abstractions which later made his

[8] *Ibid.*, p. 113.

[9] *Ibid.*, p. 108.

political philosophy so difficult. Yet without the logical apparatus his leading ideas were already there. It has been plausibly suggested that in 1802 his ambition was nothing less than to become the Machiavelli of Germany. The most striking qualities of his thought were already a firm grasp of historical actualities and a kind of hard political realism that frankly identified the state with power and estimated its success in terms of its ability to carry out a policy of national aggrandizement at home and abroad. Already he conceived the state as the spiritual embodiment of a nation's will and destiny, "the real realm of freedom in which the Idea of Reason has to materialize itself." As such it is above and distinct from the economic arrangements of civil society and from the rules of private morality that control the actions of its citizens. The realization of the nation's spiritual potentialities is a contribution of ultimate value to the cause of advancing civilization, a moment in the progressive realization of the World Spirit, and the source of the dignity and worth that attaches to the private concerns of its citizens. Already he identified the "freedom" of the individual with his voluntary dedication to the work of national self-realization, which is at the same time a personal self-realization. Already the national monarchy was pictured as the highest form of constitutional government, the unique achievement of modern politics, in which ideally there is a perfect synthesis of freedom and authority. In it Hegel believed that the outworn forms of feudal particularism could be sublimated (*aufgehoben*) into functions of a national life. So far he agreed with and accepted the consequences of the French Revolution, but he dissented absolutely from the individualism of revolutionary theory, which, like many Germans after him, he construed as a specious glorification of egoism and caprice in the individual and of plutocracy in society. Already his reference to history as the source of moral and political enlightenment was not a simple appeal to experience but was governed by the belief that the evolution of ideas and institutions reveals a necessity which is at once causal and ethical.

Second, the *Constitution of Germany* showed clearly that Hegel's conception of the dialectic was controlled by a moral rather than a scientific purpose. In the opening pages he explained that the object of the essay was to promote understanding of things as they are, to exhibit political history not as arbitrary but as necessary. The unhappiness of man is a frustration that arises from the discrepancy between what is and what he is fain to believe ought to be. It occurs because he imagines that events are mere unrelated details and not a " system ruled by a spirit." Its remedy comes with reconciliation, the realization that what is must be and the consciousness that what must be also ought to be. This is manifestly the principle which Hegel later summarized in his aphorism, " The Real is the rational." Yet no attentive reader of either the early essay or the *Philosophy of Right* can imagine that Hegel meant to teach political quietism or mere political reaction. What " must be " is not the *status quo* but the modernizing and nationalizing of Germany. The *must* is a moral imperative, not something that is physically inevitable or merely desirable, but a moral cause that can enlist men's loyalty and devotion and dignify their petty personal ends by identifying them with the destiny of civilization itself. This compounding of moral, physical, and logical necessity was the very essence of the dialectic.

DIALECTIC AND HISTORICAL NECESSITY

The Philosophy of Right[10] is a book that cannot profitably be summarized. This is true in part because of the technical elaborateness of its logical apparatus but chiefly because, from any empirical point of view, it is fundamentally ill-arranged. This was not due to confusion or carelessness on Hegel's part but precisely to the apparatus itself. The subject matter was arranged not in accord with any canon of empirical description but in accord with its "idea," by which Hegel meant its significance in the light of the dialectic. The structure of the book grew directly from the contrast of understanding and reason. The first two parts, dealing with abstract right and subjective morality, present the theory of right or law as leading to antitheses that are inevitable from the point of view of understanding. In particular, the first part has to do substantially with the rights of property, personality, and contract as these are treated in a theory of natural law. But since the under-

[10] *Grundlinien der Philosophie des Rechts,* 1821; Eng. trans. by S. W. Dyde, 1896.

standing is self-defeating, this part must issue in contradictions which understanding cannot solve and so must lead on dialectically to the third part, on Freedom or Objective Will, in which reason resolves the contradictions. It was this third part, and especially its last two subdivisions on civil society and the state, that contained Hegel's important conclusions. But the arrangement hopelessly dislocated the subject-matter. Sometimes subjects that belong together were pulled apart, as when property and contract were discussed apart from the economic order, marriage apart from the family, and crime apart from the administration of law. Sometimes subjects were inappropriately combined, as divorce and inheritance. This distortion of subject matter in the interest of a logical arrangement dictated by the notion of dialectical development tended to obscure one of the most fruitful ideas contained in Hegel's philosophy, namely, that economic, political, legal, and moral institutions are in fact socially interdependent. At the same time it must be conceded that the arrangement of the *Philosophy of Right* did accurately represent one of Hegel's most important political conclusions, namely, that the state is morally superior to civil society.

Since an exposition of Hegel's political philosophy cannot follow the order or the manner in which his ideas were developed in the *Philosophy of Right*, it will be well to break free entirely and state his arguments and his conclusions in the simplest manner possible. A critical understanding and estimate of his philosophy turns upon two points. First, it calls for a decision about the claim that the dialectic is a new method which reveals dependencies and relationships in society and history not otherwise discernible. Such a decision is important because the dialectic was adopted by Karl Marx, with considerable changes, to be sure, in its supposed metaphysical implications but with no important change in the conception of it as a logical method. Thus it became an inherent part of Marxian socialism and communism and the ground for the claim to scientific superiority that Marxism has always made. Second, Hegel's political philosophy was the classic statement of nationalism in a form which had discarded the individualism and the implicit cosmopolitanism of the rights of man. It gave to the concept of the state a special connotation which remained characteristic of German political theory throughout the nineteenth century.

Since the purpose of the dialectic was to provide a logical apparatus capable of revealing the "necessity" of history, the meaning of the dialectic depends upon the complicated meaning which Hegel attached to historical necessity. His thought on this subject started from the belief which he acquired early in his life, that the history of a people records the growth of a single national mentality which expresses itself in all phases of its culture. In contrast with this view of history Hegel set another view common to the Enlightenment, that philosophies and religions and institutions are conscious "inventions" for practical purposes. This illusion, he believed, arose because history had been regarded merely as an adjunct to the statesman's art, and it attributed to statesmen and legislators a much greater power to plan the life and growth of a society than they actually have. It depended upon the dogma that human nature is everywhere and always the same, that a relatively simple list of what Hume called "propensities" will account for all human behavior, and that accordingly conduct can be turned in any desired direction by a skillful manipulation of motives. These were in fact principles avowed by utilitarians like Helvetius and later by Jeremy Bentham. They were historically superficial, Hegel believed, because they overlook the interdependence of institutions and the momentum with which societies and institutions follow their own inherent trends. Individuals and their conscious purposes really count for very little in the total outcome. The individual is for the most part only an accidental variant of the culture that created him and in so far as he is different his individuality is more likely to be capricious than significant. Moreover individuals ought not to count for much because in general "individuals come under the category of means." Their desires and gratifications are rightly sacrificed to the achievement of the larger purposes of nations. Hegel's belief in the necessity of history, therefore, united two important elements in his philosophy. In the first place he was a logical realist. He believed that the effective realities and causes in history are impersonal and general forces, not individual persons or events. The latter are for the most part partial and imperfect materializations of social forces. In the second place his ethics assumed that the value of a person depends upon the work that he does and the part that he plays in the social drama.

These assumptions Hegel expressed by saying that the history of civilization is the unfolding or the progressive realization and materialization of the World Spirit in time. In part his philosophy was motivated by a religious sense of dependence and of the moral value of devotion to a cause greater than oneself. In part also it was motivated by a sardonic sense of humor at the vanity of human wishes, which made him delight to see the rationalist duped by the cunning of the World Spirit. From the point of view of the human actors, history is a union of irony and tragedy; from the point of view of the Whole it is a cyclic or spiral advance.

> This may be called the cunning of reason — that it sets the passions to work for itself, while that which develops its existence through such impulsion pays the penalty, and suffers loss. . . . The particular is for the most part of too trifling value as compared with the general: individuals are sacrificed and abandoned.[11]

History has its own solutions to its own problems which even the wisest men understand only in a small degree. Great men neither make nor guide it, but at the most they understand a little and cooperate with forces enormously more massive than their own will and understanding. Hegel's remark about Richelieu, quoted above, was characteristic; the political genius is such less in virtue of his own ability than because he identifies himself with a " principle," that is, with the force or trend that at the time is running. Great men are instruments of impersonal social forces that lie below the surface of history; they bow before the inherent logic of events. Hence also science and philosophy play a limited part in it. A clear understanding of any social system, Hegel thought, comes only when that system is on the road to extinction; Plato and Aristotle created a philosophy of the city-state in the fourth century, when the spontaneous creativeness of the Age of Pericles was already a thing of the past. " Minerva's owl begins its flight only in the gathering dusk." Like the Stoic God, history leads the wise man and drags the fool.

[11] *The Philosophy of History,* Introduction. Bohn Library, p. 34.

Hegel, however, did not consider history to be intrinsically inscrutable or irrational. In it resides not unreason but a higher form of reason than that of the analytic understanding. "The Real is the rational and the rational is the real." To penetrate its apparent confusion, however, and to apprehend process not as composed of discrete parts but as organic growth, a different logical apparatus is needed, and this the dialectic was designed to supply. In the abstract it was an over-simple device to open so complicated a maze. Hegel adopted, in fact, an idea as old and as vague as the first Greek speculations about nature, namely, that historical processes go by opposites. Every tendency when carried to the full breeds an opposite tendency which destroys it. This idea had always been used in defense of the mixed constitution: unrestrained democracy turns into license; unlimited monarchy degenerates into despotism. Hegel generalized the argument. Opposition and contrariety are universal properties of nature; this is at once a law of the cosmos and of thought. Everywhere forces grow into their opposites. But whereas theories of the mixed constitution had assumed that the balancing of opposites could be made a key to stability and permanence, Hegel thought of the world as an endlessly moving equilibrium. Contrary forces supply the dynamic of history but balance can never be permanent; it merely gives a continuity and direction to change. Consequently, as he thought, the opposition is never absolute. The destruction of one position in a controversial situation is never complete. Both sides are partly right and partly wrong, and when the rights and the wrongs have been properly weighed, a third position emerges which unites the truth contained in both. This Hegel believed to be the fundamental insight that Plato had embodied in his dialogues, and accordingly he adopted Plato's word, dialectic, as the name of the process.

This principle of an opposition of forces, moving in orderly equilibrium and emerging in a pattern of progressive logical development, appeared to Hegel general enough to supply a formula for all nature and all history. He applied it perhaps most plausibly to the history of philosophy. It accounts, as he supposed, for the apparent unsuccess of all systems, while it provides for the increasing meaning and growing truth of the whole. Every philosophy grasps a part of the truth, none grasps it all. Each supplements the other, and the eternal problem is to restate the questions in such a way as to include the apparent contradictions between opposing systems. In any absolute sense the problems are never solved; in a relative sense they are always being solved. The discussion begins again around a new point which takes account of all that has gone before. Consequently, as Hegel said, the history of philosophy literally *is* philosophy; it is absolute truth projected, so to speak, in time and progressing toward a consummation which, however, it can never reach. It is like a spiral that mounts as it turns. The driving force he called contradiction, thus giving to an ancient logical term a meaning which it never had in formal logic. In Hegel's logic contradiction means the fruitful opposition between systems that constitutes an objective criticism of each and leads continually to a more inclusive and a more coherent system. The dialectic, however, as Hegel conceived it, was not applicable to the development of philosophy alone. It was a method applicable to every subject matter in which the concepts of progressive change and development are relevant, and in such subjects it is indispensable, for the analytic understanding works only with the mechanical juxtaposition of discrete parts and cannot grasp the necessity inherent in process. The dialectic, therefore, was a method applicable *par excellence* to the social studies. Society itself and all the principal parts of its structure — its law, its morals, its religions, and the institutions that embody them — advance under the continual tension of internal forces and their endless readjustment by thought. This is the reason why there is a real historical method. By grasping *der Gang der Sache selbst,* the inner " go " of events, one perceives that there is a logical next step or manifest destiny inherent in the state of affairs.

When the dialectic is considered as the key to a theory of social change, it suggests two interpretations that can easily be opposed to each other. From the point of view of the dialectic, every act of " thought " contains two movements. On the one side it is negative; every affirmation or thesis has implicit in it contradictions that must become explicit and in so doing must destroy the original affirmation. On the other side it is also affirmative or constructive; it is a restatement at a higher level on which the contradictions are sublimated (*aufgehoben*) and combined in a new synthesis. Since Hegel regarded all social evolution as a development of "thought," this twofold property of the dialectic characterizes also the progressive changes that take place in social institutions. Every change is at once continuous and discontinuous, carrying forward the past and also breaking with it in order to create something new. A practical application of the dialectic to social history may with equal logic be given either of two opposite constructions. The emphasis may be upon continuity or "gradualness"— the impossibility of making a radical and voluntary departure from norms and practices long established. Or it may be upon discontinuity or negation — the necessity that change must be subversive and destructive of accepted norms and practices. Which emphasis any given thinker adopts depends as much upon the total bias of his thought, perhaps even upon his temperament, as upon logic. Hegel on the whole, and conservative Hegelians generally, tended to emphasize continuity. He tended to think of revolutions as occurring in the past. Karl Marx tended to think of them as occurring in the future, but in Marxism also the continual swing of socialist theory between revolutionism and revisionism reflected the two-sidedness of the dialectic. In general, it suggested that social history as a whole should be construed as a succession of periods of development punctuated by periods of revolution. The stresses and strains inherent in any settled situation build up to a breaking point at which the whole system undergoes a violent change of phase.

CRITICISM OF DIALECTIC

In forming a critical judgment of Hegel's dialectic it is necessary to remember that it was put forward not as a mere description of the contrary tendencies that are in fact compromised and adjusted in social history but as a law of logic. Hegel intended nothing less than a complete revision of that subject, or as he himself expressed it, the creation of a logic of reason to supplement or to supersede the logic of the understanding. The dialectic purported to revise the "laws of thought," particularly the law of logical contradiction, as this was understood in logic at any time after Aristotle. Abstractly stated this would mean that a logic ought to be constructed on the principle that one and the same proposition can be at once both true and false. No logician after Hegel can really be said to have taken this proposal with entire seriousness.[12] But the utility of such a logic, if it were constructed, must depend upon there being a definite methodology for its use. Otherwise either its acceptance or its rejection remains subjective. Historians and other social scientists have as a rule been justifiably reluctant to face the supposition that their subjects require a logic radically different from that used by the other sciences. In philosophy, where such a supposition has sometimes been entertained, it has usually taken the form of overt irrationalism, the assertion that some faculty other than reason (Bergson's "intuition," for example) is needed to grasp the nature of organism and of continuous organic growth. But this view, which was exploited in German national socialism, is in effect an acceptance of subjectivism and really means that rational or scientific standards cannot be applied to social problems. The peculiarity of Hegel's philosophy, and of the Marxian reconstruction of it, was that it claimed to be genuinely rational, while at the same time it professed to supersede the theory of logical propositions by which alone logic has been able to give precise meaning to propositions. In the last resort its claim to be scientific depends on the very dubious feasibility of this project.

When Hegel's actual use of the dialectic is examined, its most obvious characteristic is the extreme vagueness, not to say the ambiguity, of his use of terms, and the extreme generality that he attributed to words which are notoriously hard to define. Two examples of key importance for his philosophy will serve to illustrate this tendency, his use of the words "thought" and "contradiction." According to Hegel, any progressive social change — in religion, philosophy, economics, law, or politics — takes place by an advance in "thought." This usage was not accidental but was required both by his metaphysics and by the dialectic. His idealism depended upon an identification of process in mind with process in nature, and the dialectic depended upon the applicability of what he regarded as a law of thought to all subject-matters

[12] The most elaborate work in English written from a generally Hegelian standpoint is Bernard Bosanquet's *Logic or the Morphology of Thought* (1888; 2nd ed., 1911). The "modern" logic that grew out of the work of Whitehead and Russell was quite definitely what Hegel would have called a logic of understanding. Its historical antecedents were in Leibniz and Hume, not in Hegel.

of which process is an essential characteristic. All change takes place under the impulsion of thought to eliminate inherent "contradictions" and in pursuit of a higher level of coherence or logical consistency. But if these words are given any precise meaning, the theory simply is not true. Even in science or philosophy, to say nothing of less highly intellectualized social products, new discoveries and the emergence of new points of view cannot plausibly be construed as always due to self-contradictions in earlier systems of ideas. In all branches of social evolution, including philosophy, it is true as Justice Holmes said of the law that experience counts for more than logic. Hegel's determination to universalize thought had a twofold effect upon the Hegelian writing of history: either recalcitrant facts were forced into molds that were antecedently decided to be logical or else words like coherence and consistency were given a meaning so vague that they ceased to be useful. Similarly the word "contradiction" as Hegel used it had no precise meaning whatever but referred to any vague form of opposition or contrariety. Sometimes it meant merely physical forces that move in different directions or causes that tend toward opposed results, like living or dying. Sometimes the opposition referred to moral desert, as when he said that punishment "negates" crime and that evil is self-contradictory. In its actual use the dialectic was largely an exploitation of ambiguities in terminology and not in any proper sense a method. In Hegel's hands it worked out to conclusions that he had reached without it and the dialectic contributed nothing to their proof.

The special merit claimed for the dialectic was its capacity to display and clarify the "necessity" which Hegel attributed to historical development. The word necessity, however, remained as ambiguous as Hume had proved it to be. It might, of course, refer merely to the relation of cause and effect in history, and in that sense all events might be regarded as alike necessary. But this was emphatically not what Hegel meant when he said that "the real is the rational," because he always distinguished between the real and that which merely exists.[13] The real is the

[13] His contrasted terms were *Wirklichkeit* for reality and *Dasein* for existence.

permanent inner core of meaning in history in comparison with which particular events are casual, transient, or apparent. Consequently the dialectic was essentially a selective process. It was a way of discriminating what is relatively accidental and insignificant from what is important and effective in the long run. What exists is always momentary and to a large degree accidental, the mere surface manifestation of deep-lying forces which alone are real. But the basis for this discrimination of the significant and the casual was again ambiguous. It might refer to the obvious fact that some events have more weight than others in bringing about an historical result. Or it might amount to assuming that a result comes about because it is important, that its value operates as an effective cause. Hegel systematically fused these two meanings by identifying right and force. This could be justified metaphysically because he imputed to nature an ideal constitution that inevitably gives the greatest power to right, but in effect it meant that he regarded might as the criterion of right. Thus the necessity that he saw in history was at once a physical and a moral compulsion. When he said that Germany *must* become a state, he meant that it ought to do so, that the highest interests both of civilization and of its own national life require such a result, and also that there are causal forces that impel it in that direction. Hence the dialectic combines at once a moral judgment and a causal law of historical development. Germany must become a state not because Germans wish it, and not because it will do so in spite of what they wish. The *must* expresses at once a volition and a fact—a will that is more than a caprice because the growth of Germany into a state is in line with the whole direction of political development and a fact that is more than a casual event because it sums up what is objectively valuable in that development. The distinctive claim of the dialectic was that it unites intelligence and will. It purported to be, as Josiah Royce said, a " logic of passion," a synthesis of science and poetry.

The dialectic was in truth much easier to understand as ethics than as logic. Without being overtly hortatory it was a subtle and effective form of moral appeal. The sense of moral " reconciliation " which Hegel saw at the foundation of all effective human action was at once passive and active; it is both resignation and cooperation. It can cure the intolerable sense of futility and impotence to which the isolated self-consciousness is a prey precisely because it is not merely a feeling but a real identification with a higher power. In nothing was Hegel so unmeasured as in his condemnation of sentiment and mere good feeling, what he called bitingly "the hypocrisy of good intentions," which he believed to be always either weak or fanatical and in both cases futile. In nothing did he disbelieve so completely as in the power of unorganized good will to accomplish anything in a world where effectiveness is the final criterion of right. It is not sentiment that makes nations but the national will to power translating itself into institutions and a national culture. And it is the acceptance of the national task as a moral cause and of the duties imposed by one's station in it that releases the individual's creative efforts and raises him to the level of a freely acting moral person. For Hegel the individual's sense of duty, which Luther and Kant had conceived as arising from his relation to God, became concrete in his vocation as a member of his nation. And the nation itself attained an aura of sanctity as a manifestation of the divine essence. However effective this may be as a moral appeal, it does not set aside Kant's fundamental contention that moral obligation and cause are logically different.

The form of the dialectic, however, imparted its own peculiarities to its interpretation of duty. The divergent interests and values represented by thesis and antithesis were assumed to stand in a relation of flat contradiction to each other, a relation of struggle and opposition. Each must be developed to its last consequences before the contradictions can be sublimated in the synthesis. Conciliation and compromise occur indeed and emerge with the evolution of the Idea. But as matters of conscious prevision and effort on the part of human participants they tend to be pictured as marks of sentimental weakness and caprice, a kind of treason against the majesty of the Absolute. The effect was to represent society as a constellation of opposed forces that work out to an inevitable conclusion rather than as a body of human relations to be conciliated and harmonized. On the assumptions of the dialectic, also, communication itself becomes peculiarly difficult, for no proposition is ever exactly true or exactly false. It always means more or less than it seems to mean. For it was the special claim of the dialectic to unite relativism with absolutism. Every stage carries, for the time being, the whole weight and force of the Absolute, even though in the end it is transitory. It is, so to speak, absolute while it lasts, and its duty is to achieve complete self-expression, though its ultimate defeat in the further advance of the World Spirit is assured. Hence the dialectic implied a moral attitude which is at once completely rigid and completely flexible, and it offered no criterion of the rightness of either except the success of the outcome. It was for this reason that Hegel's critics, Nietzsche for example, saw in the dialectic only an opportunism which is in practice an adoration of "the whole series of successes."

Hegel's dialectic was in truth a curious amalgam of historical insight and realism, of moral appeal, romantic idealization, and religious mysticism. In intention it was rational and an extension of logical method, but the intention defied exact formulation. In practice it played upon vague contrasts of popular speech, like real and apparent, essential and accidental, permanent and transitory, to which it could assign no precise meaning and for which it supplied no clear criteria. Hegel's historical judgments and moral evaluations, to which the dialectic was supposed to lend objectivity, were in fact as much conditioned by time and place and personality, as those of other philosophers with no such elaborate apparatus. To unite purposes so diverse and factors so incapable of definition or empirical verification into a method, and to give that method scientific precision, was in fact impossible. What the dialectic accomplished was to give a specious air of logical certitude to historical judgments which, if true, can be based only on empirical evidence, and to moral judgments which, if sound, depend upon ethical insights open to everyone. By attempting to combine the two it tended rather to obscure than to clarify the meaning of both.

INDIVIDUALISM AND THE THEORY OF THE STATE

The importance of the *Philosophy of Right* did not depend upon the formal structure of its argument but upon its reference to political realities, a reference which the formalism sometimes made almost surreptitious. It dealt with two subjects of fundamental importance, the relationship between the human individual and the social and economic institutions within which he lives his personal life and the relationship between these institutions and the state, which Hegel regarded as unique among institutions. With his theories of these two relationships the remainder of this chapter will be concerned. Before taking up his theories, however, it should be made clear that Hegel's point of view, though it was opposed to the point of view of French and English political thought, had substantial reasons behind it and that its injection into political theory was timely and important. The *Philosophy of Right* was in fact permeated by the same qualities of thought that marked Hegel's early political writings, a firm grasp of political philosophy and a realistic understanding of political history. Indeed, in a limited sense his purpose might be described as an attempt to test political theory by constitutional history. The philosophy in question was of course the doctrine of inalienable individual rights and the meaning of that doctrine as revealed by the French Revolution. To his estimate of the Revolution Hegel brought a point of view that was typically German and that reflected the political experience of Germans. The philosophy of natural rights had been cut, so to speak, to fit the political experience of the French and English. Hegel's rejection of natural rights and his theory of the state was cut to fit the political experience of Germany. In a broader sense, however, Hegel's criticism was a thoroughgoing philosophical analysis of individualism and of its validity as a theory of society. Hence it served as a starting point for re-examining the whole range of psychological and ethical problems involved in a social philosophy. In this respect Hegel's philosophy was perhaps more important outside Germany than within, precisely because it brought to light considerations that individualism had neglected.

There had been and there continued to be little in the politics of Germany that could give to the idea of individual rights a hold upon the political consciousness of Germans such as it had upon the minds of Frenchmen and Englishmen. As a theory the philosophy of natural rights was of course fully known to Germans but it remained for them in a sense esoteric and academic, as German liberalism proved itself to be in 1848. In France and England the theory had been forged as the defense of a minority's claim to religious toleration against a majority that could wield against them the power of a government already comparatively well centralized and largely nationalized, while Germany was the one country in which religious differences could be made to coincide reasonably well with political boundaries. In France and England natural rights had become the defense of a national revolution against monarchy, but in Germany there had been no revolution. The defense of private judgment and individual freedom of action against the state had never been felt by Germans as a vital interest of the nation itself. Finally, in England individual rights became an adequate philosophical support for commercial and industrial expansion under a policy of *laissez faire*. Germany, on the other hand, in Hegel's day and later, had achieved no such unity of national feeling as had long existed in France and England. Its mentality was filled with provincialisms and with antagonisms against its imperfectly assimilated minorities. Its economy was backward in comparison with the national economies of England and France, and its governments in Hegel's day had just demonstrated their political and military incompetence before the onslaught of Napoleon. When Hegel died it would still be a full generation before Germany achieved a political unity consonant with its cultural nationalism, and Hegel was quite right in predicting that this would not occur on the lines that had been followed by French or English liberalism. Its government would be a federalism created by imposing a strong state upon local units; its ministry would be responsible to the monarch rather than to a national parliament; and its economic modernization and expansion would take place not by *laissez faire* but under strong political guidance. The aura of sanctity that Hegel's philosophy threw around the word "state," which to an Englishman might seem pure sentimentality, expressed for Germans real and compelling political aspirations.

The difference in point of view between Hegel's theory of the state on the one hand and French or English individualism on the other might be construed as a difference between two ways of estimating the political accomplishment of the French Revolution, and indeed Hegel did so construe it. But this difference in interpreting the Revolution depended on differing estimates of the permanently important factors in the whole evolution of constitutional government. From a liberal point of view the Revolution was a triumph of the rights of man over the irresponsible or dictatorial powers of the French monarchy. Its permanent achievements were individual liberty, government by the consent of the governed, constitutional limitations to safeguard the civil liberties of subjects, and the responsibility of officials to a nation-wide electorate. From Hegel's point of view some of these supposed achievements were incidental and some were mischievous illusions. The constructive achievement of the Revolution, he believed, might have been the consummation of a national state, a direct continuation of the process begun when the monarchy established its control over the nobility, the cities, the estates, and the other feudal institutions of the Middle Ages. The Revolution merely swept away the debris of feudalism which had been outdated but not actually destroyed with the rise of the monarchy, and its Jacobinism was an aberration. As in his essay on the *Constitution of Germany,* Hegel continued to interpret the difference between the feudal and the modern state in terms of the contrast between public and private law. Feudalism he conceived to be typically a system in which public functions were treated as private sinecures to be bought or sold as if they were private property. A state, on the contrary, comes into being when there arises a genuine public authority, recognized as higher in kind than the civil society which embodies private interests and also as competent to guide the nation in the fulfillment of its historic mission. Essentially the process is one of nationalizing the monarchy. The summit of political evolution, therefore, is the emergence of the state and the acceptance of the state by its citizens as a level of political evolution above civil society. Ethically Hegel construed this as producing a higher level of personal self-realization also, a form of society in which the modern man rises to a new height of freedom and in which there is a new synthesis of his interests as man and citizen. As a new emanation of the World Spirit the national state really is divine. Hegel's thought was well expressed by the historian Ranke when he said that states are "individualities, analogous to one another but essentially independent of each other . . . spiritual beings, original creations of the human spirit—one might say, thoughts of God."

On the other hand Hegel condemned the Revolution because, in so far as it pursued its ideals of liberty and equality, he thought that it really perpetuated the old fallacy of feudalism in a new form. It leveled down the functional differences between men in their social capacities to a common and abstract political equality, which made their relation to the state a mere matter of private interest. It reduced the institutions of both society and the state to utilitarian devices for satisfying private needs and gratifying personal propensities, which as individual passions are merely capricious. In order to attain true ethical dignity these individual motives must be absorbed and transmuted first in the institutions of civil society and then at a higher level in the institutions of the state. The philosophy of the Revolution was therefore fundamentally false in two respects. It failed to recognize that the citizen's personality is a social being which requires as a condition of its moral significance a part to be played in the life of civil society and it failed to recognize that the institutions of civil society are organs of the nation, which must be embodied in a public authority consonant in dignity with the nation's moral significance. Neither society nor the state can be said to depend merely on individual consent; they are too deeply ingrained in the whole structure of needs and satisfactions that make up personal self-realization. The highest of all human needs is the need for participation, to be an organ of causes and purposes larger than private wants and satisfactions. The fundamental error of the revolutionary philosophy, as Hegel saw it, was its abstract individualism. The fundamental error in its policy was its attempt to erect paper constitutions and political procedure on the assumptions of individualism.

The importance of this attack on individualism and the Revolution lay in the fact that it expressed not only the political experience of Germany but also profound changes that were coming about in the political and intellectual climate of opinion in all Europe. It was this which gave to German philosophy in the first half of the nineteenth century a position of leadership which it had never had. The French Revolution closed an intellectual as well as a political era. The theory of natural law, which had dominated political thought throughout the whole preceding period of modern thought, became obsolete in an astonishingly short time. Its plausibility as an intellectual construction had depended upon the great systems of philosophical rationalism inherited from the seventeenth century, which had lost their authority in the nineteenth. In France Rousseau's radical idealization of citizenship and in England Burke's conservative idealization of tradition had already suggested the lines of thought that Hegel's philosophy systematized. The completely rational individual, pursuing ends set wholly by propensities native to his own personality, was a conception that could hardly withstand historical or psychological scrutiny. And the dogma that his political and civil rights are imprescriptible and unchangeable fitted badly with a nationalism that continually set a higher value on its own collective purposes and with an ethics that became continually more aware of conflicts between individual and social values. Thus the nature of the individual person and his relation to his society — the psychological and ethical intermeshing of individual need with social purpose — which had seemed a matter to be settled by a few self-evident generalities, became a problem, indeed the central problem of social science and social ethics. The importance of Hegel's political theory consisted largely in the fact that it set this problem. In so doing it both crystallized the anti-liberal tendencies of developing nationalism and forced a thoroughgoing re-examination of the individualism of current political liberalism. Accordingly, as was said above, Hegel's political philosophy dealt with two principal subjects. The first was his ethical theory of freedom and its relation to authority, which coincided roughly with his critique of individualism. The second was his theory of the state, its constitutional structure and its relation to the institutions of civil society.

FREEDOM AND AUTHORITY

Hegel's critique of individualism was directed against two different conceptions. In the first place he identified individualism with the provincialism and particularism which had prevented Germany from achieving modern national statehood. This national trait he attributed largely to the influence of Luther, who had made Christian liberty a mystical independence of the soul from all secular conditions. In the second place Hegel identified individualism with Jacobinism, the violence, fanaticism, terrorism, and atheism of the French Revolution. This type of individualism he attributed to philosophical rationalism. The common fallacy in both types he found in the detachment of the human being from his position in and dependence upon an organized society in which he has a part to play, duties to perform, and the status belonging to such a position. Considered by himself the individual is merely capricious, an animal governed by brute instinct, as Rousseau had said, with no rule of action higher than his own impulses, appetites, and inclinations and with no rule of thought higher than his subjective fancies. To be correctly understood the individual must be regarded as a member of society. But in the modern world he must be regarded also as a member of the state. For the national state, together with Protestant Christianity, is the unique achievement of modern civilization, which has learned to combine the highest authority with the highest degree and form of freedom for its citizens.

> The essence of the modern state binds together the universal and the full freedom of the particularity, including the welfare of individuals.[14]

For no very good reason other than his concern with German culture, Hegel identified this highest form of state not only as Protestant but also as "Germanic."

Individualism in both its mystical and its rationalist form merely posits the individual, as soul or as rational being, without regard for the historical conditions which have produced him or the social and economic conditions without which his religious and moral and rational nature cannot support itself. It falsifies both the nature of the individual and the nature of society. It falsifies the first because the individual's spirituality and rationality are the creations of a social life. Hegel accepted them as metaphysical beings, but not in the way that theology or rationalism had imagined them; they are moments or phases of the World Spirit, which has created them in its immanent development. But individualism falsifies the nature of social institutions, because it regards them as accidental and indifferent to the moral and spiritual development of personality, as merely utilitarian aids invented to satisfy men's irrational desires. This

[14] *Philosophy of Right,* Section 260, addition.

is historically false, for language, government, law, and religion are not invented but "grow." It is also ethically false because it sets freedom off against the restraints imposed upon the inclinations by custom, law, and government. These are conceived as burdens which in the interest of liberty must be reduced to a minimum and which ideally might be reduced to no restraint at all in a Golden Age or "state of nature" which would permit everyone to do as he liked. But the Golden Age is historically a fiction and morally and politically it would be simply anarchy, which is not freedom but despotism.

This critique of natural rights and of individualist liberalism was, of course, dialectical. Hegel knew as well as anyone that neither Locke nor any other serious exponent of the theory had believed civilization as such to be foreign to or repressive of individual freedom, however oppressive a given society might be. The criticism developed what Hegel regarded as an implicit "contradiction" in Locke's philosophy. In point of fact it is much more effective if it is understood as calling attention to a neglected aspect of social psychology and social ethics. It amounted to pointing out the important fact that the psychological structure of individual personality is intimately related to the structure of the society in which a person lives and to his position in that society. The laws, customs, institutions, and moral valuations of a people reflect its mentality, but they also shape that mentality and continuously reshape it as they develop. The individual's moral and even his intellectual outlook is inseparable from that of the society of which he is a unit and from the relationships within that society in which he participates through citizenship, social class, or religious affiliation. Thus, for example, in his account of civil society Hegel protested against identifying economic wants with biological needs. Wants are really states of mind and are therefore dependent upon social interpretation, the economic system, the accepted mode of life in a social class, and moral valuations. The essence of pauperism, he said, consists in social rejection and loss of self-respect; poverty "does not of itself make a pauper." It depends upon the estimation in which the poor man is held and in which he holds himself.

In England even the poorest man believes that he has his right, and with him this standard is different from that which satisfies the poor in other lands. . . . In social conditions want assumes the form of a wrong done to one or other class.[15]

Passages such as this obviously contain the germ of Marx's theory that ideology depends on social position. Hegel's argument suggested an economic interpretation of social position, though it did not imply an exclusively economic interpretation. It did imply, however, that society, or perhaps more properly culture, is an indispensable category for explaining human behavior.[16] The culmination of this idea is to be found not only in Marx but in all present-day social psychology and cultural anthropology.

Hegel, however, was less concerned with psychology and sociology than with ethical and political theories of individual freedom. Freedom, he believed, must be understood as a social phenomenon, a property of the social system which arises through the moral development of the community. It is less an individual endowment than a status which is imparted to the individual through legal and ethical institutions that the community supports. In consequence it cannot be equated with self-will or the following of private inclinations. Freedom consists rather in the adjustment of inclination and individual capacity to the performance of socially significant work; or as F. H. Bradley put it, in finding "my station and its duties." It is these which impart moral worth to inclination, for no claim to liberty or happiness can be morally defended except as desire coincides with some phase of the general good and is supported by the general will. The individual's rights and liberties are those which correspond to the duties imposed by his station in society. Even private happiness requires the dignity that attaches to social status and the consciousness of having a share in socially valuable work. Hegel always believed that self-consciousness *per se* is painful, a mark of frustration and futility. This conception of happiness, and of the rights and duties essential to it, clearly depended in part, as had Rousseau's, upon the classical revival. Hegel's theory of free citizenship, like that of Plato and Aristotle, ran

[15] *Philosophy of Right,* Section 244, addition.

[16] The history of this phase of Hegel's thought is developed at length in Herbert Marcuse's *Reason and Revolution: Hegel and the Rise of Social Theory,* 1941.

not in terms of private rights but of social functions. But as Hegel imagined, the development of Christian morals and of citizenship in the modern state made possible a more complete synthesis of personal right and public duty than had been possible in a society that depended on slavery. In the modern state all men are free, and in their service to it they can find ideally the highest form of self-realization. In the state the negative freedom of self-will is supplanted by the "real freedom" of citizenship.

The dialectical form of Hegel's argument was largely responsible for the paradoxical consequences that he drew from this contrast of freedom and real freedom. The theory becomes merely a play of logical abstractions. Thus Hegel characteristically equated individual choice with caprice, sentimentality, or fanaticism, thus obscuring the fact, which is fundamentally important both for psychology and ethics, that no actual human being ever regards his "desires," however fleeting or however profound, as all on the same level of importance or allows them the same weight in affecting his behavior. Corresponding to this undiscriminating estimate of individual motives, civil society was described by Hegel as a realm of mechanical necessity, a resultant of the irrational forces of individual desire, which is governed by laws, particularly on its economic side, that he likened to the laws of planetary motion. Thus society considered apart from the state was represented as governed by non-moral causal laws and hence as ethically anarchical. The result was, so to speak, a criticism of individualism by caricature: the individual was pictured as controlled by self-seeking motives and social motives were denied to him, while society without the state was pictured as a mechanical balancing of these non-moral drives. It easily followed, of course, that the state, which "overrules" the anarchy of civil society, was credited with being the only genuinely moral factor in the entire social process. It monopolized moral purposes simply by definition, because these had been excluded analytically from individual personality and from society. Obviously, therefore, the state ought to be absolute since it and it alone embodies ethical values. Obviously also the individual attains moral dignity and freedom only as he devotes himself to the service of the state.

Just what this logical *tour de force* would have meant if Hegel had translated it into actual civil rights and liberties is difficult if not impossible to say. His statements about concrete political rights were vague to the last degree and were often flatly inconsistent with one another. Starting as he did with the assumption that individual choice is merely capricious, he fell easily into the implication that private judgment, even conscience, is merely a "superficial" thing. From passages such as this it might be inferred that he regarded duty as simply obedience, or that good citizenship consisted for him in merely conforming to the existing state of affairs and the rules that governments lay down. In the Preface to the *Philosophy of Right* he apparently denied to political philosophy even the right to criticize the state. Again, starting from the general proposition that individual good requires the finding of a significant station in society, he often spoke as if no genuine conflict of interest could ever arise between individuals and the society to which they belong. Yet from another point of view Hegel's whole social philosophy depended upon the personal frustration that he believed must result from a society that gives its members no significant work to do. In spite of his tendency to idealize the Prussian monarchy, Hegel was in fact a sharp or even a bitter critic of the actual state of German politics. As an historian he admired the successful iconoclast rather than the conformist. Quite certainly Hegel believed that, in some way which he never made clear, modern constitutional government creates a higher kind of personal liberty and respects more highly the individual's independence and right of self-determination than any form of government in the past. Quite certainly also he believed that this implied respect for human rights rather than merely the safeguarding of a functioning unit of society.

> Man must be accounted a universal being not because he is a Jew, Catholic, Protestant, German, or Italian, but because he is a man.[17]

But the belief that man as a man has value is certainly incompatible with the belief that his moral judgments are merely capricious or that his value is derived from his station in a society whose moral end is supplied by a national state.

[17] *Philosophy of Right,* Section 209, note.

The same kind of uncertainty and confusion attends the meaning of Hegel's belief that the state embodies the highest values. Even on metaphysical grounds, where he chose to place the question, it is not clear how any single state, which after all is only one manifestation of the World Spirit, could include all the values of art and religion, or account for the transference of these values from one national culture to another. Hegel's statements about art and religion were in fact notably inconsistent. Sometimes he regarded them as creations of the national spirit, yet he certainly did not consider Christianity to be the prerogative of any single nation, nor did he believe that art and literature are always exclusively national. On the other hand there was, from his point of view, no general European or human society to which they could belong, since a modern culture without a state would be a contradiction in terms. This confusion probably accounted for the fact that, on a concrete political level, Hegel had nothing clear to say about the relation of churches to the state or about freedom of conscience, though he certainly did not believe in religious coercion. His hostile estimate of Roman Catholicism and of German pietism and his admiration for Lutheran Protestantism were equally uncritical. No clear line of thought connected the metaphysical supremacy attributed to the state with the political functions of an actual government. Consequently Hegel's theory of freedom implied nothing definite in the way of civil or political liberties. The idealization of the state and the low moral estimate of civil society, however, combined to make political authoritarianism inevitable.

THE STATE AND CIVIL SOCIETY

Hegel's theory of the state, as was said above, depended upon the peculiar nature of the relationship existing, as he supposed, between the state and civil society. The relation is at once one of contrast and mutual dependence. The state as Hegel conceived it is no utilitarian institution, engaged in the commonplace business of providing public services, administering the law, performing police duties, and adjusting industrial and economic interests. All these functions belong to civil society. The state may indeed direct and regulate them as need arises, but it does not itself perform them. Civil society depends upon the state for intelligent supervision and moral significance. Considered by itself society would be governed only by the mechanical laws resulting from the interaction of the acquisitive and self-centered motives of many individuals. The state, however, depends upon civil society for the means of accomplishing the moral purposes which it embodies. But though mutually dependent, the two stand on distinct dialectical levels. The state is not means but end. It represents the rational ideal in development and the truly spiritual element in civilization, and as such it uses, or perhaps in a metaphysical sense creates, civil society for the achievement of its own ends.

> The state is the divine will as a present spirit, which unfolds itself in the actual shape of an organized world.[18]

Whereas civil society is a realm of blind inclination and causal necessity, the state "acts in obedience to conscious ends, known principles and laws, which are not merely implied but expressly before its consciousness." Quotations of this sort might be multiplied indefinitely: the state is the absolutely rational, the divinity which knows and wills itself, the eternal and necessary being of spirit, the march of God in the world.

It is important to observe, however, that the moral superiority thus attributed to the state implied no contempt for civil society or its institutions but in a sense the very opposite. Hegel, in his personal character and also in his political thought, was before everything else a good bourgeois, with rather more than the usual bourgeois respect for stability and security. The relationship between the state and civil society, as he understood it, was mutual, even though it was also a relationship of superiority and inferiority and even though the authority of the state was absolute. The economic life of society gained moral significance — in a sense it was glorified — by the fact that the state and its cultural mission depend upon it. But though the regulative power of the state is absolute, this does not extend to abolishing the institutions or the rights upon which the performance of economic functions depends. Property, according to Hegel's theory, is not created by the state or even by society but is an indispensable condition of human personality, much as it had been

[18] *Ibid.*, Section 270, note.

for Locke. Hegel's account of civil society was in fact a careful, even an elaborate, analysis of the guilds and corporations, the estates and classes, the associations and local communities that made up the structure of the German society with which he was familiar. These or some equivalent he regarded as humanly indispensable. Without them the people would be merely a formless mass and the individual would be merely a kind of human atom, since it is the context of economic and institutional ties that gives substance to his personality. From Hegel's point of view, therefore, the state is not composed primarily of individual citizens. The individual must be "mediated" through a long series of corporations and associations before he arrives at the final dignity of citizenship in the state. Jacobinism, which makes government depend upon the will of the people expressed through the suffrage, means in practice government by a rabble. "The people," Hegel said, "does not know what it wills." Its action is "elemental, void of reason, violent, and terrible."[19]

This view of civil society, it should be noted, had several aspects. On the one hand it might be regarded as reactionary. Undoubtedly it reflected the point of view of a society that was still securely stratified, that retained an unquestioning respect for rank and station, and that had never felt the leveling effects of industrialization. It attached little or no value to equal citizenship which, in the light of French and English politics, appeared to be a condition of free government. Hegel's view of civil society, however, was not merely reactionary. It did not share the illusion of the utilitarian economists that *laissez faire* is part of the unchangeable order of nature but suggested rather Marx's treatment of it as a special phase of social development. Hegel's point of view, moreover, was well adapted to a form of nationalism in which the state was assumed to have the function of fostering trade and industry as part of its general mission of extending national power. It must be admitted also that many of Hegel's criticisms of French Jacobinism were well taken. In the name of liberty it often destroyed quite recklessly forms of social organization that served a useful purpose and that in one form or another had to be reinstated in the interest of liberalism

[19] *Ibid.*, Section 301, note; 303, note.

itself.[20] In general Hegel's view of civil society embodied a sound principle: that when the individual is regarded merely as a citizen, the state tends to absorb all forms of human association. And in effect this is not liberty but despotism, as all forms of political totalitarianism prove. The arguments of the political Pluralists at the end of the nineteenth century could very largely have been constructed out of Hegel's theory of civil society. The importance that Marx attached to economic forces in politics quite definitely had its roots there, even though Marx doomed Hegel's state to extinction.

The theory of civil society and its relation to the state largely determined the meaning that Hegel attached to constitutional government. The state's power as he conceived it is absolute but it is not arbitrary. Its absolutism reflected its superior moral position and the fact that Hegel permitted the state to monopolize the ethical aspects of society. The state, however, must always exercise its regulative powers under the forms of law. It is an embodiment of reason and law is "rational." This meant for Hegel that the acts of a public authority must be predictable because they proceed from known rules, that the rules limit the discretionary powers of officials, and that official action expresses the authority of the office and not the private will or judgment of the office-holder. The law must bear equally on all the persons to whom it applies because, being general, it cannot consider individual peculiarities. The essence of despotism is lawlessness, and the essence of a free and constitutional government is that it excludes lawlessness and produces security.

> Despotism is a condition of lawlessness, in which the particular will, whether of monarch or people (ochlocracy) counts as law, or rather instead of law.
>
> The fact that everything in the state is firm and secure is a bulwark against caprice and positive opinion.[21]

Hegel's state, therefore, was what later German jurisprudence came to call a *Rechtsstaat*. It had to achieve a high order of internal administrative efficiency and its judicial system in par-

[20] See the essay on "Man and Citizen: Applications of Individualism in the French Revolution" by R. R. Palmer in *Essays in Political Theory*, ed. by Milton R. Konvitz and Arthur E. Murphy (1948), pp. 130 ff.

[21] *Philosophy of Right*, Sections 278, note; 270, addition.

ticular had to give security to rights of property and of the person, which Hegel regarded as indispensable to the economic functions of civil society. His theory of constitutional government was therefore in accord with that of liberalism in distinguishing between legal authority and personal power, but it acknowledged no relationship between the rule of law and democratic political processes.

The key to this phase of Hegel's constitutionalism was the high importance that he attached to an official governing class, the "universal class" as he called it, which by birth and training is fitted to rule and which embodies a long tradition of hierarchical authority and orderly procedure. Such a class he regarded as detached from and impartial toward the private and social interests which it regulates. In a special sense, therefore, it represents the general will and the "reason" of society, in contrast with acquisitive self-interest or special and partial interests, and is the guardian of the whole public interest. The bureaucratic organization of civil society is its apex, the point at which it makes contact, so to speak, with the still higher institutions of the state. The essential property of the whole system is that it is rooted in immemorial custom, in long accepted grades of rank and authority, and yet that these grades are functions in the total life of the nation. This conception of constitutional government was contrasted in Hegel's mind with French experiments in the making of paper constitutions and also with English parliamentary government. For the former he had an historian's deep-seated contempt. To ask who makes a constitution, he said, is nonsense, for constitutions are not made. "A constitution is not a mere manufacture, but the work of centuries." It must be "thought of as above and beyond what is made, as self-begotten and self-centered, as divine and perpetual."[22] Bills of rights, the separation of powers, checks and balances, therefore, are mere apparatus. Constitutionalism depends on a tradition of self-government, and in Hegel's opinion this tradition is inseparable from differences of social rank, an acceptable balance between a governing class and the lower orders of society, and an aristocracy characterized by its loyalty to the crown. The principal

[22] *Ibid.*, Sections 274, addition; 273, note.

function of the monarchy is to maintain this balance. But the balance depends not on a separation of powers but on a distinction of functions, and the purpose of the distinction is not to weaken but to strengthen the state. The English parliamentary system, on the other hand, appeared to Hegel to be a degenerate remnant of feudalism. In it political power had remained the private perquisite of an aristocratic oligarchy which had no national function. Hence England had never achieved the dignity of a state. Perhaps in the year of Hegel's death this was a not unrealistic, if somewhat shortsighted, estimate of English government. Hegel's earliest political conviction was a thoroughgoing dislike of government by a vested aristocratic interest as he saw it exhibited in the city of Bern. His maturest judgment, set down almost at the time of his death, was that English government belonged to that type. It lacked, he said, *der grosse Sinn von Fürsten,* and he predicted that the Reform Bill would merely add the fallacies of Jacobinism to those of feudalism.[23] According to Hegel's reading of constitutional history the significant step was the rise of national authority under the monarchy, not the control of the executive by the legislature.

In comparison with the part assigned to officialdom, both representative institutions and the monarchy played a minor rôle in Hegel's theory of constitutionalism, in spite of the mystical reverence that he gave to the monarchy. For reasons already made clear Hegel regarded representation on the basis merely of territory and population as meaningless, since the individual in his relation to the state figures as a member of one or more of the many associations supported by civil society. The legislature is the point at which these associations meet the state. What needs to be represented, on the side of civil society, are the significant spheres (*Kreise*) or interests or functional units. The difficulties that this idea of functional representation have encountered in the last quarter century make clear the reason why Hegel never arrived at any practicable plan of representative

[23] On Hegel's judgment of aristocracy in Bern, formed during his residence in that city (1793–1796), see H. Falkenheim, "Eine unbekannte politische Druckschrift Hegels," *Preussische Jahrbücher,* Vol. 138 (1909), pp. 193 ff. On English government see his essay, *Über die englische Reformbill* (1831), *Werke* (ed. by Lasson), Vol. VII, pp. 291 ff.

government on that principle. On the other hand he considered it essential that the official class, which must regulate civil society, should be represented in the legislature by the ministers. But the latter are in no sense responsible to the legislature. On the contrary the legislature, as Hegel conceived it, stands in substantially an advisory or consultative relation to the ministry, which is responsible to the crown. The monarch, however, according to Hegel, has no considerable power and such power as he has ought, in a well regulated monarchy, to flow from his legal position as head of the state.

> In a well-ordered monarchy only the objective side of law comes to hand, and to this the monarch subjoins merely the subjective "I will."[24]

The monarch is in fact a kind of visible symbol for abstractions like national spirit, national law, and national state which Hegel conceived to be the real forces in the background of politics and history.

THE LATER SIGNIFICANCE OF HEGELIANISM

Despite the technicalities in which Hegel cloaked his thoughts and the apparent abstraction of his conclusions, few political theories had a more intimate relationship to political realities. It reflected in a very real way the state of affairs in Germany at the close of the Napoleonic Wars, her bitter national humiliation at the hands of France, and her aspiration for political union and the creation of a national state corresponding to the unity and greatness of German culture. To a remarkable degree also it grasped the main lines of development by which that aspiration was to be realized in the generation following his death. It gave a special meaning to the concept of the state and invested that concept with connotations for which there was no analogue in the political thought of France and England but which made it throughout the nineteenth century the central principle of German political and juristic philosophy. After the middle of the century the concept of the state detached itself from the philosophical technicalities of the dialectic in which Hegel had wrapped it, but it retained its essential characteristics without the technical form. In substance it was an idealization of power which

[24] *Philosophy of Right,* Section 280, addition.

united curiously an almost Philistine contempt for ideals apart from force with a moral respect for force as almost self-justifying. It placed the nation on a metaphysical pinnacle above control by international law and even above moral criticism. In its political implications the theory of state was anti-liberal — a highly sublimated form of monarchical authoritarianism in which nationalism took the place of dynastic legitimacy — but it was not anti-constitutional. It conceived constitutionalism, however, in a way quite different from any that was possible in countries where liberalism and constitutionalism were phases of the same political movement. Almost its whole meaning was summed up in the aphorism "a government not of men but of laws." Hence it implied nothing in respect to democratic procedures but much in respect to orderly bureaucratic administration. It assumed security of person and property and governmental care for public welfare, but to protect these it depended not on political responsibility to popular opinion but on the public spirit of an official class assumed to stand above the conflicts of economic and social interests. In practice it represented the hazardous venture of leaving politics to those who by birth and profession are fitted to rule. But this was a venture which was intelligible in a society where the creation of political unity and the extension of national power eclipsed the concern for political liberty. In all these respects Hegel's political philosophy reflected with surprising accuracy the Germany of the Second Empire.

The importance of Hegel's political thought, however, is only feebly represented by its relation to Germany alone. His mind had an extraordinary breadth of grasp, and his philosophy as he conceived it was not only in the current of all modern thought but was intended to be its summation and its consummation. Viewed in this light its central idea was the concept of universal history, and this he designed to be a new unifying principle to take the place held by the system of natural law in the seventeenth and eighteenth centuries. In it Hegel united the idea of the general will incoherently set forth by Rousseau — a vital principle inherent in nations but also the manifestation of a larger spiritual force that forms the core of reality itself — and Burke's religious vision of history as a "divine tactic." To these vague speculations Hegel aspired to give the certainty and precision of logic and to create in the dialectic an instrument of scientific investigation which would actually display "the march of God in the world." In place of the eternal system of unchangeable natural law he put the rational unfolding of the Absolute in history.

Nothing is easier than to dismiss this grandiose structure of speculation as a vagary of the romantic imagination. Yet it was the germ of a new point of view that came to affect, both for good and bad, almost every phase of social philosophy in the nineteenth century. The significant change lay in the fact that Hegel's unfolding cosmic force, though like the philosophers of the Enlightenment he called it Reason, is manifested in social groups, in nations and in national cultures and institutions, rather than in individuals. If for Hegel's World Spirit is substituted the forces of production, the result is in principle similar. In either case society became a system of forces rather than a community of persons, and its history became a development of institutions that belong to the community as a collective entity. These forces and institutions, like the community they belong to, are conceived to follow the trends and tendencies inherent in their own nature. Institutional history — of law, constitutions, morals, philosophy, religions — became a permanent and indeed a dominant part of the intellectual equipment of social studies. To the action and development of these social forces the individual's moral judgments and his personal interests became almost irrelevant, since the real agents in society are forces which are self-justifying because their course is inevitable. Ideas such as these, which contained at once so much truth and so much exaggeration, became the climate of opinion in the social philosophy of the nineteenth century. To the study of politics they brought at once enrichment and impoverishment. Politics was enriched and made vastly more realistic when legalism and individualism were supplemented by the historical study of institutions and by a more concrete understanding of social and economic factors in government and in human psychology. Yet in a sense the very existence of politics as an independent activity was threatened by a view that reduced it to a "reflection" of social forces, of rivalries between nations or antagonisms between economic classes. For such a view tended to minimize the area of negotiation in human relations, and to obscure the fact that political institutions often are more truly agencies by which negotiation can take place than agencies for exerting power. It obscured also the fact that the art of negotiation and therefore political intelligence cannot be summed up altogether in the shrewd calculation of forces. Evidently it was a liberal conception of politics that was most likely to be lost to sight with this shift in point of view. All these tendencies existed in the germ in Hegel's philosophy, though they did not grow directly from it alone. But it was a powerful statement of the changes in social and intellectual outlook on which they depended.

Of the developments in political theory which grew directly from Hegelianism three will call for special consideration. The direct line of development was undoubtedly from Hegel to Marx and so to the later history of communist theory. Here the point of connection was the dialectic, which Marx accepted as the epoch-making discovery of Hegel's philosophy. Hegel's nationalism and his idealization of the state Marx regarded as merely " mystifications " that infected the dialectic because of the metaphysical idealism by which the system was vitiated. By transforming it into dialectical materialism and construing the dialectic as the economic interpretation of history Marx supposed that he could retain the method as a genuinely scientific way of explaining social evolution. That civil society (apart from the state) is mainly economic in its structure was a conclusion that Marx could take ready-made from Hegel. In the second place Hegelianism was an important factor in the revision of English liberalism by the Oxford idealists. Here, however, the dialectic had negligible importance. The important influence was Hegel's searching and on the whole sound critique of individualism, to which the progress of industrialism lent an urgency that Hegel never felt. The anti-liberal bias of Hegel's political theory was so remote from the realities of English politics that it passed almost unobserved. Finally, in Italy Hegelianism was adopted in the early stages of fascism to provide a philosophy for that highly pragmatic movement. In fact, however, fascist Hegelianism was almost admittedly an *ad hoc* rationalization.

SELECTED BIBLIOGRAPHY

History of Political Thought in Germany from 1789 to 1815. By Reinhold Aris. London, 1936.

The Philosophical Theory of the State. By Bernard Bosanquet. London, 1899. Chs. 9–10.

Der Begriff des Volksgeistes bei Hegel, zugleich ein Beitrag zur Geschichte des Begriffs der Entwicklung im 19. Jahrhundert. By Friedrich Dittmann. Leipzig, 1909.

"The Growth of Historical Science." By G. P. Gooch. In *Cambridge Modern History,* Vol. XII (1910), ch. 26.

The Decline of Liberalism as an Ideology, with Particular Reference to German Politico-legal Thought. By John H. Hallowell. University of California Publications in Political Science. Berkeley and Los Angeles, 1943.

The Social and Political Ideas of some Representative Thinkers of the Age of Reaction and Reconstruction. Edited by F. J. C. Hearnshaw. London, 1932. Ch. 3.

Hegel und der nationale Machtstaatsgedanke in Deutschland. By Hermann Heller. Leipzig, 1921.

The Metaphysical Theory of the State. By L. T. Hobhouse. London, 1918.

Reason and Revolution: Hegel and the Rise of Social Theory. By Herbert Marcuse. New York, 1941.

An Introduction to Hegel. By G. R. G. Mure. Oxford, 1940.

Hegel und der Staat. By Franz Rosenzweig. 2 vols. Munich, 1920.

The Philosophy of Hegel. By W. T. Stace. London, 1924. Part IV, Second Division.

Studies in the History of Political Philosophy. By C. E. Vaughan. 2 vols. Manchester, 1925. Vol. II, chs. 2–4.

Hegels Gesellschaftsbegriff und seine geschichtliche Fortbildung durch Lorenz Stein, Marx, Engels und Lasalle. By Paul Vogel. Berlin, 1925.

CHAPTER XXXI

LIBERALISM: PHILOSOPHICAL RADICALISM

The reaction against the philosophy of natural rights which began with Rousseau and Burke and received its first systematic statement from Hegel by no means superseded the tradition of individualism which formed the main strand of political thinking throughout the seventeenth and eighteenth centuries. On the contrary this philosophy produced its chief practical consequences in the nineteenth century. Its history was an example of the paradox of which Hegel was so fond, that a philosophy is fully developed in its details and applications only when its main principles have come to be taken for granted and, to that extent, have become retarded in their speculative development. The principles of the Revolutionary Era, first clearly stated by Locke and embodied in great political manifestoes like the American Declaration of Independence and the French and American bills of rights, summed up political ideals which in the nineteenth century seemed certain of progressive realization in the politics of all countries where the culture of Western Europe prevailed and might probably come to be realized throughout the world. These ideals included the civil liberties — freedom of thought, of expression, and of association — the security of property, and the control of political institutions by an informed public opinion. Everywhere, as it seemed, these ends were to be practically realized by the adoption of the forms of constitutional government, by the acceptance of the rules that government must work within the limits set by law, that the center of political authority should fall within representative legislatures, and that all branches of government should be responsible to an electorate that tended to include the entire adult population. These ideals, and this type of political agency for realizing them, had been defended in the name of natural rights and they continued to sum up the purposes and, broadly speaking, the achievements of nineteenth-century liberalism. At the core of this mode of political thought was a fundamental postulate about the nature of value, viz., that all value inheres ultimately in the satisfactions and the realizations of human personality. It was this postulate which Kant had expressed in his famous dictum that morality consists in treating persons as ends and not as means, and which Jefferson had affirmed when he said that governments exist to protect and realize the inalienable rights of man.

Yet between the philosophy of natural rights in the Revolutionary Era and the liberalism of the nineteenth century there was a profound difference of temper and spirit. The philosophy of natural rights was in essence a revolutionary creed; it could brook no compromise where a fundamental right was invaded. But the French Revolution bred in many quarters a reaction against revolution. On the Continent the imperial ambitions of Napoleon left the constitutional traditions of every western nation in ruins. Even in England, where this was not the case, the progress of parliamentary reform was checked by reaction and was resumed only with difficulty after 1815. Everywhere the Revolution produced, as revolutions are wont to do, a revulsion against its excesses, and it became the fashion to attribute these excesses to the *philosophes* and the rights of man. Chateaubriand expressed the temper of liberalism everywhere when he said, " We must preserve the political work which is the fruit of the Revolution . . . but we must eradicate the Revolution from this work." At a later date the same idea was expressed by idealizing evolution as the antithesis of revolution.

In part this moderating of the liberal attitude was due to philosophical reasons. The ethical theory upon which the philosophy of natural rights had depended was necessarily intuitional. There is no way to defend a theory of imprescriptible individual rights except to affirm, as both Locke and Jefferson had done, that such rights are self-evident. But the drift of science in general and of social thought in particular was pretty steadily toward empiricism, and therefore away from the faith that a proposition may be taken as axiomatic because it appears to be obvious. In short, the authority of rationalism steadily diminished, and the theory of natural rights had always been an element of philosophical rationalism. More influential than any theoretical consideration, however, were no doubt the changes that naturally occurred in the outlook of the commercial and industrial middle class as its position and influence became more assured. This class everywhere formed the spearhead of liberal political reform in the nineteenth century, and the trend of industrial and commercial development made the expansion of its political power a foregone conclusion. Correspondingly, the influence of the landed gentry was relatively declining, and wage earners, at least during the first half or two-thirds of the century, had as yet attained little political self-consciousness and no effective organization. It is a gross exaggeration to say, as Marxian critics of liberalism often do say, that the ideals of constitutional government and personal liberty represented nothing but the interests of the middle class. It is a fact, however, that in the beginning this class was the main spokesman for these ideals and it is also a fact that the social position of this class made it progressively less revolutionary in its outlook and methods. When Francis Place could assure the passage of the Reform Bill of 1832 by threatening a run on the Bank of England, he was clearly not addressing a class which must exert its influence at the barricades.[1] It was also true as time went on that liberal political reform passed more and more out of the region of ideology and into that of institutional reconstruction. The modernizing of administration, the improvement of legal procedure, the reorganization of the courts, the creation of sanitary codes and factory inspection — all characteristic liberal reforms — were effected not by revolutionary enthusiasm but by hard, matter-of-fact research and the careful drafting of legislation. The ideals of liberalism were an aftermath of the Revolutionary Era but its achievements were largely the outcome of a high level of practical intelligence applied to specific problems. Its theory was still rationalistic but its rationalism was qualified by the realization that ideals have to be made effective in a multitude of concrete cases. Very naturally its philosophy tended to become utilitarian instead of revolutionary.

Political liberalism as a whole was a massive movement that made itself felt in all the countries of Western Europe and in America but its most characteristic development took place in

[1] Graham Wallas, *Life of Francis Place* (1898), pp. 309 ff.

England. In Germany liberal philosophy remained for the most part academic, not deeply rooted in popular thought, and in 1848 the cause of parliamentary government and ministerial responsibility was definitely lost. The issue of liberal constitutionalism was overshadowed in the minds of Germans by the issue of national unification, and this was accomplished under the non-liberal auspices of Bismarck and the Hohenzollerns. Only in the German judicial system were such liberal values realized as security of property and a considerable measure of civil liberty, and German liberal theory was accordingly juristic rather than political. In France the most significant social consequence of the Revolution was perhaps the creation of five or six million peasant proprietors who were politically inert, except in their power to obstruct, and who felt their interests to be identical with those of the bourgeoisie. In opposition to both there grew up for the first time in Europe a proletarian working-class movement that was socialist and radical in its political outlook rather than liberal, a social development of momentous importance that was at once incorporated in Marx's theory of the class struggle. French liberalism, therefore, far more than English, tended to be the social philosophy of a class, rather aristocratic in its attitude toward " the masses," and mainly critical in function, since it could hardly aspire to carry through a national policy.[2] Only in England, which throughout the nineteenth century was the most highly industrialized country in the world, did liberalism achieve the status at once of a national philosophy and a national policy. Here, contrary to the expectation implied by Marxism, it provided the principles for an orderly and peaceful transition, first to complete freedom for industry and the enfranchisement of the middle class and ultimately to the enfranchisement of the working class and their protection against the most serious hazards of industry. This was possible because the cleavage between social and economic classes in England never coincided exactly with the lines between political parties. Even in its earlier stage, when its economic theories in particular represented clearly the interest of industrialists, English liberalism in intention at least was always a theory of the general good of the whole national

[2] On Continental liberalism see Guido de Ruggiero, *The History of European Liberalism*, Eng. trans. by R. G. Collingwood, 1927.

community. In its later stages this intention became conscious and explicit, when it became apparent that other interests, especially those of labor and agriculture, had to be considered along with those of industry and commerce.

As an effective political movement liberalism in England was composed of many elements which learned to cooperate for specific purposes without insisting upon ideological agreement. Most striking of all, perhaps, was what Graham Wallas called "the tradition of a working alliance" between Evangelical Christianity and the non-religious radicalism of Jeremy Bentham and the Philosophical Radicals. The disparity of their philosophical beliefs was more than offset by the essential similarity of their moral and social purposes. The backbone of political liberalism, as Gladstone remarked, was the nonconformist religious sects.[3] At the start they had every motive to safeguard and extend their religious liberty and their participation in political rights. Though sometimes deficient in intellectual enlightenment they provided an element of Christian charity and humanitarianism which was lacking in the grim egoism of utilitarian ethics and of the classical economics. Moreover, the nonconformists as a body were not at all revolutionary or even radical in their political views. Because it held in suspension these and other groups with diverse ideologies, political liberalism was from the start less doctrinaire than its theory, and with time the conciliation of many interests became an overt part of its philosophy. It was the Philosophical Radicals, however, who provided the intellectual structure of early liberalism and therefore its program. They were at all times a group of intellectuals rather than a political party, but their influence was never measured by their numbers. As so often happens in politics the intellectuals provided ideas, which politicians used piecemeal, or sometimes not at all, according to the exigency of circumstances.

For the purpose of emphasizing this conciliatory and synthetizing phase of English liberal philosophy it is desirable that it should be divided into two periods and yet that the historical continuity of the two periods should be kept clearly in view. For

[3] On the importance of nonconformity in the political life of England early in the century see Elie Halévy, *A History of the English People in 1815,* especially Vol. I, Book III. Eng. trans. by E. I. Watkin (1924).

the distinguishing characteristic of its history was its development from a philosophy which at the start could not unjustly be branded, as its critics generally have branded it, as the ideology of middle-class interests, into the philosophy of a national community whose ideal was to protect and conserve the interests of all classes. The development was possible because the criticism, though not unjust, was never wholly true. The early liberals, though they were often provincial and doctrinaire, were also profoundly and sincerely public-spirited men who turned a defective social philosophy to purposes which in a large measure were socially beneficent and were never in intention merely exploitative. It was for this reason that liberalism could transform itself into an intellectual bridge between the individualism of its earlier period, which was its heritage from the philosophy of the Revolutionary Era, and a recognition of the reality and the value of social and communal interests, which tended in general to put themselves forward in anti-liberal forms. Thus the purpose of later liberalism could become at once the conservation of the political and civil liberties which individualism embodied and the adaptation of them to the progressive changes of industrialism and nationalism that bred philosophies which threatened to nullify them. Acknowledging political freedom as an addition of permanent value to modern culture, liberalism could still accept the task of making it a good more accessible to a larger number of persons and hence a genuine social good. The division of liberalism into two periods is, therefore, somewhat more than an expository convenience. It is intended to suggest a change of great importance coupled with a continuity of equal importance. The dividing line can best be drawn, perhaps, at John Stuart Mill because his philosophy stood curiously on both sides of the line. Accordingly this chapter will deal with the classical version of liberalism, that of the Philosophical Radicals, the next with the revision and modernization of liberalism.

THE GREATEST HAPPINESS PRINCIPLE

The social philosophy of the Philosophical Radicals was in essence a program of legal, economic, and political reforms connected as they supposed by the fact that they are all derivative from the principle of the greatest happiness of the greatest number. This principle they held to be the only rational guide both to private morals and to public policy, and the more theoretical part of their philosophy was designed to make this principle more accurately applicable to practical problems. In point of fact no member of the group, including Bentham himself, was in any way remarkable for philosophical originality or even for a very firm grasp of philosophical principles. The formal and deductive manner of presentation which they affected gave an appearance of system to their thought that turns out upon analysis to be deceptive. The order in which the several parts of the system appeared is significant of the fact that their relationship was practical rather than logical. Originally and indeed until he was nearly sixty years old Bentham was interested wholly in legal reforms, and he expected that these would be accomplished sooner by enlightened despotism than by political liberalism. Accordingly, after the publication of the *Principles of Morals and Legislation* in 1789, he preferred to address himself to a Continental public by publishing his later works on jurisprudence in French. It was not until the 1820's that his ideas came home to England by the translation of his French works or by the publication of new works such as the *Rationale of Judicial Evidence,* which John Stuart Mill edited from his manuscripts and published in 1827. In the meantime, about 1808, James Mill convinced Bentham that legal reform in England depended on the liberalizing of representation in Parliament, and it was only then that he abandoned the Tory politics in which he had been reared. The change was in no sense due to the logical dependence of liberalism upon the greatest happiness principle but solely to the hope that it might prove a more practicable agency of legal reform than aristocracy or enlightened despotism.

In a somewhat similar manner the economic theory of the Philosophical Radicals, which was mainly the work of Ricardo and was developed without any close relation to the legal reforms that interested Bentham, was directed from the start toward the practical purpose of freeing commerce from the restrictions imposed on it by a protective tariff on foodstuffs and by the navigation laws. These reforms also, like legal reform, could be achieved only by breaking down the political monopoly enjoyed by the English landowning class. It was not until practical purposes such as these were by way of being realized that James Mill undertook a theoretical examination of the psychological and philosophical principles upon which the group had always professed to rely. His *Analysis of the Phenomena of the Human Mind* was published in 1829, when he was already fifty-six years old. This book, which logically should have been the cornerstone of the system, was in truth little more than a systematization, in a deductive and highly dogmatic manner, of the associational psychology developed eighty years before by David Hartley, by the English moralists of the eighteenth century, and by French thinkers like Condillac and Helvetius. To this psychology Mill contributed little that was original and nothing that tended to bring it into line with a realistic study of human behavior based upon observation. The alleged empiricism of the Utilitarians was in fact filled with unexamined presumptions. The greatest happiness principle in ethics might have been adopted, as it often had been in the past, without the hedonistic psychology which was supposed to support it, and the reforms advocated in the name of the greatest happiness were implied only if the principle was supplemented by a large number of premises unrelated to the system.

The general outline of utilitarian thinking, apart from economics, was announced in Bentham's earliest work, the *Fragment on Government,* which he published in 1776. This was a criticism of Blackstone's *Commentaries* and through him an attack upon the whole legal profession and upon the Whig conception of English government. Bentham thus announced his major interest, the cause of legal reform, and presented in outline the point of view which he was later to develop in a long series of books on jurisprudence. Blackstone's account of English law, he said, is at best merely expository — it describes the law as it is — or at worst it is an apology for the *status quo* disguised as an exposition. The true function of jurisprudence is "censorial," the criticism of the legal system with a view to its improvement. For such criticism a standard of value is required, and that can be supplied only by the principle of utility. "It is the greatest happiness of the greatest number that is the measure of right and wrong." This insight Bentham attributed to Hume; when he had first read Hume's ethical works, he said, he felt as if the scales had fallen from his eyes. Hume's criticism demolished the whole apparatus of indefeasible rights and contractual limitations on the power of government by showing them to be either meaningless or else confused references to the clear principle of utility. The basis of government is not contract but human need, and the satisfaction of human needs is its sole justification. In consequence, Bentham concluded, relying perhaps as much on Hobbes as on Hume, Blackstone's glorification of the British Constitution and its supposed division of powers moves in the realm of myth. Legal power by its very nature cannot be legally limited, and somewhere in every political society authority must head up in some person or persons whom others are accustomed to obey. This holds true, Bentham argued, of free as well as of despotic governments. The two are indeed different in respect to the responsibility of rulers for their acts, the liberty of subjects to criticize and to combine for political purposes, and in the freedom of the press, but not in respect to the power they exercise. The *Fragment on Government* thus laid down the chief ideas that actuated the Philosophical Radicals: the greatest happiness principle as a measure of value, legal sovereignty as an assumption necessary for reform by legislative process, and a jurisprudence devoted to the analysis and "censure" of the law in the light of its contribution to the general happiness.

The *Fragment on Government* was in the main critical but Bentham proceeded at once to construction. The *Introduction to the Principles of Morals and Legislation*, privately printed in 1780 and published in 1789, united psychology, ethics, and jurisprudence upon the lines already suggested by Helvetius. Pleasure and pain, Bentham argued, provide not only the standard of value needed for a "censorial" jurisprudence but also the causes of human behavior by which the skillful legislator can control and direct it.

> Nature has placed mankind under the governance of two sovereign masters, *pain* and *pleasure*. It is for them alone to point out what we ought to do, as well as to determine what we shall do. On the one hand the standard of right and wrong, on the other the chain of causes and effects, are fastened to their throne.[4]

[4] Ch. 1, Sect. 1.

Accordingly Bentham now included in his theory a somewhat lengthy and highly schematic account of pleasure and pain as motivating forces, designed to show how a calculation of their amount and influence is possible. He assumed, as had commonly been done by the hedonist moralists, that pleasure and pain are commensurable, a given amount of the one offsetting a like amount of the other, and also that they can be added, so that a sum of pleasures may be calculated, which will define the greatest happiness both of an individual and a group of individuals. In this calculation four "dimensions" or phases of a pleasure or pain must be considered: its intensity, its duration, the certainty with which it will follow a given kind of action, and the remoteness of the time at which it will occur. Since one pleasure or pain is likely to induce another, this tendency also must be taken into account, and in any social calculation the number of persons affected must be considered. Usually Bentham spoke as if he believed that human beings really do act in accordance with some such mental parallelogram of forces as this, though occasionally he acknowledged that the notion of adding pleasures, and especially the pleasures of different persons, is fictitious. What is certainly true was that he considered the fiction to be "a postulatum without the allowance of which all political reasoning is at a stand." He had in fact no skill in psychological observation and no interest in it for its own sake. But he aspired to be the "Newton of the moral sciences" and he considered his psychological fictions to be no more violent than some that had proved serviceable in the science of mechanics.

The theory of pleasure and pain, and also the sensationalist psychology associated with it, had for Bentham another value besides that of enabling him to calculate the effects of legislation. He believed that by using this psychology he could track down and neutralize the "fictions" which he saw everywhere in social studies and in political reasoning. Bentham's theory of knowledge was rigidly nominalist, a quality which it probably owed to Hobbes more than to Hume. Now a name is the name of something, and that something must in the end be a concrete bit of sensuous experience. The meaning of a name is determined by the experience to which it points, its "referent," as it would now be called. Consequently, in so far as names refer to real entities, they are, so to speak, "masses of proper nouns"; as general terms they run the risk at least of becoming fictitious if this fact is overlooked. Fictitious entities are indeed necessary for "convenience of discourse" ("relation," for example, instead of "objects related"), but clarity requires that the factual reference should be precisely known. "Lamentable have been the confusion and the darkness produced by taking the names of fictious for the names of real entities."[5] It must always be possible to put one's finger on the tangible experience referred to. As William James said many years later, for an empiricist every difference must make a difference. For Bentham, the utility of this theory of fictions lay chiefly in the spheres of politics and legislation. Both are filled with fictions, and legal fiction, he was convinced, "has never been employed to any purpose but the affording a justification for something which otherwise would be unjustifiable." Terms like rights, property, the crown, the general welfare, are all liable to fictional use, and usually for defending vested interests. From Bentham's point of view any corporate body, such as society or the state, is evidently fictitious. Whatever is done in its name is done by someone, and its good, as Bentham said, is "the sum of the interests of the several members who compose it." The utility of the greatest happiness principle, therefore, consists in the fact that it is the great solvent of fictions, for it means that the real significance of a law or an institution must be judged in terms of what it does, and so far as possible by what it does to specific individuals. It is of course not possible, as Bentham knew, to trace out in all cases just where the effects fall, but anything short of this is a makeshift. Since value is identical with pleasure, and pleasure can occur only in the experience of some individual human being, the worth of law and government must lie in their effects upon the lives and fortunes of actual men and women. Some such principle is a postulate of any liberal philosophy, but it does not, of course, imply accepting the crudities of Bentham's psychology.

[5] See *Bentham's Theory of Fictions,* edited by C. K. Ogden (1932), with Ogden's Introduction.

BENTHAM'S THEORY OF LAW

The greatest happiness principle, as Bentham believed, placed in the hands of the skillful legislator a practically universal instrument. With it he can "rear the fabric of felicity by the hands of reason and law." For it provides a theory of basic human nature, both its valuations and its motivations, which Bentham supposed to be applicable at all times and all places. The legislator needs to know only the special circumstances of time and place that have produced peculiar customs and habits and he can then control behavior by allocating pains and penalties to produce the most desirable results. The only limitations upon the method which Bentham recognized were psychological and ethical, fixing on the one hand what the law can do and on the other what it can wisely try to do. In the nature of the case, he believed, there can be no legal limitations upon it. Even the massive limitations imposed by long established custom or long accepted institutions were construed by Bentham as psychological, since he regarded custom and institutions as merely habits. Like all habits they contain many threats to an intelligent adjustment of means to ends; they are the source of the technicalities and fictions which the greatest happiness principle was designed to obviate. This distrust of custom and its complete subordination to legislation were among the principal characteristics of Bentham's jurisprudence. With them was connected an indifference to, or rather a contempt for, history as a factor in social studies. From Bentham's point of view history was for the most part a compendium of the crimes and follies of mankind. This temper of mind was perhaps the principal reason why his social philosophy seemed antiquated in the second half of the nineteenth century. Even his own disciple, John Stuart Mill, came to regard it as a weakness, and certainly it was often responsible for a superficial understanding of the profound differences between men reared in different cultural heritages.

Bentham's jurisprudence, which was not only the greatest of his works but one of the most remarkable intellectual achievements of the nineteenth century, consisted in the systematic application of the point of view just sketched to all branches of the law, civil and criminal, and to the procedural law and the organization of the judicial system.[6] In all cases its purpose was critical rather than descriptive, "censorial" rather than expository, as he had urged at the start against Blackstone. In all branches of jurisprudence, therefore, he distinguished what he called a natural method from a technical method. The latter consists in taking at their face value the classifications and technical procedures accepted by the law and embodied in its customary terminology, its writs, and processes. The effect of such a jurisprudence is at most to reduce legal concepts to some sort of formal order. A natural method, on the contrary, conceives of all legal prohibitions and all procedures for giving them effect in terms of their utility, as means to the greatest happiness of the greatest number. A juristic problem is essentially the correct allocation of penalties to produce desirable results.

In the field of the civil law this method required an analysis of legal rights and obligations in terms of the help or hindrance that their enforcement causes in the exchange of goods and services upon which utility depends. In the nature of the case every legal obligation must impose a limitation upon the freedom of such exchanges. A right in one person implies that his freedom of action is guaranteed by a penalty which prevents another person from invading it, and this can be justified only by the relative utility of such a limitation in comparison with what would happen if the acts of both persons were left to voluntary choice. In all cases the utility of legislation is to be measured in terms of its effectiveness, the costliness of its enforcement, and in general by its consequences in producing a system of exchanges which on the whole is advantageous to most members of the community. Utility is the only reasonable ground for making action obligatory. Property rights are justified in general by the need for security, for making the consequences of action calculable, and for avoiding the frustrations that follow uncertainty and disappointment, certainly a limited conception of social security. In Bentham's judgment security of property is a major condition of achieving the greatest happiness, but it is, as he perceived, a highly conservative principle. It implies the legal protection of the distribution of property which at any given time exists.

[6] See Elie Halévy, *The Growth of Philosophic Radicalism*. Eng. trans. by Mary Morris (1928), especially Part I, ch. 2, and Part III, ch. 2.

As a matter of policy he was convinced that the law should aim at a comparatively equal distribution of property, or at least not at the creation of arbitrary inequalities. In practice it must strike some kind of workable balance between security and equality. Similarly the sanctity of contract, which Bentham believed had been treated by jurisprudence as a kind of incantation, like transubstantiation in theology, is really justified only because it contributes to the maintenance and reliability of commercial transactions.

In the field of the criminal law the principle of utility provided, as Bentham believed, a natural method for arriving at a rational theory of penalties. The technical method starts from the assumption that crime "deserves" punishment, but the concept of desert is essentially indefinable except in terms of existing practices and ideas. The natural method, on the contrary, starts from the principle that punishment is always an evil, since it causes pain, and is justified only in so far as it either prevents a greater future evil or repairs an evil already done. Criminal jurisprudence must provide a realistic classification of crimes, not in terms of the customary categories of the law, which Bentham justifiably regarded as contradictory and largely unintelligible, but in terms of the injury that certain modes of action inflict and the incidence of these injuries on assignable individuals or on classes and on the general public. It must provide also an analogous classification of punishments in order to apportion the penalty to the crime and prevent or redress the injury as effectively as possible. In general the rule is that the pain occasioned by a punishment must exceed the profit gained by committing the offense but must exceed as little as possible the evil caused by the offense. This part of Bentham's work was much like the conclusions already reached by Beccaria, another follower of Helvetius, though it was more systematic and rather curiously did not repeat Beccaria's sound conclusion that certainty of punishment is a more effective deterrent than severity. It is true, however, that in practice Bentham was favorable to proposals, like those of Sir Samuel Romilly, for eliminating the savage and quite ineffective penalties that disfigured English criminal law at the beginning of the nineteenth century. In his criminal jurisprudence, as in most of Bentham's reformatory projects, it appears that he was more moved by a love of order and efficiency than by humanitarian motives, though it is only fair to say that he expended large amounts both of his time and his private fortune to bring about the improvement of prisons. The driving force of his personality was enlightenment, and he was more concerned about the interests of the general public than about the interests of the unfortunate or the reformation of delinquents.

It was in his theory of legal procedure and judicial organization, perhaps, that Bentham developed his most characteristic ideas, and it was certainly here that he departed farthest from the liberal tradition as it had been before him. In his desire to simplify procedure and improve the efficiency of the courts he proposed to abandon almost entirely the checks and safeguards which had been deemed necessary to protect the subjects' rights. Bentham here extended to procedural law the principles which he had already adopted relative to constitutional law in the *Fragment on Government*. He pointed out correctly that legal formalism and artificial rules about the admissibility of evidence were largely predicated upon a belief that the substantive law is bad and that government is dangerous, and he argued that, if this belief is indeed true, the reasonable remedy is to improve the law, not to weaken the courts. Formality, obscurity, and technicality in the law, he urged, result in a maximum of expense, delay, and vexation to litigants, in withholding justice from great numbers of persons, and in rendering the outcome of legal processes capricious and uncertain. This technical system, as Bentham called it, he regarded as nothing short of a conspiracy on the part of the legal profession to mulct the public. Even in the *Fragment on Government* he had paid his respects to lawyers and he pursued them throughout a long life with a reformer's rancor.

> A passive and enervate race, ready to swallow anything, and to acquiesce in anything; with intellects incapable of distinguishing right from wrong, and with affections alike indifferent to either; insensible, short-sighted, obstinate; lethargic, yet liable to be driven into convulsions by false terrors; deaf to the voice of reason and public utility; obsequious only to the whisper of interest, and to the beck of power.[7]

[7] Preface; ed. by F. C. Montague (1891), p. 104.

Bentham's ideal was "Every man his own lawyer." To this end he urged the substitution for formal pleading of informal proceedings before an arbiter who would aim at conciliation, the universal admissibility of any kind of relevant evidence, and a large measure of judicial discretion, rather than rigid rules, to exclude irrelevance. In respect to the organization of the courts Bentham attacked especially the practice of paying judges and other officers of the courts by fees rather than salaries; the divided, overlapping, and contradictory jurisdictions of the existing English courts; and the jury system, which he thought enjoyed a quite unmerited popularity.

Bentham's theory of law established the point of view of analytic jurisprudence, which was almost the only system of the subject generally known to English and American lawyers throughout the nineteenth century. This School is usually associated with the name of John Austin, but in fact Austin did little more than bring together systematically ideas that were scattered through Bentham's voluminous and not always very readable works.[8] In political theory the chief effect of Austin's work was to attach an exaggerated importance to the theory of sovereignty, which was in fact incidental to Bentham's plan for reforming the courts by Parliamentary control. Clarity of organization does indeed imply that responsibility should be definitely located somewhere, but Bentham's idea that a government is merely certain determinate persons set apart to rule, and toward whom subjects have merely a habit of obedience, is grossly inadequate to explain the part that institutions play in politics. Of vastly more historical importance than the theory of sovereignty was the fact that Bentham's work on jurisprudence provided the plan according to which the administration of justice in England was completely revised and modernized in the course of the nineteenth century. It is true that Bentham's ideas were never systematically adopted and put into effect at a single time and also that some of his ideas, notably a general codification of English law, were

[8] His lectures on jurisprudence were delivered between 1828 and 1832 at University College, London, then newly founded under Benthamite auspices. They were published in the *Province of Jurisprudence Determined,* 1832, which was later incorporated in the more extended *Lectures on Jurisprudence,* 1861–63. Selections edited with notes by W. Jethro Brown under the title, *The Austinian Theory of Law,* London, 1906.

never adopted. But in a long succession of acts a thoroughgoing reform of the law and the courts was brought about, and in an astonishing number of cases the reforms followed the direction that Bentham's criticisms had indicated.[9] Sir Frederick Pollock has said rightly that every important reform of English law during the nineteenth century can be traced to the influence of Bentham's ideas.

It is certainly true, however, that Bentham's jurisprudence was not so completely determined by the principle of utility as he supposed. In fact utility is an utterly indefinite word until one specifies utility for what and for whom. The liberal elements in Bentham's philosophy resided largely in its tacit premises. When he said that "One man is worth just the same as another man," or that in calculating the greatest happiness each person is "to count for one and no one for more than one," he was obviously borrowing the principle of equality from natural law. He did not in fact rely merely on the unprovable assumption that one man's pleasure is like another man's. Behind his love for order and efficiency there were genuinely liberal postulates, particularly the value of a humane form of living for all persons, that efficiency or the greatest happiness principle did not cover. It is also true that his jurisprudence, by reason of its individualism, had an unintended bias. The rule that a law must be judged by the incidence of its effects on human beings, and so far as possible on assignable individuals, was a sound liberal principle, but it was vastly easier to apply in some types of law than in others. The restriction of a property right is apparent, but the precise consequences of a law to protect public health cannot easily be shown in the better health of any single person. As was to become apparent, the extension of freedom of contract to as many private relations as possible resulted in quite specious senses of freedom. The connotations of Bentham's jurisprudence

[9] See the essay of Sir Charles Synge Christopher Bowen on "The Administration of the Law, 1837–1887" in *The Reign of Queen Victoria* (1887), ed. by T. H. Ward, Vol. I, p. 281; reprinted in *Select Essays in Anglo-American Legal History,* edited by a Committee of the Association of American Law Schools, Vol. I (1907), p. 516. For a contemporary appreciation of Bentham as a legal reformer see Lord Brougham's speech "On the Present State of the Law," February 7, 1828, and the Introduction, in *Speeches* (1838), Vol. II, p. 287.

no doubt made social legislation more difficult. Far more than he realized his thought was influenced by *ad hoc* considerations, especially by the fact that legal reform in his day was so largely a matter of getting rid of obsolete practices. Nevertheless, despite obvious inadequacies in his thought, there are few thinkers in the history of social philosophy that have exercised so wide and so beneficent an influence as Bentham.

THE ECONOMIC THEORY OF EARLY LIBERALISM

The liberal philosophy of law was almost wholly inspired by Bentham. Its economic theory — the so-called classical economics or the theory of *laissez faire* — formed another strand of liberal thought which owed little to Bentham but was similar in purpose and point of view. Like Bentham's own views on economic subjects it was derived from Adam Smith's *Wealth of Nations.* To this had been added the work of a generation of English writers, as well as that of the French successors to Quesnay and the Physiocrats. The classical economics received its most important statement in David Ricardo's *Principles of Political Economy* (1817), which incorporated the theory of population associated with the name of T. R. Malthus and also the theory of economic rent which Malthus had stated and to which Ricardo's own name has been attached. Thus economics emerged as an independent social study beside Bentham's jurisprudence and beside the study of politics. Like these it was conceived to depend upon the general laws of human nature stated by the associational and hedonistic psychology that Bentham had used. Hence it purported to state the laws of any economic society irrespective of time and place and without reference to prescriptions set up by systems of law or government. In its intellectual temper and point of view, therefore, the classical economics was quite in accord with the philosophy of Bentham. It was a kind of social Newtonianism which regarded institutions and their history as scientifically irrelevant, because they are reducible to habits of thought and action which can be fully explained by rather simple laws of individual behavior. This assumption that economics and government are mutually independent, or are only indirectly related through individual psychology, was one of the most characteristic elements in the point of view of early liberalism. It is also the characteristic which now makes the classical economics appear most seriously antiquated. This is due not only to the fact that the associational psychology itself was thoroughly inadequate, or to the fact that the policy of *laissez faire* espoused by liberal economists became progressively impossible in the latter part of the nineteenth century, though both these statements are true. The fundamental fact, made progressively clearer by social psychology and anthropology, is that both political and economic institutions are always related factors in a culture, and that the institutions of a culture shape from birth the innate characteristics of the individuals who compose it. Whatever the laws of human behavior turn out to be, they will certainly be far too general to correlate with the practices of any given time or place.

Though the classical economics aspired to be a science and therefore to be independent of the particular social and political circumstances in which it originated, it was marked, like Bentham's jurisprudence, by the practical reformatory purposes of its creators. The peace of 1815 produced a serious depression in the market for English manufactured goods both at home and abroad. It accordingly brought to the surface the radical disparity of interests between English landowners and English manufacturers which had been kept under cover by the crisis of the Napoleonic Wars. English agriculture had long enjoyed a market protected by the tariff on grain, while the interests of English merchants and manufacturers were all on the side of cheap food. The manufacturers themselves, having a technology superior to that of any other country, were for the time being without any need of governmental support. Under the circumstances a policy of free trade was clearly in their interest, and the stringency that followed the close of the War touched off a controversy that brought about the reform of Parliament in 1832 and culminated in the repeal of the Corn Laws in 1846. The outcome was the emergence of England as the first of the modern industrial nations, committed to the typical liberal policies of unrestricted trade, the extension of representative government at home, and the ideal of an international concert of nations all alike liberal in politics and all following their national self-interest in an international division of labor. Ricardo's economics was characteristic of the years of controversy in which his theories were formulated.

Though the classical economics purported to be a rigidly logical system, it in fact embraced two points of view that were diverse and that issued in very different ideas of economic society.[10] This diversity reflected two conceptions of nature that had been implicit in modern philosophy from the start. On the one hand was a belief that the natural order is inherently simple, harmonious, and beneficent, on the other the belief that it is devoid of ethical attributes and that its laws have no relation to justice, reason, or human welfare. Even in Bentham's jurisprudence, as has already been said, there were rudiments of natural right which contrasted with the pure naturalism or utilitarianism that he derived from Hume and professed to follow. In the case of Ricardo's economics the contrast was between what he called the static theory and the dynamic. From the point of view of social statics economic science is the theory of the exchange of goods in a freely competitive market in which prices are fixed by the condition of the market itself, unobstructed by any forces other than the choices of the individuals involved. An economic society is conceived to be composed of individual producers each bringing his products and exchanging them with other producers, each buying as cheaply as possible and selling for the best price he can get. From the point of view of social dynamics, however, economics is a theory of the distribution of total product among the producers — as Ricardo puts it, "an enquiry into the laws which determine the division of the produce of industry amongst the classes who concur in its formation." The chief components of this part of the science are the theories of rent, profits, and wages, these being the principal kinds of income into which the product of industry must be divided. From this point of view an economic society consists of classes rather than of individuals.

The difference between these two points of view is in fact very considerable. For a free market, relieved of all factors of monopolistic restraint, was conceived, in the long run at least, to serve the interests of all alike and therefore the greatest good of the greatest number. By what Adam Smith had called "the

10 This disparity is developed by Halévy, *The Growth of Philosophic Radicalism,* especially Part III, ch. 1.

simple principle of natural liberty," the operations of the market continually tend to produce prices as low as is consistent with maintaining the service and yet yielding a fair return for the effort expended. In short, complete freedom of exchange produces automatically a natural harmony of interests, which only needs to be let alone in order to produce as much economic advantage to everyone as the circumstances permit. The picture is, however, extremely different when one considers the laws of distribution. Not only do these laws run in terms of a system of economic classes in which the fate of any individual is largely determined by the portions of wealth which economic forces allot to his class, but they also make it logically inevitable, as Ricardo believed, that the interests of each class must in general always be adverse to the interests of the other classes. From this point of view the state of an economic society is typically one of class conflict. Moreover, the direction in which Ricardo expected the dynamic laws to carry a developing economy was by no means toward a natural harmony of interests.

The first of these two contrasting points of view depended upon the labor theory of value, the supposition that in a free market the value of a commodity is fixed by the amount of labor necessary to produce it. By Ricardo this theory was probably intended to provide an absolute economic standard behind the confusing array of prices that occur in an actual market. In general, as he supposed, prices would fluctuate around value according to temporary conditions of supply and demand. This purpose was not achieved, as Ricardo regretfully admitted, because the argument was in effect circular: prices are themselves the only thing that gives a definite measure of the amount of labor in a commodity. But a strictly naturalistic meaning of this sort was far from the connotations that had usually been attached to the labor theory of value. Locke had used it in an ethical sense to justify the right of property which a man acquires when he "mixes" his labor with the goods he produces, and Adam Smith had used the theory to develop the concept of a "natural" price, which in general he regarded as a just price. For if goods are exchanged according to the amount of labor that produces them, it seems to follow that in general (temporary aberrations being neglected) buyers and sellers must put in and take out equivalent amounts of value. On the whole everyone would keep a value equivalent to the amount of labor he had expended, and in effect he would retain the whole value that he had produced. Perfectly free exchange would therefore produce a system of "natural" justice. There is no doubt that the labor theory of value commended itself to Ricardo's disciples, J. R. MacCulloch, for example, less because of its use in economics than because it provided an ethical justification for free trade and an argument against "artificial" obstructions to it by legislation. The free play of human motives, all in themselves egoistic, works out to the greatest good of the community and the nearest practicable approach to justice for all its members. As Ricardo himself said, paraphrasing Adam Smith's famous expression about the "unseen hand," "The pursuit of individual advantage is admirably connected with the universal good of the whole."

This argument was not, however, utilitarian and it was glaringly at odds with Bentham's use of pleasure and pain in his jurisprudence. Utility, according to Bentham, does indeed require a harmony of interests and the greatest happiness of all, but such a condition is not natural. It can be produced only by legislation, and the significance of pleasure for a jurist is that, in addition to providing a standard of value, it makes possible the control of human behavior. Moreover, Bentham had consistently refused to name liberty as the object of law, because law exists solely to force men to do what they would not do voluntarily. From Bentham's point of view social harmony is produced by legislative coercion; from the economists' point of view the harmony of economic interests is produced by the absence of legislation. There can be no doubt that, for a utilitarian, Bentham's position was the more consistent, though possibly, in an effort to secure the repeal of a tariff, the economists' argument was the more persuasive. For even though coercion is always an evil, as Bentham believed, it is a necessary evil, and the limits of its use are set only by its power to prevent a greater evil. It is of course possible to argue on utilitarian grounds against particular restraints of trade, but some legal regulation of it is inevitable, and the principle of utility can justify any amount of "interference" with trade, provided only it does less harm than good.

Laissez faire, however, was often defended on the ground that any legal control is intrinsically productive of inequalities of exchange, and this argument apparently assumes that the condition which prevails in the absence of regulation is one of natural liberty and natural equality.

The dynamic laws which govern the distribution of the social product presented a picture very different from the harmony and justice implied by the system of natural liberty. The distribution is between social classes, and the interests of the classes are in general antagonistic. The dynamic laws, moreover, are laws of social evolution, and the normal expectation which they establish for an expanding economy is, as Ricardo described it, very far from optimistic. The crucial factor among the dynamic forces is the property which Malthus had attributed to population in his *Essay,* first published in 1798.[11] Malthus's point was that human fecundity, if uncontrolled, sets an inevitable limit to the possibility of social progress anticipated by Condorcet and in England by William Godwin. Any improvement in the standard of living results in an increase of population which nullifies the improvement, and since in general population increases faster than the production of food, population tends always to press hard upon the means of livelihood. Apart from temporary fluctuations, therefore, the standard of living for the mass of mankind will stand at about the level of subsistence. It cannot, of course, permanently fall below this minimum, but neither can it permanently rise higher, for a further increase of population will always overtake any increase in the supply of food. The economic consequences of this sociological law were formulated in the second dynamic law, the law of rent, which Malthus had stated and which Ricardo elaborated. Food is the product of land, and land is peculiar in that it is limited in amount and differs in its productivity. Clearly a cultivator can afford to pay a higher rent for fertile than for infertile land, since larger crops can be produced at equal cost. If land produced enough barely to pay the costs of production no rent could be paid for it; for more fertile land the rent which the owner can exact will

[11] In fact, so many earlier writers had approximated Malthus's conclusions that his originality consisted chiefly in his pseudo-mathematical statement of the principle. See Halévy, *op. cit.,* pp. 225 ff.

be greater as the productivity rises. Rent, therefore, is the differential between the productivity of any given piece of land and that of land which, at prevailing prices of food, would just fail to pay the cost of using it.

From these two laws of population and rent Ricardo deduced important consequences. It follows in the first place that the landlord is a monopolist, or indeed a kind of economic parasite, who can collect a tribute from all other economic classes, since rent contributes in no way to production. As Ricardo said, "The interest of the landlord is always opposed to the interest of every other class in the community." Moreover, any increase in the price of food, because it brings less fertile land under cultivation, will increase rents, and an increase of population will increase prices. In the second place, the laws of rent and population imply a law of wages, viz., that except temporarily wages cannot rise above or fall below the level of subsistence. As Ricardo said, the "natural price of labour is that price which is necessary to enable the labourers, one with another, to subsist and perpetuate their race, without either increase or diminution." Finally, since the total product of industry is in general distributed as rent, wages, or profits, it follows that any increase in the first two is subtracted from the portion that goes to the capitalist. The normal tendency of a progressive economy, therefore, in which production is rising, will be for landlords to receive a larger share, though they contribute nothing to progress, for capitalists to receive a smaller share, and for labor to receive as always only so much as will replace the labor force. Even the most determined optimist would hardly describe this as a system of natural justice. In Ricardo's dynamic laws nature figures merely as the brute instinct of procreation without regard for consequences.

What held together the idea of a naturally harmonious economic society and the idea of naturally conflicting classes was not logic but the fact that both appeared to converge on a policy of free trade and more specifically on the repeal of the tariff on grain. This conclusion would follow obviously from the theory that economic society is naturally self-regulating by competition. On the other hand, if rent is an unproductive drain on the economy, it would follow that rent ought not to be increased by legislation that artificially raises the price of food. This concentration on the immediately practical purpose of repealing a single kind of taxation had the effect of narrowing the interest of the classical economics in a manner that depended very little upon the logic of the system. Any taxation is bound to affect the economy in some way, and from a purely utilitarian point of view there is no reason why a legislator should not direct taxation to increasing the general welfare, provided only that his measures would work. James Mill, for example, admitted that it might be directed to increasing capital, though he believed the attempt would probably not succeed. Moreover, there are many forms of economic rent besides the rent of land, and even if the state were to confiscate them all, the legislation, according to the theory, would in no way hamper production. Henry George's *Progress and Poverty* (1879), which affected so powerfully the young Englishmen who were about to found the Fabian Society, reflected a change of interest more than a change of theory, namely, a desire to explore the possibilities, within existing economic theory, of using legislation to regulate the economy for the general good. The opposition of many of the classical economists to all forms of social legislation, possibly excepting the public support of education, reflected their concern with a single problem of the English economy and an unconscious bias in favor of the class they represented. The alleged impossibility of improving the lot of wage earners by legislation depended on Malthus's sociological law of population, which turned out to be the least reliable part of the system. The opposition to social legislation was never shared by humanitarian liberals. The English legislation of the 1820's began the removal of restraints on trade, but it included also the beginning of the factory acts and of the removal of limitations on the right of labor to organize. It is true, however, that the emphasis of liberal legislation, until after the middle of the century, was on the side of *laissez faire*.

The extent to which liberal economics was controlled by practical considerations rather than by logic is curiously illustrated by the ease with which Karl Marx turned its arguments to a quite different purpose. Ricardo had emphasized the antagonism of the landlord's interest to the interests of labor and capital, but it was equally easy to argue that the interests of the capitalist were similarly antagonistic to those of labor, since whatever share of the product went to profits was withdrawn from wages. And if the landlord could exact rent because he monopolized land, it could equally well be held that the capitalist in an industrialized economy monopolizes the means of production and that his profits are a kind of surplus value or, in essence, an economic rent, as the Fabians argued. Moreover, it is far from obvious that Ricardo's laws for a developing economy are the only ones or the correct ones. Ricardo might pessimistically expect that capitalists would be impoverished in the interest of landlords, but it was equally open to an optimist to hope that they might be expropriated in the interest of wage earners. The truth is that the classical economics provided Marx with a ready-made picture of the exploitation of labor. The economist, to be sure, imagined that he was describing a system that was rooted in the nature of things. But having the Hegelian dialectic in hand, Marx could readily think of it as rooted in history and ascribe the exploitation to the capitalist system.

THE POLITICAL THEORY OF EARLY LIBERALISM

The political theory of Benthamite radicalism was less significant than Bentham's jurisprudence or the classical economics. In part this was due to the fact that the dogma of a self-regulating economy left to government a rôle of very restricted importance. In part it was due to the fact that the direction which liberal political reforms must take in England had long been evident and that such reforms were long overdue. Quite evidently the political monopoly of the landed interests in Parliament must be broken, if either legal or economic reform was to be possible. James Mill, in an article contributed to the newly founded organ of the radicals, the *Westminster Review,*[12] estimated that effectively the House of Commons was chosen by some two hundred families, to which the clergy of the Established Church and the legal profession were substantially adjuncts. Between the two existing political parties there was, he said, practically no difference except that the one in opposition was bent on securing the patronage enjoyed by the one in power, without changing the monopoly by which both profited. English govern-

[12] Vol. I (1824), p. 206; on the *Edinburgh Review.*

ment, he charged, was absolutely an organ of class interests. Both parties represent a small ruling class, mostly landowners, with some small infiltration of influence by moneyed interests mostly through bribery. The remedy, as he naively supposed, consisted simply in extending representation to the whole community and especially to the industrial middle class. "In the grand discovery of modern times, the system of representation, the solution of all difficulties, both speculative and practical, will perhaps be found."[13]

The original parts of the early utilitarian political theory were all suggested by Bentham's jurisprudence and had indeed been outlined in the *Fragment on Government*. They consisted in an extension to constitutional law of the same ideas which he used in his plans for the reorganization of the judicial system.[14] The fundamental principle is that liberal government cannot be equated with weak government. Devices for legal limitations on sovereignty, such as bills of rights, the separation of powers, and checks and balances, Bentham regarded as confused in theory and self-defeating in practice, like the building up of formality and technicality in the law. Accordingly he accepted the complete legal sovereignty of Parliament and the need for relying upon an enlightened public opinion to insure responsibility. Ultimate political sovereignty, he believed, should inhere in the people, since only so can the interest of government be made to coincide with the general interest. To make the interest of the people effective he believed in universal suffrage, with only temporary disqualifications until education can produce an enlightened electorate. And to make Parliament responsive to the electorate he would have reduced its legal life to a year. The significance of these political ideas lies not so much in the fact that they were more radical than any scheme of reform that was practicable in Bentham's lifetime as in the fact that he jumped, so to speak, quite over the stage of liberal thought that regarded constitutional limitations as the chief guaranties of freedom. Conceptions of government which he had originally applied to enlight-

[13] The article on Government in the Supplement to the *Encyclopædia Britannica,* 1820; reprinted in *Essays on Government,* etc., 1825.

[14] The principal work is the *Constitutional Code* (1830), *Works* (ed. by Bowring), Vol. IX.

ened despotism he applied forthwith to liberalism. His belief in enlightenment was such that he had no misgivings about the possible tyranny of a majority. As John Stuart Mill later said, the early utilitarians were liberals not so much because they believed in liberty as because they believed in good government. Bentham was, no doubt, inclined to underestimate the importance of institutional safeguards for political and civil liberty, and this was of a piece with his deficient sense of the reality of institutions in culture. At the same time his position was sound in so far as it depended on the principle that liberal government need not be defended by accepting its inefficiency.

James Mill's ideas of government and reform differed in no important respect from those of Bentham, but his *Essay on Government* exposed somewhat more clearly the philosophical basis of those ideas. In particular it showed that the political thought of the Benthamite liberals depended more on Hobbes than on Hume. Like Hobbes, Mill believed that all men are driven by a restless desire for power which institutional limitations cannot check. Like Bentham he rejected, for liberal as well as for autocratic governments, any conception of the division or balancing of powers, though he asserted broadly that the only difficult questions in government have to do with restraining the power which rulers must have. The problem, as he supposed, could only be solved by securing a legislature whose interests are identical with those of the country, so that its members have no motive for using their power otherwise than in the general interest, and by giving the legislature control over the executive. As has been said, he imagined, rather fatuously, that such a result would automatically be brought about by a representative system with universal suffrage and short terms of office. In spite of his tendency to state every argument as if it embodied a universal and eternal principle, Mill's political thinking was in fact dominated by the immediate purpose which he considered important, namely, the enfranchisement of the industrial middle class. This class he described quite frankly as "the wisest part of the community," and he supposed that the "lower classes" would always be guided by it. He never contemplated the possibility that the middle class might itself use political power for its own advantage.

Like classical economics, Mill's political thought united in an uneasy combination an egoistic theory of individual motivation with a belief in the natural harmony of human interests. His argument for universal suffrage depended upon the premise that all human beings, at least with a moderate amount of education, can be brought to a clearsighted understanding of their interests and that, understanding their interests, they will infallibly act in accordance with them. It depended also on the tacit assumption that, if all men reasonably seek their individual interests, the greatest good of the greatest number will result. In short he succeeded, after some manner known only to a doctrinaire, in combining a rather pessimistic estimate of human nature with some remnant of that sublime faith in reason which had made revolutionary radicals like Condorcet and Godwin look forward to limitless human progress. John Stuart Mill described his father's point of view quite accurately as follows:

> So complete was my father's reliance on the influence of reason over the minds of mankind, whenever it is allowed to reach them, that he felt as if all would be gained if the whole population were taught to read, if all sorts of opinions were allowed to be addressed to them by word and in writing, and if by means of the suffrage they could nominate a legislature to give effect to the opinions they adopted. He thought that when the legislature no longer represented a class interest, it would aim at the general interest, honestly and with adequate wisdom.[15]

Manifestly a belief such as this could have been logically supported only upon the assumption that reasonable action issues naturally in social harmony and could never have been reached on empirical or utilitarian grounds.

The liberalism of the Philosophical Radicals was an intellectual force of enormous practical importance in nineteenth-century politics. Without themselves attaining the proportions of a political party, they disseminated ideas in the light of which a vast amount of antiquated political lumber was swept away, and legislation, administration, and judicial process were made both more efficient and more democratic. The reform of Parliament, the repeal of obsolete restrictions on trade and industry, and the reorganization of the judicial system were the most conspicuous examples of this process but they were not the only ones. The

[15] *Autobiography* (1873), p. 106.

reform of Parliament in 1832 amply justified Bentham's belief that liberal reform would not limit the power of government but would invigorate its action. Parliamentary reform initiated within a few years a long series of administrative reforms in which men trained in the ideas of Bentham played an important though not always a conspicuous part. Almost at once a centralized administration for the Poor Law was begun, and the moving spirits were Edwin Chadwick and George Grote. The organization of services for protecting public health and of centralized administration for the county police and the inspection of factories followed soon, and again Chadwick played a leading part. In 1840 J. A. Roebuck and other Benthamites secured the passage of an inadequate but still substantial bill looking to a universal system of primary education. Lord Durham's Report in 1839, prepared in part by Charles Buller and Edward Gibbon Wakefield, began a revision of colonial policy and introduced in Canada a liberal constitution which was the first constitution granted to a colony. This, with Wakefield's plan for the colonization of Australia, was in effect the inception of the British Commonwealth of Nations.[16] In the patient drudgery of these utilitarians the faith in reason which they inherited from the Enlightenment was combined with an ideal of professional competence which they learned from Bentham, and the two together issued in reforms that made government both more liberal and more efficient.

The criticisms commonly passed upon Philosophical Radicalism and given currency even by liberal successors like John Stuart Mill were that it neglected institutions and their historical growth and that it worked with a falsely schematic conception of human nature and motives. Both criticisms were true. Often however they were taken to imply that it was clear, rigidly logical and systematic, and merely based on premises too narrowly limited. This was not true. Its fundamental weakness was rather that as a philosophy it was never clear and never critical of its assumptions or its deductions. In certain respects it was a system of " nature " like the rationalist philosophies of the seventeenth

[16] See B. W. Richardson, *The Health of Nations, a Review of the Works of Edwin Chadwick* (1887), especially the Biographical Dissertation and Vol. II, Parts I and II. J. A. Williamson, *Short History of British Expansion* (2nd ed., 1930), Part V, chs. 3 and 4.

century, but it had no theory of knowledge that made an appeal to nature intelligible. It claimed to be empirical but it made little effort to check its premises by observation, and in effect its empiricism stopped with a crude form of sensationalism that had been derived from Locke two generations before. Hence it easily fell a victim to criticism as soon as it faced thinkers less impressed than Mill with its characteristic dogmas. Philosophical Radicalism was in truth largely an *ad hoc* philosophy, and it was also largely the spokesman for a single social interest which it identified, hastily though not hypocritically, with the well-being of the whole community. The consciousness of this fact, together with a perception of the intolerable consequences of its social policy, tended to discredit it as a social philosophy, even before the legal reforms for which it stood were accomplished. Its weakness as a social philosophy can be summed up by saying that it had no positive conception of a social good, and that its egoistic individualism made it look with suspicion on the validity of any such conception, at a time when the total welfare of the community was becoming a principal object of concern. Its weakness as a political philosophy was that its theory of government was almost wholly negative, at a time when it was becoming inevitable that government should assume a larger responsibility for the general welfare. In a long view of political evolution, therefore, Philosophical Radicalism tended to be carried by inertia instead of projecting itself upon the growing lines of development. Its importance as an agent of political obsolescence was inestimable but by limiting itself to that function it dated itself as the organ of a period.

SELECTED BIBLIOGRAPHY

The Austinian Theory of Law. By W. J. Brown. London, 1906.

Political Thought in England from Bentham to J. S. Mill. By William Davidson. New York, 1916.

The Growth of Philosophic Radicalism. By Elie Halévy. Eng. trans. by Mary Morris. New York, 1928.

The Social and Political Ideas of some Representative Thinkers of the Revolutionary Era. Ed. by F. J. C. Hearnshaw. London, 1931. Ch. 7.

The Social Problems of an Industrial Civilization. By Elton Mayo. Boston, 1945. Ch. 2.

Bentham's Theory of Fictions. By C. K. Ogden. London, 1932. Introduction.

"Benthamism in England and America." By P. A. Palmer. *Am. Pol. Sci. Rev.*, Vol. XXXV (1941), p. 855.

Three Criminal Law Reformers: Beccaria, Bentham, Romilly. By Coleman Phillipson. London, 1923. Part II.

A History of European Liberalism. By Guido de Ruggiero. Eng. trans. by R. G. Collingwood. Oxford, 1927.

French Political Thought in the Nineteenth Century. By Roger Soltau. New Haven, 1931.

The English Utilitarians. By Leslie Stephen. 3 vols. London, 1900.

The Life of Francis Place, 1771–1854. By Graham Wallas. London, 1898.

Select Essays in Anglo-American Legal History. Compiled and edited by a Committee of the Association of American Law Schools. 3 vols. Boston, 1907–09. Vol. I, Part IV.

CHAPTER XXXII

LIBERALISM MODERNIZED

The greatest legislative success of Philosophical Radicalism was coeval with the beginning of its recession. The high water mark of its influence was reached in 1846 with the repeal of the Corn Laws and the establishment of free trade as British national policy. But even before that date the social effects of unregulated industrialism began to excite grave misgivings in the minds even of liberals, and they produced a reaction in classes whose vested interests or traditional ways of living were threatened. In 1841 the report of a Royal Commission, appointed to investigate the coal-mining industry, shocked all England with its revelation of the brutality that existed in the mines: the employment of women and children, barbarously long hours of work, the absence of safety devices, and the prevalence of revolting conditions both sanitary and moral. The discussion of this report and of similar revelations in other industries was reflected almost at once in English literature, in novels of industrialism such as Mrs. Gaskell's *Mary Barton,* Disraeli's *Sybil,* and Kingsley's *Alton Locke,* all published in the 1840's. Throughout the remainder of the century a steady stream of criticism, partly on moral and partly on esthetic grounds, continued to be leveled at industrialism by Carlyle, Ruskin, and William Morris. Even as early as the 1830's Parliament had begun hesitatingly to pass factory acts regulating hours and conditions of work, though all such legislation limited freedom of contract and was therefore contrary not only to the trend of earlier liberal legislation but also to the commonly held theory of what liberal policy should be. As the nineteenth century advanced the volume of social legislation steadily increased until, in the opinion of competent observers, by the end of the third quarter of the century Parliament had in effect discarded individualism as its guiding principle and had accepted "collectivism."[1] Liberalism as it had been understood was on the defensive, and by a curious anomaly legislation passed in the interest of social welfare, and therefore of the greatest happiness, ran counter to accepted liberal ideas.

This reaction against economic liberalism did not proceed from any antithetical social philosophy nor did it imply any philosophical agreement among those affected by it. What Dicey called "collectivism" was certainly not a philosophy. It might be more accurately described as a spontaneous defense against the social destructiveness of the industrial revolution and the recklessness of a policy that encouraged industrialization without safeguards against the wreckage that it entailed. The controlling motive was a sense, not very clearly formulated, that unregulated industrialism and commercialism carried a threat to social security and stability, a threat which was not much mitigated even if it were true, as the economists argued, that there had been on the whole an increase of prosperity and a rise in real wages. As a matter of fact restrictions upon *laissez faire* were enacted in all countries and by political parties that professed widely different social philosophies.[2] This reaction can be attributed partly to humanitarianism aroused by the inhumane conditions imposed on industrial workers. Liberalism as a political movement could ill afford to part company with humanitarianism, for this had always been a powerful motive among liberals even though it got little overt recognition from the Philosophical Radicals. Over and above this general reaction, however, the very success with which liberalism had pleaded the cause of the industrialists stimulated the political self-consciousness of two other economic interests whose position liberalism threatened. In the first place the adoption of free trade reversed a long-standing policy of tariff protection for British agriculture and therefore on its face amounted to sacrificing the interests of farmers to the expansion of commerce and industry. The agri-

[1] A. V. Dicey, *Law and Public Opinion in England during the Nineteenth Century* (1905), Lecture VII. Herbert Spencer, alarmed at what he considered to be the anti-liberal trend of legislation passed by the Liberal Party, compiled in *The Man versus the State* (1884) a long list of acts which interfered with the operations of a free market. They included not only labor legislation but sanitary regulations and public support of education.

[2] Karl Polanyi, *The Great Transformation* (1944), pp. 145 ff.

cultural interest had always been mainly conservative, and in so far as conservatism had a political philosophy it was derived from Burke. By conviction it stressed the values of social stability and the historical continuity of the community, and this made it the natural critic and opponent of industrialism. The result was anomalous, at least from the point of view of a liberal like James Mill, who had imagined that workers would always follow the lead of "the wisest part of the community," namely, the industrial middle class. A workingman whose trade was threatened by a new technology might very easily feel that his interests were safer with a party controlled by landlords than with one that was the spokesman of his employers. Disraeli's "Tory democracy" became a real, if only a temporary, political force. In the second place the political self-consciousness of industrial employers inevitably bred a like consciousness on the part of labor. The enfranchisement by a Conservative government of a considerable portion of English workingmen, which occurred in 1867, marked the beginning of a political change of permanent importance. It meant the appearance of a group of voters who were more concerned to protect wages, hours of labor, and conditions of employment than to extend business enterprise, and who were well aware that their strength lay not in freedom of contract but in collective bargaining. One of two things must happen: either liberalism would meet these requirements or the working class would not be liberal.

As was said in the last chapter, the distinctive characteristic of English liberalism was that it developed into a national political movement and did not remain, as it began, the spokesman of middle-class industrial interests. England was indeed the most highly industrialized country in the world, and its industrialists had gained a degree of political power not enjoyed by any similar class elsewhere. But they were also part of a society that was profoundly convinced of its national solidarity and of the community of its national interests. This public had learned by long experience with representative government that, as Halifax had said at the time of the Revolution, "There is a natural reason of state . . . which . . . still preserveth its original right of saving a nation, when the letter of the law would perhaps destroy it." Consequently liberalism, if it was not to lose its public, had to revise the letter of its law, and this in fact was what it did. As a party it had to revise its policy but in order to maintain its position as a factor in social thought it had also to revise its theory. Of the two the first was the easier, depending as it did upon political expedience. It was necessary only to discard the dogma, never very convincing except to those already convinced, that society always progresses "from status to contract," and that, as Dicey said, had been done by 1870. But the dogma had behind it not only an immense weight of sentiment but the impressive system of Bentham's jurisprudence and the claim of the classical economists that their own policy was based upon well established laws of human behavior. A thoroughgoing revision of liberal theory, therefore, required a re-examination of the nature and functions of the state, the nature of liberty, and the relationship between liberty and legal coercion. And such a re-examination opened up the prior question of the relationship between individual human nature and its social *milieu*. To deal with this last question the old ready explanations, in terms of self-interest, pleasure, and utility, proved steadily less convincing. Both in ethics and in social science the current was away from individualism and toward exploring some kind of collectivist concept. In short, a modernizing of liberal theory depended upon breaking down the intellectual isolation of Philosophical Radicalism, which was largely responsible for its dogmatism, and bringing it into touch with the outlook of other social classes, with Continental strains of thought, and with new fields of scientific investigation. Only so could liberalism claim to be a social philosophy and not merely the ideology of a special interest.

The revision occurred in two waves, so to speak. The first was chiefly the related but contrasting philosophies of John Stuart Mill and Herbert Spencer; the second was the philosophy of the Oxford idealists, especially that of Thomas Hill Green. The work of the first two men is the clearest proof of the urgency, not to say the inevitability, of the revision. Both were bred in the native philosophical tradition and in important respects each in his own way remained faithful to it. Yet the most obvious characteristic of each was his reaching out toward intellectual influences that the tradition lacked. In the case of Spencer this was the effort to bring his social philosophy into the context of organic evolution and the whole body of the natural sciences. In the case of Mill it was the effort both to revise utilitarianism and the conception of personal liberty and also to take account of the social philosophy of Comte. It was Oxford idealism, however, that finally broke by its criticism the hold of the empirical tradition on Anglo-American philosophical thought and based itself avowedly on post-Kantian German philosophy. Yet in respect to its political philosophy idealism maintained its continuity with liberalism. Green submitted to drastic criticism the sensationalism and hedonism upon which the older liberalism professed to be based, but he was more clearly and more coherently liberal in his political theory than John Stuart Mill. And while idealism called itself neo-Hegelian, it contained no more than a trace, and not that in Green, of the political authoritarianism that Hegelianism connoted in Germany.

JOHN STUART MILL: LIBERTY

The general outlook of John Stuart Mill's social philosophy, and especially his ethics, was determined perhaps as much by personal experience as by intellectual considerations. From birth he was destined by his father to carry on the crusade of the Philosophical Radicals, and certainly the elder Mill never envisaged the possibility that the objectives of that crusade could change. The younger Mill from an early age was subjected to the most dogmatic indoctrination and the most extreme educational "forcing" ever suffered by a man who afterward attained intellectual independence. It was not until after his father's death in 1836 that Mill was able to strike out his own line of approach to ethical questions, though by that time (at the age of thirty) he had long been before the public as an editor and as a contributor to the liberal reviews. In the meantime this enforced precocity had induced a period of nervous exhaustion from which he finally escaped, as he tells in his *Autobiography,* by absorbing himself in the reading of Wordsworth's poetry, certainly not a method contemplated in his father's philosophy of education. Thus Mill's intellectual life became ambivalent. He retained an exaggerated allegiance, enforced by an intense sense of personal loyalty, toward the philosophy which he had learned from his father and from Bentham and of which he had been predestined to be the exponent. At the same time he achieved a considerable degree of sympathy and appreciation, but hardly a critical understanding, for an antithetical philosophy derived from German idealism which he associated with Wordsworth. In the first third of the nineteenth century this philosophy was represented in England chiefly by the rather formless metaphysical speculation and the personal influence of Coleridge. Mill's mind was characterized by a very high quality of candor and intellectual honesty which made him almost nervously anxious to do justice to a philosophy opposed to his own. Thus he was inclined to make concessions which implied far more than he realized and which were often more generous than critical. The companion essays on Bentham and Coleridge, which he published in the *London and Westminster Review* in 1838 and 1840 respectively and which were a kind of declaration of independence from his father's influence, did rather more than justice to Coleridge and somewhat less than justice to Bentham. With rare intellectual perceptivity Mill sensed in Coleridge's philosophy a regard for the institutional nature of society and for the historical evolution of institutions which he felt to be lacking in the tradition of British Empiricism. At a later date he was attracted by similar qualities in the French philosophy of Auguste Comte. In a broad sense, therefore, Mill's philosophy was an effort to modify the empiricism in which he was bred by taking into account the very different point of view of Kantian and post-Kantian German philosophy.

Unfortunately Mill's candor and open-mindedness were not matched by the grasp or the originality required to bring about a really coherent synthesis of philosophies so widely divergent, a task which in truth occupied almost the whole attention of English and American philosophers in the later nineteenth century. Mill's thought had all the marks of a transitional period in which the problems have outgrown the apparatus for their solution. Without much exaggeration it might be said that his books followed a formula. On nearly every subject he was likely to begin with a general statement of principles which, taken literally and by itself, appeared to be as rigid and as abstract as anything that his father might have written. But having thus declared his allegiance to the ancestral dogmas, Mill proceeded to make concessions and restatements so far-reaching that a critical reader was left in doubt whether the original statement had not been explained away. Thus, for example, his *Logic* was by profession empirical, though it went to surprising lengths in recognizing the scientific importance of deduction and it tried to reduce inductive procedure to rules analogous to the rules of the syllogism. Yet Mill's theory of knowledge had no way of explaining the logical coerciveness of formal reasoning except "indissoluble association" which, as A. D. Lindsay said, became a philosophical maid-of-all-work called in to explain any discrepancies between the facts and what ought to be the facts on the assumption of a crude empiricism. Mill was never able to achieve critical detachment toward the philosophy in which he was bred. On its face his psychology was still a sensationalism in which the association of ideas provided the only law of mental structure. The theory of motivation and of value in his ethics was still overtly the hedonistic calculus, and his utilitarianism was still in strict logic the egoistic individualism of Bentham. Yet in no case would these statements correspond with the actual meaning of Mill's philosophy. The qualifications and not the theory were what carried his meaning. For this reason systematic criticism is fatally easy and practically useless. The importance of Mill's philosophy consisted in its departures from the system which it still professed to support and hence in the revisions that it made in the utilitarian tradition.

The ethical theory which Mill set forth in his *Utilitarianism* illustrates this defect of his philosophy, yet it is also the root of his revision of liberalism. He began by accepting apparently *in toto* the greatest happiness principle as it had been stated by Bentham. The desire for one's own greatest pleasure is the individual's only motive, and the greatest happiness of everyone is at once the standard of social good and the object of all moral action. Mill united these propositions by an argument so patently fallacious that it became a standard exhibit in textbooks of logic. He then qualified his hedonism by asserting that pleasures can be graded as superior or inferior in moral quality. This put him in the indefensible logical position of demanding a standard for the measurement of a standard, which is a contradiction in terms, and also reduced his utilitarianism to complete indefiniteness, since the standard for judging the quality of pleasures was never stated and if stated could not itself be a pleasure. The root of all this confusion was that Mill was not willing to accept Bentham's greatest happiness principle for what in effect it was, namely, a rough and ready criterion for judging the utility of legislation. Used for this purpose, which was the only purpose that had interested Bentham, it was logically independent of Bentham's theory of psychological motives and might be equally applicable to legislation no matter what standards of personal morality individuals might follow. The distinctive characteristic of Mill's utilitarianism, on the other hand, was that he tried to express a conception of moral character consonant with his own personal idealism. From this point of view Bentham's famous pronouncement, that "pushpin is as good as poetry" if it gives one the same pleasure, is simply vulgar nonsense, while Mill's own pronouncement, that it is "better to be Socrates dissatisfied than a fool satisfied," states a normal moral reaction but is certainly not hedonism. Mill's ethics was important for liberalism because in effect it abandoned egoism, assumed that social welfare is a matter of concern to all men of good will, and regarded freedom, integrity, self-respect, and personal distinction as intrinsic goods apart from their contribution to happiness. Moral convictions of this sort underlay Mill's whole conception of a liberal society.

It was therefore natural that his most characteristic and also most lasting contribution to political thought should have been contained in the essay *On Liberty* (1859). This essay struck a definitely new note in utilitarian literature. As Mill himself said in another place, the utilitarians of his father's generation had desired liberal government not for the sake of liberty but because they thought it would be efficient government, and it was indeed true that Bentham had changed nothing but details when he turned from benevolent despotism to liberalism. For Mill freedom of thought and investigation, freedom of discussion, and the freedom of self-controlled moral judgment and action were goods in their own right. They aroused in him a warmth and a fervor that hardly appeared in his other writings but which placed the essay *On Liberty* beside Milton's *Areopagitica* as one of the classical defenses of freedom in the English language. Mill believed as a matter of course that intellectual and political freedom are in general beneficial both to the society that permits them and to the individual that enjoys them, but the effective part of his argument was not utilitarian. When he said that all mankind has no right to silence one dissenter he was really affirming that freedom of judgment, the right to be convinced rather than coerced, is an inherent quality of a morally mature personality and that a liberal society is one which both acknowledges that right and shapes its institutions in such a way that the right is realized. To permit individuality and private judgment, as if they were tolerated vices, is not enough; a liberal society puts positive value on them as essential to well-being and as marks of a high civilization. This valuation of free personality affected profoundly Mill's valuation of liberal government. He did not defend popular government because it is efficient. He had grave doubts whether it always is, and he had quite lost his father's confidence that the apparatus of liberal government, such as the suffrage, would always be rationally used for beneficial ends. The real argument for political freedom, he thought, is that it produces and gives scope to a high type of moral character. To hear public questions freely discussed, to have a share in political decisions, to have moral convictions and to take the responsibility for making them effective are among the ways in which reasonable human beings are produced. The reason for constructing this kind of character is not that it serves an ulterior end but that it is an intrinsically humane, civilized kind of character.

> If it were felt that the free development of individuality is one of the leading essentials of well-being; that it is not only a co-ordinate element with all that is designated by the terms civilization, instruction, education, culture, but is itself a necessary part and condition of all these things; there would be no danger that liberty should be undervalued.[3]

It is a striking characteristic of Mill's argument for liberty, and even of his essay on *Representative Government,* that strictly

[3] *On Liberty,* ch. 3.

political questions are no longer in the foreground. His argument was addressed not to the state but to society. The essay *On Liberty* was an appeal not for relief from political oppression or for a change in political organization, but for a public opinion that is genuinely tolerant, that values differences in point of view, that limits the amount of agreement it demands, and that welcomes new ideas as sources of discovery. The threat to liberty which Mill chiefly feared was not government but a majority that is intolerant of the unconventional, that looks with suspicion on divergent minorities, and is willing to use the weight of numbers to repress and regiment them. This was a possibility that had never troubled the older generation of liberals, indeed that they had never thought of, as long as their problem had been to take government out of the hands of an intrenched minority. The elder Mill had supposed that the reform of representation and the extension of the suffrage, given a moderate degree of public education, would solve all serious problems of political liberty. By 1859 it was apparent that even after substantial reforms the millennium did not follow, and that the achievement of liberty was more than a problem in the mechanics of political organization. What Mill recognized, and what the older liberalism had never seen, was that behind a liberal government there must be a liberal society.

This recognition that political institutions are part of a larger social context which largely determines the way in which they work was in itself an important discovery and it indicated an important addition to political concepts. Society or the community becomes a third factor, and a preponderating factor, in the relationship between the individual and government and in securing the individual's liberty. Mill's fear of an oppressive and intolerant public opinion was in part a realization that the individualism of early liberal theory was inadequate. At the same time it is difficult to say what precisely this phase of Mill's thinking connoted. That it was a note of disillusionment, as compared with the high hopes of his father's generation, is evident. Probably in part it reflected also the shrinking of a sensitive, fastidious, and highly intellectual personality from the contact with mediocrity implied by practical politics. Perhaps it indicated also a half-expressed fear that the democratizing of society might prove to be incompatible with individual distinction. Such a fear was common enough in the mid-nineteenth century. Yet it is quite certain that Mill had not lost faith in the traditional lines of liberal reform, that on the contrary he valued some of them, like the enfranchisement of women, out of all proportion to their importance. In his *Representative Government* he hailed as a great discovery that *ignis fatuus* of doctrinaire liberalism, proportional representation. The total impression produced by Mill's theory of liberty is therefore a little indefinite or perhaps even negative. While he affirmed an ethical valuation of liberty that had been quite lacking in earlier liberal writing, he identified liberty with no new lines of approach to political problems. In particular he never really faced the problems of individual freedom that are peculiarly characteristic of an industrial society or the problems of freedom that press most heavily on wage earners in such a society.

When Mill went on from his general estimate of the moral worth of freedom to his practical rule for deciding what limitations either society or the state is justified in imposing on it, his essay was at its weakest. What he proposed was that it is possible to distinguish a class of self-regarding action which " affects the interests of no persons besides " the agent and with which neither society nor the state ought to interfere. Taken literally this would reduce freedom to a triviality, since an act that affects no one but a single person probably will not affect him very much. Mill's argument avoided the appearance of triviality only because it was circular, as no doubt Bentham would have pointed out. For an act which " concerns " only an individual really means an act for which he ought to take the responsibility and which therefore ought to be left to his own decision. But it was just this area of private decision that Mill proposed to define. His argument would be convincing only if there were a body of natural rights which belong intrinsically to individuals and of which they ought never to be deprived, but obviously no such line of reasoning was open to a utilitarian. On the other hand, it was equally clear, in view of the intrinsic value which he had attached to freedom, that Mill could not fall back on Bentham's reasoning and hold that rights are creatures of the law and that individuals have only such liberties as the state gives them. The fundamental difficulty with Mill's argument was that it never really analyzed the relationship between freedom and responsibility. At times he retained the traditional view derived from Bentham that any compulsion or even any social influence is an abridgement of liberty. Yet he never supposed that there could be any important freedom without law and when he identified liberty with civilization, he did not imagine that there could be civilization without society. What Mill's theory of liberty required was a thoroughgoing consideration of the dependence of personal liberty on social and legal rights and obligations. It was this which T. H. Green tried to add to liberalism.

The unclearness of Mill's criterion for defining the proper limits of legislation became apparent when he went on to discuss actual cases. His conclusions conformed to no rule at all but depended on quite subjective habits of judgment. Thus he regarded prohibition of the sale of alcoholic liquors as an infringement of liberty though compulsory education is not — a conclusion that certainly could not be justified on the ground that a man's education affects other persons more than himself — and he was prepared to accept a large and ill-defined regulation of business and industry in the interest of public health and welfare. However unclear the principle, the important result emerged that Mill had abandoned economic *laissez faire*. Even Bentham's maxim that legislation is inherently bad and so must be kept at a minimum has lost the connotation that it had for Bentham. For all practical purposes Mill simply laid aside the dogma of earlier liberalism that the largest amount of freedom coincides with the absence of legislation and accepted the evident fact that there are many forms of coercion other than that exercised by the law. But one of two results must follow: either legislation cannot be judged at all by the liberal purpose of diminishing coercion or liberal theory must be extended to considering the relation of legal coercion to the effective though non-legal coercion that would exist if the state abstained from acting. This was the issue that Green tried later to meet with the theory of "positive freedom." So far as Mill was concerned, he merely accepted the need for social legislation, probably on humanitarian grounds, with no clear theory of its justifiable limits.

Mill's economic theories showed like deficiencies of logical clarity and therefore are subject to like criticism. He started indeed from the economics of Ricardo and the classical theorists and in principle he never definitely abandoned this position. He became convinced, however, that the classical economists had confused certain general and inescapable conditions of production with conditions of distributing the products of industry which arise from the historical development of economic and social institutions. The latter, therefore, he conceived to be matters of public policy and hence within the province of legislative control. Indeed in his later years he was willing to contemplate a degree and kind of control which he called socialism. This criticism of classical economics indicated one aspect of a general deficiency which Mill came to attribute to the social philosophy of the early liberals, namely, that it neglected the institutional nature of society and the historical growth of institutions. His criticism of classical economics was sound in so far as it merely pointed out a tendency to regard all economic concepts as absolutely general, without regard for historical conditions, and therefore as derived from universal properties of human nature and unchangeable physical conditions of human life. Mill's distinction between historical institutions and general psychological laws of human behavior, however, or between institutions and unchangeable physical conditions, did not coincide with the economic distinction between production and distribution. Consequently it did not really bear upon the economic difficulties of combining a capitalist system of production with a socialist system of distribution. The significant feature of Mill's economics was that he substantially abandoned the conception of natural economic laws and in consequence the dogma of a self-regulating competitive economic system. Thus he opened the whole question of the relation between legislation and the economy, even its relation to the maintenance of a free market. The practical implications of this change, however, were far from clear. Like liberals in general Mill retained a considerable suspicion of government and all its ways. What it did, he suspected, would probably be done badly. Hence he preferred individual initiative and feared paternalism, though his objection to the latter was ethical and not economic. Mill's economic thought, like his social philosophy in general, was really directed by a generous moral indignation against the injustices of a capitalist society which, as he said, distributed the product of labor "almost in an inverse ratio to the labor."

A just and at the same time a sympathetic estimate of Mill's liberalism is very difficult. Nothing is easier, for reasons that have been explained, than to represent it as a typical example of the futility of putting new wine into old bottles. His expressly stated theories — of human nature, of morals, of society, and of the part to be played by government in a liberal society — were always inadequate to the load that he made them carry. Yet this kind of abstract analysis and criticism is neither sympathetic nor historically sound. The clarity of his writing, though it was too often a superficial clarity, his manifest generosity and candor, which often made the worst of his deficiencies, and his almost hereditary position as the successor of the first generation of liberals, all gave weight or influence to his opinions out of proportion to the philosophical argumentation that he was able to put behind them. Paradoxical as such a judgment seems when applied to a thinker who concerned himself continually with the rationale of evidence, Mill's most important insights were intuitive, the outcropping of a fine moral sensitiveness and deep consciousness of social obligation. Without reference to the defects of coherence that marred Mill's systematic philosophy, his contribution to a liberal philosophy may perhaps be summed up under four heads. First, his version of utilitarianism rescued that form of ethics from the desiccation to which it was condemned so long as its theory of moral value ran in terms only of a calculation of pleasures and pains. The central moral idea in Mill's ethics, like Kant's, was really respect for human beings, the sense that they must be treated with a due regard for the dignity that moral responsibility deserves and without which moral responsibility is impossible. Mill's ethics was utilitarian chiefly in the sense that he thought of the value of personality not as a metaphysical dogma but as something to be realized in the actual conditions of a free society. Second, Mill's liberalism accepted political and social freedom as itself a good, not because it contributed to an ulterior end but because freedom is the proper condition of a responsible human being. To live one's own life, developing one's own native traits and capacities, is not a means to happiness; it literally is a substantive part of happiness. A good society must, therefore, be one which both permits freedom and opens up the opportunity for free and satisfying ways of life. Third, liberty is not only an individual good but also a social good. To silence an opinion by force both does violence to the person who holds it and also robs society of the advantage it might have had from a free investigation and criticism of the opinion. In fact these two claims, that of individual right and of public utility, are closely connected. For a society in which ideas live or die by a process of free discussion is not only a progressive society but is in truth the only kind of society that can produce persons fit to enjoy the rights of free discussion. Fourth, the function of a liberal state in a free society is not negative but positive. It cannot make its citizens free merely by refraining from legislation or assume that the conditions of freedom exist merely because legal disabilities have been removed. Legislation may be a means of creating, increasing, and equalizing opportunity, and liberalism can impose no arbitrary limits upon its use. Its limits are fixed by its ability, with the means at its disposal, to preserve and to extend to more persons those conditions which make life more humane and less coercive.

THE PRINCIPLES OF SOCIAL STUDY

Mill's theory of political and ethical liberalism, developed chiefly in his *Utilitarianism,* the essay *On Liberty,* and the *Representative Government,* remained for the most part within the circle of subjects and of ideas native to his English tradition. The very important changes which he made were considered by him, mistakenly, to be amendments and additions. But Mill came also to believe that there were general deficiencies in this social philosophy, and with his usual open-mindedness he tried to understand and make use of other points of view. These deficiencies he believed could be summed up under two principal heads. First, the politics and economics of Bentham's age tried to proceed from a few general laws of human nature, believed to be universally the same in all times and places, directly to the political and economic behavior of men in specific societies, at specific times, and within the framework of specific systems of legislation. Hence the older utilitarians had not sufficiently recognized the importance of institutions or the fact that institutions are, so to speak, a third reality between individual psychology and the concrete practice of a given time and place. Second, because institutions were not recognized as independent realities, the factor of historical growth or development was not given the importance it deserved. Mill associated both these additions to social philosophy with foreign influences, somewhat vaguely with German idealism and the " Coleridgeans," definitely with the philosophy of Auguste Comte. What was needed and what Mill thought that Comte supplied was a general science of society, to support more limited sciences like politics and economics, and the formulation of a general law of social growth. These were, in short, sociology and the law of the " three stages."

These two projects were highly characteristic of social thought in the mid-nineteenth century and in the event they led to important consequences but for the time being they signified a change in point of view rather than any specific achievement. In one sense Comte's philosophy was a culmination of social speculation that had begun with Rousseau's enigmatic idea of the general will, the concept of society as a collective entity which has its own properties and values and which overarches the purposes and wills of its members. The reaction against the French Revolution gave this conception a central place in the social philosophy of the early nineteenth century. Comte himself encountered this reaction primarily in Roman Catholic traditionalists such as Bonald and de Maistre. The social philosophy of Hegel, however, was actuated by the same general tendency in a different form, and Marxism was still a further elaboration of it. What Comte contributed was not so much a new discovery as the hope that speculation might be replaced by science, that the concept of society might be analyzed and its laws discovered by methods that would conform to canons of empirical verification, and that the relationships might be traced in detail between social institutions and human nature. In another sense, therefore, Comte's philosophy was not a culmination but a beginning, the midpoint from which might be dated the whole vast effort to bring the social studies within the sweep of modern science. Considered in this light it merely opened up a task whose complexity was only dimly realized and which even yet has achieved no startling success. Its history from Comte's time to the present has been one of new problems and new methods, new fields of investigation, and even of whole new sciences such as cultural anthropology or social psychology. This fundamental purpose of Comte's philosophy was one that for obvious reasons appealed strongly to Mill. It was an enlargement of a belief that had always been central in liberal doctrine, the conviction that human relations are amenable to intelligent understanding and control.

For the time being Comte's general plan for a science of society appeared to be bound up with his second and, as it turned out, very dubious idea that the main result of such a science would be the discovery of a "law" governing the growth and development of societies. Such a law, it was assumed, would mark out a normal or standard line of evolution to which every society might be expected in general to conform, allowing for some degree of variability according to circumstances. This fascinating speculation, which Léon Brunschvicg called the "darling vice" of social thought in the nineteenth century, drew support from several different and indeed logically discrepant sources. It was already assumed by the belief in progress which had been inherited from pre-revolutionary thinkers like Turgot and Condorcet. In a different form it was implicit in Hegel's philosophy of history and in the historical method which Hegelianism introduced into social studies. And as Herbert Spencer was to show, it at least seemed to join hands with biological evolution, which after Darwin became a scientific preoccupation of the nineteenth century. Under the guidance of these several ideas, which appeared for the moment to converge upon a single point of view, the "comparative method" became a commonly accepted procedure in nearly all branches of social study. In general the result, though it enormously extended the range of information about varieties of social and political organization, was wholly disappointing so far as concerned the main purpose. Probably few if any anthropologists would now accept the presumption that cultures do in fact follow any normal line of growth or that, in view of what is known of the causes of social change, there is any reason to expect them to do so.[4]

When Mill encountered the philosophy of Comte, however, speculations of this sort were quite definitely a part of the climate of opinion. He was eager to supplement and fill out an inherited social philosophy which he had come to regard as limited and insular. Accordingly he accepted, with some reservations, both the idea of a general social science and the hope for a philosophy of history, though they came to him too late to be interwoven with the older native strands of his thought. In his *Autobiography* he enumerated the most important conclusions to which Comte and the " Coleridgeans " led him.

> That the human mind has a certain order of possible progress, in which some things must precede others, an order which government and public instructors can modify to some, but not to an unlimited extent: that all questions of political institutions are relative, not absolute, and that different stages of human progress not only *will* have, but *ought* to have, different institutions: that government is always either in the hands, or passing into the hands, of whatever is the strongest power in society, and that what this power is, does not depend on institutions, but institutions on it: that any general theory or philosophy of politics supposes a previous theory of human progress, and that this is the same thing with a philosophy of history.[5]

To write a complete gloss on this sentence would require a commentary on a substantial portion of the evolutionary ethics and evolutionary sociology of the second half of the nineteenth century, much of which was undertaken from the point of view of a liberal social philosophy derived from Mill and Green.[6] In that sense Mill's thought was programmatic. Liberalism had always claimed that it rested on an empirical foundation, but empiricism had been understood to mean an individual psychology developed from the " new way of ideas " that Locke had consid-

[4] On the methodological difficulties in the concept of historical laws see Karl Popper, " The Poverty of Historicism," *Economica,* N.S., Vol. XI (1944), p. 86; p. 119; Vol. XII (1945), p. 69.

[5] *Autobiography* (1873), p. 162.

[6] The best instance of a coherent combination of liberalism and evolution, together with a careful attempt to test the generalizations by thoroughgoing historical induction, was the sociology of Leonard Hobhouse; especially *Mind in Evolution* (1901) and *Morals in Evolution,* 2 vols. (1906). There were later editions of both books.

ered to be the original insight of his *Essay*. Now it appeared that an individual psychology was not enough but must be supplemented by a study of social institutions and particularly of their growth. The method would still be empirical but the empiricism would be on a much larger scale. The program therefore had tremendous scope, and certainly Mill had little conception of all that was involved. If the mind has "a certain order of possible progress" it must be possible to show by historical induction what that order has been. If there are "different stages of human progress," it must again be possible to show an evolution of moral ideas and a growth of the social institutions in which moral ideas are expressed. And finally it must be possible to show by far-reaching comparisons that the growth of mind is correlated with the advancement of civilization. If all this were accomplished, it would then indeed be proved that liberalism depended upon a "theory of human progress," that it was a culmination and a summation of political development. In nineteenth-century Europe it was possible, perhaps even plausible, to entertain the expectation that political institutions everywhere would be liberalized by a process of gradual evolution. And as yet anthropological investigation had not revealed the difficulties, not to say the fallacies, that lurked in the comparative method.

However little of this ambitious project Mill may have foreseen when the passage quoted was written in 1873, he had grasped two ideas that were both sound and important. The first was the dependence of political upon social institutions and the second was the psychological nature of society. The first point corresponded to his general criticism of the older liberals, that they had been unaware of the extent to which general laws of individual psychology are adaptable to a wide range of institutions and historical circumstance. Thus in jurisprudence they had construed sovereignty as a mere "habit of obedience" to specific persons, and in economics, as Mill believed, they had erroneously referred the practices of a capitalist society to unchangeable psychological necessities. In his essay *On Liberty* Mill had tacitly developed the same criticism by regarding liberal government as dependent on a social and moral respect for individuality. The awareness of society and the sense that individual behavior always is in some sense socialized was in fact an important property of Mill's thought, even though he did not always see clearly how much was implied. The second main idea, that psychology (rather than biology) is the basic science of social behavior was one in which Mill differed from Comte. In this respect he adhered to the position which had always prevailed in English social studies. Possibly his conclusion was in part determined by the fact that his thought took form before biological evolution was a factor to be considered, but in any case it was sound. The attempt to tie social and moral development directly to organic evolution was an error that served to confuse both, as Spencer's evolutionary philosophy demonstrated. On the other hand, it is impossible to see how Mill could have explained the " certain order of possible progress " that he attributed to the mind by the associational psychology which he always professed. For the association of ideas meant substantially that the sole process required to explain mental development was the formation of habits, and what ideas habit associated depended not on the mind but on circumstances. At this point also any effective development of Mill's thought would have involved complete reconstruction.

Mill inserted in his *Logic* a special section, the Sixth Book, dealing with scientific method in the social studies. The mere inclusion of the subject in a work on logic which dealt mainly with the methodology of the inductive natural sciences was significant. It showed the need that Mill felt for enlarging the scope of social studies, of making their methods more rigorous, and particularly of giving them a place besides the natural sciences. In general he took the position that the method of the social sciences involved a twofold use of induction and deduction, which was no doubt true but did not distinguish social studies from other subjects. This conclusion was at once a concession to criticisms directed at the deductive procedure of the Philosophical Radicals and a reaffirmation of the necessity and justifiability of that procedure. In 1829 Macaulay had printed in the *Edinburgh Review* a rather contemptuous article on James Mill's *Essays on Government,* attacking the book for its highly rationalistic method and apparently taking the position that political science ought to be purely empirical. Mill in the *Logic* rejected both exclusive views in favor of one which used both deduction and induction. Politics required, he argued, psychological laws of behavior which can rest only on induction, but the explanation of political events must be largely deductive since their explanation means referring them to psychology. Mill followed the same line of argument in trying to make his own procedure accord with that of Comte. He accepted the possibility of establishing inductively some laws of historical development, though with some traces of skepticism about the extent and certainty of this procedure, but he still regarded such laws as explainable only by their deduction from psychology. Mill's general conclusion, therefore, was that there are two methods of procedure for social studies which should supplement each other. The one he called the direct deductive method, which was his own, and the other the indirect deductive method, which he credited to Comte.

HERBERT SPENCER

For the purpose of gauging the state of liberal theory in the third quarter of the nineteenth century, it is both interesting and instructive to compare the philosophy of Mill with that of Herbert Spencer. The two men were generally recognized as the most important exponents of the philosophy of political liberalism and of the native British philosophical tradition. Both had their intellectual origins in Philosophical Radicalism. In the case of Spencer this was not quite as evident as in the case of Mill because he put at the center of his philosophy the new conception of organic evolution. Yet all of Spencer's important ethical and political ideas were derived from utilitarianism and had no close logical dependence on either biology or evolution. The *Social Statics* was published nine years before Darwin's *Origin of Species,* and to a considerable degree Spencer's later evolutionary ethics consisted in constructing speculative psychological ties between pleasure and biological survival The fact that both Mill and Spencer went back to Philosophical Radicalism and yet differed very widely from each other reinforces the conclusion reached in the preceding chapter that two strains of thought had been incoherently joined in that philosophy. Mill was in the main the intellectual descendant of Bentham, an empiricist who put few *a priori* limitations on the social functions of legislation.

Spencer carried on into the latter part of the nineteenth century the rationalist tradition of the classical economists and utilized evolution to reconstruct the system of a natural society with natural boundaries between economics and politics. Yet a substantial part of what both Spencer and Mill did for social philosophy was to reach out for new intellectual connections and to break down the insularity of the older liberalism. In the case of Spencer this consisted in bringing it into relation with biology and sociology and with biological and social evolution.

Spencer's Synthetic Philosophy was an astonishing system of nineteenth-century rationalism (covering the whole range of knowledge from physics to ethics) worked out through thirty-five years and in ten volumes, and constructed with no important change of plan between the prospectus and the concluding volume. Nothing analogous to it can easily be found short of the great systems of natural law that flourished in the seventeenth century, and indeed the intellectual affinities between these and Spencer's philosophy were close. For Spencer the modernized version of "nature" was evolution. From von Baer's embryology he took the law of differentiation and integration, "from an indefinite incoherent homogeneity to a definite coherent heterogeneity," and erected it into a cosmic principle which manifests itself in a thousand subject-matters while preserving identity of pattern. Assuming "the instability of the homogeneous" Spencer undertook the amazing task of "deducing" organic evolution from the conservation of energy. And from this beginning the system proceeded successively to the principles of biology, of psychology, of sociology, and of ethics. Allowing for temporary eddies of "dissolution," nature advances upon a straight line from energy to life, from life to mind, from mind to society, from society to civilization and to more highly differentiated and integrated civilizations.

It need hardly be said that this kind of logical *tour de force* was not notable for its scientific rigor or for the cogency of its deductions. In a large measure it was in its own day an astonishingly successful popularization, and it has suffered the fate of obsolete popularizations. In a sense it was typical of its period, even though few thinkers attempted a philosophical synthesis so broad. Spencer's evolution was another version of the philosophy of history already mentioned. It expressed again the hope that the growth of society would provide clear criteria of lower and higher stages of development by which to distinguish the obsolete from the suitable, the fit from the unfit, and therefore the good from the bad. With Spencer this hope was given the appearance of having behind it the established fact of organic evolution, since moral improvement was made to seem merely an extension of the biological concept of adaptation, and social well-being appeared to be equated with the survival of the fittest. In addition to involving many logical ambiguities, this conflation of ideas was a source of serious scientific confusion. The only way in which Spencer could pass from biological adaptation to moral progress was by supposing that socially valuable behavior, once established by moral prescription as habits, is translated into anatomical changes that are transmitted by inheritance. This belief, of which Spencer was a lifelong exponent, was not only biologically baseless but was the source of endless confusion about the nature of culture and of social change. Yet when all this has been said about the deficiencies of Spencer's philosophy, it must still in fairness be added that it contributed to important changes in the social studies, quite without reference to the validity of particular conclusions. It brought psychology into relation with biology, and this was a first step toward breaking down the dogmatism of the old associational psychology. It also brought politics and ethics into the context of sociological and anthropological investigation and therefore into the context of cultural history. The age of the Synthetic Philosophy was also the age of the scientifically more original and important work of E. B. Tylor and L. H. Morgan.[7] Spencer like Mill, though in a different way, broke down the intellectual isolation of the older utilitarian philosophy and of social studies in general, making them a part of the broad sweep of modern science. In this respect his philosophy, like that of Comte, had in its day a profound intellectual significance.

Spencer's political philosophy on the other hand was merely reactionary. He remained a philosophical radical after philosophical radicalism had been obsolete for a generation. The

[7] Tylor's *Primitive Culture* was published in 1871 and Morgan's *Ancient Society* in 1877.

theory of evolution provided him with the concept of a "natural" society, and this turned out to be only a new version of the old system of natural liberty. The deduction presented some difficulties, since it might seem that evolution would make the state, like society, more complex and more highly integrated, while Spencer had to prove that a society which grew steadily more complex would support a state that simplified itself practically out of existence. He solved the paradox by supposing that most functions exercised by government originated in a military society and that war would become obsolete in an industrialized society. Hence he inferred that, with increased industrialization, more and more would be left to private enterprise. Indeed Spencer's theory of the state was very largely a list of functions that the state should at once abandon, since they had been assumed in the first place by some of the innumerable "sins of legislators," or of functions that will be made unnecessary by the progress of evolution. Most legislation is bad, because it mars the perfection which nature tends to produce by the survival of the fittest, and virtually all legislation will be rendered obsolete as evolution approaches a perfect adaptation of the individual to society. Hence Spencer opposed consistently all regulation of industry, including sanitary regulations or the requirement of safety devices, all forms of public charity, and public support for education. Indeed, in the *Social Statics* he proposed that the state should turn over the mint and the post office to private enterprise.

The philosophies of Mill and Spencer taken together left the theory of liberalism in a state of unintelligible confusion. Mill restated its philosophy in such a way as to suggest that he departed in no important way from the principles of his father and of Bentham, but he so qualified the conclusions that they gave little or no support to what had always been deemed to be the characteristic line of liberal policy, namely, the limitation of control by governments, the encouragement of private enterprise, and the widest possible extension of freedom of contract. Spencer on the contrary had given to liberalism a new philosophy that purported to depend upon a scientific discovery unknown to any generation before his own, but the new philosophy turned out to teach more rigidly than ever before a policy that practical liberals, who were not overly concerned about logical consistency, had already discovered to need substantial modifications. In either case the French proverb seemed to apply: *Plus ça change, plus c'est la même chose.* Liberalism seemed to be a set of formulas that had ceased to mean what they had always been thought to mean and a set of policies that corresponded to no formulas at all. Yet two facts were evident to any clear-thinking person of liberal sympathies. One was that the enfranchisement and organization of labor were giving political power to a class that had no intention of accepting without a struggle anyone's demonstration that its standard of living was fixed permanently at the level of existence and reproduction, without the amenities that industrialism was producing in ever larger volume. The other was that public opinion, whether on ethical or religious or humanitarian grounds, was prepared to countenance and support this claim. With the results of unregulated industrialism before it, a new generation of liberals was not prepared to acquiesce in the belief that government has only a negative rôle to play in making men free. It was this frame of mind that made John Stuart Mill, despite the insufficiency of his formal philosophy, the most convincing liberal of the middle period of the nineteenth century. What was evidently needed was a re-examination of the philosophy which supported the ideals of a liberal society and the function in it of a liberal government.

THE IDEALIST REVISION OF LIBERALISM

This revision of liberal theory was accomplished in the two decades following 1880 by the Oxford idealists of whom Thomas Hill Green was the most important representative, at least in political philosophy. In the United States there was an analogous and related movement in philosophy of which Josiah Royce was the best known representative; the pragmatism of John Dewey was a later development from idealism which carried on its liberalism but rejected its metaphysics. With the exception of Dewey this loosely related group of thinkers was usually described as neo-Hegelian, though no very exact meaning ever attached to this description. Certainly none of them ever regarded the dialectic as an exact instrument of logical analysis, as Hegel and after him Marx imagined it to be, and none of them accepted the authoritarian strain in Hegel's political theory. If some leaned toward conservatism, as contrasted with liberalism, it was still a conservatism that had no misgivings about representative political institutions, and the most radical of them were quite without any leaning toward a theory of class antagonism like Marx's. What related their social philosophy to that of Hegel was chiefly the very general idea that human nature is fundamentally social. Oxford idealism was the culmination of the vague body of intellectual influences that came from outside the British empirical tradition, chiefly from post-Kantian German philosophy, and that had been associated with the names of Coleridge and Carlyle. But there was one important difference. This earlier idealism, because it was largely a criticism of industrialism and its social effects, had never been liberal in its political outlook. What Green accomplished, then, might be described as a twofold reversal of position. On the one hand he captured for liberalism a movement of thought which was to dominate Anglo-American philosophy for a full generation at the turn of the century. On the other hand he revised liberalism to meet the valid objection that, as a one-sided statement of class interests, it had stood for a conception of liberty which, in fact if not in intention, amounted to a reckless disregard for social stability and security. To a considerable degree this revision had only to make coherent and explicit the qualifications by which Mill had in effect explained away the individualism and the egoism of Bentham's form of liberalism.

The principal purpose of idealism was to reconstruct a system of philosophy, while the purpose of directing a political movement was incidental. Looked at after the event it is easy to see that its main achievement in philosophy was critical.[8] It released British thought once and for all from what had become a burdensome tradition: the associational psychology and its supposed implications for logic, and in ethics the pleasure-pain theory of

[8] In this sense the books of critical historical importance produced by Oxford idealists were a long and tedious Introduction that Green wrote for his edition of Hume's *Treatise* (1874), his *Prolegomena to Ethics* (1883), F. H. Bradley's *Ethical Studies* (1876), and the chapters of criticism in his *Principles of Logic* (1883). Better known and on the whole more characteristic works such as Bradley's *Appearance and Reality* (1893) and Bernard Bosanquet's *Principle of Individuality and Value* (1912) were metaphysical constructions based on the criticism.

motivation and value with its individualist implications for social philosophy. With respect to the latter the idealists developed and made coherent the criticism of individualism that began with Rousseau's theory of the general will, and that they found still further elaborated in Hegel's theory of freedom. The fundamental philosophical problems of idealism, therefore, were the nature of personality, the nature of the social community, and the relationship between the two. Its purpose was to show that personality is "realized" by finding a significant part to play in the life of society. Its problems were conceived in terms of logical analysis and metaphysical construction, which was responsible for some of the strength and a good deal of the weakness of idealism. On the one hand it was a fairly effective critic of a form of mechanistic dogmatism that was commoner in science fifty years ago than it is now. On the other hand the idealist argument moved on a high level of abstraction that often prevented it from exerting its due influence either on scientists or on persons primarily engaged in politics. Idealism tended always to be an academic philosophy and to be stated in a cumbersome, Germanized terminology that kept it esoteric. Nevertheless its central problem — the mutual dependence between the structure of personality and the cultural structure of its social *milieu* — was one that has steadily increased in importance over the whole range of social studies. Idealism was the agency through which this problem emerged into social psychology and impinged upon a more concrete conception of a liberal society.

There were special circumstances that make the study of T. H. Green's philosophy difficult. He died relatively young and the only books which he completed and published hardly mention any political or concrete social question. His *Lectures on the Principles of Political Obligation* was put together and edited after his death from his notes and from those of his students. Moreover, Green's own experience was in the main academic, though he was concerned throughout his life with the improvement of secondary education. He had at first hand almost no acquaintance with the social problems created by industrialization, though he had been able to observe something of its indirect effects on agricultural labor, and his remarks upon them are always a little remote. Green's direct influence, therefore, was measured almost wholly by the effect of his teaching upon his students, and while this was very great it could hardly be inferred from his published writings. At its root lay a strong sense of the moral injustice of a society that withheld from large portions of its members the goods, partly material but chiefly spiritual, which the culture of that society created. As Green once said, the " underfed denizen of a London yard " has hardly more share in the civilization of England than a slave had in that of Athens. In some measure this feeling was like that which actuated Mill's rejection of a competitive economy but it was also different. There was in Green's ethics, and in idealism generally, a religious element that had no counterpart in utilitarianism, and also Green did not think of the deprivation as primarily economic. Abject poverty, he felt, is likely to entail some measure of moral degradation. Full moral participation in a social life was for Green the highest form of self-development, and to create the possibility of such participation was the end of a liberal society. The source of this conviction with Green was not Hegel. It represented on the one hand his understanding of Christian brotherhood and on the other hand a liberalized conception of Greek citizenship, not reserved as in Aristotle for a privileged few but made available to all men. Accordingly for Green politics was essentially an agency for creating social conditions that make moral development possible.

> We content ourselves with enacting that no man shall be used by other men as a means against his will, but we leave it to be pretty much a matter of chance whether or no he shall be qualified to fulfil any social function, to contribute anything to the common good, and to do so freely.[9]

The most concrete statement of his liberalism that Green ever made was in a lecture which he delivered in 1880 entitled " Liberal Legislation and Freedom of Contract." [10] The lecture was occasioned by Gladstone's proposal to regulate contracts between Irish tenants and landlords. This plan posed a question which, as Green said, had arisen repeatedly in respect to liberal legislation: it purported to be liberal and yet it abridged the right of contract. Earlier liberal policy had in general followed the rule

[9] *Political Obligation,* Section 155.

[10] *Works,* Vol. III, p. 365.

that freedom of contract ought, for the purpose of diminishing legal restraint, to be extended as far as was compatible with public order and security. Is liberalism then inconsistent in pursuing opposite policies in different cases? The question clearly must be answered in the affirmative if the position taken by Bentham is correct, namely, that all legislation is intrinsically a restriction of freedom and that freedom is always greater where a relationship is not regulated by law but is left to voluntary agreement between the parties. But as Green said, Bentham's position tacitly assumed that law is the only restriction on liberty, and this is not true unless freedom is arbitrarily identified by definition with the absence of legal restraint. Against this conception, which Green called "negative freedom," he set up a "positive" definition: liberty is "a positive power or capacity of doing or enjoying something worth doing or enjoying." Freedom must therefore imply not merely a legal but an actual possibility, in view of existing circumstances, of developing human capacities, a genuinely increased power on the part of an individual to share in the goods which a society has produced and an enlarged ability to contribute to the common good. Freedom of contract may be a means to this end and, if so, is a good, but it is not an end in itself. It may, for example, in cases where the bargaining power of employer and employee is grossly unequal, merely reduce the general practice in a trade to that of the least scrupulous employers. The freedom of an Irish tenant to contract with the owner of his land becomes a mere formality when eviction means starvation. In such cases the actual coercion which an employer or a landlord can exert under the legal form of a contract is in fact, Green argued, far more oppressive and far more destructive of effective freedom than the legal coercion exerted by the state when it abridges the right of contract to protect the weaker party. The choice of the latter course is not, Green argued, a reversal of liberal policy. For the law has always recognized that some contracts are subversive of the general good and hence are to be prevented as contrary to public policy, and there is nothing illiberal in putting other contracts into this category if they too jeopardize general interests such as public health or a respectable standard of public education.

Green's argument in this lecture was an effective analysis, on a limited scale, of liberal purposes in legislation. It brought out the fact that liberal theory in the past had been largely *ad hoc,* controlled by the purpose of repealing obsolete legislation, and it argued cogently that liberalism could not be placed permanently on so narrow a foundation. Liberal policies have to be flexible to meet changes of circumstance and if they are genuinely liberal they have always to follow the guidance of moral purposes. They are essentially an effort to open a humane way of living to a larger number of persons. Consequently, he inferred, at the center of a liberal philosophy is the idea of a general good or common human well-being which is capable of being shared by everyone and which provides a standard for legislation. This standard cannot be individual liberty alone, or the least possible legal restriction of free choice, because free choice has always to be exercised in a situation, and some situations are such that they reduce choice to a mockery. Choice means opportunity, and opportunity means a society that is not coercive beyond need either in its legal and political structure or in its economic and social structure. Freedom is really a social as much as it is an individual conception; it refers at once to a quality of society and a quality of the persons that make up a society. Hence it is impossible that a government should be liberal merely by standing aside and refraining from legislation, or that a liberal society should come into being merely, so to speak, by political inadvertence. The function of a liberal government is to support the existence of a free society, and while government cannot make people moral by law, it can remove many of the obstacles that may stand in the way of their moral development. Green's ethics and political philosophy were an elaboration and reinforcement of these ideas, which his Lecture on Liberal Legislation applied to the specific case in hand.

The central principle of Green's ethics was the mutuality of the relationship between the individual and the social community of which he is a member. As he put it, "the self is a social self." By this he meant, much as Aristotle might, that the highest form of community is one in which equal is associated with equal and in which the bond that holds the community together is the loyalty of the members for the group and its purposes. At the same time to be a member of such a group, to share its work and have a significant part to play in it, is both the condition of achieving a well-rounded personality and also the highest satisfaction that a human being can gain. Within limits, Green believed, any social group is of this sort. Even the most powerful and the most despotic government cannot hold a society together by sheer force; to that extent there was a limited truth in the old belief that governments are produced by consent. Government, Green said, depends on will and not on force, because the tie that binds a human being to society is the compulsion of his own nature and not the penalties of the law or the calculation of ulterior advantages. The unanswerable argument for a liberal society is that it recognizes this fundamental social impulse in human nature, which is at the same time a moral impulse, and tries to give it realization in a form adequate to the full ideal meaning of morality. This ideal requires that the members of a society meet as moral equals, that they treat each other with respect, that all are free to think and act for themselves, and that their thought and actions are guided and controlled by full moral responsibility. For this reason coercion ought to be reduced to a minimum, and this is no truer of coercion exerted by the state than of any other form of coercion which has the effect of making persons less than free moral agents. For Green as for Kant a community of persons is a "Kingdom of ends" in which everyone is treated as an end and not merely as a means. Because this is inherently the ideal nature of a community and of a person, the opportunity ought to be open to everyone to realize such a life up to the limit of his capacities. Hence a really liberal society cannot aim at less than to give to all men the right to moral self-determination and to the moral dignity which is at once the condition and the due of personality.

Green developed this conception chiefly in his analysis of right. A right, he argued, has always two elements. It is in the first place a claim to freedom of action which is in substance the assertion of an individual's impulse to realize his own inner powers and capabilities. A hedonist psychology, he argued, is fundamentally false because human nature is a mass of desires and tendencies to actions which are directed not toward pleasure in general but toward concrete satisfactions. The claim, however, is never morally justified merely by the desire, but only by rationalized desire, which takes account of the claims of other persons. What justifies it is the fact that the general good itself allows of such freedom of action. It is a claim to participate and contribute. In consequence the second element in a right is a general social recognition that the claim is warranted, that the individual's freedom really does contribute to the general good. A moral community from Green's point of view, therefore, is one in which the individual responsibly limits his claims to freedom in the light of general social interests and in which the community itself supports his claims because the general well-being can be realized only through his initiative and freedom. Ideally it is, as Rousseau said, " a form of association which will defend and protect with the whole common force the person and goods of each associate, and in which each, while uniting himself with all, may still obey himself alone." There is, therefore, a general social good or welfare which is the criterion of the individual's rights and duties — what Plato called the " health " of the community — but it is neither distinct from nor opposed to the happiness of the individual, because it is one in which the individual can share and because the participation is itself a significant part of the individual's happiness. The fundamentally liberal element in Green's ethics consisted in his refusal to contemplate a social good which demanded merely self-sacrifice or self-abnegation on the part of the persons who share and support it. The obligation and the right of the community matches the right and the obligation of its members. Green's meaning was well stated by Leonard Hobhouse, in a book designed to refute what Hobhouse regarded as the illiberal, or Hegelian, tendency to lift society or the state above the interests of its members which he attributed to Bernard Bosanquet, Green's most distinguished student.

> The happiness and misery of society is the happiness and misery of human beings heightened or deepened by its sense of common possession. Its will is their wills in the conjoint result. Its conscience is an expression of what is noble or ignoble in them when the balance is struck. If we may judge each man by the contribution he makes to the community, we are equally right to ask of the community what it is doing for this man. The greatest happiness will not be realized by the greatest or any great number unless in a form in which all can share, in which indeed the sharing is for each an essential ingredient. But there is no happi-

> ness at all except that experienced by individual men and women, and there is no common self submerging the soul of men. There are societies in which their distinct and separate personalities may develop in harmony and contribute to a collective achievement.[11]

This mutual interdependence of individual claim and social recognition was with Green an ethical and not a juristic conception. He explicitly rejected Bentham's definition of rights as "the creatures of law." The reason for this lay in Green's conviction that a liberal government is impossible except in a society where legislation and public policy are continuously responsive to a public opinion which is at once enlightened and morally sensitive. This was the truth which, he believed, was contained in the theory of natural law; it held up to the law an ideal of justice and equity and humanity to which it ought to approximate. By this he did not mean that law can try to make men moral, because morality, being mainly a matter of character, cannot be produced by legal coercion. Law necessarily deals with the externals of conduct and not with the spirit and the intention behind it. Yet in order that government may be truly liberal there must, Green believed, be a continuous reciprocity between law and morals. This interchange is twofold. On the one hand the rights and obligations that are actually enforced by law are never up to the level of what would be possible. The moral judgment of society is the indispensable means of holding government up to the best that it might accomplish. On the other hand, though the state cannot make men moral, it can do much to create social conditions in which they are able to develop a responsible moral character for themselves. At the very least it can remove many hindrances to such development, as it does, for example, by recognizing that children have a right to education. Governments that profess to be liberal have in fact, Green argued, fallen far short of what they ought to undertake in this respect. The moral obligation of the state to create opportunity is not diminished because men cannot be compelled to make the best use of opportunity, and it is both idle and cruel to hold men to a moral standard that they have no opportunity to meet. The most characteristic element in Green's liberalism was his belief

[11] *The Metaphysical Theory of the State* (1918), p. 133.

in the reality of a social conscience which both regulates law and is supported by law. This was the meaning which he attached to Rousseau's general will. But he argued that Rousseau was merely confused when he tried to find out where in a society the general will is located. Moral judgment cannot in the nature of the case be located anywhere, because no man and no social institution is infallible. Every man must follow his intelligence and his conscience, and a liberal society is one which both respects his right to judge and also enhances the probability that his judgments will be socially trustworthy.

This moral freedom, which Green conceived to arise from the metaphysical nature of the self or personality, was for him the foundation of political liberalism. It is meaningless to inquire in general, he argued, why a human being is subject to rules created by social institutions or why as a member of society he has rights. His liberties and his obligations are two sides of the same social relationship which gives him at once the duties of his place in the social structure and provides him with a personality that can be invested with rights. A human society, therefore, is a complex of institutions within which human beings live their personal lives, and their personalities consist largely in the sharing and participation which such membership implies. The part to be played by government in this social complex is that of regulation and control in the light of this ideal of free participation. A liberal government aims at minimizing coercion, but coercion is of many kinds and can depend on many circumstances. In general any situation is coercive when it frustrates the spontaneous self-expression of native capacities and substitutes compulsion for moral self-control. The justification of legal coercion is precisely that it offsets and neutralizes other forms of coercion which are less tolerable. The right to freedom of judgment and action Green extended to all men, without distinctions of rank or wealth, in so far as they rise to the acceptance of social responsibility, and he believed that all men do rise more or less to this level in so far as they are given the opportunity to share in the moral culture provided by civilization. Hence he regarded education as the most important social function, and he conceived that the chief difference between ancient and modern civilizations lay in the degree in which the modern nation opens to all men goods which in antiquity were reserved to an aristocracy. For the present, Green thought, the nation is probably the largest unit that has the social cohesiveness needed to make the idea of a common good effective, but he was convinced that states ought to direct their policy with due regard for the general human welfare. War, he argued, can never occur without moral fault somewhere, and while it may sometimes be unavoidable, it is always a confession of moral failure.

LIBERALISM, CONSERVATISM, SOCIALISM

Green's restatement of liberalism did away with the rigid line between economics and politics by which the older liberals had excluded the state from interfering with the operation of a free market. From Green's point of view even a free market was a social institution rather than a natural condition, and quite possibly it might require legislation to keep it free. The political and the economic, instead of being distinct areas, are interlaced institutions which are certainly not independent of one another and which ought ideally both to contribute to the ethical purposes of a liberal society. In political theory this change implied a radical departure from the attitude toward the state and legislation which had been characteristic of liberalism. Liberalism had always looked with suspicion on the state and had kept its activities within narrow limits, whether by a rigid list of constitutional guaranties or by the assumption that legislation is likely to be an undesirable " interference " with freedom. Green's liberalism, on the contrary, was a frank acceptance of the state as a positive agency to be used at any point where legislation could be shown to contribute to " positive freedom," in short, for any purpose that added to the general welfare without creating worse evils than it removed. It is true that Green himself, and indeed the whole generation of liberals to which he belonged, made no sudden shift of attitude to conform with their change of theory. They remained even nervously fearful of " paternalism " and the undermining of individual responsibility by social legislation. But from Green's point of view this issue no longer implied a difference of principle but became one merely of fact and of the probable effects of legislation. The major purpose of his revision was to force the state into lines of legislation from which it had previously abstained on principles avowedly liberal. Thus Green himself was convinced that the state must go further than it had in financing public education and making it compulsory, though in this area almost no liberal except Spencer had stood on a platform of *laissez faire.* He was convinced also of the need for an extension of sanitary regulation in the interest of public health, of standards of housing in the interest of decent living conditions, and of control over labor contracts. And since he argued in general that all rights of private property can be defended only if they contribute to the common good, his theory opened up very wide possibilities of legislative regulation. To be sure, he believed that no great change in property rights was needed, because he argued, rather vaguely, that the growth of large-scale capitalism does not interfere with a parallel growth of small-scale capitalism. But this too was a question of fact, and if he had been convinced that he was mistaken, he could have altered his belief quite logically.

This quality of Green's liberalism tended to obscure or to blur any sharp lines of distinction between alternative political theories, as long as they were not incompatible with his ethical conception of a liberal society. Or to put the case a little differently, Green's liberalism ceased to imply any single and invariable line of political and legislative policy and implied rather a combination of different lines of policy to safeguard a variety of social interests all accepted as contributing to the general welfare. Thus the differences between liberalism and conservatism, or even between liberalism and a liberal form of socialism, cease to be matters of principle. Green's social philosophy, like Mill's, might be described as an enlarged and idealized form of utilitarianism. In one sense this change was not contrary to the general temper and bias of liberalism, but was merely an enlargement of the concept of the greatest happiness. In point of fact, however, Green really appropriated for liberalism a body of social values and policies which in the tradition of English politics had characteristically belonged to conservatism. It was this which caused some of his contemporaries, Mark Pattison for example, to regard his political philosophy as merely confused. The conservatism of Disraeli, derived substantially from Burke, had publicized itself as the protector of stability and security against too rapid and too drastic change, the principal cause of change being the expansion of trade and industry which was a typical policy of liberalism. The revision that Green made in liberal theory amounted in part to an insistence that stability and security are themselves important elements of general welfare and are necessary conditions of liberty. Green's philosophy attempted to state a moral platform so broad that all men of social good will could stand on it, and in a measure he succeeded. Its purpose was to transform liberalism from the social philosophy of a single set of interests seen from the point of view of a particular class into one which could claim to take account of all important interests seen from the point of view of the general good of the national community.

Obviously, however, this purpose could not be wholly successful. The generality, not to say the vagueness, of Green's ethical terms, was such that it did not obviate differences in view even among younger men all of whom considered themselves to be in substantial agreement with him. Idealist political theory was capable of two constructions, the one more authoritarian or possibly more conservative, the other more definitely liberal. To a considerable extent the difference depended upon the closeness with which Green's philosophy was regarded as following Hegel. The Hegelian elements in Green's philosophy were selected and emphasized, in part with the purpose of correcting Green, by his most distinguished student, Bernard Bosanquet, in *The Philosophical Theory of the State* (1899). Under the stress of the First World War this book was subjected to a drastic criticism by Leonard Hobhouse, himself strongly under Green's influence, in his *Metaphysical Theory of the State* (1918). In substance what Hobhouse did, under the stimulus of the War, was to throw into relief some of the anti-liberal implications of Hegelianism that English and American Hegelians had considered to be of only passing importance. The issues between Bosanquet and Hobhouse turned chiefly upon two points, both obscure in Green: the ethical relationship between the individual and the community and the relation of society to the state.

Green's assertion that the self is a social self was indeed an important statement as long as anyone was inclined to neglect it, but once it was admitted the question still remained, what exactly did it mean and in particular what did it imply in cases where an individual came into conflict with accepted social beliefs or practices. Bosanquet, like Hegel and unlike Green, attached little value to the social criticism of the moral dissenter but assumed that changes in institutions take place by "the inherent logic of social growth." Accordingly, as Hegel had identified individual inclinations with "caprice," so Bosanquet tended to identify them with "ordinary trivial moods" and the "narrow, arbitrary, contradictory will." And as Rousseau sometimes represented the general will as that which "gave men's actions the morality they had formerly lacked," so Bosanquet ascribed to society a "real will" with which the individual's will would be identical if he were fully moralized and fully intelligent. Taken literally this would amount in practice to the assumption that society is always right and the individual is always wrong, or to the practical conclusion that private conscience ought merely to conform and be submissive to authority. Some such view was in fact implied if not asserted when F. H. Bradley said in his chapter on "My Station and its Duties":

> We should consider whether the encouraging oneself in having opinions of one's own, in the sense of thinking differently from the world on moral subjects, be not, in any person other than a heaven-born prophet, sheer self-conceit.[12]

A conclusion of this kind is consistent with much of Hegel but certainly not with Green, who always regarded the give and take between private judgment and social institutions as mutual. Social pressure of course, as Bosanquet argued, continually holds individuals up to higher standards of conduct than they would achieve if left to themselves, but it is equally true that personal ideals constantly hold law and government up to standards that they would not achieve without criticism A political philosophy which denied the second of these two statements would certainly be very defectively liberal, for without it free thought and free speech would largely lose their political significance.

The introduction into English usage of the word "state," overtly as a technical term, with connotations drawn from Hegel, was uniformly unfortunate. Before the idealists no English political thinker had used the word in any special sense or indeed

[12] *Ethical Studies* (1876), 2nd ed., p. 200.

had made any common use of it at all. Nor for that matter did the idealists give it any exact meaning; in Green, and still more in Bosanquet, it was a source of constant confusion not only in terminology but also in thought. Sometimes it meant government, sometimes it meant nation, sometimes it meant society — all vague words but certainly not interchangeable — and sometimes it meant an ideal entity which, like Rousseau's general will, is " always right " but which cannot be identified with anything on earth. This last meaning in particular, when combined with the others, had the effect of investing some institution with a moral dignity and authority to which it need have no claim, and it was this which Hobhouse attacked as a " metaphysical " use, or misuse, of the word. He showed that it might be used to justify either political regimentation or long established social stratification, and in either case it would contravene the spirit of liberalism. In another work Hobhouse argued that one mark of a liberal society is that the claim of every man to a morally significant place in the community is admitted to rest on justice and not on charity and that in consequence there is a broad moral distinction between liberalism and philanthropy.[13]

Though Green's liberalism might thus be bent toward conservatism, it was consistent also with a liberal form of socialism, provided the latter did not depend on a theory of class antagonism. No sharp difference of principle separated Green's liberalism from the socialism of the group of young men who organized the Fabian Society in 1884. This does not appear to have been due to a direct influence of Green's teaching upon the Fabians, or indeed to the influence of abstract philosophical theories of any kind. Both Green and the Fabians reflected, probably independently, an important change in the climate of British political opinion, namely, a loss of confidence in the alleged social efficiency of private enterprise and an increased willingness to use the state's legislative and administrative power to correct its abuses and to humanize it. Like Green the Fabians defended their program as an extension of liberalism. In the *Fabian Essays* (1889) Sidney Webb asserted that, " The economic side of the democratic ideal is, in fact, socialism itself," and Sydney Olivier

[13] *Liberalism* (1911), ch. 8.

said that "Socialism is merely individualism rationalized"; its morality "is only the expression of the eternal passion of life seeking its satisfaction through the striving of each individual for the freest and fullest activity." Socialism is not the suppression but the realization of personality and individuality. Indeed, it would not be difficult to represent Fabian socialism as an effort to implement Green's "positive freedom" on the basis of a much wider knowledge of economics and of industrial and political administration than Green possessed. And while the Fabians proposed to go much farther than Green in the direction of nationalizing basic industries and controlling production and distribution, they based their plans, as Green did, on the observed bad effects of leaving the economy uncontrolled, and not like Marx on the dialectic of economic development and the inevitability of the class struggle. Fabian economics was for the most part not Marxian but an extension of the theory of economic rent to the accumulation of capital, on lines already suggested by Henry George. Fabian policy was based on the justice and the desirability of recapturing unearned increment for social purposes. These purposes depended on the conviction, essentially similar to Green's, that liberty is impossible without a reasonable degree of security and that in consequence social security and stability are as much an object of political policy as liberty. Accordingly, the socialist principles for the reorganized British Labor Party, stated in Sidney Webb's *Labor and the New Social Order* (1918), took the form of national minima — of leisure, health, education, and subsistence — below which it was contrary to public policy that any large proportion of the population should fall. This purpose has continued to be defended as an extension of liberty. In 1942 the Party Executive reaffirmed its confidence that a planned society can be "a far more free society" than a competitive one, because it can "offer those who work in it the sense, on the one hand, of continuous opportunity for the expression of capacity, and the power, on the other, to share fully in the making of the rules under which they work."

THE PRESENT MEANING OF LIBERALISM

An estimate of the meaning of liberalism and its present position in political theory must take account of the fact that the word is used, with some consistency, in two contrasted senses. On the one hand it may be identified almost by definition as the social philosophy of the industrial middle class and hence as nearly equivalent to *laissez faire* or economic imperialism. In general this meaning corresponds more nearly to Continental than to English or American usage, and it is the meaning characteristically adopted by Marxian or fascist critics of liberalism. On the other hand liberalism may be understood, with good historical justification, as the present-day culmination of the whole "Western political tradition" and as "the secular form of Western civilization."[14] In this broad sense liberalism would be practically identical in meaning with what, in popular political usage, is more likely now-a-days to be called "democracy." It would take for granted not only political and civil liberty but also opportunity and a considerable measure of social and economic security for the whole population. The principal thesis of such a philosophy is that all these purposes fall within the conception of the general good or the total social welfare, which ought to be the object of public policy, and that such a conception can measurably be agreed upon despite diversity of interests. If liberalism is understood in this sense, it cannot be described as the ideology of a social class, unless indeed its purpose is dogmatically declared to be impossible and its profession to be hypocritical. Marxists commonly take some such position, which really brings discussion to an *impasse*. It has been largely the purpose of the present chapter to show that the identification of liberalism with *laissez faire* or the description of it as merely the social philosophy of the middle class has a very limited historical justification. Measurably it was true for the earlier period of liberalism, roughly the first two thirds or three quarters of the nineteenth century. During that period liberalism was largely a movement to make the political power of the industrial and commercial middle class correspond to its economic and social importance, and its theory conceived the functions of government from the point of view of persons whose freedom of action was more likely to be hampered than helped by legislation. In spite of the enormously valuable effects of Bentham's

[14] This is the theme of Frederick M. Watkins' *The Political Tradition of the West: A Study in the Development of Modern Liberalism,* 1948.

jurisprudence, the political theory of early liberalism tended to be doctrinaire and its policy reckless. Its theory was doctrinaire precisely because liberal economists did in fact, though not in intention, rationalize a limited class interest as a total social interest and imputed a spurious generality to concepts that had in fact a limited and temporary applicability. Its policy was reckless because it took for granted an unlimited backlog of social security and stability, without which political liberty is impossible, and overlooked the disintegrating effects of the new industrial technology.[15] It could do this only because it was so largely the philosophy of persons for whom security was no problem and who lacked the imagination to appreciate the position of persons for whom it was the primary problem. The point of greatest historical importance, however, is that this state of affairs was temporary and that the liberalism which corresponded to the stereotype began to evaporate with its success. From John Stuart Mill on no important liberal thinker except Herbert Spencer held a theory of the relation between economics and government that could be at all accurately described as *laissez faire* or assigned to the state functions so largely negative as were in general assumed by Bentham's jurisprudence.

This development of liberal thought was neither accidental nor incidental. It was not accidental because behind it were two powerful causes that have already been mentioned: the reaction against *laissez faire* of a public opinion that included many diverse stripes of ideology and the rise to political influence of labor unions with an ideology of their own. Political liberalism had to assume the rôle of conciliator or resign leadership. Its choice of conciliation was not incidental, at least in England, because its success in evolving into a national movement was precisely its outstanding historical characteristic. This may have been anomalous from the point of view of Marxism, since it might have been thought that in the most highly industrialized country in the world, where industrialists had achieved a degree of power not matched anywhere else, exploitation would have been the order of the day and the class struggle would have been correspondingly intensified. Yet the direction in which liberal

[15] Cf. Karl Mannheim, "The Crisis in Valuation" in *Diagnosis of Our Time,* 1944.

thought developed was toward inclusiveness, toward the appreciation of social interests other than those for which it had spoken, toward a more sympathetic and humane ideal of the relations between classes, toward a mitigation of the brutalities of unregulated industrialism, and in consequence toward a more positive conception of the function of a liberal state in a liberal society. This development was due neither to political opportunism nor to unclearness of thought. It was not intellectual confusion that caused Mill and Green to think of themselves as liberals. The later form of liberalism in important respects was continuous with its early form. Neither the greatest happiness of the greatest number nor utility needed to have the limitations that Bentham and the classical economists tacitly put upon their connotations, any more than the rights of man had to be, as Marx said, the rights of the middle class. Even when it was most definitely a middle-class philosophy, liberalism had always claimed to stand for the greatest social good and, except in its economic theory of distribution, it had not conceived of society in terms of permanently antagonistic social classes. Rather it had supposed that classes would tend to disappear with the abolition of political privilege. Bentham had argued as strongly as Mill and Green, and on the whole more effectively, that jurisprudence is essentially a criticism of the working of the law in terms of a moral standard. And Green, in spite of his criticism of the individualism of early liberalism, was as far as Bentham from a really collectivist or "organismic" theory of either society or the state. Whatever values society achieves must from Green's point of view accrue to individuals in terms of a more satisfying experience and a higher development of character. The differences between the liberalism of Bentham and that of Mill and Green, important as they were, did not amount to a solution of continuity. The later liberals corrected, enlarged, and made explicit, but they did not reverse the meaning of liberalism.

At all stages of its development quite as much as with Bentham the center of liberalism remained a "greatest happiness principle." The later liberals added that the greatest good must be also a common good. The addition embodied an insight that emerged as liberalism developed. As theory and as political practice liberalism depended on the supposition, first, that a sense of the public good or the general welfare is an effective motive in politics and, second, that the concept of such a good can be a matter of reasonably general agreement. Behind any liberal government there must be a society sufficiently cohesive so that a consciousness of the good of the community overlaps in the minds of its members the diversities of interest, of social position, or of economic class that tend to divide them. The will to keep the whole community together and to make it operate effectively and without too much friction does not extinguish differences of interest or party but it does hold them within limits. The forces operate, so to speak, within the rules of the game, which is the practical meaning of Green's aphorism that a community depends not on force but on will. From this it follows that the primary obligation of a liberal government is to protect all essential interests and that its primary function is to maintain the conditions or the agencies by which conflicts of interest can be adjusted with as little coercion as possible. It follows also that political parties cannot regard themselves simply as the exponents of an interest or a class, for parties in a liberal government are largely agencies to effect the compromises by which a conciliation of interests takes place. Liberalism is the antithesis of the Marxian theory that politics can only reflect an irreconcilable class struggle which must lead to the dominance of one class and the exploitation of the others. Political liberalism is manifestly impossible unless political issues and political parties are not divided strictly on lines of social class or of economic advantage and unless, when the lines are so drawn, the conflicts are mitigated and kept within limits. As a political movement liberalism succeeded because these assumptions were in general true in English politics. Obviously, also, they were true in part precisely because these ideals permeated all English parties and set standards of political ethics. Quite possibly the dependence of liberal government on a strong sense of common interest may mean in practice that liberalism is a political ideal of limited applicability, though neither Mill nor Green was perhaps aware of this. The required solidarity has never existed in a unit larger than a nation and often not there. Whether it can exist in larger units and whether it can be brought into being where it does not exist are the unsolved problems of liberalism.

The evolution of liberal theory might from one point of view be described as a progressive realization of the dependence of politics on the intangibles, or perhaps as a progressive transference of liberal concepts out of the field of political organization into the less definite field of moral ideas and social influences. This was in part a recognition, induced by political experience, of the difficulty of giving effect to any liberal ideal, and in part a recognition that the common good itself is no simple formula but a workable adjustment of many diverse and often conflicting interests. In essence it is a matter of human relations and not of political formulas. This tendency in liberal thought was illustrated by the astonishment with which in his later life John Stuart Mill looked back upon his father's simple trust in the apparatus of representation and in the inherent "reasonableness" of human behavior in voting. It was illustrated also in the evolution of the conception of freedom and the problem of giving constitutional protection to freedom. The faith that a few inalienable and unchangeable natural rights could be preserved forever by listing them in bills of constitutional guaranties had already been abandoned by Bentham, who pointed out the fallacy of supposing that a weak government is *ipso facto* liberal. Green however rightly saw that Bentham's predilection for efficiency did not necessarily imply any respect whatever on the part of government for citizens' rights. He therefore regarded his own philosophy as reaffirming in some sense a theory of natural law. But he had no notion whatever of going back to natural rights as these were understood in the seventeenth-century systems of rationalism. His own idea of positive freedom — the capacity of doing something worth doing — was as he himself saw largely formal, since what is regarded as worth doing must always depend on the concrete opportunities and possibilities of achievement that can be opened to human beings. If Green reinstated natural law, it was what has since been called "natural law with variable content."

Green's reaffirmation of natural law meant for him not a distinction between two kinds of law but what can perhaps be described as the "naturalness" of law — its importance as part of the social structure of a community and its intimate relationship with morals. Unlike Bentham he could not regard law as merely a clever matching of behavior with pleasures contrived by an expert legislator, and similarly he could not regard the distinction between law and morals as principally consisting in the kind of penalties by which each is "sanctioned." The distinction is one rather between two sets of social institutions that mutually support one another but are fundamentally different. There is a structure of character, of moral intention and socialized attitude, which is a part of educated and civilized human nature, and there is a structure of settled and fixed patterns of behavior that can be enforced and that prescribes limits to individual choice. Both are involved in what Green called positive freedom but neither can be a substitute for the other. Freedom is possible only if there are at once areas of choice and free decision and also definite understandings and expectations that put limits to those areas. The validity of each of these — the area of individual judgment and that of legal necessity — depends on their being at any given time reasonably distinct and on a kind of tacit agreement that the one will not trespass on the other. For a theory of liberal politics there were two important implications. On the one hand government has to operate within definite legal or constitutional limits. It is this which distinguishes executive discretion within the law from dictation and arbitrary power, and so makes it possible to say that government rests on will and not on force. On the other hand wide ranges of social behavior have to be left to individual judgment, free decision, and voluntary association. A liberal government cannot even contemplate a policy of universal regimentation which would bring legal coercion and political organization into all the private arrangements of individual and social life. The lines cannot be drawn once for all but there must always be a line. The ultimate support for the constitutional guaranties is, as Mill said, a public conscience that sincerely believes privacy and individuality and personal responsibility to be valuable.

Implicit, therefore, in the evolution of liberal thought about the social foundations of government was the recognition of another fundamental principle which in Green was perhaps assumed rather than clearly stated. A liberal government depends not only on a community imbued with a sense of its common good but also upon a community which permits within it a wide range of lesser communities that are largely autonomous and self-directing within a framework of legal rights and duties imposed by the state in the interest of the whole community. In this sense the antithesis of liberalism is totalitarianism, the regimentation under government of all associations such as churches or labor unions. A liberal government is one that respects the rights of communities as well as the rights of individuals. Indeed the two are not distinct, for the rights of individuals as they are concretely exercised very largely are rights of free association, and individual liberty very largely is the right of membership in groups that can responsibly make their own rules in performing significant social functions. The word personality never quite lost the connotation of its origin: *persona,* the actor who plays a variety of rôles, and the insight of idealist ethics, that self-realization involves finding " my station and its duties," was a recognition of the fact that personality means neither isolation nor eccentricity but participation. It was for this reason that the ambiguous use of the word " state " in the idealist theory of liberalism, to which reference was made above, was so injurious. Liberal theory really required a clear distinction between society or the community on the one hand and the political or legal organization of society on the other. In truth Green usually made that distinction even though he sometimes obscured it by the way in which he used the word " state." He argued explicitly that in its historical development the state does not supersede social institutions, many of which are older than it, and that in general it does not make rights but recognizes and regulates them. A fuller recognition of the fact that " society " is really a collective name for a vast multiplicity of intricately connected associations and that human beings are normally members of many such associations came with the extension of sociological knowledge after Green's time. An adequate recognition of its ethical importance for political liberty came perhaps only as a result of the violence that totalitarian governments did to this property of social organization. A free society and one that can support free government must be what R. M. MacIver has called a "multi-group society."[16]

The liberal plan of free government and the liberal defense of its procedures, such as suffrage, representation, party organization, and party control of government follow naturally from and depend upon the liberal conception of a free society as one that has found a workable relationship between the common good and a multiplicity of private, sectional, and class interests. The procedures are the practical devices which experience and experiment have found efficacious in producing and giving effect to that meeting of minds about controversial questions upon which free government depends. They provide the apparatus through which discussion of opposing ideas, deliberation about contrary policies, and negotiation between conflicting interests can take place, and by which a reasonably general consensus can be approximated. The devices and the apparatus depend at every step upon the possibility of the consensus, for it is the belief that consensus is possible which creates the will to make the apparatus work, and it is the belief that a consensus has been sought that takes from its execution the sense of being merely coercive. But the apparatus is after all more than machinery, for it requires, if it is honestly used, pecular and difficult moral restraints. The system presumes on the part of government a fair recognition of the fact that it acts on a consensus which is practically never complete and hence that it is obligated, even in carrying out the will of a majority, to retain a decent respect for the minorities it does not represent. It must concede the right to organize and propagandize, and it must honestly try to avoid contaminating the sources of public information. The system requires of its parties a strategy which sincerely accepts the fact that their tenure of power ought not to be eternal and that they must use only limited and legitimate means to keep their opponents out of power. For this reason they must seek, within the limits of human frailty, the moral victory not only of tolerating opposition but of admitting that opposition is an essential function in government. And the system requires from those who

[16] *The Web of Government* (1947), pp. 421 ff. Cf. Pendleton Herring, *Politics of Democracy* (1940), pp. 427 ff.; George H. Sabine, "Beyond Ideology," *The Philosophical Review,* Vol. LVII (1948), pp. 1 ff.

work its apparatus a combination of intellectual honesty and partisanship, of inflexibility and willingness to compromise, of loyalty to principle and loyalty to a compromise agreed upon, which can be appreciated but not defined even by those who have lived long in its climate of opinion.

SELECTED BIBLIOGRAPHY

Political Thought in England from Herbert Spencer to the Present Day. By Ernest Barker. London, 1915.

Reflections on Government. By Ernest Barker. London, 1942.

The Political Ideas of the English Romanticists. By Crane Brinton. Oxford, 1926.

English Political Thought in the Nineteenth Century. By Crane Brinton. London, 1933.

"Thomas Hill Green, 1836–1882." In *Studies in Contemporary Biography.* By James Bryce. New York, 1903.

Morals and Politics: Theories of their Relation from Hobbes and Spinoza to Marx and Bosanquet. By E. F. Carritt. Oxford, 1935.

The Political Theory of Thomas Hill Green. By Y. L. Chin. New York, 1920.

Fabian Socialism. By G. D. H. Cole. London, 1943.

What is Liberty? A Study in Political Theory. By Dorothy Fosdick. New York, 1939.

The Neo-Idealist Political Theory: Its Continuity with the British Tradition. By Frederick P. Harris. New York, 1944.

The Social and Political Ideas of some Representative Thinkers of the Age of Reaction and Reconstruction. Ed. by F. J. C. Hearnshaw. London, 1932. Chs. 6, 7.

The Social and Political Ideas of some Representative Thinkers of the Victorian Age. Ed. by F. J. C. Hearnshaw. London, 1933. Ch. 7.

The Metaphysical Theory of the State. By Leonard T. Hobhouse. London, 1918.

Social Evolution and Political Theory. By Leonard T. Hobhouse. New York, 1911.

"Bernard Bosanquet's Philosophy of the State." By R. F. A. Hoernlé. In *Pol. Sci. Quarterly,* Vol. XXXIV (1919), p. 609.

The Victorian Critics of Democracy. By Benjamin E. Lippincott. Minneapolis, 1938.

England in the Eighteen-eighties: Towards a Social Basis for Freedom. By Helen M. Lynd. New York, 1945.

The Web of Government. By R. M. MacIver. New York, 1947.

The Service of the State: Four Lectures on the Political Teaching of T. H. Green. By J. H. Muirhead. London, 1908.

Carlyle and Mill: An Introduction to Victorian Thought. By Emery Neff. 2nd ed. rev. New York, 1926.

History of the Fabian Society. By Edward R. Pease. 2nd ed. London, 1925.

The Political Tradition of the West: A Study in the Development of Modern Liberalism. By Frederick M. Watkins. Cambridge, Mass., 1948.

States and Morals: A Study in Political Conflicts. By T. D. Weldon. London, 1946.

CHAPTER XXXIII

MARX AND DIALECTICAL MATERIALISM

Liberal political thought developed largely as an elaboration of two fundamental social or moral ideas, that politics is distinctively an art of reaching non-coercive adjustments between antagonistic interests and that democratic procedures are the only effective ways for making such adjustments. Consequently, though its later history undertook to take into account Hegel's valid critique of individualism, it never accepted the two major assumptions in Hegel's social philosophy. These were, first, that society is a moving balance of antithetical forces which generate social change by their tension and struggle, and second, that social history is an internal or quasi-logical evolution of the forces themselves. These elements of Hegel's thought, however, played a large part in the political theory of the nineteenth century and later. This was due in the main to the transformation of Hegel's philosophy effected by Karl Marx. Marx removed from Hegel's theory the assumption that nations are the effective units of social history — an assumption that never had any close logical relation to his system — and replaced the struggle of nations with the struggle of social classes. Thus he took away from Hegelianism its distinctive qualities as a political theory — its nationalism, its conservatism, and its counterrevolutionary character — and transformed it into a new and very powerful type of revolutionary radicalism. Marxism became the progenitor of the more important forms of party socialism in the nineteenth century and ultimately, with very important modifications to be sure, of present-day communism. In two respects, however, Marx's philosophy was continuous with Hegel's. He retained the dialectic as a method and by reinterpreting it as economic determinism he expanded into the modern concept of ideology Hegel's scattered suggestions about the dependence of thought on social position. The intrinsically anti-liberal implications of Hegel's point of view were largely submerged in Marx's radicalism. This was due partly to the fact that his career as an active revolutionist ended about 1850 and partly to a conviction, which he transmitted to most nineteenth-century Marxists, that socialism would be a continuation and not a reversal of political liberalism. Nevertheless the assumptions that economic forces are not amenable to legislative control and that social history is a record merely of class struggle were in principle incompatible with the belief that politics can effect peaceable adjustments of antagonistic interests. This latent opposition became fully explicit in the communist version of revolutionary Marxism.

THE PROLETARIAN REVOLUTION

Marx's social philosophy depended upon and first clearly brought into the focus of attention a social change of absolutely first-rate importance which occurred in the nineteenth century: the rise to political self-consciousness and finally to political power of an industrial working class. This, as was said in the preceding chapter, became responsible for changing the course of liberal thought, but Marx perceived its importance far sooner than the liberals. Especially in the historical studies which formed an integral part of his philosophy he presented capitalism for the first time in what might be called its human aspect, as an institution that had produced and was continually enlarging a class of men who must live wholly from wages and who were therefore related to their employers only by a cash-nexus. Their power to work is a commodity, the only economically valuable commodity they have, which must be sold in a competitive market where the only obligation of the purchaser is to pay the current price. The relationship of employer and employee in industry tends thus to be stripped of human significance and of moral obligation and becomes simply one of power. Marx rightly saw in this situation potentially the most revolutionary fact in modern history — on the one hand a class defined by its ownership of the means of production and motivated chiefly by the necessity of creating profits, on the other an industrial proletariat having no power except through the pressure of well-organized masses and obliged to set as its end not political liberty but the maintenance or improvement of its standard of living. Understanding this as an historical fact, Marx was aware of capitalism as an institution, not the result of timeless economic laws but a phase in the evolution of modern society. Starting therefore from the fact of divergent class interests, already made abundantly clear by the classical economists, he set himself both to interpret political liberalism as the ideology characteristic of the middle class and also to create a social philosophy for the rising proletariat, suitable for its use in the struggle for power.

The purpose of Marx's social philosophy was therefore twofold, as Hegel's had been. Both men combined a theory of social development with a plan for taking part in it and influencing it. Marx's philosophy like Hegel's was a philosophy of history, setting forth "the natural phases of evolution" which proceeds under the internal drive of the dialectic. Whereas Hegel had supposed that European history culminates in the rise of the Germanic nations and anticipated the rise of Germany to a position of spiritual leadership in European civilization, Marx believed that social history had culminated in the rise of the proletariat, and he looked forward to the advance of that class to a dominant place in modern society. In Hegel's philosophy of history the driving force was a self-developing spiritual principle that embodied itself successively in historic nations; in Marx's it was a self-developing system of productive forces that embodied itself in basic patterns of economic distribution and in the social classes consequent thereto. For Hegel the mechanism of progress was warfare between nations; for Marx it was antagonism between social classes. Both men regarded the course of history as rationally necessary, a pattern of stages unfolding according to a logical plan and advancing toward a predetermined goal. At the same time, however, Marx's philosophy even more explicitly than Hegel's was a plan for intervening in the course of development, an incitement to action, a peculiar but under proper circumstances a highly appealing form of moral exhortation. Whereas Hegel appealed to national patriotism, Marx appealed to the fidelity of workers to their class. In both cases the appeal was in a sense collective; it was addressed rather to loyalty than to self-interest, to duties rather than to rights, yet it could powerfully enlist the feeling and the action of individuals. It called on men to repress their capricious self-will, to subordinate their petty self-interest, and to take their place in the inevitable march of civilization. In Marx's philosophy this meant providing the working class with the understanding, the plan, and the motive needed to prepare and consummate a social revolution.

This union in Marx of a program of revolutionary action with a philosophical theory of the necessary course of social development has been a standing puzzle to commentators, though it was in truth not different from the union of similar factors in Hegel. Unsympathetic critics have usually separated the two and described, first, Marx the social philosopher and, second, Marx the founder of party socialism. This kind of interpretation never fails to provoke from Marxists the charge of being superficial and "bourgeois." It is certain that Marx himself had no consciousness of playing a double rôle. The necessity that he attributed to history was like Hegel's in that it invited cooperation and participation; a theory of party tactics was its natural supplement. With both Hegel and Marx the secret of this union was believed to lie in the dialectic. The dialectical necessity that makes communism the end of social evolution is much like that which Calvinists attributed to divine predestination. The compulsion is not a matter of desirability, nor of cause and effect, nor of moral obligation but of all three at once — a kind of cosmic imperative. Human calculation and human interests are factors in achieving the result, yet the process predetermines the calculation for its own end and sets the direction that the interests must take.

Marx's social philosophy fell into two parts, corresponding to two periods of his life and the outcome principally of two historical influences. The earliest was his study of Hegel during his years as a student in Bonn and Berlin. By this time the School was divided into an idealist wing, largely concerned with religious apologetics, and a materialist wing led by Ludwig Feuerbach. In later years Marx described Feuerbach as a small figure compared with Hegel but epoch-making after Hegel, because he freed Hegelianism from its bondage to idealist "mystifications." After Marx left Germany his contact with French socialism turned his attention toward economics but convinced him that socialist philosophy was superficial because it lacked a grasp of economic theory and economic history. To these subjects the rest of his life as a scholar was devoted. The earlier and more general outcome of Marx's studies was dialectical or economic materialism: the theory that social development depends upon the evolution of the means of economic production. The later and more specific result of his study of the classical economics was his theory of surplus value. The first part of Marx's work corresponds roughly to the writings of his earlier years down to about 1850, which were mainly controversial tracts occasioned by the revolutionary outbreaks that came to an abortive end about 1848; the second corresponds to the theoretical (as distinguished from the historical) part of his great work on *Capital,* which took economic materialism for granted but nowhere stated it. This division was unfortunate. The latter half of the nineteenth century was strangely free from revolutionary movements and in consequence Marx's earlier tracts tended to drop out of sight. The first volume of *Capital* (1867) made the theory of surplus value the distinguishing mark of what Marx considered to be " scientific " socialism and turned the discussion of Marx's economics almost wholly toward the internal consistency of that theory. It was not until nearly the end of the century, after Marx's death, that economic materialism began to be widely discussed. Yet everyone would probably now agree with Lenin, that economic materialism is " the central point around which the entire network of ideas, expressed and discussed, turns." The unfortunate fact is, therefore, that the most significant part of Marx's social philosophy was never systematically expounded by him and is contained in a few very compact passages in occasional writings which were not discussed during his lifetime, while the bulk of his systematic theorizing belongs to the category of economic scholasticism. In this chapter it will be assumed that the most important part of Marx's social philosophy was dialectical materialism: the thesis that the dialectical evolution of the system of economic production determines the institutional and ideological superstructure of society. The primary philosophical question is the meaning and validity of this theory. The theory of surplus value may be dealt with in a much briefer discussion.

DIALECTICAL MATERIALISM

The sources for the study of dialectical materialism in Marx and Engels fall into two groups. There is, in the first place, a number of brief works by Marx, polemic writings produced while he was formulating his theory of social revolution or occasional pamphlets analyzing the failures of revolutionary efforts in France. In the second place there are several works by Engels, including a number of important letters, written after Marx's death, elaborating and explaining Marx's ideas on the subject and objecting to misuses of the theory by younger socialist writers in Germany toward the close of the century. In neither case was there anything that can be called a systematic exposition of it. When Marx was dealing with a specific problem of historical development and especially in his later life, he clearly distrusted efforts to turn dialectical materialism into an explicit philosophy of history. In spite of dogmatic-sounding generalizations about "tendencies which work out with an iron necessity towards an inevitable goal," such as occur in the Preface to *Capital,* in practice he was interested in the theory largely as a suggestive working hypothesis, first, to aid in formulating the tactics proper for a revolutionary proletarian party and, second, as a guide to historical studies and to the criticism of economic and social theory. The reduction of dialectical materialism to a formula and the more or less mechanical application of it to history was contrary to Marx's practice and also to his express injunctions. Thus for example in 1882, in an introduction which he wrote for Vera Zasulich's Russian edition of the Communist Manifesto, he affirmed the possibility that socialism in Russia might develop out of the *mir* instead of running through the standard stages of feudalism and capitalism.

Marx first formulated the theory of dialectical materialism in a series of works published between 1844 and 1848 in which he both developed his own ideas of philosophy and jurisprudence, first formed during his years of study in the universities of Bonn and Berlin, and reformulated French socialism in the light of

Hegelian principles.[1] His original purpose was twofold, having to do with German philosophy on the one hand and socialism on the other. An industrially and politically backward country like Germany, Marx believed, could contribute nothing to the advance of European civilization except abstract philosophical analysis, in short, the dialectic. This supposition was in itself an extraordinary commentary on the hypothesis that the superstructure can rise only upon the foundation of the system of economic production. The Hegelian philosophy, properly understood, Marx regarded as revolutionary in its implications, in spite of the reactionary uses to which conservative Hegelians put it. The only way to bring to light its real significance would be to make it the intellectual organ of a revolutionary party. The revolutionary quality of Hegelianism is most apparent in its criticism of religion. The dialectic shows that all supposed absolute truths and transcendent religious values are in fact relative. They are merely social products that spring up in the life of a community in the course of its temporal and historical growth. More specifically they supply imaginary or fantastic satisfactions for real human needs and thus fend off rational efforts to find real satisfactions. Thus Christianity imputes to man a double life as spirit and body and offers the imaginary solace of heaven as an off-set to the real misery of life. A radical use of critical Hegelianism shows the true nature of religion as a merely illusory satisfaction and hence as "the opium of the people." Hegel's idealization of the state Marx regarded as another form of illusory satisfaction. To abandon these illusions is the first step toward an effective demand for the means of real happiness here and now. In the first instance, therefore, the dialectic was for Marx a critical method of deflating dogmatically asserted abso-

[1] *Deutsch-französische Jahrbücher,* 1844; *Die heilige Familie,* 1845; Selections from these are translated by H. J. Stenning under the title, *Selected Essays by Karl Marx,* New York, 1926. *Die deutsche Ideologie,* 1846 (first published in full in the *Gesamtausgabe*); *The German Ideology,* Eng. trans. of Parts I and III by R. Pascal, New York, 1939. *La misère de la philosophie,* 1847; Eng. trans., *The Poverty of Philosophy,* ed. by C. P. Dutt, New York, 1936. *The Communist Manifesto,* 1848. The standard edition of the works of Marx and Engels (which is not complete) is *Karl Marx, Friedrich Engels, historischkritische Gesamtausgabe, Werke, Schriften, Briefe.* Im Auftrage des Marx-Engels-Instituts, Moskau, hrsg. v. D. Rjazanov. Frankfurt a. M., 1927—.

lutes and a way of enforcing the Hegelian distinction between the real and the apparent. Its materialist interpretation meant first and foremost secularism, a release from the symbolic meanings of religious dogma and ecclesiastical authority, and more generally a way of undermining religion as one of the great conservative or reactionary forces in society.

In the *Holy Family* Marx made somewhat more explicit the sense in which his philosophy was materialist. He distinguished sharply between his own dialectical materialism and the French materialism of the eighteenth century. The latter he identified with mechanical explanation, which he regarded as suitable to natural sciences like physics and chemistry, where the subject-matter presents no problems of historical development, but unsuitable where such problems occur. Like Hegel he considered dialectic to be a more powerful method precisely because it can deal with a continuous, evolving subject-matter and can reveal the necessity inherent in historical development. With a book like Holbach's *System of Nature* Marx's materialism had nothing in common except a detestation of religion. At no time had he any belief that a method of explanation borrowed from the physical sciences would serve any useful purpose for social studies, and he had a low opinion of the excursions of natural scientists into history and economics, which he expressed in no uncertain terms in *Capital*. It is true that he compared his own work to that of Darwin, because it presented an evolutionary morphology of the modes of production and exchange, which he regarded as the keys to all social phenomena, analogous to evolutionary anatomy. It is quite certain, however, that Marx regarded Darwin as merely furnishing an external support to the theory of the class struggle. What impressed him on a first reading of the *Origin of Species* was "the crude English method of development,"[2] the only possible reaction of an Hegelian to Darwin's strictly empirical method. The truth is, of course, that except as Marx escaped from the connotations of the dialectic his method was not empirical, and his use of the word materialism was mis-

[2] Letter to Lasalle, January 16, 1861; *Marx-Engels Correspondence, 1846–1895* (1934), p. 125. Cf. *Capital,* Vol. I, Eng. trans. by E. and C. Paul, p. 392, n. 2.

leading in the light of its current meaning. His philosophical theory of social development could be far more accurately described as a kind of naturalistic vitalism, not unlike Aristotle's, and in that sense it was prescientific. The forces of production unfold from within by their own inherent momentum and create their own expression in the institutions and the ideology of a society. With Marx as with Hegel the controlling figure of speech was an expanding metaphysical force that forms the hidden reality behind a multiplicity of more or less unreal appearances. "Reality" is not what exists or occurs but the underlying force, which is essentially a depersonalized purpose.

The rejection of religion, however, was not the only consequence which Marx drew from a critical application of Hegel's dialectic. Substantially, Marx believed, Hegel's rejection of the French Revolution and the revolutionary rights of man will stand, for in the light of dialectic these cannot be absolute any more than religious beliefs but are only the ideological expression of a single stage of social development. But since the implications of the dialectic were for Marx revolutionary, Hegel's criticism must be reinterpreted; a spiritualized state cannot be the final term or the ultimate synthesis. What is implied by the dialectic is rather a new revolution at a higher level, a social revolution as contrasted with a political revolution. The latter transferred power from one class to another; the former will abolish class entirely. In the past revolutions have taken the power to exploit from one social class and have given it to another, but they have always left the fundamental fact of an exploited class. Hence the civil and political liberties sought by a political revolution are no real liberation; its rights are bourgeois, not human. Though religious liberty be gained, the religion of private caprice is left standing; though the freedom to control property be granted, property itself remains as a private right; though civil equality be assured, society itself is still stratified. Like Christianity, political revolution leaves man still with a double life, real servitude and imaginary freedom. No solution can be final which does not completely unite the man and the citizen, the individual's private and social capacities, and only a revolution by the proletariat, the final class below which no exploited class remains, can achieve this end. The classless society which will result will abolish the division of labor and indeed all compulsory labor.

> The division of labor implies the contradiction between the interest of the separate individual or the individual family and the communal interest of all individuals who have intercourse with one another. . . . For as soon as labor is distributed, each man has a particular, exclusive sphere of activity, which is forced upon him and from which he cannot escape . . . while in communist society, where nobody has one exclusive sphere of activity but each can become accomplished in any branch he wishes, society regulates the general production and thus makes it possible for me to do one thing today and another tomorrow.[3]

The classless society is at once the ultimate goal of social development and the logical next step beyond the era of the bourgeois revolutions. Like Hegel's philosophy, therefore, Marx's theory of social revolution achieved the logical paradox of crowning a system of apparently thoroughgoing relativism with a capstone of absolutism and utopianism. Both systems of thought exhibit the same curious combination of realism and amoralism in respect to the present with a kind of moral romanticism in respect to the future.

ECONOMIC DETERMINISM

Each of the two types of revolution reflects the social position and therefore the social purpose of the class that causes it. The political revolution is a bourgeois revolution produced in the main by the middle class and designed to establish the power of that class to exploit. A social revolution, which will aim to abolish classes and exploitation and which will equalize not only civil liberties but also economic privileges, can be the objective only of the proletariat. The French Revolution, as Marx interpreted it, was a bourgeois revolution. In it the middle class destroyed the political superiority of the nobility and the clergy, won political rights for itself, and swept away the remnants of feudal law and government which hampered the rising system of capitalist production. It rationalized and sanctified its purposes in the name of the rights of man. From the point of view of a working class, however, the civil liberties and the forms of demo-

[3] *The German Ideology,* Eng. trans. by R. Pascal, p. 22.

cratic government are not eternal verities or self-evident principles, as the system of natural law imagined them. They are the rights of the middle class. But this does not mean that they are negligible, because they are a prior condition to increasing the political self-consciousness and the power of the proletariat. In general Marx always regarded political liberalism as an antecedent stage necessary to the realization of socialism, and he assumed that the latter would continue and extend political freedom.

Thus Marx arrived at an evolutionary theory of society in which the whole system of natural law fell into place as the ideology appropriate to a specific stage of development. The normal course of social development is feudalism, capitalism, socialism, with a form of political organization fitted to each. Moreover, his theory of revolution made evident the mechanism by which political change takes place: it is the incompatible interests of social classes and the struggle between them to dominate society in their own interest. The French Revolution relieved the middle class from exploitation by the older classes but left it an exploiting class. The wage-earning proletariat is an inevitable product of capitalism which rises *pari passu* with the bourgeoisie. The success of the bourgeois revolution opens the way for the more thoroughgoing proletarian revolution which in the end will sweep away the new exploiting class. But the final step will complete the process by abolishing classes and exploitation altogether.

Marx made it quite clear that he did not regard himself as having originated the theory of class antagonism. He took over and extended a theory created by French historians to explain the Revolution. In a letter to Engels he referred to Augustin Thierry as "the father of the class struggle in French historical writing."[4] What Marx objected to in the middle-class historians was the presumption that the class struggle had ended with the rise to power of the bourgeoisie, just as he objected to the economists' presumption that the laws of a capitalist economy were eternal and immutable. In the revolutions of his own day Marx believed that he saw a new type of revolutionary up-

[4] July 27, 1854; *Marx-Engels Correspondence, 1846–1895,* p. 71.

rising which had as its spearpoint not a middle class intent upon political rights but a working class rising to the consciousness of its own degradation and confusedly determined to alter not the political superstructure but the underlying economic causes of social inequality.

> What I did that was new was to prove: (1) that the *existence of classes* is only bound up with *particular, historic phases in the development of production;* (2) that the class struggle necessarily leads to the *dictatorship of the proletariat;* (3) that this dictatorship itself only constitutes the transition to the *abolition of all classes* and to a *classless society.*[5]

The final step in Marx's argument, therefore, is that the structure of classes that exists in a society at any given period is itself an historical product which changes with the forces of economic production that the society is able to utilize. This he regarded as the ultimate cause to which the whole social, legal, and political framework of society can be traced back, while changes in this framework are to be correlated with changes in the methods of economic production. Writing in 1859, in one of the few autobiographical passages that occur in his works, Marx explained how a brief editorial experience with economic questions, for which he felt inadequately prepared, drove him back to a reconsideration of his Hegelian studies in philosophy and jurisprudence.

> I was led by my studies to the conclusion that legal relations as well as forms of state could neither be understood by themselves, nor explained by the so-called general progress of the human mind, but that they are rooted in the material conditions of life, which are summed up by Hegel . . . under the name of "civic society"; the anatomy of that civic society is to be sought in political economy.[6]

This then was the final significance which Marx attached to materialism in contrast with Hegelian idealism. Hegel's civil society and not his state is the primary factor in social evolution. The legal and institutional relations that make up the state, and all the moral and religious ideas that accompany them, are only

[5] Letter to Weydemeyer, March 5, 1852; *ibid.,* p. 57. The italics are Marx's.

[6] *Critique of Political Economy,* Preface; Eng. trans. by N. I. Stone (1904), p. 11.

a superstructure built upon the underlying economic foundation of civil society.

> The phantoms formed in the human brain are also, necessarily, sublimates of their material life-process, which is empirically verifiable and bound to material premises. Morality, religion, metaphysics, all the rest of ideology and their corresponding forms of consciousness, thus no longer retain the semblance of independence. They have no history, no development; but men, developing their material production and their material intercourse, alter, along with their real existence, their thinking and the products of their thinking. Life is not determined by consciousness, but consciousness by life.[7]

The order of importance and of causal efficacy is reversed: it is the economic order that " produces " while the mind merely " reflects." As Marx said later, in Hegel " dialectic stands on its head "; dialectical materialism " turned it right way up " by removing the " mystifications " of idealism and substituting for them the substantial and tangible realities of the industrial system. Thus the dialectic no longer moves in the realm of logical abstractions but in the realm of real forces.

It is important to note, however, that it was not the dialectic which Marx changed but rather a metaphysical interpretation of it. The dialectic was a method, and it is quite clear that he meant to retain the main outline of Hegelian methodology. The purpose of the method in Hegel had been the essentially metaphysical one of establishing an order of precedence or of " degrees of reality " by which thought can rise from appearances to the Absolute Idea. What Marx " turned right way up " was the order of precedence, while his forces of production remained a kind of material analogue to Hegel's Absolute Spirit. Thus the actual facts and events of social, legal, and political history were still conceived by him as the " phenomenal forms," the appearances or manifestations of this underlying reality, a kind of surface-play of transient and largely accidental circumstance which draws its necessity from the hidden force out of which it arises. On purely empirical grounds the fact that political institutions and moral ideas are " products " of economic conditions would in no way entail the conclusion that they cannot in turn affect these conditions. In short, economic factors in dialectical

[7] *The German Ideology,* Eng. trans. by R. Pascal, pp. 14 f.

materialism do not act merely as scientific causes which produce empirical consequences. They are more nearly creative energies that operate like semi-personalized agents, though it is only fair to say that when Marx dealt with an actual problem of historical analysis he was almost always better than his method. But the important critical question still remains, whether the dialectic was not a pseudo-method. In fact the sociological importance of Marx's materialism depended on the degree in which it ceased to be in any definite sense dialectical and became simply empirical and causal.

In the *Poverty of Philosophy* Marx applied his new point of view to the criticism of economic science, both the classical economics and the economics of contemporary socialism. For the former he had a high admiration, being convinced that a revolutionary philosophy must make use of the most exact results of economic analysis. His objections against it were aimed largely at the incredible naiveté of the economists in respect to the historical aspects of their subject. As Engels said later, they argue as if Richard the Lion Hearted, had he only known a little economics, might have saved six centuries of bungling by adopting free trade, instead of wasting his time on the crusades. As theologians divide religions into true and false, viz., their own and all others, so the economists treat all economic systems as if they were blundering approximations to capitalism, while they treat capitalism as if its relations and categories were natural and eternal. Against this Marx defended the thesis that economics is an historical science. Its laws are applicable only to the stage of economic production to which they belong; its categories, such as profits, wages, and rent, are "theoretical expressions, the abstractions, of the social relations of production."

> These ideas, these categories, are as little eternal as the relations they express. They are *historical and transitory products*.[8]

Thus economics became for Marx a combination of history and analysis: analysis of the relations prevailing in any given system of production, supplemented by the history of the rise and development of that system.

Toward humanitarian, utopian, and reformist criticisms of

[8] *The Poverty of Philosophy,* Eng. trans. edited by C. P. Dutt, p. 93.

classical economics Marx was less tolerant. Such projects, in his opinion, offer palliatives, sentimentality, and idealist dreams without either history or analysis. In substance they all reduce to some plan for separating the good from the bad in capitalism, usually to some impossible way of uniting capitalist production with socialist distribution. The fallacy in them is revealed, Marx believed, by the fact that any system of production, by an inexorable logic of its own, must determine the distribution of the social product. Consequently it determines the class structure of the society and ultimately its whole institutional and political organization. In fact, Marx was much less than just to the utopian socialists, though his irritation with some of their schemes is not hard to understand. The classless society was as utopian as anything in Proudhon, its principal advantage being that it could always be deferred to an indefinite future. Moreover, Marx's theory of economic causation logically implied that any legislative control over the industrial system, whether utopian or not, must be only a palliative. Liberal reform was excluded, so to speak, by definition, with the result that revolution was the only solution left.

IDEOLOGY AND THE CLASS STRUGGLE

It was characteristic of Marx that he was interested less in perfecting dialectical materialism as a philosophy of history than in applying it to concrete situations, especially with the purpose of finding a program of action for a consciously revolutionary proletariat. Thus in 1848 he and Engels used the class struggle as the key to "all hitherto existing society" in the *Communist Manifesto*, which became one of the great revolutionary tracts of all times. A little later he wrote two pamphlets to explain the failure of the revolutionary struggle which had just occurred in France. They applied the economic interpretation to a problem in contemporary history.[9] These pamphlets give a very able and incisive analysis of the economic affiliations of the several parties

[9] *Die Klassenkämpfe in Frankreich, 1848–1850,* articles in the *Neue Rheinische Zeitung,* 1850, published by Engels, 1895; Eng. trans., ed. by C. P. Dutt, *The Class Struggles in France* (1848–50), New York, 1934. *Der achtzehnte Brumaire des Louis Bonaparte,* 1852; Eng. trans., ed. by C. P. Dutt, *The Eighteenth Brumaire of Louis Bonaparte,* New York, 1935.

in the revolution and also a clear insight into the inchoate state of the proletarian parties. They are indeed much the kind of analysis of a revolutionary situation which any first-class journalist would now try to make, a clear indication of the extent to which Marxian interpretation has gained general acceptance. At the same time they certainly do not justify the extravagant claims which Marxists often make for the dialectic as a means of prognosis. Marx's prophecy, that the recurrence of a business depression like that of 1847 would start the revolution anew, was mistaken and, as Engels candidly admitted later, Marx quite failed to appreciate the possibilities for development contained within the capitalist system.

The pamphlets serve also to make clearer Marx's conception of the relation of social classes both to the course of history and also to their own mentality. The class had for Marx a collective unity as the nation had for Hegel. It acts in history as a unit and it produces its characteristic ideas and beliefs as a unit, acting under the compulsion of its place in the economic and social system. The individual counts mainly through his membership in the class, because his ideas — his moral convictions, his esthetic preferences, even the kind of reasoning that seems to him convincing — are in the main a reflection of the ideas generated by the class.

> Upon the different forms of property, upon the social conditions of existence rises an entire superstructure of distinct and characteristically formed sentiments, illusions, modes of thought and views of life. The entire class creates and forms them out of its material foundations and out of the corresponding social relations. The single individual who derives them through tradition and education may imagine that they form the real motives and the starting-point of his activity.[10]

This passage suggests the peculiar sense in which Marx used the word ideology. Ideas reflect and more or less misrepresent an underlying economic reality; they are " mystifications " of it, at least in so far as their origin has not been unmasked. As ideal motives or reasons for conduct they are merely appearances or manifestations of something which is in its real nature quite different. And though they seem valid and compelling to their unsophisticated possessor, their compulsive force is really some-

[10] *The Eighteenth Brumaire,* Eng. trans., pp. 40 f.

thing which is not in his consciousness at all but is concealed in the social position of his class and in its relations to economic production. The explanation quite evidently ran in terms derived from the Hegelian contrast between appearance and reality. The forces of production, like Hegel's World Spirit, are infinitely cunning and produce all manner of illusions and mystifications which can be discounted only by someone who understands their origin. Marx's classes also were personifications which produce their appropriate ideologies much as Hegel imagined that the spirit of the nation produces the national culture. The conception of ideology was at once one of Marx's most pregnant ideas and also one of the vaguest and most subject to abuse in application. It was a powerful controversial weapon but one that could be used with equal force by every side, until all theories and beliefs, including Marxism itself, would have no more meaning than the multiple reflections in a gallery of mirrors. A scientific use of it would require an adequate theory of the way in which economic factors do in fact affect the mind, an empirical problem of the utmost difficulty about which there has been much speculation but very little reliable information.

The two pamphlets on the revolutionary movement in France laid down also the main outline of Marx's theory of class structure in modern industrial societies. This theory was pretty clearly suggested to him by his observation of French society and his experience with French socialism, and it assumed that these provided a type to which other capitalist societies would more or less approximate. The theory postulated a middle class mainly urban and commercial in its interests and devoted politically to the civil and political liberties of the Revolution, and an industrial proletariat also mainly urban but concerned more with economic security than with political liberty. These classes Marx regarded as the active political forces in a modern society, the forces between which the class struggle mainly takes place, so that the issue is fundamentally the dominance of one or the other. The other classes that the theory recognized, the peasantry and the petty bourgeoisie, he regarded as politically inert though they may, under proper circumstances, be able to affect what the two active classes can do. Marx also considered the ideology of the peasant class to be characteristically petty bourgeois. If

Marx had taken England as his type, with its history of capitalist agriculture and of political preponderance by the gentry, it is not certain that his analysis of classes would have been the same. Since he pictured the class struggle as a dialectical opposition of "contradictory" forces, he was compelled in any case to have two major opponents. Hence his theory of classes was over-simplified, and some of his predictions were quite erroneous. Thus his theory implied that the lower middle class would be absorbed into the proletariat, whereas the increase of salaried employees, middlemen, professional people, and small stockholders — groups that can only be classified as petty bourgeois in Marx's scheme — has been a marked characteristic of industrial societies. Fascism showed that such people resist absorption into the proletariat with a savagery that Marx could hardly have imagined. Moreover the position of agriculture in an industrial society was by no means merely the problem of a peasant class; farmers throughout the nineteenth century were the despair of Marxian theorists and socialist organizers. Even as regards a genuine peasantry, in Russia for example, Marx's theory tended to be misleading. Lenin's success as a revolutionist depended in no small degree on the fact that he did not overlook the peasants, as most Russian Marxists were inclined to do. The truth of course is that the class structure of any society, and of an industrial society in particular, is incredibly complicated and is not fully explained by economic factors only. Marx's theory was at best no more than a first approximation, and it was constructed by him largely *ad hoc* and for controversial purposes.

MARX'S SUMMARY

The fragmentary manner in which Marx worked out the theory of dialectical materialism justifies the quotation at some length of the only summary he ever made of his conclusions, a passage which could not be improved for clarity and force:

> In the social production which men carry on they enter into definite relations that are indispensable and independent of their will; these relations of production correspond to a definite stage of development of their material powers of production. The sum total of these relations of production constitutes the economic structure of society — the real foundation, on which rise legal and political superstructures and to which

correspond definite forms of social consciousness. The mode of production in material life determines the general character of the social, political, and spiritual processes of life. It is not the consciousness of men that determines their existence, but, on the contrary, their social existence determines their consciousness. At a certain stage of their development, the material forces of production in society come in conflict with the existing relations of production, or — what is but a legal expression for the same thing — with the property relations within which they had been at work before. From forms of development of the forces of production these relations turn into their fetters. Then comes the period of social revolution. With the change of the economic foundation the entire immense superstructure is more or less rapidly transformed. In considering such transformations the distinction should always be made between the material transformation of the economic conditions of production which can be determined with the precision of natural science, and the legal, political, religious, aesthetic, or philosophic — in short ideological forms in which men become conscious of this conflict and fight it out. . . . No social order ever disappears before all the productive forces, for which there is room in it, have been developed; and new higher relations of production never appear before the conditions of their existence have matured in the womb of the old society. Therefore, mankind always takes up only such problems as it can solve; since, looking at the matter more closely, we will always find that the problem itself arises only when the material conditions necessary for its solution already exist or are at least in the process of formation.[11]

Marx's theory of cultural development, then, as presented in this passage, included four principal propositions. First, it is a succession of stages each of which is dominated by a typical system of producing and exchanging goods. This system of productive forces generates its own characteristic and appropriate ideology, which includes law and politics together with the ideal or so-called spiritual products of the civilization, such as morals, religion, art, and philosophy. As an ideal pattern each stage is complete and systematic, a coordinated whole in which the ideological factors are adjusted to the underlying forces of production and to each other. In actual use, as for example in the descriptive and historical chapters of *Capital,* Marx relaxed the logical rigidity of the theory. At any given time the development of the forces of production has run unequally in different countries and in different industries of a single country; there are remnants of

[11] *Critique of Political Economy,* Preface; Eng. trans. by N. I. Stone, pp. 11 ff.

the older economy and beginnings of the newer. Consequently there are correspondingly different ideologies in different strata of population. Second, the whole process is "dialectical"; its motive force is supplied by the internal tensions created by disparities between a newly evolving system of production and the persisting ideology appropriate to an older system. A new method of production finds itself in a hostile ideological environment which must be dissolved before it can grow. The ideology appropriate to the old system becomes more and more restrictive of the new, and the internal stresses and strains build up until they reach a breaking point. A new social class, with an ideology appropriate to its social position in the new system of production, comes into sharper conflict with the older classes having ideologies bred by the obsolescent system. The general pattern of development, therefore, is cyclical, an alternation of periods of evolution, in which a new system of production is gradually formed and new ideologies are gradually created, and periods of revolution in which the whole constellation of forces breaks down and recrystallizes, so to speak, in another pattern. Third, the forces of production — the methods of producing goods and of distributing the products of industry — are always primary as compared with their secondary, ideological consequences. The material or economic forces are "real" or substantial, while the ideological relations are only apparent or phenomenal. This does not mean, however, that the latter do not exist nor does it altogether preclude the possibility that the appearances may affect the reality, though the relation between them is described metaphysically rather than causally. The distinction is the Hegelian distinction of degrees of reality or significance, except for the fact that Marx regards the material rather than the ideal as substantial. Fourth, the dialectical development is an internal process of unfolding or of vitalistic realization. The productive forces inherent in any society develop completely before the dialectical transformation or re-crystallization of forces takes place. And since the ideological superstructure merely reflects the internal growth of the underlying metaphysical substance, the problems that appear upon the level of consciousness will always be soluble with the further unfolding and the progressive realization of the substratum behind them. Quite obviously this metaphysical conclusion is not susceptible of any empirical proof.

ENGELS ON DIALECTIC

The theory of dialectical materialism was completed by Marx about 1850. From that time forward it was presumed in all that he wrote but even in *Capital* it was nowhere stated; the treatment of socialism in that work turned discussion toward intrinsically less important economic theories such as surplus value. It was not until later in the nineteenth century that the economic explanation of history began to assume the importance it deserved and to extend its influence beyond the circle of professed Marxists. In the meantime the public had been prepared to take an interest in it by the spread of biological evolution, though inherently there was little if any logical relation between the two. Anthropologists like Lewis Morgan, apparently without depending upon Marx, had stressed the importance of technology in primitive cultures. The development of historical scholarship among socialists, especially in Germany, caused the economic interpretation of history to be applied and re-examined. By this time Marx was already in failing health (he died in 1883) and the further exposition of his theory fell to his friend, Friedrich Engels.[12] Unfortunately, Engels, though he was a man of strong common sense and transparent candor, was philosophically not very acute and in no sense original. He elaborated Marx's fragmentary texts but he left the underlying obscurities in the theory almost exactly where they were.

In their understanding of the general nature of dialectic and the kind of necessity which it discloses in history, it is clear that both Marx and Engels relied on Hegel. They objected to particular uses of it by Hegel, which Engels said were nearly always arbitrary, and they rejected of course the idealist interpretation

[12] *Herrn Eugen Dührings Umwälzung der Wissenschaft,* 1878 (Usually referred to as "Anti-Dühring"; Marx cooperated in writing this work); Eng. trans. by E. Burns, *Herr Eugen Dühring's Revolution in Science,* New York, 1935. *Ludwig Feuerbach und der Ausgang der deutschen Philosophie* (1884); Eng. trans. *Ludwig Feuerbach and the Outcome of Classical German Philosophy,* New York, 1934. Letters to Conrad Schmidt, August 5 and October 27, 1890, July 1 and November 1, 1891, *Marx-Engels Correspondence, 1846–1895,* pp. 472, 477, 487, 494; to J. Bloch, September 21, 1890, *ibid.,* p. 475; to Franz Mehring, July 14, 1893, *ibid.,* p. 510.

of it as a self-development of thought. It is, on the contrary, a self-development of nature itself reflected in thought. But this implied no very serious change of Hegel, since he also believed that the dialectic revealed a development implicit in reality. Hegel's metaphysical logic, therefore, was an assumed major premise in the whole Marxian argument, with this difference only, that Marx and Engels substituted a materialist for an idealist metaphysics. For Engels as for Hegel the value of dialectic lay in the fact that it permitted the discovery of a necessary evolution in history:

> From this standpoint [of Hegel's philosophy] the history of mankind no longer appeared as a confused whirl of senseless deeds of violence, all equally condemnable before the judgment seat of the now matured philosophic reason . . . but as the process of development of humanity itself.[13]

In his *Feuerbach* Engels attributed rationality to nature in exactly the Hegelian sense. The real or rational cannot be equated with existence because much of what exists is irrational and therefore unreal; for example, in 1789 the French monarchy existed but was not real. In other words, for Engels as for Hegel "real" means not existent but significant or valuable. The process of history is inherently selective and self-realizing rather than causal, and in effect the important is regarded as bringing itself into existence simply because it is important, after the manner of an Aristotelian entelechy. The whole conception was fundamentally vitalistic or mystical, just as it was in Hegel. Despite their so-called materialism, the necessity of history for Marx and Engels as for Hegel was really a moral necessity, the "progressive development," as Engels calls it, of civilization by the expansion of its inner forces. The supposed necessity reflected their faith in the inevitable success of the proletarian revolution, as for Hegel it reflected his faith in the mission of Germany.

According to Engels' account of the dialectic in his *Feuerbach* the important difference between Marx and Hegel lay in the fact that Marx adopted a materialist version of dialectic; ideas are not forces, as Hegel supposed, but "pictures of real things,"

[13] *Anti-Dühring,* Eng. trans. by E. Burns, p. 30.

"the conscious reflex of the dialectic evolution of the real world." Engels' account of ideas as "pictures" got a posthumous importance when it was reproduced by Lenin in his *Materialism and Empirio-Criticism.* Quite obviously the word "picture," used as a collective term for every kind of idea from a scientific theory to an hallucination, was nothing but a meaningless figure of speech. Apparently it was intended to have two connotations. It suggested, first, that ideology is relatively insubstantial as compared with economic forces and that any form of philosophical idealism is a "mystification" whose real purpose is to support reaction. It suggested, second, that ideas do have real counterparts in the world; in this sense it was a figurative way of denying subjectivism. And while subjectivism has never been a serious philosophical position, it was convenient for Engels to regard Kant and Hume in that light. His treatment of modern philosophy was therefore summary in the extreme. He merely assumed that every philosophy must be either idealist or materialist, and thus with hardly more than a sentence he dismissed the whole anti-metaphysical tradition from Hume to Kant. Apparently Engels really believed that their argument could be refuted merely by pointing out that there is such an operation as empirical confirmation! The truth is, of course, that the critical question about dialectic was not metaphysical at all. The question was whether Hume and Kant were right in making the methodological distinctions they did between causal sequence and valuation.

Engels made it clear in the *Feuerbach* that what chiefly commended the dialectic to him and to Marx was its power as a solvent of dogmatism. It was this, he said, which made Hegelianism a revolutionary philosophy.

> Truth, the cognition of which is the business of philosophy, became in the hands of Hegel no longer an aggregate of finished dogmatic statements, which once discovered had merely to be learned by heart. Truth lay now in the process of cognition itself, in the long historical development of science, which mounts from lower to ever higher levels of knowledge without ever reaching, by discovering so-called absolute truth, a point at which it can proceed no further and where it would have nothing more to do than to fold its hands and admire the absolute truth to which it had attained.[14]

[14] *Ludwig Feuerbach,* Eng. trans., p. 11.

There are neither self-evident truths in science nor natural and inalienable rights in society; nothing is absolute, final, or sacred. The most that can be said is that a scientific theory or a social practice is "suitable" to its time and conditions, and all theories and practices that prevail are suitable, as is shown simply by the fact that they do prevail. But it is certain that with the passage of time and change of conditions they will pass away and be supplanted by something "higher." Nothing remains but the endless process of passing from lower to higher. The difficulty with Engels' argument is that it provides no criterion of "higher," except his own presumption that the proletarian revolution will of course be a step in advance, and no reason why a later stage of society must always be an improvement on what preceded it except his confidence in progress.

Both Marx and Engels occasionally played with the idea that dialectic is merely a working hypothesis which implies no substantive conclusion whatever. This was perhaps a mark of deference to Kant that was hard to avoid in Germany in the third quarter of the nineteenth century. It was also a "deviation" that revisionist Marxists were prone to and that Lenin felt it necessary to refute in 1909 when it occurred among Russian Marxists, for if the dialectic were only a working hypothesis, its moral appeal would largely evaporate. Thus Engels in *Anti-Dühring* said that the dialectic proves nothing but is merely a way of advancing to new spheres of research, and that it does away with the need for a metaphysics or a philosophy of history. Marx was even more explicit. In a letter which he wrote in 1877 to a Russian correspondent he said that the account of primitive accumulation in *Capital* did not pretend to do more than trace the path by which capitalism emerged from a feudal economy in Western Europe, and he protested against a critic who, in applying his account to Russia, had metamorphosed an historical sketch into "an historico-philosophic theory of the *marche générale* imposed by fate upon every people."

By studying each of these forms of evolution separately and then comparing them one can easily find the clue to this phenomenon [different historical results from apparently similar conditions], but one will never arrive there by the universal passport of a general historico-philosophical theory, the supreme virtue of which consists in being super-historical.[15]

If this statement were taken literally, the dialectic would mean about the same as the "comparative method" so popular in anthropology during the last quarter of the nineteenth century. In the same strain Engels in his letters criticized the younger German socialists who, he said, used historical materialism as an excuse for not studying history. Yet it is certain that Marx did not regard the history of capitalism merely as empirical history. Had he done so he would hardly have spoken in the Preface to *Capital* of "tendencies which work out with an iron necessity toward an inevitable goal," or of "the natural phases of evolution," or said that a country more highly industrialized than others "simply presents those others with a picture of their own future." Either the dialectic is a method that makes historical prediction possible or else the Marxian historian has at his command only the same methods that other historians use. Certainly if the dialectic is only a working hypothesis, it does not warrant the assertion that the proletarian revolution is "inevitable."

ENGELS ON ECONOMIC DETERMINISM

Apart from the philosophical principles entering into the dialectic, Engels' elaboration of dialectical materialism dealt mainly with the use of economic interpretation in history. In the letters already referred to, written between 1890 and 1894, he discussed the extent to which such interpretation is possible or useful, his main purpose being to correct what he thought to be the exaggerated claims made for it by younger members of the party. He acknowledged that he and Marx, in putting forward a new idea, had overstated the extent to which economic causes could be found for political and legal institutions. He asserted that it would be pedantic to seek economic causes for all history, instancing the High German consonant-shift as one for which no economic origin could probably be given. The example was a little strange and one wonders whether he realized that he was taking the history of language, with all its implications for differences of national culture, quite out of the region of economic explanation. He suggested that in the case of religion and

[15] *Marx-Engels Correspondence, 1846–1895,* pp. 354 f.

mythology economic forces may act negatively rather than positively. He admitted that, within a general framework of economic forces, political or even dynastic relationships may exert a large historical influence, as in the rise of Prussia from Brandenburg rather than from some other small German state. And he acknowledged that legislation " can close some paths of economic development and open others," though it cannot alter its main course. It had never been Marx's belief, he said, that economic forces are the sole causes of historical change, but only that they are " ultimate " or " fundamental." The economic factor is " the strongest, most elemental, and most decisive." Finally, Engels now argued that it was the special merit of dialectic to take into account the interaction of all the different factors that are present together in an historical situation.

> According to the materialistic conception of history the factor which is *in last instance* decisive is the production and reproduction of actual life. More than this neither Marx nor I have ever asserted. But when anyone distorts this so as to read that the economic factor is the sole element, he converts the statement into a meaningless, abstract, absurd phrase. The economic condition is the basis, but the various elements of the superstructure — the political forms of the class contests, and their results, the constitutions — the legal forms, and also all the reflexes of these actual contests in the brains of the participants, the political, legal, philosophical, the religious views . . . all these exert an influence on the development of the historical struggles, and in many instances determine their form.[16]

With all these concessions it is hard to see what there is about the economic explanation of history that the most bourgeois historian would have any concern to deny or that calls for dialectic to explain it. What Engels says in substance is that Marx brought into prominence a hitherto neglected factor in social studies, namely, the interdependence of political and legal institutions with the prevalent modes of producing and exchanging goods. This was certainly a notable discovery and Marx very largely deserved the credit for it. The importance of economic factors in history has steadily been rated higher as time has passed, and the recognition of it has long since ceased to be peculiar to Marxists. Probably it would now be generally granted

[16] Quoted by E. R. A. Seligman, *The Economic Interpretation of History* (1902), pp. 142 f. From a letter published in *Der sozialistische Akademiker,* October 15, 1895.

that this was one of the most fruitful principles of interpretation brought into social studies in the nineteenth century. It is difficult to see, however, what Engels thought he was saving for dialectical materialism when he said that the economic factor in a social complex is the "most elemental and most decisive." If, as he admitted, law and politics can open some doors of economic development and close others, they must be "decisive" as far as they go and the fact that they are not omnipotent does not make them indecisive. A word such as "elemental" merely reflected the metaphysical origin of the dialectic. The productive forces of society, the human relations produced, the structure of classes and their antagonisms, and the ideas of art, religion, and morals bred within each class are stages of remoteness from reality like a series of Neo-Platonic emanations. It is to the credit of Marx's realism that this mythological aspect of the dialectic did not much hamper him in actual historical analysis. Its possibilities for producing nonsense are suggested by Engels' assertion that historical personalities are mere accidents; if Napoleon had never existed, the dialectical process would have created a substitute.

Engels also expanded somewhat in his letters the brief accounts which Marx had given of ideology and its relation to the economic system. The striking part of Engels' discussion was that, without making the division explicit, he in effect separated ideology into two parts which he treated in entirely different ways. One part of the whole ideal superstructure raised by a society is its science and technology, the other is its law, morals, art, philosophy, and religion. Obviously the first of these is a factor of first-rate importance in shaping the forces of production, since technology depends largely on scientific knowledge. The most that Engels claimed for the economic determination of science was that the problems investigated by scientists are largely set by industry and that their discoveries are socially important largely because they react on technology. The truth of a scientific theory is explained, he supposed, by the fact that it is an accurate "picture" of things as they are. In so far as ideology meant science, therefore, Engels' philosophy presented the paradox, from a Marxian point of view, of explaining the objective forces of production by the subjective ideology. Apparently it did not occur to him that anyone would try to find an economic derivation for the concept of scientific truth itself, though this is what a consistent Marxian relativism ought to undertake if it treated science in the same way as morals, art, and religion. From this point of view the criteria of truth accepted in a society ought to depend on the class structure of the society. Proletarian science might be different from bourgeois science, as later Marxists have occasionally maintained for controversial purposes. Carried to its logical conclusion this view would seem to imply that communication between persons of different social classes is impossible. Less rigidly applied the idea that standards of truth may sometimes and in certain subjects depend upon social position has produced the rather large body of theory now known as the sociology of knowledge.[17] The importance of this subject has been enhanced by the extraordinary position in society that Leninism attributed to the class of intellectuals. There is no reason to suppose, however, that Engels perceived these possible implications of regarding science as a branch of ideology.

The other parts of the ideological superstructure Engels treated very differently. The validity which men claim for law, morals, politics, art, religion, and philosophy is a "false consciousness" or a deceptive reflection of the interests which the system of production assigns to the various classes engaged in it. Here the thinker is not clearly aware of the motives that actuate him but imagines that his ideas are true merely in and for themselves. To this category Engels attributed especially abstractions like justice, liberty, and supposed esthetic, moral, and religious verities when these are not recognized as belonging in some specific social context. These are what have more recently been named "rationalizations" — specious defenses of wishful thinking or the covert idealization of class interests. At the same time Engels certainly did not regard all ideologies as equally false. The ideology of the proletariat is superior to that of the bourgeoisie presumably for two reasons. In the first place, the philosophy of Marx makes it clear to the proletarian that his ideas of morality,

[17] See for example Karl Mannheim's *Ideology and Utopia: An Introduction to the Sociology of Knowledge,* Eng. trans. by Louis Wirth and Edward Shils, 1936, which contains an extensive bibliography.

art, and philosophy do depend upon his class and its position in the class struggle. This argument seems to assume that a preference rationally understood and responsibly accepted, with a clear understanding of its implications, is on a higher moral level than a mere prejudice. This is a perfectly respectable principle, accepted and defended by most systems of ethical idealism, but it figures rather curiously in a system that makes a virtue of being materialist. In the second place, the proletariat is the "rising" class which the present historical epoch is bringing to a position of dominance, so that its ideology is to be the prevailing one in the immediate future. This argument is as sound as its major premise, viz., that in any period some class has to be dominant and that the proletariat is now the predestined class.

The Marxian conception of ideology was a highly suggestive hypothesis but like many valuable hypotheses it brought problems to light rather than solved them. If the statement that beliefs and ideas "reflect" the social position and economic status of those who hold them meant no more than that men are misled by their interests, it would hardly be a discovery. In fact Marx intended nothing so commonplace. The importance of the conception depended upon the fact that the influences concerned are subtle and act in ways that are not obvious. The inferences that can be justifiably drawn depend upon knowing how in fact such influences do affect men's minds. Moreover, the effects of social class depend upon human interrelationships and interpersonal influences that again operate upon the mind in subtle and often very unexpected ways. "Rationalization" is therefore an extremely difficult and complicated psychological conception, in spite of the facility with which psychological amateurs use it. The problem concerns what may roughly be described as psychological causation, or of the ways in which social influences affect the structure of individual personality as it grows.[18] The most important scientific consequence of the conception of ideology was that it helped to open up problems of this sort for social psychology, but only psychological investigation can provide reliable answers.

In general the tendency of Marxism was simply to personify

[18] The dependence of personality on economic conditions is discussed in Gardner Murphy's *Personality* (1947), chs. 33–35.

classes and attribute to them a kind of collective personality analogous to that of an individual. Apparently Marx and Engels assumed that a social class will normally act in its own interest and produce an ideology favorable to its rise and continuance in power. Indeed a Marxian class sometimes seems to pursue its own self-interest with the same unerring certainty that the classical economics attributed to the economic man. Once the rise of an ideology is conceived in terms of cause and effect, there is no evident reason why this should be so. The ideas and the behavior induced in a class might easily be disadvantageous, just as individuals under stress often act in highly irrational ways. On the other hand the dialectic requires that classes, like everything else, should have the seeds of their own dissolution within them. At some point therefore the behavior of a class ought, so to speak, to become suicidal. Lenin's argument about the part played by intellectuals in formulating Marxian theory in fact required some such assumption. He was obliged to suppose that the middle class, for some unexplained reason, produces intellectuals who devote themselves to creating a theory that will destroy their own class. The truth of course is that either assumption, that classes are usually self-preservative or that they are sometimes self-destructive, is too vague to have any explanatory value. What is needed is a thoroughgoing psychological examination in detail of the ways in which social conditions, economic and other, affect the structure of human mentality. In such an examination there is no reason to start from the hypothesis that economic forces play a predominant part. The psychology of Freud provides a whole arsenal of motives, in no specific sense economic, that give rise to rationalizations substantially like the "false consciousness" which Engels attributed to ideology. Up to the present time psychoanalysis appears to have contributed more to social psychology than economic interpretation.

The importance for political and social theory of Marx's economic interpretation of history can hardly be exaggerated.[19] It

[19] See the estimate and critique in Max Weber's essay, "Die 'Objektivität' sozialwissenschaftlicher und sozialpolitiker Erkenntnis." This essay was a statement of editorial policy written in 1904 upon Weber's assumption of the editorship of the *Archiv für Sozialwissenschaft und Sozialpolitik*. It is translated in *Max Weber on the Methodology of the Social Sciences*, by Edward A. Shils and Henry A. Finch (Glencoe, Illinois, 1949), p. 50.

made evident the enormous influence that economic factors like technology, transportation, the supply of raw materials, the distribution of wealth, and finance have exerted upon the structure of social classes, on politics past and present, on law, and on the formation of moral and social ideals. It erased once for all the artificial line that the earlier forms of liberal theory had drawn between the utilitarian adjustments of political institutions and the "natural" laws of economic production. Thus it opened up far more realistic lines of approach to political problems than were possible within the prevailing legalism of earlier political theory. It was one of the earliest and one of the most important factors in bringing political thought into the context of sociology, anthropology, and social psychology. The fact that Marx's hypothesis was not the only factor in these developments does not diminish his originality. The economic interpretation of history was certainly one of the most important additions made to social theory in the nineteenth century. The conventional criticism, that Marx exaggerated the importance of economic factors in history, is really of little moment; their importance is certainly great and no one knows how great. The exaggerations were largely due to a tendency, much more characteristic of Marxists than of Marx, to think of economic causes as metaphysical essences. The much more serious criticisms of Marx's procedure were two. First, he greatly oversimplified an exceedingly complex body of social and psychological phenomena, and second, by forcing them into the *a priori* form supplied by Hegel's dialectic he drew political conclusions from them that are not really implied.

The defect of oversimplification was in part the normal deficiency of a scientific hypothesis in its early stages. In Marx's case it resulted also from the fact that dialectical materialism was first formulated and was subsequently used largely for controversial purposes and was based *ad hoc* on his observations of the revolutionary disturbances, mainly in France, during the 1840's. It was upon this situation that Marx based his analysis of the class structure of a modern society. But the generalization of this analysis raises questions that cannot be answered summarily. How typical was the situation that Marx analyzed? Would he have reached the same conclusion if he had been as deeply involved in the politics of England or Russia as he was in the revolutionary movement of the 1840's in France and Germany? If not, why should the French situation be more typical than some other? Or if it is typical, does this imply that all industrialized societies will develop approximately on the same lines? Marx's letter quoted above, relative to the development of socialism in Russia, shows that he did not seriously believe this to be true, even though he sometimes spoke as if he did. But even if the emergence of socialism is "inevitable," must it occur through the mechanism of a social revolution? Marx himself entertained the possibility that socialism might be achieved in England by peaceful means, though England was the most highly industrialized of all countries. But granting that the lines of modern industrialism are relatively similar in all countries, is it certain that this similarity will override the admitted diversity of other factors in the several national cultures? Finally, is it credible that social classes should disappear and give place to a classless society? Engels regarded the division of labor as the reason for the differentiation of society into classes and for differences of social outlook or ideology produced by specialization of function. But division of social labor is a phenomenon found in all societies, from the most primitive to the most developed, and certainly does not diminish with industrialization. One might therefore expect that even a society organized on completely socialist principles would still develop its own structure of social classes. But does this sociological fact (if it is a fact) imply that the ethical relations between classes must be exploitative and discriminatory?

Marx's acceptance of the dialectic as the pattern of relationship between classes forced upon him two assumptions which are far from obvious. First, the relation between classes is prevailingly one of antagonism or struggle, and second, in any given period of social development a single class must be dominant and the exploiter of the other classes. These assumptions caused him to place a low valuation upon all forms of social legislation, except in so far as they tend to increase the fighting power of the proletariat. They were responsible also for the contemptuous attitude that he took toward the moral criticism of social abuses and for his belief that all important social changes are accomplished by force. But even though classes always do have special interests and though these interests conflict, it is surely impossible, even according to Marx's own theory, that they should merely conflict. If they arise from a division of social labor, their special interests cannot be *per se* antagonistic and injurious to the general welfare of the society of which they are functioning parts. The cooperative side of the relationship must be at least as normal as the antagonistic. Moreover, in any functioning social system special interests must in general be limited by some considerations of public good and sound public policy, else the system would simply disintegrate. The regulation of special interests is just as normal a part of society as the existence of the interests themselves, and it is a function that any responsible government must perform in some manner. A communist government in Russia is obliged to assume that relations between the proletariat and the peasantry are "friendly," but the assumption does not alter the fact that the advantage of the one is the disadvantage of the other in respect to the relative prices of manufactured goods and agricultural products. The theory that states are merely agents of exploitation is essentially the propaganda of a revolutionary minority; it is not a theory upon which any government in power can operate.

CAPITALISM AS AN INSTITUTION

Marx regarded historical materialism and the class struggle as general theories applicable to all societies and all periods, unless perhaps to a period of primitive communism which Engels at least thought had existed in prehistoric times. The main concern of Marx's life as a scholar after 1850 was not to apply them to a wider range of societies and periods but to give them a deeper and stronger foundation as interpretations of contemporary industrial society in Western Europe. This involved an intensive study of the economic origins of existing social classes and a thoroughgoing economic analysis of the nature of the antagonism between these classes. These two lines of investigation formed the principal subjects of his work on *Capital*. The first took him into extensive historical research into the origins of the capitalist organization of industry, the rise of the middle class, and the formation of its counterpart, the industrial wage-earning class, which Marx rightly regarded as the major development in modern European society. The second undertook to back history with a precise economic analysis of capitalism, upon lines already set by the classical economists, to show at once the mechanism by which capitalism produces the two chief classes and the grounds for their inevitable and growing antagonism. This part of Marx's work issued in the theory of surplus value, which unfortunately tended to monopolize the discussion of Marxian socialism in its earlier stages.

The historical chapters of *Capital,* especially those which deal with the earlier history of the capitalist organization of industry, prior to the eighteenth century, and with the formation of a class dependent solely upon its wages were the finest of all Marx's writings. They have scarcely been superseded even yet, despite the attention given to economic history by later writers, who were in no small degree inspired by the beginning Marx made. He opened up the main avenues of approach to the historical study of capitalism, especially as the new industrial system affected social history: the formation of a proletariat by the divorce of the peasantry from common rights in the land, the destruction of household industry by the growth of capitalist organization, the steady increase in the size and power of the units of such organization, and the acceleration of these processes by the expropriation of the church and the colonial exploitation of America and the Indies. The distinctive feature of Marx's treatment was his stress upon the changes in human and social relations that result from industrial and commercial changes, and particularly upon the cramping, even the distorting, of the workers' lives by the steady advance of the division of labor. Marx's general thesis was that the working class has been subjected by industrial organization to a regimentation at odds with the profession of liberty and equality in the bourgeois democratic philosophy.

> In manufacture, the enrichment of the collective worker, and therefore of capital, in the matter of social productivity, is dependent upon the impoverishment of the workers in the matter of their individual powers of production.[20]

[20] *Capital,* Vol. I, Eng. trans. by E. and C. Paul, p. 382 f.

The same thesis was developed in the descriptive chapters of *Capital* which dealt with the contemporary history of capitalism and its effects upon wage earners as a class. Here Marx opened up most of the criticisms of capitalist industry which are current even today and reinforced his criticisms with much statistical and other factual data drawn from public reports. This part of his work was probably assisted by Engels, who had published his book on the *Condition of the Working-Class in England* in 1844. Marx dealt realistically with such subjects as the periodic recurrence of crises, the existence even in prosperous times of chronic technological unemployment, the destruction of the skilled crafts by new machines, the displacing of skilled by unskilled labor, the sweating of non-industrialized trades, and the growth of an unemployable slum-proletariat. As with his historical studies, the novel and distinctive characteristic of Marx's treatment was his stress upon the social repercussions of industrialization, its tendency to weaken primary social groups like the family, and therefore upon the human problems that it created. The upshot was the conclusion that capitalism is essentially parasitic and devours the human substance of society. The contradictory quality of capitalism seemed to him, as it had to Hegel, to be its paradoxical union of organization and anarchy: the technological organization of production united to an anarchy of exchange, an elaborate social coordination of the units of production united with an almost complete disregard for the adaptation of industrial means to human ends. Though the ideal received only occasional and passing statement, Marx had always in mind the contrast between capitalism and a planned and socialized economy, designed to produce and distribute goods when and where a legitimate need exists for them. Fundamentally, therefore, his criticism of capitalism was ethical. It depended upon a contrast between the actual condition of an industrial society and an ideal condition which he projected as a possible moral improvement of it. The most effective part of Marx's criticism was his assumption that any moral ideal, in order to be effective, must depend upon the social situation within which it arises. It must depend upon a realistic understanding of the situation as it is and upon a careful analysis of the possibilities of change that it contains. This of course does not alter the fact that the ideal itself is a moral valuation nor does it eliminate the factor of moral choice, since every situation contains many possibilities. Every situation has its policy-making dimension, and this is the ultimate reason why politics is a phase of it.

SURPLUS VALUE

Because Marx regarded any overt acknowledgment of a moral ideal as a confession of utopianism and also because, like Hegel, he conceived his ideals under the guise of the inevitable, he was obliged to show that the capitalist system must, with dialectical necessity, give rise to the opposed system of socialism because of its own internal contradictions This part of his argument took roughly the following form. The appropriation of surplus value by capitalist owners of the means of production supplies the underlying economic ground for the observed tendency of capitalism toward large-scale production and monopoly. Marx inferred that this must result in a continuous concentration of wealth in fewer hands and a sharper division of society into capitalists and proletarians. In the end this must produce a revolutionary situation in which the expropriators will be expropriated and production will be socialized. Apparently Marx believed that the general tendency would be both toward putting a larger and larger proportion of the population into the wage-earning class and also toward severer poverty in that class. The validity of this forecast proved to be a matter of long and not very fruitful controversy, for the factors involved turned out to be considerably more numerous and more complicated than the argument assumed. The concentration of industry into larger units took place, but this was not exactly the same thing as the concentration of ownership, since ownership and control are not identical. Capitalism assumed international proportions but working-class mentality did not break over national barriers to produce a class struggle on an international scale. The economic condition of workers apparently improved over what it had been earlier in the century. The number of salaried employees increased enormously but this was not at all the same thing as the growth of the proletariat, for the lower middle class showed no inclination whatever to accept the status of proletarians. From the point of view of practical politics this was probably the most disastrous aspect of

Marx's prophecy, for salaried workers simply could not be attracted into Marxian parties with the arguments that had seemed convincing to the older generation of wage earners.[21] At the very least the course of development toward the revolution was far longer and far more complicated than Marx anticipated. Toward the close of the century Engels admitted that the capacity for internal development within the capitalist system had been greatly underestimated.

The theoretical basis for Marx's argument was his theory of surplus value. The controversy over this theory almost monopolized the discussion of Marxism after the publication of the first volume of *Capital* in 1867. This controversy had in general no satisfactory outcome. None but those who were already professed Marxists accepted the theory, and they held to it in the face of criticism. In the meantime the Ricardian theory of value from which Marx took his start became antiquated for non-Marxian economists. This left little to discuss except the internal consistency of Marx's differences from Ricardo, which was not a matter of major importance in any case. The controversy was in fact an excellent example of an argument conducted at cross purposes; neither side recognized the tacit assumptions of the other side. One suspects that even for Marxists surplus value is today an object of respect as being a relic of the master rather than a serious part of the system. Lenin, for example, hardly mentioned it.

The theory of surplus value was professedly an extension of the labor theory of value held by the classical economists. Commodities exchanged in the market have the single common property of being the products of labor. But labor as here used, Marx explained, is " homogeneous " — that is, it is bare, abstract labor of no particular quality, measured solely by its duration, so that skilled labor may be counted as a multiple of it. The inclusion of labor in a commodity gives it value. The labor, however, must also be " socially necessary "; that is, it must be performed

[21] The feebleness of the Weimar Republic was due in part merely to the age of its clientele. In 1931 only a quarter of German salaried employees were organized in Marxian unions and only ten percent of Social Democrats were under twenty-five years old. See William Ebenstein, *The German Record* (1945), p. 216.

with the technical means normal to the prevailing conditions of production. Moreover the goods must be produced in such quantities that they can enter into exchange, for if the market refuses to take all the goods produced, too much labor time has been put into them, exactly as if they had been made by an antiquated technology. The power to labor is itself a commodity and its value is fixed in the same way as that of any other commodity. That is to say, its value in exchange is fixed by the labor needed to produce it; in other words the exchange value of labor amounts to the commodities needed to support the laborers and to enable them to reproduce their kind. But labor is unique among commodities because in being used up it creates more value. The two quantities of value, however, are not equal, and the employer sees to it, by the regimentation and organization of his workers, that the amount produced when their labor power is consumed is greater than the amount paid for it as a commodity. The labor power used produces value beyond the replacement of the labor power consumed. From this surplus value arise all profits, interest, and rent, since the mere exchange of labor or any other commodity adds nothing to its value.

The first puzzle about this argument is to find out what it was intended to explain. Marx's critics assumed that he was trying to explain the prices of commodities in a competitive market. This had been Ricardo's purpose when he formulated the labor theory of value, and in the first volume of *Capital* Marx apparently assumed that the prices of commodities would fluctuate, under the influence of supply and demand, a little above or below their value. But on that assumption the notion of socially necessary labor time reduced the whole theory to a tautology, because the price which a commodity will bring is the only measure of the time that is socially necessary to produce it. This objection might apply to any labor theory of value, but Marx's theory was open to other lines of attack. If surplus value is produced only by the consumption of labor power, an industry in which the capital invested goes mainly to buy labor ought to produce a large amount of surplus value and should return a large profit as compared with one in which capital goes mainly to buy machinery. But as Marx knew, the return on all capital, however invested, tends to be equal. In the third volume of *Capital* he explained this by competition between capitalists for the more profitable forms of investment. But such competition can equalize profits only by its effect upon prices, and accordingly Marx now explained prices as fixed by the cost of production *plus* an average return on the capital invested. Nothing but sheer accident would make the two theories coincide, that is, cause a price fixed by cost of production to be the same as one fixed by the value which labor power has put into the commodity. This celebrated discrepancy between the first and the third volumes of *Capital* was the subject of a long controversy and was exhaustively discussed by the Austrian economist, Böhm-Bawerk.[22] On the assumption that Marx's theory of value was merely an attempt to explain prices, his argument was unquestionably self-contradictory.

This criticism of surplus value, however, postulated a degree of economic positivism more characteristic of the end of the nineteenth century than of either Marx or the classical economists. In fact the labor theory of value never altogether lost the ethical connotation that it had in Locke; it remained in some degree the theory of a just or natural price. Considered from this point of view the theory of surplus value was in substance a dialectical refutation of the bourgeois economists' defense of capitalism, and it was in truth not an ineffective one. In spite of Marx's disclaimer of any moral presuppositions, his argument is more powerful when it is regarded as ethical than when it is taken as purely economic. It really sought to accomplish two purposes: first, to bring to light the ethical bias implied in the bourgeois defense of a competitive economy and to show that this bias is incompatible with the moral professions of individualist liberalism, and second, to pose the question of the nature of social justice in a highly organized society where individualism has ceased to be a tenable moral position. In short, Marx's social philosophy was the first realistic attack on a purely "acquisitive society," and there is little doubt that this, far more than its fine-spun dialectic, was what made it acceptable to his followers.

[22] *Karl Marx and the Close of his System,* Eng. trans. by Alice M. Macdonald, New York, 1898.

Considered in the light of the first of these two purposes, the theory of surplus value might be rephrased somewhat as follows. In a defense of capitalism labor power figures in two very different senses. It is at once a commodity for which the wage earner gets a bare subsistence and at the same time a creator of value which the capitalist receives entire after he has paid for the subsistence of the workers. All the initiative, skill, and creative intelligence that workers put into production, over and above what would keep them alive, goes to the capitalist, who at the same time is supposed to be paid precisely for his own superior enterprise, foresight, thrift, and capacity to organize. As Marx says, the whole social productivity of labor is made to assume "the specious semblance of being the productivity of capital." The theory of surplus value thus served the same critical purpose for Marx that the theory of economic rent later served for the Fabian Socialists.[23] It showed that, on the one hand, capitalism gives to the owners of the means of production an advantage of position that permits them to take a larger share of the product than their contribution to the process warrants. And it showed, on the other hand, that labor power, by reason of its disadvantageous position, is treated merely as a commodity on a level with other non-human commodities. Thus according to Engels the upshot of what Marx's theory of value proved was that "labor *can* have no value," because such an expression as the value of labor is as tautological as the value of value. The form of Marx's argument of course required him to present this difference of position as a logical contradiction which makes the capitalist system dialectically self-destructive. The removal of the contradiction will produce socialism, "which will emancipate human labor power from its position as a *commodity*."[24] This whole apparatus of alleged contradiction was confusing in the last degree. What it amounted to was essentially a moral judgment that it is objectionable to treat labor merely as a commodity. The contradiction is between the position actually assigned to labor in a competitive system and the

[23] George Bernard Shaw in Fabian Tract No. 41 (*The Fabian Society: Its Early History,* 1892) emphasized this transition.

[24] *Anti-Dühring,* Eng. trans. by E. Burns, p. 228.

moral profession of liberalism that human beings ought to be treated as ends and not as means.

THE COLLECTIVE WORKER

The second aspect of Marx's theory of value set a problem rather than offered a solution. The ethical force of the labor theory of value lay in the argument that in a system of perfectly free exchange every individual would bring to the market the product of his own labor and receive in return for it an equivalent value. The distribution of products would therefore be just, in the sense that everyone would draw out as much as he put in; in effect every individual would enjoy the full product of his own labor. The argument was individualist in two senses: it assumed that every person produces by virtue of his own effort and skill, without any important consequences from cooperation and organization, and it assumed also that the total social good is a summation of individual advantages. These assumptions in a highly industrialized society are, as Marx perceived, highly questionable if not absolutely fictitious. In a system of highly socialized production, which has become cooperative to the point where no one by himself makes any usable commodity, there is no way of telling what any individual produces. The product is literally a social product, and the true productive unit is society itself, or as Marx put it, the "collective laborer," organized for joint cooperative production. This is the "reality" around which the capitalist economy wraps "mystifications" like prices and profits and wages. The coexistence in the same system of two incompatible elements — socialized production and capitalist appropriation — is the underlying contradiction that drives society toward a revolutionary readjustment of forces. In such a readjustment a fully socialized economy must create a social system consonant with its own fully cooperative nature.

Fundamentally, therefore, the purpose of Marx's theory of value was ethical and not purely economic; it was a theory of social good and not a theory of prices. And the fundamental difference between Marx's theory and the Ricardian theory of value from which he derived it was a difference of standard for measuring social justice and well-being. Essentially Marx's criticism of capitalist economics was that it construed human relations in terms of a cash-nexus which conceals the human problems involved. And in so far as these economic concepts describe what actually exists, the relationships must be for the worker stultifying and distorting. The technical perfection of the collective worker is purchased at a moral cost to its human elements.

> It [manufacture] transforms the worker into a cripple, a monster, by forcing him to develop some highly specialized dexterity at the cost of a world of productive impulses and faculties . . . To begin with, the worker sells his labor power to capital because he himself lacks the material means requisite for the production of a commodity. But now his individual labor power actually renounces work unless it is sold to capital.[25]

Against the conception of a society in which the economy is assumed to be automatically self-regulating through the operations of the market and in which human relations are conceived in terms of price, Marx sets up the ideal of a planned and completely humanized economy: "an association of free individuals who work with jointly owned means of production, and wittingly expend their several labor powers as a combined social labor power."[26] A society in which the social control of production had become consonant with the actual social nature of production would be one in which the economy is consciously regulated to supply commodities where needed and in the quantity needed and in which the whole social power to produce is intelligently directed to yield a socially desirable result.

> Only when production will be under the conscious and prearranged control of society, will society establish a direct relation between the quantity of social labor time employed in the production of definite articles and the quantity of the demand of society for them.[27]

It was not in Marx's nature, or indeed in the nature of the dialectic, to acknowledge this criticism of an acquisitive, capitalist society for what it was, a moral objection against the human consequences of such a society. Marx had derived from Hegel a kind of contempt for any belief in the efficacy of moral convictions and a tendency to think of moral ideals as if they were merely individual caprices bred in the mind by the operation of

[25] *Capital,* Vol. I, Eng. trans. by E. and C. Paul, p. 381.
[26] *Ibid.,* p. 52.
[27] *Capital,* Vol. III, Eng. trans. by Ernest Untermann, p. 221.

substantial but non-moral social forces. With both men this was a temperamental perversion of the sound idea that moral criticism, in order to be effective, has to depend on a realistic analysis of what is criticized. One consequence of this bias was that, when Marx criticized the notion that social justice consisted in giving to every man the fruits of his labor, he directed the criticism not against economic and ethical individualism but against the utopian socialists or the amateurs whom he called "vulgar economists." All such speculations, he thought, amounted to sentimental schemes for accepting the advantages of capitalist production and then manipulating distribution in some arbitrary way alleged to give the laborer the whole product of his industry. Against all such schemes Marx argued, quite in the manner of the classical economists, that capitalism or indeed any system of economic production carries with it its own mode of distributing the product. His own "scientific socialism" he conceived as differing from utopianism in accepting to the full the conclusions of economic science, by which he meant the classical economics, but supplementing the conclusions with a proof that they are dialectically self-defeating. The consequence was that Marx, like the *laissez-faire* economists, tended to regard any legislative regulation of the economy as utopian, or at best as a mere palliative which is useless unless it hastens or facilitates the revolution. This bias was a cause of continual difficulty in the strategy of Marxian parties toward social legislation, which became a factor of steadily increasing importance in all political programs, and also a fruitful cause of revisionist deviations and reinterpretations of Marx.

On the other hand the very determination to be relentlessly realistic introduced into Marxism a factor that was itself essentially utopian. Quite obviously, "the conscious and prearranged control of society," which at the revolution is supposed to take over the direction of industry, was in substance a figure of speech. It personified "society" in order to contrast control exercised in the public interest with control in the interest of a class, but under no social system will "society" ever literally control anything. The result of this personification was a tacit assumption that it is necessary to plan the revolution but not necessary to consider anything that will happen thereafter. In Marx's theory of value there was a similar disposition to assume that an organization runs itself. In his anxiety to show that labor produces everything and capital nothing, he was willing to concede only grudgingly that direction and management are themselves productive. But even if production were completely socialized, the function of making policies in industry would remain at least as important as it is in a system of private enterprise. Possibly it might be more important, since in a planned economy there must be some effective substitute to do the work that the price system is supposed to do in a free market. The passages quoted in the second paragraph above convey the impression that, with the coming of socialism, the effects of the industrial division of labor will simply disappear. In fact a socialist government could no more dispense with questions of policy, and therefore of political expedience and social justice, than any other government. How very rudimentary the ideas of revolutionary Marxists about government and management often were may be seen from Lenin's sketch of what he thought a post-revolutionary government in Russia would be like. Few utopian socialists have planned a state that was farther from what in fact it turned out to be.[28]

The utopian element of Marxism was concentrated, so to speak, in the classless society which is the goal of the whole dialectical process in history. The classless society was the element of apocalyptic vision which is perhaps indispensable for any revolutionary theory — the glittering hope for the future that compensates for the disillusionments of the present and the disappointments of the revolution itself. It was characteristic of both Marx and Engels that neither man was interested to envisage what this ideal would be like if it were realized or to draw the outlines of a truly cooperative commonwealth and describe the steps by which it might be realized. Perhaps they felt that the documenting of a vision is little short of impertinence, or with Lenin that the ideal was none the worse if it should never be realized. In this sense the classless society was a kind of myth, designed to give cohesion and volitional drive to a revolutionary party, like the myths that Sorel made an important part of the

[28] *State and Revolution,* ch. 5.

theory of revolutionary syndicalism. What was typical is that the ideal, conceived as a far-off event, was not intended to serve as a guide in any day-to-day process of improvement. In so far as Marxism remained a revolutionary theory, it centered upon producing the revolution. In so far as it became evolutionary and revisionist, as to a large extent it did in the years before World War I, its purposes became largely those of left-wing liberalism. As an ideal the classless society meant substantially a form of wholly noncoercive association, in respect both to political authority and to the authority of direction and management in industry. In such a society every person would contribute voluntarily according to his ability and would receive without price according to his needs. The state will, in Engels' famous expression, "wither away," since it is essentially the repressive organ of a society based upon exploitation and would have no purpose in a classless society. In it also management and administration in industry will vanish. Again as Engels said:

> The government of persons is replaced by the administration of things and the direction of the process of production.[29]

Just how the socializing of industry can diminish the authority of management, or indeed remove the stultifying effects of the division of labor, neither Marx nor Engels undertook to say.

Of far more practical importance than the classless society was the transitional stage, the dictatorship of the proletariat, envisaged by Marx and Engels as the immediate consequence of a proletarian revolution. In this stage, by a violent uprising, the proletariat is conceived to have seized power and thus to have created a state which uses coercion in its own behalf. The dictatorship of the proletariat, therefore, like the bourgeois state that it supplants is an instrument of class domination. Its function is to destroy the bureaucracy of the displaced capitalist state, to convert the means of production into public property and to repress any effort by the bourgeoisie toward a counter-revolution. Only after these purposes have been accomplished, presumably, will the process of "withering away" begin, and

[29] *Anti-Dühring,* Eng. trans. by E. Burns, p. 315. Cf. Engels' letter to Bebel, March 18–28, 1875; *Marx-Engels Correspondence, 1846–1895,* p. 332 ff.

the probable duration of the dictatorship is left entirely to conjecture. Neither Marx nor Engels developed the dictatorship of the proletariat into an important part of their social philosophy. The principal references to it concern the revolutionary disturbances in France in 1848–50. It was of course obvious that the classless society, if it were ever to become a reality, would not spring into existence over night. Some transitional stage must be supposed. The lapsing of European politics after 1850 into a state of non-revolutionary calm made it unnecessary to pursue the subject very far. It was Lenin who seized upon the conception in 1917 and made it the instrument for a revival of revolutionary Marxism, and it was the success of Lenin's revolution that made it a matter of vital importance for present-day political thought.

SELECTED BIBLIOGRAPHY

Karl Marx's Interpretation of History. By Mandell M. Bober. 2nd ed. rev. Cambridge, Mass., 1948.

The Marxian Theory of the State. By Sherman H. M. Chang. Philadelphia, 1931.

What Marx Really Meant. By G. D. H. Cole. London, 1934.

The Materialist Conception of History: A Critical Analysis. By Karl Federn. London, 1939.

"The Social Philosophy of Karl Marx." By Abram L. Harris. In *Ethics*, Vol. LVIII (1948), No. 3, Part II.

History of Economic Doctrines. By Eduard Heimann. New York, 1945. Ch. 6.

Towards the Understanding of Karl Marx: A Revolutionary Interpretation. By Sidney Hook. New York, 1933.

From Hegel to Marx: Studies in the Intellectual Development of Karl Marx. By Sidney Hook. New York, 1936.

Reason, Social Myths, and Democracy. By Sidney Hook. New York, 1940. Chs. 9–12.

Karl Marx: an Essay. By Harold J. Laski. London, 1922.

Karl Marx's Capital: An Introductory Essay. By A. D. Lindsay. London, 1925.

Karl Marx: The Story of his Life. By Franz Mehring. Eng. trans. by Edward Fitzgerald. New York, 1935.

The Open Society and its Enemies. By K. R. Popper. 2 vols. London, 1945. Chs. 13–21.

An Essay on Marxian Economics. By Joan Robinson. London, 1942.

Democracy and Socialism: A Contribution to the Political History of the Past 150 Years. By Arthur Rosenberg. Eng. trans. by George Rosen. New York, 1939.

Karl Marx, his Life and Work. By Otto Rühle. Eng. trans. by E. and C. Paul. New York, 1929.

The Economic Interpretation of History. By E. R. A. Seligman. 2nd ed. rev. New York, 1924.

The Theory of Capitalist Development: Principles of Marxian Political Economy. By Paul M. Sweezy. New York, 1942.

Human Nature: The Marxian View. By Vernon Venable. New York, 1945.

CHAPTER XXXIV

COMMUNISM

Karl Marx once said of himself that he was not a Marxist. This remark referred in part to his own comparative indifference to the doctrinal completeness of his social philosophy and the misgivings with which he and Engels in their later life regarded the dogmatism of some of their disciples. It referred also to the wide variety of influences both theoretical and practical that flowed from his thought. These influences were exerted upon historians, sociologists, and political scientists, and also upon every form of political radicalism, socialist, syndicalist, and anarchist. Even within larger Marxian parties, like the German Social Democracy, Marxism never stabilized itself as a single generally accepted system of ideas. As socialist parties grew in size and influence, they tended to put aside the revolutionary elements in Marx, and to become evolutionary or "revisionist" in their philosophy and reformist in their policy. But there never ceased to be theorists who regarded Marxism as revolutionary, and the shades of difference between interpretations of Marx were endless.[1] With the rise of Russian communism, however, all these differences receded into a position of merely historical importance. Russian Marxism, on the other hand, which down to World War I had been little more than a backwash, became Marxism *par excellence.* In the main this restatement of Marxism was the work of Lenin, though Trotsky contributed more to it than its official interpreters admit. Stalin, after Lenin's death and Trotsky's exile, made additions that were more notable for being opportune than for being dialectically adroit. In order to understand this body of ideas it is important to keep in view its dependence on Marxism and still more to appreciate its very wide departures from the Marxian tradition in Western Europe.

[1] See Francis W. Coker's *Recent Political Thought* (1934), chs. 3–9.

THE RELATION OF LENINISM TO MARXISM

Lenin's Marxism was by profession utterly dogmatic and orthodox, to be supported in all contingencies by a kind of scholastic exegesis of the master's *ipsissima verba*. The bitterest and most constant condemnations that he hurled at his opponents were charges of " adulterating " Marx's meaning as revealed by a literal and correct interpretation. In this respect Lenin followed a tradition already set by Russian Marxists, who, as Engels said ironically in 1893, " interpret passages from Marx's writings and letters in the most contradictory ways, just as if they were texts from the classics or the New Testament." At the same time, however, Lenin always described theory as a guide to action. It is not a body of static doctrines but rather of suggestive ideas to be used in assessing concrete situations and to be modified in application. Some of Lenin's fiercest struggles with his own followers resulted from his effort to lead them on paths that were generally believed to be bad Marxism. His dogmatism was in fact far more a profession than a practice, and when he practiced it, it usually served his purposes. Much of his genius as a leader consisted in this curious combination of rigidity and suppleness, his ability to take instantaneous advantage of an opportunity, to make a change of front appear as the logical next step, to change direction without abandoning his course, and in general to combine opportunism with what no doubt he himself sincerely regarded as rigid adherence to principle. Marxian theory played in Lenin's thought, and continues to play in communism, two diverse parts. On the one side it was dogma, an absolute and unassailable creed or quasi-religious symbol, whose principal function was to elicit unreserved devotion to a cause. On the other it was a body of interpretations and hypotheses intended to direct political policy and to be modified in the light of experience. Between the two there stood an elaborate exegesis to prove that no policy, however unexpected, was really a departure from Marxism but only a better understanding of what Marxism always really meant.

The official definition of Lenin's philosophy, laid down by Stalin in his *Foundations of Leninism* (1924), is that " Leninism is Marxism in the epoch of imperialism and of the proletarian revolution." According to this definition Lenin's work consisted in bringing Marxism down to date, taking account of the evolution of capitalist society after Marx, and reformulating its theory and its tactics in the light of developments of which Marx saw only the beginning. At the same time Stalin took note of a different but, as he said, incorrect interpretation of Lenin's philosophy which regarded it as an adaptation of Marxism to the state of affairs in Russia. For obvious reasons this latter interpretation could not be accepted without abandoning the claim that Leninism is a social philosophy generally applicable to all countries, which would amount to admitting that Lenin's work as a Marxian theorist was, from his own point of view, a failure. In point of fact, however, the changes that Lenin made in Marxian theory conform only in small part to Stalin's official account of his work. In certain respects, it is true, Lenin's revision did supplement Marxism in the light of changes that occurred in the development of capitalism. These changes, as was quite reasonably urged by both Lenin and Trotsky, greatly altered the position of the Russian revolution as compared with the revolutions that Marx had observed in the 1840's. It is also true, however, that Lenin had made changes in Marxian theory of much more profound importance long before the international situation became a matter of concern to Russian Marxists. In general these changes grew naturally out of the internal situation in Russia and the position of a revolutionary party under the Czar. The adaptation of Marxism to the state of affairs in Russia was a primary condition for the success of a Russian Marxian party, and in the end Lenin's career as a revolutionist depended far more on his understanding of Russia than on a theory about the evolution of capitalism.

When Marxism was first adopted as the philosophy of a Russian socialist party in the 1880's, it supervened upon a native Russian socialism which was in general agrarian and humanitarian. The main principle of this philosophy was the belief that socialism in Russia might develop directly from the communism of the *mir* or village, without passing through the stages of social development characteristic of industrialism. It followed that socialist propaganda in Russia should be addressed to the peasantry. The Marxists on the other hand held that the evolution from feudalism to capitalism to socialism was "inevitable" and that the hope of socialism in Russia as in all countries depended upon the urban proletariat. Curiously, the position of the Russian Marxists was not the position that Marx himself had taken with respect to Russia, as has been indicated in the preceding chapter. No Marxist, naturally, was unaware of the political and economic backwardness of Russia, but the general tendency of their theory was to make them minimize the part of the peasantry in a Russian revolution. One source of Lenin's strength as an organizer of revolution was that he never succumbed to this tendency of Russian Marxism or lost sight of the peasantry and the question of the land. In 1917 his success depended on his clear perception of the fact that no revolution could succeed without at least the acquiescence of the peasants and on his readiness to postpone his own preferred policy of nationalizing the land. Lenin's Marxism was always flexible enough in practice to permit him to take a line that Russian Marxists commonly regarded as not Marxian at all.

Another problem of crucial importance for Russian Marxism and one that emerged early in its history concerned the organization of an effective socialist party and its relation to conspiratorial and extra-legal activities. This question of party organization in turn was closely related to the acceptance or rejection of democratic political principles and practices in the state. In the end the party proved to be the decisive factor in settling the political character of Russian communism, but it had been a matter of keen debate between Russian Marxists for years before 1917. Here again, as in the case of the land and the peasantry, Marx and Engels provided little direct guidance to Russian Marxists. After 1850 they had simply severed their connections with the underground, a course that a Russian revolutionist could not imitate under the Czar. Nor was it possible to imitate in Russia the tactics of the great Marxian parties such as the Social Democrats in Germany. In general these parties had always assumed that the success of a socialist program depended upon the liberalizing of government, that the extension of social control over industry would retain and extend political freedom, and that socialist parties would as a matter of course be more rather than less democratic in their internal organization than bourgeois parties. In Russia it proved to be far easier to profess allegiance to principles like these than to put them effectively into practice. Indeed it may well be doubted whether a socialist revolution could ever have succeeded on these lines.

At all events Russian Marxists had been divided and subdivided on these questions, and especially on questions of party organization and tactics, since the beginning of the twentieth century. Lenin's first appearance in the rôle of a Marxian theorist was as the proponent of a type of party organization, and he figured until the end of his life as the leader of the Bolshevik faction of the Marxian Social Democratic Labor Party.[2] This combination of party organizer and theorist was characteristic of Lenin and also a source of his strength, since no other Russian Marxist united the two qualities in an equal degree. But Lenin was first an organizer and second a theorist. Everything that he wrote, except his *Development of Capitalism in Russia*, which was written during a period of exile in Siberia, had reference to a specific situation and was occasional in its purpose. Indeed Lenin might almost be said to have had no existence except as a party member, and he was notorious among socialists for years before the Revolution because of the dictatorial nature of his leadership. Nothing satisfied him in his associates short of unquestioning obedience, and he combined a perfect assurance of the rightness of his policies with perfect devotion to the cause of revolution and a complete lack of personal self-seeking. His theories, in spite of their constant reaffirmation of Marxian generalizations, always had reference to a specific course of action in a definite situation. Lenin's Marxism, therefore, was at once intensely dogmatic and highly pragmatic, a combination that can be as puzzling to historians as it often was to his Marxian associates.

[2] The words Bolshevik and Menshevik, meaning respectively majority and minority, were assigned to the two factions first by the accident of their relative strength in a party convention in 1903. Lenin continued to call his faction "the majority," because of the prestige value of the name, though usually it was not a majority and sometimes it almost ceased to exist as a party. The split which began in 1903 did not become permanent and complete until 1912. In the interval there was a bewildering series of "unifications" and redivisions. The history of these and of Lenin's part in them can be followed in Bertram D. Wolfe's *Three Men Who Made a Revolution* (1948), chs. 14 and 30 and *passim*.

The long and bitter controversy between Lenin's faction and his Menshevik opponents extended through some fifteen years before the Revolution and was conducted with all the dialectical subtlety long characteristic of Russian Marxism. Behind the two factions there was, however, a fundamental difference in point of view that was perfectly intelligible and entirely practical in its significance. The issue turned upon the kind of organization that was suitable and effective for a revolutionary socialist party in Russia in the period that led up to World War I. Between the two factions there was no difference in their general profession of Marxian principles but profound differences about the way to make them effective. In general the Bolsheviks saw the center of the movement in a conspiratorial underground and in the extra-legal activities of such an underground. It followed logically that the nucleus of the party should be an inner group of professional revolutionists, absolutely and fanatically devoted to the revolution, rigidly disciplined and tightly organized, not too large for secrecy, and acting as the "vanguard" of all the potentially though not actually revolutionary elements in trade unions and among the workers. Lenin's opponents, on the other hand, tended to see the purpose of the revolutionary movement as the organization of the working class for legal political action. Hence the party was for them a mass-organization aiming to be as inclusive as possible of trade unions and other forms of working-class institution. Of necessity, therefore, its form of organization would have to be decentralized or perhaps federalized and at least potentially "democratic." The ideologies of the two groups corresponded in general to these two points of view. They reflected on the one hand the relation of a revolutionary conspirator toward an extra-legal secret society and on the other hand the relation of a working man toward his union.[3] And these attitudes implied, as will appear, marked differences of opinion about the course which the revolution would pursue once it had achieved its first success. It is evident that the point of view of Lenin's faction had a definite affinity with the outlook long characteristic of Russian revolutionary and even terrorist organizations whether Marxian or not, while that

[3] Wolfe, *op. cit.*, p. 367.

of his opponents was an attempt to imitate the course marked out by the Marxian parties in Western Europe. In this sense Lenin's Marxism was thoroughly Russian and was sharply in contrast with the main line of Marxian tradition. There can be little doubt that his success as a Russian leader was largely due to this fact. But his success exacted its price in the course that it dictated in 1917 for the Revolution.

This question of the organization of the party was the subject of Lenin's first important theoretical work, a pamphlet entitled *What is to be done?* which he published in 1902 in *Iskra,* a new journal largely planned and founded by him. The thesis of the work is stated succinctly in the following passage.

> A small, compact core, consisting of reliable, experienced and hardened workers, with responsible agents in the principal districts and connected by all the rules of strict secrecy with the organizations of revolutionists, can, with the wide support of the masses and without an elaborate set of rules, perform *all* the functions of a trade-union organization, and perform them, moreover, in the manner the Social Democrats desire.[4]

TRADE UNIONIST AND SOCIALIST IDEOLOGY

It was not Lenin's way, however, to advocate a form of party organization on grounds merely of political expedience. He was quite aware, and his opponents were aware, that a party such as he described in the passage just quoted was not planned upon the lines followed by the Social Democracy in Germany. He was also aware that it ran counter to accepted principles of Marxism. No passage from Marx had been quoted more frequently than the famous sentence, "The emancipation of the working class is the work of the working class itself." This sentence summed up the principle of economic materialism, that the relations of production create the characteristic revolutionary ideology of the proletariat and that this ideology is the mainspring of an effective social revolution. It was upon this principle that Marxists had always distinguished their own "scien-

[4] *Collected Works,* Vol. IV, Book II, p. 194. *Selected Works,* Vol. II, p. 133. The English edition of Lenin's *Collected Works,* translated from the Russian edition published by the Lenin Institute in Moscow, is not complete. The *Selected Works,* 12 vols., follows a selection made by the Lenin Institute. Both are published by International Publishers, New York.

tific" socialism from utopianism, and the "inevitable" revolution from the "made" revolutions of idealist dreamers. The social revolution simply cannot be made by force or exhortation to run ahead of the underlying industrial development upon which a proletarian mentality depends. Knowing all this, Lenin was quite aware that his conception of party organization was logically untenable without a corresponding change in the Marxian theory of ideology. Accordingly he made perhaps the boldest and most drastic change in Marxian theory ever made by a Marxist who was concerned to preserve his orthodoxy. The usual Marxian argument, he asserted, confused the mentality or ideology of trade unionism with that of socialism. Spontaneously the workers do not become socialists but trade unionists; socialism has to be brought to them from the outside by middle-class intellectuals.

> We said that *there could not yet be* Social-Democratic consciousness among the workers [in the Russian strikes in the 1890's]. This consciousness could only be brought to them from without. The history of all countries shows that the working class, exclusively by its own effort, is able to develop only trade-union consciousness, i.e., it may itself realize the necessity for combining in unions, to fight against the employers and to strive to compel the government to pass necessary labor legislation, etc.[5]

The socialist philosophy of Marx and Engels, Lenin argued, was as a matter of historical fact created by representatives of the bourgeois intelligentsia and it was introduced into Russia by a similar group. A trade-union movement is incapable of developing a revolutionary ideology for itself. Hence the choice for a revolutionary party lies between allowing the trade unions to fall a prey to the ideology of the middle class or indoctrinating it with the ideology of socialist intellectuals.

This conception of socialist ideology was obviously not that of the Western Marxist but that of the Russian revolutionary intellectual, who had always regarded the revolution as something that must be brought to the masses "from without" and who assumed that the people, except under the leadership of revolutionary intellectuals, were somnolent, inert, and incapable of

[5] *Collected Works,* Vol. IV, Book II, pp. 114 f. *Selected Works,* Vol. II, p. 53. The italics are Lenin's.

helping themselves. Lenin's reasoning about the Russian trade unionist was analogous to Marx's reasoning about the petty bourgeoisie and the peasantry, which are politically impotent except as they follow either the bourgeoisie or the proletariat, but by an astonishing paradox Lenin applied the reasoning to the proletariat itself. Being unable to create its own ideology, the working class is hung between the parties that represent a bourgeois ideology and those that represent a revolutionary socialist ideology. It can only be captured by one or the other, but it is the party intellectual who creates the ideology on which the revolution depends. Few political philosophies have given to intellectuals a rôle as world-shaking and none has assigned to the proletariat so small a share in the proletarian revolution. Quite obviously, however, Lenin's theory of the party and its ideology, propounded in 1902, prefigured very accurately the meaning of the proletarian dictatorship.

Nevertheless it might easily be construed as a dialectical refutation of Marxism. If, as numberless Marxian dialecticians have argued, "New social ideas and theories arise only after the development of the material life of society has set new tasks before society,"[6] and if the working class by reason of its industrial experience develops the mentality of trade unionism but nothing farther, why should not that mentality be taken as the final step in the evolution of a working-class ideology and why should not trade-union tactics be the final answer of the proletariat to capitalism? Or again, if socialist ideology must be produced and disseminated among the proletariat by middle-class intellectuals, what remains of the principle accepted by all Marxists, that new relations of production arise within society "not as a result of the deliberate and conscious activity of men, but spontaneously, unconsciously, independently of the will of man"? And finally by what nicety of economic materialism does a productive system that has created bourgeois and proletarian classes and made them irreconcilably antagonistic to each other also produce out of the middle class an intelligentsia whose social function is the making of an ideology to destroy the middle class? And if the revolution cannot occur except in consequence of an ideology

[6] Stalin, "Dialectical and Historical Materialism," *Leninism: Selected Writings* (New York, 1942), pp. 417 f.

provided through the party, was not Marx unduly modest when he said that his philosophy could only " shorten and lessen the birth-pangs "? Russian Marxism being a foreign importation, the one tie that could preserve its logical continuity with Marxism as a general social philosophy was, as Trotsky perhaps saw sooner than Lenin, the assumption that international capitalism operates everywhere to produce a single integral system of ideology.

Manifestly, however, Lenin in 1902 was not mainly concerned with making a philosophical system. What interested him was a strong party and an effective type of party organization. Viewed in this light his theory of socialist ideology was intelligible and dealt with a problem which no revolutionary party, least of all a Russian party, could avoid if it was seriously bent upon success. The Marxian doctrine that the revolution must mature, that no society can " overleap the natural phases of evolution," had always been an invitation to revisionism and therefore deadly in its effect upon revolutionary parties. The revolutionist who waits for the revolution to ripen can easily miss his chance. As Lenin said in 1917, " At the decisive moment and in the decisive place you must prove the stronger one. You must be victorious." At some point the dialectical development of the social system passes over into the revolutionary will of a leader and a party prepared to gamble on the chances of success. The reason Marx never met this change of phase with more than vague phrases about proletarian dictatorship was that his revolutionary ventures were never close enough to success to make it more than a speculative question. But Lenin's belief in the dialectic of history was more than matched by his will as a practical revolutionist. And within three years of the date when he issued his plan of party-organization the Russian Revolution of 1905 turned the proper tactics to be followed by a socialist party during a bourgeois revolution into an important practical problem. This question will come up for further examination in a later section of this chapter. At present it is important to see clearly the assumptions with which Lenin approached a working-class revolution. Stripped of its Marxian technicalities it amounted to this. Working-class people, whether peasants or industrial workers, do not naturally have much inclination for revolution. Since Lenin never doubted that revolution is inevitable, this was nearly the same as saying that they have very little capacity to think for themselves, that they learn very little from their experience with the economic system, and that their ideas about what is good for them are not really of much importance. Hence, left to themselves, they have little motive or spontaneous capacity for self-government. "Aside from the influence of the party, there is no *conscious* activity of the workers." Consequently they must take their ideas from the Marxian professionals, who alone know the dialectic of history and can predict what the revolution can and must bring forth. It was this conception of the educational function of socialism that put Lenin farthest outside the tradition of Marxism in Western Europe. It called out the sharpest criticism, not from anti-revolutionists, but precisely from revolutionists like Rosa Luxemburg. What Lenin called "proletarian discipline," she said, is discipline by the Central Committee of the party, not "the voluntary self-discipline of social democracy."

THE PARTY

The clue, therefore, to Lenin's revision of Marxism, and indeed to the course which he ultimately followed in the Russian Revolution, lay in his theory of the party. The party as Lenin conceived it is a carefully picked body of the intellectual and moral *élite,* an intellectual *élite* in the sense that its Marxian scholarship preserves the purity of Marxian doctrine and provides the guide to policy in the party and, once the party has attained power, in the state as well; a moral *élite* in the sense that selection and a rigid party training gives it complete, wholehearted, and devoted absorption in the purposes of the party and the revolution. Such a conception of the party was no novelty in socialist theory, but it had belonged not to Marx but to the French syndicalist Blanqui. The party, as Lenin thought of it, is in the midst of all working-class movements, providing the guidance and the leadership which such movements require, but it is always distinguishable from the body of workers. It was not the case, of course, that Lenin ever had any desire to exclude workers from membership, but such as were admitted must be carefully selected and carefully trained for their duties as members. It is also true that the purpose of the party is the good of the proletariat and of the whole people, but the party is definitively the judge of what is good for them. The party thus becomes the staff organization in the struggle of the proletariat to gain power and to retain it after it has been gained. It is the "vanguard" of the proletariat, the most class-conscious and at the same time the most devoted and self-sacrificing part of the working class. Marxism is the creed that holds it together and organization is the principle that makes it powerful.

From the beginning of his career as a leader, therefore, ideal union through Marxism as a creed and material union through rigid organization and discipline were the two foundation stones upon which Lenin proposed to build a revolutionary movement. Two passages may be placed side by side to show how constantly he adhered to this purpose. The first is from his pamphlet, *One Step Forward, Two Steps Back,* published in 1904.

In its struggle for power the proletariat has no other weapon but organization. Divided by the rule of anarchic competition in the bourgeois world, ground down by slave labor for capital, constantly thrust back to the "lower depths" of utter destitution, savagery and degeneration, the proletariat can become, and will inevitably become, an invincible force only when its ideological unity around the principles of Marxism is consolidated by the material unity of an organization, which unites millions of toilers in the army of the working class.

The second is from a resolution adopted at a congress of the Communist International in 1920:

The Communist Party is part of the working class, namely, its most advanced, class-conscious, and therefore most revolutionary part. The Communist Party is formed of the best, most intelligent, self-sacrificing and far-seeing workers. . . . The Communist Party is the organized political lever by means of which the more advanced part of the working class leads all the proletarian and semi-proletarian mass in the right direction.[7]

The latter passage became the basis for the description of the party in its charter of 1934 and its amended charter of 1939 and also for the clause in the Constitution of 1936 which for the first time gave it legal status. According to the last the party "rep-

[7] The first passage is in the *Selected Works,* Vol. II, p. 466. The Theses and Statutes of the Communist International, adopted in 1920, are printed in *Blueprint for World Conquest* (Washington, 1946); the quotation is on pp. 73 f.

resents the leading nucleus of all organizations of the working-people." In the Convention which adopted the Constitution of 1936, Stalin, after praising its "consistent and thoroughgoing democratism," since it is free from the reservations and restrictions of bourgeois-democratic constitutions, added:

> I must admit that the draft of the new Constitution does preserve the regime of the dictatorship of the working class, just as it also preserves unchanged the present leading position of the Communist Party of the U.S.S.R. . . .
>
> A party is part of a class, its most advanced part. Several parties, and, consequently, freedom for parties, can exist only in a society in which there are antagonistic classes whose interests are mutually hostile and irreconcilable. . . .
>
> In the U.S.S.R. there are only two classes, workers and peasants, whose interests — far from being mutually hostile — are, on the contrary, friendly. Hence there is no ground in the U.S.S.R. for the existence of several parties, and, consequently, for freedom for these parties.[8]

Thus the conception of the party which Lenin formulated in 1904 has remained the conception of the party in Russia, and with the success of the Revolution the party became the mainspring of the government itself. As Stalin said in 1928:

> In the Soviet Union, in the land where the dictatorship of the proletariat is in force, no important political or organizational problem is ever decided by our soviets and other mass organizations without directives from our party. In this sense, we may say that the dictatorship of the proletariat is substantially the dictatorship of the party, as the force that effectively guides the proletariat.[9]

Lenin's idea of the party was the counterpart or supplement of his idea of philosophical Marxism. Both play a twofold part. Marxism is a dogma and a symbol that elicits the deepest loyalty and at the same time a scientific guide to action. Similarly the party is the semi-priestly custodian of a truth whose purity must at all times be preserved against the "deviations" with which uninstructed or evil-minded persons try to corrupt it and at

[8] *Leninism: Selected Writings* (New York, 1942), p. 395.

[9] Quoted in *Social-Economic Movements* (1946), ed. by Harry W. Laidler, p. 428. On the present conception of the party see Julian Towster, *Political Power in the U.S.S.R.* (1948), ch. 6.

the same time a body of expert tacticians equipped with a scientific theory of history and society. Nothing could surpass the dogmatism with which at all times Lenin asserted the integrity of the Marxian philosophy and the solidarity of the party.

To belittle socialist ideology *in any way, to deviate from it in the slightest degree means* strengthening bourgeois ideology.

Freedom of criticism is opportunism, eclecticism, lack of principle, "Bernstein revisionism," and hence a form of disloyalty.

We are marching in a compact group along a precipitous and difficult path, firmly holding each other by the hand. We are surrounded on all sides by enemies, and are under their almost constant fire. We have combined voluntarily, especially for the purpose of fighting the enemy and not to retreat into the adjacent marsh. . . . And now several in our crowd begin to cry out — let us go into this marsh! [10]

At the same time the theory makes possible scientific predictions so accurate that politics becomes practically a kind of engineering. The official *History of the Communist Party* asserts:

The power of the Marxist-Leninist theory lies in the fact that it enables the Party to find the right orientation in any situation, to understand the inner connection of current events, to foresee their course and to perceive not only how and in what direction they are developing in the present, but how and in what direction they are bound to develop in the future.[11]

Accordingly it is equally the function of the party to decide questions of policy and to pass upon the "correctness" of opinions in the light of the "Marxist-Leninist theory." From this double function follows the curious combination of free discussion and closed decision that Western observers have found puzzling in Russian politics. Within the whole body of opinion possible at a given time some questions are still open for discussion and are therefore legitimate matters of "self-criticism." Other questions have been decided and have taken their place among the dogmas that are closed to discussion. There is perhaps no analogue in Western European thought for this combination of fixed prin-

[10] *What is to be done? Collected Works,* Vol. IV, Book II, pp. 123, 97. *Selected Works,* Vol. II, pp. 62, 33. The italics are Lenin's.

[11] *History of the Communist Party of the Soviet Union* (*Bolsheviks*). Short Course (New York, 1939), p. 355.

ciples and free controversy within set limits except the medieval distinction between revelation and reason. In this sense communism is a kind of political clericalism and its philosophy is a kind of secular scholasticism. However much it may change, the changes must always be derived by a complicated reinterpretation from the unchangeable principles of Marxism. The party, when it speaks *ex cathedra,* also speaks infallibly.

It follows as a matter of course from the purposes assigned to the party that its organization must be strongly centralized or hierarchical, "from the top downward." Democracy in party organization Lenin described as "a useless and harmful toy." He consistently opposed any form of decentralization or federalism that left freedom to local groups or autonomy to the constituent elements of the party. From 1904 until 1917 he was frequently engaged in polemics on this subject, since it was one of the most important points at issue between Bolsheviks and Mensheviks. Sometimes criticism forced him to give ground temporarily but he never changed his view. For his position he invented the name, "democratic centralism," though no one but Lenin was able to perceive its democracy. In 1904, in the pamphlet *One Step Forward, Two Steps Back,* he put the issue bluntly.

> Bureaucracy *versus* democracy is the same thing as centralism *versus* automatism, it is the organizational principle of revolutionary political democracy as opposed to the organizational principle of the opportunists of Social-Democracy. The latter want to proceed from the bottom upward and, consequently, wherever possible and to the extent that it is possible, it supports automatism and "democracy." . . . The former proceed from the top, and advocate the extension of the rights and powers of the center in respect of the parts.[12]

In the course of this dispute Leon Trotsky, then a Menshevik and hence in opposition to Lenin, uttered the following remarkable prediction:

> The organization of the Party takes the place of the Party itself; the Central Committee takes the place of the organization; and finally the dictator takes the place of the Central Committee.[13]

[12] *Selected Works,* Vol. II, pp. 447 f.
[13] Quoted by Wolfe, *op. cit.,* p. 253.

In 1917 Trotsky was willing to forget this prophecy made twelve years before, though he must have been rudely reminded of it after 1927. By that time he was explaining the evolution of the dictatorship as a " Thermidorian reaction " and a " betrayal of the revolution." On the whole his earlier insight was the better. It was Lenin's party that made the revolution and it was Lenin's theory of the party that settled the political philosophy of the proletarian dictatorship.

LENIN ON DIALECTICAL MATERIALISM

The quasi-clericalism of Lenin's intellectual outlook was perhaps best illustrated by what was ostensibly his principal theoretical work, his *Materialism and Empirio-Criticism,* published in 1909. On its face this book dealt with general philosophical problems, the nature of dialectic, its relation to the natural and social sciences, the validity of materialism, idealism, and scientific positivism as philosophical systems. In point of fact it was written as an incident in one of the innumerable party controversies in which Lenin was perpetually engaged.[14] Ostensibly Lenin's purpose was to refute an attempt by some of his party associates and fellow editors to bring Marxism into line with the scientific positivism of Ernst Mach. On philosophical grounds such a change would have been possible only if Marx's affiliation with Hegelianism were abandoned and if his philosophy were interpreted in the light of the occasional passages, mentioned in the preceding chapter, in which Marx and Engels had described dialectical materialism as merely a working hypothesis. This, to say the least, would have required a drastic reconstruction which Lenin might very reasonably have questioned. In fact he saw in the books which he attacked chiefly a deviation from Marxian orthodoxy, which he reaffirmed in the most dogmatic fashion.

> You cannot eliminate even one basic assumption, one substantial part of this philosophy of Marxism (it is as if it were a solid block of steel) without abandoning objective truth, without falling into the arms of the bourgeois-reactionary falsehood.[15]

Everything essential in Lenin's argument was taken out of Engels' *Anti-Dühring* and *Feuerbach,* but the differences between

[14] Wolfe, *op. cit.,* ch. 29.
[15] *Collected Works,* Vol. XIII, p. 281. *Selected Works,* Vol. XI, p. 377.

Lenin's way of arguing and Engels' were more striking than the similarities. Engels attacked his opponents' theories and not their characters. With Lenin a difference of opinion became a moral issue, and his opponents' philosophy was for him the mark of a "guilty conscience." "The philosophy of Mach, the scientist, is to science what the kiss of Judas is to Christ." What Lenin refuted was not what his opponents had said but what he chose to think they implied, or the ulterior purpose that he chose to impute to them. Even the desire to find a new point of view in philosophy, he said, "betrays some poverty of spirit." Since Lenin's book, though ostensibly a philosophical discussion, was in fact an attack on men whom he had read out of his faction, it is hardly possible to tell how far its rancor represented his actual belief and how far he was merely exercising the prerogative, which he elsewhere candidly avowed, of not allowing either truth or fairness to interfere with the discrediting of an opponent whom he placed outside the pale of the party.

The philosophical argument of *Materialism and Empirio-Criticism* was quite simple and thoroughly superficial. He adopted from Engels the dogma that every philosophy must be either idealist or materialist, any third form being merely a confusion or a pretense. Idealism is clericalism, since non-spatial and non-temporal beings were inventions of the clergy to deceive the masses — a bad product of a bad social order. But idealism is not nonsense. Scientific positivism, on the other hand, is merely "a pseudo-erudite pretense to transcend idealism and materialism," and is in reality covert clericalism, "conciliatory quackery," "a bourgeois, Philistine, cowardly tolerance" of dogmas. Lenin traced correctly the scientific positivism of Mach to the philosophical tradition of Hume and Kant, and like Engels he regarded it as refuted by the fact that statements can be empirically verified. Throughout he represented positivism as merely a modified form of Berkeleyan idealism and therefore equivalent to solipsism, or the denial that there is any such thing as objective truth or any reality other than states of consciousness. Its only purpose is to offer a confused or hypocritical defense of religious faith. Characteristically Lenin simply neglected the historical fact that Hume's philosophy was the most potent solvent of religious dogmatism produced by modern thought.

Materialism, on the other hand, was reduced in Lenin's exposition to the not very profound proposition that objective reality (that is, matter) exists independently of our knowing it, which he stated as meaning indifferently that perceptions give us correct impressions of things, that we directly know objects themselves, and that objects act causally on our senses. Hence our ideas "reflect" objects or give us "pictures" or "images" of them. His account of dialectic ran in almost the same terms used by Engels. Truth is at once relative and absolute, that is, partly incorrect but an "approximation" to absolute objective truth. Every ideology is historically conditioned but it is an unconditional truth that there is an objective truth corresponding to every scientific theory. This, he said, has the merit of being indefinite enough to prevent science from becoming dogmatic, but definite enough to exclude any form of faith or agnosticism. Throughout Lenin's argument there ran a curious sympathy for clericalism and a moral abhorence for scientific positivism. He hated clericalism, or idealism as he called it, but he did not fear it because he knew the answer. It was intelligible to him as an honest enemy that does not conceal the dogmatic and authoritarian purpose which he tacitly imputed to every philosophy. As he wrote in his notebook, clericalism is indeed "a sterile flower, yet one growing on the living tree of a prolific, true, powerful, omnipotent, objective, and absolute human knowledge." On the other hand the indifference of a scientist like Mach to metaphysical disputes, and the empirical and non-authoritarian temper of his philosophy, produced in Lenin's mind a sense of profound moral repulsion. It was so foreign to his way of thinking that he could not believe it honest.

In one important respect Lenin's treatment of dialectical materialism and of its relation to science differed from that of Marx and Engels, though the difference was not, apparently, occasioned by an intentional change of view on Lenin's part. Marx, following Hegel, had regarded the dialectic as a method especially suited to the social studies, because these have to do with a subject-matter in which development or growth is an important factor. Sciences that deal with inanimate nature like physics and chemistry, Marx assumed, are sufficiently well served by a materialism of the non-dialectical type, like that of Holbach.

Lenin, on the other hand, in criticizing Mach had to deal with the "new" physics of non-Newtonian mechanics and non-Euclidean geometry. These, he argued, appear to be puzzling merely because the physicists and mathematicians have not taken the trouble to instruct themselves in dialectical materialism. Had they learned that dialectic proves all distinctions to be relative rather than absolute, they would not have been surprised and confused to find that matter can sometimes be interchanged for energy and *vice versa.* The discoveries of modern physics merely confirm Engels' statement that there are no fixed lines of demarkation in nature and Marx's criticism of pre-Revolutionary French materialism. By following the direction laid down by Marxian theory it is possible to draw nearer and nearer to objective truth; by following any other path one arrives only at confusion and falsehood.[16] In short, dialectical materialism, as Lenin conceived it, became a universal method applicable in every field of science and the only safe guide in any. In effect this turned it into a higher form of knowledge — a species of theology — that can act as arbiter of all the moot questions of all the sciences. Hence it can discover heresy in the most surprising places, as when Lenin said that Mach's doubts about three-dimensional space caused him to abandon science for theism. Thus dialectical materialism can set the mathematician right about Euclidean and non-Euclidean geometry and can instruct the physicist about the "correct" relations between matter and electricity. In 1948 it did settle, by decision of the Central Committee of the Communist Party, the question of the inheritance of acquired characters in biology, Mendelism being a "bourgeois fraud" jointly perpetrated by an Austrian priest and an American geneticist under capitalist influences.[17] Dialectical materialism is equally valid in determining the esthetic merits of art and literature. That Lenin intended consequences such as these was probably not the case. The few persons who heard of *Materialism and Empirio-Criticism* in 1909 knew it for what it was, a tactical move in an obscure party quarrel among

[16] *Collected Works,* Vol. XIII, p. 114. *Selected Works,* Vol. XI, p. 205.

[17] *The New York Times,* August 25 and 28, 1948. Cf. "The Destruction of Science in the U.S.S.R.," by H. J. Muller, *Saturday Review of Literature,* December 4, 1948.

an insignificant group of Russian exiles in Geneva. Today it is a basic philosophical text in Russia, and it has Lenin's party, now metamorphosed into the Russian state, to implement its pseudo-scientific dogmas.

The relationship of dialectical materialism to the social studies, as Lenin conceived them, is of course much closer than its relationship to the natural sciences, though not different in kind. Philosophy and social studies, Lenin candidly asserted, are inevitably partisan. Professors of economics, he said, are nothing but scientific salesmen of the capitalist class, and professors of philosophy are scientific salesmen of theology. The most that a scientific theory of society can discover is a general outline of the objective logic of economic and historical evolution, and this is provided by dialectical materialism. In philosophy, economics, and politics impartiality or scientific detachment, therefore, is merely a pretense adopted to cover a defense of vested interests. Within the framework of dialectical materialism there are two systems of social science, the one produced in the interest of the middle class, the other produced in the interest of the proletariat. A similar division exists between bourgeois and proletarian art and literature. The superiority of proletarian social science does not consist in its being formally more exact or even in its being empirically more reliable but in the fact that the dialectic proves the proletariat to be the " rising " class which is in the forefront of social progress. The middle class, on the contrary, is engaged in a hopeless struggle to hold back the inevitable transition from capitalism to communism. Hence its science is at least static and more probably decadent and reactionary. Thus the ineradicable class struggle becomes a factor, over and above scientific evidence, in determining the truth of scientific conclusions, and over and above esthetic appreciation in determining the esthetic value of art. It follows that objectivity of judgment, at least over the whole range of social and humanistic studies, is not only difficult (which every scholar would admit) but is impossible and not even to be striven for. Whether he is a proletarian or a bourgeois, every social scientist is, *volens nolens,* a special pleader. If he is honest he begins with a profession of faith, and no conclusion that he reaches is logically independent of his starting point. For practical purposes, within a system dominated by an organization like the communist party, this means that at some point or other his criterion of truth is the party line.

If this is true of the scientific study of society, it is true *a fortiori* of political negotiation and of the dealings of social group with social group. The policy of a party in conducting its relations with other parties, or of a nation in conducting its relations with other nations, must, as Trotsky said, be deduced from the class struggle. For the class struggle is an ultimate principle which can at most be temporarily obscured but can never be set aside. This follows from the dialectic itself, because the dialectical progression, in society and in nature, takes place through the "contradictions" inherent in the system, and even a temporary cessation of the struggle can occur only because one party has become for the time being dominant. Hence the purpose of negotiation is not conciliation or compromise or a meeting of minds, which is really impossible, but is a strategic move to win an advantageous position when the struggle shall begin again. In 1938 Stalin also produced an authoritative account of "Dialectical and Historical Materialism" which followed closely the models set by Engels and Lenin but emphasized the relations between dialectic and policy.[18]

> The dialectical method therefore holds that the process of development from the lower to the higher takes place not as a harmonious unfolding of phenomena, but as a disclosure of the contradictions inherent in things and phenomena, as a "struggle" of opposite tendencies which operate on the basis of these contradictions.
>
> Hence, in order not to err in policy, one must pursue an uncompromising proletarian class policy, not a reformist policy of harmony of the interests of the proletariat and the bourgeoisie, not a compromisers' policy of "the growing of capitalism into socialism."

IMPERIALIST CAPITALISM

Down to the beginning of World War I Lenin's attention had been almost wholly devoted to the internal concerns of Russian socialism, and his additions to Marxian theory had all been in the direction of adapting it to his own conception of party strategy in Russia. In 1914 he was so forgetful of international politics

[18] *Leninism: Selected Writings* (New York, 1942), pp. 406–433. It was originally Chapter 4 of the *History of the Communist Party of the Soviet Union.* The quotations are on pp. 410 and 412 respectively.

that the outbreak of war found him in Austrian Poland and he narrowly escaped internment as an enemy alien. The war, however, and more especially the defection of socialists everywhere from their internationalist and antipatriotic professions, forced him to attend to broader aspects of Marxian theory. This was responsible for the formulation of his theory of imperialist capitalism, his interpretation of the war as an imperialist war, and his theory of correct socialist tactics in the emergency.[19] These constitute his principal claim to having restated Marxism in the light of later capitalist evolution, which, as was said above, is the official interpretation of his work as a theorist. Lenin, living for the most part as an exile in Switzerland, stood nearly alone, his own Russian faction reduced to a handful, while the anti-nationalist socialists of other countries consisted only of a few dissenters like Karl Liebknecht and Rosa Luxemburg in Germany. Lenin was one of the very few socialists who followed his international theory to the point of accepting the defeat of his own nation as a thing to be desired. "From the point of view of the laboring class and the toiling masses of all the peoples of Russia, the lesser evil would be the defeat of the Czarist monarchy and its army." From the beginning Lenin argued that the apportionment of guilt among the belligerent nations was nonsense, that all were dominated by the same kind of economic motives, that the war was merely a phase in the evolution of capitalism, and that the tactics of an intelligent socialist party must be based on these facts. In a quarrel about the division of booty the working class of no nation has any vital concern. Certainly, he said, Russian workers have no interest in taking away the spoil of one young robber (Germany) in order to give it to two old ones (England and France). The great hope of Lenin's life was that it might be possible to "turn the imperialist war into a civil war," that is, into a proletarian revolution. He undoubtedly believed that such a revolution, on a worldwide scale, was imminent.

The "betrayal of socialism" by the socialists was obviously

[19] See the *Collected Works,* Vols. XVIII and XIX; *Selected Works,* Vol. V. Especially *Under a Stolen Flag, Socialism and War,* 1915 (with G. Zinoviev); *Imperialism: The Highest Stage of Capitalism,* 1916; also Bukharin's *Imperialism and World Economy* (New York, 1929). These were published after the March Revolution in 1917.

an anomaly from the point of view of Marxism. For according to the theory the class struggle ought to have been growing sharper and society more clearly divided into bourgeoisie and proletariat as capitaiism developed. And as the proletariat became more class-conscious, it ought to be less influenced by national patriotism. Hence the theory must be revised to account for what seemed to be a gross exception. Lenin began with an unquestionable historical fact. In the period after 1871 the socialist parties had grown by legal means to a size where they could put their trust wholly in parliamentary methods. In consequence they had been infiltrated with petty bourgeois members and ideology, and the tactics of trade unionism had displaced the tactics of revolution. But since ideology follows the relations of production, this fact itself ought to be traceable to some peculiarity in the development of capitalism during the period. This Lenin found by supposing that, in the successful imperialist countries, an expansion of markets and an increase of production had enabled a small part of the workers, especially in the skilled trades, to better their economic position. This produced between 1871 and 1914 a kind of backwash in the class struggle. A small but influential part of the working class joined with capitalists to exploit the great mass of unskilled workers, especially workers in backward countries and colonies. The ideology of this movement was petty bourgeois. It fell a victim to the illusion that economic evolution could be peaceful and that a harmony of interests between the proletariat and the bourgeoisie was possible. Hence the year 1914 found "the proletarian mass entirely disorganized and demoralized by the shifting of a minority of the best-situated, skilled and unionized workers to liberal, i.e., bourgeois, politics." This theory was probably suggested to Lenin by Engels' conclusions about the effect of foreign trade upon the British labor movement.

Having related the peculiar form of the class struggle to the typical qualities of capitalism in the period after 1871, Lenin proceeded to show that the latter corresponded to a certain stage in the development of the capitalist system as a whole. His account of the imperialist stage of capitalism brought together a number of characteristics noted by many authors before him, both socialist and non-socialist.[20] It amounted to expanding Marx's theory of capitalist accumulation. As the units of industry grow in size and become monopolistic, either over a whole industry or over a vertical string of related industries, a point is reached where monopoly plays a decisive part in the whole economy. The market becomes worldwide and prices both of commodities and of labor tend to be fixed in the world market. Within national units competition practically ceases and free competitive capitalism virtually disappears, but at the same time competition more and more assumes the form of rivalry between national monopolies. Tariffs cease to nourish infant industries and become weapons in national trade wars. With the formation of industrial combinations the control of industry passes out of the hands of the producers of commodities and into the hands of financiers and bankers; commercial capital is fused with banking capital in the hands of a financial oligarchy. Capital itself becomes a significant item of export. The steady pressure for larger markets and the demand for raw materials, both inherent in the expansion of capitalist production, result in an international scramble for undeveloped territory and the control of backward peoples. In international politics the vital question becomes the partition among the powers of exploitable territory and population. In internal politics capitalist control over political institutions becomes more direct and parliamentary liberalism becomes more and more a sham. Reduced to its essentials, therefore, an imperialist war, such as that begun in 1914, is merely a struggle between syndicates of German capitalists, with their subsidiaries, and syndicates of allied French and English capitalists, with their subsidiaries, for the control of Africa. To be sure, eddies and backwashes occur. Smaller groups of capitalists skirmish, so to speak, around the edges of the main struggle for such limited advantages as they can gain. Thus Russian capitalists hope to get Constantinople and the Japanese hope to exploit China. In the backward nations there are even *bona fide* nationalist movements, as in Serbia or India. Fundamentally, however, monopoly- and finance-capitalism is the logical outcome of free competitive capitalism, political imperialism is the logical outcome of mo-

[20] See E. M. Winslow, *The Pattern of Imperialism* (1948), especially ch. 7.

nopoly-capitalism, and the war is the logical outcome of imperialism. Imperialism is "the highest stage of capitalist development" and a part of the process by which a still higher, non-capitalist or communist, economy and society are evolving.

> Imperialism emerged as the development and direct continuation of the fundamental attributes of capitalism in general. But capitalism only became capitalist imperialism at a definite and very high stage of its development, when certain of its fundamental attributes began to be transformed into their opposites, when the features of a period of transition from capitalism to a higher social and economic system began to take shape and reveal themselves all along the line.[21]

THE IMPERIALIST WAR

Lenin's theory of the stages of capitalist evolution required also a new analysis of the ideological and institutional superstructure based upon it. Such an analysis was required to bring him to the end of his task as a theorist, namely, to give him a reasoned foundation for his attack on the Second International and for his conclusions about correct socialist tactics. Accordingly Lenin supplemented his theory of finance-capitalism with a theory of the relative positions of the proletariat and the bourgeoisie in a period of imperialist war. This required a theory of the development of European society under capitalism and of the significant periods into which its history should be divided. The turning points Lenin took to be 1871 — fixed by the last important revolutionary outbreak in the Paris Commune — and 1914, the beginning of the first imperialist war. Between the French Revolution and 1871 capitalism, he held, had been on an ascending curve and the bourgeoisie had been a progressive class compared with the remnants of feudalism which it displaced. In this period it produced its characteristic — and, in their time and place, its valuable — social and political consequences, notably the democratization of government and the liberation of nationalities. There is no doubt that Lenin, down to the time when the exigences of the Revolution in 1917 forced him into a position of virtual dictatorship, retained the belief generally held by Marxists, that political liberalism was a necessary stage in the

[21] *Imperialism: the Highest Stage of Capitalism; Collected Works,* Vol. XIX, p. 159. *Selected Works,* Vol. V, p. 80.

evolution of communism. At all times, also, he was sympathetic toward a liberal view of national development, even though he never regarded nationalism as a fundamental cultural phenomenon. During the period down to 1871, he argued, the proletariat was in process of formation and was therefore obliged to adjust itself to the expanding power of the bourgeoisie. Hence it was sound socialist tactics to inquire whether the international interests of the proletariat would be best served by one or another outcome of a national controversy, as Marx did in 1859 when he took a stand on the issue between Austria and France. War in this period was, by and large, an agency in the forming and freeing of nationalities, and socialists could logically cooperate with this process. The period from 1871 to 1914 was, so to speak, the flat top of the curve, the age of capitalist domination and incipient decay, in which the class struggle was obscured in the more progressive European countries by a false appearance of harmony and in which the capitalist organization of society took on the monopolist and imperialist characteristics just described. In 1914 World War I signalized the end of this period and the beginning of a precipitate fall in the curve of capitalism. The bourgeoisie had now become a decaying and reactionary class devoted to protecting its vested interests, concerned not with production but with consumption, and having the typical ideology of the *rentier*.[22] Bourgeois policy, therefore, does not reflect the real tendencies of the system of production but is imposed on the system by finance-capitalism. In this period there must occur a series of imperialist convulsions, of which the war is the first but not necessarily the last, and in it the European situation has again become definitely revolutionary from the point of view of a proletarian party. In 1914 a progressive bourgeoisie is a contradiction in terms and there can be no valid reason for an alliance between the proletariat and any group of national imperialist capitalists. The socialist-nationalists of the Second International, who profess to see an advantage in the victory of

[22] Cf. Bukharin's analysis of Böhm-Bawerk's theory of value as representing the ideology of a consuming class; *The Economic Theory of the Leisure Class,* New York, 1927. The book was written in 1914 before the war and first published in 1919. Bukharin was executed in the purges of 1937–38, but in 1914 he was closely associated with Lenin.

one side or the other or who argue, like Kautsky, that a world economy can develop within the capitalist system, are simply misleading their followers and are in reality traitors to the cause of the proletariat. The policy of the working class must be the revolutionary overthrow of international finance-capitalism.

There can be no doubt that Lenin's theory was a very able supplementation and extension of Marx's analysis of capitalism. It enabled him to interpret the existing national and international situation by means of the categories provided by the Marxian system. The opposing interests of imperialist national groupings could be construed as "contradictions" between the productive forces of industry and the restraints imposed on them by an outworn ideology. Lenin's theory was designed indeed to refute all the principal objections urged against Marxism by two generations of revisionists and "opportunists" during the period when proletarian thought had been corrupted by the mirage of peaceful development and conciliation. The theory conceded, as Engels had conceded in 1895, that Marx had failed to appreciate the possibilities of internal development within the capitalist system. But it reaffirmed, as Engels also had done, that Marx had been essentially right in estimating the general direction of capitalist development. In substance what Lenin's theory undertook to do was to bring war itself, as a social phenomenon at a definite stage of capitalist evolution, into the sweep of the Marxian conception of an expanding capitalist economy. This enabled him to set aside all the hair-splitting inquiries of the revisionists about the relative or the absolute increase of poverty through the appropriation of surplus value. As the Second Communist Manifesto, adopted by the Communist International in 1919, affirmed, the spectacle of human suffering provided by World War I settled "the academic quarrel among socialists over the theory of increasing misery." By implication at least Lenin was able also to correlate war with the increasing frequency and severity of crises, since from his point of view war itself was only a crisis on a magnified scale. Most important of all for the practical purpose that Lenin had in mind, his theory restored and revivified Marxism as a philosophy of social revolution and took it out of the hands of cowards and sentimentalists, of pacificists, reformists, conciliationists, and democrats. The class struggle was once more clearly inevitable, the "reality" behind the false appearance of peace, of freedom for the working class within the framework of parliamentary liberalism, and of national self-determination within the framework of imperialism.

Obviously a fundamental factor in Lenin's theory of capitalist development was his belief in the imminence of a worldwide proletarian revolution, which could be deduced from the situation in 1914 as Marx had more than once deduced it from the situation in the 1840's. The fundamental contradiction in 1914 is between the international nature of industry and the restraints imposed by national political divisions. The ruling class which controls production, and labor as well, is divided into national groups with competing interests that have no counterpart in the system of production. The policies of national states, under the control of these artificial groupings, have become a clog upon the normal development of production. The ideology of national solidarity and political self-determination, with the corresponding policies of tariff-exclusion and national monopoly, stands square across the path of expansion appropriate to the economic system, and this expansion is forced into the perverted form of imperialist annexation. Inevitably the underlying forces of production must assert their mastery. The immediate effect of the war, Lenin believed, would be to centralize political power, destroy small states, and expand monopoly. But its most important effect would be to reinstate the class struggle as the permanent force in capitalist society and to convince an international proletariat that its interests can be served only by an international social revolution.

The War severs the last chain that binds the workers to the masters, their slavish submission to the imperialist state. The last limitation of the proletariat's philosophy is being overcome; its clinging to the narrowness of the national state, its patriotism. The interests of the moment, the temporary advantage accruing to it from the imperialist robberies and from its connections with the imperialist state, become of secondary importance compared with the lasting and general interests of the class as a whole, with the idea of a social revolution of the international proletariat which overthrows the dictatorship of finance capital with an armed hand, destroys its state apparatus and builds up a new power, a power of the workers against the bourgeoisie.[23]

It was, therefore, with a firm belief in the imminence of a world-wide proletarian revolution that Lenin approached the situation in Russia when he returned to Petrograd in April, 1917, and began a series of choices which determined both the success and the nature of the Revolution.

THE BOURGEOIS AND THE PROLETARIAN REVOLUTIONS

The success of the March Revolution in Russia at once plunged Russian Marxists back into a theoretical and a tactical controversy which had been simmering since the Revolution of 1905. No principle of Marxism was better settled than the proposition that revolutions cannot be made by naked force but only by a revolutionary ideology, which in turn can be produced only as the workers are disciplined in the relations of capitalist production. Marx himself had said that it was the final purpose of *Capital* to show that no nation could "overleap the natural phases of evolution," and Engels had used no less than three chapters of the *Anti-Dühring* to prove that force can never do more than supplement a revolutionary situation already prepared by economic development. Any doubt on this article of belief would at once have labeled the doubter an anti-Marxist. It had been apparent also to all Marxists that the Russian Revolution of 1905 was a middle-class revolution, not one made by the proletariat for socialist purposes. The same was true of the March Revolution in 1917. And the theory required that the bourgeois revolution should be "completed," as a stage that must be passed through, before the situation could "ripen" for a proletarian revolution. The theoretical problem was matched by serious questions of tactics. For a proletarian party must decide what line it would take toward bourgeois revolutionary parties. The class struggle makes it absurd to aid the bourgeoisie in an effort to become the exploiter of the proletariat. Yet a socialist revolution is dependent on the political democracy which the bourgeois revolution produces, and in any case the proletariat cannot hope to attain power until the time is ripe.

[23] Bukharin, *Imperialism and World Economy,* Eng. trans., p. 167.

Confronted by this dilemma Russian Marxists in 1905 had constructed two antithetical theories which continued to divide them during the dozen years that elapsed until 1917. The Menshevik faction held a straightforward if somewhat unimaginative Marxism based upon the ideas of radical socialist parties in Western Europe. According to this theory a proletarian party cannot " seize power " but will ultimately grow into a majority, when the political freedom established by the bourgeois revolution and the growth of the working class make this possible. It can in general support the bourgeois struggle for power but once a bourgeois government is established, a proletarian party can be only a left-wing opposition. This theory was unexceptionable Marxism but it would be hard to imagine a program better calculated to take the heart out of a revolutionary party. Against this Menshevik position Trotsky, though himself loosely affiliated with the Mensheviks, developed in 1905 the line of reasoning not very accurately described as the theory of " permanent " revolution. Twenty years later this was to become the principal ground for denying the orthodoxy of his Leninism. Trotsky boldly attacked the Menshevik theory as unintelligent Marxism.

> To imagine that there is an automatic dependence between the dictatorship of the proletariat and the technical and productive resources of a country is to understand economic determinism in a very primitive way. Such a conception would have nothing to do with Marxism.[24]

Any revolution in Russia, Trotsky argued, will be different from revolutions in the past because of the international development of capitalism and because Marxism already exists as an ideology among Russian intellectuals. The Russian bourgeoisie is timid and will not boldly attack the system of landownership. Consequently the proletariat must take the lead, " leaning upon " the peasantry, and in so doing it will inevitably go beyond the limits of political liberalism. Thus the two revolutions will coalesce or be concurrent; Trotsky called this " the law of combined devel-

[24] Trotsky developed his theory in several essays written between 1904 and 1906. Some selections, under the title " Prospects of a Labor Dictatorship," were published in English translation in *Our Revolution* (New York, 1918), pp. 63–144. The quotation is on p. 85. For a summary see " Three Concepts of the Russian Revolution " in Trotsky's *Stalin* (1941), Appendix. Cf. his essay entitled *The Permanent Revolution* (1930), Eng. trans., New York, 1931. The several theories are summarized by Wolfe, *op. cit.*, ch. 17.

opment." The strength of the proletariat depends not on its numbers but on its position in the national economy, and the outcome of revolution in Russia depends on the state of international capitalism. Hence the only guaranty against a bourgeois reaction will be success in fostering genuine proletarian revolutions in " over-ripe " capitalist countries outside Russia. In 1905 the controversial part of this theory was the coalescence of the two revolutions, since no one was concerned to deny that a revolution in Russia would depend on the international situation. The question of tactics Trotsky handled with equal boldness; an armed uprising or a general strike is immediately indicated. After the *coup* succeeds, " political power necessarily passes over into the hands of the class that has played the leading rôle in the struggle, the working class." In other words, the government becomes a dictatorship of the proletariat, with " hegemony over the peasants," which in substance means a dictatorship of the party that has led the revolution.

Down to 1917 Lenin never allied himself with either of the two opposed theories just described but held a middle position. Like Trotsky he was convinced that the policy proposed by the Mensheviks meant resigning leadership to middle-class liberals who would make the fewest political reforms possible. Consequently a socialist revolutionary party must not only take part in the revolution but so far as possible must take the lead. It could not hope to make a socialist revolution, though Lenin said that the two revolutions would be " continuous." But by encouraging the revolutionary tendencies of the peasants, it may force the middle class to go the full length of replacing the monarchy with a republic. This program he called a " revolutionary dictatorship of the proletariat and the peasantry." Then as always Lenin was clear that any revolutionary movement in Russia could succeed only if it had at least the passive support of the peasants. For this reason, perhaps, he could not convince himself that Trotsky's idea of an immediate proletarian dictatorship would certainly result in " hegemony " over the peasants. Consequently in 1905 Lenin still supported the traditional Marxist position, that political democracy is an essential precondition of socialism, and consigned the permanent revolution to the category of " absurd semi-anarchist ideas." In short, Lenin was not yet ready to accept the implication of Trotsky's theory, that a socialist revolution in Russia could purchase success only by abandoning democracy.

> We Marxists must know that there is not, nor can there be, any other path to real freedom for the proletariat and the peasantry than the path of bourgeois freedom and bourgeois progress. We must not forget that there is not, nor can there be at the present time, any other means of bringing socialism nearer than by complete political liberty, a democratic republic, a revolutionary-democratic dictatorship of the proletariat and the peasantry.[25]

Thus the years between 1902 and 1905 presented the grimly humorous spectacle of Trotsky rejecting Lenin's theory of the party because it implied a form of organization that would lead to dictatorship and of Lenin rejecting Trotsky's theory of revolution because it implied a procedure that would abandon democracy. The two men and the two theories joined hands in the Revolution of 1917.

When Lenin returned to Russia in April, 1917, and assumed the leadership of a socialist party in the midst of a revolutionary situation, he immediately perceived — as Trotsky had been led to perceive by his experience as leader of the St. Petersburg Soviet in 1905 — that a socialist who waits for the revolution to mature will miss his chance. Within a week of his arrival in Petrograd, Lenin astonished his followers by relegating to " the archive of ' Bolshevik ' pre-revolutionary antiques " the idea that a time of preparation must elapse between the bourgeois and the proletarian revolutions. The " antique " in question was of course the position that Lenin himself had taken in 1905. The concrete situation, he said, has proved to be more " original " than theory had anticipated — which was a formula for saying that Lenin had changed his mind — and " living Marxism " consists in keeping pace with the facts.

> It is necessary to acquire that incontestible truth that a Marxist must take cognizance of living life, of the true facts of reality, that he must not continue clinging to the theory of yesterday, which, like every theory, at best only outlines the main and the general, only approximately embracing the complexity of life . . . Whoever questions the

[25] *The Two Tactics of Social-Democracy in the Democratic Revolution* (1905), *Selected Works,* Vol. III, p. 122; cf. p. 52.

"completeness" of the bourgeois revolution from the old viewpoint, sacrifices living Marxism to a dead letter. According to the old conception, the rule of the proletariat and peasantry, their dictatorship, can and must follow the rule of the bourgeoisie. In real life, however, things have turned out otherwise; an extremely original, new, unprecedented interlocking of one and the other has taken place.[26]

This "interlocking" of the two revolutions was substantially identical with "the law of combined development" which Trotsky in 1905 had made the basis of his theory of permanent revolution. When Lenin accepted it in 1917 he doubted no more than Trotsky its fundamental premise, namely, the imminence of a worldwide proletarian revolution and the merely temporary isolation of a revolutionary government in Russia. This was the principal reason why the theory could be regarded as an amendment to Marxism rather than a denial of it. Neither Lenin nor Trotsky intended to commit their party to "jumping over the bourgeois revolution." They merely took account of the international situation and the existence in Russia of a minority already imbued with a Marxian revolutionary ideology. The important fact in 1917 was that Lenin and Trotsky had found common ground in a position essentially like that taken by Trotsky in 1905.[27]

Lenin, however, had still to find a way around the anti-democratic implications which had caused him to reject Trotsky's theory in 1905. When he returned to Russia in 1917 he found that the actual situation presented the anomaly which he described as "Dual Power," the existence side by side of the bourgeois Provisional Government and the soviets. This state of affairs posed serious problems both of theory and tactics. The

[26] *Letters on Tactics* (April, 1917). *Collected Works,* Vol. XX, Book I, p. 121. *Selected Works,* Vol. VI, pp. 34 f. The translation in the *Selected Works* has been revised and the word "interlocking" has been replaced with "interlacing."

[27] After Stalin adopted the policy of "socialism in one country" the theory of permanent revolution became, so to speak, retroactively heretical. Consequently the coalescence of Trotsky's and Lenin's views about revolution is no longer admitted and cannot even be discussed. See "Some Questions concerning the History of Bolshevism" in Stalin's *Leninism: Selected Writings* (New York, 1942), p. 232. The "correct" interpretation of Lenin's writings in 1905 and 1917 can be found in the notes to the *Selected Works,* Vol. III, pp. 547 ff. According to Souvarine, Lenin admitted that Trotsky had been right in 1905; *Stalin* (1939), p. 79.

Provisional Government admittedly stood for constitutionalism and political reform on the lines of democratic liberalism. Repeatedly during his first three months in Russia Lenin still insisted that he was opposed to a seizure of power by a minority and to changes in government not ripe "in the consciousness of an overwhelming majority." He also continued to assert that "The most powerful and advanced type of bourgeois state is that of a parliamentary democratic republic." Yet the soviets presented the only possibility for a revolutionary seizure of power, and "All power to the soviets" was the only practicable slogan for a revolutionary party. But from Lenin's point of view the soviets themselves were not a simple problem. Marxists had been and still were a small minority among their members, and Bolsheviks were a small minority among Marxists. Moreover, the revolutionary spontaneity of the soviets was in principle far closer to Menshevik ideas about local autonomy and the federal organization of the working class than to Lenin's theory of a centrally administered party. It was Trotsky who in 1905 had made his revolutionary reputation as leader of the St. Petersburg Soviet and had described it as "an embryo of a revolutionary government," while Lenin's party (prior to Lenin's return from exile) had looked askance at both the soviets and the trade unions. Lenin himself in 1906, summing up the experience of the preceding year, had indeed recognized the value of non-party groups as "organs of direct mass struggle," but had emphasized chiefly their insufficiency for "organizing the insurrection."[28] In 1917 the practical difficulty was solved when the soviets themselves came under Bolshevik leadership, which opened the way for amalgamating the power of the party, as Lenin had always conceived it, with a *pro forma* soviet organization. In effect this was the beginning of the end, so far as the soviets had stood for any real element of popular government. The dictatorship of the proletariat was on the way to becoming the dictatorship of the party. The theoretical difficulty Lenin solved by virtually abandoning the Marxian theory, which had kept him apart from

[28] *The Dissolution of the Duma and the Tasks of the Proletariat* (1906), *Selected Works,* Vol. III, pp. 378 ff. Cf. Wolfe, *op. cit.,* pp. 368 ff. On the soviets in Russian government see Julian Towster, *Political Power in the U.S.S.R.* (1948), chs. 9–11.

Trotsky in 1905, that political democracy is necessarily a precondition of socialism. For it he substituted the theory that the soviets are themselves "the highest type of democratic state" which in a revolutionary situation spontaneously replaces the forms of parliamentary representation by a direct people's government.

Viewed from one angle this new theory merely recognized more clearly what Lenin had always seen, that no revolutionary situation is resolved by constitutional or democratic formulas. Like Marx himself Lenin always saw that a revolution is necessarily terminated by an extra-legal, and in that sense dictatorial, settlement. To this he now added the somewhat more general argument that, for a social philosophy which regards the class struggle as the fundamental and permanent property of society, a democratic concept like majority rule is virtually meaningless. Except under a special condition, he argued, a majority cannot prevail, and the necessary condition is that the interests of the class in power should coincide with the interests of the majority. If this happens, the majority prevails merely because the ruling class allows it to; otherwise the ruling class merely suppresses or deceives the majority. Hence majority rule is a "constitutional illusion," a dialectical mystification of the underlying reality, which is class dominance.[29] Specifically this means in Russia that the peasantry, which is politically inert, will necessarily be attached either to the proletariat or the bourgeoisie. As a matter of tactics it implies that the revolutionary proletariat must destroy its bourgeois opponent and the apparatus of the bourgeois state, and must attach its majority to it by satisfying the economic needs of the non-proletarian masses. In short, a revolutionary party seizes power and gets its majority afterward. In all revolutions there are innumerable examples of the fact that "the more organized, more class conscious, better armed minority forces its will upon the majority." In substance this amounted to practically the same thing as what Trotsky in 1905 had called the dictatorship of the proletariat with "hegemony" over the peasants. It clearly foreshadowed the dissolution of the Constituent Assembly five months later, an act which Trotsky to the

[29] *On Constitutional Illusions* (August, 1917). *Collected Works,* Vol. XXI, Book I, pp. 66 ff. *Selected Works,* Vol. VI, pp. 180 ff.

day of his death believed " struck formal democracy the beneficent blow from which it will never again recover." [30] On the other hand the theory that the dictatorship of the proletariat is " true " rather than formal democracy had still to be brought under the aegis of Marxian theory. This required the elaborate exegesis which Lenin undertook in *State and Revolution.*

THE DICTATORSHIP OF THE PROLETARIAT

Lenin's pamphlet, *State and Revolution,* despite the fact that it remained unfinished and was planned merely as an occasional piece, may very probably stand as the classic ideological defense of the November Revolution.[31] It summed up the principal ideas about the European War that Lenin had been issuing since 1914 and it brought the contemporary situation in Russia, the imminent seizure of power by the soviets, into the framework of Lenin's Marxism. Granting the point of view and the habitual modes of thought imposed by the dialectic, it was undoubtedly one of the most convincing and persuasive political tracts ever written. In form it was merely an examination, in chronological order, of all the principal passages in which Marx and Engels had dealt with the nature of the state and the revolution. In truth the essay followed a pretty rigid plan of construction and interpretation, and it was this which gave it force as a revolutionary document. Marx and Engels apparently tell their own story, and out of the simple chronological arrangement there emerges a dialectical necessity. Their thought develops; it comes to grips with a problem; it triumphantly reaches a solution. The exegesis exhibits Marxism as a growing theory of revolutionary tactics: the inevitable struggle of classes and the movement toward the seizure of power by the proletariat, the failure of the first fumbling efforts in '48, the slow learning of the lesson that the capitalist bureaucracy must not be captured but destroyed, the first confused crystallization of genuine proletarian institutions in the Paris Commune of 1871, the painstaking elab-

[30] *Stalin* (1941), p. 343.

[31] *Collected Works,* Vol. XXI, Book II, pp. 147 ff. *Selected Works,* Vol. VII, pp. 3 ff. The pamphlet was written in August and September, 1917, while Lenin was living in Helsingfors. Only the first part was finished because the writing was interrupted by the Revolution. It was not published until 1918.

oration of Marx's insights by Engels, the development of proletarian government at a higher level in the soviets of 1905, and finally, of course, its triumphant realization in 1917. As history it was all highly imaginative, as history in apologies for revolution is likely to be. As exposition of Marx, though accurate in what it included, it was highly selective and on the whole a distortion. For anyone habituated to dialectical reasoning and convinced at the start that the communist revolution was inevitable, Lenin's argument was in a high degree persuasive.

State and Revolution may be said to have had two general and major purposes. It brought to a climax Lenin's lifelong effort to resuscitate Marxism as a philosophy of social revolution relieved of all the perversions with which revisionist and evolutionary socialism had " adulterated " it, and it provided the proletarian revolution with a theory of its own state suitable to its needs in a period of successful revolution. The pamphlet therefore took for granted or summarized Lenin's theories of finance-capitalism, the imperialist war, and of social evolution under capitalism which have already been explained. So far as concerns a theory of the state, the fundamental fact is that any form of state merely reflects the class struggle, and the class struggle is inevitable and irreconcilable short of the classless society. The capitalist state is inherently and essentially an instrument of exploitation used by the dominant class to enforce its interests at the expense of the exploited classes. Consequently it is impossible that it should be overthrown except by force, and any theory of peaceful social evolution or any policy of conciliating the class struggle is an illusion. Lenin's argument was largely developed in the form of an analysis of Engels' famous sentence about the " withering away " of the state under socialism. This, he argued, was falsely turned into a support for evolution and gradualness, whereas the correct meaning was that the capitalist state is overthrown by a revolutionary uprising of the proletariat, that a transitional form of state — the dictatorship of the proletariat — thus comes into being, and that this state, or semi-state, then gradually withers away as the proletariat produces the conditions of genuine communism. Lenin's argument was wholly exegetical in so far as it concerned the meaning of Marx and Engels and wholly *a priori* in so far as it concerned the facts. He gave not the slightest attention to such historical questions as whether there have actually been peaceful transferences of power from class to class or whether violent revolutions have characteristically produced such transferences. At no point did Lenin really meet the fundamental assumption of Marx and Engels, that the dictatorship of the proletariat would eventuate in political democracy.

The second main point of Lenin's argument was a frank acceptance of the fact that the new state produced by the revolution is itself an instrument of power and repression, quite as much as the capitalist state which it replaces. In it "the proletariat organized as a ruling class" creates its own appropriate apparatus of violence to enforce its purposes on the non-proletarian or semi-proletarian elements of society. The workers cannot accomplish their revolution merely by taking over the existing forms of bourgeois democracy but must destroy and replace them with a government of their own. Consequently a victory over the bourgeoisie requires a long, persistent, life-and-death struggle which can be carried through only by inflexible determination and by the use of force. The two purposes to be accomplished by the dictatorship of the proletariat are, first, "to hold down the exploiting class," whose resistance increases tenfold after its overthrow, and so to prevent any attempt at a counter-revolution, and second, to organize the new economic and social order. The latter is especially the function of the party, which is the teacher, guide, and leader of all the exploited classes which have not as yet become class-conscious. Though Lenin did not say it in so many words, this meant essentially, as Stalin said later, that the dictatorship of the proletariat is the dictatorship of the party, which becomes the "nucleus" of all working-class organizations. The point which Lenin clearly established, however, is that the dictatorship of the proletariat is a state, the organ of a class and an organ of suppression. It not only suppresses the exploiters but it exercises an "iron discipline" over the workers and the whole population. Reduced to its simplest form Lenin's argument amounted to this. Any state, bourgeois or proletarian, is an instrument of class dominance. Wherever there is dominance there is neither freedom nor democracy. Consequently political freedom must be postponed to the utopian stage of communist society when social classes have disappeared. For the present the proletarian dictatorship, being a state, makes no profession of being either free or democratic. As Trotsky said, democracy is merely the "ultimate hypocrisy of the bourgeois social order."

These two general purposes of *State and Revolution* merely led up to the more immediate purpose which it had in September, 1917. It had still to bring the seizure of power by a minority within the limits of Marxian theory, and more especially to tone down the by-passing of political democracy and representative institutions. This Lenin accomplished in two ways. First, he systematically denigrated parliamentary practices as merely agencies of bourgeois domination and hence as having little real value to workers, a precise reversal of the position he had taken in 1905. Second, he elaborated the theory of a more advanced "proletarian democracy" which had first appeared in the Paris Commune and which, as Lenin now claimed, Marx had recognized as such in his *Civil War in France*. This higher form of democracy had been continued and developed in the Russian soviets of 1905 and 1917.

With respect to the nature and value of political democracy, Lenin retained indeed the Marxian formula that the democratic republic is the highest type of government achieved by a bourgeois society. But he now asserted that any capitalist government requires "the greatest ferocity and savagery of repression" and he systematically represented democracy as "hypocritical and false to the core," having no value for any except a small exploiting minority.

In capitalist society, under the conditions most favorable to its development, we have more or less complete democracy in the democratic republic. But this democracy is always bound by the narrow framework of capitalist exploitation, and consequently always remains, in reality, a democracy for the minority, only for the possessing classes, only for the rich. Freedom in capitalist society always remains just about the same as it was in the ancient Greek republics: freedom for the slave-owners. The modern wage-slaves, owing to the conditions of capitalist exploitation, are so much crushed by want and poverty that "democracy is nothing to them," "politics is nothing to them"; that, in the ordinary peaceful course of events, the majority of the population is debarred from participating in social and political life.[32]

In 1919 Lenin wrote a similar estimate of the worth of political democracy for the working class into the revision of the Communist Manifesto adopted by the Communist International:

> If the finance-oligarchy considers it advantageous to veil its deeds of violence behind parliamentary votes, then the bourgeois state has at its command, in order to gain its ends, all the traditions and attainments of former centuries of upper-class rule multiplied by the wonders of capitalist technique: lies, demagogism, prosecution, slander, bribery, calumny, and terror. To demand of the proletariat in the final life-and-death struggle with capitalism that it should obey lamblike the precepts of bourgeois democracy would be the same as to ask the man who is defending his life against robbers to follow the artificial rules of a French duel that have been set by his enemy but not followed by him.[33]

This depreciation of liberal political institutions was a complete reversal of the valuation set upon them by the tradition of Western Marxism. Karl Kautsky was certainly right when he said in criticism that modern socialism had always been understood to mean not only a social organization of production but also a democratic organization of society. But Lenin's reversal of Marxism remained the position of communism, for which political and civil liberty became merely " fulcra " to bring about a single-party dictatorship.

The affirmative part of Lenin's argument, that which tried to discover in the Commune and the soviets a purer and higher type of democracy, was really a logical *tour de force*. It was an effort to extract from a dozen short passages in Marx something that simply was not there, namely, an outline of a form of government and a sketch of a post-revolutionary society. So far as the government of the Commune was concerned, Lenin was able to find in Marx only the vaguest generalities. The people in arms displaces the army and the police; the communes are representative without being parliamentary; they are working assemblies and not talking shops; their members execute the laws as well as

[32] *State and Revolution,* ch. 5, Section 2. *Collected Works,* Vol. XXI, Book II, p. 217 f. *Selected Works,* Vol. VII, p. 79.

[33] The Manifesto is printed in Appendix II to R. W. Postgate's *The Bolshevik Theory* (1920); the quotation is on p. 185.

make them. What these phrases might mean if they were translated into actual institutions or governmental practices Lenin made no attempt to show. So far as concerned the economy and the society that was to follow the revolution he was almost equally vague, and where he was not vague he was wrong, if his predictions are judged by the later course of the revolution itself. Its principle was to be simple, work for everyone and from everyone and equal pay for all. Officials and technical experts were to receive the wages of moderately paid clerks. This was possible, he imagined, because capitalism has already rationalized the organization of business and the public services to a point where it can be made to work by anyone who is able to read and write. All industrial administration, he supposed, is analogous to the post office. Years after Lenin's post-revolutionary experiments in this direction had proved impractical and disastrous, he still regarded the enforced reversal of his policy as "a defection from the principles of the Paris Commune and of any proletarian rule." On one point only was Lenin explicit. A political organizer always, he insisted that government by the soviets cannot be federal. It is "voluntary centralism," but how centralized control could be made compatible with any real autonomy of the soviets he never explained. Centralism was the term with which Lenin had long described the rôle which his theory assigned to the party. Certainly it was the party dictatorship and not his belated espousal of the soviets that Lenin's political philosophy contributed to the theory of communist government.

The history of the communist economy in Russia had, of course, no important relation to these speculations. Lenin himself and his successors met problems as they arose with experimentation and improvisation. The idea of equal pay came later to be described as a "slander on Marxism," and the functions of management in industry came to be substantially those which are exercised in capitalist industry. Stalin in 1931, in one of his addresses to business executives, mentioned as their principal duties the recruiting of labor, the reduction of labor turn-over, the adoption of wage-differentials that would provide effective incentives, the improvement of housing, the supervision of labor organizations, the enlargement of technical and administrative staff, and the improvement of accounting.[34] The one concrete claim made in behalf of "non-exploitative" communist industry is that it has eliminated unemployment. Against this substantial (if actual) achievement must be set an unknown amount of enforced and disciplinary labor and also the fact that management, in performing the duties enumerated, is not obliged to consult autonomous labor organizations. On the side of political freedom the development was substantially similar. Proletarian democracy continued to be described "a million times more democratic than the most democratic bourgeois republic." The Constitution adopted in 1936 contained full guarantees of free speech, free press, and free meeting and assembly, and in presenting it Stalin described it as "the only thoroughly democratic constitution in the world." But at the same time he pointed out that it left the powers of the party unchanged, and it also left unchanged the powers of the political police, which are in no way limited by the Constitution. What rights proletarian democracy guarantees or concretely secures to its citizens is therefore indefinite. The net effect of Lenin's substitution of "real democracy" for the democracy of the bourgeois republic was to rob that already vague term of whatever definite meaning it formerly had. The claims and counter-claims of communism and democracy became almost inaccessible to rational evaluation.

State and Revolution ended, apart from a chapter attacking the "opportunists," with a distinction between two stages of communist society. The first or lower stage, sometimes called socialism as distinguished from communism, was to be the period of proletarian dictatorship in which exploitation has been substantially eliminated. It is the official view that this stage has now been reached in Russia; the Constitution of 1936 describes the U.S.S.R. as "a socialist state of workers and peasants." No class struggle or conflict of interest between peasants and urban industrial workers remains. With the abandonment of equal pay, the principle of socialism is now said to be, "From each ac-

[34] "New Conditions, New Tasks in Economic Construction," *Leninism: Selected Writings* (New York, 1942), pp. 203 ff. On Russian practice relative to wages and management see Abram Bergson, *The Structure of Soviet Wages* (Harvard Economic Studies, Vol. LXXVI, 1944); *Management in Russian Industry and Agriculture* (1944), ed. by Arthur Feiler and Jacob Marschak, chs. 2 and 3.

cording to his ability, to each according to his work." Beyond this first stage Lenin placed the second or highest stage, the classless society, in which it will be possible to realize the communist ideal, " From each according to his ability, to each according to his needs." At this stage the state and all coercion will have " withered away." A vast expansion of production, Lenin imagined, would follow the abolition of capitalism, and a long habituation to a planned social life would create a state of mind in which an occasional unsocial individual will be as easily repressed as any crowd of civilized people would part two fighters. In it all distinction between work with the hands and work with the brain will disappear, and all can take their turn at managing and working. Thus Lenin retained the utopian capstone of the Marxian system but, a realist to the end, he was careful to point out that the end may never be realized and, the " unthinking " population being what it is, cannot now be definitely imagined. What is certain is that, at the lower stage, " socialists demand the *strictest* control, *by society and by the state,* of the quantity of labor and the quantity of consumption."

At this point, with all the more significant aspects of communist philosophy in hand, it is worth while to pause and inquire what precisely Lenin's interpretation did to the Marxism from which it started and to which it professed to adhere. The outcome has been aptly described as " inverted Marxism." Indeed, if piety toward the master permitted, Leninism might claim to have stood Marxism on its head, as Marx claimed to have stood the Hegelian dialectic on its feet. First, an economic structure, supposed by Marx to evolve independently of men's wills and by the internal development of its productive forces, is to be introduced by conscious planning and the will of the proletariat into the least industrialized of European countries. Second, the working class, supposed by Marx to have its mentality formed by its social and economic position in industrial society and to be emancipated only by its own efforts, is to receive its ideology from the outside by the instruction of middle-class intellectuals. Third, a socialist party, supposed to draw together the workers of the world, becomes a closed organization of professionals hierarchically organized from the top down and composed of a self-selected and self-perpetuating *élite*. Fourth, the social revolution, envisaged by Marx as supervening upon a bourgeois revolution that had already created the institutions of political democracy, " interlocks " with the bourgeois revolution and in half a year absorbs it. And finally, the accomplished revolution, supposed to conserve and extend all the political and civil liberties of the democratic republic, becomes the dictatorship of a single party which refuses to tolerate the activity or even the existence of any second party. The simple truth, which requires no dialectical explanation, is that the Marxian dogmas which Lenin piously held were simply abandoned when they came into conflict with his profounder belief in organization and his will as a revolutionist. Lenin's formulas remained the formulas of Marx; the meaning of Leninism departed very widely from the meaning of Marxism.

CAPITALIST ENCIRCLEMENT

The principal addition to Leninism as it has been described was occasioned by Stalin's abrupt acceptance in 1924 of the conclusion that socialism is possible in a single country. This change of position might well have occasioned a re-examination of the theory of the revolution and its dependence upon international developments both political and economic. In 1924, however, the theoretical issue was obscured by the rivalry between Stalin and Trotsky for Lenin's place and the desire of each to figure as the only true exponent of Leninism. Trotsky accordingly insisted that Stalin's change of front was simply defection from Lenin's position and the beginning of a counter-revolutionary reaction. It is by no means certain, however, that Lenin, had he lived, would not have made some shift of position analogous to Stalin's, in view of statements in his latest writings which seem to regard the evolution of socialism in Russia as depending on internal cultural and industrial development rather than on international politics.[35] No doubt if Lenin had made the change it would have been done with more dialectical subtlety than Stalin's heavy-handed method displayed. Stalin in effect denied that any change had occurred. He argued that Lenin and Trot-

[35] See, for example, " Better Fewer, but Better " (1923), *Selected Works*, Vol. IX, p. 400; " On Cooperation," *ibid.*, p. 409.

sky had always held incompatible theories of the revolution, even in 1917 when all communists expected an early outbreak of proletarian revolutions in Western Europe, that Trotsky's theory of permanent revolution had never been anything but a Menshevik fallacy, and that in 1917 Lenin had continued to hold the same view of the relation between the bourgeois and proletarian revolutions that he had held in 1905.[36] The effect of these propositions was not only to give to the theory of permanent revolution a doctrinal importance that it lacked in 1917 but also, by implying that the possibility of revolution in a single country had always been part of Leninism, to obscure really serious questions about the dependence of the proletarian revolution on the evolution of the international economy. In view of the care with which Lenin had developed his theory of imperialism, it seems certain that he would never have entertained the idea that communism could detach itself from the state of the world economy. Yet Stalin's theory of socialism in one country, with capitalist encirclement, in effect regarded the relationship as political rather than economic. It amounted to assuming that a socialist economy in Russia could insulate itself and could pursue political tactics alternatively of cooperation or intervention as circumstances dictated, while it waited for capitalism to collapse. Such a policy would be practically indistinguishable from Russian nationalism or imperialism and would have no logical relation to Marxism.

The only phase of the theory of capitalist encirclement that Stalin elaborated was its bearing upon Engels' famous prediction that in a socialist society the state would " wither away." If the evolution of society toward communism can go on in one country and if Russia by 1936 had already achieved the first or socialist stage of this evolution, some modification of that prediction was evidently required, and even some revision of Lenin's restatement of Engels' prediction in *State and Revolution.* For Engels said in the *Anti-Dühring* that the seizure of the means of production would be the " last independent act " of the state, and Lenin said that when the socialist phase of communism was complete, the highest or communist phase would begin, with the gradual dis-

[36] " The October Revolution and the Tactics of the Russian Communists," *Leninism: Selected Writings* (New York, 1942), pp. 9 ff.

appearance of all instruments of suppression. Accordingly at a Party Congress in 1939 Stalin discussed "some questions of theory," especially the following:

The exploiting classes have already been abolished in our country; socialism has been built in the main; we are advancing towards communism. . . . Why then do we not help our socialist state to die away? [37]

The question, Stalin said, shows that those who ask it have "conscientiously memorized" the doctrine of Marx and Engels but "have failed to understand the essential meaning of this doctrine." It proves that

They have failed to realize in what historical conditions the various propositions of this doctrine were elaborated; and, what is more, that they do not understand present-day international conditions, have overlooked the capitalist encirclement and the danger it entails for the socialist country.

What the question overlooks is the "espionage nets" with which capitalist countries surround a socialist government and the value of its "intelligence services," that is, the political police, in combating them. Engels' theory is true only if one considers what would happen in the internal development of a single country, abstracting from the international situation, or if one assumes that socialism is already victorious in all countries. This interpretation amounted to saying that Engels' prediction was merely an exercise in logic, with stipulated premises that need have no relation to the facts. As for Lenin, if he had finished *State and Revolution*, he would have covered the question. Since nothing is known about Lenin's intentions for the second part of his book, beyond the fact that he would have dealt with the Russian revolutions of 1905 and 1917, this statement claimed Lenin's authority for the conclusion but did not provide Lenin's premises if he had made the argument. The two functions of the communist state, according to Stalin, are defense against foreign intervention and internally the economic organization and cultural education of the country, and these are required in perpetuity, short of the worldwide realization of the classless society. "The

[37] Report to the Eighteenth Party Congress. *Leninism: Selected Writings* (New York, 1942), p. 469.

state will remain in the period of Communism also" unless the capitalist encirclement is liquidated.[38]

The theory of capitalist encirclement is hardly important because it postpones the disappearance of the Russian state, which might have been assumed in any case. Its importance consists rather in the fact that it severs the last link of logic that connected politics and ideology with international economic evolution. According to the theory the development of a communist economy in Russia and of the communist culture appropriate to it is simply a function of the communist state. Moreover, a socialist government in a single country can not only achieve socialism but can progress toward communism in spite of a permanently hostile international capitalism. It cannot indeed achieve complete security, but the risk appears to depend wholly on the chances of political intervention. Seemingly, according to this theory, a socialist economy in a country with adequate natural resources can achieve virtual independence of the economic causes that operate in a world economy. If this is true it is difficult to see what remains of Marx's theory of economic determinism.

THE TEMPER OF COMMUNISM

In spite of the elaborate, semi-scholastic structure of Leninism as a system, its distinguishing characteristic consists not so much in logic as in a kind of temper or moral bias, just as the paradox of Lenin's Marxism was the astonishing suppleness of its dogmatism. What really tied Lenin to Marx was not the logical cogency of Marx's arguments but the intense devotion to the cause of social revolution which Lenin found in Marx's revolutionary pamphlets and which both men regarded as the only road to human progress. The historical continuity between Marx and Lenin was far less one of scientific ideas than of moral attitude between two periods both of which were revolutionary in temper and method. Consequently the temper of communism — the moral attitudes and presumptions which Lenin bequeathed to it — is at least as important as its intellectual content. It was this which made communism a creed and a faith, true beyond the per-

[38] Cf. the official textbook of constitutional law edited by Andrei Y. Vyshinsky, *The Law of the Soviet State,* Eng. trans. by Hugh W. Babb (1948), p. 61.

adventure of a doubt, that afforded at once the sense of a unique insight and a moral imperative for every contingency. In his own personality this created for Lenin a kind of egocentric selflessness — a wholehearted devotion to the revolutionary cause, a sense of his own inevitable rightness, and complete freedom from any sense of self-seeking or personal ambition. It also left his judgments of policy and tactics, which were largely intuitive, extraordinarily untrammeled by the logic of the system that he professed. This amounted to a consciousness of vocation very like that which in the seventeenth century made up the peculiar moral quality of Calvinism. It was the unique achievement of Hegel's dialectic to convert this sense of vocation from devotion to individual liberty into devotion to the aggrandizement of a social class, and to rename it the logic of history for a generation no longer moved by allegiance to the will of God. This sense of vocation Lenin transmuted into the ethics of communism — an ethics of selfless devotion, of militant partisanship, of rigid adherence to principle coupled with a good deal of practical opportunism, of the exaltation of one principle above all others and of casuistry in behalf of the supreme principle.

Especially in Russia this moral attitude reflected a frame of mind normal to the devoted revolutionist in a country where political reform by legal means had long been hopeless, where reform by any means was a purpose shared by a small proportion of the population, and where the reformer was perpetually confronted by the social, economic, and political backwardness of his country. In such a case it is questionable whether a revolution could ever set itself the task of constructing democratic political institutions. Apart from the formidable difficulty of creating such institutions and making them function in a population almost wholly lacking in the experience or the ideology that such institutions require, the urgency of rapid industrialization was too great. Political democracy is a dubious instrument for coercing along the road of industrialization a population which lacks the skills and the ideology of industry. It is the fact that this state of affairs existed not only in Russia but is duplicated over large parts of Eastern Europe and Asia that gives force to communism. The ideology of the Russian revolutionist is far more suitable than that of either the Westernized capitalist or the Westernized working man to become the ideology of a new ruling class, devoted to the introduction of modern technology, accumulating its capital by taxation, and manipulating a population that is economically and politically helpless. Such a ruling class may be public-spirited according to its lights and benevolent in its intentions, but it can hardly be democratic in its methods. Considered in this light communism is peculiarly the ideology of an industrially backward country rather than of a country in which labor is already well organized and has attained strong political influence.

For this reason it may easily happen, in spite of logic, that there is no very clear line between communism, as a driving force in politics, and nationalism, that other great driving force of modern politics. The enthusiasm and the devotion of the revolutionist can merge, by a quite simple emotional transfer, into the enthusiasm and devotion of the patriot. Or conversely the motives of the nationalist may overrule or redirect the avowed purposes of the proletarian revolutionist. Quite conceivably the combination might work out to new and important results in countries where the character of nationalism is not already fixed. Lenin himself, so far as appears from his biography, had never been much interested in nationalism until a short time before the beginning of World War I, when a period of residence in Austrian Poland brought the subject to his attention and interested him in the relationship between Marxism and the nationalist minorities. His conclusions, based on the state of affairs in the multi-national states of Eastern Europe, were decidedly different from the doctrinaire internationalism of the old-line Marxists, who had tended simply to disregard nationalism.[39] Lenin sympathized deeply with the aspiration of minorities for cultural equality and regarded this as a progressive tendency in society which Marxism ought to accept and encourage. The precise ground for this conclusion was perhaps not quite clear, apart from the incompatibility of Marxism with any racial theory of culture. Apparently he never abandoned the traditional position

[39] See Stalin's *Marxism and the National Question* (1913); Eng. trans., New York, 1934. It seems clear that Stalin's conclusions were largely inspired by Lenin; see Wolfe, *op. cit.*, ch. 33. On the position of the nationalities in Russian government see Julian Towster, *Political Power in the U.S.S.R.* (1948), chs. 4–5.

of Marxism, which looked on national patriotism as a bourgeois virtue that depended ultimately on economic causes. Moreover, he was quite aware that a policy of cultural autonomy for national minorities might cut across his firmly held belief in "centralism." In fact communist government in Russia found a middle course that enabled it to evolve toward a kind of national federalism, without giving up Lenin's belief in centralized organization. Its policy towards national and racial minorities after the Revolution, largely under Lenin's leadership, was humane and enlightened and markedly successful. Essentially this policy was an experiment in cultural autonomy and equality, with local political autonomy but with a strong, integrated central power. If this should prove to be permanently feasible in Eastern Europe and other multi-national areas, it would modify profoundly the political significance of nationalism. On the other hand, the inheritance of acquired characters, which seems to have become a communist dogma, could be turned into a new defense of racial discrimination.

The essential and distinctive quality of Leninism was the rôle that it assigned to the communist party. The moral attitude which Lenin passed on to the class-conscious Marxist — the attitude of a man with an insight and a mission — was far more that of a militant religious order than that which democratic countries associate with a political party. The communist is a self-confessed intellectual and moral aristocrat. If his position carries privileges and opportunity, as it undoubtedly does in Russia, it carries also a heavy load of responsibility, inculcated by an intensified training and enforced by a relentless party discipline. His ethical code includes an unshakable conviction of the rightness of the party and of his own rightness as an agent of the party. With this moral attitude go naturally contempt for conciliation and compromise and the belief that men of other principles are insincere and hypocritical. And like most men who believe that life can be organized by a single supreme principle, the communist is prone to believe, and to act on the belief, that only the principle matters and the means of its attainment are morally indifferent. This kind of moral attitude reflected qualities of Lenin's personality which he ingrained in communism. Years before the Revolution of 1917 he was known to friend and foe alike as a leader who often evoked the loyalty of his followers but who also demanded their unquestioning agreement and submission. Hence he was an inveterate maker of party divisions when such agreement was not forthcoming. In 1906 his practice as a party "splitter" was regarded as so outrageous that he was tried by a party court for "conduct impermissible in a Party member," specifically for publicly charging the Central Committee with bad faith and corruption. Lenin's defense was both peculiar and revealing. He admitted that he had used language "calculated to evoke in the reader hatred, aversion, and contempt" and also that this was "impermissible among members of a united party." But, he argued, a split had occurred and the seceding factions were no longer members of a united party.

> It is wrong to write about Party comrades in a language that systematically spreads among the working masses hatred, aversion, contempt, etc., for those who hold different opinions. But *one may and must write* in that strain about a seceded organization. Why must one? Because when a split has taken place it is one's duty to *wrest* the masses from the leadership of the seceded section.
>
> The limits of the struggle based on a split are not party limits, but general political limits, or rather general civil limits, the limits set by the criminal law and nothing else.[40]

A political struggle between the party and a faction is "a fight of extermination." Obviously a political struggle between the party and any outsiders "who hold different opinions" will not be conducted by methods more scrupulous about truth and fair play. The limits are the criminal law, and if the party makes the law, there are no limits except those of power.

This conception of the duty of political leadership and of the ethics of political controversy — thus candidly stated in 1906 as controlling the relationship between the party and dissident members — inevitably controlled also the relationship of the party to persons and groups outside the party. It was decisive in defining once for all the diversity between the ethical presumptions of communism and those of political democracy. It determined, in the first place, the concrete meaning of proletarian democracy and the rôle played by the party as the vanguard

[40] Lenin's speech in full is in *Selected Works,* Vol. III, pp. 486–498. The quotations are on pp. 490 f. and 494.

and nucleus of the non-proletarian and semi-proletarian masses. A party which conceives itself as the guardian of unquestionable truth — a truth which is authoritatively announced by the party leaders and which, if properly understood, insures a correct answer for every question practical and theoretical — can hardly understand its educational function otherwise than as a duty of indoctrination or coercion. The party's purpose is of course by definition, and often no doubt quite sincerely, to secure "the interest of the exploited majority." But this does not imply that the majority ought to have any voice in deciding what its interest is, or that its opinion has any validity that the party ought to consider. On the contrary the theory assumes that the vanguard already knows what the uninstructed non-party proletarian would know if he had enjoyed the advantages of a perfect communist education. The moral attitude which the theory reflects is that of a righteous minority wholeheartedly devoted to saving a world which for the most part is too lazy or too stupid to know that it needs saving. However effective this attitude may under certain circumstances be, it is the antithesis of a democratic idea of political education. It was this educational phase of communism perhaps more than any other that repelled the German Marxists who assumed, as Karl Kautsky said in criticism, that "the education of the masses, as well as of their leaders, in democracy is a necessary condition of socialism." The part which communism assigned to the vanguard left no place for the two most important elements in a democratic theory of political education, the belief that education in political practices comes by participating in them and that participation is meaningless unless the participants, by reason of their own experience, can contribute something which an intellectual cannot tell them.

In the second place the moral attitude which Lenin impressed upon communism settled the terms upon which the party is willing to cooperate with other groups or organizations. Here too there is a fundamental distinction between the ethical point of view of communism and that of democracy. The difference amounts to a totally different estimate of the moral worth of compromise or cooperation or the conciliation of opposed parties in interest. For democracy these are ends; for communism they are means. In all Lenin's ample vocabulary of vituperation no other word had quite the bitterness that he gave to "opportunist" — a person who makes any concession in respect to the Marxian dogmas, who relaxes in any degree the program of revolution, or who enters into any agreement with one "who holds different opinions" except to further the cause of the revolution. Yet he also denied that he was a "doctrinaire." In August, 1917, after he had already declared his intention to make a revolutionary *coup* when he could, he wrote a revealing little essay on the utility of compromise.

The task of a truly revolutionary party is not to declare the impossible renunciation of all compromises, but to be able *through all compromises*, as far as they are unavoidable, to remain true to its principles, to its class, to its revolutionary task, to its cause of preparing the revolution and educating the masses of the people for victory in the revolution.[41]

According to Lenin's ethical code a compromise was always morally questionable, though it might sometimes be necessary. It was a sign of weakness, not of a willingness to admit any possible virtue in an opposing point of view. Hence it was a temporary expedient, a truce or a maneuver in readjusting the power-relationships between parties. As Lenin said elsewhere, a revolutionary party does not "support" its allies. It "utilizes" them. For its own ends, being fixed by the eternal principle of the class struggle, cannot change short of their complete accomplishment. It was in this sense that he construed his own concessions to the peasants in 1917, which he defended as "democratic." It was in this spirit that the Communist International in 1935 advocated a United Front.

As long as we cannot replace bourgeois democracy by the dictatorship of the proletariat, the proletariat is interested in retaining every scrap of bourgeois democracy in order to use it to prepare the masses for the overthrow of the power of capitalism and to achieve proletarian democracy.[42]

Or as Stalin said of the use of legal methods by communist parties, "parliamentary struggle is only a school, a fulcrum, for the

[41] "On Compromises," September, 1917. *Collected Works,* Vol. XXI, Book I, p. 152. *Selected Works,* Vol. VI, p. 208. Lenin's italics.

[42] Remarks by the Chairman of the Executive Committee at the Seventh World Congress. Quoted in *Social-Economic Movements* (1946), ed. by Harry W. Laidler, p. 468, n. 19.

organization of the extra-parliamentary struggle of the proletariat." In practice, therefore, communist tactics of cooperation amount to a policy of rule or ruin. The underlying moral assumption of the policy is the belief that any meeting of minds across the barrier of social class, except temporarily and superficially, is impossible and that accordingly a profession of conciliation is foolish or hypocritical. " Great questions in the life of nations," Lenin wrote in 1906, " are settled only by force."

SELECTED BIBLIOGRAPHY

Dialectical Materialism: The Theoretical Foundation of Marxism-Leninism. By V. Adoratsky. New York, 1934.

World Communism: A History of the Communist International. By Franz Borkenau. New York, 1939. (Published in England with the title, *The Communist International.*)

A Philosophic Approach to Communism. By Theodore B. H. Brameld. Chicago, 1933.

The Soviet Impact on the Western World. By Edward H. Carr. New York, 1947.

The Russian Revolution, 1917–1921. By William Henry Chamberlin. 2 vols. New York, 1935.

The Russian Enigma. By William Henry Chamberlin. New York, 1943.

Toward an Understanding of the U.S.S.R.: A Study in Government, Politics, and Economic Planning. By Michael T. Florinsky. New York, 1939.

The Political Theory of Bolshevism: A Critical Analysis. By Hans Kelsen. University of California Publications in Political Science. Berkeley and Los Angeles, 1948.

Russia in Flux. By Sir John Maynard. Edited and abridged by S. Haden Guest from *Russia in Flux* and *The Russian Peasant and Other Studies.* New York, 1948.

" Freedom of Artistic Expression and Scientific Inquiry in Russia." By Philip E. Mosley. In *Annals Am. Acad. Pol. and Soc. Science,* Vol. CC (1938), p. 254.

A History of Bolshevism from Marx to the First Five Years' Plan. By Arthur Rosenberg. Eng. trans. by Ian F. D. Morrow. London, 1934.

Power: A New Social Analysis. By Bertrand Russell. New York, 1938.

The Spirit of Post-War Russia: Soviet Ideology, 1917–1946. By Rudolf Schlesinger. London, 1947.

Soviet Philosophy: A Study of Theory and Practice. By John Somerville. New York, 1946.

Political Power in the U.S.S.R., 1917–1947: The Theory and Structure of Government in the Soviet State. By Julian Towster. New York, 1948.

The Law of the Soviet State. Ed. by Andrei Y. Vyshinsky. Eng. trans. by Hugh W. Babb. New York, 1948. Introduction.

To the Finland Station: A Study in the Writing and Acting of History. By Edmund Wilson. New York, 1940.

Three Men who made a Revolution: A Biographical History. By Bertram D. Wolfe. New York, 1948.

"The Soviet Union since World War II." *Annals Am. Acad. Pol. and Soc. Science,* Vol. CCLXIII, May, 1949.

CHAPTER XXXV

FASCISM AND NATIONAL SOCIALISM

The political philosophy of communism represented on the whole a coherent and carefully developed point of view. Even in change it was meticulously careful to preserve its continuity with Marxism, which in turn had been elaborated by two generations of scholarship. Lenin and Trotsky were men of settled convictions and long experience in party leadership before World War I. By comparison fascism in Italy and national socialism in Germany were mushroom growths. The parties were non-existent until they sprang up out of the demoralization that followed the war. Their leaders were men with neither the interest nor the aptitude for philosophical construction. Though the beliefs and ideas and prejudices that went into the making of their ideologies had been long in existence, they had never been part of a coherent body of thought. And when they were put together to make a "philosophy," their combination was largely opportunist. They were chosen with a view to their emotional appeal rather than to their truth or their compatibility, and often with a cynical indifference to intellectual honesty.

Both in Italy and in Germany opportunism was inherent in the process by which the parties extended their power. Discordant groups with incompatible interests had to be held together by appealing not to common purposes or principles but to common hatreds and fears. Peasants and large landowners, small shopkeepers and large industrialists, white-collar salaried workers and trade unionists were brought precariously together by the politician's device of promising everything to everybody, where a straightforward and definite program of any sort would surely have repelled some group that the party wished to attract. In both countries the leaders adopted this strategy consciously and purposefully. Mussolini in his early speeches adopted the pose of the practical man, of the empiricist or the intuitionist without theories, the man whose motto is "Action not talk." "There is no need for dogma, discipline suffices." Thus in an article written in 1924 he said:

> We Fascists have had the courage to discard all traditional political theories, and we are aristocrats and democrats, revolutionaries and reactionaries, proletarians and anti-proletarians, pacifists and anti-pacifists. It is sufficient to have a single fixed point: the nation. The rest is obvious.[1]

Similarly in Germany the twenty-five articles which the National Socialist party adopted in 1926 and declared to be its unchangeable principles had in fact nothing to do with its policies.[2] In the electoral campaign of 1933 Hitler refused to state a program.

> For all programs are vain; the decisive thing is the human will, sound vision, manly courage, sincerity of faith, the inner will — these are the decisive things.[3]

A leader of the party in Dresden, writing to an industrialist in 1930, was franker.

> Do not let yourself be continually confused by the text of our posters . . . There are catch words like "Down with capitalism," . . . but these are necessary . . . We must talk the language of the embittered socialist workman . . . We don't come out with a direct program . . . for reasons of diplomacy.[4]

Moreover, when Mussolini decided in 1929 that fascism must "provide itself with a body of doctrine," it was done almost by decree; the work must be finished in two months, "between now and the National Congress."

Under these circumstances many persons reached the conclusion that fascism and national socialism simply had no philosophy. Their methods appeared to be a mixture of mob psychology and terrorism, and their leaders appeared to have no purpose except to get and keep power. To some degree, of course, this was true but it was not the whole truth. Fascism and na-

[1] Quoted by Franz Neumann, *Behemoth* (2nd ed., Oxford University Press, 1944), pp. 462 f.

[2] They are enumerated, with comment, in the English translation of *Mein Kampf* (New York, 1939), p. 686, note. References are throughout to this edition.

[3] Quoted by Konrad Heiden, *Der Fuehrer* (1944), p. 554.

[4] Quoted by Edgar A. Mowrer, *Germany puts the Clock Back* (1933), p. 149.

tional socialism were genuine popular movements that elicited the fanatical loyalty of thousands of Germans and Italians. Even in the case of the higher leaders, who were most obviously cynical, it would be hard to say whether they were the masters or the slaves of the ideology they had helped to create.[5] A plausible argument might be made to prove that anti-Semitism, in which they believed as sincerely as they believed anything, was in fact their most disastrous handicap. And though the fascist "philosophy" was in many respects synthetic and *ad hoc,* it was put together largely out of elements that had long been current and that had the emotional force not only of familiarity but of passionate prejudice and sometimes of passionate aspiration. This philosophy, it is true, was not a rational plan for reaching limited and clearly defined ends. But then it made no such claim for itself. It professed to be "creative," to depend on "sound vision" and the "inner will." And when it tacitly or expressly assumed that creativeness and vision are antithetical to intelligence and reason, it was merely echoing an idea that had been current in European philosophy for a century. When it made creativeness the prerogative of a Leader charged with charismatic virtue, it was saying only what romantic hero-worshipers had been saying since the days of Thomas Carlyle. The fascist hero, especially in defeat, was a tawdry figure, and the fascist philosophy was no doubt a vulgarization and a caricature, but like all caricatures it resembled something real. For better or worse it belonged to the evolution of European political ideas and practice, and in that sense it was a philosophy.

The hypothesis that fascism and national socialism were merely the creatures of personal ambition forced on Italy and Germany by propaganda and terrorism would be more plausible if it were certain that they died with Mussolini and Hitler, or that they will have no counterparts in other countries. Few thoughtful

[5] Cf. H. R. Trevor-Roper, *The Last Days of Hitler* (The Macmillan Company, 1947), especially chs. 1–3. Goebbels, who was the only national socialist leader with any pretension to unusual intellectual capacity and who would no doubt have been willing to devote his talents to communism, monarchy, or even democracy if Hitler had adopted any of these, was completely duped by his hero-worship for Hitler and by anti-Semitism. See, for example, *The Goebbels Diaries, 1942–1943.* Eng. trans. by Louis P. Lochner (1948), pp. 16, 62, 116, 180, 241, 354, 370, 377.

men would assert that this is so, however much they may wish it. Fascism and national socialism were reactions to a real state of affairs, and the fact that they were intellectually mediocre and outraged the moral convictions of the civilized world is not, unfortunately, a guaranty that they may not have their analogues. The only guaranty for that would be a more intelligent and a less barbarous way of dealing with the problems inherent in the situation that produced them. Fascism and national socialism depended for their driving force on national patriotism, which is admittedly the most powerful sentiment in the political world today and which also has elements of genuine cultural value. Yet they moved in a European society — in fact in a world-society — in which absolute national self-determination and sovereignty are manifestly impossible. Their " new order " professed to resolve the disparity between a political world in which the governing units are nations and an economic world in which only a handful of great powers can aim at even approximate self-sufficiency. Their solution postulated the proposition that any international order must be an imperialism under the forcible control of a dominant nation. And the disproof of that proposition can never be complete until an effective international order on some more liberal principle is in sight. In their domestic policy fascism and national socialism professed to stabilize an economy in which inflation and depression had largely wiped out the security of both property and labor. They offered what they claimed were peaceful and orderly and just means for resolving the tensions between management and workers, which may jeopardize production and national security itself. They promised full production and full employment in an economy which has never utilized its full productive power except in preparing for war. Their " solution " in fact destroyed the civil liberties of workingmen without securing the rights of property or the freedom of industrial management. Its price was indeed ruinous, but the only assurance that it will not be paid again would be a more intelligent way of fulfilling the promises. The recurrence of fascism in some form will never be impossible so long as any important part of the public can be persuaded that intelligence in politics is barren, disputatious, timid, and incapable of action, or that democratic procedures are feeble, decadent, and plutocratic.

NATIONALIST SOCIALISM

The fact that fascist and national socialist philosophy was so largely a synthetic product put together out of diverse and long familiar elements has made its proper historical antecedents difficult to locate. Its " sources " have been found, both by its friends and its enemies, in Italian history as far back as Dante and in German history as far back as Martin Luther. This kind of historical explanation, by the assembling of isolated ideas out of context, is unenlightening. No European literature since the sixteenth century has lacked apologies for political absolutism, which is indeed the simplest of political ideas and the readiest defense against the threat of insecurity and disorder. For obvious reasons both fascism and national socialism ransacked history for ideas and heroes that could be called into service. In itself this process would have caused the two movements to develop quite different philosophies, since a German and an Italian public would hardly be amenable to the same emotional appeals. As a matter of pure logic it would be easy to contrast the philosophies of *Mein Kampf* and of Mussolini's article in the *Enciclopedia Italiana*. The contrasts would, however, prove very little, since no one has ever doubted that the substance was the same, no matter how different the language. The differences, even if they amount to logical contradictions, are easy to account for. The place to begin is the overt and not too highly rationalized identity between the two philosophies.

Fascism in Italy and national socialism in Germany both put themselves forward as socialist regimes adapted to national purposes, or as what figured in Goebbels' propaganda as " true socialism." In both countries they finally attained power by the alliance of a professedly socialist party with a nationalist party. This occurred in Italy early in 1920 when Mussolini suddenly adopted nationalism, despite a long record of violent anti-nationalism,[6] and when the Nationalist party made at least a token acceptance of syndicalist socialism. In Germany a corresponding event occurred when Hitler finally gained a majority in the Reichstag by a coalition with Hugenberg's Nationalists, despite

[6] The record is fully covered by Gaudens Megaro, *Mussolini in the Making* (1938), especially pp. 246 ff.

his announced determination to forego all compromises and alliances.[7] Alfredo Rocco, long a leader of the Italian Nationalists, who became Minister of Justice in the new coalition, thus stated the principle of fascism as a nationalist form of socialism in the Chamber of Deputies in 1925.

> Fascism understood that the problem of the organization of social groups — that is, of syndicalism — was by no means necessarily connected with the movement designed to destroy capitalist economy, which is based on the private organization of production, so as to substitute for it a socialist economy, based on the community organization of production. It saw the necessity of isolating the syndical phenomena from socialism, which had complicated it with all the anti-national, international, pacificistic, humanitarian, rebellious ideologies of its political doctrine, that had nothing to do with syndical organization. Thus fascism created a national-syndicalism, inspired wholly by sentiment for the fatherland and by national solidarity.[8]

The idea was simple enough and appealing enough so that its origin hardly needs looking for. Society ought to be cooperative rather than torn by strife; the nation is the society to which everybody belongs; therefore every class and every interest ought to work together in the interest of the nation. The idea also implied the main lines of strategy for a party that meant to seek power on so utopian a platform. It must be socialist, at least in name, because in Italy and Germany popular politics had long run in terms that were in some sense socialist. Yet it had at the very least to neutralize and sterilize the political influence of labor unions that were in general socialist whether they were Marxian or not. A nationalist socialism was well calculated to appeal to the lower middle class — the small shopkeepers and salaried employees — who had suffered most from inflation and depression and who were terrified at the prospect of being degraded to the ranks of the proletariat, a fate that Marxism had long promised them. In every country this class finds itself precariously balanced between organized labor on one side and large-scale business on the other, and since it is defenseless by its own efforts against both, the prospect of help from a national government is correspondingly welcome. The larger industrialist and businessman might hope that in the new combination na-

[7] *Mein Kampf*, pp. 759 ff.

[8] Quoted by Herbert L. Matthews, *The Fruits of Fascism* (1943), p. 96.

tionalism would take the curse off socialism. At least he might be free from any effective pressure by union labor, and while in accepting socialism he gave up the dream of escaping regulation by the government, that was after all more than he really expected. On the whole it seemed more realistic to believe that he might control government, while government in turn controlled labor, and in any case he needed the support of government for commercial expansion abroad. Thus a nationalist version of socialism promised happiness for everyone, and while the prospect on careful analysis might have seemed utopian, it was at least a welcome relief in a society that suffered from the psychological aftermath of the war, whose middle class had been expropriated by inflation, and whose economy offered no reasonable opportunity to large numbers of young men. The proposed partnership was indeed very unequal, at least for those who seriously believed that socialism meant a redistribution of national income and substantial improvement in the general standard of living. It was also very precarious. But every side could always hope that the next turn would be in its favor, and the leadership could always throw the advantage now one way and now another. And as the party consolidated its power it became progressively independent of all sides.

A program of nationalist socialism determined also the main lines of political theory by which such a program must be supported. In essence it meant a complete control of the national economy by national government in the national interest. Hence it was equally opposed to any form of liberalism that tended to limit political control over the economy and to Marxism which regarded politics as determined by the economy. A fascist political philosophy must therefore put itself forward as an exalted form of political idealism. It must condemn alike the brutality of Marxian materialism and the egoism and plutocracy of liberalism. Against the rights of liberty, equality, and happiness it must set the duties of service, devotion, and discipline. Since it was intrinsically nationalist it must identify internationalism with cowardice and lack of honor, and it must interpret all self-governing associations as agencies of the class struggle, which it claimed to supersede. It must as a matter of course brand parliaments as mere "talking shops" and all forms of democratic procedure as futile, weak, and decadent. It must set up the glory and power of the nation as a moral end that includes or overrides all individual goods and it must magnify the will of the nation as a force capable of surmounting all obstacles both material and spiritual. These were in fact the principles that Mussolini put into the Italian Labor Charter promulgated in 1927. The ends of the Italian nation are "superior to those of the separate individuals or groups of individuals which compose it." "Work in all its forms . . . is a social duty." Production "has a single object, namely, the well-being of individuals and the development of national power."

PRUSSIAN SOCIALISM

In Germany also the idea that all the nation's resources, both economic and cultural, might be consolidated for national purposes was old and familiar. It had in fact been more nearly realized in German than in Italian history. Sometimes the idea had been exploited mainly in the interest of nationalism, sometimes of socialism, but whatever the emphasis the idea itself was no novelty. It was essentially the principle that the philosopher Fichte had developed in *Der geschlossene Handelsstaat* as far back as 1800. The economic philosophy of Friedrich List had departed from the non-political tradition of English economics in being quite definitely a plan for national economic development, with political regulation of both capital and labor in the interest of national expansion.[9] Though German party socialism had been in general Marxian, socialist speculation had always included figures like Rodbertus, Lassalle, and Eugen Dühring, whose philosophy leaned toward some kind of state socialism rather than toward internationalism. The idea that the class struggle might be supplanted by some form of cooperation between capital and labor had been almost a characteristic heresy of Marxian revisionists.

It was in no way surprising, therefore, that an idea so simple and so familiar should have been enticing to Germans in the

[9] *Das nationale System der politischen Ökonomie,* 1841; Eng. trans. by S. S. Lloyd, *National System of Political Economy,* London, 1885. National socialism resuscitated List by regarding him as the discoverer of *Lebensraum.*

period of economic and political demoralization that followed World War I. Two writers, of no great philosophical importance but of considerable literary brilliance, did much to popularize the idea of "Prussian Socialism" among German intellectuals, Oswald Spengler and Arthur Moeller van den Bruck.[10] History, according to Spengler's philosophy, is a record of the struggle between "culture areas." Sometimes a culture area was described as "Europe" in contrast with "Asia," sometimes it was the "white race" in contrast with the "colored races." In either case the conclusion was drawn that it is the historical mission of Germany to defend the frontier of European civilization against Asia and the colored races. Political democracy is a form of degeneration which is due partly to industrialization and partly to the debauching of the will to power by intellectualism. Consequently it must be superseded by an era of dictatorial leadership and of competition for world empire. In this process national states will be absorbed as tribes and peoples were conquered and absorbed by Rome. Democracy and freedom rest on the illusion that men are rational, and intellectualism is a "weed of the pavement," a typical corruption produced by the urban proletariat. Only in the peasantry and the aristocracy does the healthy will to possession and power survive, and these have always been the driving forces of history. For man is by nature a beast of prey; justice, happiness, and peace are dreams, and the ideal of physical betterment is boring and senile. Hence it followed that socialism must be purged of the Marxian dogmas of internationalism and the class struggle. In Germany this means that it must be incorporated with the Prussian tradition of discipline and authority. Political parties and parliamentary institutions must give way to political and economic hierarchy, and the industrial working class in particular must be reduced to obedience. The fundamental question, as Spengler saw it, was

[10] Spengler's *Preussentum und Sozialismus* was published in Munich in 1920. His *Decline of the West* (Eng. trans. by C. F. Atkinson, New York, 1926–28) and his *Hour of Decision* (Eng. trans. by C. F. Atkinson, New York, 1934) were better known but had less political importance. Moeller van den Bruck's *Das dritte Reich* was published in Hamburg in 1923. There is an abridged translation by E. O. Lorimer entitled *Germany's Third Empire*, London, 1934. See Gerhard Krebs, "Moeller van den Bruck: Inventor of the 'Third Reich,'" *Am. Pol. Sci. Rev.*, Vol. XXXV (1941), pp. 1085 ff.

whether trade rules the state or the state rules trade. The first idea is British and the second German. Spengler's conception of a healthy society was in important respects identical with that which actuated national socialism: a Junker-industrialist political class, a settled peasant agricultural economy, enough industry to provide the sinews of military power, and a working class disciplined to obedience and deprived of the independent labor unions that give it political influence. By these devices, if only they could be made compatible with one another, Spengler hoped to see Germany raised to the headship of a continental empire that should rival or eclipse Britain.

The thought of Moeller van den Bruck was substantially similar. The recurrent theme of *The Third Reich* was that "Every people has its own socialism," but ideally it is a socialism that "begins where Marx ends." Being a Jew, Marx lacked the appreciation of any ideal values and in particular of national values. A true national socialism is not materialist but idealist. It is not proletarian, for "proletarians are what remains at the bottom." It has been purged of every element of liberalism, which is a false front for plutocracy, and of liberal democracy, which is the death of nations. It depends upon "the will of a nation that knows what it wills" under the guidance of a great leader who can express the nation's will. In it the class struggle has been replaced by national solidarity, for only a united nation is strong enough to stand in the European chaos.

> The only question is whether the national elements in the German working classes will have the power and the will to wheel the proletarian battle front in a national-socialist direction; or rather, to wheel it right about, so that the forces which were directed to class war against our own nation shall face the foreign foe.[11]

The expression "national-socialist" in this passage did not refer to Hitler's party, but its use suggests the reasons that led Hitler to adopt the name.

Whether Hitler was influenced by "Prussian socialism" is hard to tell and not very important. *The Third Reich* was republished with Goebbels' endorsement in 1931, but after the expulsion of the socialist members of the party, it became proper to depre-

[11] *Germany's Third Empire,* Eng. trans., p. 167.

ciate Bruck as a mere "literary man." What is quite certain, however, is that Hitler's plan for organizing his party, as he described it at the end of the first volume of *Mein Kampf*, depended on combining nationalists and socialists.[12] Germany in 1918, he said, was a people "torn into two parts." Its nationalist part, which "comprises the layers of national intelligence," is timid and impotent because it dare not face its defeat in the war. The great mass of the working class, on the other hand, which is organized in the Marxian parties, "consciously rejects any promotion of national interests." Yet it "comprises above all those elements of the nation without which a national resurrection is unthinkable and impossible." The highest aim of the new movement is "the nationalization of the masses," "the recovery of our national instinct of self-preservation." It is also certain that Hitler's propaganda was cleverly designed to appeal to a working class steeped in Marxian ideology. The nation played the same utopian part as the classless society, and the class struggle was displaced by the struggle of the "have-not" nations against the forces of Jewish democratic plutocracy. His promises of economic betterment were limitless but altogether vague, as was necessary if the anti-Marxists were not to be repelled.

Fascism and national socialism, therefore, were attempts to draw together the whole population of the nation, eliminating or suppressing all rivalry between groups and interests, and to marshal the total resources of the country behind its government. They were socialist in a twofold sense: they appealed to a public in which popular political movements had usually been socialist, and they required a thoroughgoing political control over business and industry. They were not socialist in the sense that they included any serious intention of redistributing national income in the interest of the working class. They were nationalist also in a twofold sense: no sentiment except nationalism was general enough and powerful enough to control the divergent interests that had to be united, and nationalism was the antithesis of parliamentarism and internationalism. They were not nationalist in any sense that implied respect for nationalism as a cultural value or as the moral prerogative of all peoples. Their suc-

[12] Cf. the autobiographical passage in his speech at Wilhelmshaven, April 1, 1939; *My New Order* (New York, 1941), pp. 619 ff.

cess, therefore, could have only one outcome. The only condition that submerges the divergent social and economic interests of a modern nation is preparation for war. Accordingly fascism and national socialism were in essence war governments and war economies set up not as expedients to meet a national emergency but as permanent political systems. In a situation where national self-determination was not a feasible plan for political order in Europe, they meant the regimentation of national resources for imperialist aggression against other nations and the organization of the Italian and German peoples for imperialist expansion. They assumed that the only feasible form of international organization is, as Spengler had said, internationalism "not by compromise or concession but by victory and annihilation." They were socialist and nationalist in a form antithetical to individual liberty and democracy, "endowed," as Mussolini said on the eve of the Abyssinian War, "in an ever higher degree with the virtues of obedience, sacrifice, dedication to the fatherland." They signified that "the whole life of the nation, political, economic, spiritual, should concentrate on those things which form our military necessities."

IRRATIONALISM: THE PHILOSOPHIC CLIMATE OF OPINION

A philosophy whose immediate political implication was national expansion by war must of necessity be an adventurer's philosophy. By no rational calculation either of individual happiness or of tangible national benefit could such a purpose be made plausible. It must assign a mystical rather than a calculated value to national greatness, some remote and glittering goal of national "creativeness" that would at once allay the individual's moral scruples and persuade him to accept discipline and heroism as ends to which no rational purpose need be assigned. In short, it must set up will and action as self-justifying. In the thought of the nineteenth century there was no lack of ideas that contributed to such a philosophy. The enemies of fascism and national socialism generally described these movements as a "revolt against reason," and its theorists not only accepted but underscored this description. Their writings were filled with assertions that "life" controls reason, not reason life; that the great deeds of history were performed not by intelligence but by the heroic will; that peoples are preserved not by thought but by a herd-instinct or a racial intuition inherent in the blood; that they rise to greatness when their will to power surmounts its physical and moral handicaps. Similarly they consistently represented the desire for happiness as a despicable motive, in comparison with heroism, self-sacrifice, duty, and discipline. The democratic ideals of freedom and equality, and the civil and political liberties of constitutional and representative government, were represented as the outworn remnants of philosophical rationalism, which reached its culmination in the French Revolution. "Barren intellectualism" was the standard term of contempt by which fascism and national socialism described all rival political theories, whether liberal or Marxian.

Philosophic irrationalism had formed a persistent strand in European thought throughout the nineteenth century but it had been marginal, in the sense that it had appealed to artists and literary men rather than to scientists or academic scholars, and it had been critical, in the sense that it had reflected a mood of dissatisfaction and maladjustment. Modern industrialized society has rarely been a congenial home for artists or mystics. Irrationalism was born of the experience that life is too difficult, too complex, and too changeable to be reduced to a formula, that nature is driven by dark and mysterious forces opaque to science, and that a conventionalized society is intolerably rigid and superficial. Against intelligence, therefore, it set up some other principle of understanding and action. This might be the insight of genius, or the inarticulate cunning of instinct, or the assertiveness of will and action. However described, this force was contrasted with reason as being creative rather than critical, profound rather than superficial, natural rather than conventional, uncontrollable and demonic rather than methodical. The patient weighing of evidence and the systematic search for fact are bourgeois virtues beneath the dignity of the genius or the saint.

Though an irrationalism of this sort had rarely had any positive political or social implications, it had combined two tendencies that were at once logically opposed and emotionally compatible. It had been a cult of the folk or the people or the nation, and it had been a cult of the hero or the genius or the great man. Sometimes it had imagined the folk collectively as the bearer and source of civilization; from its spirit emerges mystically art and literature, law and government, morals and religion, all marked with the spiritual qualities of the national soul. In Germany especially this cult of the *Volk* had been characteristic of literary romanticism. Long before the French Revolution Herder had contrasted "genuine folk-thought" with the cosmopolitan rationalism of the French and English Enlightenment. The cult of the *Volk* had been implied in the conscious idealization of medieval art in contrast with the pseudo-classicism of the Eighteenth Century, in the revived appreciation of folk poetry and folk music, and in the "Germanism" of historical theories of constitutional law and political institutions. In its capacity as the creator of culture the folk was imagined to act collectively rather than by individual invention. Yet this same romantic tendency of thought might take the form of the most extreme individualism, since all that is really great in art or politics was often imagined to be created by the heroes or the rare great minds that from time to time emerge from the soul of the *Volk*. Hero-worship was an authentic quality of romantic thought from Carlyle and Nietzsche to Wagner and Stefan George.[13] In this form of individualism reverence for the folk collectively was curiously combined with contempt for the masses individually. The individualism of the hero is the opposite of democratic egalitarianism. He despises the utilitarian and humanitarian virtues of ordered bourgeois life; he has a pessimistic contempt for comfort and happiness; he lives dangerously and in the end he meets inevitable disaster. He is the natural aristocrat, driven to creation by the demonic powers of his own soul, and after the inertia of commonplace minds has destroyed him the people worship him.

The intellectual progenitors of this type of irrationalist thought in nineteenth-century philosophy were Schopenhauer and Nietzsche. Schopenhauer saw behind both nature and human life the struggle of a blind force which he called "will," an endless striving without purpose, a restless and meaningless effort that desires all things and is satisfied with nothing, that creates and destroys but never attains. In this swirl of irrational

[13] There is a sympathetic but critical account in Eric R. Bentley's *A Century of Hero-worship* (Philadelphia, 1944).

force only the human mind builds up a little island of apparent order in which the illusion of reasonableness and purpose has a precarious footing. Schopenhauer's pessimism was based upon a moral intuition of the vanity of human wishes in such a world, the littleness of human effort, and the hopelessness of human life. In particular it was rooted in contempt for the little values and virtues of the Philistine, the smugness, self-satisfaction, and complacency of the undistinguished and the vulgar, who imagine that they can bind the incomprehensible forces of life and reality with rules of convention and logic. This purblind spiritual pride Schopenhauer believed, not altogether justly, to be embodied in his rival Hegel. Against the logic of history he set up the creativeness of genius, of the artist and saint, who master the will not by controlling it but by denying it. The hope of mankind lies not in progress but in extinction, in realizing that struggle and achievement are illusions. This release he imagined to be attained either through religious asceticism or the contemplation of beauty, which is consciousness without desire. The morality of everyday life Schopenhauer derived from pity, the sense that suffering is inevitable and that all men are essentially equal in their misery.

This curious blending of irrationality and humanitarianism, of will and contemplation, was broken apart by Nietzsche. For if life and nature are truly irrational, irrationality ought to be affirmed morally as well as intellectually. If achievement is meaningless, in any sense other than that human nature is blindly driven to strive, men can only accept, and if possible accept joyfully, the striving in place of the achievement; the value lies in the struggle and even in the very hopelessness of the struggle. Not pity and renunciation but the affirmation of life and the will to power are the inner forces of personality. The commonplace, the smug, and the hypocritical, Nietzsche agreed, are as contemptible as Schopenhauer had said, but it is the hero rather than the saint who transcends them. All moral values must be "transvalued" accordingly: in place of equality, the recognition of innate superiority; in place of democracy, the aristocracy of the virile and the strong; in place of Christian humility and humanity, hardness and pride; in place of happiness, the heroic life; in place of decadence, creation. This, indeed, as Nietzsche insisted, is no philosophy for the masses, or rather, it assigns the masses to their proper place as beings of a lower order whose healthy instinct is to follow their leader. Once this healthy instinct is corrupted, the masses create only a slave morality, a fiction of humanity, pity, and self-abnegation, which in part reflects their own inferiority but is more truly a subtle poison, an invention of servile cunning, to sterilize the powers of the creators. For there is nothing that the common man hates or fears so much as the disruptive force of originality. The two great embodiments of such a slave morality Nietzsche found in democracy and Christianity, each in its own way an apotheosis of mediocrity and a symbol of decadence. Nietzsche ransacked the vocabulary for terms of violence to describe his hero, the superman, the "Big Blond Beast," who tramples down opposition, despises happiness, and creates his own rules. But what commended his philosophy to revolutionists of all kinds, and especially youthful revolutionists, was his indictment of the Philistinism and vulgarity of the modern bourgeois.

Despite the obvious similarity of Nietzsche's ideas to the philosophy of fascism and national socialism, the relationship was not so simple as has often been supposed. Critics were often disposed to see in him the sources from which the ideas of the two movements were mainly drawn. Fascists and national socialists themselves were not unwilling to admit this derivation, partly because some of the affinities were genuine and even more, perhaps, because they needed the prestige of a great writer to supplement their own literary production, which was not in fact very distinguished. Neither Mussolini nor Hitler was averse to being regarded as a superman and both sincerely felt and indeed professed contempt for the masses whom they led. Both could find in the "transvaluation of values" a politer phrase for moral cynicism. Fascists and national socialists alike were not inaptly cast in the rôle of "new barbarians," not softened by over-civilization or moral renunciation, and both publicized themselves as the redeemers of a decadent civilization. They shared with Nietzsche a sincere hatred of democracy and Christianity. In important respects, however, they had to use him with caution, and his writings could be safely circulated only in carefully selected anthologies. Few writers in the nineteenth century had been so contemptuous of nationalism, which he regarded as little better than a vulgar prejudice. Nietzsche's chief pride was in being a "good European." No German writer had been so bitterly critical of the Germans of the Second Empire, whom he described as "slave-souled" and who needed, he thought, an intermixture of Slavic blood to redeem them. The only periods of European history that Nietzsche admired were the Italian Renaissance and the France of Louis XIV. Finally, though he often said harsh things about Jews, he was not altogether anti-Semitic. He once described the Jews as "the strongest, toughest, and purest race now living in Europe."[14] No national socialist quoted Nietzsche's aphorism, "Gut deutsch sein, heisst sich entdeutschen."

The irrationalism of Schopenhauer and Nietzsche was almost wholly moralistic. There existed in nineteenth-century philosophy, however, other tendencies more closely related to science which were also in some sense irrationalist. These were often designated by such vague words as pragmatism and positivism. They grew in general from two sources: the biological discovery that reason or intelligence, like other mental faculties, could be regarded as a vital process that had a naturalistic origin in organic evolution, and the logical discovery that scientific procedure, even in the exact sciences, included postulates and assumptions that were not self-evident in any rationalistic sense but could be more easily described as matters of convention or convenience. These two tendencies were common properties of much philosophy in the nineteenth century but they found their most popular exponent in the French philosopher Henri Bergson. Unlike Nietzsche's aphoristic moralizing Bergson's irrationalism was a systematic use of reason to undermine reason and a highly intelligent criticism of the pretensions of scientific intelligence to be a source of truth. On its critical side Bergson's *Creative Evolution* was an analysis designed to show that intellect is merely a factor in biological adaptation which has a pragmatic or instrumental use in the struggle for life and the control of man's environment. Utility rather than the attainment of truth is the function of science. This negative criticism, however, merely cleared the ground. Bergson's main purpose was to show that

[14] *Beyond Good and Evil,* Section 251.

intelligence is the servant of the "life-force," an obscure cosmic drive not unlike Schopenhauer's will or Hartmann's "Unconscious." Only intuition can directly apprehend the world as what it really is — an indefinable, unpredictable, superrational creative force. Bergson supposed the mind to be natively endowed with such an intuition, akin to instinct and more deeply rooted in life than is reason, but largely atrophied in human development by man's over-dependence on intelligence. He also imagined that the intuitive powers might be recovered and made a methodical instrument for attaining metaphysical truth, but he was quite unable to say what the methods were. In point of fact his appeal to intuition was simply an invitation to a kind of vitalist mysticism in biology and psychology as well as in philosophy.

PHILOSOPHY A MYTH

Until about the close of the nineteenth century philosophic irrationalism was notable for lacking any very specific applications to politics. It had been on the whole an artist's philosophy, viewed askance by academic philosophers and neglected by political theorists. There was, indeed, a steadily growing reaction in psychology and sociology against intellectualist or rationalist explanations of human behavior and a corresponding emphasis on "non-logical" factors, whether in the form of instinctive sentiments and drives or pseudo-logical rationalizations of them. In the sociology of Pareto this contrast of the logical and the non-logical had produced a cyclical theory of social change which has been believed, on rather flimsy evidence, to have influenced Mussolini. Political power must of necessity be concentrated in a ruling class and this class rises to power in the first instance because it is dominated by a social ideal which it is prepared to realize by force. The possession of power and the need to stabilize and perpetuate it renders the ruling class effete; the "lion" is displaced by the "fox." And in the end the old ruling class is displaced by younger, more virile, and more ruthless candidates for power. Psychological and sociological theories, however, were not scientifically irrationalist. Pareto's sociology was bred of a desire to give to social science an exactness comparable with that of the natural sciences.

A direct application of Bergson's ideas to social philosophy, however, was made by Georges Sorel in his *Réflexions sur la violence* (1908).[15] Sorel had long been a violent critic of the "illusions of progress" and of democracy. So long as his syndicalism had made any profession of being Marxian, it had selected those elements of mystical evolutionism that Marx had carried over from Hegel, which are not hard to find if one looks for them. Capitalism in Marx, Sorel said, behaves like Hartmann's Unconscious; it is a blind but cunning force that evolves higher forms of social life without intending them. Sorel recognized correctly that Bergson's "vital force" belonged in the same philosophical tradition, which was in principle antithetical to Hegel's belief in a universal logic of history. Consequently it could be used to expunge from Marx all traces of economic determinism or indeed of any theory of social change by rational causes, leaving the class struggle as a manifestation of sheer creative "violence" on the part of the proletariat. Bergson's intuition, being a direct insight into creative evolution, could also be used to provide a philosophy for revolution, and such a philosophy could justify direct action and the general strike (in contrast with the political action advocated by the Marxian socialist parties) which had always been main instruments of syndicalist strategy. For Sorel, therefore, social philosophy became a "myth," a vision or symbol to unite and inspire the workers in their struggle against a capitalist society. All great social movements, he believed, like Christianity for example, have come about by the pursuit of a myth. To analyze a myth or to inquire whether it is true — even to ask whether it is practicable — is meaningless. For it is essentially an image that can evoke sentiment and that supplies the cohesion and the drive which enables a group to bring its energies into play. A political philosophy is not a guide to rational action but an incitement to fanatical determination and blind devotion. The general strike, which was Sorel's version of a myth for the proletariat, was too lacking in emotional overtones to be very effective, but his idea that any social philosophy is

[15] *Reflections on Violence,* Eng. trans. by T. E. Hulme, New York, 1914. Bergson's earlier work was singularly lacking in any applications of his philosophy to ethics. *Les deux sources de la morale et de la religion* was not published until 1932.

some kind of myth became part of the revolutionary syndicalism in which Mussolini was for years an agitator and an editor. He reviewed at length the Italian translation of Sorel's book in 1909. The fascist conception of the nature and purpose of a philosophy was substantially identical with Sorel's conception of the myth. In it the irrationalism of the philosophical tradition from Schopenhauer to Bergson gained social and political expression. Sorel himself, however, never arrived at any final definition of the myth. In his later years he was about equally attracted to fascism, Bolshevism, and reactionary nationalism, without precisely identifying himself with any of them.

Conceived as a myth philosophy is a vision of life but not a plan, and still less is it a theory that depends on reason. It is rather a release of the deep-lying instincts of a people, inherent in the "life-force" itself, or in their "blood" or "spirit." Mussolini said in a speech at Naples in 1922, using words that obviously echoed Sorel:

> We have created our myth. The myth is a faith, it is passion. It is not necessary that it shall be a reality. It is a reality by the fact that it is a goad, a hope, a faith, that it is courage. Our myth is the nation, our myth is the greatness of the nation! [16]

This fascist myth was sedulously built up by Italian nationalists like Alfredo Rocco in the doctrine that modern Italy is the spiritual heir of the Roman Empire. Rocco proposed nothing less than a complete rewriting of European history to show that democracy is a culmination of the decadence and anarchy that began with the fall of Rome. The liberal idea of individual rights was merely the last step in setting aside the Roman idea of the right and authority of the state, a consequence, according to Rocco, of the influx of "Germanic individualism." But even through the dark ages of national dissolution, Italy clung to the legacy of Rome, for liberalism is foreign to the "Latin mind." The purpose of fascism is "to restore Italian thought in the sphere of political doctrine to its own traditions, which are the traditions of Rome." [17] The astonishing feats of interpretation that Rocco

[16] Quoted by Herman Finer, *Mussolini's Italy* (1935), p. 218.

[17] *Dottrina politica del fascismo* (1925); Eng. trans. by Dino Bigongiari, "The Political Doctrine of Fascism," in *International Conciliation*, No. 223.

performed on eminent Italians like Thomas Aquinas and Mazzini can hardly be criticized, since they were intuitions of the "Latin mind." It is hardly necessary to say that his notion of "Germanic individualism" did not survive the German alliance.

There was of course no such direct relationship between Hitler and Sorel as between Sorel and Mussolini, but this was not necessary. Hitler already had a model in Mussolini and the fascist myth. The meaning that he put into the nearly untranslatable word *Weltanschauung* in *Mein Kampf* came to practically the same thing. A "view of life" never compromises; it demands complete and absolute acceptance to the exclusion of every alternative view; it is intolerant like a religion; and it fights its opponents with every available means. It does not argue or concede any validity to an opposing view but is completely dogmatic and fanatical. Hence it supplies the "spiritual foundation" without which human beings cannot be as ruthless and as unscrupulous as they must be to win the battle of life. Politics is fundamentally a battle to the death between "views of life."

> Only in the struggle of two views of life with each other can the weapon of brute force, used continuously and ruthlessly, bring about the decision in favor of the side it supports.[18]

In national socialism this "spiritual foundation" was provided by "blood and soil," and it played the same part in Germany as the myth of imperial Rome in Italy. In spite of the imposing façade of pseudo-biology and pseudo-anthropology built around it, it was as impervious to scientific criticism as Rocco's revision of European history was to historical criticism. Alfred Rosenberg's use of the word "myth" in the title of his *Myth of the Twentieth Century* was clearly borrowed from Sorel.

> The life of a race or people is not a philosophy that is logically developed and consequently is not a process that grows according to natural laws. It is the construction of a mystical synthesis or activity of soul which cannot be explained by rational inferences or made comprehensible by exhibiting causes and effects. . . . In the last resort every philosophy that goes beyond formal, rational criticism is not so much knowledge as affirmation (*Bekenntnis*) — a spiritual and racial affirmation, an affirmation of the values of character.[19]

[18] *Mein Kampf,* p. 223; cf. p. 784.

[19] *Der Mythus des 20. Jahrhunderts* (1930), pp. 114 f.

Purity of blood speaks louder than reason or fact. Another national socialist philosopher, Ernst Kriek at Heidelberg, asserted the contrast as follows.

> There has arisen . . . blood against formal reason; race against purposeful rationality; honor against profit; unity against individualistic disintegration; martial virtue against bourgeois security; the folk against the individual and the mass.[20]

FASCISM AND HEGELIANISM

According to the preceding interpretation, the intellectual affinities of fascism and national socialism were with philosophic irrationalism. This conclusion makes it necessary to consider their relation to Hegelian nationalism and the Hegelian theory of the state. The relation was in fact somewhat complicated. Hegel's philosophy had been regarded throughout the nineteenth century as the logical antithesis of Schopenhauer's irrationalism. Yet the version of fascist philosophy that Mussolini adopted after he decided that fascism needed a philosophy was obviously borrowed from Italian Hegelianism. It utilized to the full, in its attack on liberalism and parliamentarism, the Hegelian critique of individualism, though this had long been taken into account by the later English theorists of liberalism. On the other hand, German philosophers of national socialism usually ignored Hegel or, like Rosenberg, explicitly rejected him. Moreover, German critics of national socialism usually regarded it as incompatible with most of what the Hegelian theory of the state had concretely meant in German politics during the nineteenth century.[21] The clues to this apparent discrepancy are to be found partly in the opportunist nature of the philosophy professed by Mussolini and partly in internal differences between Italy and Germany and in the position of the two movements in their respective countries.

That Hegel's system, in intention at least, was the very opposite of irrationalism is too obvious to require elaboration. The center of the system was logic, and its several parts were all supposed to be bound together by a dialectical argument that was rigidly rational. It is true that Hegel's conception of reason

[20] Quoted by Franz Neumann, *Behemoth* (1944), p. 464.

[21] See, for example, Herbert Marcuse, *Reason and Revolution* (1941), especially pp. 402 ff. Cf. Franz Neumann, *Behemoth* (1944), pp. 77 f., 462.

was largely "romanticized" and that his dialectic lacked the precision which he claimed for it and which would be needed to make it a reliable method of scientific investigation. But this does not affect his intention, nor does it affect his view of social change. This, according to Hegel, is strictly necessary and logical. It offers little scope to the heroic or to what Rocco called "the intuitiveness of rare great minds," since Hegel was notoriously skeptical of the influence of great men in history. In this respect the closest modern analogue of Hegel's social philosophy is Marxism, and dialectical materialism is, metaphysics apart, essentially Hegelian in origin and in conception. There was more than a little philosophical ineptitude therefore in an effort to use Hegel to refute Marx. But the economic interpretation of history, at least as much as political liberalism, was an opponent that fascism and national socialism had to refute. Both in Italy and in Germany at the close of World War I it was necessary to argue that the national will, by a sheer act of affirmation or assertion, could rise superior to a lack of material resources and create its economic opportunity by political means. The superiority of political to economic forces was an article of faith for both fascism and national socialism. Both movements were, in fact and by profession, revolutionary, or more truly counter-revolutionary. But the revolutionary possibilities of Hegelianism had long since been exploited by the Marxists, and while Hitler undoubtedly admired and imitated the rabble-rousing tactics of Marxian agitators, he was quite aware that national socialism could not borrow the philosophy of Marxian theorists.

Hegel's political philosophy and the political philosophy of fascism and national socialism agreed in being nationalist and anti-liberal. This agreement, however, implied less unity in philosophical outlook than has often been supposed. Hegel's nationalism had been logically the weakest part of his system. He never gave any sound reason why the nation, rather than any one of a dozen other possible social groups, should be endowed with the moral pre-eminence that he assigned to it. Moreover, Hegel's nationalism, though it included a moral glorification of war, had not been imperialist, for imperialism is incompatible with any genuine moral respect for nationality as a cultural value. On the other hand, long before World War I, nationalism had ceased to depend in any definite way on Hegel. Nationalists everywhere tended to be anti-liberal and anti-parliamentarian — in contrast with the nationalists of the period after the French Revolution — on the ground that representative institutions and popular government are incompatible with a strong national policy. Everywhere they tended to be militarist and to exalt the alleged spiritual value of the warlike virtues. Everywhere they availed themselves of Hegelian arguments against the value of individual liberty and equality, but this implied no knowledge of Hegel's philosophy. A German who had read Treitschke's *Politics* or a Frenchman who knew monarchists like Maurras or Barrès had little to learn about nationalism from Hegel. Hegelianism in its day may well have played its part in imbedding such ideas in the European political tradition, but if so, its work had long since been done.

When Mussolini decided that fascism needed a philosophy, he apparently entrusted the task to Giovanni Gentile who, like Benedetto Croce, had long been identified with an Italian school of Hegelian philosophy. Gentile had at hand the Hegelian theory of the state and not having much time he used it. Mussolini took what Gentile offered him, and in consequence the theory of Italian fascism was a theory of "the state" and of its supremacy and sanctity and all-inclusiveness. Its motto became

> Everything for the state; nothing against the state; nothing outside the state.

Since Mussolini was already in control, it was easy to equate the power of the state with the power of his government. Since the state is the embodiment of an "ethical idea," fascism could be presented as a form of lofty political idealism, in contrast with the self-proclaimed materialism of the Marxists, and as a moral or religious conception of society, in contrast both with the class struggle and with political liberalism, which was described as merely selfish and anti-social individualism. This was in fact the line that Mussolini took in his *Encyclopaedia* article.[22]

[22] *Enciclopedia Italiana,* Vol. XIV (1932); reprinted under the title *La dottrina del fascismo,* Milan, 1932; in English, under the title *Fascism, Doctrine and Institutions,* Rome, 1935. The article is in two parts, a statement of general principles, perhaps prepared by Gentile, and a set of less abstract observations on political and social theory. The first is translated

Fascism, now and always, believes in holiness and in heroism; that is to say, in actions influenced by no economic motive, direct or indirect. And if the economic conception of history be denied, according to which theory men are no more than puppets, carried to and fro by the waves of chance while the real directing forces are quite out of their control, it follows that the existence of an unchangeable and unchanging class-war is also denied — the natural progeny of the economic conception of history. And above all fascism denies that class-war can be the preponderant force in the transformation of society. . . . Fascism denies the materialist conception of happiness as a possibility, and abandons it to its inventors, the economists of the first half of the nineteenth century: that is to say, fascism denies the validity of the equation, well-being happiness, which would reduce man to the level of animals, caring for one thing only — to be fat and well fed — and would thus degrade humanity to a purely physical existence.

Fascism, therefore, is really " a religious conception in which man is seen in immanent relation to a higher law, an objective will, that transcends the particular individual and raises him to conscious membership in a spiritual society." And it is the state rather than the nation which creates and embodies this spiritual society.

It is not the nation which generates the state; that is an antiquated naturalistic concept. . . . Rather it is the state which creates the nation, conferring volition and therefore real life on a people made aware of their moral unity. . . . Indeed, it is the state which, as the expression of a universal ethical will, creates the right to national independence.

In these passages there is no doubt a good deal of Hegelian language but there need be very little genuine Hegelianism. Certainly the syndicalist socialism in which Mussolini grew up contained nothing of Hegel and not much of Marx. In 1920 his editorials were still branding the state as the " great curse " of mankind, and in 1937 he adopted the racial theory as an incident of the German alliance. In the hands of Gentile the theory of a fascist " state " sometimes became little more than an apology for terrorism. The fascist squads that broke up the meetings

with a running commentary by Herman Finer in *Mussolini's Italy* (London, 1935), pp. 165 ff. The second was translated by Jane Soames in *The Political Quarterly,* Vol. IV (1933), p. 341; reprinted in *International Conciliation,* No. 306. Of the three quotations following the first is from Part II (*International Conciliation,* No. 306, p. 9); the second from Part I, Section 5; the third from Part I, Section 10.

of anti-fascist labor unions, he said, "were really the force of a state not yet born but on the way to being." Moreover, according to Gentile, might is simply right, and liberty is simply subjection.

> Always the maximum of liberty coincides with the maximum force of the state. . . . Every force is a moral force, for it is always an expression of will; and whatever be the argument used — preaching or black-jacking — its efficacy can be none other than its ability finally to receive the inner support of a man and to persuade him to agree to it.[23]

Gentile's fascist theory of the state was in truth hardly more than a caricature of Hegelianism. Benedetto Croce, the most distinguished of Italian Hegelians, was also the most important opponent of fascism among Italian philosophers. Long before the rise of fascism he had pointed out that even Gentile's metaphysics contained elements of irrationalism derived from Nietzsche and was doubtfully Hegelian.

In contrast with the Hegelian façade that Gentile provided for Italian fascism, national socialism never put itself forward as a theory of "the state." *Mein Kampf* contains many passages in which Hitler asserted that the state is not an end but a means, that it ought to be resisted if its policy jeopardizes the well-being of the *Volk*. Nothing in national socialist philosophy was better settled than the proposition that the racial folk is the creator and bearer of culture and provides the standards of morality and politics. In other words, Hitler's philosophy was an example of the "antiquated naturalistic concept" that Mussolini rejected in favor of the "ethical" idea of the state.

> Consciousness of duty, fulfillment of duty, and obedience are not ends in themselves, just as little as the State is an end in itself, but they all are meant to be the means to make possible and to safeguard the existence in this world of a community of living beings, mentally and physically of the same order.[24]

It would of course be futile to try to draw definite conclusions from the use of two words as vague as the fascist "state" or the

[23] *Che cosa è il fascismo* (1925), p. 50. The translation is taken from Herbert W. Schneider's *Making the Fascist State* (1928), Appendix, No. 29. The passage occurred in a speech delivered at Palermo in 1924, and the explanation about the fascist squads was put in a footnote when the book was printed. The word translated "black-jack" is *manganello*.

[24] *Mein Kampf*, p. 780; cf. pp. 122, 195, 579 f., 591 ff.

national socialist "folk." Nevertheless the difference of usage did conform to certain historical realities in the two cases. When Hitler wrote *Mein Kampf* he was in prison as the leader of a discredited band of unlawful revolutionists. Nothing would have been more inept than to argue that Germany needed a "state," when Germans had been convinced for two generations that they already had one. Moreover it was an important fact about the German Revolution of 1918 that, though it had displaced the Kaiser, it had not greatly weakened the official governing class or seriously dislocated the bureaucratic processes by which day-to-day government was carried on. As has been said in the earlier chapter on Hegel, these processes were the concrete meaning that attached to the word "state" in Hegel's theory of constitutional government. The word had not implied political liberalism but it had connoted a considerable degree of civil liberty and certainly a high degree of orderly legal procedure. In Italy Mussolini could plausibly represent fascism as an attempt to create such a governing machine, because it had in fact never existed in Italian politics. The whole apparatus of the corporative state as it was brought into existence might be so rationalized. But it would have been absurd for Hitler to imitate this strategy in Germany, where his problem was in part to undermine the bureaucracy. In the minds of most Germans the word "state" connoted the bureaucratic procedures of the Second Empire. The theory of the racial folk was far more in accord with the purposes of national socialism, with the national socialist conception of leadership, and with the totalitarian regime that national socialism instituted. The philosophy characteristic of the national socialist dictatorship, therefore, was not the artificial Hegelianism of the Italian movement but the theory of the racial folk constructed to support the German movement. This consisted essentially of two parts: first, the related theoretical ideas of blood and soil, of race and *Lebensraum,* and second, of the practical applications of these in totalitarian government.

THE FOLK, THE ÉLITE, AND THE LEADER

No figure of speech recurred more frequently in national socialist writing than that of the organism and its organs to express the relationship between the individual and the nation of which he is a member. Mussolini had written it into the Italian Labor Charter in 1927 which began

The Italian nation is an organism having ends, life, and means of action superior to those of the separate individuals or groups of individuals which compose it.

The analogy was of course very old. It had been used by the critics of individualism from Rousseau on and often it had been expanded in fantastic ways. Usually it had meant nothing definite except the obvious ethical statement that persons who have rights also have obligations. But the word "organic" had long had mystical and vitalistic connotations that had little or no foundation in biology. The national socialist conception of the racial folk developed these obscure suggestions into a philosophy and claimed for them a scientific — in fact a pseudo-scientific — support. The result was the mystical concept of the *Volk* and the parallel theories of blood and soil in which the concept was elaborated. The concept of the Leader and his relation to the folk was for practical purposes the most important element in the complex. National socialist political theory was a philosophy of the *Volk* and of the state which is appropriate to the *Volk*. Thus in *Mein Kampf* Hitler repeatedly proclaimed national socialism as the theory of the "folkish" state.

The highest purpose of the folkish state is the care for the preservation of those racial primal elements which, supplying culture, create the beauty and dignity of a higher humanity. We, as Aryans, are therefore able to imagine a state only to be the living organism of a nationality which not only safeguards the preservation of that nationality, but which, by a further training of its spiritual and ideal abilities, leads it to the highest freedom.[25]

The use of the invented word "folkish" in this passage is a recognition on the part of the translators that there is in English no word that has the connotations of the German word *Volk* and its derivatives, especially those which national socialist theory exploited. The central idea in this theory was that of the racial folk or the "organic people." The folk cannot be described as a race, in any sense that accords with the biological meaning of race, because it refers to culture, which is in fact always learned

[25] *Mein Kampf,* p. 595.

or acquired and cannot be inherited. It is not equivalent to nation because it is assumed by national socialist theory to be biological. It is not people because it is collective, a real but quite non-empirical essence of which any actual person is merely for the time being the bearer. Stefan George called it the "dark womb of growth," and on the whole some such figurative expression would be the best rendering of the word, since the meaning is essentially inexpressible. From the dark womb of growth, the racial folk, the individual emerges; to it he owes all that he is and all that he does; he shares in it by virtue of his birth and he is important only because for the moment he embodies its infinite potentialities. He is united to his fellows by the "mystic holiness of the blood tie." His highest training is discipline for its service and his highest honor is to be expended for its preservation and growth. His values — whether of morals, of beauty, or of scientific truth — are derived from the folk and have no meaning except as they maintain and foster it. Consequently individuals are in no sense equal in dignity or worth, for they embody the reality of the folk in varying degrees. Rather they make a hierarchy of natural superiors and natural inferiors, and the institutions of the folk must distinguish these grades of worth with corresponding degrees of power and privilege. At the center stands the Leader, surrounded by his immediate following, and at the margin is the great body of undistinguished individuals whom he leads. The national socialist theory of society and politics thus included three elements, the masses, the ruling class or *élite,* and the Leader.

The picture which national socialism drew of the people in the mass appears at first sight strangely contradictory. Neither Hitler nor Mussolini ever concealed his contempt for them. The great body of any nation, Hitler said, is capable neither of heroism nor intelligence; it is not good and not bad but mediocre. In a social struggle it is inert but falls in behind the victor. Its instinctive reaction is to fear originality and hate superiority, yet its highest desire is to find its leaders. It is unmoved by intellectual or scientific considerations, which it cannot understand, and it is swayed only by gross and violent feelings like hatred, fanaticism, and hysteria. It can be approached only with the simplest arguments, repeated again and again, and always in a manner fanatically one-sided and with unscrupulous disregard for truth, impartiality, or fair play.

> The great masses are only a part of nature. . . . What they want is the victory of the stronger and the annihilation or the unconditional surrender of the weaker.[26]

On the other hand neither Hitler nor Mussolini ever doubted that his position depended on the fanatical devotion and self-sacrifice which he inspired. That they did inspire it was simple matter of fact. When every allowance is made for the use of terrorism, and they used it continuously and systematically, national socialism and fascism were authentic mass-movements and owed their power to that fact. Terrorism was merely a logical extension of propaganda, since as Gentile cynically said, national socialist " argument " was itself a kind of intellectual blackjack. The characteristic quality of national socialist propaganda was its alternating resort to abuse and flattery — perhaps psychologically an appeal to some primitive sense of sin and redemption — and this method was quite in accord with the theory. For in the mass the people are endowed not with intelligence but with a more elemental capacity of instinct and will. Deep in human nature is " that sure herd instinct which is rooted in the unity of the blood and which guards the nation against ruin, especially in dangerous moments." Or as Mussolini is said to have expressed it, in different words but to the same effect, " The capacity of the modern man for faith is illimitable." And it is, of course, faith that removes mountains. Both men no doubt believed, as sincerely as they believed anything, that

> All great movements are movements of the people, are volcanic eruptions of human passions and spiritual sensations, stirred either by the cruel Goddess of Misery or by the torch of the word thrown into the masses.[27]

From the masses, who merely follow and under stimulus provide the weight and force of the movement, national socialist

[26] *Mein Kampf,* p. 469; cf. Vol. I, ch. 12, *passim.* See also the revealing entry in Goebbels' *Diaries,* p. 56, in which he recorded a conversation with his mother, who " to me, always represents the voice of the people."

[27] *Mein Kampf,* p. 136. The preceding quotation is on p. 598. The quotation from Mussolini is reported by Emil Ludwig, *Talks with Mussolini* (1933), p. 126.

theory distinguished the natural aristocracy, the leading and ruling class or *élite,* which provides intelligence and direction. Because it depended on the masses, national socialism claimed to be "truly democratic," but it imputed to them no judgment that lent value to their political opinions nor did it assume that any process of popular education would alter the case. In this respect its theory followed the line already taken by most revolutionary philosophies of the twentieth century, by the syndicalism in which Mussolini grew up and by Lenin's theory of party organization. Long before he was a fascist Mussolini described the party as "the small, resolute, audacious nucleus." [28] National socialism merely construed this idea of revolutionary strategy as a universal biological fact. The process of selecting the *élite* takes place through the eternal struggle for power which is characteristic of nature. The national socialist ruling class emerges as the racially fittest, or perhaps more truly are thrown up from "the dark womb of growth" as the natural leaders of the folk.

> A view of life which, by rejecting the democratic mass idea, endeavors to give this world to the best people . . . has logically to obey the same aristocratic principle also within this people and has to guarantee leadership and highest influence . . . to the best heads.

The selection of the *élite* is therefore a natural process, quite different from the mechanical device of vote-counting. They represent the folk simply by embodying more clearly and explicitly its inner will to power.

> World history is made by minorities whenever this numerical minority incorporates the majority of will and determination.[29]

At the head of the national socialist *élite* is the Leader in whose name everything is done, who is said to be "responsible" for all, but whose acts can nowhere be called in question. The relation of leader to folk was essentially mystical or irrational. It was what Max Weber called "charismatic," which might be expressed less learnedly by saying that the leader was a kind of mascot, the "luck" of the movement.[30] He is an offshoot of the

[28] Megaro, *op. cit.,* p. 187; cf. pp. 112 ff.

[29] *Mein Kampf,* pp. 661, 603, respectively.

[30] Even a man as "emancipated" as Goebbels regarded Hitler in this way; see the *Diaries,* p. 62. In defeat Hitler remained the undisputed master of his party; see Trevor-Roper, *op. cit.,* ch. 1.

folk, bound to his people by the mystic tie of blood, deriving his power from his roots in the race, guiding them by a sure intuition that is akin to animal instinct, and drawing them to him by an affinity that has nothing to do with the power to produce intellectual conviction. He is the genius or the hero conceived as the man of pure race. In the florid language that seems appropriate to the idea, the leader "soars heavenward like some strong and stately tree nourished by thousands and thousands of roots." He is "the living sum of untold souls striving for the same goal." Less poetically but to like effect Hitler in *Mein Kampf* characterized the leader in terms of propaganda. The leader is neither a scholar nor a theorist but a practical psychologist and an organizer — a psychologist in order that he may master the methods by which he can gain the largest number of passive adherents, an organizer in order that he may build up a compact body of followers to consolidate his gains. The only parts of the book that can be called methodical are those which deal with propaganda and the steps by which the author perfected himself in the art. No trick was overlooked: the advantage of oratory over written argument; the effects of lighting, atmosphere, symbols, and the crowd; the advantage of meetings held at night when the power to resist suggestion is low. Leadership works by a skillful use of suggestion, collective hypnosis, and every kind of subconscious motivation; the key to its success is "clever psychology" and the "ability to sense the thinking processes of the broad masses of the population." [31] The leader manipulates the people as an artist molds clay.

THE RACIAL MYTH

This idea of the *Volk* and the leader was supported by a general theory of race and of the relationship between race and culture, or more specifically by the myth of the Aryan or Nordic race and its place in the history of Western Civilization. Hence the racial theory and the parallel and supporting theory of *Lebensraum* formed the central elements of national socialist ideology. The race problem was held to be the fundamental social problem and also the key to history. Hitler in *Mein Kampf* attributed

[31] *Mein Kampf,* pp. 704 ff.; cf. Vol. II, ch. 11, *passim.* The quotations are from Goebbels' *Diaries,* p. 129.

the collapse of the Second German Empire to its failure to realize the importance of race, and Alfred Rosenberg, who became the official philosopher of national socialism, made the struggle between races and their characteristic cultural ideas into a principle for explaining the evolution of European civilization. Upon this philosophy of history, alleged to be supported by scientific biological and anthropological evidence, the policy of national socialism as a political or social movement was supposed to be based. In point of fact the theory of race as it was developed by national socialism had no dependence whatever on any scientific study of genetics or of race as a biological phenomenon. It was pseudo-scientific throughout. Essentially it was a myth invented to support political chauvinism, and it depended for its effect on race prejudice, especially anti-Semitism.

Like other parts of national socialist ideology its version of the racial myth was put together from ideas that had long been current. The word "race," used without any precise biological meaning, and a spurious claim of descent from an alleged Aryan master race had been used to bolster the national pride of Frenchmen and Americans as well as Germans. Possibly it may be said to have originated with the Frenchman Gobineau at about the middle of the nineteenth century, who used it however not to support the claims of nationalism but of aristocracy against democracy. At the turn of the century a Germanized Englishman, Houston Stewart Chamberlain, and his father-in-law Richard Wagner, popularized the Aryan myth in Germany.[32] The important difference between Gobineau and Chamberlain was that the latter made Germanism into a claim of national superiority. In the period that followed World War I it was a ready salve for national humiliation. This literature of racism, though it supported widely different movements in many countries, was in general anti-liberal, imperialist, and anti-Semitic. Anti-Semitism had been vociferous in Germany since the time of

[32] Gobineau's book was published in Paris, 1853–55; the first volume was translated under the title, *The Inequality of Human Races,* by Adrian Collins, London, 1915. Chamberlain's book, published in 1899, was translated as *The Foundations of the Nineteenth Century,* by John Lees, London, 1910. For other books that purported to be part of a scientific literature on the relations between race and culture, see F. W. Coker, *Recent Political Thought* (1934), pp. 315 ff.

Martin Luther; the standard charges that national socialism brought against the Jews — that capitalism and Marxism are Jewish and that a Jewish conspiracy exists to gain world-power — had been current for decades. The national socialist notion of the racial folk, therefore, capitalized a vast amount of familiar dogma backed by violent prejudice and the inclination that every nation has to believe in its own superiority.

The basic postulates of the race theory were stated clearly though not very systematically in *Mein Kampf*.[33] They can be summarized briefly as follows. First, all social progress takes place by a struggle for survival in which the fittest are selected and the weak are exterminated. This struggle occurs within the race, thus giving rise to a natural *élite*, and also between races and the cultures that express the inherent natures of different races. Second, hybridization by the intermixture of two races results in the degeneration of the higher race. Such racial mixtures are the cause of cultural, social, and political decay, but a race can purify itself because hybrids tend to die off. Third, though culture and social institutions directly express the inherent creative powers of race, all high civilizations or important cultures are the creation of one race, or at most of a few. Specifically races may be divided into three types: the culture-creating or Aryan race; the culture-bearing races which can borrow and adapt but cannot create; and the culture-destroying race, namely, the Jews. The culture-creating race requires " auxiliaries " in the form of labor and services performed by subject-races of inferior quality. Fourth, in the culture-creating Aryan self-preservation is transmuted from egoism into care for the community. Dutifulness and idealism (honor) rather than intelligence are the Aryan's outstanding moral qualities. These propositions merely express in generalized form the characteristics which national socialism attributed to the *Volk*, the *élite*, and the Leader.

The race theory was elaborated by Alfred Rosenberg into a philosophy of history in *Der Mythus des 20. Jahrhunderts* (1930), which was the principal statement of national socialist ideology. All history, according to Rosenberg, must be rewritten

[33] Especially in Vol. I, ch. 11.

and reinterpreted in terms of the struggle between races and their characteristic ideals, or more specifically as a struggle between the Aryan or culture-creating race and all the lower breeds of mankind. Rosenberg supposed that this race had spread from some point of dispersion in the north, had migrated to Egypt, India, Persia, Greece, and Rome, and had become the creator of all these ancient civilizations. All the ancient cultures declined because the Aryans interbred with lower races. The Teutonic branches of the Aryan race, engaged in an age-long struggle against the "racial chaos" in which Rome ended, have produced all that has moral or cultural value in the modern European states. All science and all art, all philosophy as well as all great political institutions, have been created by Aryans. In contrast with them stands the parasitic anti-race, the Jews, who have created the modern race-poisons, Marxism and democracy, capitalism and finance, barren intellectualism, the effeminate ideals of love and humility. All that is worth saving in Christianity reflects Aryan ideals, and Jesus himself was an Aryan, but Christianity in general was corrupted by "the Etruscan-Jewish-Roman system" of the church. A true Germanic religion, without dogma or magic, Rosenberg believed he could find in the German mysticism of the Middle Ages, especially that of Eckhart. The great need of the twentieth century is for a new reformation, a renewed belief in honor as the supreme virtue of the person, the family, the nation, and the race.

The philosophy upon which this imposing reconstruction of history was based might be called a kind of racial or biological pragmatism. All mental and moral faculties are "race-bound" (*rassengebunden*). "Soul is race seen from within." They depend upon insights or forms of thought that are innate, and whatever is a problem or a solution for a race depends upon its racial cast of thought. The questions posed by a Nordic are without meaning for a Jew. "The most completely developed knowledge possible to a race is implicit in its first religious myth." Hence there are neither general standards of moral and esthetic value nor general principles of scientific truth. The very idea of a truth, a goodness, and a beauty that is open to understanding and appreciation by men of different races is a part of the degeneracy of intellectualism. Every race is under an iron necessity to suppress what is foreign, because it does violence to the mental structure of the racial type. Since truth is "organic" — a realization, that is, of innate racial faculties — its test is the power of science or art or religion to enhance the form (*Gestalt*), the inner values, the vital power of the race. Any creative philosophy is an affirmation or a creed (*Bekenntnis*) which expresses at once an intuition inherent in the racial type and an act of will directed toward the dominance of the type. Among the declarations issued in support of Hitler by the National Socialist Teachers Association was one by the philosopher Martin Heidegger. In substance it was a paraphrase of Rosenberg.

> Truth is the revelation of that which makes a people certain, clear, and strong in action and knowledge. From such a truth springs the real will to know, and this will to know circumscribes the claim to know. And it is by the latter finally that the limits are set within which genuine problems and genuine investigation must be established and certified. From such an origin we derive science, which is bound up in the necessity of self-responsible existence by the Folk. . . . We have rid ourselves of the idolatry of a baseless and impotent thought.

Rosenberg's argument for the identity of his Aryan race ran in terms of vague resemblances between styles in art, moral ideals, and religious convictions which were largely fanciful and wholly subjective. Moreover, his philosophy was by profession a myth. Once national socialism established itself in Germany, however, the racial theory was developed as "scientific" anthropology, especially under the direction of Hans F. K. Günther, who was made Professor of Social Anthropology at Jena.[34] In general no biologist or anthropologist not already committed to the theory was ever convinced either that there are biological criteria of racial superiority or that racial characters are correlated with culture, and these propositions have been refuted times without number. Unfortunately scientific refutation is almost powerless against a theory that depends on the will to believe or an intuition that is rooted in the blood. Very often also the racial theory, in national socialism and elsewhere, lay in the region of

[34] See for example his *Racial Elements of European History,* Eng. trans. by G. C. Wheeler, London, 1927. For a scientific criticism of the racial theory and a history of it before national socialism, see Ruth Benedict, *Race: Science and Politics* (New York, 1940), which gives references to many other criticisms by biologists and anthropologists.

what Thorstein Veblen called "applied psychiatry," the art of exploiting a prejudice for an ulterior purpose. This does not mean, of course, that it was not sincerely believed — anti-Semitists are sincere enough — but only that irrationalists make a virtue of wishful thinking. Even the notoriously fictitious Protocols of the Wise Men of Zion were sufficiently believed so that Goebbels could write in his diary: "The nations that have been the first to see through the Jew . . . are going to take his place in the domination of the world."[35] The racial theory has to be judged not by its truth but by the consequences which it produced and the purposes which it served.

The practical effects of the racial theory on national socialist policy were threefold. In the first place it led to a general policy of encouraging increase of population, particularly of the supposed Aryan elements, by subsidizing marriage and large families, even though the need for territorial expansion was at the same time urged on the ground that Germany was already overpopulated. Secondarily the policy eventuated in a virtual encouragement of illegitimate births. In the second place the racial theory produced the eugenic legislation of 1933. Ostensibly this was designed to prevent the transmission of hereditary disease but in practice it represented a general policy of sterilizing or exterminating physical and mental defectives. Apparently this policy was pursued with barbarous severity. The eugenic gain, it must be supposed, was more than offset by the ethical and social demoralization produced, but the racial theory was of course based on the ethical postulate that humanity and mercy for the weak are not virtues. In the third place and most characteristically the racial theory produced the anti-Jewish legislation of 1935 and 1938. This legislation also purported to aim at increasing or maintaining purity of race. By it marriages were outlawed between Germans and persons of one fourth (or more) Jewish ancestry, the property of Jews was expropriated, Jews

[35] *Diaries,* p. 377. Cf. the curious passages in which Goebbels records his astonishment that his anti-Semitic "arguments" should not have been suppressed by the British and American press; pp. 241, 353 f., 370. It is even possible that the picture of "Jewish world-domination," was a kind of model for national socialism, as Konrad Heiden suggested; see *Der Fuehrer* (1944), p. 100 and *passim.* On the history of the Protocols see John S. Curtiss, *An Appraisal of the Protocols of Zion,* New York, 1942.

were excluded from the professions and from business, and they were reduced to an inferior civil status as "state-subjects" rather than citizens. These measures culminated in a policy of outright extermination, which Hitler predicted in 1939 would be the result of a new war, and of reducing Jews not exterminated to forced labor.[36]

The anti-Jewish policy of national socialism can only be described as the acme of inhumanity in a century that has not been notably humane. Logically, however, the application of the racial theory to the Jews was incidental. It could be applied and, as Hitler's policy developed of expanding German territory toward the east, it was applied to other peoples. Thus in occupied Poland the Ukrainians were given preferential treatment as compared with the Poles though they were not given equal status with Germans; the Poles retained at least nominal freedom, and the Jews were reduced to virtual slavery. What the racial theory implied in general was a gradation of civil and political status, with power and privilege reserved for those counted as racial Germans and with various subject-peoples ranged in a descending series under them. In short it meant, as Hitler had said in *Mein Kampf,* a master race with "auxiliary" races to serve it. But since race (as the theory used it) was fictitious, this meant in fact that a national socialist government could suppress and exploit on racial grounds any group that it chose. Logically the racial theory was merely a way of rationalizing dominance by the national socialist *élite.*

The ulterior purposes that the racial theory and anti-Semitism served in national socialist philosophy are more speculative since they fall within the cloudy region of mass-psychology. It seems clear, however, that they did in fact help to solidify national socialism in at least two ways. First, anti-Semitism made it possible to transmute a variety of hatreds and fears and resentments and class antagonisms into the fear of a single tangible enemy. The fear of communism became fear of Jewish Marxism; resentment against employers became hatred of Jewish capitalism; national insecurity became fear of a Jewish plot to dominate the world; economic insecurity became hatred for the Jewish con-

[36] The eugenic and anti-Jewish legislation is analyzed by Franz Neumann, *Behemoth* (1944), pp. 111 ff., Appendix, pp. 550 ff.

trol of big business. That all these allegations of Jewish dominance were fictitious was irrelevant. The Jews were in a position that fitted them ideally to play the part that the racial theory assigned to them. They were a minority against whom there was a long accumulation of prejudice; they were strong enough to be feared but weak enough to be attacked with impunity. Considered in this light the racial theory was merely a psychological device to unify German society by redirecting all its antagonisms toward a single enemy that could be easily exterminated. To this must be added the fact that Jewish property supplied substantial rewards for the party and its supporters. In the second place the racial theory supplied an excellent ideological support for the particular form of imperialism that Hitler's policy contemplated, namely, expansion to the east and south at the expense of the Slavic peoples. It was only in this region that compact Jewish communities existed, and anti-Semitism as a psychological force was hardly distinguishable from a belief in the racial superiority of Germans to Poles, Czechs, and Russians. The racial theory, which had often been allied to Pan-Germanism, could easily be used to foster the idea of a Germanic state in Central Europe surrounded by an expanding ring of non-Germanic satellite states. Thus the racial theory joined hands with the second element of national socialist ideology, the idea of " soil " which was the natural supplement to the idea of " blood."

LEBENSRAUM

The national socialist theory of territory or space, like the theory of race, was put together from ideas that had been current in Europe for a century. Fundamentally it was merely an enlargement of plans for a powerful German state in Central and Eastern Europe, which should expand as far as its military powers permitted. Like the racial theory also it was not exclusively German. In fact it was a Swedish political scientist, Rudolf Kjellén of the University of Uppsala, who expanded the plan into a philosophy and gave it the name under which national socialism popularized it, *Geopolitik*.[37] In origin Kjellén's geo-

[37] For a general account see Robert Strausz-Hupé, *Geopolitics: The Struggle for Space and Power,* New York, 1942. There is a longer summary of Kjellén's work in Johannes Mattern, *Geopolitik: Doctrine of National*

politics was a development of an old subject, political geography, especially as that subject was understood by Friedrich Ratzel. Its fundamentally sound scientific idea was that a realistic study of the history and growth of states must include such factors as physical environment, anthropology, sociology, and economics, as well as their constitutional organization and legal structure. In its development it almost lost touch with its geographic starting point. Behind Kjellén's theorizing there was also a fear of the western extension of Russian power. The national socialist expansion of geopolitics was associated especially with the name of Karl Haushofer, though many other German writers and scholars had a part in it. Haushofer added little to the scientific definition of the subject, though he and his associates accumulated vast masses of information from all parts of the world about geography or social, economic, and political matters. What tied this miscellaneous material together was not its scientific organization but its possible use by a military general staff to lay out lines of strategy or by a government that was bent on extending its power. Haushofer also made geopolitics into an effective organ of propaganda designed to make Germany "space-conscious." These two characteristics were in general what distinguished geopolitics from political geography. According to the definition of the subject formulated by the editors of Haushofer's *Zeitschrift für Geopolitik*, it was "the art of guiding practical politics" and "the geographic conscience of the state," practical politics being in substance imperialist expansion. Like the racial theory, geopolitics combined erudition with a pseudo-scientific justification of imperialist politics.

The distinctive idea in the national socialist theory of imperialism was supplied by an English geographer, Sir Halford J. Mackinder. Earlier imperialist theory, like that for example of Admiral A. T. Mahan, had stressed in the main the importance of naval power and had depended largely on the history of the British Empire. Mackinder in 1904 put forward the idea that much European history could be explained by the pres-

Self-Sufficiency and Empire (Baltimore, 1942), chs. 5 and 6. Many extracts from Karl Haushofer and other national socialist *Geopolitiker* are given by Derwent Whittlesey, *German Strategy of World Conquest,* New York, 1942, and by Andreas Dorpalen, *The World of General Haushofer,* New York, 1942.

sure of landlocked peoples in Eastern Europe and Central Asia on the coastal peoples. This vast area he called the pivotal area or "the heartland," the core of the "world-island" (Europe, Asia, and Africa) which makes up two thirds of the world's land area. Australia and the Americas are merely outlying islands. Consequently, if any state could command the resources of this territory and thus combine sea power with land power it could dominate the world. Mackinder summed up his argument in a kind of aphorism: "Who rules East Europe commands the Heartland. Who rules the Heartland commands the World-Island. Who rules the World-Island commands the World."[38] His immediate purpose was to urge the advantages to England of an alliance with Russia, but the meaning of his aphorism was equally clear to Germans. It outlined a project that resolved the uncertainties of German imperialist thought since the Tirpitz naval expansion in 1900, its ambivalence between naval and land power, and the differing points of view of East German Junkers and West German industrialists. In essence both were right, but expansion by land into contiguous territory on the Continent had priority. Initially the problem is Russia, and in theory the problem might be solved either by a Russian alliance or by conquest. France as a land power is decadent, in terms of the racial theory "negroid" in its ethnic character, and the pattern of British imperialism is outmoded. The object of German diplomacy and strategy must be to immobilize the western powers, but against Russia its object must be dominance. Substantially this was the theory of German politics that Hitler outlined in *Mein Kampf*,[39] reputedly under the prompting of Haushofer. The fundamental error of the Second Empire, he said, was in choosing the policy of expanding its industries and its exports instead of expanding its territory. The most decisively important events in a thousand years of German history were the colonization of the Ostmark and the area east of the Elbe. The national socialists will "terminate the endless German drive to the south and west of Europe, and direct our

[38] *Democratic Ideals and Realities* (1919); reissued 1942, p. 150. Cf. Mackinder's earlier article, "The Geographical Pivot of History," *The Geographical Journal*, Vol. XXIII (1904), pp. 421 ff.

[39] Especially Vol. II, ch. 14; cf. Vol. I, ch. 4. Apparently Haushofer had fewer illusions than Hitler about the practicability of Russian conquest.

gaze towards the lands in the east . . . We can think primarily only of Russia and its vassal border states."

The lines of reasoning upon which the national socialist theory of *Lebensraum* overtly depended were, like the racial theory, a curious mixture of sentiment and dubious science. In part they were addressed to the long-standing tendency of Germans to idealize the medieval empire, which existed "long before the American continent had been discovered," and to the myth that all the political and cultural achievements of Central Europe, or even of pre-communist Russia, were the work of German minorities. Hence the Germans are the "natural" leaders and rulers of this region. The generalized and professedly scientific argument of geopolitics largely took the form of a biological analogy. States are "organisms" and the relation between them is one of natural selection. So long as they are vigorous they grow, and when they cease to grow they die. A non-expanding state is either decadent or the product of a people that is "space-bound" and lacks the genius for political construction. Vitally strong states are compelled "under the categorical imperative" to enlarge their space. The frontiers of a state are its "peripheral organs" or growing edges. In nature a state has no fixed boundary but only a temporary front line, a "point of calm in a running development." A "good" frontier is one that favors expansion, in short, one that makes infiltration and border incidents easy. Treaties and international law are powerless to limit the mighty natural forces inherent in a *Volk,* and in general its constitution and its legally created institutions are merely aids to organize and increase its power. Any voluntary limitation of the competitive struggle by birth-control or pacifism merely resigns the future to the inferior races, since struggle is the law of progress.

> The culturally superior, but less ruthless, races would have to limit, in consequence of their limited soil, their increase even at a time when the culturally inferior, but more brutal and more natural, peoples, in consequence of their greater living areas, would be able to increase themselves without limit. In other words, the world will, therefore, some day come into the hands of a mankind that is inferior in culture but superior in energy and activity.[40]

[40] *Mein Kampf,* pp. 174 f.

The idea of *Lebensraum,* therefore, was an adjunct of the idea of the racial folk. Scientifically indeed the two ideas were divergent, for if culture depends on race, it cannot depend on geography. But what united the two was not science. The tie was essentially mystical or emotional. Phrases like the "cultural landscape" or the "folkish soil" combined two universal and powerful human feelings, the love that every people feels for its homeland and the love that it feels for its way of living, and they marshaled these feelings behind a plan of military conquest.

Stripped of these sentimental factors the effective reasoning behind the geopolitical concept of *Lebensraum* relied on the presumption that economic prosperity depends on political control and that both depend on military power. Added to these was the strategical theory outlined above, that military power under modern conditions is land power rather than sea power. The primary consideration was not territory as such, but access to raw materials and a market for manufactured exports. Hitler's repeated comparisons between population and area — such for example as that the United States has fifteen inhabitants per square kilometer while Germany has a hundred and forty — between "the nations that have and the nations that have not" or between proletarian and possessing nations, were obviously meaningless except in terms of markets. And the argument that over-population called for expansion depended on the proposition that markets can be gained only by political power. The geopolitical concept of "space," therefore, was a figure of speech derived from the advantages that large areas undoubtedly have for military strategy. Literally it meant simply power extended by the conquest of land-areas contiguous to Germany, for purposes of economic exploitation. In this sense also the geopolitical concept of self-sufficiency must be understood. The development of internal resources and of substitutes for missing raw materials were not policies, though some national socialists (Gregor Strasser, for example) thought they were. They were measures to gain relative independence of world markets during war. The geopolitical principle that self-sufficiency is an attribute of successful states meant that preparedness for war is a permanent necessity, because on it depends a state's commercial prosperity.

Probably the clearest statement ever made of the meaning of

Lebensraum was contained in the remarkable speech which Hitler delivered in 1932 before the German industrialists of Düsseldorf. The success of the speech probably marked the turning point in his political fortunes. German prosperity and the relief of unemployment, he said, depend on foreign trade, but the idea that one can conquer the world by purely economic means is "one of the greatest and most terrible illusions."

> It was not German business which conquered the world and then came the development of German power, but in our case, too, it was the power-state (*Machtstaat*) which created for the business world the general conditions for its subsequent prosperity. . . . There can be no economic life unless behind this economic life there stands the determined political will of the nation absolutely ready to strike — and to strike hard.

Behind all imperialism stands the will of the white race to exercise "an extraordinarily brutal right to dominate others."

> The white race, however, can in practice maintain its position only so long as the difference in the standard of living in different parts of the world continues to exist. If you to-day give to our so-called export-markets the same standard of living as we ourselves possess, you will find that it will be impossible for the white race to maintain that position of superiority which finds expression not merely in the political power of the nation but also in the economic fortune of the individual.[41]

Two years before, commenting on self-sufficiency, Hitler had said:

> Our task is to organize on a large scale the whole world so that each country produces what it can best produce while the white race, the Nordic race, undertakes the organization of this gigantic plan. . . . That must not, it is true, be bound up with any exploitation of the other race, for the lower race is destined for tasks different from those of the higher race: the latter must have in its hands the control, and this control must remain with us in common with the Anglo-Saxons.[42]

In substance, therefore, the national socialist theory of *Lebensraum* was the crudest, if also logically the simplest, possible solution of the problems of international trade and politics. It meant political dominance by military power and the maintenance of a

[41] The address is printed in full in *Speeches* (London, 1942), ed. by Norman H. Baynes, pp. 777 ff. The quotations are respectively on pp. 804 f., and 794.

[42] *Ibid.*, p. 775.

high standard of living for the dominant power by a system of exploitation that would perpetuate a low standard of living for the subject-peoples. Short of world dominance by a single power, which might of course be the ultimate goal of a power controlling the world's Heartland, the theory meant regionalism. The world would be divided into a few great "orders" or spheres of control each governed by its own dominant power. This was the meaning attributed to the American Monroe Doctrine, to which the theorists of geopolitics assigned a place of high importance as the first recognition of their principles. American insistence on the rights of nations outside the American sphere they construed as imperialism. Their own plan they often described as a Monroe Doctrine for Europe. Between regions the relations were assumed to be merely those of power, since no treaty could be more than a temporary compromise, and no boundary could be more than a "point of calm" where two powers were for the time being balanced. Within each region the dominant power, in theory the dominant racial group, would assign to the subordinate groups their economic function and their political status. Juristically, therefore, *Lebensraum* like the racial theory would work out to systems of folk-law and extraterritoriality. International law would disappear in a twofold sense. There would be no equal rights of nations and there would be no equal rights of persons or minorities irrespective of race. In any legal sense nationality would disappear along with internationalism. Though national socialism drew its support from German national sentiment, its theory implied a form of world organization substantially like that of the pre-national empires.

TOTALITARIANISM

Both Italian fascism and German national socialism were intrinsically efforts to submerge all differences of class and group in the single purpose of imperialist aggrandizement. The myths which constituted their philosophy were designed to further that purpose. Hence the practical outcome of both, however justified, was the totalitarian internal organization of the state. For reasons already explained, the national socialist theory of the racial *Volk* provided a more adequate philosophy for such a movement than Mussolini's Hegelianism, but in either case the conclusion was the same. Government may, indeed must, control every act and every interest of every individual or group in order to use it for enhancing national strength. According to the theory of totalitarianism, therefore, government was not only absolute in its exercise but unlimited in its application. Nothing lay outside its province. Every interest and value — economic, moral, and cultural — being part of the national resources were to be controlled and utilized by government. Except by permission of government there could be neither political parties, labor unions, industrial or trade associations. Except under its regulation there could be neither manufacture, business, nor work. Except under its direction there could be neither publication nor public meeting. Education became its tool and in principle religion was also, though neither fascism nor national socialism succeeded in getting more than unwilling acquiescence from the churches.[43] Leisure and recreation became agencies of propaganda and regimentation. No area of privacy remained that an individual could call his own and no association of individuals which was not subject to political control. Membership in the folk absorbed alike his personality, his capacities, and his intimacies.

As a principle of political organization totalitarianism of course implied dictatorship. It rapidly brought about the abolition of German federalism and of local self-government, the virtual destruction of liberal political institutions such as parliaments and an independent judiciary, and the reduction of the suffrage to the level of carefully managed plebiscites. Political administration became not only all-pervasive but "monolithic," as national socialists liked to call it, the implication being that the whole social organization had been reduced to a system and all its energies directed single-heartedly toward national ends. As a matter of fact there was a large amount of fiction in this representation of totalitarianism. There was, of course, an absolute concentration of power in the leader, that is, on the highest policy-making level. But the leader's power depended on his personal ascendancy, and the administrative organization by which a policy had to be

[43] Goebbels regarded priests as "the most loathsome riffraff" except the Jews, but he had to postpone making them "see the light" until after the war; *Diaries,* p. 146; cf. 120 f., 138.

carried out was "in fact a confusion of private empires, private armies, and private intelligence services."

> In truth, irresponsible absolutism is incompatible with totalitarian administration; for in the uncertainty of politics, the danger of arbitrary change, and the fear of personal revenge, every man whose position makes him either strong or vulnerable must protect himself against surprise by reserving from the common pool whatever power he has managed to acquire. Thus there is, in the end, no common pool at all.[44]

If this was true on the administrative level, it was doubly true on the constitutional or legal level. National socialist totalitarianism never achieved a rational division of functions in any branch of government, or an organization into governing agencies with legally defined powers that acted predictably according to known rules. These bureaucratic qualities, which far more than political liberalism had been connoted by German constitutionalism, were in fact destroyed by the rise of national socialism to power. Existing administrative and judicial agencies were left standing but they were infiltrated by party personnel, often for the express purpose of breaking down their customary procedures. They were supplemented also by a bewildering array of new agencies that partly took over old duties and partly took on new duties as occasion arose. Hence Goebbels could complain that "we are living in a form of state in which jurisdictions are not clearly defined . . . As a result German domestic policy completely lacks direction."[45] National socialism in fact completely wrecked the German ideal of a *Rechtsstaat*, and for this reason its German critics often denied that it was a "state" at all.

The jumbling of functions and the lack of clear-cut legal relationships were thoroughly characteristic of totalitarianism. Thus, for example, there could never have been any clear constitutional theory of the National Socialist party or of its relation to the government, though it was by law the only party permitted to exist. Legally the party was a corporation but it was certainly

[44] Trevor-Roper, *op. cit.*, p. 2; cf. p. 233.

[45] *Diaries*, p. 301. On the organization of national socialist government see Franz Neumann, *Behemoth* (1944), pp. 62 ff.; Appendix, pp. 521 ff. Cf. John H. Herz, "German Administration under the Nazi Régime," *Am. Pol. Sci. Rev.*, Vol. XL (1946), p. 682.

not amenable to any legal or political control, and its acts were indifferently legislative, administrative, and judicial. Similarly the Élite Guard (*Schutzstaffel*), the Storm Troops (*Sturmabteilung*), and the Hitler Youth, though they were nominally agents of the party and not of the government, all had legislative and judicial powers and enjoyed extra-legal privileges. The judiciary, on the other hand, completely lost its independence and security, while at the same time judicial discretion was extended practically without limit. The law itself was made studiously vague, so that all decision became essentially subjective. The penal code was amended in 1935 to permit punishment for any act contrary to " sound popular feeling," even though it violated no existing law. Similarly a journalist might lose his license for publishing anything that confused selfish with common interests, that might weaken the unity of the German people or was offensive to the honor or dignity of a German, that made any person ridiculous, or that was for any other reason indecent. Obviously no rational administration of such statutes was possible. Equality before the law and due process were supplanted by complete administrative discretion. What totalitarianism meant in practice was that any person whose acts were regarded as having political significance was quite without legal protection if the government or the party or one of their many agencies chose to exert its power.

The results were similar in the social and economic structure. Totalitarianism undertook to organize and direct every phase of economic and social life to the exclusion of any area of permitted privacy or voluntary choice. But it is important to observe what this type of organization concretely meant. First and foremost it meant the destruction of great numbers of organizations that had long existed and that had provided agencies for economic and social activities. Labor unions, trade and commercial and industrial associations, fraternal organizations for social purposes or for adult education or mutual aid, which had existed on a voluntary basis and were self-governing, were either wiped out or were taken over and restaffed. Membership became virtually or actually compulsory, officers were selected according to the " leadership principle," and the rules by which they operated were decided not by the membership but by the appointing agency. The "leadership principle" meant everywhere the substitution of personal authority for authority working through regular channels and the substitution of imposed regimentation for self-government. The result was in a sense paradoxical. For though totalitarian society was "organized" in a bewildering number of ways and for every conceivable purpose, the individual stood more alone than ever before. He became helpless in the hands of the organizations to which he nominally "belonged," and he had virtually nothing to say about their purposes or their management. In spite of national socialist contempt for the "atomic individualism" of democratic society, totalitarian society was far more genuinely atomic. The people as a whole became literally "the masses" and consequently ideal material for propaganda to work on. The distinctive feature of totalitarianism was not organization as such, for every complex society is intricately organized. It was the nature of the organization, the fact that organization was designed to be an agency of regimentation.

In respect to economic organization there was superficially a considerable difference between Italian fascism and German national socialism. In accord with ideas long familiar in Italian syndicalism, fascism took the form of what was called the "corporate state." In Germany the corporate state was talked about in the earlier days of national socialism but was dropped along with the other socialist elements of the party's program. The idea of the corporate state was simple and long antedated fascism. It was merely that workers and owners should cooperate for the purpose of increasing production and should negotiate wage contracts rather than resort to strikes or lockouts. The corporate apparatus was brought into being piecemeal in Italy over a period of fourteen years. It consisted of vertical syndicates of employers and employees in the main branches of the economy organized locally, regionally, and nationally, and of horizontal corporations also uniting both employers and employees in the several industries. The system headed up in the Chamber of Corporations, which was not created until 1939. In theory the Chamber constituted functional representation by industries on lines long advocated by syndicalists and guild socialists. In theory also the syndicates were autonomous unions of employers and employees for collective bargaining. In fact, though membership was not compulsory, dues were withheld from the wages of members and non-members alike, and wage contracts were binding on non-members. In Germany the Labor Front was a division of the party and was not organized by occupations except for administrative purposes. Membership was compulsory and occupational unions were abolished. Hence the Labor Front made no pretense of collective bargaining; wages were adjusted by labor trustees chosen by the government. Employers' trade associations were not destroyed but they were covered into national groups organized according to the leadership principle.

Ostensibly, therefore, the Italian system was one of self-regulation by associations in which employers and employees were equally represented, while the German system was an outright regulation of industry by government. In reality there was little or no difference between the ways in which the two systems worked. Both management and labor lost their freedom of association and independence of action. The supposed equality of labor and management in the Italian plan was never actual. In both countries ultimate control was in the hands of persons appointed by government (or by the party, which amounted to the same thing) and such persons were in general much closer to management than to labor. In both countries also the general tendency was to increase the size of industrial units and to absorb small independent producers into cartels. The one substantial benefit that labor received was full employment, but as a whole it got a smaller fraction of the national income. In short, both in its fascist and national socialist form totalitarianism had the characteristics and the tendencies normal to a controlled war economy, which essentially was what it was.

The control which totalitarianism exercised over the economy was extended as a matter of course to the press, to education and scholarship, and to art, indeed to every part of the national culture that might be a factor in the national strength. When Goebbels' ministry was created in 1933 it became "responsible for all factors influencing the mental life of the nation." No channel of influence was to be neglected, as Hitler had said, "from the child's primer down to the last newspaper, every theater and every movie." Instruction in every subject, including science, was to become "a means for the promotion of national pride." And it must reach its "culmination in branding, through instinct and reason, the race sense and race feeling into the hearts and brains of the youth."

> No boy or girl must leave school without having been led to the ultimate knowledge of the necessity and nature of the purity of the blood.[46]

This was the program as it was projected and as it was carried out, at all levels of the educational system and in all fields of intellectual work. In respect to art an important textbook on law declared,

> The totalitarian state does not recognize the separate existence of art. . . . It demands that artists take a positive position towards the state.[47]

Many plans existed for new Teutonic cults to replace Christianity or for purifying it of supposed non-Aryan elements, though for reasons of prudence the government never identified itself with any of these. What Rosenberg called "the old vicious freedom of teaching without limitation" disappeared from the German universities, to be replaced by "true freedom," the freedom "to be an organ of the nation's living strength." Jewish scholars were displaced, faculties and students were organized according to the "leadership principle," and the purpose of German higher education became, in accord with national socialist principles, the training of a political *élite*. In this respect the typical educational institutions were not the universities but the technical schools and the party leadership-schools. Social studies like history, sociology, and psychology, became substantially branches of propaganda adapted to elaborating and spreading the racial myth. Possibly the apex of absurdity was reached when a treatise on physics declared that "science, like every other human product, is racial and conditioned by blood."[48]

[46] *Mein Kampf*, pp. 636 f. See for example *The Nazi Primer*, Eng. trans. by H. L. Childs, New York, 1938, a textbook issued for the Hitler Youth.

[47] Quoted by William M. McGovern, *From Luther to Hitler* (Boston, 1941), p. 655.

[48] For this and other similar statements see Edward Y. Hartshorne, *The German Universities and National Socialism* (Cambridge, Mass., 1937), pp. 112 ff.

It was probably true that ideas as bizarre as Aryan physics did not much affect the professional teaching of science and engineering. Nevertheless they cast a high light on what may well be one of the insoluble dilemmas of totalitarian government. A government that aims at a maximum of military power and also a maximum of intellectual control commits its educational system to a peculiar experiment. Essentially it has to find out whether it can debauch the social studies and the humanities and yet keep the natural sciences vigorous enough to support the technology. If it fails of the former the government loses its own self-assigned reason for existence; if it fails of the latter it loses the basis of its power. To combine the two is no doubt possible for a time but whether it can be done permanently is another question. In the case of Germany there is no way to tell how far the loss of Jewish mathematicians and physicists demoralized research that was needed to carry on the war.

NATIONAL SOCIALISM, COMMUNISM, AND DEMOCRACY

Any account of the political theories of the last quarter century must inevitably end with a comparison of national socialism and communism and of both with liberal democracy. For within this period these three have been the rivals for men's loyalty and each has exacted from its followers miracles of effort and self-sacrifice. The end of the period saw the defeat of national socialism by a temporary cooperation between believers in the other two, a cooperation however that left communism and democracy more sharply contrasted than ever before. And only a very optimistic thinker would predict that the essential purposes of national socialism may not be revived in a new form. The contrasts and similarities, therefore, are matters of present concern and indeed of perennial concern for political theory. For at bottom they depend upon contrasting views of politics, its nature and the part that it can play and ought to play in societies both national and international.

Many of the similarities between national socialism and communism lie upon the surface and are manifest. Both throve on social and economic demoralization, which was partly an aftermath of war but which reflected also inherent maladjustments of Western society. Both were political dictatorships. Both discarded with scorn the parliamentary aids to deliberation and negotiation which centuries of European political experience, under the guidance of liberal principles, had created as stabler and more workable substitutes for dictatorship. Both were obliged to reinstate the purge as a political institution. Both tolerated only a single political party which was allowed to maintain its own coercive apparatus. According to the theory of both the party was a self-constituted aristocracy which has the mission partly of leading, partly of instructing, and partly of coercing the bulk of mankind along the road that it is good for them to follow. Both were totalitarian in the sense that they obliterated the liberal distinction between areas of private judgment and of public control, and both turned the educational system into an agency of universal indoctrination. In their philosophy both were utterly dogmatic, professing, the one in the name of the Aryan race the other in the name of the proletariat, a higher insight capable of laying down rules for art, literature, science, and religion. Both induced a frame of mind akin to religious fanaticism. In strategy both were reckless in their assertions, boundless in their claims, abusive toward their opponents, prone to regard any concession on their own part as a temporary expedient and on a rival's part as a sign of weakness. The social philosophies of both agreed in regarding society as in essence a system of forces, economic or racial, between which adjustment takes place by struggle and dominance rather than by mutual understanding and concession. Both therefore regarded politics as a method of implementing forces and hence an expression of power.

Despite these similarities, however, it is certain that communism was on a far higher level, both morally and intellectually, than national socialism. Initially at least the underlying purpose of communism was generous and humane. Its sincerity was unquestionable. Its theory was an outgrowth of two generations of Marxian scholarship with which it claimed both moral and intellectual continuity. Indeed it erected its identity with Marx into a dogma. National socialist theory, on the contrary, was the product of opportunism and sometimes of cynicism and downright intellectual dishonesty; its ethics was the ethics of the *déclassé*. Marxism had been born of the knowledge that modern technology and capitalism were dehumanizing and demoralizing in their consequences, as liberalism itself came to see, and though it minimized it did not deny the substantial values achieved in the development of liberal politics. Traditionally it claimed to extend rather than to restrict democracy. The circumstances of its development in Russia and not a conscious intention forced Lenin to expunge from Marxism most of its democratic implications. Even so its aims remained on the whole benevolent though its methods were sometimes brutal. Fascism and national socialism, on the contrary, derived their strength from an effort to maintain and perpetuate a system of social and economic privilege. To peoples that were to be forced permanently onto a lower standard of living they offered the sentimental reward of participating in a grandiose national mission, which was in substance economic imperialism, and of sharing in prospective material rewards that were never to be realized. The structure of power and privilege which national socialism envisaged as the form of the national community was projected in the picture of an international community with a similar structure. The end revealed the insubstantial and visionary quality of the project. Not only did it lead to war, which was certain in advance, and not only did war bring incredible loss and suffering, which could have been anticipated, but the nature of national socialist government turned defeat as nearly as possible into destruction. A government that had transformed itself into a personal dictatorship could not even resign power in order to leave the national economy and the national political structure intact.

The philosophies of national socialism and communism both tended to become intellectually unapproachable by one who was not a devotee. Both demanded full surrender and based their claim to inevitable and total rightness on a kind of insight that an outsider could not have and that was impervious to evidence. Neither philosophy conceived itself as a medium of intellectual and moral communication. The national socialist claim to an Aryan science and an Aryan art was matched by the communist claim to a proletarian science and a proletarian art, and both claims were liberally backed by charges of degeneracy against the non-Aryan and the bourgeois. Yet even here, in philosophic principle at least, the two dogmatisms and the two dictatorships were potentially not on the same level. Communist philosophy was never overtly irrational; it honestly believed that the dialectic was an instrument of logic yielding results that could be rationally evaluated. Perhaps it had too much rather than too little faith in logic; its dogmatism was a little naive in trusting its ability to read off from its Marxian formulas the course of history, the working of human motives, and the nature of institutions. National socialism on the contrary avowed that its philosophy was a myth which was made "true" by the will to believe. Between nations it set the insurmountable barrier of race, and even for its devotees it supplied no basis for agreement except emotional intoxication. It must be admitted, however, that the potential difference between the two dogmatisms may wear very thin, when the implicit irrationalism of the dialectic comes to the surface. If no conflict can be resolved until its oppositions have been driven to the last extreme, if intelligence and with it science and art and philosophy are inextricably bound to social class, if proletarian and bourgeois never meet until both are sublimated in the utopia of the classless society, the result is the same as if the differences were innate. But certainly it is true that the national socialist *élite* would never have acknowledged its own extinction as an ideal.

The fundamental difference in point of view between the philosophy of liberal democracy and that of either communism or national socialism is that democracy always believed in the possibility of general communication. Whether in terms of universal natural rights or of the greatest happiness or of the common good, its theory purported to be a medium through which men of reasonable intelligence and normal good will could communicate across the boundaries of nation and of social class and so could reach by negotiation as much understanding and agreement as was needed to serve the purposes of a limited public authority. For this reason a democratic social philosophy conceived a community not as a constellation of impersonal forces — either racial or economic — but as a complex of human beings and of human interests. Such interests, it conceded, are always more or less antagonistic and always stand in need of mutual adjustment and readjustment. It was the fundamental assumption of democracy, however, that such adjustments were possible, because communication is possible, and consequently that human relations are conducted on the whole more characteristically by negotiation than by force. Force it conceived, in a civilized society at least, to be rather a last resort than a universal characteristic of social relationships. Hence the ethics of democracy regarded mutual concession and compromise not as defections from principle but as ways of reaching agreements which on the whole were more satisfactory than any that could be reached by the dominance of one interest or one party over all the others. The purpose of a democratic philosophy was to extend rather than to limit the scope of negotiation. This purpose it supposed to be based on a sound and a generally admitted observation, which indeed required no high degree of psychological penetration. It depended on the fact that coercion is at best a crude method of controlling mechanisms as delicately constructed as human personalities and the social ties between personalities, a method that is likely to fail of its purposes, and when it does not fail, is likely to leave in its train accumulations of resentment, frustration, and aggressiveness that lay the foundation for future failure. In general, therefore, democratic theory moved toward the conclusion that politics, by definition, ought to be conceived as the area of negotiation and its institutions as agencies to make possible the interchanges of opinion and understanding on which successful negotiation depends. Such a view attributes to politics a degree and a kind of social importance that is impossible according to a theory that regards it as merely a reflection of social forces or a way of giving effect to the strongest force.

Communication and negotiation, however, have moral as well as semantic presuppositions. They assume in society a factor of free intelligence, not bound either to race or to social position, that can take cognizance of social forces and within limits can direct them. They assume in addition a factor of good will, not unrelated to intelligence and also not bound to race or social position, that intends in the direction of social forces to adjust them to one another with a minimum of friction and coercion. In this last assumption resides, perhaps, the political meaning of the traditional democratic virtues — the belief which has never since Aristotle been absent from liberal thought that on the political level human beings have to meet as free men and equals.

Politically speaking liberty and equality are neither inherent natural rights nor extrinsic aids to happiness, but they can quite reasonably be regarded as moral attitudes without which communication and negotiation become in any complete sense of these words impossible. A genuine meeting of minds may result if both parties in interest will concede to the other side the honor of believing, at least as an initial assumption, that its point of view is not merely vicious or silly. Without that attitude understanding will almost certainly not result, and in a very real sense to assume that attitude is the meaning of treating another person as an equal. Agreement may follow when each side can speak its mind freely without fear of reprisal. Granted a residue of good faith and good will, it becomes possible to accept the fact that free politics is inescapably, but on the whole beneficently, partisan because it is not partisan without limit or scruple. These attitudes make it possible that communication should issue in understanding and that negotiation should end in agreement. They are not guaranties that the process will succeed but their absence is a guaranty that it will fail. Purely as individual attitudes these moral presumptions of democracy are, it must be admitted, weak. For their effective operation in politics they depend on institutions and procedures which conduce to their exercise. The discovery of such procedures — and they are discoveries as truly as any technological discovery — is a work of first class human intelligence applied to the art of human relations. The philosophy of a democratic society is, therefore, as its critics have said, a form of intellectualism. But it need not be an intellectualism that perpetuates an obsolete psychology. It is rather an intellectualism which assumes that understanding is not beyond the range of possibility and that it not only depends on but extends good will and tolerance.

SELECTED BIBLIOGRAPHY

Rosenberg's Nazi Myth. By Albert R. Chandler. Ithaca, New York, 1945.

Fascist Italy. By William Ebenstein. New York, 1939.

The Nazi State. By William Ebenstein. New York, 1943.

Mussolini's Italy. By Herman Finer. New York, 1935.

The Dual State: A Contribution to the Theory of Dictatorship. By Ernst Fraenkel. Eng. trans. by E. A. Shils. New York, 1941.

The Crisis of the National State. By W. Friedmann. London, 1943.

A History of National Socialism. By Konrad Heiden. New York, 1935.

Der Fuehrer: Hitler's Rise to Power. By Konrad Heiden. Eng. trans. by Ralph Manheim. Boston, 1944.

Freedom and Order: Lessons from the War. By Eduard Heimann. New York, 1947. Ch. 2.

The Educational Philosophy of National Socialism. By George F. Kneller. New Haven, 1941.

The Third Reich. By Henri Lichtenberger. Eng. trans. by Koppel S. Pinson. New York, 1937.

The Fruits of Fascism. By Herbert L. Matthews. New York, 1943.

Mussolini in the Making. By Gaudens Megaro. Boston, 1938.

What Nietzsche Means. By George A. Morgan, Jr. Cambridge, Mass., 1941.

The Nazi Economic System: Germany's Mobilization for War. By Otto Nathan, with the Collaboration of Milton Fried. Durham, N. C., 1944.

Behemoth: The Structure and Practice of National Socialism, 1933–1944. By Franz Neumann. 2nd ed. New York, 1944.

Permanent Revolution: The Total State in a World at War. By Sigmund Neumann. New York, 1942.

The Rise of Italian Fascism, 1918–1922. By A. Rossi. Eng. trans. by Peter and Dorothy Wait. London, 1938.

The Plough and the Sword: Labor, Land, and Property in Fascist Italy. By Carl T. Schmidt. New York, 1938.

The Corporate State in Action: Italy under Fascism. By Carl T. Schmidt. London, 1939.

The Last Days of Hitler. By H. R. Trevor-Roper. New York, 1947.

INDEX

INDEX

If there is a single chief treatment, this is cited first; otherwise the citations are in the order of their occurrence.